The New Criterion Reader

The first five years

The New Criterion Reader

The first five years

Edited,
with an introduction,
by Hilton Kramer

The Free Press
A Division of Macmillan, Inc.
New York
Collier Macmillan Publishers
London

The Free Press
A Division of Macmillan, Inc.
866 Third Avenue, New York, N.Y. 10022

Collier Macmillan Canada, Inc.

Printed in the United States of America

printing number
1 2 3 4 5 6 7 8 9 10

Library of Congress Cataloging-in-Publication Data

The New criterion reader: the first five years/edited by Hilton Kramer.
p. cm.
Articles previously published in the New criterion.
Includes bibliographical references.
ISBN 0-02-917641-7
1. Arts, American. 2. Arts. I. Kramer, Hilton. II. New criterion (New York, N.Y.)
NX503.N49 1988
700—dc19

Contents

IV. Artists & Ideas

V. Figures of History

VI. The Contemporary Scene

Acknowledgments

I want to make grateful acknowledgment to all those at *The New Criterion* for the many ways in which they worked on this *Reader:* Samuel Lipman, Erich Eichman, Robert Richman, Donna Rifkind, and Maria Garvey. Thanks, too, to those former members of the staff who made important contributions to the preparation of the writings contained here: Jeanne Wacker, Colleen Babington, Beth Vickery, Kim Ohnemus, and Leslie Beran. (A note about the role of the late Eva Szent-Miklosy is contained in the introduction to this book.) Gratitude is due also to our designers, Alvin and James Eisenman, for the attention they have given this project, and to our esteemed colleagues at Eastern Press: Bill Joslin, Paula Joslin, Mike Malmad, Bohdan Dziubina, and Terry Olenoski. We are indebted as well to Erwin Glikes of The Free Press, who has been an extraordinarily attentive and encouraging editor, and to Edward Rothstein, who oversaw this book in its first stages before leaving The Free Press to write a book of his own.

H.K. May 1987

The first five years: an introduction
by Hilton Kramer

It is now five years since *The New Criterion* published its first issue. From the outset, this monthly review devoted to the arts and contemporary culture was intended to serve as "a dissenting critical voice," as the editors wrote in our inaugural issue, and to this critical task the magazine has continued to give its principal energies.[1] By way of introducing the present *Reader*, which is drawn from the first five years of *The New Criterion* (1982–1987), it is appropriate to recall the situation that prompted the creation of this new publication in the first place. For the cultural impulses that *The New Criterion* set out to question and combat have by no means disappeared. On the contrary, they remain a powerful force in the artistic and intellectual life of our society today. And the kind of achievement that *The New Criterion* was—and is—concerned to elucidate and to honor remains acutely vulnerable to the baleful influences so often discussed in our pages. To appreciate what *The New Criterion* has set out to accomplish—what, in effect, the magazine stands for—it is important to understand the situation that moved its founders to take such a strong dissenting view.

American cultural life in the early 1980s was characterized by an odd combination of social euphoria and critical entropy. In many fields, we were confronted with the dismaying spectacle of rapid institutional growth taking place in an environment of creative inertia. In the visual arts, for example, the atmosphere of public celebration generated by new museum construction, the hurly-burly surrounding "blockbuster" exhibitions, the expansion of the art audience and the art market, and the runaway vogue for "post-modern" skyscraper architecture was everywhere accompanied by an accelerating sense that standards had collapsed and art had entered upon a period of decadence. In the literary world, the impulse to elevate a handful of mediocre writers to an unearned stardom while ignoring the calamitous decline of literary culture in the educated classes became a firmly established practice, and in the world of serious music there was likewise a widespread tendency to look for salvation in celebrity performance and the writing of spuriously romantic ("popular") compositions. Even in the realm of television, which had never been noted for its intellectual standards, it was no longer possible to speak seriously of "educational TV"—clearly a lost cause—as the vulgarities of the Public Broadcasting Service, an enterprise increasingly devoted to popular entertainment and political journalism, made a mockery of the few artistic or "highbrow" subjects it condescended to program.

None of these developments was or could have been considered marginal. They repre-

1 See "A Note on *The New Criterion*," which introduced the first issue of the magazine in September 1982, on page 3.

sented what had now become the mainstream of cultural life. They were routinely praised in the media, they received the respectful attention of the academy, and they enjoyed the unstinting and uncritical support of a new and powerful system of patronage emanating from the philanthropic organs of government and business. What it all added up to, more often than not, was an establishment culture devoid of serious artistic standards, and in some cases devoid of serious artistic interests. Increasingly, indeed, the only standard that counted was a publicity standard, and this, in turn, produced a familiar roster of OK names in every field. To these names an uncritical obeisance was paid—and was expected to be paid—by critics, patrons, and the institutions that nowadays play so large a role in shaping public opinion in the arts. Which is another way of saying that criticism, which had once contributed so much to our understanding of the arts, had all but defaulted on its essential task. Criticism thus surrendered its standards before the juggernaut of the new cultural establishment and became, in effect, an adjunct to the very enterprise it had once been its function to question.

It was in the context of this situation of artistic and critical dissembling that *The New Criterion* raised its dissenting voice. In doing so, the magazine was obliged to confront another of the powerful impulses that was shaping the established culture of the 1980s—the political impulse that derived from the radical movements of the 1960s and was now an institutionalized component of cultural life. So pervasive had this leftist political influence become in the cultural life of the early 1980s that it constituted a kind of establishment within the establishment. In the arts it enjoyed an immense prestige. In the colleges and universities it reigned without significant opposition. In the media it determined not only the objects of discussion but the judgments to be made of them. Even in the world of corporate and government patronage, which might have been expected to take a skeptical, if not indeed a hostile, attitude toward an ideological impulse that is anti-capitalist in its very essence—and that had categorically condemned capitalism and the democratic institutions supporting it as the enemy of all cultural enlightenment—even in this bastion of the establishment, the ideas of the political Left met with consistent and considerable favor. The result was a cultural establishment eager to adopt the rhetoric and often the programs of its political adversaries. As political standards came to replace artistic standards, the net effect was to make the life of culture more and more hostage to the influence of the Left. For the more the Left denounced our cultural institutions as reactionary, elitist, sexist, racist, or whatever, the harder these institutions worked to satisfy the Left's political criteria and the more respectable and established these criteria became.

Given this situation, it was not to be expected that *The New Criterion*—which set out to take a hard look at the contemporary cultural scene—would ignore the political component of the subjects it confronted, and it didn't. On this, as on other compelling issues that play a significant role in shaping the agenda of American cultural life, we have not hesitated to take a sharply dissenting view. The editors of *The New Criterion* never made any secret of the fact that they looked upon the radical legacy of the 1960s as a cultural calamity. However opinions might differ on certain aspects of this subject—and there are certainly differences even among our own writers—there was no denying the reality of this radical influence, and it was our firm conviction that it had to be addressed.

The critical attention we paid to this political component of the contemporary cultural scene did not pass unnoticed, to say the least. It was promptly noted and much debated. While in some quarters our critical stance on this issue was welcomed with a sigh of relief and an enthusiastic show of support, elsewhere—in what can only be described as the citadels of established opinion—it was greeted as an intellectual scandal, and the uproar it caused was surely one of the reasons why *The New Criterion* was instantly regarded as something of an event. From its very first issue, the magazine met with a spirited and often hostile response—especially on the political Left, which had long had reason to regard the publication of critical journals as a prerogative that was not to be shared by opposing points of view. That a new monthly review devoted to the criticism of literature, the arts, and the social currents of cultural life need not subscribe to the shibboleths of the political Left, that it might even question and criticize the role played by political radicalism in the arts and offer an alternative to the leftward drift that had come to dominate American cultural life—this was an unexpected development at a moment when a great many artists and intellectuals took it for granted that the Left defined the only possible standard of enlightenment in matters having to do with art and culture. In the face of this assumption, the appearance of *The New Criterion* was bound to cause a good deal of consternation and commotion, and it did. "Not since H. L. Mencken and *The American Mercury* has literary America seen so much fur fly," Adam Gussow wrote in the liberal *Boston Review*, and on this point at least he was right.

The howls of protest that greeted the publication of *The New Criterion* varied, of course, both in the intensity of their wrath and in the kind of abuse they heaped upon the magazine and its writers. For some of our critics, our worst offense lay in our energetic defense of modernism—which, because of the disfavor it now met with in radical circles, had itself become a political issue. Coming at a time when widespread manifestations of a "postmodern" temper had acquired the momentum of an irresistible fashion, this defense of modernism caused considerable shock and indignation. In the academy, in the museums, and in the media, modernism was in the process of being unmasked and "deconstructed" as either a bourgeois plot or an outmoded aesthetic idea or both, and anything said in its defense—especially anything that claimed, as *The New Criterion* often did, that modernism continued to represent our most vital and essential cultural tradition—was taken to be a threat to the prevailing orthodoxy.

For others, it was our commitment to capitalism that could not be forgiven. Not only on the extreme Left but even among many liberals, capitalism is so firmly established in the demonology of intellectual debate as the enemy of an enlightened culture that all questions having to do with the relation obtaining between capitalism and contemporary cultural life are regarded as settled—settled, that is, in the judgment that capitalism is to be regarded as the primary obstacle to whatever it is we may wish to achieve in both society and art. With this view—an essentially Marxist view that had come to occupy a sacrosanct place in the new cultural orthodoxy—*The New Criterion* categorically disagreed, and we left our readers in no doubt as to where we stood on this crucial issue.

From certain of our critics, however, what drew the fiercest response was precisely an espousal of the idea that modernism and capitalism, notwithstanding the tensions that had marked their past history, had now evolved in a way that made them natural and inevitable allies in a modern democratic society; and that it is indeed upon the survival and prosperity of both, no matter how troubled their relation to each other might sometimes be, that the future vitality of a democratic society and a free cultural life is henceforth likely to depend.

It was to be expected that this idea would meet with opposition from the hard-line opponents of capitalism, and there was no shortage of opposition from that quarter. More interesting (because of what it signified) was the critical response this idea met with among liberals who had more or less reconciled themselves, however warily, to an acceptance of capitalism but who were unprepared to modify their view of modernism. For liberals of this persuasion, capitalism might somehow be accommodated, if only because it guaranteed their own prosperity and freedom, but certain myths—or should we call them pieties?—surrounding the modernist movement were not on that account to be surrendered simply because they had been rendered obsolete by history. For these liberals, the very conception of modernism has remained so inextricably bound up with the idea of insurrection and revolution that they cannot bring themselves to think about modernism in any other terms. Modernism-as-insurrection is the last remaining remnant of the radicalism they forfeited when they made their uneasy peace with capitalism, and it is all the more precious, of course, as a token of the *révolté* impulse they have largely abandoned.

"Insurrection" was thus, not surprisingly, the word repeatedly invoked by Leon Wieseltier, the literary editor of *The New Republic*, to describe *his* conception of modernism when he sought to set his readers straight about the outlook of *The New Criterion*. While reluctantly conceding that "capitalism certainly has the best record on democracy," Wieseltier nonetheless recoiled in horror at what he called *The New Criterion*'s "marriage" of "modernism to capitalism and to the middle class." "Modernism *was* a cultural insurrection," Wieseltier insisted, "and sometimes also a social insurrection, and sometimes even a political insurrection." As, indeed, it *sometimes* was—but, as Wieseltier failed to point out, it often wasn't. Was Impressionism a mode of insurrection? Was Cubism? Can we find in the great achievements of the modern masters—in the paintings of Cézanne, Matisse, and Miró; in the poetry of Eliot, Stevens, and Valéry; in the fiction of Proust, Joyce, and Mann; in the music of Schoenberg and Stravinsky; or in the architecture of Wright, Corbusier, and Mies—any warrant to support this notion of insurrection? We cannot, and it is the sheerest sentimentality to believe otherwise. It is also bad history to suppose that modernism can somehow be isolated, as if by political quarantine, from the high culture of capitalism and the middle class.

The point is, what has remained of permanent value in the culture of modernism is not one or another of the alliances it sometimes formed with movements of social and political revolt. Those alliances, after all, have consistently proved to be highly perishable, and in retrospect often turned out to be peripheral to the mainstream of modernist endeavors. What has remained of permanent value in the culture of modernism is the quality and scope of its artistic achievements. It is these that *The New Criterion* has made a concentrated critical effort to clarify and reclaim, and this effort has inevitably obliged us to pay a good deal of critical attention, too, to the many attempts now being made to obscure and discredit those achievements in the name of one or another radical ideology. To subordinate the achievements of art to a radical political agenda, or indeed to any political agenda; to claim that art itself is to be understood merely and mainly as the coefficient of some political objective—this is, indeed, to de-legitimize the function of art and to deny it the autonomy it has so arduously won for itself in the modern era.

It is precisely in the autonomy accorded to art by the tradition of modernism that we find the freedom of spirit that is the cultural analogue of the political freedoms guaranteed to us by capitalist democracy. This is one reason why all attempts to establish the culture of modernism in nondemocratic, anticapitalist societies have proved to be tragically short-lived. To deny modernism its aesthetic autonomy is to deny its very essence. Like it or not, it is only in democratic capitalistic societies—which is to say, in the world of the bourgeois democracies—that modernism has flourished *as* a cultural tradition. No doubt the relation in which modernism stands to these bourgeois societies will continue at times to be a troubled one. It is in the nature of modernism to be critical of its own conventions. But to characterize that critical impulse as insurrectionist is to misunderstand it in the most fundamental way.

On this subject, at least, the radicals who reject modernism as insufficiently revolutionary are actually a good deal closer to the truth than the liberals. That modernism has proved not to be a mode of insurrection is a matter the radicals understand very well, which is why they have labored so diligently to discredit the whole modernist enterprise. The liberals, on the other hand, though fundamentally indifferent to the aesthetics of modernism—see any issue of *The New Republic* or *The New York Review of Books* for confirmation—nonetheless cling to the myth of modernism-as-insurrection as an article of faith. Why? Primarily, I think, because it is only *as* a political fiction that modernism holds any interest for them. As an artistic actuality it hardly exists in their eyes. Which is why liberalism has had nothing to say about the life of art in our time. There is no liberal criticism of the arts today that can be taken seriously because there is no liberal criticism of the arts today that *takes art seriously*. And what is true of the liberals in this respect is also true of those who still claim to be socialists. Thus, an article in Irving Howe's *Dissent* ("Culture and the Neoconservatives" by Oliver Conant, Spring 1987) attacks *The New Criterion*, its editor, and its writers for their views on the arts; but it is only when mounting a political assault on *The New Criterion* that Howe's socialist journal pays even the slightest attention to the life of art. From the socialist perspective, as from that of the liberals, art today exists solely as a political datum.

For all the attention we have lavished on the politicization of the arts and their institutions, it is no paradox to say that *The New Criterion* is not primarily a political magazine. It is not we who have accorded the political Left its immense influence in current cultural affairs. We have found this influence to be there, deeply entrenched, in fact, and have been obliged to deal with it accordingly, as an important part of our effort to specify where the real achievements of contemporary culture are to be found and what the principal obstacles to genuine achievement now consist of. It has never been our purpose to mount, via the back door of cultural criticism, an explicit defense of capitalism, for example—nor, for that matter, of any other political credo—in the pages of *The New Criterion*. Our primary interest lies in the arts and in the ideas that govern them. It is because politics of a certain kind has come to figure so prominently among these ideas that politics has so often been dealt with in the magazine and in this book. But in no case, I think it is fair to say, has this attention to the politicization of the arts led to political judgments about the art under discussion.

It has naturally been gratifying to us that our approach to this critical task has met with so much interest, for it has confirmed our belief that the time was ripe for a serious challenge to the reigning pieties—artistic as well as political—that now disfigure so much of our cultural life, and for that challenge to be mounted, indeed, in the name of a serious and disinterested criticism. In this respect, the response to the first five years of *The New Criterion* has been everything we could have wished for. Opposition—mainly on political grounds—has sometimes been fierce, of course, but that has come as no surprise. No cultural establishment can be expected to welcome a dissenting view of its ideas or a challenge to its influence. What we have proved, however, is that the voice of serious criticism still has a significant role to play in the life of the arts today and that it is indeed only by the application of a sustained critical intelligence that we can hope to penetrate and comprehend the terrible miasma of contemporary cultural life and discover some alternatives to the reckless and debilitating course it is now pursuing.

On a more personal note, a word about the founding of the magazine. The origin of *The New Criterion* dates from a couple of years prior to the appearance of the first issue—to some time in 1980 when the idea of publishing a new monthly review of the arts began to take shape in conversations between the two writers who in 1982 became, respectively, its editor and publisher.[2] One of them, myself, had for some years been the art news editor and chief art critic of *The New York Times*. The other, Samuel Lipman, was a pianist—a former student of Pierre Monteux, Darius Milhaud, and Rosina Lhévinne—who since 1976 had been the music critic for *Commentary* and a regular contributor to the London *Times Literary Supplement*. I had been writ-

2 These conversations were joined in 1981 by Michael S. Joyce, at that time the executive director of the John M. Olin Foundation. It was *The New Criterion*'s—and our—great fortune to find in Mike Joyce a wise friend, and a perceptive and dedicated supporter of our ideas and our work.

ing criticism for thirty years, contributing to *Partisan Review, The Hudson Review, Arts Magazine, The New York Review of Books, The New Republic, The Nation,* and other journals before moving to *The Times* in 1965. In the Fifties I had served as the editor of *Arts Magazine*, in the Sixties as an editor and critic for *The New Leader*, and in the Seventies as visiting professor of criticism at the Yale University School of Drama. Sam Lipman had been performing the classical music repertoire in concerts since his childhood in San Francisco, and for some years had been a member of the faculty of the Aspen Music Festival. He had also taken a master's degree in political science at the University of California at Berkeley and had played in Carnegie Hall the first New York performance of the Elliott Carter Piano Concerto. It was as a result of his becoming the music critic for *Commentary,* to which I had also been a contributor for many years, that we met.

Although our backgrounds and professional experience were distinctly different, we soon found that our interests were remarkably similar. Foremost among them was a deep and abiding commitment to the traditions of high art, an acute awareness of the ways in which those traditions were being compromised and betrayed by the artists and institutions who had them in their keeping, and a keen understanding of the role played by politics in the crisis (as we saw it to be) that had overtaken contemporary cultural life. It was out of our many conversations about these issues that *The New Criterion* was born. We shared a conviction that a new critical effort was needed to deal with these issues and that such an effort could effectively be made only under nonacademic auspices since the academy had itself become so large a part of the problem we wished to confront.

From the outset, we were fortunate in recruiting a splendid staff. Erich Eichman had been an editor first at *The American Spectator* and then at *Harper's Magazine* before joining *The New Criterion* as managing editor. He has skillfully presided over the magazine's daily editorial operations since its inception, and has won the admiration and gratitude of the many distinguished writers with whom he has worked. Robert Richman had served on the staffs of Basic Books and Random House before coming to the magazine, and had also contributed some noteworthy criticism—mainly of contemporary poetry—to *Commentary*, the London *Times Literary Supplement*, and *The Village Voice*. Jeanne Wacker, who came to us from *National Review*, was invaluable as our first assistant managing editor before leaving for a position in Washington. The late Eva Szent-Miklosy, who died this year at the age of fifty-three, was in some respects the most remarkable of our founding editors. Although English was her second language—Eva was a native of Germany—her versatile editorial talents set a high standard for us all, and her courage and humor in the face of adversity were an inspiration. It is a great sadness to us that Eva did not live to see the completion of this *Reader*, to the contents of which she contributed so much.

It was also our good fortune to have in Alvin and James Eisenman the ideal designers for the kind of magazine we wished to publish. It is they who have given *The New Criterion* its distinctive and much admired graphic style.

Finally, a word about the selection of this anthology. From its very first issue, *The New Criterion* undertook to address a broad range of subjects, and these I have endeavored to represent as fully as possible within the limits of a single volume. The *Reader* is thus designed to provide a comprehensive account of the magazine's interests as well as a critical history of the period it covers. It is also intended to be representative of the writers we have published. Of the twenty-nine contributors whose work is included in this volume, some have long been renowned, of course, while a fair proportion of the others can be said to have made their reputations in our pages. I have tried to represent both groups as fully as possible. To start a magazine like *The New Criterion* is inevitably something of a gamble, and one of the things the editors gamble on is the hope that their enterprise will prove to be sufficiently compelling to attract the best new talent. In this respect, too, we have been extremely fortunate. Of the writers who now contribute to the magazine on a regular basis, the majority were unknown to the editor when he brought out his first issue; some had never before been published. And since aspiring writers often wonder what the chances are for an "unknown" to get published, it may be worth noting that when we launched *The New Criterion* I was personally acquainted with fewer than half the writers now included in this book. I deeply regret having to omit a number of outstanding contributions that it had been my hope to include, but there was clearly a physical limit that had to be met. One general principle of exclusion has been observed, however: I have included no contributions that have already appeared in book form. Hence the omission of, among other distinguished writers, Gertrude Himmelfarb, Ada Louise Huxtable, Frederick Crews, and Norman Podhoretz, whose essays for *The New Criterion* have now been published in books of their own.

One further point. The *Reader* contains none of the poems that *The New Criterion* has published in every issue since the April 1984 number. As it happens, the magazine's poetry editor, Robert Richman, is preparing for publication a new anthology of American and British poetry written since 1975, and this volume—to be called *The Direction of Poetry*—will include some of the finest poems to have appeared in our pages.

I. Culture & Politics

A note on *The New Criterion*: September 1982

There are no doubt many reasons for wanting to start a new review, but the primary one was long ago stated with exemplary candor by Sir Walter Scott while he was involved in preparations for launching *The Quarterly Review*. Writing to Gifford in October 1808, on the eve of the *Quarterly*'s initial appearance, Scott declared that "The real reason for instituting the new publication is the disgusting and deleterious doctrines with which the most popular of our Reviews disgraces its pages." The journal Scott had in mind was, of course, the *Edinburgh Review*. But he—fortunate man!—lived in a tidier and more fastidious intellectual universe than ours. Today we know to our sorrow that there are many worse disasters to be visited upon the life of culture than the *Edinburgh Review*. We are surrounded by the evidence wherever we turn. The feeling of dissatisfaction with existing journals, and with the ideas and practices that govern them, is therefore likely to be especially acute just now for anyone capable of recalling a time when criticism was more strictly concerned to distinguish achievement from failure, to identify and uphold a standard of quality, and to speak plainly and vigorously about the problems that beset the life of the arts and the life of the mind in our society.

Today, more often than not, the prevailing modes of criticism have not only failed to come to grips with such tasks, they have actually come to constitute an obstacle to their pursuit. A multitude of journals of every size and periodicity—quarterlies, monthlies, fortnightlies, weeklies, and even the daily papers to the extent that they concern themselves with matters of the mind—lavishes upon the life of culture a vast amount of attention. Yet most of what is written in these journals is either hopelessly ignorant, deliberately obscurantist, commercially compromised, or politically motivated. Especially where the fine arts and the disciplines of high culture are concerned, criticism at every level—from the daily newspaper review of a concert or a novel to the disquisitions of critics and scholars in learned journals—has almost everywhere degenerated into one or another form of ideology or publicity or some pernicious combination of the two. As a result, the very notion of an independent high culture and the distinctions that separate it from popular culture and commercial entertainment have been radically eroded. Far from resisting this erosion, criticism has lately been responsible for hastening it on its downward course. Not only have our critics assisted in blurring the kinds of distinctions that were once fundamental to their vocation. In many cases they have openly celebrated the demise of such distinctions.

This fateful collapse in critical standards—and in the very idea of critical disinterestedness—is only a part, of course, of a more general cultural drift that has brought some woeful consequences in its wake. It has changed, and changed very much for the worse, the way the arts and the humanities are now studied in our universities. It has changed the way art museums and other cultural institutions now conceive of their programs and priorities—and indeed, the very reason for their existence. It plays a role in the way government agencies, private foundations, and corporate sponsors dispense funds for cultural projects. In many cases it has condemned true seriousness to a fugitive existence even in realms, such as the world of scholarship, where it was once highly prized. It has thus altered the conditions of artistic and intellectual life in this country, and made it infinitely more difficult for the voice of informed intelligence to make itself heard, and almost impossible for it to prevail.

A very large part of the reason for this sad state of affairs is, frankly, political. We are still living in the aftermath of the insidious assault on mind that was one of the most repulsive features of the radical movement of the Sixties. The cultural consequences of this leftward turn in our political life have been far graver than is commonly supposed. In everything from the writing of textbooks to the reviewing of trade books, from the introduction of kitsch into the museums to the decline of literacy in the schools to the corruption of scholarly research, the effect on the life of culture has been ongoing and catastrophic. Yet the subject is one that has scarcely been studied. It would probably take the combined talents of a Gibbon and a Tocqueville to tell the whole shabby story on the requisite scale, but one does not have to be a genius to recognize some of the more egregious results of this flight from intelligence and intellectual scruple. The cultural landscape is littered with its casualties and debris.

Consider, for example, what now passes for the writing of contemporary art history in the offices of the Oxford University Press in New York:

> When the Philip Morris Company sponsored a concert of Arnold Schoenberg's *Pierrot Lunaire* to accompany the Guggenheim [Museum's] presentation [of German Expressionist painting], the musical director included a parody of *Pierrot Lunaire* composed by Hanns Eisler, a former student of Schoenberg's who had fled Nazi Germany in 1933, worked in Hollywood as musical assistant to Charlie Chaplin, and was so savagely persecuted as a Communist that he was forced to flee America in 1947 during the worst of the red witch hunts. Eisler's brilliant parody, composed to the poems of another rebellious German, Christian Morgenstern, went unnoticed by both the corporation and those reporting the event. But while the directors of museums insist that the benign supercompanies never attempt to influence judgments in high artistic matters, had Philip Morris only known . . .

The knowing ellipsis is in the original, by the way, which is to be found in the closing pages of Dore Ashton's recently published *American Art Since 1945,* a book clearly intended for classroom use. Apparently we are to regard the life of art in the United States as existing under some kind of dire political threat from big business—even when big business does *not* interfere in the artistic activities it sponsors. No wonder a reviewer in *The Nation,* though he found *American Art Since 1945* to be neither "a brilliant [n]or a profound text," praised its author for seeing "art as a political as well as an esthetic activity."

Needless to say, it is never explained why it is right and proper for Hanns Eisler, Dore Ashton, and reviewers in *The Nation* to see "art as a political as well as an esthetic activity" while it is somehow wrong—and indeed sinister—for corporate patrons of the arts to evince the least curiosity about the social implications of the artistic programs they are invited to sponsor. Incidentally, nowhere in *American Art Since 1945* is it pointed out that Hanns Eisler, after he left the United States in 1947, went on to become the privileged composer laureate of the Communist regime in East Germany that, among much else, built the Berlin Wall. Opinions will differ as to whether an account of a career like Eisler's even belongs in a history of American art since 1945. But if it is to be included, does there not exist some elementary obligation to the reader—who, more often than not, is likely to be a student without any detailed knowledge of the period—to tell the whole story?

Elsewhere the tendency to substitute political fantasies for the writing of art history has become even more programmatic. Thus, in a journal called *Art History* (September 1980) we find the following contribution to historical enlightenment. The authors—Fred Orton and Griselda Pollock of the University of Leeds—are discussing the mammoth "Post-Impressionism" exhibition mounted at the Royal Academy in London in 1979-1980 and afterwards shown, in somewhat modified form, at the National Gallery in Washington. They are particularly concerned to discredit John Rewald's definitive *Post-Impressionism: From Van Gogh to Gauguin,* published by the Museum of Modern Art in 1956 and still the most comprehensive study of its subject today. This is what they say about it:

> Those of us who are neither indebted to Rewald nor convinced of the possibility or desirability of writing definitive histories do, however, believe that it is important to note the historical specificity of the reassertion of 'Post-Impressionism' in Rewald's view of history, the date of the book's publication (1956), the institution which published it (Museum of Modern Art, New York), and the *dramatis personae* acknowledged as Trustees of the Museum of Modern Art (1950s hegemonists, power elitists and upper class Americans with interests in shaping foreign policy). Rewald's *The History of Impressionism* (New York, 1946) and *Post-Impressionism* must be recognized for what they are, symptoms of, and contributions to, the construction of a history of art from the mid-nineteenth century to the present which was conceived by that Cold War warrior and ideologue Alfred H. Barr Jr., Director of the Museum of Modern Art. Rewald's conception of the history of art fits snugly into Barr's grand design, modernism, into that creation of an autonomous linear development which obfuscates the changing conditions of production in art practices and the real social relations in which they are embedded in favour of those abstractions, style and genius.

And while our authors modestly acknowledge that this article "is not the place to begin the deconstruction of modernism as one of the corner-stones of American cultural imperialism," in a footnote we are promised "a historical study of Alfred H. Barr and the role of the Museum of Modern Art in the construction of modernism" for the future.

It would be comforting, perhaps, to suppose that such manifest and malevolent misrepresentations of art, of history, of scholarship, and of the institutions that have been created in democratic societies to secure their integrity, are isolated or eccentric occurrences on the cultural scene today. But such, alas, is not the case. For more than a decade now there has been an active school of criticism at work promoting the notion that the New York School, for example, was little more than a political instrument conjured up by those "1950s hegemonists" for the purpose of fighting the Cold War. This line was introduced into criticism by the English Marxist writer John Berger in the Fifties, when the paintings of Pollock, Rothko, de Kooning, et al. were first exhibited in Europe on a large scale and began to exert a tremendous influence on the rising generation of artists there. It was not taken seriously on this side of the Atlantic, however, until the political shifts of the Sixties created an intellectual environment more conducive to its reception. Since that time, Berger's own writings have acquired a cult status in this country, and there have been some notable conversions to the same Marxist line by critics and scholars who once knew better.

One of the saddest of many such cases is that of the critic Lucy Lippard. Here is a writer who began her career in the Fifties as a serious student of modern art, and went on to produce important monographs on the work of Eva Hesse and Ad Reinhardt and valuable anthologies of the writings of the Dadaists and the Surrealists. There was every reason to suppose that a writer of this quality would one day become one of our leading historians of the modern movement. Yet in the Seventies Miss Lippard fell victim to the radical whirlwind. The scholarship and discrimination that won her the respect of the art world is a thing of the past. Nowadays, she writes in defense of ideas that, if triumphant, would require all her earlier work to be placed under a permanent political ban.

This, to be sure, is an extreme case. The descent into straight-out political propaganda is not usually so crude. But the same ideological impulse can be observed, too, in the realm of academic scholarship. It is by no means confined to the world of *révolté* journalism. At Harvard University, for example, the study of nineteenth-century French art history—still the fulcrum of any systematic study of the whole modern period—is now presided over by the English Marxist scholar T.J. Clark, the author of two influential texts, *Image of the People: Gustave Courbet and the Second French Republic, 1848-1851* and *The Absolute Bourgeois: Artists and Politics in France, 1848-1851.*[1]

In the literary world, similar political distortions are now so commonplace that they defy easy summary. Not since the 1930s have so many orthodox leftist pieties so casually insinuated themselves into both the creation and the criticism of literature, and remained so immune to resistance or exposure.

Part of this is, of course, sheer trendiness. Writers seeking readers' favor inevitably—and not always very thoughtfully—tend to conform to whatever views seem at the moment to be "in." They merely follow where the fashion seems to lead. But how, then, are we to account for a trend that elevates such views to a position of unquestioned modishness? What it seems to come down to is a fervent wish on the part of many writers to dissociate themselves from the capitalist society in which we live. Everything in their intellectual upbringing has disposed them to identify the literary vocation with the conventions of radical criticism, and thus made them acutely vulnerable to the pressure exerted by the special political intensities of the Left.

Many writers on the Left—and this includes a good many of our prominent critics, too—have never forgiven history for failing to conform to the fictions of radical prophecy. They have never forgiven American society for failing to live up to their critique of it. In some tender sanctum of the soul, socialism remains their moral and social ideal—but a socialism so immune to historical contingency and moral reality that it is now indistinguishable from a religious dogma. It would therefore break their hearts and shatter every illusion they have inherited from the sacred traditions of radicalism to have to acknowledge that capitalism, for all its many flaws, has proved to be the greatest safeguard of democratic institutions and the best guarantee of intellectual and artistic freedom—including *their* intellectual and artistic freedom—that the modern world has given us. How profoundly they despise this elementary fact of their existence, and how energetically they work to disguise and distort its reality!

The time has surely come for criticism to turn its back on this intellectual vaudeville act, which wears a fancy radical face when performing for the public while at the same time—backstage, as it were—availing itself of all the advantages and preferments that our society offers in such abundance. It is time to apply a new criterion to the discussion of our cultural life—a criterion of truth. This is by no means a simple or an easy task. The defense of high art in a democratic society has never been a simple or an easy task. It is in the very nature of democracy, with its multiplicity of interests and tastes,

1 Something of the flavor of Professor Clark's outlook may be gleaned from the following exercise in translation. In a passage (page 171) in *The Absolute Bourgeois,* first published in 1973 and lately reprinted in paperback, he writes of Baudelaire: "The revolution [of 1848] would destroy his family, so Baudelaire hoped. Hence the famous slogan he shouted in February, clutching his looted flintlock: *'Il faut fusiller le général Aupick!'* (equals, roughly, 'Up against the wall Motherfucker')." Translation is a notoriously inexact science, of course. It allows a writer many liberties. But there is obviously something more than the creative interpolation of a text at work in this particular effort.

for the task to be difficult. Yet it is imperative that we recognize, as the first condition for any serious criticism of the arts in the contemporary world, that it is now only in a democratic society like ours that the values of high art can be expected to survive and prosper. The dishonesties and hypocrisies and disfiguring ideologies that nowadays afflict the criticism of the arts are deeply rooted in both our commercial and our academic culture. They govern much that is written about the arts in the media, and much that is taught about them in the classroom. For all practical purposes, indeed, they constitute a very large part of the mainstream of our cultural life today. It is therefore all the more urgent that a dissenting critical voice be heard, and it is for the purpose of providing such a voice that *The New Criterion* has been created. —*The Editors*

Modernism and its enemies

by Hilton Kramer

Nowadays, for anyone who takes a keen interest in the arts and has acquired the habit of making them an object of critical thought, there is one issue—or perhaps I should say, one debate—which is more and more found to overshadow all others, and that is the debate over the nature and destiny of modernism. This debate takes many forms and addresses itself to a great many aspects of cultural life, from the most purely aesthetic to the most explicitly political. Moreover, the participants in this debate are extremely diverse. They include not only the expected artists and critics and patrons of the arts, and the administrators and publicists who preside over our arts institutions, but also specialists in the social sciences, political activists and theorists, journalists and editorial writers, and philosophers, intellectuals, and academics of all kinds—all of whom have lately discovered in the problem of modernism a subject they deem to be central to the cultural and political life of our time. All tend to enter into this debate with strong feelings, and indeed pronounced passions, which are not always based on a mastery of the materials under discussion but which nonetheless derive from a sense that something important has changed in the relation of culture to society in our world, the world of the bourgeois democracies, and that the key to this change is to be found in that complicated conjunction of historical developments which generally goes under the name of modernism.

A debate which elicits the fierce polemical participation of so many diverse parties and interests is not easily summarized, to be sure, yet its salient features are, I think, now sufficiently clear to be identified and examined, and it is to this task that I wish to address myself here. I do not come to this subject as a neutral observer, of course. The most striking feature of this debate about modernism is—as the title of this paper suggests—the extraordinary degree of *enmity* it exhibits toward modernism itself; and in relation to this fierce enmity I wish to speak here as something of a champion and defender of the phenomenon that is now under attack. For it seems to me that in this attack on modernism by its enemies what is really at stake is something essential to the vital cultural life of our democratic society.

At the outset of this discussion, it will help us to understand both the intensity of this attack on modernism and its amazing scope if I offer some examples which can be held in the mind, as it were, as specimen citations from what is already a vast critical literature. Examples that commend themselves for this purpose abound, alas, as every publishing season for years now has added new and ever more vehement contributions to the fray. From Tom Wolfe's *The Painted Word* and *From Bauhaus to Our House,* on the one hand, to T. J. Clark's *The Painting of Modern Life* and Serge Guilbaut's *How New York Stole the Idea of Modern Art,* on the other, all shades of political opinion are represented, and in the case of at least one book, Suzi Gablik's *Has Modernism Failed?*, which calls for nothing less than a reformation of human nature itself, this literature has even acquired something akin to a religious dimension. Since the subject is now close to constituting a virtual subdivision of the book-publishing industry, it was inevitable that college textbooks would also be issued, and the alert firm of Harper & Row has been quick to establish its priority in the field with three titles widely used in the classroom: *Modern Art and Modernism*; *Modernism, Criticism, Realism*; and *Pollock and After*; all published in the last four years and all organized to promote a more or less Marxist interpretation of the subject.

From this large and burgeoning literature I shall offer only three representative citations drawn from very different political perspectives. The first and longest comes from an essay by a critic immensely influential in academic circles, Fredric Jameson, who, after much competition among the universities for his intellectual favors, has lately settled into a chair at Duke University. Jameson's text is entitled, "Postmodernism and Consumer Society," and appears, incidentally, in another of those anthologies designed for the classroom—*The Anti-Aesthetic: Essays on Postmodern Culture.*[1] In this essay Jameson is concerned to explain why, as he says, "classical modernism is a thing of the past and why postmodernism should have taken its place." The reason for this historic shift, Jameson writes, is to be found in what he calls "the end of individualism as such." And on this subject he offers the following commentary:

> The great modernisms were . . . predicated on the invention of a personal, private style, as unmistakable as your fingerprint, as incomparable as your own body. But this means that the modernist aesthetic is in some way organically linked to the conception of a unique self and private identity, a unique personality and individuality, which can be expected to generate its own unique vision of the world and to forge its own unique, unmistakable style.
>
> Yet today, from any number of distinct perspectives, the social theorists, the psychoanalysts, even the linguists, not to speak of those of us who work in the area of culture and cultural and formal change, are all exploring the notion that that kind of individualism and personal identity is a thing of the past; that the old individual or individualist subject is "dead"; and that one might even describe the concept of the unique individual and the theoretical basis of individualism as ideological. There are in fact two positions on all this, one of which is more radical than the other. The first one is content to say: yes, once upon a time, in the classic age of competitive capitalism, in the heyday of the nuclear family and the emergence of the bourgeoisie as the hegemonic social class, there was such a thing as individualism, as individual subjects. But today, in the age of corporate capitalism, of the so-called organization man, of bureaucracies in business as well as in the state, of demographic explosion—today, that older bourgeois individual subject no longer exists.
>
> Then there is a second position, the more radical of the two, what one might call the poststructuralist position. It adds: not only is the bourgeois individual subject a thing of the past, it is also a myth; it *never* really existed in the first place; there have never been autonomous subjects of that type. Rather, this construct is merely a philosophical and cultural mystification which sought to persuade people that they "had" individual subjects and possessed this unique personal identity.

Jameson then goes on to identify the aesthetic dilemma which follows from this analysis. The older models, as he calls them, naming Picasso, Proust, and T. S. Eliot, "do not work anymore (or are positively harmful), since nobody has that kind of unique private world and style to express any longer." The only thing now possible, in this view, is for culture to turn to pastiche and parody, and this means, he adds, that "con-

1 *The Anti-Aesthetic: Essays on Postmodern Culture,* edited by Hal Foster (Bay Press, 1983) pages 111-125.

temporary or postmodernist art is going to be about art itself in a new kind of way . . . that its essential messages will involve the necessary failure of art and the aesthetic, the failure of the new, the imprisonment of the past," etc.

The second passage I want to cite approaches the debate from a very different perspective—one that takes abstract art, especially the kind of abstract painting that was produced in New York in the heyday of the Abstract Expressionist movement, as emblematic of the evils caused by the spirit of modernism. Here the writer is not an academic but a journalist, Roger Starr, a member of *The New York Times* editorial board and formerly the housing commissioner of New York City. In Starr's view, many of the catastrophes which have overtaken New York City in recent decades can be traced to, of all things, abstract painting and the modernist impulse as he understands it to be embodied in that painting. Thus in his new book on *The Rise and Fall of New York City* he writes as follows:

> It would surely be overreaching to suggest that the spirit of nonobjective art forced New York into its financial difficulties of 1975, or that it continues to hold before the city the specter of other severe difficulties that it may face in the future. But it is not overreaching to suggest that when the institutional leaders of the city make modern painting and sculpture their most prized art form, and when they devote as much time, intelligence, and, not least, money to its pursuit as the New York leaders of the postwar world have done, they demonstrate a set of values that endangers those needed to keep an urban polity on a firm, reasonable, and safe course.
>
> . . . Accepting as a form of high and serious art an arrangement of colors and shapes that has no relationship at all to objects of the world outside the canvas inferentially denies the value and importance of understanding the relationships between those objects and the observer. It offers the viewer instead spatial relationships that relate the paints . . . to each other within the canvas and nowhere else.[2]

By this reasoning the turn away from abstraction and toward various modes of representation which has been the single most conspicuous feature of contemporary art in New York for a decade now would have to be taken as a sign that "severe difficulties," as Roger Starr calls them, can now safely be consigned to the past as far as New York City is concerned. But I doubt if he would agree with that. It is not, in any case, the merit of Starr's criticism which interests me here—in my opinion, it has no more merit than Fredric Jameson's—but the fact that a writer in his position feels compelled to make it—that is, to seize on modernism as the source of so many of our social ills.

Clearly the "institutional leaders of the city" whom Roger Starr has in mind are mostly named Rockefeller, although he never comes right out and says so. No such reticence is to be found in yet another writer who traces many of our social ills to the influence of modernism—Daniel Bell, who in a recent article entitled "The Revolt Against Modernity," essentially a rehash of the book he first published in 1976 called *The Cultural Contradictions of Capitalism,* speaks of the Museum of Modern Art in New York as "a satrapy of the Rockefeller family."[3] (One somehow doubts that Professor Bell would ever refer to Rockefeller University, that citadel of scientific research, as a "satrapy of the Rockefeller family," but that's the way it goes with the enemies of modernism. Which is to say, anything goes—even if a word like "satrapy" in this context evokes nothing so much as the pages of the old *New Masses.*) That for Daniel Bell modernism *is* the enemy we can have no doubt, for he had already confided to us in *The Cultural Contradictions of Capitalism* that "I see Modernism as the agency for the dissolution of the bourgeois world view."[4]

---

2 *The Rise and Fall of New York City* by Roger Starr (Basic Books, 1985), page 219.

3 "The Revolt Against Modernity" by Daniel Bell, in *The Public Interest* (Fall 1985), page 57.

4 *The Cultural Contradictions of Capitalism* by Daniel Bell (Harper Torchbooks edition, 1978), page xxi.

What makes the discussion interesting, of course, is that Jameson rejects modernism because it has proved so conclusively to be, in effect, a *coefficient* of the bourgeois world view. The Left rejects modernism because it is seen to be an integral part of bourgeois democracy; the Right, if that is the word for these writers, rejects modernism because it is seen to subvert bourgeois democracy.

Jameson is, I suppose, a Marxist of some sort—let us call him a post-structuralist Marxist. He is certainly anti-capitalist and anti-bourgeois. Bell likes to call himself a socialist—and, as we have seen, he does have a fondness for the old socialist rhetoric. Whether he is really anti-capitalist or anti-bourgeois, however, I have my doubts. Roger Starr has sometimes been called a neoconservative, and this is a position close to my own (at least on matters other than modernism and culture). Starr is certainly pro-capitalist and pro-bourgeois. Yet despite these differences in the content of their respective criticisms, such distinctions play little or no role in the passion and prejudice which these writers (and so many others) bring to this debate.

Now this is quite the most remarkable thing about this debate, and what really identifies it as marking a new development in the history of modernism—the way it has ignited passions and confounded all the old alignments. What we are witnessing is, among much else, an historic breakdown in the divisions which once separated radicals from conservatives, for instance, or the avant-garde from the philistines—divisions which served for so long to chart the course of modern cultural life.

As a result of this altered situation, the old terms have lost much, if not quite all, of their meaning. Those who pride themselves on being either radicals, on the one hand, or philistines, on the other, need no longer, at least on the question of modernism, necessarily find themselves in adamant opposition (as, of course, they once would have been). As for the champions of modernism—who, not so long ago, would have been universally regarded as the opponents of reaction—they, or I should say *we,* now often find ourselves described, and not unjustly either, as representatives of a conservative impulse. We are indeed in a new historical situation in which positions once easily stigmatized or praised as radical or conservative, avant-garde or philistine, no longer always serve as a reliable guide to the beliefs and commitments which govern cultural life.

How, then, does it happen that on this question the old alignments have so completely broken down, and there is now arrayed against modernism and its achievements such a vigorous and wide-ranging campaign of deconstruction and disinformation?

The essential precondition of this campaign was, of course, the absorption of modernism into the mainstream of American cultural life. Not until modernism achieved—and was clearly seen to achieve—its mainstream status in the academy, in the marketplace, in the media, and in our institutions generally, did it begin to come under the current critical assault. Virtually all of the earlier attacks on modernism had emanated from a fundamentally middlebrow cultural establishment concerned to defend and reaffirm its own legitimacy in the face of what were looked upon as upstart or malevolent challenges to its authority. These earlier attacks on modernism had failed to be effective, as we know—and largely, I believe, because they finally had nothing to offer as an alternative to the modernist tide. When that failure came to be widely recognized, then the way was clear for modernism to itself become the established culture, and that is what it did become.

This is a development we can date with a fair degree of precision, even if we cannot wholly account for the rapidity with which it occurred when it did occur. It happened in the early 1960s, in the Kennedy period, and in my view we cannot really expect to understand the current assault on modernism if we fail to grasp that it was in the Sixties that modernism first established its authority as mainstream culture. For both modernism as mainstream culture and the accelerating assault on modernism, which began in the Seventies and has reached a point of crisis in the Eighties, are together part of what the Sixties bequeathed to American culture and American society.

This aspect of the Sixties has been very little understood, I believe, for its beginnings predate the developments we generally associate with the Sixties—the emergence of the counterculture and the antiwar movement and the tremendous changes they brought in their wake. In our preoccupation with the consequences of that upheaval we tend to forget that the Sixties witnessed an extraordinary expansion in the cultural life of the nation, and that this expansion occurred largely, though not exclusively, in those areas which brought high culture—high culture as distinguished from popular culture—to a public larger than any which had theretofore been receptive to it.

We need only recall that this was an era that saw the building of a great many new museums and the expansion of a great many existing museums. It brought us Lincoln Center in New York, and many similar complexes around the country. It was in this period, too, that dance emerged for the first time as a mainstream artistic interest, and there were similar developments in other fields.

What has not been much remarked upon, however, is that it was in the Sixties, too, that the media underwent a drastic change in attitude toward the arts, and especially in its attitude toward modernism in the arts. We tend to forget that it wasn't until the Sixties that a living painter or sculptor of modernist persuasion could expect to receive a sympathetic response from the principal art critics on such publications as *Time* and *Newsweek* and *The New York Times*. On this matter I can speak from personal experience, for it was in the fall of 1965 that I was invited to join the staff of *The New York Times,* and the editors who offered me the job made it very clear that they now felt obliged for the first time to employ a critic who could be counted upon to be more informed and up-to-date about modern art than those they had generally employed in the past. (They had already made one or two attempts at this, but none had worked out.) For they weren't looking for a cheerleader, and, I might add, they certainly didn't get one when they hired me. But they were looking for a writer who took the subject with the requisite seriousness. As the then executive editor of *The Times,* Turner Catledge, explained to me (with something of a sigh): "Our readers are now a lot smarter about all this than we are." To keep these readers and win still others the managers of the paper felt it necessary to redress the balance, and this meant—in some fields at least—joining the modernist tide instead of opposing it.

To redress the balance—in fact, to catch up on the artistic and cultural reality of the moment—was very much what this shift in the early Sixties was about. Tremendous changes had taken place in American cultural life in the Fifties which were accorded little, if any, sympathetic representation in mainstream cultural institutions and almost none in the mainstream media. In the visual arts, for example, the New York School had established itself in the Fifties as the leading international art movement of the post-World War II period, yet it was accorded no recognition in such institutions as the Metropolitan Museum or the National Gallery in Washington. Even the Museum of Modern Art, which in principle specialized in such developments, gave the movement only sporadic recognition until 1959 when it mounted a major exhibition, called "The New American Painting," for the first time. There were exceptions, of course—a critic here, a curator there, an adventurous collector or two—but for the most part what might be called mainstream highbrow taste—elite taste—in the Fifties still favored French painting over anything American and representational art over anything abstract.

By the early Sixties there existed in this country a public that was large and growing which felt very keenly this discrepancy between what I have called the cultural reality of the moment—anyone who had been to school in the Fifties understood that modernism in one form or another was at the heart of it—and the paucity of its representation in the mainstream institutional life of culture. Out of an interest in their own survival and prosperity, it was thus in the early Sixties that these mainstream institutions set about closing the gap. How it was done, and whether the doing kept faith with the original impulse, whether something valuable and important got lost in the process—all these are questions worth exploring on another occasion. The point to be grasped here, however, is that it was *not* the institutional life of culture which initiated the change—the institutions responded to a change which had already occurred. They initiated nothing in the realm of artistic creation; they were attempting to catch up with and keep abreast of what had already been created and had already elicited a significant response. It was out of this situation, moreover, that the National Endowment for the Arts first emerged in 1965—as a response to a cultural development already in progress.

How this shift of modernist culture into the mainstream would have turned out if, as the Sixties developed on its headlong course, there had been no war in Vietnam, no rock music or birth-control pill, no military draft or drug culture or antiwar movement or Woodstock, etc., we are not in a position to know. All of these upheavals did occur—they swamped us, and we are still, in a sense, digging our way out of the debris which they left in their wake.

What, we may ask, was the fate of modernism in this historical upheaval? What role, if any, was it seen to have played in the counterculture and the antiwar movement and the sexual revolution of the Sixties and early Seventies? This, I think, is the crucial question, for it is in relation to the role assigned to modernism at this turn in our history that the current crop of modernism's avowed enemies has emerged.

By and large, and allowing for differences in emphasis and nuance, the roles assigned to modernism in the upheavals of the Sixties by its current enemies derive from two very distinct interpretations of what modernism was and is. The first, which is now clearly identified with the political Left, rejects modernism out of a sense of bitter disappointment and betrayal. (This is the position of Jameson and his numerous academic brethren.) This view may be summed up as follows: Modernism claimed to be revolutionary, it claimed to be anti-bourgeois, it promised us a new world, but it turned out to be a coefficient of bourgeois capitalist culture, after all, and we therefore reject it as counterrevolutionary and indeed reactionary. And further, since modernism is in some sense the only high culture which currently exists in living form, we also reject the claims of high culture and must work to destroy the privileged status it enjoys in the cultural life of the bourgeois democracies. Hence the new role assigned to popular culture as an agency of political deconstruction.

That, I think it is fair to say, just about sums up the judgment which the intellectual Left has made on modernism as a cultural movement.

It is more difficult to characterize the second categorical interpretation of modernism made by its enemies on the basis of its role in the upheavals of the Sixties—the interpretation which unites Roger Starr, Daniel Bell, and a good many others. As I said, Bell claims to be a socialist and Starr has been called a neoconservative. Lionel Trilling, upon whose ideas Bell and other writers of this persuasion so much depend, regarded himself as a liberal but was regarded by many others as a conservative. So what can we call this interpretation? Despite what I have said earlier about the fallen status of the word, I am afraid we must fall back, after all, on the term *philistine*—it is the one that will have to do until we can come up with a better one.

This philistine view, then, may be summed up as follows: Modernism was largely responsible for all the upheavals of the Sixties. What we saw happen in the Sixties was the ethos of modernism translated into action, modernism brought into the streets, so to speak, and enacted in every aspect of the sexual revolution and the whole counterculture.

In this view, Woodstock was in some sense the culmination of the modernist dream of a society in a permanent state of orgy and ecstasy. Above all, modernism promised us the destruction of capitalism and bourgeois life, and the Sixties showed us just how subversive modernism could be if its governing ideas were acted upon.

But how much of the culture of modernism was it that dreamed of a society in a permanent state of orgy and ecstasy? In actuality, the counterculture of the Sixties derived from ideas which were deeply inimical to the fundamental modalities of modernist thought if we take the latter—as I think we must—to be represented by such figures as Flaubert and Henry James and Marcel Proust, T. S. Eliot and Wallace Stevens and even the early Ezra Pound, Manet and Cézanne and Matisse and Picasso and Brancusi and Miró and the painters of the New York School, Igor Stravinsky and Arnold Schoenberg, etc. It wasn't the works of James Joyce or Thomas Mann or Ernest Hemingway or Gertrude Stein which were carried in the rucksacks of the antiwar marchers, and it wasn't to the music of Stravinsky or Schoenberg that they marched.

Now the exact relation in which the high culture of modernism stands to the cultural upheavals of the Sixties and the exact relation in which the high culture of modernism stands to capitalism and bourgeois democracy are both questions of a far greater complexity than the enemies of modernism can bring themselves to acknowledge. The Left position wishes to delegitimize modernism for failing to fulfill a revolutionary function; the philisitine position wishes to delegitimize modernism by making it the scapegoat for social developments it regards as calamitous. Both, I submit, are based on caricatures of history.

That there has been from the beginning of the modernist movement a *révolté* element is not to be denied, of course, but it was rarely, if ever, the dominant element, and in each case where a group or movement, such as Futurism or Dada, allied itself with a politically revolutionary cause, it was the aesthetic component—not the politics—which proved to be enduring, and which came to play a role in shaping the sensibility of high culture in bourgeois societies. That, of course, is what is so frustrating about modernism for the ideological Left—that the principal achievement of modernism always turns out to be aesthetic rather than political. And as the Left has no way of accommodating the aesthetic either as a mode of cognition or as an autonomous cultural enterprise—both of which may be said to constitute the very foundations of what modernism finally represents—it must consign it, either literally or figuratively, to the so-called superstructure. But the philistine position cannot accommodate the notion of an independent aesthetic impulse, either, and so aesthetic achievements must likewise be stigmatized as ideological if they are to be discussed at all.

Something more than modernism is also being caricatured in these attacks—namely, the bourgeoisie, in other words, you and me, and the life of the mind in middle-class, capitalist society. Reading through this vast literature on the failures and/or crimes of modernism, one would scarcely suspect that bourgeois life had been changed more than a little, and by and large for the better, since Balzac and Flaubert wrote about it in their novels, or that the culture of modernism has played a decisive role in making bourgeois life a more liberal, a more enlightened, and a spiritually more spacious environment than it once was. The truth is, the culture of modernism has served all along as the aesthetic and spiritual conscience, and sometimes even the moral conscience, of middle-class life, and it is this which has made it pre-eminently the culture of democratic capitalist society, however many the conflicts it may still have with that society, and it is this which has made the culture of modernism so anathema to anti-democratic political regimes. Isn't what is really at stake, then, in this attack on modernism something central to the vital cultural life of our democratic society? Central, that is to say, to democracy itself? I think it is.

(*March* 1986)

"But today the struggle": Spain and the intellectuals

by Ronald Radosh

Coming to terms with the truth about the Spanish Civil War seems more than ever to pose insurmountable difficulties for those intellectuals—perhaps the majority—who were brought up to believe that Spain in the Thirties was the one great cause in that "low dishonest decade," as Auden called it, which need never be either reconsidered or repented. Yet the publication of two new anthologies on the fiftieth anniversary of the war—Valentine Cunningham's *Spanish Front* and John Miller's *Voices Against Tyranny*—together with the discussion they have generated come as a sober reminder that this is a subject that remains part of the unfinished business of recent intellectual history.[1] "No episode in the 1930s," Paul Johnson has aptly observed, "has been more lied about than this one, and only in recent years have historians begun to dig it out from the mountain of mendacity beneath which it was buried for a generation."[2] Judging from some recent commentaries on Spain in the Thirties, there are still many intellectuals who would prefer—even today—to let the terrible truth remain buried rather than have their fantasies of a noble past destroyed.

For most Left intellectuals, in fact, Spain in the Thirties is a cause to be reaffirmed rather than investigated. Reviewing *Spanish Front* and *Voices Against Tyranny* in *The New York Times*, for example, Herbert Mitgang wrote that for all the doubts caused by the actions of Soviet commissars in Spain, George Orwell and other intellectuals "never regretted that they had gone to Spain" in support of the Republican side.[3] In the same vein, Christopher Hitchens, writing about Spain in *Grand Street*, asserts that there is "something creepy about the 'compulsion' to chuck Old Left causes [like the Spanish Civil War] over the side."[4] Despite all that Hitchens claims to understand about the betrayal of the Spanish Republic by the Soviets and the Communists, he cites Orwell to support his conclusion that Spain in the Thirties "was a state of affairs worth fighting for." And writing in *The New Republic*, the distinguished literary critic Alfred Kazin offers the same quotation from Orwell—who was talking about the libertarian-anarchist revolution of 1936—and comments that "truth would always be Orwell's ace in the hole." To Kazin, the "truth" is that the Civil War is simply "the wound that will not

1 *Spanish Front: Writers on the Civil War*, edited by Valentine Cunningham, Oxford University Press, 388 pages, $7.95; and *Voices Against Tyranny: Writing of the Spanish Civil War*, edited by John Miller, Charles Scribner's Sons, 227 pages, $7.95.

2 Paul Johnson, *Modern Times: The World from the Twenties to the Eighties*. Harper & Row, 1983, pages 321-340. Other citations from Paul Johnson are from these pages.

3 Herbert Mitgang, *The New York Times*, August 18, 1986, page C18.

4 Christopher Hitchens, "Re-Bunking," *Grand Street*, Summer 1986, pages 228-231.

heal"; hence, the "destroyers of the Spanish Republic would always be my enemies."[5]

To those like Kazin who still consider Spain "their" war, it was the one pure cause of the 1930s. "It was the passion of that small segment of my generation," Murray Kempton has written, "which felt a personal commitment to the revolution."[6] The cause was easily definable—support of a legally elected democratic government battling reactionary generals who fought to install a Spanish version of fascism. The democratic Republic stood alone: the Western democracies stayed neutral and refused to sell it arms, while the regimes in Germany and Italy rushed men, airplanes, and weapons to aid General Franco's rebellion. Defense of the Republic became a symbol for all that was good and decent, as the "progressive" world organized against the tides of reaction and Nazism.

The truth, of course, is not so simple. The Civil War took place because indecisive elections in February 1936 revealed a nation divided in half; the irresponsible militancy of sectors of the more extreme Left fed the aims of the insurgent generals. Once civil war broke out, both sides were responsible for unspeakable and equally repugnant atrocities. The foreign intervention of Germany prevented Franco's defeat, just as Soviet military aid allowed the Republic the means to beat back the initial advance of Franco's forces.

The problem was that the Soviet Union exacted a harsh price from the Spanish Republic for receipt of that military aid. Stalin's involvement came rather late in the war, by way of a policy of cautious military intervention. Soviet tanks, planes, and artillery did not reach Spain until October and November of 1936, and they were of a limited caliber—no match for the heavy equipment supplied by the Germans and Italians. Even so, Stalin insisted upon payment in advance; he took the valued gold reserves of the Republic out of Spain and into Russia. Fearing involvement in a war with Germany and Italy, Stalin limited his aid to bolstering the resistance of the anti-Franco forces in the hope that Britain and France might be induced to abandon their policy of non-intervention.

Stalin's cynical goal was to steer internal developments in Spain to coincide with the foreign policy objectives of the Soviet Union. He wanted to prolong the existence of the Republic until the Western democracies joined him in supporting the Republicans. It was a strategy of stalemate: Stalin purposely never gave the Republic enough arms with which to win. At the same time, he secretly began to negotiate with Nazi Germany, hedging his bet lest the first course fail to produce results.

The price paid by the Republic for the much-heralded Soviet aid was the factor that led to the ultimate betrayal. In exchange for military aid, Stalin demanded the transformation of the once free Republic into a prototype of what became the People's Democracies in the postwar world. The findings of historians have helped us to understand just how total Soviet control of the Spanish Republic had become. Indeed, the most recent contributions starkly confirm the validity of the revelations of General Walter Krivitsky, the very first defector from the NKVD (the forerunner of the KGB). At the time—in 1938—much of the left-wing world treated Krivitsky's confession as anti-Bolshevik paranoia—most especially his revelation that Stalin was already dealing with the Nazis, but also his detailed accounts of the torture and police-state methods brought to Spain by the Soviets as part of their program of "assistance." We know now that Krivitsky was telling the truth.

When Hugh Thomas published the first edition of his now classic work, *The Spanish Civil War,* in 1961, he warned readers that "Krivitsky's evidence must be regarded as tainted unless corroborated." By 1966, when he brought out the second edition of his history, Thomas had revised that early

5 Alfred Kazin, "The Wound That Will Not Heal," *The New Republic,* August 25, 1986, pages 39-41.

6 Murray Kempton, *Part of Our Time.* Dell, 1955, page 317.

judgment, and wrote that "Krivitsky's evidence can generally be accepted."[7] But it was left to Burnett Bolloten, author of the majestic historical study—forty years in the making—*The Spanish Revolution* (1979), to give Krivitsky's work a close reading, and to conclude not only that this NKVD general was telling the truth but that "Krivitsky's revelations have proved to be amazingly accurate, including many of the smallest details, and they constitute a major contribution to our knowledge of Soviet foreign policy aims and Soviet intervention in the Spanish civil war."[8] Regarding torture, Krivitsky had written that what the Russians brought to the Republic was unmitigated repression and terror—a civil war against the Spanish Left. The regular police corps was reorganized. Communists secured the pivotal positions in the newly rebuilt police, which became a formal part of the Soviet apparatus in Spain. The NKVD, Krivitsky wrote in his memoirs, "had its own special prisons. Its units carried out assassinations and kidnappings, filled hidden dungeons and made flying raids. It functioned . . . independently of the Loyalist government . . . . The Soviet Union seemed to have a grip on Loyalist Spain, as if it were already a Soviet possession."[9]

At the time, of course, these comments were treated as smears by an untrustworthy renegade who was said to be in league with the Nazis. Just how accurate Krivitsky actually was, however, can best be appreciated by looking at the conclusions reached by the dean of left-wing British historians, E. H. Carr. Carr was as sympathetic to the Soviet Union as any historian could be, yet he declared in his posthumously published book, *The Comintern and the Spanish Civil War,* that by 1937 the Russians had brought to Spain an institution known as SIM, "a new body whose professed function was counter espionage," and that it "quickly spread its tentacles to all parts of Republican Spain, occupying itself with repression and torture." Spain, Carr wrote, had become "what its enemies called it, the puppet of Moscow."[10]

Another British historian, Antony Beevor, writes in his book *The Spanish Civil War* that the torture introduced was of a new and quantitatively different caliber.[11] It went beyond "beatings with rubber piping, hot and cold water treatment, splinters inserted under nails and mock executions." Under Soviet direction, Beevor tells us, "cell floors were specially constructed with the sharp corners of bricks pointing upward so that the naked prisoners were in constant pain. Strange metallic sounds, colours, lights and sloping floors were used as disorientation and sensory-deprivation techniques."[12]

The evidence is unmistakable that, by 1937, the Spanish "Red" Republic had more in common with Franco's territories in Spain, or with the authoritarian regime after his victory, than it did with the libertarian revolt of 1936 that had been heralded by the much-quoted George Orwell. As Beevor so aptly writes, the Communists were in "many ways the counterpart of Franco . . . practitioners of statecraft [who] . . . exploited the war emergency to label any opposition . . . as treasonable to the cause." As one Anarchist militant put it: for the people of Spain, "whether Negrin won with his communist cohorts, or Franco won with his Italians and Germans, the results would be the same for us."[13]

What if the Republic, and not Franco, had won? In *The Spanish Revolution,* the historian

---

7 Hugh Thomas, *The Spanish Civil War.* Eyer and Spottiswood, 1961, page 263; revised edition, Penguin, 1965, page 337. A third edition was published by Harper & Row last month.

8 Burnett Bolloten, *The Spanish Revolution: The Left and the Struggle for Power during the Civil War.* University of North Carolina Press, 1979, page 110.

9 Walter G. Krivitsky, *In Stalin's Secret Service.* Harper, 1939, pages 102-107, 291.

10 E. H. Carr, *The Comintern and the Spanish Civil War.* Pantheon, 1984, page 44; page 31.

11 Antony Beevor, *The Spanish Civil War.* Orbis Publishing, 1982, pages 211-212.

12 Beevor, page 281.

13 The anarchist militant is Abad de Santillan, quoted in Beevor, page 194.

Stanley G. Payne judges that if one goes by left-wing policy during the Civil War, there is little reason to assume that a Communist-dominated Republic would have shown any tolerance for dissent or even led to a subsiding of brutal internal terror. Indeed, Payne writes, "there was nothing in Franco's zone to equal the almost constant interparty murder that went on under the People's Republic." This reality, Payne argues, accounted for much of the "final collapse of morale" within the Republican ranks.[14]

Even one former Spanish militant in the PCE (Spanish Communist Party), the future novelist and screenwriter Jorge Semprun (who was a leader of the Communist underground between 1959 and 1964), admits that, under Franco's authoritarian reign, Spain reached a higher level of material and social progress, along with industrial and military strength, than existed in any "socialist" regime under Soviet control. And, he adds, under Franco the working class in Spain had more freedom than their counterpart in any country "improperly called Socialist." In the Eastern European states, "it is not allowed to strike. It can organize itself only in labor unions that are mere transmission belts of the state apparatus and the single party, compared to which the vertical unions of the Franco dictatorship were genuine democratic paradises."[15] One can honestly agree with the judgment of Joaquín Maurín, once an intellectual activist with the Communist-syndicalist Worker Peasant Bloc, who wrote a full quarter of a century later, in 1966, that "from the moment in which the alternative was posed, beginning in June 1937, between the Communist party, at the orders of Moscow, or the opposing military regime, reactionary but Spanish, the conclusion of the Civil War was predetermined."[16]

14 Stanley G. Payne, *The Spanish Revolution.* Norton, 1970, page 313.

15 Jorge Semprun, *The Autobiography of Federico Sanchez and the Communist Underground in Spain.* Karz, 1979, page 133.

16 Cited in Payne, page 374.

Understanding some of this history is a prerequisite for evaluating the story of the Western intellectuals and their response to the Civil War. As we have seen, Alfred Kazin and others make much of Orwell's statement that though there was much he did not understand and did not even like about revolutionary Barcelona, "I recognized it immediately as a state of affairs worth fighting for." The quotation is accurate, but those who cite Orwell tend to omit the careful distinction he made between the original revolt and the very different reality after 1937. Orwell recognized this new reality full well, and he did not like what he saw. While he heralded Spain of August 1936 as a people's revolt, he had reached the sad conclusion that by January of 1937 "the Communists were using every possible method, fair and foul, to stamp out what was left of the revolution." He went on to cite, as one of his reviews reprinted in *Spanish Front* reminds us, "the ceaseless arrests, the censored newspapers and the prowling hordes of armed police," comparing the situation to a "nightmare."[17] Does anyone really think that this was the Spain that Orwell saw as worth defending and fighting for?

Spain, as Mr. Kazin has so eloquently reminded us, became the central metaphor for artists, intellectuals, and writers of the 1930s. Hemingway immortalized the conflict in *For Whom the Bell Tolls,* although the veterans of the International Brigades were angered by his critical portrayal of the fanatic French commissar, André Marty. Nicknamed "the butcher of Albacete" because of his murder of at least five hundred of his own men for desertion or Trotskyism, Marty is believed to have killed, by a minimum count, one-tenth of all the volunteers who died in Spain.

"Madrid is the heart," of a world, a civilization and an ideal, Auden opined in his poem "Spain" (1937). He spoke for a generation when he said one had to put aside "the

17 George Orwell, "Spanish Nightmare," from *Time & Tide,* July 31, 1937; reprinted in Cunningham, pages 316-317.

walks by the lake . . . the bicycle races." There was only one task: "But to-day the struggle."[18] These two new anthologies devoted to writings about the Spanish Civil War remind us of just how much the attitude epitomized by Auden's poem (which he subsequently—to his honor—repudiated) was typical of the intellectual response at the time. They also serve to remind us, as Paul Johnson wrote, that "the intellectuals of the Left did not want to know the objective truth; they were unwilling for their illusions to be shattered. They were overwhelmed by the glamour and excitement of the cause and few had the gritty determination of Orwell to uphold absolute standards of morality."

In this respect, the role of Stephen Spender is particularly instructive. Spender has written the introduction to John Miller's anthology, *Voices Against Tyranny,* and he uses the opportunity to reflect on what Spain meant to the writers and artists of his generation. Spender now says that Auden, who had been criticized by Orwell for the poem on Spain, "came to agree with Orwell to the extent of feeling that his conscientious attempt to politicize his poetry in support of 'Spain' led him into very alien territory"; it opened him, Auden felt, to the grave charge of "using poetry to tell lies." Hence, because of the concluding lines of "Spain," Auden never allowed it to be reprinted during the remainder of his lifetime. The last lines of the poem had declared that

> History to the defeated
> May say Alas but cannot help nor pardon.

Auden commented that "[T]his is a lie." As for himself, Spender now admits that "there were atrocities on the Republican side perhaps equalling those committed by the rebels." On the subject of atrocities, however, he never refers to Arthur Koestler's account, in *The Invisible Writing,* of the way Comintern propagandist Otto Katz manufactured phony fascist atrocities out of his office in Paris.[19] This is an important part of the story, for Stalinism was thus aided, as Paul Johnson writes, "not only by superb public relations but by the naïveté, gullibility and, it must also be said, the mendacity and corruption of Western intellectuals, especially their willingness to overlook what W. H. Auden called 'the necessary murder.'"

One might hope that, fifty years later, Western intellectuals would have more perspective on the events that once moved them into such tight corners. Yet, judging from Spender's introduction to *Voices Against Tyranny,* Spain still appears to be what Spender calls a simple "direct confrontation between good and evil, right and wrong, freedom and tyranny." In this view, there was only one bad side—that of Franco. Spender does observe that Auden and he too curbed their true shock over things like the destruction of the churches. Looking back, he reflects, there was an authentic Wordsworthian recognition of the joys of rebellion, but he bemoans the fact "that we could not see any of the terrible murders happening behind this scene of revolution." He now acknowledges "that there is no trust to be placed in travellers' impressions of popular rejoicing soon after revolution."

Spender, however, is still being disingenuous. His own career is a salutary reminder of how total identification with the "right" side corrupts intellectual integrity. One of the documents reprinted in Valentine Cunningham's *Spanish Front* is Spender's "I Join the Communist Party"—printed in the London *Daily Worker* in 1937—in which Spender apologized for first doubting that the Moscow trials were anything but honest, and explained that he now understood the nature "of the gigantic plot against the Soviet Government." This early heresy, Spender told his new comrades, occurred because he was then only "a liberal approaching com-

---

18 W. H. Auden, "Spain," from *The English Auden: Poems, Essays and Dramatic Writings 1927-1939,* reprinted in Miller, page 211.

19 Arthur Koestler, *The Invisible Writing.* Macmillan, 1954, page 327.

munism." Now that Spender understood that Stalin was right, he was ready to join the Party, evidently a necessity if one desired to go to Valencia to engage in anti-Fascist propaganda.[20]

Having joined the Party, Spender became an ardent spokesman for it. In that capacity, he took part in the International Writers' Congress held in Madrid in 1937. This was the prototype of those events that were later to occur with regularity in Havana during the 1960s and Nicaragua in the 1980s—events in which Western intellectuals reaffirm their closeness to the revolutionary struggle by partying in its midst. In Spain, Spender recorded, he and other delegates were "treated like princes or ministers . . . riding in Rolls Royces, banqueted, fêted, sung and danced to," all while the battle raged around them. The same Writers' Congress was noted for its conclusion, which consisted of a massive attack on André Gide, who was excoriated as a "fascist monster" for the book he had recently published criticizing the USSR.[21]

Spender's 1937 account tells how they were "woken up at 4 a.m. by the air-raid alarms," as the reality of the war intruded upon the Congress. Evidently, it did not intrude too much for Spender to proclaim that the Spanish writer José Bergamín was the right man to rebuke Gide, because Bergamín had a "mind which sees not merely the truth of isolated facts which Gide observed in the USSR, but the far more important truth of the effect which Gide's book is going to have."

If Spender bought the classic rationale of the Stalinized intellectual, it was this affair that caused another participant in the Congress, the Dutch Communist Jef Last, to suffer a severe disillusionment. Proud that the Congress condemned the murder of writers by Franco and other Fascists, Last asked, "why this conspiracy of silence around the cultural reaction in Russia . . . ?" Last could not accept the argument, presented to him by Egon Erwin Kisch, that when you hear of a Fascist bombing of a school you have "to defend everything that has been done on our side, *even the trials!*" Acting alone, Last protested against the Soviet delegates' demands that Gide be attacked by the Congress. Indeed, he pointed out, few in attendance had even read the book they were being asked to condemn. Gide had not been translated into Spanish and his book was not available anywhere in Spain.[22]

Spender then stood with the regular Communists. Later, of course, he broke with them, and today he writes that there is a "'truth' of 'Spain' that remained independent of, and survived the mold of, Communism into which successive Republican governments were forced." Even anti-Communists who supported the Republic, Spender writes, "nevertheless retained their belief in the justice of the Republican cause."

But when Spender was in Spain—at the very time he was attending the 1937 Congress and spoke in Britain on behalf of aid for the International Brigades—he privately held to a different "truth." It is to the credit of Valentine Cunningham that he includes the remarkable letter which Spender wrote to Virginia Woolf on April 2, 1937, in which the poet reflects that "politicians are detestable anywhere," and that Spain has shown him "the lies and unscrupulousness of some of the people who are recruiting at home" for the International Brigades, including those "of the *Daily Worker.*" He had not seen the poet Julian Bell, her nephew, Spender wrote to Woolf, and he assumed that "he has not joined the Brigade." While Spender himself spoke in England in favor of the volunteers, he told Woolf that he

20 Stephen Spender, "I Join the Communist Party," London *Daily Worker,* February 19, 1937, in Cunningham, pages 7-9.

21 Stephen Spender, "Spain Invites the World's Writers," from *Notes on the International Congress, Summer 1937* from *New Writing,* Autumn 1937, in Cunningham, pages 85-91. Gide's book, *Retour de l'U.R.S.S.,* was published in 1936.

22 Jef Last, from *The Spanish Tragedy.* Routledge and Kegan Paul, 1939; in Cunningham, pages 94-100.

hoped Bell "will not do so," since participating in the Brigades called for "terrific narrowness and a religious dogmatism about the Communist Party line," as well as "toughness, cynicism and insensibility."[23]

Since Spender never said anything similar in public—and does not say anything like this in print even today—his letter is riveting. "The sensitive, the weak, the romantic, the enthusiastic, the truthful live in Hell," he wrote to Woolf, "and cannot get away." The Hell he spoke of was not that of Franco. "The political commissars . . . bully so much that even people who were quite enthusiastic Party Members have been driven into hating the whole thing." Spender told the story of one veteran he spoke with, who "complained to me bitterly about the inquisitional methods of the Party." Noting that it was a lie that the men were volunteers who could leave when they liked, Spender wrote Woolf that actually they were "trapped there," and wounds or mental collapse were not considered grounds for leaving, "unless one belongs to the Party élite and is sent home as a propagandist to show one's arm in a sling to audiences." Bitterly, Spender revealed that his closest friend fought in an offensive in which the men were sent to be slaughtered, with only olive groves for protection. After his friend's mental collapse, Spender tried to hire him as his personal secretary. The Party refused, and sent the man back to battle. He sought to escape, and was then put in a labor camp. Spender asked that nothing he had written be repeated, particularly "the more unpleasant truths about the Brigade."

Privately, Spender sought to help such men leave Spain, and he condemned the total fanaticism of the Party leaders who were really "unconcerned with Spain" and were intolerant of any dissent. But such truths had to be carefully guarded. Thus, Spender asked Woolf to quote his letter anonymously "to any pacifist or democrat who wants to fight." Privately, he hoped they would refrain from enlistment with the International Brigades. Publicly, Spender towed the line, and his published poems supported the cause. Of the martyred John Cornford, he said, in a review written in September of 1938, that he exemplified "the potentialities of a generation" that was fighting "for a form of society for which [it] was also willing to die."[24] When Spender wrote the letter to Virginia Woolf, was he secretly hoping that she would show it to Cornford before he made the fatal decision to join the battle, as Cornford wrote, "whether I like it or not"?

How are we to judge a writer who says one thing to a friend in private and quite the opposite to an innocent and credulous public on such a momentous issue? It is no wonder that Richard Gott was recently moved to observe that, the more we gain some historical perspective on Spain, "the more blurred becomes the morality."[25] It is worth remembering, however, that there *were* some writers who grasped the morality of the situation at the time, and showed an exemplary bravery and candor in acknowledging the villainy of their chosen side. The Catholic writer Georges Bernanos, once a supporter of the rightist and anti-Semitic Action Française, saw firsthand the horror of the atrocities perpetrated by the Franco forces and sanctified by the Catholic priests. In his searing account from *A Diary of My Times* (1938), which appears in the Cunningham anthology, Bernanos tells of "the organizing of Terrorism" by the Italian Black Shirts brought to Majorca by Franco.[26] Bernanos recoiled in horror at the figure of three thousand killed by right-wing death squads, as we would call them today, in a

---

23 Stephen Spender to Virginia Woolf, April 2, 1937, Henry W. and Albert A. Berg Collection, New York Public Library, Astor, Lenox and Tuden Foundations, in Cunningham, pages 307-309.

24 Review of *John Cornford: A Memoir*; *New Statesman & Nation*, November 12, 1938, in Cunningham, pages 328-330.

25 Richard Gott, "The Spanish Tragedy," *Manchester Guardian Weekly*, July 27, 1986, page 22.

26 Georges Bernanos, *A Diary of My Times*. The Bodley Head, 1938; in Cunningham, pages 145-152.

brief seven-month period. On that small island, he wrote, one could "witness the blowing-out of fifteen wrong-thinking brains per day." Hating "the sound and sight of it," Bernanos told the world the truth, despite the fact that it meant he was criticizing his own side. Bernanos saw that civil war meant "there is no longer any justice," and he pointed out that even moderate Republicans were shot "like dogs just the same," even though they had nothing to do with the Red Terror of Barcelona. To this Catholic intellectual, civil war meant terrorism had become "the order of the day."

On the Left, Simone Weil was Bernanos's counterpart. "[H]oping every day," she wrote in a letter to Bernanos, ". . . for the victory of one side and the defeat of the other," Weil went to Spain in August 1936.[27] After two months there, Weil no longer saw the war as one "of starving peasants against landed proprietors and a clergy in league" with them, but instead she viewed it as "a war between Russia, Germany and Italy." Almost witnessing an unjustified execution of a priest by Republican militants was enough to push Weil toward pacifism. Seeing the famed anarchist Durruti execute a young Falangist soldier, who had been conscripted against his will, never stopped weighing on her conscience. What Weil objected to was the relentless pleasure in murder that occurred on all sides. Killing "Fascists" and seeing them as beasts made the Republicans, in Weil's view, no better than the enemy; they too were excluding "a category of human beings from among those whose lives have worth." Such behavior, she wrote in her letter to Bernanos in 1938, soon obscured "the very purpose of the struggle." She had her sympathies with the anarchists and their cause, but Weil put her finger on what made the soldiers—as it made the Marxist guerrillas of the 1960s—a new elite. "An abyss separated the men with the weapons," Weil wrote, "from the unarmed population," an abyss Weil saw as similar to that which separated "the rich from the poor." Hence Weil felt that Bernanos, a monarchist, was closer to her than the proletarian comrades of the Aragon militia she had come to Spain to support.

If the Spanish War was a "People's War," as Valentine Cunningham claims, "the most potent and emotionally engaging focus of thirties democratic struggles and progressive working-class ambitions," it was also a writers' war, in which almost all writers felt the need to take sides. It is true that most writers of merit were on the Republican side. But can one say with a clear conscience that the forces of the Republic were fighting, as Cunningham suggests, for the survival of art and culture in free societies, when, had the Red side won, such a free society would have been just as much at risk as it was after the Franco victory?

Orwell had warned, in the concluding pages of *Homage to Catalonia*, that one should beware of partisanship, and of the distortion caused by his having seen only one corner of events. And he warned that readers should "beware of exactly the same things when you read any other book on this period." What happened, of course, was that writers went to Spain and, on the basis of brief tours, committed themselves and their art to the cause. Weil noted that it was "in fashion to go on a tour down there, to take in a spot of revolution, and to come back with articles bursting out of your pen." She noted such endeavors had to be superficial, especially since in the gale of civil war and revolution "principles get completely out of phase with realities," and the criterion for judging events disappears. How, she queried, could one "report something coherently on the strength of a short stay and some fragmentary observations?"

The problem continues into our own day. As Paul Hollander has lately reminded us, scores of modern-day political pilgrims continue the journeys to "socialist" countries and bring back their enthusiastic accounts of revolution, despite the realities

27 Simone Weil, "Lettre à Georges Bernanos," *Écrits Historiques et Politiques*. Editions Gallimard, 1960, in Cunningham, pages 253-257.

that somehow evade their notice.[28] As even Cunningham acknowledges, Spain does not "sustain the earliest lyrical and romantic readings of the war as the zone where the necessary evils and terrors of revolution and war might after a temporary outing prove the gateway to happy conclusions."

We need to be especially alert to the accounts of the International Brigades in Spain, for on this subject particularly a great deal of emotion has been invested and a great many lies told. When, some years ago, Orwell condemned a memoir by the International Brigidista John Sommerfield as "sentimental tripe," he wrote that "we shall almost certainly get some good books from members of the International Brigade, but we shall have to wait for them until the war is over."[29] Such a book was in fact written, and it is far more powerful, honest, and moving than many of the didactic excerpts to be found in either of the new anthologies. William Herrick's novel *Hermanos!,* first published in 1969, is again available from Second Chance Press.[30] Herrick has given us what is perhaps the first honest portrayal of the war from within the Brigades in Spain, a searing, tough indictment, filled with the bitter reality of youthful bravery and idealism crushed by the agenda of the Comintern and its decision to allow so many thousands to die for nothing. Given that Herrick's novel is virtually the only critical account of the Civil War experience from the inside, an excerpt from it would have strengthened both of the new anthologies immeasurably. And another, younger novelist, David Evanier, continues the tradition with his forthcoming novel of the Old Left; a recently published excerpt pertaining to the International Brigades traces one veteran's destruction as part of his experience with the Soviet tank corps.[31]

Reading the committed partisans of the Left so many years later cannot but leave one with a bitter taste. How weak seem the partisans, and how prescient seem those who had doubts and expressed them. Indeed, one is struck by the intellectual courage it took to give anything but the expected answer, particularly when the question was framed, as it was in 1937 in a declaration "To the Writers and Poets of England, Scotland, Ireland and Wales" by Auden, Spender, Neruda, and Aragon: "Are you for or against . . . the People of Republican Spain? . . . it is impossible any longer to take no side." Those who answered by insisting that no side be taken must be given high marks for intellectual fortitude, and for refusing to ride with the herd.

Aldous Huxley spoke a simple truth when he replied, to those who demanded he side with the Reds, that dictatorial Communism would produce "results with which history has made us only too sickeningly familiar." T. S. Eliot replied that, while he was sympathetic to the Republicans, "it is best that at least a few men of letters should remain isolated." Condemned as a Fascist for these sentiments, Eliot at least was able to stay aloof from the foolish chorus of Stalinist hosannas in which the rest of the intellectuals joined. Was he not correct, then, to claim that, were the Left to win, it would "be the victory of the worst rather than of the best features . . . a travesty of the humanitarian ideals which have led so many people" to work for the Republic?[32] Eliot was wrong, I think, to have opposed lifting the embargo on arms. Despite the tragedy of

---

28 Paul Hollander, *Political Pilgrims: Travels of Western Intellectuals to the Soviet Union, China and Cuba.* Oxford University Press, 1981.

29 George Orwell, review of John Sommerfield's *Volunteer in Spain,* from *Time & Tide,* July 31, 1937, in Cunningham, page 19.

30 William Herrick, *Hermanos!* Second Chance Press, 1983.

31 David Evanier, "How Sammy Klarfeld Became a Vacillating Element in Spain," *The Journal of Contemporary Studies,* Summer/Fall 1985, pages 89-106.

32 Quotations from Aldous Huxley and T. S. Eliot are from *Authors Take Sides on the Spanish War, 1937.* Lawrence and Wishart Ltd., 1937, in Cunningham, pages 51-57.

the conflict—and the evils of Communism—the main threat to the world in the Thirties was that of the menace of aggressive Hitlerism. But Eliot was right, after all, on the moral issue involved, that democracy had little to do with supporting either "Berlin or Moscow."

Those who argued that the Fascists killed Lorca—and therefore all writers must stand with the Republic—would be hard pressed to refute the argument of Salvador Dali that Lorca's "death was exploited for propaganda purposes," and that personally the poet was "the most a-political person on earth."[33]

Undoubtedly, some did side with the Republic because of a valid opposition to Fascism, and because the Republic had the support of the populace. But who can question the accuracy of Vita Sackville-West, who addressed the hypocrisy of the call to support "the *legal* Government of Spain"? "Is this because it is the *legal* Government," she asked, "or because it is a Communist Government?"[34] (One is reminded of the pro-Sandinista writers today who ask that we not oppose the "legal" government of Nicaragua—something they did not hesitate to do when Somoza represented its legitimacy.) Noting that, if legality were the issue, these writers would have to support the existing regimes in Italy and Germany if rebellion broke out against them, Sackville-West identified the real issue: ". . . you want to see Communism established in Spain as well as in Russia, and you do not care a snap of the fingers whether a Government is 'legal' or not." Demanding frankness, Sackville-West challenged what she called the "subterranean forms of propaganda."

It was apparent that defenders of the Republic would use almost any argument to gather support. Virtually all honest observers knew about the brutal assassinations ordered by the Comintern for socialists, anarchists, and POUM revolutionaries after 1937. Yet Ernst Toller, whose propagandistic appeal to Americans started the campaign on behalf of Spain in the United States, emphasized the humanity of the Republic's troops toward its worst enemies. He had seen with his own eyes, Toller wrote, "the humane treatment of war prisoners, of Nazi pilots and Italian Fascist flyers who have killed dozens of children, dozens of women."[35] How false was the picture painted by Toller, of a free society in which Syndicalist, Communist, and parliamentary liberal were totally free and cooperated in word and deed for one aim—the destruction of the armed rebellion. It was Toller who orchestrated the false defense of Spain, and assured the worried liberals in the United States that "it is a lie that the fight is going on between Communism and Fascism." After all, he assured American liberals, Negrin had said that "private property is protected in Spain," and was simply trying to do "the same things that President Roosevelt strives to do: free the country from the power of economic Royalists." It was precisely these directives, forced upon Negrin by the Comintern, as Bolloten writes, that antagonized "other parties of the left and eventually" undermined the war effort "and the will to fight."[36] Having lost its reason and inspiration to fight, the Republic found itself with low morale among its would-be defenders and dependent upon the most treacherous of allies, Joseph Stalin and the Comintern apparatus.

How appropriate, then, that Cunningham ends his collection with "Crusade in Spain" by Jason Gurney,[37] who speaks the clear truth when he writes that "nobody, from either side, came out of it with clean hands." A member of the British section of the

33 Salvador Dali, *The Secret Life of Salvador Dali.* Dasa Ediciones, 1942, in Miller, pages 203-210.

34 Vita Sackville-West's comment is also from *Authors Take Sides on the Spanish War,* in Cunningham, page 229

35 Ernst Toller, "Transcript of Broadcast to the USA," *New Statesman & Nation,* October 8, 1938, in Cunningham, pages 72-75.

36 Burnett Bolloten, *The Spanish Revolution,* page 173.

37 Jason Gurney, *Crusade in Spain.* Faber and Faber Ltd., 1974, in Cunningham, pages 379-380.

International Brigades, Gurney noted that he and his comrades "had wilfully deluded ourselves into the belief that we were fighting a noble Crusade because we needed a crusade—the opportunity to fight against the manifest evils of Fascism . . . which seemed then as if it would overwhelm every value of Western civilization."

Gurney felt, writing in the mid-1970s, that "[W]e were wrong, we deceived ourselves and were deceived by others." But he argues as well that their fight was not in vain, and he does not regret his own part in that fight. "The situation," he says, "is not to be judged by what we now know of it, but only as it appeared in the context of the period." But much *was* known then, and suppressed by those who knew. Gurney would have it both ways. History has taught him the truth about Communism. But he still insists that because "others took advantage of our idealism in order to destroy it does not in any way invalidate the decision which we made." And this man who claims to understand history gives his last word to the blabbering of "La Pasionaria," Dolores Ibarruri. This famous Communist deputy, who sang the praises of the departing brigidistas as they were suffering the consequences of her betrayal, went immediately thereafter to Moscow, where she remained in exile until Franco's death. Those brave men who gave their lives had allowed themselves to be part of an ideological and propaganda instrument forged by the Comintern for its own purposes. Had they looked closer, they could have discerned the truth at the time. In 1986, those who still respond to the Spanish Civil War as simply "our cause" have no excuse.

(*October* 1986)

II. The Decline of the Academy

Destroying literary studies

by René Wellek

At least since the time of Aristarchus in Alexandria, who died one hundred forty-five years before Christ, a body of knowledge or, if you prefer, a "science of literature" has been built up over the centuries. The Renaissance revived and codified it and the Romantic movement gave impetus to its enormous expansion and institutionalization in the later nineteenth century. Though deep changes in methods and emphases came about in the first half of this century, one can say that literary scholarship has flourished uninterrupted—at least in all Western countries—for roughly two centuries.

One can distinguish among three main branches of literary study. First, there is theory, which is concerned with the principles, categories, functions, and criteria of literature in general. Theory is the term now preferred to the older "poetics," since "poetics" seems limited to writing in verse and has not shed the implication of prescriptive rules. Second, there is the study of concrete works of literature, which is sometimes identified with criticism or called "practical criticism" and which attempts to describe, analyze, characterize, interpret, and evaluate individual works of literature or groups of works, for example, of one author or in one genre. Interpretation is only one step in this process of criticism, though it has developed an enormous debate about its theory, for which the old theological term *hermeneutics* has been revived. And third, there is literary history, seen most frequently in the setting of political, social, and intellectual history. Literary biography is an established subgenre within literary history. These three branches of literary study implicate each other. There can be no literary theory without concrete criticism and without history; there is no criticism without some theory and history; and no literary history is possible without theoretical assumptions and without criticism.

This growing body of knowledge, immense in its ramifications, anticipates and parallels the establishment of similar disciplines, such as the study of the fine arts (sometimes included in aesthetics or developed as history of art) and the study of music, musicology, the history of music, and so on. The study of the relationships among the arts and of their common traits has been a growing concern. It leads to aesthetics and to a philosophy of art.

Today this whole edifice of literary study has come under an attack that is not merely the normal criticism of certain aspects of a changing discipline but an attempt to destroy literary studies from the inside. The attempt seems to have succeeded in certain academic circles; it has enlisted the support of a number of journals and has affected many students, apparently all over the country. It has hardly dislodged or even modified up till now the practice of the vast majority of teachers and students of literature. But it has had considerable publicity and, if it should be generally effective and find many adherents among the younger generation, may spell the breakdown or even the abolition of all traditional literary scholarship and teaching.

I shall try to distinguish among the different motifs and aims of the attack, which is by no means uniform or directed from a single center, either institutional or ideological.

One rather old view that has gained new prominence is the simple denial of the aesthetic nature of literature. One can doubt the very existence of aesthetic experience and refuse to recognize the distinctions, clearly formulated in Immanuel Kant's *Critique of Judgment,* between the good, the true, the useful, and the beautiful. This attack on aesthetics goes back at least as far as the German theory of empathy, as Croce's intuition-expression doctrine, as Dewey's account of art as the experience of heightened vitality, and, in the Anglo-American critical tradition, as I. A. Richards's claim that there is no "aesthetic mode or aesthetic state" or "aesthetic emotion" and that there is no difference between reading a poem and "dressing in the morning." Richards held, in *Principles of Criticism,* that "the world of poetry has in no sense any different reality from the rest of the world and it has no special laws and no other-worldly peculiarities." Since this argument abolishes the distinction between plays, poems, and novels on the one hand and didactic, expository, informative prose on the other, we arrive at the conclusion that literary study includes everything in print.

Long before Richards, of course, the study of literature was often conceived as the study of the whole history of civilization. In *Province of Literary History* (1931), for example, Edwin Greenlaw stated forcibly that "we [literary historians] are not limited to *belles lettres* or even to printed or manuscript records." This expansion of literary study has been justified, in part at least, by the fact that the branches of learning which should be studying the history of thought and sensibility and of social change have at least temporarily neglected to do so. English and American technical philosophy is notoriously anti-historical and has practically abandoned the study of the history of philosophy to English departments, to the "history of ideas" in Lovejoy's sense. And for a long time academic history departments have been preoccupied with diplomatic, military, and political events, though in recent decades one can speak of a strong revival of social and cultural history, partly under the influence of Marxism and the *Annales* group in France. Most of my own historical work is concerned with the history of ideas, with Immanuel Kant's influence in England, with the history of critical ideas, with the history of historiography and of specific key terms and concepts. There is nothing wrong with this except the danger that imaginative literature might be neglected.

But the old apprehension that literary study might be absorbed in general cultural and social history is now being replaced by a very different worry. The new theory asserts that man lives in a prison house of language that has no relation to reality. It seems to be suggested, or at least buttressed, by a few passages in Nietzsche where, for example, he speaks of "truth as a mobile marching army of metaphors, metonymies, and anthropomorphisms, illusions of which one has forgotten that they are illusions," and by an interpretation of the *Cours de linguistique générale* of Ferdinand de Saussure, who considered the referential function of language irrelevant for a science of linguistics but who did not doubt language's relation to experience and reality. In its extreme formulation, which looks for the abolition of man, denies the self, and sees language as a free-floating system of signs, the theory leads to total skepticism and ultimately to nihilism. This accusation is not simply an invention of the detractors of "deconstructionism," as it is called. It has been expressly confirmed by its practitioners: by J. Hillis Miller writing in *Critical Inquiry* (1977, no. 3); by Paul de Man, who in *Blindness and Insight* elaborates in gloomy existentialist terms the view that poetry names the void, asserts itself as "pure nothingness"; and by Jacques Derrida, who describes the new theory as a "Nietzschean affirmation," as the joyous affirmation of this play of the world, a world of signs, "without truth, without origin beyond man and humanism" (in *Écriture et la différance* [1967]).

The view that there is "nothing outside of text," that every text refers or defers only to another text, ignores that texts—political, juridical, religious, philosophical, and even imaginative and poetic—have actually shaped the lives of men and thus the course of history. Denying the self and minimizing the perceptual life of man, the theory deliberately refuses to acknowledge that the relation of mind and world is more basic than language.

For literary studies, some consequences have been drawn that would spell their doom. If there is no distinction between imaginative literature and any other writing, if everything is a language game, the inclusive words *écriture* and "text" allow the claim that the critic is equal to the creative writer. A critic can feel himself to be on the level of Dante or Shakespeare. Actually, some of the new critics compare themselves and their friends constantly with the greatest names of the past, speaking in the same breath of themselves and of Carlyle, Ruskin, or Pater. They revive the idea of "creative criticism" propagated by Oscar Wilde. No doubt there are aesthetic features in much critical writing: composition, style, evocative skill, and so on. And there were and are critics who feel strongly that they are artists expressing or displaying their personalities. Friedrich von Schlegel, William Hazlitt, and Sainte-Beuve are obvious examples, and Oscar Wilde flaunted ostentatiously the view of the critic as artist. But the new view goes much further: it wants to make criticism indistinguishable from fiction and it does not recognize that there is a definite work of literature out there (whatever its mode of existence may be) which has to be understood, which challenges and imposes on us. In the new theories there is no object but only an event in the mind—or, rather, in the language—of the critic. The critic engages in a free play with language.

Jacques Derrida is the philosopher who, for American students, has formulated this view most impressively. He rejects the whole tradition of Western thought, which he labels a "metaphysics of presence," by "presence" meaning its reliance on ultimate concepts such as Being, God, consciousness, self, truth, origin, and so on. He propounds the preposterous theory that writing precedes speaking, a claim refuted by every child and by the thousand spoken languages that have no written records. His view can be defended only by giving "writing" a deliberately deceptive new meaning. He argues that all philosophy is shot through by metaphors, ambiguities, "undecidables," as is all literature and criticism. This view was welcomed by some literary critics and students as a liberation, since it gives license to the arbitrary spinning of metaphors, to the stringing of puns, to mere language games. The model praised to the sky is Derrida's *Glas,* which presents, in two columns, a string of quotations from Hegel's *Philosophy of the Right* alongside Genet's *Journal of a Thief.* As even an admirer admits, it is "a purely speculative chain of words and associations." In practice, it is a series of puns, beginning with the French pronunciation of Hegel as *aigle* (eagle) and wandering off to *seigle* (rye), the field the thief crosses, and to *sigle* (sign). The book falls between three stools: it does not give an aesthetic experience, it is not literary criticism, and it is not good philosophy. It is at most a display of ingenuity and wit, inspired (possibly) by Heidegger's etymologizing punning, by *Finnegans Wake,* Dada, and Surrealism. If this were an isolated instance of the whim of a learned man, it might be harmless. Unfortunately, it has been widely imitated, with less wit and learning, and has encouraged utter caprice, extreme subjectivity, and hence the destruction of the very concepts of knowledge and truth.

In practice, of course, these absurd consequences are often avoided by theorists inventing new techniques or by their diverting attention to newly formulated problems. Thus, "deconstruction" is often an ingenious uncovering of ambiguities, contradictions, and inconsistencies in diverse texts, along with the monotonous conclusion that every work of literature is only "words about words," literature about literature. These writers have only just discovered an old and simple truth—that words are not things. Some time ago, Jonathan Swift satirized the project of carrying around "such things as were necessary to express the particular business they are to discuss on." These new critics refuse to understand that words designate things and not only other words as they argue.

I am no defender of the Realist dogma. I have advocated the view that Realism is only one possible style of literature and I have always recognized the fantastic, the Utopian, the grotesque, the symbolic, and many other modes of representing reality. But literature does represent reality, however distorted and transformed. It both projects a world of its own creation and tells us something about our world. The deconstructionist theory is a flight from reality, and from history. Paradoxically, it leads to a new, anti-aesthetic ivory tower, to a new linguistic isolationism. Actually, the deconstructionists often ignore modern technical linguistics. In the writings of Paul de Man, for example, "deconstruction" amounts to a study of rhetoric, understood not as a technique of persuasion but as a study of figures and tropes, metaphors and metonymy. The entire question of meaning is bracketed. Thus, at least the rudiments of literary study are preserved, as the texts of a few suitable authors are attended to: Rousseau, Nietzsche, Proust, Mallarmé, and Rilke. There is no pretense here of creative criticism.

The second prominent motif of the new trends is abolition of the authority of the text, the rejection of the whole ancient enterprise of interpretation as a search for the true meaning of a text. We have learned since the New Criticism to look for ambiguities and paradoxes, and Ingarden and others (myself included) have defended the view that an accrual of meaning occurs in the course of history. The possibility exists of a conflict of interpretations that cannot be completely resolved in some cases, though there is always a limit to the freedom of interpretation. All this has been endlessly debated by E. D. Hirsch, who defends the criterion of the author's intention and the prescriptive role of genre, by J. P. Juhl, who believes that there is only one correct interpretation, and most learnedly by Hans Georg Gadamer in *Wahrheit und Methode* (1960) and a whole new German school of hermeneutics. The so-called *Rezeptionsaesthetik* or reader-response criticism has shifted attention away from the work of literature to the process of reading, to the audience. In the theory propounded by the Konstanz group (mainly Hans-Robert Jauss, a learned student of medieval French literature, and Wolfgang Iser, a specialist in the English novel) we hear of a "fusion of horizons" between that of the reader or interpreter and that of the work of art. It is a compromise between the present-day assumptions and the historical definiteness of a work. *Rezeptionsaesthetik* recommends some good things: paying attention to the history of taste and criticism (which, needless to say, I fully approve) and to the implied reader addressed in the text. But the theory is unable to bridge the gulf between these two problems: the reader reactions and the signs of historicity—parody, imitation, allusion, conventions—embodied in the works themselves. In practice, *Rezeptionsaesthetik* lands in extreme relativism, though the emphasis on certain neglected aspects of readers' reactions seems to me welcome. But the theory of this school is not as new as it claims and is hardly a panacea for the presumed ills of literary history.

The most influential American reader-response theory, that of Stanley Fish, is another matter. It comes in several versions: in its most radical formulation it assumes that a work is completely contained in the sequential, linear reading process. It is a protest against what Fish regards as the reification and illegitimate spatialization of such concepts—or, rather metaphors—as the "verbal icon" or "the well-wrought urn." It has led him to make—in *Self-Consuming Artifacts* (1972)—farfetched, forced, and sometimes demonstrably mistaken readings of seventeenth-century texts. It is restated theoretically in his 1980 collection *Is There a Text in this Class?* There we are told that texts are so undetermined that we cannot decide their meaning at all, that "no interpretation can be said to be better or worse than any other." Thus, "interpretation is not the art of construing but the art of constructing. Interpreters do not decode poems: they make them." More recently Fish has seen that his theory leads to complete anarchy and extreme subjectivism, a consequence he tries to obviate or circumvent by an appeal to "interpretive communities." But he merely worsens the situation. By absolutizing the power of assumptions, he empties literature of all significance. Great critics have fortunately eluded "interpretive communities," resisted or contradicted them. Fish's theories encourage the view that there are no wrong interpretations, that there is no norm implied in a text, and hence that there is no knowledge of an object.

A few reflections should refute this view. There are patently absurd and wrong interpretations, for example, that Hamlet is a woman in disguise or that Hamlet is "mainly King James I," as Miss Winstanley argued. There are interpretations that can be shown to be wrong. For instance: D. H. Lawrence in his comment on Dostoevsky's "Legend of the Grand Inquisitor" in *The Brothers Karamazov* interprets Christ's kissing the Grand Inquisitor as meaning his acceptance of the Inquisitor's views, "Thank you, thank you, you are right, old man." But the kiss is rather the silent answer of religion that rejects and refutes the Inquisitor's diatribe. Alyosha immediately afterwards kisses Ivan, forgiving him for his atheism and Ivan reacts, "This is plagiarism from my poem." The rest of the book, the story of Zosima and Brother Markel, confirms this. Dostoevsky's journalistic writings confirm it and so do all the later novels. One can thus correct mistaken interpretations by appealing to the context of a book, of an author's work, and finally of a whole tradition. There are also, one should admit, puzzling cases. The end of *King Lear* has led to opposite conclusions. Blake's "Tiger" and Wordsworth's Lucy poem "A Slumber Did My Spirit Steal" have excited heated disagreements. But even here it is possible to adjudicate the differences: to explain them by the different approaches and implied assumptions of the interpreters. The Hegelian concept of tragedy assumed in A. C. Bradley will lead to different conclusions than will the Sartrean existentialist concept assumed in Jan Kott's *Shakespeare Our Contemporary.* Still, there are works or passages that are ambiguous, indeterminate, and even opaque and incomprehensible; but that should be a spur to discovering meaning rather than an argument for surrender. The otherness of a text, removed in time or place or both, or simply alien to our way of thinking, is a challenge to interpretation. To draw completely skeptical conclusions is simply to doubt the very possibility of knowledge, to deny the ideal of man ever understanding himself or other human beings and their creations. The world may be dark and ultimately mysterious, but the mind of man is not so narrowly limited that it cannot understand and illuminate its own creations. Vico, in the early eighteenth century, knew that, while nature may be impenetrable to man, we can have certain knowledge of our own works in history, in poetry, and in institutions. The recent attempts to increase our self-consciousness, to make us aware of our own situation in time and place, to see the "presenticentric predicament," to use the unlovely coinage of A. O. Lovejoy, is valuable if it diminishes rampant subjectivity and makes us more tolerant of other viewpoints. But it can also have a paralyzing effect, turning us into the famous centipede that did not know which foot to put first and thus encouraging the suppression of personality, which, whatever its excesses, is after all the source of insight and judgment.

This ideal of impersonal objectivity is only one of the motives for the current dismissal of evaluation in literary criticism. Evaluation used to be criticism's central task. It has been dismissed by a new group of students of literature with completely different assumptions: by would-be scientists, mainly linguists, by semioticians and some structuralists, and by Northrop Frye, who erected a complex system of archetypes that obliterates the distinction between the most trivial detective story and a play by Shakespeare. Evaluation seems especially irrelevant to these system builders, who are looking for examples of structures to incorporate in their schemes, scientific or imaginative. Recently evaluation has also been attacked as "elitism," as a defense of the tradition, and even as a method of oppression. But a little reflection should show that evaluation is a basic task of literary study. There is an insuperable gulf between great art and real trash.

The day-to-day task of criticism is the sifting of the enormous production of books, and even the ranking and grading of writers. That we teach Shakespeare, Dante, or Goethe rather than the newest best-seller or any of the romances, Westerns, crime, and detective novels, science fiction, and pornography on the racks of the nearest drugstore is an act of evaluation. We exercise choice the minute we take up even a classical text whose value is certified by generations of readers, in deciding what features we shall pay attention to, what we shall emphasize, appreciate, and admire, or ignore and deprecate. It is now unfashionable to speak of a love of literature, of enjoyment of and admiration for a poem, a play, or a novel. But such feelings surely must have been the original stimulus to anyone engaged in the study of literature. Otherwise he might as well have studied accounting or engineering. Love, admiration is, I agree, only the first step. Then we ask why we love and admire or detest. We reflect, analyze, and interpret; and out of understanding grows evaluation and judgment, which need not be articulated expressly. Evaluation leads to the definition of the canon, of the classics, of the tradition. In the realm of literature the question of quality is inescapable. If this is "elitism," so be it.

Recently, arguments have been advanced in favor of subliterature, of *Kitsch,* colportage, *Trivialliteratur,* or however we may call it. Nobody can deny that a study of subliterature throws light on the history of taste, or that detective stories, science fiction, and all the other genres can be studied for structural properties and even graded by aesthetic criteria. One may very well distinguish between good, mediocre, and bad science fiction, detective novels, and even pornography. Even the most vociferous enemies of evaluation judge and rank. In his *Anatomy of Criticism,* whose "Polemical Introduction" denounces value judgment and hopes for a "steady advance toward undiscriminating catholicity," Northrop Frye speaks of Aristophanes's *Birds* as "his greatest play" and of Burton's *Anatomy of Melancholy* as "the greatest Menippean satire in English before Swift." The mere fact that Frye and others have elected to study Milton rather than Blackmore, Shakespeare rather than Glapthorne, is sufficient to show that there is no criticism or even literary history without choice and judgment. Recently, we also find an influential critic, Leslie Fiedler, advocating in *What Was Literature?* a reversal of the canon, praising pulp science fiction, hard-core pornography, and fiction "not accepted in the canon of o.k. art": Conan Doyle, Bram Stoker, Rider Haggard, Margaret Mitchell. Fiedler is convinced that narrative skill and mythopoeic power are independent of formal excellence. Despising "upper-class" art and embracing "pop" art, Fiedler rejects his early admirations as so much hypocrisy. But even he has to make distinctions and evaluations. Though he tends always to side with the underdog, the proletarian, and the black man, he condemns Alex Haley's *Roots* as "prefabricated commodity *schlock.*" But he has not told us why there should be, in what he considers upper-class art, no masterpieces to be pointed out and ranked, as he has ranked the examples of pop art he admires.

The need for evaluation is also obvious in literary history. In recent decades, literary history has often been dismissed as concerned only with the accumulation of external facts: bibliography, biography, influences, reputations, and so on. It has been ridiculed as a catchall of information on all subjects, as trivial antiquarianism. I count myself among the severest critics of literary histories (in reviews of Legouis-Cazamian's, A. C. Baugh's, and Grierson's histories of English literature and R. Spiller's *Literary History of the United States*). Many attempts have been made to remedy this situation. I must sketch the history of literary historiography to make the present situation comprehensible. There is a romantic tradition of nationalistic histories that sees literature as the expression of the national mind; there is a school of social explanation formulated memorably in Hippolyte Taine's triad—*race, milieu, moment*; finally, there are the schemes of internal evolution devised by Ferdinand Brunetière on the analogy of biology and by the Russian formalists and Czech structuralists who saw literary evolution as a dialectical process of shifts in structure. Little to my mind has been added to these schemes that is really new. T. S. Eliot's interpretation of the tradition has changed the evaluation of specific periods, styles, and groups of writers in the history of English poetry but has not changed the practice of literary history. The numerous writings of Harold Bloom have recently given a new twist to old problems. He is obsessed by the "burden of the past" (a phrase used in the title of W. J. Bate's book on the English romantics) and by what he calls "the anxiety of influence," the poet's revolt against his predecessors. Bloom restates the old convention-revolt problem in psychoanalytical terms: the poet has an Oedipus complex; he wants to slay his poetic father. "True poetic history is the story of how poets have suffered other poets," Bloom says in *The Anxiety of Influence*. He makes elaborate distinctions among the ways a poet handles his relation to older poets, inventing fancy terms—*tessera, kenosis, daemonization, askesis,* and *apophrades*—and describing the whole history of poetry as "an endless civil war, indeed a family war." His criticism is "antithetical, revisionist," carried by prophetic pathos in defense of "visionary" poetry, the line he construes—in conscious antithesis to T. S. Eliot's—from Milton via Blake and Shelley to Whitman and Wallace Stevens. Unfortunately, this very individual scheme is marred by Bloom's adherence to the view that all interpretation is misreading ("misprision") and that "the true poem is the critic's mind." But Bloom cannot share the deconstructionists' rejection of poetry's relation to reality. "The theory of poetry is for him the theory of life," to borrow his quotation from Wallace Stevens.

The abolition of aesthetics, the blurring of the distinction between poetry and critical prose, the rejection of the very ideal of correct interpretation in favor of misreading, the denial to all literature of any reference to reality are all symptoms of a profound *malaise*. If literature has nothing to say about our minds and the cosmos, about love and death, about humanity in other times and other countries, literature loses its meaning. It is possible to account for the flight from literary studies in our universities. I am of course aware of other reasons, mainly economic, but the emptying of human significance, the implied nihilism, must be contributing to the decline of the appeal of subjects like English and foreign languages and encouraging the preference for more palpable and palatable subject matter not only in the sciences and their utilitarian applications but also in the social sciences, which are still concerned with a nonlinguistic reality.

I would be misunderstood if I were seen simply as a *laudator temporis acti,* as recommending a return to the unreflective literary history that dominated the American universities when I first came to this country in 1927. After all, I wrote (with Austin Warren) *Theory of Literature* (1948), the first book in English with this title. In it I discuss the Russian formalists, Ingarden's phenomenological analysis of the work of art, Czech structuralism, German *Geistesgeschichte* and stylistics, and other Continental developments. Long before, in 1937, I got involved in a controversy with F. R. Leavis whom I had criticized for his boastful empiricism, for being suspicious of any theory. In the last chapter of *Theory* (later deleted), I criticized the American academic situation quite harshly. I cannot be suspected of enmity toward theory or Continental developments.

There is a recent book by an Englishman, Geoffrey Strickland, *Structuralism or Criticism?* which puts the choice bluntly, voting for criticism in Leavis's sense and rejecting structuralism mainly for its ambition to construe a closed system of literary signs. I agree with him on this point and can quote Hugo Friedrich, the eminent German *Romanist,* who wrote in 1967: "there cannot be a scheme or system, which would consider all phenomena of literature as limited by internal relations and combinations." But I don't see what can be said against the less universal structural analyses of Mukařovský, Genette, Todorov, and Lotman. There is a new poetics in the making, particularly of the novel, called "narratology," which has profited from the structuralist approach. Strickland's *Structuralism or Criticism?* poses a false dilemma. The enterprise of structuralism, first clearly formulated by the Prague Linguistic Circle in about 1935, seems to me fully justified. It is inconceivable, however, without the criticism of concrete works, without analysis, interpretation, and ultimately evaluation. I cannot agree with Jonathan Culler, an enthusiast for structuralism, who says in *The Pursuit of Signs* that "the interpretation of individual works is only tangentially related to the understanding of literature." Only the collaboration, the exchange and necessary interaction of criticism and poetics, can guarantee a healthy development of literary studies. I reject the theories of some structuralists and post-structuralists who advocate "the abolition of man" (whatever that may mean), who are content with the presumed "prison house of language" and claim a complete systematization of all literature. Nor can I sympathize with the blurring of the difference between imaginative literature and criticism. I cannot advocate either a return to the anti-theoretical, almost instinctive kind of criticism practiced, say, by F. R. Leavis or Yvor Winters. I sometimes feel guilty of having helped to propagate the theory of literature. Since my book, theory has triumphed in this country and has, possibly, triumphed with a vengeance. Still, I approve the basic impulse behind theory of literature, the need for clarification of principles and methods, for an articulated rationale of literary study. But some of the recent developments in their extreme skepticism and even nihilism would destroy this ideal, "deconstruct," as they say, all literary study, interrupt tradition, dismantle an edifice built by the efforts of generations of scholars and students. Fortunately, one may hope that this new "absurdist" wave, as Hayden White has called it, has already crashed on the shore, even though its propounders still believe that they ride its crest.

(*December* 1983)

Debating the humanities at Yale

by Roger Kimball

Early this April, the Whitney Humanities Center at Yale University sponsored a one-day, public symposium entitled "The Humanities and the Public Interest." The symposium convened at nine o'clock on a Saturday morning and consisted of three sessions. The purpose of the event, in the words of a University press release, was "to re-examine the traditional association between the study of the humanities and the guardianship of humanistic values in the context of contemporary American society." Peter Brooks, director of the Whitney Humanities Center and professor of the humanities at Yale, expanded on this: "The symposium will ask whether the case for the humanities can rest on traditional assumptions," he was quoted in the press release as saying, "or whether a new rationale is needed if the humanities are to claim a major place in contemporary modes of thought and analysis."

One might think this a tall order for a single day's discussion. But the Yale community proved itself undaunted by the prospect. Even the symposium's first session, which was devoted to "Technology in the Humanities, the Humanities in Technology," drew an audience of over a hundred people; and the second two sessions—"The Social Mission of the Humanities" in the late morning and "A New Rationale for the Humanities?" after lunch—both filled the house with an audience of some three hundred or more. Each session featured two speakers and two respondents, with a member of the Yale faculty serving as moderator.

The symposium opened with some introductory remarks by Professor Brooks, who noted that the original impetus for the symposium was Secretary of Education William J. Bennett's report on higher education in the humanities, *To Reclaim a Legacy*. Though it appears over Secretary Bennett's name, the report is in effect a committee document. It reflects the findings and recommendations—and also, one feels, the concessions and compromises—of a study group that included some thirty teachers, administrators, and experts on higher education. Undertaken when Secretary Bennett was chairman of the National Endowment for the Humanities, the thirty-two-page pamphlet was published by the Endowment in November, 1984, and has excited considerable consternation in the academy. In part, this is because the report criticizes the way in which the humanities are being taught—or left untaught—in many American colleges and universities. But more importantly, the report has been controversial because of the frankly conservative vision of the humanities that informs its analysis.

In brief, *To Reclaim a Legacy* defends precisely those "traditional assumptions" of the humanities that Professor Brooks hoped the Yale symposium would question. For himself, Professor Brooks declared his "profound disagreement" with the conclusions and general outlook of Secretary Bennett's report, taking issue especially with what he described as its "intellectual fundamentalism." Professor Brooks's opening remarks were very brief, but in many ways they established the tenor for the day's discussion; and since he identified Secretary Bennett's report as the catalyst for the symposium, we may begin by taking a closer look at its argument.

To Reclaim a Legacy begins by reaffirming the traditional role of the humanities as the chief instrument of our cultural self-definition. Its presiding deity is Matthew Arnold, whose faith in the ennobling effects of high culture, of "the best that has been thought and said," is patent throughout the report. Elaborating Arnold's famous phrase, Secretary Bennett describes the humanities as "the best that has been said, thought, written, and otherwise expressed about the human experience." The humanities are important, he writes, because

> they tell us how men and women of our own and other civilizations have grappled with life's enduring, fundamental questions: What is justice? What should be loved? What deserves to be defended? What is courage? What is noble? What is base? . . .
>
> These questions are not simply diversions for intellectuals or playthings for the idle. As a result of the ways in which these questions have been answered, civilizations have emerged, nations have developed, wars have been fought, and people have lived contentedly or miserably.

Against the background of this faith in the importance of the humanities, the statistics that are marshaled in *To Reclaim a Legacy* cannot but give one pause. For example, according to Secretary Bennett, since 1970 the number of students majoring in the humanities has declined by about half, by nearly two-thirds in the case of history. Similarly, fewer than half of all colleges and universities now require foreign language study for the bachelor's degree—down from ninety percent in 1966, we read—and a student can now graduate from seventy-five percent of our colleges and universities without having studied European history, from eighty-six percent without having studied classical Greece and Rome, and from seventy-two percent without having studied American literature or history. In other words, in the past two decades American higher education has suffered a wholesale flight from the humanities.

But the source of the controversy surrounding Secretary Bennett's report does not lie in its litany of dispiriting statistics. The real issue lies rather in his prescriptions for "reclaiming" the legacy he finds threatened and, in the end, in his understanding of the substance and definition of that legacy. In the simplest terms, he calls for a reshaping of undergraduate curricula "based on a clear vision of what constitutes an educated person." In his view, the goal of the humanities should be a "common culture" rooted in the highest ideals and aspirations of the Western tradition. Thus, while he urges the study of other cultures, he asserts that "the core of the American college curriculum . . . should be the civilization of the West . . . ." Along the way, Secretary Bennett also criticizes the widespread tendency to politicize the humanities, to make them "the handmaiden of ideology," as well as the penchant for radical subjectivism that would have us view the meaning and value of the humanities as intractably relative. Indeed, central to Secretary Bennett's view of the humanities is an adherence to traditional criteria and standards for educational excellence and scholarly accomplishment. He believes, for example, that the tradition provides us with a generally recognized canon or body of "great works" that should form the basis for a humanistic education. And though he acknowledges that there will always be differences of opinion about the details of this canon, he insists that its basic lineaments are clear and ought to be preserved.

Despite accusations to the contrary, Secretary Bennett does not advocate restoration of a previous state of affairs. He insists that the solution to the current crisis in the humanities "is not a return to an earlier time when the classical curriculum was the only curriculum and college was available to only a privileged few." Given the charges of elitism and reaction that his proposals have occasioned, it seems well to emphasize this point. "American higher education today serves far more people . . . than it did a century ago," Secretary Bennett writes.

> Its increased accessibility to women, racial and ethnic minorities, recent immigrants, and students of limited means is a positive accomplishment of which our nation is justly proud . . . . But our eagerness to assert the virtues of pluralism should not allow us to sacrifice the principle that formerly lent substance and continuity to the curriculum, namely, that each college and university should recognize and accept its vital role as a conveyor of the accumulated wisdom of our civilization.

It is of course this final affirmation that has troubled Secretary Bennett's opponents. For one thing, who decides what counts as "the accumulated wisdom of our civilization"? In Arnold's terms, why should the humanities be concerned primarily with the *best* that has been thought and said? Does that not exclude a large portion of human experience? And does not that mass of experience deserve "equal time" in our institutions of higher education? Here again, who is to say what counts as "best"? Perhaps the Arnoldian injunction has been interpreted too narrowly, too "ideologically," too exclusively? Furthermore, why should the humanities focus so intently upon the past? Why should they not concern themselves as much with the *creation* as with the *preservation* of culture? Such questions are at the heart of Professor Brooks's "profound disagreement" and charge of "intellectual fundamentalism"—a charge that has been loudly echoed in the academy and that was to be advanced with great zeal that Saturday at Yale's Whitney Humanities Center.

The symposium's first session, however, on technology and the humanities was notable mostly for its lack of focus. Alan Trachtenberg, professor of American Studies and chairman of the American Studies Program at Yale, served as moderator. He opened the session by noting that the antagonism between technology and the humanities has become something of a "cliché." The antagonism might be overcome, he suggested, if we were to invert the terms of the discussion and try to show how technology and the humanities are at bottom "interrelated systems" that point to a "common destiny." This sounds lovely, of course—who wouldn't wish to show that the rationalistic imperatives of modern science and technology are somehow compatible with the intrinsically value-laden life of the humanities? Unfortunately, though, Professor Trachtenberg failed to specify what it might mean for technology and the humanities to be "interrelated systems," and in default of such specification his dream of their "common destiny" can be little more than wishful thinking. Clichés rarely provide one with an "interesting" interpretation of phenomena, but it sometimes happens that they express an obvious truth.

The principal speakers in this first session were Elting Morison, professor emeritus at MIT, and Daniel C. Dennett, professor of philosophy at Tufts University. Professor Morison offered us some rather commonplace reflections on the disintegration of the "received scheme of things" in the modern world and on the academy's accompanying shift away from the humanities as traditionally conceived toward more technical subjects. In a formidable phrase that captured the imagination of the other speakers, he called for the establishment of a "laboratory for the study of epistemological disorders" that could bring the humanities and technology together. Professor Dennett read part of a paper on ethics in which he discussed some of the special ethical quandaries with which our modern, technological society confronts us. He was especially concerned with analyzing the increased moral responsibility we feel in the face of our greater knowledge of the world's miseries. Given that knowledge and our immense technical capabilities, he asked, where does our responsibility end? At the same time, he criticized our "misbegotten reliance" on technology and—in the session's second arresting phrase—lobbied for "a moral first-aid kit" that would be more responsive to particular ethical problems.

The respondents added little to the discussion. Jules Chametsky, professor of English and director of the Institute for Advanced Study in the Humanities at the University of Massachusetts, wondered whether Professor Dennett's proposals were capable of addressing "real problems" and made the novel observation that the prospect of a nuclear holocaust weighs heavily on modern consciousness. Professor Chametsky also offered us some wandering reflections on the moral wisdom expressed in Wallace Shawn's play *Aunt Dan and Lemon* and concluded by noting that in "Reagan's America" it is difficult to make the humanities "relevant." The other respondent in the first session was Leo Marx, professor of American cultural history at MIT. Professor Marx began by reminding us how difficult it is to establish compelling criteria for moral action. He liked the notion of a "laboratory for epistemological disorders," he told us, but in general felt that the proposals made that morning were too "sanitized," too abstract and detached from real-life problems. He emphasized the "embedded" quality of moral problems, observing that for moral guidance most people rely not on abstract cogitation but on inherited belief systems. The real function of the humanities, he suggested, was not to provide us with "instrumental values" but to help us distinguish and discriminate among belief systems, to reflect critically on inherited values.

While the question of the relation between technology and the humanities is undoubtedly a pressing one, the contributions that morning rarely proceeded beyond assorted—and often dubious—platitudes, on the one hand, and fairly abstract speculation about ethics, on the other. The discussion became considerably more concrete in the second, and most publicized, session of the symposium, "The Social Mission of the Humanities." This session featured a "dialogue" between Yale President A. Bartlett Giamatti and Norman Podhoretz, the well-known writer and editor of *Commentary* magazine; the respondents were Henry Rosovsky, professor of social science at Harvard, and Cornel West, associate professor of the philosophy of religion at the Yale Divinity School. It was in this session that the real issues facing the humanities in contemporary American society were most clearly set forth.

Mr. Podhoretz spoke first. The humanities, he said, cannot be justified on practical grounds. Because the knowledge and culture they represent are "good in themselves," their ultimate justification is simply their intrinsic value. From this it follows that the humanities cannot directly help us in the formulation of public policy; nor do they yield any particular political position; nor indeed does acquaintance with the humanities necessarily make us morally more upright or more humane—think only of the cultivated Nazi commandants who also savored Mozart. Echoing the sentiments expressed in Secretary Bennett's report, Mr. Podhoretz identified the chief function of the humanities to be the creation of a "common culture." Central to this view of the humanities is the idea of a more or less generally recognized canon of works that define the tradition. Mr. Podhoretz admitted that there will always be disagreement about the composition of the canon at, as it were, its edges; but he claimed that, at least until recently, there has been a widely shared consensus about the core body of works that constitute "the best that has been thought and said."

In one sense, of course, this view of the humanities can be said to be exclusive or "elitist," since it presupposes a rigorously defined notion of what it means to be an educated person. But in another sense, it is deeply democratic, for it locates authority not in any class or race or sex, but in a tradition before which all are equal. Indeed, as Mr. Podhoretz observed, to the extent that the humanities are crucial to the maintenance of civilized life, it is essential that as many people as possible be exposed to the canon: only thus is high culture preserved and transmitted. Furthermore, as the transmitter of the canon, of what Mr. Podhoretz described as our "intellectual patrimony," the humanities have traditionally instilled a sense of the value of the democratic tradition we have inherited. And it is in this respect, he noted, that the humanities *do* have a political dimension, insofar as they rest upon a belief in the value and importance of Western culture and the civilization that gave birth to it.

With the social and political upheaval of the Sixties and early Seventies, Mr. Podhoretz continued, this entire conception of the humanities came under radical assault. Not only the idea of a common culture founded upon a recognized canon of great works, but the very notion of a politically autonomous realm of culture, was dismissed as naïve, ethnocentric, or somehow repressive. Even the fundamental belief in the value of Western culture and civilization—the value, that is to say, of the whole humanistic enterprise—was undermined. And while it is true that the more extreme manifestations of this revolt have disappeared, Mr. Podhoretz maintained that the radical attitudes espoused in the Sixties and Seventies live on in attenuated form in the academy—even, or rather especially, in the humanistic disciplines, in the values and assumptions that typically inform the teaching and study of the humanities. For the most part, he said, a study of the humanities now tends at best to encourage a feeling of "mild contempt" for culture as traditionally defined and at worst to inspire outright hatred of our civilization and everything it stands for. And because of this sedimented radicalism in the academy, the humanities, however much they may still add to an individual's enlightenment and culture, no longer really contribute to the common good.

It cannot be said that Mr. Podhoretz's diagnosis was sympathetically received. I overheard the idea of a "common culture," for example, variously described as "moribund," "imperialistic," and "fascist." It was considered to be equally "sexist," I gathered, judging from the knowing looks that his use of the phrase "intellectual patrimony" occasioned. President Giamatti began by telling us that he found Mr. Podhoretz's talk "internally contradictory," for is there not a contradiction between asserting the essentially private nature of the humanities and then lamenting that they no longer conduce to the commonweal? In fact, though, President Giamatti's charge depended upon distorting Mr. Podhoretz's description of the humanities. It is one thing to say that the humanities cannot be justified on instrumental grounds, as Mr. Podhoretz did, quite another to say that they are a private affair entirely without social consequence, which no one but President Giamatti thought to propose.

The President of Yale University, himself a scholar of Renaissance literature, also came out strongly against the idea of a canon. Instead, he thought that the humanities should encourage "modes of thinking that would discipline the imagination without pretending to direct it"—the idea being, I suppose, that it doesn't much matter what one learns so long as one learns something. President Giamatti even claimed that this was the "Greek view" of education. Perhaps he meant the view current in contemporary Greece; certainly, the idea that education should seek "to discipline the imagination without pretending to direct it" is completely foreign to the teachings of Plato and Aristotle—think, for example, of the quite definite ideas that Plato had about what should and should not be taught in his discussion of education in the third book of *The Republic.* But leaving the Greek view of education to one side, President Giamatti's reservations about the importance of the canon do help us understand his central charge against Mr. Podhoretz: that his view of the humanities is "solipsistic" and "spiritually selfish." Basically, President Giamatti presented Mr. Podhoretz as an elitist who wanted to keep culture for himself. But as I understand it, the real difference between them was that Mr. Podhoretz wanted the *humanities* to be as widely available as possible, whereas President Giammatti was happy with what we might call universal schooling—the substance, the content, of what was taught was for him more or less up for grabs.

If nothing else, President Giamatti exemplified the strategy that Henry Rosovky, the session's first respondent, identified as the prime imperative for academic administrators—"Be vague." Professor Rosovsky, himself a social scientist, began his response with some amusing reflections on the difference between the humanities and the social sciences. For example, he found it "very humanistic" that there should be no formal papers at the session; and thinking over the discrepancy in income and prestige between faculty in the social sciences and the humanities, he couldn't but wonder whether the true social mission of the humanities "may in fact be sacrificial." About the humanities themselves, Professor Rosovsky suggested that their hallmark was "an eternal dissatisfaction," that they ought in fact to "engender a kind of dissatisfaction," and hence that they "should not be conservative." Against Mr. Podhoretz's vision of a "common culture," Professor Rosovsky sided with President Giamatti in questioning the desirability of adhering to a canon and in extolling the ideal of a "multi-culture" nourished by disparate sources and traditions.

But the most articulate, as well as the most histrionic, response to Mr. Podhoretz came from the Yale Divinity School Professor Cornel West. Professor West's performance, approximating the fervor of a political rally or revival meeting, clearly won the hearts and minds of the Yale audience. They thrilled to his rhetoric, punctuating his impassioned speech with enthusiastic applause. Professor West warmed up with a few words about "decolonization," "the eclipse of European dominance" in the world, and the disintegration of "white, male, WASP hegemony" in the academy. (I had thought that WASPs were white by definition, but no matter: "white, male, WASP hegemony" has an edifying ring to it.) He pictured the evolution of the humanities in recent years as a reflection of a world-wide struggle for freedom against what it has pleased him to describe elsewhere as "the final fruits of bourgeois humanism: North Atlantic ethnocentrism."[1]

In Professor West's view, the "collapsing consensus" that Mr. Podhoretz spoke of tokened not decline but liberation. The Sixties, far from being a debacle, was a "watershed" for the humanities. For one thing, the "onslaught" of popular culture that began then has helped undermine elitist notions of high culture. Then, too, the attention lavished on the history and literature of blacks, women, peasants, and other groups has revealed the traditional canon to be the biased, ethnocentric construction that it is. Hence the "self-contempt" that Mr. Podhoretz said a study of the humanities tended to instill these days is really "a deeper self-critique" that mirrors important changes in the world ("the eclipse of European dominance," etc.), changes that must be recognized and accommodated "if we are not to blow up the planet."

I hasten to add, though, that in criticizing Mr. Podhoretz, Professor West by no means sought to align himself with President Giamatti. On the contrary, he criticized both men for their "lack of historical sense" and for their conservatism. (The term "conservative," one notes, has degenerated into a negative epithet; in many circles, to describe something or someone as "conservative" is simply a politicized way of signaling one's disapproval.) Distinguishing between the "battle-ridden neoconservatism" of Mr. Podhoretz and the "more charming" conservatism of President Giamatti, Professor West wondered whether the "dynamism" championed by President Giamatti didn't at bot-

---

1 See his "Afterword: The Politics of American Neo-Pragmatism," in *Post-Analytic Philosophy,* edited by Cornel West and John Rajchman, Columbia University Press, 1985, pp. 259-275.

tom merely represent "the recovery of highbrow classical humanism." He can rest easy on that score, I think, even if it must be admitted that, in comparison with Professor West's vision of the humanities, President Giamatti's does seem conservative.

To my mind, however, the real clue to Professor West's view came with his celebration of the incorporation of the New Left into the university. Among other things, he championed the New Left for creating "combat zones" that could challenge the entire ethos of bourgeois humanism that stands behind the humanities as traditionally conceived. And taking issue with Mr. Podhoretz's severe criticism of the intellectual, moral, and political effects of the New Left, Professor West described writers like Herbert Marcuse and the post-World War II French Marxists as "the best of Western civilization."

Now, it is worth pausing for a moment over Professor West's identification of Herbert Marcuse and the "French Marxists" as representatives of "the best of Western civilization." Just what do these individuals stand for? What have they contributed to furthering the fundamental principles of the humanities? Consider Louis Althusser, one of the most influential among the French Marxists whom Professor West admires. In an interview that he gave in 1968,[2] this example of the "best of Western civilization" explained that he had come to philosophy through his attempt to "become a Communist militant" during and after World War II. Having finally understood that "philosophy is fundamentally *political*"—more specifically, that it is a tool of "class struggle"—Althusser also realized that "it was not easy to resist the spread of contemporary 'humanist' ideology, and bourgeois ideology's other assaults on Marxism." Being an intellectual, a philosopher, made things especially difficult, he confided: "Proletarians have a 'class instinct' which helps them on the way to proletarian 'class positions.' Intellectuals, on the contrary, have a petty-bourgeois class instinct which fiercely resists this transition." Most would agree, however, that Althusser succeeded rather well in overcoming the specified resistance, even if he finally fell prey to "contemporary humanist ideology" when he confessed to murdering his wife in 1980. In any case, it is quite clear that Althusser's view of intellectual life is deeply inimical to the ideal of disinterested scholarly inquiry, an ideal that is at the heart of the humanist tradition.

Then there is Marcuse. One could turn to any number of his works for an introduction to his view of the value of the humanities—to the "Political Preface" that he added to the 1966 edition of *Eros and Civilization*, for example, where he calls for a thoroughgoing revolt against "the political machine, the corporate machine, the cultural and educational machine" of "affluent Western society." What he calls for, in short, is a revolt against just those political, social, and intellectual traditions that define the humanistic endeavor. But perhaps the best précis of Marcuse's thinking about such matters is to be found in his notorious 1965 essay, "Repressive Tolerance."[3] Unable to deny that modern Western democracies offer their citizens an unparalleled degree of personal and political liberty, Marcuse is nevertheless able to denounce the West as essentially "totalitarian" by the simple device of declaring its brand of liberty "repressive" and a product of "false consciousness." (What a versatile tool of obfuscation the notion of "false consciousness" has been, utterly exempt from subservience to mere "empirical reality"!) Indeed, he offers a simple formula for distinguishing between the "repressive tolerance" that expresses itself in the real world in such phenomena as freedom of speech and freedom of assembly and the "liberating tolerance" that would seem to occur chiefly in his imagination: "Liber-

2 "Philosophy as a Revolutionary Weapon," reprinted in *Lenin and Philosophy and Other Essays*, translated by Ben Brewster, Monthly Review Press, 1971, pp. 11-22.

3 Reprinted in *A Critique of Pure Tolerance*, by Robert Paul Wolff, *et alia*, Beacon Press, 1969, pp. 81-123.

ating tolerance," he writes, "would mean intolerance against movements from the Right, and toleration of movements from the Left."

In brief, then, what Marcuse wants is "not 'equal' but *more* representation of the Left," and he blithely sanctions "extralegal means if the legal ones have proved to be inadequate." In one of the more extraordinary passages of the essay, Marcuse admits that "extreme suspension of the right of free speech and free assembly is indeed justified only if the whole of society is in extreme danger," but continues immediately to note that

> I maintain that our society is in such an emergency situation, . . . Different opinions and "philosophies" can no longer compete peacefully for adherence and persuasion on rational grounds: the "marketplace of ideas" is organized and delimited by those who determine the national and the individual interest. In this society, for which the ideologists have proclaimed the "end of ideology," the false consciousness has become the general consciousness—from the government down to its last objects.

There is no escape, apparently—unless of course one happens to be blessed, as Marcuse believed himself to be, with the "true consciousness" that allows one to penetrate such nearly universal mendacity.

It is in the context of such passages from Professor West's intellectual heroes, I believe, that we must understand the conception of freedom that underlies his view of the humanities. Like his heroes, Professor West finds the "ideology of pluralism" suspect because it "domesticates" radical thought. And like them, too, he questions the traditional "bourgeois" notion of the citizen as a "bearer of rights." Instead, he lobbies for an idea of citizenship that would incorporate "collective action," that would "undermine the liberal protection of rights" in favor of a more encompassing ideal. In response to an objection from Mr. Podhoretz, Professor West admitted that the New Left faced the "temptation" to nihilism and totalitarianism. But he did not seem to think the temptation very serious, and stressed the promise of freedom over such obstacles. Given the record of utopian thinking in this century, however, Oscar Wilde's boast that he could resist anything but temptation seems perhaps less a piece of wit than a solemn admonition.

Since the second session of Yale's symposium on the humanities and the public interest had sought to dispose of the traditional rationale for the humanities, it seemed only appropriate that the final session should address itself to the question of formulating a new rationale for its discredited predecessor. The session was moderated by Professor Brooks, and featured presentations by Jonathan Culler, professor of English and comparative literature at Cornell University, and Vincent Scully, professor of the history of art at Yale. Responding to Professors Culler and Scully were Carolyn G. Heilbrun, professor of English at Columbia University, and J. Hillis Miller, professor of English and comparative literature at Yale.

Professor Culler began by criticizing the traditional rationale for the humanities as "universalist" and "foundationalist." The pretension to be "universalist," he said, was primarily a political consideration: the humanities as traditionally conceived had presumed to speak universally to the human condition, but had in fact represented a narrow "white male" viewpoint. The attempt to be "foundationalist" involves epistemological considerations: the humanities had pretended to provide a foundation for both thought and values, but radical criticism in the last decades had exposed the fictional, and ideologically motivated, ground of that pretense. Professor Culler did not, however, attempt to formulate the new rationale for the humanities that he demanded, but merely offered a list of "divided imperatives" that he thought the humanities ought to heed. The list was fairly vague, even banal, unfortunately—the humanities ought to "assume unity" but also assert the value of other cultures, and so on—though it was full of appropriately combative rhetoric and wonderful-sounding, Nietzschean proclamations like his suggestion that thought really becomes valuable "only when it is extreme."

As an example of the kind of retrograde thinking he disparaged, Professor Culler cited a letter he had recently received from a dean at St. John's College in Annapolis, Maryland, inviting him to lecture there. St. John's offers a traditional "great books" curriculum—tailored to include classic developments in modern science and mathematics—and the dean, explaining the nature of the curriculum, described it as based on the "greatest books" of the Western tradition. This Professor Culler and his audience found quite risible, for after all what did the good dean from St. John's mean by the "greatest books"? Only books written by "white Western males before 1900," of course, something that for Professor Culler seemed to demonstrate how parochial—not to say ethnocentric and sexist—his correspondent's notion of education must be. (For the record, one does read women authors and beyond 1900 at St. John's.) Professor Culler never really specified his own idea of a good college curriculum. But one can bet that it wouldn't be "ethnocentric"—indeed, it's not even clear that it would be anthropocentric, since Professor Culler wondered in passing whether a view of the humanities based exclusively on a study of mankind wouldn't be guilty of "speciesism."

Mercifully, Professor Culler did not pursue this absurdity, though it was taken up by Vincent Scully, who began his talk by suggesting that what we needed was not so much a new rationale for the humanities as a new rationale for "animality." Professor Scully then treated us to a slide show that opened, as such slide shows must, with a picture of the snow shovel Marcel Duchamp presented as a work of art in 1915. What won't be taken as a work of art today, Professor Scully reflected, and then went on to share with his audience a number of other truly novel ideas: that the movies and television have emerged as the dominant style of modern life, for example, or that the artist must be "open-minded, pluralistic, poised for surprise." One began to understand why Professor Scully is most successful in a lecture hall full of undergraduates: when entertainment with a dash of edification about the wonderfulness of art is the goal, one needn't worry about the details.

Carolyn Heilbrun began her response on a melancholy note by observing that even now, even at a symposium on the humanities at Yale in 1986, she was the only woman on the panel. And I was surprised, I must confess, that Professor Brooks could have made this blunder. Surely he must have known that such a discrepancy in numbers would be held up for criticism. And as an academic administrator, he must also have known that the important thing in such situations is not to get the appropriate speakers for the occasion but to assemble a panel with the correct ethnic, social, and sexual mix. In any case, Professor Heilbrun went on to note that, though she was also the oldest person on the panel, it was the symposium's youngest representatives, Professors Culler and West, who spoke for her. She, too, believed that college should "teach us to be dissatisfied" and that thought is really valuable only when it is extreme. In addition, as the panel's official feminist, she also told us that it is the questions that women can ask about the canon that are the important questions. Why only women can ask them, or indeed, what the important ones might be, she didn't really say. Nevertheless, one got a pretty good idea of the kind of thing she had in mind when she criticized Professor Scully for presenting Michelangelo's depiction of the creation of man as representative of the human condition. After all, both God and Adam were—well, there's no getting around it: they were male, and how universal can that be?

After all this, J. Hillis Miller cannot be blamed for failing to add much to the discussion: by this time, the fashionable positions had all been staked out. Professor Miller has proved himself an expert at creatively adapting fashionable positions, however, and in his talk he adroitly elaborated on several of the day's themes. Above all, he warned against attempting simply to reimpose the traditional canon and proposed, as a kind of compromise, a curriculum in which canonical works would be read alongside "non-canonical" ones. What seemed crucial to him—and this was an idea that appealed to a good number of speakers that day—was not so much the teaching of particular texts or subjects as the teaching of "reading" in general.

The session, and the symposium, ended with a few comments and questions. Two comments in particular stuck with me. The first was Professor Heilbrun's assertion that our reading of texts is inescapably "ideological." And the second was Professor Brooks's concluding observation that, because the humanities are "inherently subversive," the recent developments in the academy that people like Secretary Bennett and Mr. Podhoretz bemoan ought actually be taken as signs of health. Together, the comments seemed to me to epitomize the proceedings in New Haven that day, and it may be well to conclude by considering them in a bit more detail.

The idea that all reading is "ideological" has gained great currency in literary studies in recent years. Among other things, it implies that we are imprisoned by our point of view, that our language, our social or ethnic background, or our sex inescapably condition the way we understand things. But are we so imprisoned? Granted that such contingencies *influence* our point of view, do they finally determine it? "Ideologies," as Hannah Arendt observed years ago, are "isms which to the satisfaction of their adherents can explain everything and every occurrence by deducing it from a single premise." In this sense, she notes, an ideology differs from a simple opinion "in that it claims to possess either the key to history, or the solution for all 'riddles of the universe,' or the intimate knowledge of the hidden universal laws which are supposed to rule nature and man."[4] Yet is is precisely this sort of distinction that the contention that all reading is ideological dismisses. It dismisses, in other words, the crucial distinction *between* a point of view and an ideology, between an individual perspective on the world—which *as* a perspective is open to challenge, accommodation, correction—and an *idée fixe.* All in all, what we might call the universalization of ideology underscores the truth of Northrop Frye's observation that "it is a curious tendency in human nature to believe in disillusionment: that is, to think we are nearest the truth when we have established as much falsehood as possible."[5]

And in this context, since Matthew Arnold was invoked, whether as friend or foe, by practically every speaker at the Yale symposium, it is worth mentioning that in "The Function of Criticism" Arnold identifies "disinterestedness" as the chief mark of responsible criticism. Now in describing criticism as "disinterested," Arnold did not mean that it presumes to speak without reference to a particular point of view—though critics of the idea often so caricature it. Rather, he meant a habit of inquiry that keeps "aloof from what is called 'the practical view of things' . . . [b]y steadily refusing to lend itself to any . . . ulterior, political, practical considerations about ideas." In modern terms, Arnold looked to criticism to provide a bulwark *against* ideology, against interpretations that are subordinated to essentially political interests. Of course, the ideal of such disinterested criticism is rejected by many contemporary critics as naïve (or worse), though it is not at all clear whether the criticism they practice is more astute than Arnold's or, alas, only more ideological.

Arnold is also useful in appreciating the oft-voiced contention that education ought to instill "dissatisfaction" or, to use Profes-

4 *The Origins of Totalitarianism,* Harcourt Brace Jovanovich, 1973, *seriatim,* pp. 468, 159.

5 "The Realistic Oriole: A Study of Wallace Stevens," in *Fables of Identity: Studies in Poetic Mythology,* Harcourt Brace & World, 1963, p. 244.

sor Brooks's more dramatic formulation, that the humanities are "inherently subversive." Such sentiments were so widely shared at the Yale symposium that it was almost taken for granted that the function of education is not to impart knowledge but to subvert, to excite "dissatisfaction." Behind this idea is a deep suspicion of authority, a suspicion that, in fact, would have us collapse the distinction between authority and authoritarianism. Yet it is a nice question whether the humanities can survive without recognizing the authority of tradition. It is indeed for this reason that, in "The Literary Influence of Academies," Arnold praised the willing "deference to a standard higher than one's own habitual standard in intellectual matters" as the result of a "sensitiveness of intelligence." And thus it is, too, that Hannah Arendt suggested that "conservatism, in the sense of conservation, is of the essence of the educational activity, whose task is always to cherish and protect something." "The real difficulty in modern education," Arendt wrote,

> lies in the fact that, despite all the fashionable talk about a new conservatism [Arendt was writing in 1958], even that minimum of conservation and the conserving attitude without which education is simply not possible is in our time extraordinarily hard to achieve. There are very good reasons for this. The crisis of authority in education is most closely connected with the crisis of tradition, that is with the crisis in our attitude toward the realm of the past . . . . The problem of education in the modern world lies in the fact that by its very nature it cannot forgo either authority or tradition, and yet it must proceed in a world that is neither structured by authority nor held together by tradition.[6]

"Neither structured by authority nor held together by tradition"—in the end, this would seem to describe the goal of the "new rationale" for the humanities as envisioned at Yale. And of course the real casualties are the students and junior faculty, who often haven't the foggiest notion of the value of the tradition they have been taught to disparage. The senior faculty are at least old enough to recognize what it is they are abandoning. Champions of the "new rationale" like to pretend that they are merely thinking more critically than the tradition had allowed. In fact, though, they have as often as not degenerated from criticism to nihilism. Indeed, the whole situation reminds one of nothing so much as of Turgenev's portrait of the nihilist Bazarov in *Fathers and Sons*:

> "A nihilist," said Nikolai Petrovich. "That comes from the Latin *nihil—nothing,* I imagine; the term must signify a man who . . . who recognizes nothing?"
>
> "Say—who respects nothing," put in Pavel Petrovich, and set to work with the butter again.
>
> "Who looks at everything critically," observed Arcady.
>
> "Isn't that exactly the same thing?" asked Pavel Petrovich.
>
> "No, it's not the same thing. A nihilist is a person who does not take any principle for granted, however much that principle may be revered."

The humanities had once striven to inculcate the ability to think critically, that is, to enable one to discriminate between ideology and a point of view, between legitimate authority and authoritarianism, between genuine freedom and its tyrannical parody. The "new rationale" propounded at Yale would have us believe that thinking critically is indistinguishable from Bazarov's nihilism.

(*June* 1986)

---

6 "The Crisis in Education," reprinted in *Between Past and Future: Eight Exercises in Political Thought,* Penguin, 1978, pp. 192-3, 195.

T. J. Clark and the Marxist critique of modern painting

by Hilton Kramer

The question is, finally: how could there be an effective political art? Is not the whole thing a chimaera, a dream, incompatible with the basic conditions of artistic production in the nineteenth century—easel painting, privacy, isolation, the art market, the ideology of individualism? Could there be any such thing as revolutionary art until the means existed—briefly, abortively—to change those basic conditions: till 1919, when El Lissitzky puts up his propaganda poster outside a factory in Vitebsk; or 1918, in Berlin, when Richard Huelsenbeck has the opportunity, at last, to "make poetry with a gun in his hand"?

—T. J. Clark, in *The Absolute Bourgeois: Artists and Politics in France 1848-1851.*

"It turns out we are part of the superstructure," M. said to me in 1922, after our return from Georgia. Not long before, M. had written about the separation of culture from the State, but the Civil War had ended, and the young builders of the new State had begun—for the time being in theory only—to put everything in its proper place. It was then that culture was assigned to the superstructure.

—Nadezhda Mandelstam, in *Hope Against Hope: A Memoir.*

There are times when, owing to its larger ramifications, a single academic appointment at a leading university very quickly acquires the status of an historical event for those alert to its meaning. The appointment of T. J. Clark as professor of art history at Harvard University in 1980 was for some observers an event of this kind. For what it signified was a decisive shift in the way the study of art history—and most particularly, of course, the history of modern painting, which is Professor Clark's academic specialty—would henceforth be pursued as an intellectual discipline at this venerable seat of learning.

In an earlier generation the Harvard art history department, together with its illustrious museum-training program at the Fogg Art Museum, had won a high reputation among the *cognoscenti* of the art world as a citadel of humanistic scholarship and aesthetic connoisseurship. There had indeed developed a distinctive Fogg tradition at Harvard. It was a tradition based, above all, on the close, comparative study of individual art objects, and one of its goals was to produce a certain kind of expert intelligence—aesthetic intelligence. In the perspective of this tradition, it was assumed that for the mastery of such intelligence the cultivation of sensibility—a sensibility for objects—was quite as essential as the acquisition of historical knowledge; that, in other words, aesthetic intelligence was virtually meaningless if separated from the disciplines of connoisseurship.

This, in any event, appears to have been the ideal that once governed the Fogg tradition at Harvard, and from the influence it exerted on the museums and the universities, on art collecting and on art scholarship, there can be no question but that the art public in America had over the course of many years reaped some significant benefits. There are certainly more than a few masterpieces to be seen in our public collections today which owe their presence there—and thus their place in our experience—directly or indirectly to precisely the kind of connoisseurship that concentrates its principal interest on aesthetic quality. For this reason, the Fogg tradition may be accurately described, I think, as an example of cultural elitism that serves the public interest.

If there was also something to be said against the Fogg tradition—that it tended to be snobbish and clubby; that it was often condescending to outsiders, operating in the world of money, jobs, appointments, and preferments, as something of an old-boy network; and that it produced its full share of duffers who had all the appurtenances and pretensions of the connoisseur without any discernible trace of the sensibility or knowledge essential to the connoisseur's task—well, that too may be taken as a measure of how far the ideal often fell short of being realized in an imperfect world. The ideal itself, however, was not only a noble one, but one that had the merit of addressing itself to something at once central and indispensable to our aesthetic experience.

By the time Professor Clark came to Harvard in 1980, this Fogg tradition was already on the wane. If its demise was not quite complete, its days were nonetheless clearly numbered. The cultural insurgency of the Sixties had done its work at Harvard, no less than elsewhere in the academic world, and a new administration at the university was obviously prepared to welcome not only radical change but a change in the direction of an avowedly left-wing radicalism. Art history was by no means the only field in which this new direction made itself felt at Harvard. Its successful penetration of the law-school faculty was sufficiently dramatic in its consequences to cause articles to be written about them in *The New Yorker, The New York Times,* and other publications. For those who understood what was happening to the study of art history at Harvard, the change represented by Professor Clark's appointment was seen straightaway to be no less fateful.

What this change entailed, moreover, could never have been in doubt. Harvard certainly knew what it was getting. Professor Clark, a British scholar trained at Cambridge University and the Courtauld Institute, had in 1973 published two works—*The Absolute Bourgeois: Artists and Politics in France 1848-1851* and *Image of the People: Gustave Courbet and the 1848 Revolution*—which spelled out his philosophy of art history in unmistakable terms. They had instantly established him as one of the most programmatic and plainspoken Marxist writers then concentrating on the field of nineteenth-century French art. The author of *The Absolute Bourgeois* and *Image of the People* was not one of your new-style, hermetic Marxists, given to employing an esoteric jargon and an impenetrable syntax. There was nothing arcane in Professor Clark's vocabulary, and nothing obscure or ambiguous in his ideology. The opening chapter of *Image of the People* had been devoted to a disquisition "On the Social History of Art," which made the flagrantly political character of the inquiry altogether explicit; and lest there remain any lingering doubts on this score, Professor Clark wrote a new preface for inclusion in both volumes when these were reissued in paperback editions by the Princeton University Press in 1982.

In this preface he underscored the fact that both *Image of the People* and *The Absolute Bourgeois* "were written for the most part in the winter of 1969-70, in what seemed then (and still seems) ignominious but unavoidable retreat from the political events of the previous six years. Those events haunt the books' best and worst pages, and provide throughout the main frame of reference for the history of a distant revolution and its cultural dimension." The main purpose of the preface was thus to provide a summary of what Professor Clark called "the books' chief problem"—which is to say, their principal political objective.

> So I owe it to the reader, confronting these relics of a slightly better time, [he wrote] to state again what I took to be the books' chief problem. They wished to establish what happened to art when it became involved, however tangentially, in a process of revolution and counter-revolution: in other words, when it lost its normal place in the machinery of social control and was obliged for a while to seek out other spaces for representation—other publics, other subjects, other idioms, other means of production. As my Jamesian title [*The Absolute Bourgeois*] was meant to imply, one could hardly have expected the story, in an order already irredeemably capitalist, to be other than one of failure to find such space. Bourgeois society is efficient at making all art its own. The conditions for a rendezvous between artistic practice and the only class which henceforth could produce and sustain alternative meanings to those of capital did not exist in 1850, and have only existed in botched and fragmentary form in the century since—against the grain of the Bolshevik Revolution, around the edges of the Workers' Councils in Berlin, Barcelona or Turin, and nowadays [1981] perhaps in the struggle of the Polish working class to reimpose soviet rule.

There is much that could be said about the outlook that is revealed in these observations. One notes, for example, the easy, unargued assumption that the primary "meanings" to be gleaned in a work of art are those which derive from the economic and political situation in which it is produced. Then, too, there is the implacable hatred of capitalism and its corollary detestation of the institutions of bourgeois society (except, perhaps, where appointments to the Harvard University faculty are concerned). There is the inevitable—for a Marxist—glorification of revolution, and the cynical—indeed sickening—reference to "the struggle of the Polish working class to reimpose soviet rule." From these and other attitudes so emphatically avowed in the preface to the new editions of *Image of the People* and *The Absolute Bourgeois,* as well as in the books themselves, it will be evident that Professor Clark not only approaches the study of art history from the perspective of a doctrinaire Marxist, with everything this implies about the primacy given to politics in his entire intellectual enterprise, but that he wishes to be clearly understood to be doing just that. Somewhat less evident, perhaps, at least to the uninitiated, is what follows from this: that in the perspective of this politicized history of art, art itself is definitively consigned to what in classic Marxist parlance is called the "superstructure"—a subject to which we shall return in due course.

Now Professor Clark has given us a new book, his first since joining the Harvard faculty. It is called *The Painting of Modern Life,* and it bears the subtitle, "Paris in the Art of Manet and His Followers."[1] Once again, the ostensible subject is nineteenth-century French painting. The names of Manet, Monet, Pissarro, Degas, Seurat, and other artists of the Impressionist era appear frequently, and reproductions of their works, both in color and in black and white, adorn its pages. Yet it will come as no surprise to any reader acquainted with *Image of the People* and *The Absolute Bourgeois* to discover that the real focus of *The Painting of Modern Life* is not on the history of *art.* What interests Professor Clark is something else.

In this new book it is mainly, but not exclusively, the issue of *class.* In its fundamental concerns, *The Painting of Modern Life* is yet another contribution to the propagation of that mythic phenomenon which lies at the heart of the Marxist conception of history: class conflict. This is Professor Clark's real subject in this book. Everything else—certainly everything involving aesthetics—is placed in a subordinate relation to that sub-

1 *The Painting of Modern Life: Paris in the Art of Manet and His Followers;* by T. J. Clark. Alfred A. Knopf, 338 pages, $25.

ject. And while Professor Clark is shrewd enough not to insist on the fact that this is his principal subject in this book, he doesn't deny that it is, either. He even offers us some ruminations on the concept of class at the outset of the discussion, but at the same time cautioning the reader that these may appear to be "very general, not to say banal, propositions on the nature of society as such." He is anything but a fool. He knows exactly what he is doing. But he is also somewhat fearful—as he has every reason to be—of being seen to be an exponent of what he himself dismisses as "the worst pitfalls of vulgar Marxism." Rather than dwell on the "vulgar" concept of class conflict, then, he avails himself of the more sanitized and eminently more fashionable nomenclature of semiotics. Thus the new revised standard version is: "Society is a battlefield of representations." Behind this semiotic smokescreen, however, the same old Marxist scenarios remain firmly in place. Nothing has changed but the words.

The truth is, there are no instruments fine enough to measure the difference between the vulgar Marxism which Professor Clark professes to scorn and the particular variety of Marxist dialectics which governs every page of *The Painting of Modern Life*. In the one variety of Marxism, as in the other, neither the creation nor the experience of art is believed to enjoy the slightest degree of aesthetic independence from the iron laws of history. Everything in art is seen to be determined by the economic "base" and what are now called its "representations." As a result, art is simply—and sometimes very simply indeed—treated as a kind of epiphenomenon of the historical process, of interest mainly as a reflection of the depredations of bourgeois society and the strategies which have been devised to conceal or compensate for their outrageous moral consequences.

In keeping with this view, Professor Clark writes of Seurat's *La Grande Jatte* that "it attempts to find form for the appearance of class in capitalist society" and "that the forms it discovers are in some sense more truthful than most others produced at the time; and that it suggests ways in which class might still be painted." (There is thus an assumption here that "ways in which class might still be painted" is, or ought to be, an important item on the agenda of contemporary art today.) And just as "the intermingling of classes" is said to be "Seurat's subject," and hence the basis of his appeal for us, the real interest of Manet's *Olympia* is said to be "that class was the essence of Olympia's modernity and lay behind the great scandal she provoked." Of Manet's *La Musique aux Tuileries,* moreover, Professor Clark writes that it is "hardly a picture of modernity at all, as it is sometimes supposed to be, but, rather, a description of 'society's' resilience in the face of empire." Class is thus assumed to be the key to every aspect of painting by Manet and his followers, and Professor Clark is sometimes quite cross with those painters whose work fails to support him on this point.

Much of *The Painting of Modern Life* is devoted not so much to painting itself as it is to the work of Baron Haussmann in redesigning and reconstructing the city of Paris in the nineteenth century and to the ways in which painters depicted the life of the city as the result of this work. Professor Clark is very concerned about those artists who are deemed to have failed to grasp the real—which is to say, the class—meaning of this phenomenon. Monet and Renoir, for example, are among those who are given failing grades on this score.

> It should go without saying that this situation—Haussmann's work and its aftermath—[Professor Clark writes] presented painting with as many problems as opportunities. Naturally it offered occasions for a meretricious delight in the modern, or proposals in paint that the street henceforth would be a fine and dandy place. (I cannot see, for example, that Monet's two pictures of *Le Boulevard des Capucines* in 1873 do more than provide that kind of touristic entertainment, fleshed out with some low-level demonstrations of painterliness. Where Monet went, Renoir inevitably

followed; his image of the *grands boulevards* in 1875 is untroubled by its subject's meanings, and not helped by this innocence.)

Now it needs to be pointed out, I think, that when Professor Clark writes the words *I cannot see* in this passage, he isn't kidding. He sees only what he wants to see, and he clearly cannot find anything worth looking at in a painting if it fails to denote signs of class distinction, or other evidence of social conflict, with the requisite degree of documentary explicitness. To the extent that he can be said to have an "eye" for anything in painting, it is as an eye for "its subject's meanings." But these "meanings" are rarely, if ever, those determined by the painter. They are entirely predetermined by Professor Clark himself and his "method." Which is to say that he has eyes only for the meanings he has gone in search of, and no other meanings—least of all those which are known to have been of primary interest to the painter in question—have any reality for him.

As for the matter of how painters see their subjects, Professor Clark turns out to be a curious (and sometimes comical) guide. Consider, for example, the famous question of *flatness* in Manet's painting. Professor Clark does not deny, of course, that it is an issue in Manet, but he insists that it is not so much an aesthetic issue as an ideological and social one. Thus, the very term is rejected in the discussion of *Olympia,* for it is deemed insufficient to account for the "circuit of signs" that is held to be responsible for the radical nature of the painting's subject. Yet in speaking of Manet's *Argenteuil, les canotiers,* flatness is accepted because it is found to serve a documentary function in the painting. Taking note of "the unlikely construction of the black straw hat" in this picture, Professor Clark writes: "it has to be said . . . that Manet *found* flatness more than invented it; he saw it around him in the world he knew."

On the other hand, what Monet's eye—the most celebrated "eye" in Impressionist painting—found in the world *he* knew is judged to have little or nothing to do with visual observation and everything to do with the presuppositions of political ideology.

> There is a rule to these paintings [by Monet], and it might be stated roughly as follows [Professor Clark writes]: Industry can be recognized and represented, but not labour; the factories have to be kept still, as if that were the guarantee in an art which pretended to relish the fugitive and ephemeral above all else. Industry must not mean *work*; as long as that fictitious distinction was in evidence, a painting could include as much of the nineteenth century as it liked. The railway, for instance, was an ideal subject because its artifacts could so easily be imagined as self-propelled or self-sufficient. The train went discreetly through the snow . . . .

And so on. Nor was Monet's eye the only one to be governed primarily by social considerations of this sort. Why did Pissarro, at a crucial phase in his development as a painter, turn to the Neo-Impressionist methods of Seurat? Not, according to Professor Clark, for aesthetic reasons—which are never mentioned in this book. What prompted Pissarro's interest in Seurat's pictorial innovations was, it turns out, the burning issue of "leisure in class conflict." (Here the "battlefield of representations" is abandoned in favor of the more familiar Marxist terminology.) Of Neo-Impressionism Professor Clark writes:

> I do not believe that its vehemence (or its appeal to Pissarro) can be understood unless it is seen as deriving from an altered view of leisure, and of art as part of that leisure—which in turn derived from a new set of class allegiances.

I await with interest the monograph which either Professor Clark or one of his students must surely now be preparing for the purpose of tracing the relationship of every one of Pissarro's changes of style to the artist's shifting perception of "class allegiances" in the society of his day. Who knows? In the magical world of Marxist dialectics it might even be disclosed to us that it is in this issue of *class* that the key to Pissarro's influence on Cézanne—and perhaps on Matisse, too—is finally to be found. No doubt all will be revealed to us in the fullness of time.

It would be unrewarding to dwell further on Professor Clark's treatment of particular artists or particular works of art in *The Painting of Modern Life.* The field of inquiry which it is the purpose of this book to explore and enlarge upon contributes nothing to our understanding of painting *as art,* and is not meant to. On the contrary, its purpose is to destroy—or, as we say nowadays, deconstruct—the very idea that art is in any sense an autonomous enterprise or that its highest achievements often add up to a good deal more than the sum of the social and material circumstances of its creation. (Also deconstructed in the process—and thrown, as it were, onto the ash heap of history—is the concept of aesthetic intelligence that once governed the Fogg tradition at Harvard.) There is a striking irony in this, of course. For in denying to art the spiritual freedom that it has sought for itself and very often achieved in the modern era—most notably, of course, in precisely those bourgeois capitalist societies which Marxist criticism is most eager to condemn—writers of this persuasion inevitably exhibit a kinship with the kind of reactionary and philistine taste which led so many benighted critics to condemn modernist art in the first place.

I wonder if it isn't, after all, a sense of this kinship which has prompted Professor Clark to devote so much of his intellectual energy, in this book as in his others, to disinterring a great many of the articles and reviews which attacked Manet and his contemporaries in their own day. Professor Clark's devotion to this "lost" critical literature, which he has culled from the annals of nineteenth-century French journalism, amounts at times to an obsession. He can hardly set down three consecutive paragraphs of his own prose without inserting into them some lengthy passage from an obscure review of the exhibitions in which Manet, Seurat, and others showed their work. Excerpts from this vast reservoir of critical writing, usually given in English in the main body of Professor Clark's text and in the original French in the voluminous notes, actually make up a sizable part of *The Painting of Modern Life*—by far the more valuable part, in my opinion. Professor Clark's real gifts are those of a researcher, not a critic. Documents, not art objects, are his forte—which is yet another reason, I suppose, why he is inclined to deal with art objects as if they, too, were little more than social documents. Given his interest in nineteenth-century French art criticism, one rather regrets that Professor Clark hadn't settled for producing an anthology of critical writing along the lines of the collections given us in recent years by Elizabeth Gilmore Holt.[2] But of course it is not in the interest of his political scenario to do so. His quotations from French art criticism, like his "readings" of French paintings as sociological reports, are made to serve a purpose. Both are part of the indictment he has drawn up for the purpose of unmasking modernism itself as a failed revolutionary impulse. What is intolerable to a Marxist like Professor Clark is that modernist art, despite its many and famous conflicts with bourgeois society, has proved in the end to be an essential component of bourgeois culture, and accepted as such. For that reason alone modernism must now stand condemned as a coefficient of capitalism—than which, from a Marxist perspective, no worse crime in the realm of cultural life is conceivable. It must therefore now be discredited and deconstructed to make way for that future "rendezvous," as Professor Clark has called it, between artistic practice and "the only class"—the proletariat, of course—capable of ushering in a new golden age.

It is no wonder, really, that Professor Clark is haunted by the specter of "vulgar"

---

2 Holt's two major works on the history of art in nineteenth-century Europe are *The Triumph of Art for the Public* (Anchor Press, 1979) and *The Art of All Nations* (Anchor Press, 1981).

Marxism. Some forty-one years ago, in the aftermath of the radical movement of the Thirties, Arthur Koestler wrote an essay called "The Intelligentsia"—it was published in *Partisan Review* and then reprinted in *The Yogi and the Commissar*—in which he discussed the falsity of this Marxist mode of historical analysis. He spoke of "the fatal short cut [taken by Marx and Engels] from Economy to 'Superstructure': that is, culture, art, mass-psychology"—a shortcut that has been endlessly retraced by Marx's intellectual heirs ever since. "Marxian society," Koestler wrote, "has a basement—production, and an attic—intellectual production; the staircase and the lifts are missing." Koestler went on to point out that "it is not as simple as that: the triumphant class creating its own philosophic superstructure to fit its mode of production like a tailored suit." Now despite everything that has happened in the last four decades, and despite the new terminology that is invoked to give this famous "short cut" a new currency, this image of a basement and an attic with the staircase and the lifts missing is, as it happens, a very accurate description of the historical method employed by Professor Clark in the writing of *The Painting of Modern Life*. For much of this book, he rummages around in the basement of nineteenth-century French society, retracing and reinterpreting events in the economic life of the period. To make his ascent from this basement of "production" to the attic, where the form of "intellectual production" called painting is to be found, he is obliged to avail himself of that magic carpet he calls historical materialism. No wonder, then, that when he arrives at his destination he has some difficulty discovering—to use Koestler's other image—a "tailored suit" which entirely pleases him. History is not, after all, a fertile field for the discovery of miracles.

The question to be asked about *The Painting of Modern Life*, and indeed about Professor Clark's entire intellectual enterprise, is: Why? Why now? What accounts for its governing animus, which is a profound and unappeasable hostility to modernist art, and why has it won such a favorable response both inside the academy and out? In attempting to answer such questions, it is no longer sufficient to say that a phenomenon like Professor Clark is part of the price we continue to pay for the political upheavals of the Sixties. This is true as far as it goes—it is indeed the basic truth of the historical situation in which we find ourselves today—but it does not entirely account for the place which this Marxist critique of modern painting now occupies in contemporary cultural life or for its reception among people who believe themselves to be interested in art, people who believe art to be vitally important to their lives.

The answer, I think, lies in the sense of keen disappointment—a disappointment that amounts at times to a feeling of rage—among people of a generally liberal and leftist outlook over recent changes in our relation to the achievements of modern art. Brought up to believe that the essence of the modern movement was to be found in its *révolté* impulses, that in some sense modernism *was* revolutionary in its ultimate goals as well as in its technical and expressive innovations, these people feel betrayed by their discovery—which history has now made all but unavoidable—that they were mistaken, or at least misinformed, about the thing they loved so much and placed so high a value on. Modernism not only did *not* turn out to be, as they were for so long led to assume it was, coextensive with the impulses of political revolutionism, but was in some respects deeply hostile to those impulses and incompatible with them. Modernism really did turn out to be an essential component of bourgeois culture. And to this fact of history, which they now recognize *as* a fact of history, they cannot reconcile themselves. It leaves them bereft of a sense of cultural purpose. Never mind that these disappointed acolytes are the same people, for the most part, whose embrace of modernism has confirmed its central place in bourgeois cultural life. Such paradoxes of history do little to assuage the bitterness of their disappointment. They were brought up, after all, to believe that they could have the cake of revolution and eat it too, and now that they have discovered otherwise there is no consoling them. Their grief is great, and it has disposed them to welcome any and all attempts to discredit the achievements of the very thing in which they once placed their fondest hopes.

There remain, of course, for the people I speak of, certain sacred moments in the history of modern art that are exempt from the general condemnation. The Russian avant-garde in the early years of the Bolshevik Revolution, the German Dadaists in the upheaval of the First World War and the German revolution—these, above all, have not lost their luster. For true believers in the doctrine that modernism must remain synonymous with revolutionism if it is not to be despised and rejected, these remain the exemplary episodes in the history of artistic production (as they call it). Hence the loving references to these episodes in Professor Clark's writing. (Hence, too, the whole program of a critical journal like *October,* by the way, which draws its name and indeed its *Weltanschauung* from a similar reading of history.) Hence, above all, the need to discredit the idea of *aesthetic* achievement in art and replace it with scenarios claiming to represent an authentic *social* history of art.

Professor Clark is only one exemplar of this movement which has made such headway in the academy and the art journals (including such eminently bourgeois journals as *Art in America* and *Artforum*) in recent years, and Harvard's is by no means the only department of art history to have felt its influence. Yet precisely because Harvard for so long represented a philosophy of art that has now been made a special object of ideological deconstruction, T. J. Clark's appointment to that faculty has inevitably acquired a significance which reverberates far beyond the groves of academe.

(*March* 1985)

III. The Arts & Their Institutions

Art and patronage today

by Samuel Lipman

As far as patronage is concerned, it seems difficult to avoid the conclusion that all the arts are in pretty much the same condition today regardless of their separate developments and relative prosperities. This condition may be characterized as an inversion of John Kenneth Galbraith's famous (if not notorious) formulation about the state of American society in the late 1950s. For Professor Galbraith, America was then a land of private opulence and public squalor. For us today the arts in America are in a condition of public opulence and private decrepitude.

Clearly such a position does not represent the received wisdom. According to this quintessential distillation of past error, present self-service, and future illusion, the United States is the last haven of the private sector in culture. This supposed reality is pointed to with pride by conservative partisans of our democratic capitalistic society, but scorned by those who admire the glitter of European state culture. The proud cite the high level of private contributions to our arts institutions—made possible under a beneficent tax system—and the scornful lust after the cornucopia abroad of government largesse for such disparate artistic activities as the Berlin Philharmonic and the operas (if they can be called that) of the perennial avant-gardist Karlheinz Stockhausen.

There is no point in quoting statistics. Those available are, to put it most kindly, imperfect. But their burden is clear. In this country the preponderance of support for the arts comes from the private sector; in Europe, it comes from government. Because everywhere the role of education in making artistic activity possible is so downplayed, it must be added that both here and abroad a substantial amount of money for the arts comes in the form of school budgets; in Europe these budgets come almost totally from government sources, and here largely so. In any case, our national *per capita* arts expenditures, combining private and public contributions, stack up well against the figures for most of the major European countries. It should therefore be understood that when people extol the European state arts-support systems as a model for our country, what they desire is not a switch from private support to public, but rather an increase in total support produced by an increase in public spending.

But the issue is not just money. The issue is rather the relationship of money to art. From this perspective, our present means of supporting art is little different from that in Europe, for arts support increasingly means the same thing, whether here or abroad: support of public, not private, culture. Or put another way, the support of art, whatever the source, is not the support of the individual tastes of the givers; rather it is the support of the tastes which are held widely in the society as a whole. This formulation may be obscure; it certainly is difficult.

To understand the present relation between art and patronage, it is necessary first to describe something of the historic shift in the place of the arts in society during the four decades since World War II. In 1945, the greatest art was seen as belonging to high culture, which was the historical possession of a cultivated minority. This minority was usually of fortunate birth, mostly of economic privilege, and almost always of refined education. Whatever the art under discussion, whether visual arts, literature, music, or dance, the natural audience for it was small, self-selecting, and self-defining.

It goes without saying that although the culture favored by so restricted an audience was the leading intellectual and artistic force in society, it was not the only source of entertainment or art for the larger public. By 1945 popular culture was already carried by radio, recordings, and film (though not yet by television). It was widely seen by both its own audience and the smaller audience for high culture as an entirely separate activity, influencing more sophisticated pursuits and being influenced by them but nonetheless existing in its own world of creation and mass consumption. To use an up-to-date term, it could be said that while there was "crossover" between popular and high culture, there was very little confusion between them.

To be sure, this idea of a separate audience for an elite culture was deeply affected by the progress of what we might call the democratic ideal. European opera houses, after all, were built with many cheap seats and even with large areas for standing room, and the operas of Verdi did provide tunes for organ grinders on the streets. The emergence of public museums and public concerts in Europe occurred along with the coming of public education and universal literacy. But despite the democratic spread of culture, in the upper strata of many European societies there was deep satisfaction with the continuing reality of distinct cultures: one for the millions and another for those with the millions. These pre-industrial attitudes may be found today in the rigorously selective character of French higher education and in the impregnable career status of its graduates. An analagous phenomenon is evident in the position of Oxford and Cambridge (and their graduates) in English life. Indeed, only in the most recent years can it be said that wherever one looks in Europe—take France and England as examples—one sees enormous and troubled concern on the part of government with what in the United States is called "outreach."

In America, the situation of elite culture has always been different. This country was founded, after all, as a reaction against the continuation of those aristocratic social attitudes which bordered on the feudal. Such aristocracy as we have had—one thinks immediately of the Adams family—either made its peace with democracy or found itself in external or internal exile. The new monied elite of the nineteenth century was deeply affected by the gospel of wealth, which itself was the product of the many leveling influences, both religious and secular, at work in the expansion of the original colonies into a continental nation. The watchword, of course, was education, which meant education for the masses as well as education for the elite. Indeed, all of us are beneficiaries of the strength of our national educative impulse.

The effect of American attitudes toward education was not restricted to McGuffey's Reader and the one-room schoolhouse. There was the great growth of our public schools, the founding of our public library system, the development of land-grant colleges, and the provision (well back in the nineteenth century) of facilities for what is now called adult education. In this connection, it is also important not to forget the extraordinary flowering in this country of privately financed and controlled education; it is equally important to remember that this private education often assumed denominational forms.

But beyond—although not *above* and beyond—education in its specialized sense of teachers, classes, and students, and beyond the provision of facilities for scientific and scholarly investigation such as the Rockefeller Institute for Medical Research in New York and the Institute for Advanced Study in Princeton, culture for the masses included hefty doses of high artistic culture, regularly administered as a part of the social responsibilities of the leading figures of the community. The principle was the same whether the particular benefaction was the Metropolitan Museum or the Art Institute of Chicago in the second half of the nineteenth century or the Museum of Modern Art and the National Gallery in the first half of the twentieth, the Juilliard School in New York or the Curtis Institute in Philadelphia, the Metropolitan Opera in the East and the San Francisco Opera in the West. The duty of the lovers of high art was to provide that art in undefiled form as an *educational service* to those who by reason of birth, social position, economic status, and educational background did not, to put it in the vernacular, "know what they were missing." Both the governing taste, and the money necessary to communicate that taste, belonged to the rich, the cultured, and the powerful; only the bodies on the receiving end belonged to the masses.

Curiously, despite the comfortable patrician assumption that the rich would stay rich and the poor poor, it was never questioned that the culture the masses really wanted was exactly the high art that their betters wanted for themselves. And curiously, too, this upper-class self-confidence remained in operation well into the recent past. To cite just one example, many opera fans alive today remember the haughty yet eagerly ingratiating tones of Mrs. August Belmont as she raised funds on the air for the Metropolitan Opera Guild from the millions of Saturday radio listeners across the United States and Canada.

But after 1945 something changed. With the death of Franklin Roosevelt and his replacement by Harry Truman, the age of political leaders drawn from the patriciate came to an end. The passage of the GI Bill and the Fulbright awards program by Congress opened up college study in this country to most Americans and, for many of the brightest, even the prospect of graduate study abroad. A very few years later *Brown v. Board of Education,* along with the increasing entry of women into higher education, began the long-delayed process of making "most Americans" into "all Americans." About 1950 the CIA discovered that judicious covert aid to culture and ideas abroad might influence intellectuals, and after 1953 the Eisenhower administration realized that cultural exchange programs could be a valuable tool in foreign policy.

In the 1960s, forces within the Kennedy administration, led nominally by the president's wife but perhaps more effectively by Arthur Schlesinger, Jr., Richard Goodwin, and Michael Straight, argued for open federal support to the arts and the humanities. This support, in violation of a longtime taboo against American government interference with culture, was to be undertaken not for the purposes of foreign policy, or of social welfare (as had been the case in the 1930s with the WPA) or of ideological democratization. The arts and the humanities were to be supported for themselves, with *quality* as the sole criterion.

Yet there can be little doubt that another, and rather more complicated, reason for support was lurking in the background, surrounded by all the scrimshaw and the decorator rooms which have become a part of the cultural mythology of the Kennedy White House. This was the nagging idea that the existence in the United States of purely private culture—of a cultural life, that is, that did not receive the imprimatur of the state—robbed the state and its leaders of the legitimacy and the glory which in the great European countries was conferred by a rooted association with the imperishable monuments of civilization. There is evidence for the power of this nagging idea over Michael Straight, who later became deputy chairman of the National Endowment for the Arts during the Nixon administration. In his 1982 memoirs, *After Long Silence,* Mr. Straight wrote that his much-postponed decision to tell the FBI about his involvement with the Anthony Blunt Soviet espionage ring was forced by one fear: the exposure of his past might alter the fact that in 1963 "the United States Government accepted a limited but continuing responsibility for the advancement of the arts in America."

The legislation finally creating the National Endowment for the Arts (and the National Endowment for the Humanities) was not passed until the Johnson administration, where it took its place in the blizzard of Great Society legislation promulgated in the years following Kennedy's assassination. Small at first, the NEA grew rapidly under President Nixon and his NEA chairman, Nancy Hanks; this growth continued under President Carter and his chairman Livingston Biddle. It was not until the coming of Ronald Reagan in 1981 that the NEA budget leveled off, and indeed there are no signs today that the immediate future will see any increases for the agency. But regardless of the fact that NEA budgets are now on something of a plateau, one simple fact remains: no major arts event in the United States, and hardly a minor one either, takes place without the appearance of the telltale legend, printed in the material which accompanies the art: "this event is supported by a grant from the National Endowment for the Arts, a Federal agency."

It is the proud claim of partisans of the NEA that the increase in government arts funding, coming not just from the federal treasury but increasingly from state and local entities as well, has meant an enormous increase in private funding. It is no secret that this increase has hardly come from individual contributions or even from foundation grants; in recent years these have remained constant, and in some cases have shown signs of decreasing, as many private foundations have decided to turn their agendas toward social welfare programs and related social action. The great increase in private funding has instead come from corporate sources, from those profit-making enterprises which have become convinced that the arts are good for business.

There is little need to remind the reader who these corporate Maecenases are. The largest corporate patrons have by now firmly established themselves in our minds. If one watches public television, one will immediately recognize the role of Exxon, Mobil, and ARCO; if one follows the museum world in New York, one will immediately think of Philip Morris and Equitable; if one is interested in orchestras on tour, one will think of AT&T and perhaps Citibank; if one listens to opera on radio, one's mind will turn to Texaco. And so it goes. So great has been the success of corporate sponsorship of art that long after the art presented has been forgotten the corporate logo on the screen remains firmly fixed in our minds.

It may be taken for granted that money is a good thing. No one would like to do without it. Furthermore, no one would dispute the proposition that if more money in general is a good thing, more money for the arts is a wonderful thing. And yet one may surely be pardoned for quietly asking: "More money for what?" Just what has all this money from new forms of patronage, both governmental and non-governmental, brought us in the way of art?

In my own opinion, it has brought us very little, and what it has brought has been often harmful to the true cause of art and its lovers. It must be said at the outset that this new money has on many occasions gone to worthwhile artists, and has brought much worthwhile art to millions who might never have become part of what is now so nicely called the arts audience. It must be said, too, that under this new financial dispensation, more people than ever before are calling themselves artists—well over one million by the census bureau's last reckoning. And there are vastly more arts institutions, too, run by vastly more arts professionals working in marketing, development, publicity, community relations, personnel, accounting, and generalized mass advocacy.

More people in the audience, more people calling themselves artists, more institutions and people working in them, and everybody spreading the gospel: what, in

God's name, could be bad about all these virtues existing in such a state of plenty? The answer is that all this activity is not about the creation of art, or art education. Rather, it signifies the transformation of the art of the past into consumables for the present, along with the trivialization of what has been, and is being, created.

Let us begin with public television, the flagship of all this new patronage. Here, on the tens of millions of television sets in American homes, may be found just what in the arts governmental and corporate patrons think should be watched. In the theater, Shakespeare and schlock, both archly delivered, from England; in music, the warhorses of the European classics and American pop, both in routinized performances; in opera, the safest repertory imaginable, handled with kid gloves; in dance, only a smattering of the new developments which have made America the capital of the dance world; in the visual arts, blockbuster programs rich in glib judgments and expensive travel shots. Of the history of the modern arts in America there is almost nothing; of the history of our great literature nothing; of the arts and the humanities for small but highly educated audiences nothing; of arts education, nothing. Of the meretricious personalities in the performing arts of our day there is, however, everything.

As with public television, so with a broad range of arts today. In all too many cases the prime criterion for giving and getting help, in both government and corporate support, is not the particular character of the art being done, nor the need. It is purely and simply high visibility, or the possibility of such visibility soon. In vanishingly few cases is the criterion for support the pleasing of the *taste* of the patron. In the vast majority of cases the criterion is that the grantee, now or in the near future, bring the grantor favorable publicity.

Just because this requirement of favorable image recognition is so widely observed, it is foolish indeed to talk of a governmental or a corporate taste in culture and art. The architecture of Lincoln Center, so wrongly called "Mussolini modern" by some critics, does not represent corporate taste. It represents what the powerful in business and government believe their fellow New Yorkers and Americans of a certain substance will like. Similarly, the art in the Whitney Museum branches at the Philip Morris building and the new Equitable Life Assurance Society building in New York does not represent the artistic taste of corporate bureaucracy, any more than the grants made by the National Endowment for the Arts represent what governmental leaders think art is or should be. All these efforts represent an attempt to please important economic, social, and political constituencies. When artists are consulted, it is because a judgment has been made that they will produce or select well-liked work; when the avant-garde is supported it is out of a desire on the part of various funders to be thought up-to-date and "with it." The struggle everywhere is not so much to do substantive good in any particular art as to be seen to be doing good for the arts as a whole.

Even when corporate and governmental support is directed toward the needs of the grantee rather than the grantor, the funds are often not directed at covering the basic operating costs of the institution or at supporting the art. Instead, the money must be used to expand programming or fund-raising. Programming must be expanded to bring in audiences regardless of the artistic or financial cost, and money must be raised in ever-increasing amounts regardless of how much it costs to raise or of how much programming must be changed in order to appeal to a broader base of funders. The reality of support for the arts in this country at the present time is well described in the words of an arts-contributions officer of a major corporation who was addressing the head of a very distinguished arts institution: "We don't give anyone fish, we give a fishing rod." This oracular saying can be translated in a way every grant applicant in the arts knows only too well. Money is given primarily for the purpose of enabling more money to be raised from others. The key to such expanded fund-raising is increased visibility; such visibility is only obtained by expanded programming and activities—far-flung orchestral touring and highly publicized blockbuster museum exhibitons, to mention only two examples—which please the largest possible audience.

As the reader will have noticed, throughout my description of contemporary patronage I have yoked business and government. I have not done so because I think that the responsibility for the present situation in arts patronage falls equally on both. The pressures beating on government are pressures which arise out of our political system, out of the day-to-day legislative and administrative process which guarantees our liberties. Government personnel, after all, must be at least as much representatives as leaders. Private patrons, however, have a greater freedom and a much greater responsibility to choose their course of action.

I have yoked government and business because, despite the very real differences which should separate them, there is an intimate, and I believe deeply mistaken, link between the decision-making processes which govern their support for the arts. This link can be simply described. Government, in order to demonstrate maximum impact for its grants, finds it most convenient to support that to which corporations have been contributing; at the same time corporations, in order to avoid artistic responsibility for their decisions, rely increasingly on the "governmental good housekeeping seal of approval" as the necessary condition for their own grant-making.

It is this linkage between government and business patronage of the arts which constitutes the public opulence mentioned earlier. The private decrepitude is simply the other side of the opulence. Board members who go to the concerts or the operas which their boards oversee are scarce, as are volunteers willing to contribute their own money rather than just work endlessly to get others to give. Patrons who make individual, artistically competent, and committed decisions about what their own money—not the taxpayers' money, not the shareholders' money, not the community foundation donors' money—will suppoort are in short supply. Above all, knowing, discriminating, core audiences—and here I speak authoritatively about music, but I fear that what I am saying can easily be matched in other artistic fields—are getting smaller and less sure of themselves year by year. They are being replaced by casual and even fickle audiences who are less and less capable of understanding the art being offered to them, and who demand more and more celebrity performances and a cheapened repertory as a price for their continued presence.

Despite all the negative aspects of this story, in fairness it must be stated that the present situation is not a conspiracy, not the result of evil intentions, not even the result of political and economic opportunism, but rather the result of an *educational* failure in the arts. The problem is not bad motive; those responsible for our present system of public patronage, whether governmental or corporate, mean well. They like art. They have a general perception that art is a good thing. They are responsible citizens. They want to help. But in all too many cases they do not themselves know what to do. Their problem, like that of the audience, is insufficient knowledge. Insufficient knowledge of art, of the high culture of which we should be so proud, of the connections which civilization makes possible between a known past and an unknown future.

It must be repeated yet once more that this insufficient knowledge is responsible not just for the kind of patronage we see today but also for the behavior of the public this patronage is attempting to reach. This situation is merely the adult equivalent of the lowered scores we see everywhere in students' general comprehension of and knowledge about the arts. The scores themselves, it need hardly be stressed, are but the symptom of the state of arts education in our nation today.

What is the way out of this depressing situation? The way out can only be found through education. Perhaps now that the climate for education has changed so much in so many subjects we are ready for a new look at education in the arts. Perhaps we are now ready to understand that art, like every other intellectual activity, is composed of skills and knowledge; that art can be taught and learned; that beauty, no matter how difficult it is to define, is not merely a matter of the feelings, but partakes of the nature of objective reality.

We cannot go back, in arts patronage, to a pre-democratic era of rule by an elite few. Whatever the mix of private individuals, corporations, and government is to be—and it is very much to be hoped that individual patronage will increasingly constitute our predominant mode of support—only education can promise that informed citizens, in art as in politics, will be able to make wise choices. This will hardly be the first time in the life of democracy that education has become the saving hope: more than a century ago, the English liberal politician Robert Lowe advised those who wished to extend the franchise that "it will be absolutely necessary that you should prevail on our future masters to learn their letters." We know that these letters include literature, mathematics, and the sciences. It is now our job to convince our society that these letters include a serious and high art as well.

(*May* 1986)

The Whitney's new Graves

by Hilton Kramer

In the life of certain art institutions there sometimes comes a moment—call it the moment of truth—when, as the result of a particularly fateful and disastrous decision about their future course, they stand revealed as the unmistakable enemy of all the standards and traditions and achievements they have claimed to represent. Policies and programs which, prior to this revelatory moment, might be regarded as merely misguided or inadvertent or simply ignorant, suddenly acquire a more sinister and menacing character when their full implication is made so baldly apparent to us. It is only then that we come to understand that these institutions may now constitute a real threat to the life of art and its place in our society.

For many people concerned with the life of art in this country, the program of the Whitney Museum of American Art has now come to constitute a portent of this kind. Much has lately been happening to the Whitney to raise grave doubts about the museum's ability to perform its designated functions. It was a bad sign, for example, when Gail Levin left the Whitney's curatorial staff last year, for Miss Levin was one of the very few bona fide scholars in the field of early twentieth-century American art on the museum staff, and as far as we know, she has never been replaced by a scholar of comparable credentials. Then, too, there was the matter of the museum's unseemly actions—and inactions—on the Morgan Russell donation (about which we shall have more to say in due course). Above all, this year's Biennial exhibition was deeply shocking even to the many museumgoers who, through grim experience, had come to expect the worst from this particular enterprise. Certainly the 1985 Biennial exceeded, in its gleeful surrender to everything that is most vulgar, superficial, and meretricious on the contemporary art scene, anything that had heretofore been seen at the Whitney—and that is really saying something when one considers the recent history of the Biennials.

Yet, distressing as these and certain other developments at the Whitney have been, it was not until May 21, when the museum announced its plans to repackage the Marcel Breuer building it has occupied since 1966 as part of a new and larger museum designed by Michael Graves, that the moment of truth finally dawned even for those who had tried so arduously to make allowances for so many egregious misadventures in the past. With this announcement, the crowded record of foolish decisions could no longer be regarded as a succession of miscellaneous delinquencies. Clearly a new policy was in place, and there was now every indication that we would henceforth be dealing with an institution which cannot be trusted to serve the interests of either art or its public.

While it would not be inaccurate to claim that the new Michael Graves building, which combines an appalling poverty of architectural thought with a maximum of ornamental ostentation, is the perfect symbol of what the Whitney now aspires to be, that of course is precisely what makes this whole episode so oppressively significant. Mr. Graves has been nothing if not entirely faithful to the spirit of his client's wishes—a spirit governed by an invincible preference for glitz and specious glamour at the expense of art itself. It is for this reason that the Graves building, though in itself an object lesson in how *not* to design an art museum, cannot be separated from the Whitney program it is intended to serve.

What, then, does this program entail? Alas, there are no mysteries to be decoded in this matter. By its actions, no less than by its pronouncements, the Whitney has made its present and future goals altogether plain. In this respect, its ill-conceived branch-museum program reads like a blueprint for future operations. There are now two of these so-called branch museums already functioning —one in the Philip Morris building at Park Avenue and Forty-second Street in Manhattan, and another in the Champion International building in downtown Stamford, Connecticut. Two more are planned for Manhattan—one in the Equitable tower at Seventh Avenue and Fifty-third Street, scheduled to open this fall, and another at Federal Reserve Plaza, now set for early 1986. No doubt there are still others under discussion.

From the branches already in operation the nature of the Whitney's interest in these misnamed "museum" projects can be easily discerned, and it is not primarily an artistic or museological interest. To a serious experience or understanding of art these branch operations make no contribution whatever. In fact, they aren't in any true sense of the word museums at all and shouldn't be called by that name, but are more akin to boutiques or advertising displays in which token art objects are put on show for the purpose of conferring a spurious "cultural" image on the host companies. The real function of these branch operations is neither to educate nor to delight, but simply to provide both the Whitney and the sponsoring corporations with a mutually beneficial public relations program. The Whitney looks as if it were performing a service for the public, and the sponsoring corporations look as if they were performing a service for art, whereas in truth both are cynically using art *and* the public as a means of promoting their own respective interests.

It is in this historic shift to public relations as a priority interest, to the use of art for the purposes of institutional self-promotion and self-aggrandizement, that the branch-museum program of the Whitney affords a key to its current outlook. Given the goals implicit in that outlook, the building which Michael Graves has designed for the new Whitney is abysmally appropriate, of course. For what the Whitney program calls for isn't so much a new art museum as a new corporate headquarters, and this, more or less, is what Mr. Graves has given it. Unfortunately, for those of us who are still more interested in art than in this transformation of the museum into an arm of the public-relations business, the Graves design is hideously *in*appropriate to the function to which, for the moment anyway, the Whitney still gives lip service: exhibiting works of art. With its sherbert-colored cladding and its cookie-cutter windows, its ornamental cornices and penthouse colonnade, all topped off with one of those preposterous pergolas which serve no other function than to announce to all the world that the whole lugubrious conception is unmistakably Michael Graves's, this design belongs in one of those ballyhoo exhibitions of which the current directorship of the Whitney is so inordinately proud. It was therefore entirely apt that the Graves design should be unveiled to the public while the latest Whitney Biennial was in progress, for it is a design that inflicts on the existing Marcel Breuer building the same kind of degrading transformation which the museum invited one of its favored graffiti artists, Kenny Scharf, to carry out in the building's second-floor washrooms and telephone booths as part of his contribution to this year's Biennial.

The Whitney's blithe disregard for the building which it commissioned from Marcel Breuer scarcely twenty years ago is in itself a scandal of considerable significance. Among much else, it instantly throws into doubt the Whitney's role—which is, be it remembered, the primary role it claims for itself—in making what its director, Tom Armstrong, calls "initial judgments about the merit of current work." Why should we place any trust in the judgment of a museum that shows itself so eager to repeal the most important architectural decision it ever made and so blind—or is it merely cynical—about the implications of this eagerness?

It is true that the Breuer building has never been an easy building to live with. It makes rather too much of its own authority, and it isn't always as subtle or as commodious in accommodating itself to its functions as it might be. But it was the Whitney, after all, which gave us this high-powered, difficult building in the first place. It was the Whitney which boasted of its merits and made large claims for its excellence. And there is this to be said for the Breuer building: it unequivocably focuses attention on the seriousness of the museological enterprise, it speaks in every detail for the gravity and high purposes of art, and it does not easily lend itself to frivolity or foolishness. Which is why, I suppose, it had to be outrageously defaced to accommodate the spirit of this year's Biennial, and why the current director, with his unerring penchant for the showy and the superficial, is so eager to see it absorbed into Michael Graves's gaudy labyrinth.

We know now what we can expect from the new Whitney. In his remarks to the American Institute of Architects on July 25, Mr. Armstrong announced that in its new building the Whitney would exhibit its art in a new way. What he characterized as the "anonymous spaces" of Sixties museum architecture—meaning, of course, the Breuer building—would no longer do, he said. Which, translated from the public-relations argot used on such occasions, simply means that the Michael Graves design can be counted on to provide the same kind of non-anonymous spaces for the museum's permanent collection that Kenny Scharf and others gave us a glimpse of in this year's Biennial. Which means, in turn, that works of art will henceforth be at the mercy of the art of display at the Whitney, and that the museum will naturally favor the kind of art —of which there is no shortage on today's art scene—which is itself a form of display. No one can say that we weren't warned.

Cognizant that, despite this emphasis on fun and games, the museum must also have at least the appearance of a more serious side, the Whitney has made the claim that its new building will "[enable] the Museum to fulfill its role as a major center for scholarship in American art." For anyone familiar with the museum's record in this matter, the notion of the Whitney serving as "a major center for scholarship in American art" borders on the comical. In this regard, the case of the Morgan Russell donation tells us everything we need to know. Russell was, of course, one of the pioneer figures in the early history of abstract painting. He also happened to enjoy the patronage of Gertrude Vanderbilt Whitney, the founder of the museum. Seven years ago Henry M. Reed, who has devoted much time, effort, and expense to assembling an invaluable collection of Russell's manuscripts, studies, and works of art, donated the collection to the Whitney on the understanding that the museum would organize an exhibition of this material and publish a scholarly catalogue. But of course nothing has ever been done with it, and Mr. Reed has now been obliged to go to court in the hope of getting the collection transferred to an institution more receptive to scholarly pursuits. It is farcical for the present administration of the Whitney to claim to have any interest in or understanding of scholarship.

But farce—of one kind or another—seems to be the name of the game that is now being played at the Whitney, which looks and acts more and more like an institution that has severed whatever connections it had with the standards and achievements of high art in order to set itself up as another kind of enterprise.

(*September* 1985)

What's so great about the RSC?
by Mimi Kramer

In the context of the Royal Shakespeare Company's visit to New York this year and Terry Hands's productions of *Cyrano de Bergerac* and *Much Ado About Nothing* at the Gershwin Theater on Broadway, I have been thinking back to a conversation I had with a friend not long ago during a recent trip to London. We were sitting at a little table outside of a wine bar in Covent Garden. It was one of those clear, chilly end-of-summer evenings in London that seem to take a long time to settle down around you, and the whole world, as it went loping by us on King Street, seemed wanting to intrude: the young man who wanted to bum a cigarette, the older one who wanted to sit down at our table, the skinheads leaning noisily against a nearby car.

But we had bought a bottle of wine and were deep in conversation. We were talking about London theater and somehow the conversation seemed to keep coming back to the Royal Shakespeare Company. Alison actually works for the RSC, in their administrative offices at the Barbican Arts Centre. I had been spending a good deal of time around the Barbican myself, seeing various RSC productions. We were both excited about one or two things we had recently seen at Stratford—and a little exhilarated, the way one is on those clear, chilly, end-of-summer evenings in London. Not to mention the wine, of course. Anyway, I don't remember precisely what led up to Alison's rather abrupt question, but the talk must have gotten a little enthusiastic before she brought it back down to earth. She suddenly looked at me suspiciously and said, "Come to think of it, what *do* you think is so great about the RSC? I mean, they *are* very, very good. But surely there is something comparable in New York; there must be! Isn't there?"

I remember feeling winded and a little bit panicky. It seemed like such a big question—and so naïve. Where did one begin? How could I explain to Alison that there was virtually no repertory theater in New York at all, when London could boast not one but two huge subsidized theaters, the National and the RSC, each turning out a steady stream of plays: old, new, and forgotten! We had both just seen *Richard III* and *Henry V* at Stratford, where *Hamlet* and *The Merchant of Venice* (among other things) were also running in repertory and a production of *Love's Labour's Lost* was about to open. In London, the RSC was doing (again, among other things) *Volpone* and another Jacobean comedy, while their productions of *Twelfth Night, Measure for Measure,* and *Henry VIII* still did not quite account for all the Shakespeare being produced in London at the time. How could I describe how infrequent and inadequate productions of Shakespeare generally were in New York? And where, oh where, was someone who could corroborate my story, some native New Yorker milling about the crowds in Covent Garden Market?

Keeping an eye out for passing Instamatics and an ear cocked for accents west of Land's End, I began to tell Alison horror stories of the state of the classics and repertory theater in New York. I told her a little about how Shakespeare is produced there. I said that there was, indeed, an institution called the New York Shakespeare Festival/Public Theater which, every year, gives mediocre productions of one or two Shakespeare plays, most of them *Hamlet.* I said that a number of smaller companies occasionally attempt Shakespeare, particularly in the summer at various outdoor venues, but that most of it was fairly gimmicky and all of it far below the level of competence demanded of Michael Croft's teenagers at the National Youth Theater. I told her about a relentlessly well-meaning little production of *Measure for Measure* I had seen this summer in which most of the performances had ranged from bad television-acting to middling burlesque and the only member of the cast with any inkling of how to speak verse had been relegated to the comparatively small role of Mariana, while the performance of the actress playing Isabella would have caused concern on "Captain Kangaroo."

I said that *American* "classics" were frequently revived on Broadway, but that as often as not these productions were miscast with big-name movie stars. There was, I said, a theater called the Circle In The Square which often did productions of European "classics," but that even a first-rate production like *Heartbreak House* (which had been New York theater at its very best) was bound to have, in addition to Dana Ivey (far and away the best actress in town), one or two important roles filled apparently by someone the stage manager had hauled off the street at preview time ("Hey, mac! Ya wanna be in a play?") The Circle In The Square, I pointed out, only produces one or two plays each year anyway, and they could range anywhere from something as good as the recent revival of *The Caine Mutiny Court-Martial* to something as ghastly as the more recent productions of *Design for Living* and *Awake and Sing!* Downtown at the Public Theater, meanwhile, Joe Papp seemed firmly committed—for the next few years, at any rate—to importing contemporary work from Central Europe and Great Britain. So that the Roundabout Theater, where the direction was simple and unpretentious but not particularly inspired, was the only regular source for productions of "modern classics" in the city. Finally I said that there was, in fact, a large and prosperous center for the performing arts in Manhattan which did, indeed, boast two elegant theaters, but that for six of the last seven years those theaters had been dark.

This was, I see now, a terrible answer. It approached the question from the wrong end entirely. You cannot explain a phenomenon like the RSC by looking at what doesn't exist in New York; you can only try to isolate what RSC theater is and why it works. The Royal Shakespeare Company did not burst, fully armed, from the head of the Arts Council of Great Britain and RSC theater did not come into existence because the English are better or nicer or more sophisticated and talented people than we are. It came about because of Peter Hall and John Barton and the radical departures they made from what was the predominant approach to Shakespeare production when Peter Hall took over directorship of the Shakespeare Memorial Theatre in 1959.

Quite simply, Peter Hall did three things when he took over the theater at Stratford: along with John Barton, he revolutionized the way Shakespearean verse was spoken on stage; he established a permanent resident company at Stratford; and he fostered an approach to Shakespeare in which the shape of the production as a whole was more important than the individual performance of any single actor. Before about 1960, from the Twenties onward, Shakespeare production had focused almost entirely on the performance of a great actor. The Old Vic was the fountainhead from which most Shakespeare flowed, but what people went flocking to see there and in the West End was *a performance*—"the Gielgud Hamlet" or "the

Olivier Richard III"—and the criticism of the period reflects this. Kenneth Tynan's reviews of productions of Shakespeare, until the mid-Fifties, are almost exclusively devoted to describing great (or poor) performances. He mentions other elements of production only to say that there is nothing to say.

This state of affairs had proceeded from circumstances within the Old Vic itself as well as from developments in the wider context of London theater between the wars. But the tenacity of this style of production—the fact that it prevailed from the late Twenties well into the late Fifties—must partly be attributed to the emergence of a generation of actors who were, in fact, capable of making history in a theater in a single night. This was the Great Actor Generation—and they *were* great actors, and still are, those that are still alive. Gielgud, Guinness, Richardson: the guys whose voices you would know anywhere. And, of course, Olivier. But Olivier represented a new approach to acting Shakespeare, indeed, he was inventing it: a newfangled "naturalistic" style which many accused of lacking "poetry," but which he got away with because he was so extraordinarily good at it.

Gielgud, on the other hand, knew how to speak verse and it was primarily to hear great poetry read greatly that people went to see Shakespeare. (Even Tynan, in 1947, is only half tongue-in-cheek when he writes that "there seems to be little else, in an averagely good performance, to enrapture the mind.") Nothing in the spoken arts is quite as beautiful as the sound of Alec Guinness or John Gielgud reading Shakespearean verse. If you listen to a recording of someone like John Barrymore reading snippets from *Hamlet* in the late Twenties and then to Guinness and Gielgud in the Old Vic recordings of *Macbeth* and *Hamlet* made in the Fifties, the difference is staggering. By comparison, Barrymore sounds as though he were giving an elocution lesson. His delivery bears no relation to the lugubrious music of Gielgud's voice or to the long, slow, pounding, and funereal tones of Guinness's soliloquies. Gielgud's Hamlet, wishing that this too, too solid flesh would melt, sounds like nothing on earth. Unless it is Gielgud's Richard II invoking everyone to sit upon the ground and tell sad stories of the death of kings . . . but that's the snag. And that's where Peter Hall and John Barton come in.

What Hall and Barton aimed at was a marriage between the old style of speaking verse "poetically," exemplified by Gielgud, and the new style that Olivier and other film actors were exploring: a balance between the "naturalistic" and the "lyrical." Of course, "naturalism" in acting is a very relative term: each generation sees itself as forging a style of acting "more realistic" than the one that went before. But the balance sought by Barton and Hall was founded on more objective criteria, lodged in ideas about textual analysis and verse structure that Barton and Hall had been developing since their not-so-far-off undergraduate days studying under George Rylands and F. R. Leavis at Cambridge. The technique they evolved originated with an extraordinarily analytical approach to both the structure of Shakespeare's verse and the text of a play. It examined the logic of grammar and sentence structure and paid minute attention to the way the rhythm of an individual line can play against the pattern of pentameter verse. It tried to differentiate between a character who is speaking in a self-consciously "heightened" manner for rhetorical or self-indulgent reasons (like Richard II in the speech cited above) and one whose thoughts just happen to find the cadence of poetry (like Hamlet of the soliloquies). It worried about why Shakespeare uses prose when he does and about why a character will sometimes depart from his normal habit of speech. Above all, it sought for the actor—in the answers to such questions—some guideline to finding a middle ground between the sound of a character's words and their meaning.

Now the debate between Nature and Poetry in drama is as old as theater: Aristophanes thought the realism of Euripides's plays demanded from his actors a level of "naturalism" that was frankly turning theater into a bathhouse. Again, the terms are relative. Moreover, verse-speaking is ever in a state of flux: fashions in acting come and go even at the RSC. What we hear when Derek Jacobi plays Cyrano de Bergerac in 1984 is very different from the detached rationality that Terry Hands might have elicited from an Alan Howard ten years ago or the evenly cerebral performance that Peter Hall might have got from an Ian Richardson ten years before that. But when Derek Jacobi stands outside Roxanne's window rhapsodizing about love and his voice compels you from the beginning of each thought to its end so that your attention never wanders for a moment, part of what you are experiencing is the result of work done by John Barton and Peter Hall in the early Sixties and their efforts to find a compromise between the logic and conviction of everyday speech and the exigencies of verse.

Of course verse-speaking was only one area of Hall's new approach. More visible was the production style that he developed, along with Peter Brook and Michel Saint-Denis (briefly his co-directors), and began making a trademark of the company. Briefly, it involved three things, all of which are still recognizable aspects of the RSC style: 1) a pseudo-Brechtian style of staging and stagecraft; 2) an attempt to unite all aspects of a production—the sets, the lighting, the costumes, and the music as well as staging and performance—in the service of an idea; and 3) a reading of a play that tended to be more objective and literary critical than it was subjective and empathic. Where traditional methods of production tried to tell a story, simply and effectively, from the protagonists' point of view, offering the audience a chance to empathize with the hero, Hall's approach was able to stand back from the protagonists and judge them against the prevailing values in the play. It was the difference between presenting a character solely as he sees himself, looking only at the actual words he speaks (where King Lear, for example, *is* "a man more sinned against than sinning" because he says so) and looking also at other elements in the picture—his actions, for example, his powers of judgment, his friends and what they said about him—all with a view to teaching an audience more about a character than how to feel for him. Hall's readings of a play demanded from an actor a kind of performance in which, subtly, he was simultaneously playing a character from his own point of view and *not* from his own point of view, and then united that performance with all the other production elements around it. RSC productions looked for ways of turning staging and stagecraft into a running commentary—to make a statement, pursue an image, or present a unified vision of a play. Thus, where traditional methods had pretty much used lighting and scenery to establish atmosphere and a sense of place (respectively), costumes to evoke a time, and music to create a mood and cover scene changes, the functions of various elements of production at the RSC was not so cut and dried. And scene changes, at the RSC, were not something you wanted covered: for where the prevailing methods of Shakespeare production had sought to lessen the embarrassing inconveniences inherent in the form of theater, the RSC made use of them. Instead of using theatrical convention to apologize for the ways in which a play did not resemble films or real life, the RSC style explored new ways of using theatrical convention to create the world of the play.

It is worth noting that almost none of the "innovations" that constituted Hall's approach were in themselves new ideas. Granville-Barker, in the early part of the century, had striven to find some middle ground for the Shakespearean actor between the realistic and the stylized; Hall's predecessors at Stratford had long been aware of the need for a resident company; and Peter Brook, a lone voice in the wilderness of London theater, had been staging Brechtian productions of Shakespeare for years. Hall knew a good idea when he saw one and it could be argued that his influence on the staging of Shakespeare comes down to little more than having seen and implemented at Stratford three very good ideas. I would argue, though, that he did something more, that he managed to invent an approach to staging Shakespeare that amounts to turning practical criticism into theater.

And that, in the end, is the strength of the RSC I think: that one foot (or part of a foot) that Hall and Barton left behind, solidly planted in academia. What is so good about the RSC and about a production like Terry Hands's *Much Ado About Nothing* isn't English accents or English tailoring or "Masterpiece Theater" or the ghost of Laurence Olivier crying out in the rafters: it's the nonrealistic set and the nonrealistic lighting and the music and the staging and the way that all are used thematically to bring about a view of the play that concerns more than just what happens in it. It is the solo cellist with whom Terry Hands begins to people the stage in the first few seconds of the play so that Messina is immediately defined as a world in which it is perfectly normal for a pretty young girl wearing ringlets and wide taffeta skirts to sit down under a tree and pick out a mournful tune on a cello. It is the tree that isn't a tree but only the drawing of a tree, apparently etched in glass. It is the sense of place established by simply flying in another tree or moving some chairs or finding the slant of light that seems to alter our perspective of a view of hills. It is the self-contained world set off by the glassy, box-like frame that surrounds the stage, a world of fragile, chiming surfaces, like the lilting music whose fragile, chiming surface runs counter to an ominous and melancholy undertone. It is the long, distorted shadows cast on the masking and the proscenium arch which, like the rippling reflections of the people and places we see cast in the shining surface of the floor and walls, seem to echo the distortions in the play: a man and woman's distorted images of themselves cast by their friends; the brittle reflection of a young girl's reputation shattered by malice. It is the young men we sometimes see, at the beginning of a scene, fencing with one another in jest: a parody of some battle-in-earnest which, at the beginning of the play, has taken place somewhere. It is the beacon that sometimes gleams in the night sky from a nearby promontory, a reminder of seriousness and danger and an outside world that never impinges on Messina.

Mind you, not everything in Terry Hands's production of *Much Ado About Nothing* is as great as all that. I felt uncomfortable during the first half of the performance: Derek Jacobi seemed to be giving an unusually effeminate tinge to the role of Benedick; and Sinead Cusack's Beatrice seemed in danger of laying a few of the characters out cold on that shiny glass floor. It seems to me that what ails Benedick and Beatrice in the first half of the play is obvious enough without having to play the one as a raging queen or the other as a harpy. But then, the RSC is generally better at dealing with the enigmatic than the obvious.

Anomaly, I think, is the secret here. The best RSC productions seem to head straight for the anomalies in Shakespeare: that word or line or speech or scene or character that catches the eye because it breaks some pattern. It is a wise means of access to a play, first because it assumes that the playwright did everything he did for a reason, and second because new anomalies present themselves with every reading of a text: the short line that seems to break the rhythm of pentameter, the scene that serves no function in the plot, the nameless battle that will never come up again but for some reason begins the play, the messenger who serves no purpose in the scene but has a pompous and shallow way of talking. One time round with *Much Ado* you notice, perhaps, that Claudio is really a rather loathsome fellow, so you emphasize the contrast between his relationship with Hero and Benedick's with Beatrice. Another time you notice that Don Pedro has strange ideas about how to relate to other people: so you let him usurp from his brother, Don John, the role of Malcontent. At the end of this production Don Pedro, a lone black figure on a stage swirling with white and gold, walks offstage into the shadows in the direction of an exit no one else has ever used. It is typical of RSC staging to pick up on some crux that scholars have been worrying for generations and turn it into theater: the sprawling structure of *Antony and Cleopatra*; the abundance of music in *Twelfth Night*; that fact that there never *was* a seacoast in Bohemia; or that at the end of *Much Ado About Nothing* Don Pedro is depressed.

It is this almost unfailing instinct for finding a play's alleged weaknesses and turning them into strengths that informs as well Terry Hands's production of *Cyrano de Bergerac* and makes it such good theater. Of course, with its great theatrical set pieces and grand dramatic gestures, *Cyrano* is pretty good theater to begin with. Its fundamental weakness as a play, however, is that it uses the idiom of realism to present events that are essentially unrealistic. It asks us to accept the wildly unlikely and to take it literally. Now all literature before a certain period actually deals with unrealistic events (verisimilitude doesn't really come on the scene until the eighteenth-century novel), but most literature dealing with the magical or heroic also possesses some mechanism inherent in the conventions of its form which either smooths over the lack of verisimilitude or else absolves the audience from the necessity of taking things too literally. Cyrano doesn't—and for a very good reason. Rostand's whole point, of course, in *Cyrano* was to thumb his nose at the realism of the Dumas and Ibsens, the Strindbergs and Shaws. He wanted to put on stage the triumph of heroic idealism and romanticism. The whole point of Cyrano and his "panache" is that they *are* larger than life. Which is as good a reason as any for writing a play in which there is not one ghost of an idea, in which the psychological depth of none of the characters approaches two fingers of Scotch, and in which we are to accept that a girl intellectual enough to care about the quality of pillow-talk she gets, devoted enough to follow her lover to the front lines, and resourceful enough to get there, requires fourteen years and a very big hint to work out whom she really loves.

Still, *Cyrano* is such a wonderful mixture of the comic, the romantic, the heroic, and the burlesque, that its lack of verisimilitude is not really a problem until the last scene: Cyrano's death. This is the first instance in the course of the play in which Cyrano has not been acting a part or putting on a show for someone's benefit. Throughout the play his larger-than-life persona has gone hand in hand with some form of spectacle. Now, in his death, we see him for the first time as he is—*in extremis,* the man himself. And he isn't any different! That Cyrano dies as spectacularly and theatrically as he lived is again the whole point, of course; but for this reason, perhaps, his death always fails to move me. Cyrano never seems to have any resonance as a real person: he is just something sad that happened in a play.

Ralph Koltai's sets for *Cyrano* at the Gershwin Theater are even more beautiful than those for *Much Ado*—and more effective in dealing with the play's weaknesses. The first thing an audience sees on entering the theater is the Act I set for the Hotel de Bourgogne. It is an elaborate affair, but strangely balanced and uncluttered, full of dark, massive furniture draped in dark brocade. Cobwebs and tattered gauze seem to drip from everywhere in the room, particularly from three outsized chandeliers that hang from threadbare ropes of red velvet about ten feet straight down to the floor. Because there is no curtain, the audience has a long time to examine the set and its blend of realistic, gothic, and surreal acts as a visual preface, suggesting that the play we are about to see may be full of cobwebs, things that seem threadbare or had been put away, things that are wildly out of proportion. It suggests that an old story is about to be told and that in it we may encounter things, like the chandeliers, that are not to be taken literally.

All of the sets for Cyrano are ingeniously devised and superbly executed. But I think the most effective design decision Terry Hands made in this production has to do with the size of Cyrano's nose, traditionally hideously and grotesquely large. Derek Jacobi's wasn't really all that huge: I mean, he had a big nose, don't get me wrong. But it wasn't *unrealistic*; it did not make his a cartoon of a face. Consequently, Cyrano wasn't really ugly—he was rather distinguished looking, in fact, which put things in a new light. Jacobi's Cyrano became a man whose happiness was obstructed not so much by fate as by himself, not so much by ugliness as by an apprehension of ugliness. It amounted to a rather subtle distinction (partly because Jacobi did not play Cyrano as a pitiable or vulnerable figure), but once made, everything else began to fall into place.

Question: have you ever known a truly ugly man or woman who was aware of being ugly? No, of course you haven't; neither have I. But one can think of scores of people who regard themselves as ugly without being so. It was suddenly understandable that Cyrano should be so pathologically sensitive about his nose; and his commitment to honesty—in this light—became almost another disguise behind which he was hiding from the discovery of some ghastly truth within himself. It was suddenly believable that he should go to such lengths to deceive Roxanne as much from a desire to avoid a confrontation with failure as from more generous motives. And in the play's last moments, the symbolic host of abstractions with which Cyrano duels to the death (and which have never made any sense to me because he does not possess any of those vices—Deceit, Compromise, Prejudice, Cowardice, Stupidity) became not actual faults but the shadows of vices he had always been afraid of finding in himself.

To praise two RSC productions in New York is not to say that London theater is better than New York theater. The Royal Shakespeare Company is by no means representative of theater in London. Theater in London is not uniformly better than it is here: there is more of it and of a wider variety, and there is better value for the money. But the West End produces just as much bad theater as Broadway does and most of what one sees in "fringe" theater is more interesting than it is good. Nor is it true that the British are better actors as a rule. There are some things we do much, much better. My friend Alison, for instance, has probably never seen a really great Broadway musical —not if she was impressed by that production of *Guys and Dolls* they did at the National Theater several years ago. And the National Theater production of David Mamet's *Glengarry Glen Ross* is a complete disaster. It misses the central conflict and values of the play in very much the way that American productions of Shakespeare go astray. The actors do not even seem to understand the idiom of the language.

I could go on for pages about how much better the Broadway production of *Glengarry Glen Ross* was and why. But the style of the Royal Shakespeare Company produces a great theatrical experience in the same way that the Mamet play did. Nothing looks quite like RSC theater, nothing sounds quite like it, and nothing feels quite like it in the audience. And when, at the end of the evening, members of a New York audience with dinner reservations or a train to catch who have begun making their way purposefully up the aisles turn and stop where they are, gazing back at the stage as curtain after curtain calls the company back out until that embarrassing moment comes when the cast starts to wave good night, what makes the audience still stand there and begin waving back is something more than Anglophilia.

Of course, I didn't say any of this that night in Covent Garden: it didn't occur to me. I hadn't seen the two productions at the Gershwin Theater yet (or the audience response to them) and, to be honest, I hadn't thought much about what made RSC theater good. So I talked instead about New York theater, trying to explain how this or that had come to pass. Then the wine started flowing more freely and the conversation got a little wild as Alison and I got our great idea. We were going to form an Anglo-American theater troupe, some sort of offshoot of the RSC based in New York. We would need a second stage, of course, as a showcase for contemporary work and for a place to move the really big successes we had on the main stage with Jacobean drama, Restoration Comedy, Chekhov, Shaw, Greek tragedy, and brilliantly witty adaptations of Aristophanes. The whole point was to start a school, of course—we would ask John Barton to devise a special course for Method actors: "Learn to speak verse like you mean it without murdering the poetry!" We'd go to Trevor Nunn: "Trev," we'd say, "How would you feel about sending some of your boys back to New York with us? We feel there's work to be done there!"

A number of obstacles occurred to us, but we were thinking positively, creatively. Money? We'd go to everyone—Exxon, Ford, Mobil, OPEC—surely someone would be eager to fund so worthy a project! Or we'd go to the government agencies: NEA, NEH, the Board of Education, the arts councils. We'd go to President Reagan: he used to be an actor! Equity laws? We'd get a royal charter, a special dispensation from the Pope. Hell, we'd *build* a theater in the British Embassy and Equity could go munch its beard!

The wine had run out and as sobriety began to take its toll I managed to come up with the one really insuperable obstacle in all of this. I said there wasn't a market for that sort of theater in New York. I think that was the most outrageous thing I'd said all evening.

(*December* 1984)

Making a spectacle of architecture on PBS

by Roger Kimball

Devotees of public television will have noticed a new item on its menu of cultural delicacies these past weeks. In addition to the usual fare of romanticized Dickens, Austen, colonial India, and the other literary and historical subjects that have provided the staple for its tastefully served-up "dramatizations," we are now being offered romanticized architecture—also "dramatized," to be sure, and certainly "served up," though perhaps not quite so tastefully as one has come to expect from the programs that the Public Broadcasting Service has imported from the BBC. What we have, in short, is *Pride of Place: Building the American Dream,* an eight-part series on American architecture that is sponsored by Mobil Oil and scheduled to air weekly through the middle of May.

Our host for *Pride of Place* is the New York architect Robert A. M. Stern, a Professor of Architecture at Columbia University and Director of Columbia's Temple Hoyne Buell Center for the Study of American Architecture. Mr. Stern narrates the series, accompanying the television cameramen to more than one hundred locations across the country, from the ghettos of the South Bronx to the gaudy, stage-set splendors of San Simeon, William Randolph Hearst's "dream house" in California. Mr. Stern's tour of American architecture includes cities, campuses, resorts, suburbs, parks, and reconstructed villages like Williamsburg, Virginia, as well as individual buildings and monuments. All in all, he undertakes an ambitious itinerary that is intended to lend credibility to the series' double billing as both a documentary and a "personal view" of its subject.

"Personal" the series surely is—often to the point of idiosyncrasy. Indeed, for anyone who has sat through all eight episodes of *Pride of Place* in three days, as this writer has, there can be no doubt that it offers the viewer abundant evidence of Mr. Stern's opinions about the triumphs and failures of American architecture, including his speculations about where modern architecture went wrong and his assessment of the most pressing challenges facing contemporary architectural practice. But does *Pride of Place* also count as a "documentary" in any recognized sense of the word? Does it present us with anything like a straightforward, historically accurate account of the distinctive heritage and achievements of American architecture? Does it, at bottom, really even address itself primarily to matters of architectural interest? These are the questions one finds oneself asking again and again when contemplating *Pride of Place.*

Such questions are also provoked by the book published to accompany the series. Written by Mr. Stern with two associates, Thomas Mellins and Raymond Gastil, the book *Pride of Place* is a three-hundred-odd-page, copiously illustrated volume that faithfully reproduces the "personal view" of American architecture that Mr. Stern has provided for the PBS series.[1] The chief difference between the television series and the book is that in the former Mr. Stern interrupts his narrative once or twice an episode for a prearranged chat with a fellow architect or architectural writer about the topic at hand. Altogether, there are eighteen guests on *Pride of Place,* including such well-known figures as the architects Philip Johnson, Cesar Pelli, Peter Eisenman, Morris Lapidus, and Leon Krier, the historians Vincent Scully, Gwendolyn Wright, and Charles Jencks, and the journalist Paul Goldberger. These exchanges, which range from arcane speculations about architectural "space" to Philip Johnson's reminiscences about his cousin Theodate Pope Riddle (one of America's first women architects), would seem to be intended to impart an air of authority and credibility to the series—that, and perhaps also to add a touch of human interest to Mr. Stern's soliloquizing.

The interludes vary considerably in theme, too, from Morris Lapidus's musings about what the Mayan Indians might have built had they had our decorative resources to Peter Eisenman's misty "philosophical" observations about his attempt to "destabilize the notion of home." One of the founders of the now defunct theoretical architecture journal *Oppositions,* Mr. Eisenman is famous for abstruse, often polemical pronouncements that are full of the rhetoric of semiotics. He was comparatively straightforward for the television cameras, however, even if, like several other guests on *Pride of Place,* he liked to pretend that architecture is best understood as a "text." Mr. Stern, as *au courant* as anyone about such matters, likes to think of architecture as a text as well, though he did confide in his book that it was not until he went to graduate school at Yale that he "began to understand . . . that architecture is a narrative art, and that architectural style is analogous to poetic diction." It was sometimes easy to forget, watching *Pride of Place,* that architecture primarily has to do with building buildings—real buildings, ones that we live and work in, not ones that we read or ponder abstractly.

It has hardly been necessary to tune into PBS, let alone to turn the pages of Mr. Stern's companion volume, to know something about *Pride of Place.* Sponsored *in toto* by Mobil, the series has been the subject of the kind of aggressive advertising that is usually reserved for a big-budget Hollywood movie or Broadway show. In New York City, for example, one can hardly walk down the street without encountering a clump of posters proclaiming *Pride of Place,* and the magazines and journals here have likewise been full of notices for the show. The spate of advertising in *The New York Times* culminated just before the series began airing at the end of March in an arresting two-page spread, featuring the postmodernist *Pride of Place* logo and a précis of each episode. There was also a screening of the first episode early in March at the State Department in Washington, D.C., followed by a lavish reception in the recently redone diplomatic reception rooms on the top floor of the building. This was not your usual cheese-and-crackers-and-cheap-white-wine affair, but a buffet feast for several hundred people replete with champagne and open bar, suckling pig, and—to reinforce the ambiance of culture—a string quartet discreetly dispensing Vivaldi in the corner. One couldn't but wonder how much all this cost—eight hour-long television episodes, many of which involved a generous use of aerial photography, ubiquitous advertising, the reception—but Mobil declined to reveal the budget for this latest example of tax-exempt educational programming.

What were we actually shown after all this promotion? Did it merit the advertising, the champagne, the suckling pig? Unfortunately, the answer is "no." No matter how one looks at it—as video documentary, as architectural history, as social history, even as television entertainment—*Pride of Place* is

---

1 *Pride of Place: Building the American Dream,* Houghton Mifflin/American Heritage, 344 pages, $34.95.

a shambles. Even before Mr. Stern makes his first appearance on the screen one knows—or rather hears—that something is terribly wrong. The dreadful, and dreadfully manipulative, music leaves no doubt that we are in for something spurious. The music was composed by Carl Davis, currently the conductor for the Bournemouth Pops Symphony Orchestra and composer of the music for various television series, such as *The World at War, Churchill—The Wilderness Years,* and the Mobil-sponsored series *Praying Mantis,* as well as for the film *The French Lieutenant's Woman.* For *Pride of Place,* Mr. Davis's music features the strains of sweet nostalgia—"Home Sweet Home" plays with unbearable frequency—but is capable of achieving the mock-heroic and pop-apocalyptic when the occasion arises. And arise it does—again and again and again.

But corny as the music is, it probably provides the series with its only semblance of dramatic tension or show-business flair. And in relation to Mr. Stern's on-camera performance, the music is also responsible for a good deal of the series' unintended humor. While the music is alternately bathetic and absurdly sentimental, Mr. Stern is consistently, comically wooden. His voice is reedy and unpleasantly high-pitched; his delivery is uncertain; and the nervous staccato hand movements that accompany his every word rob even his most heartfelt pronouncements of grace. Then, too, there is Mr. Stern's manner. He tends to maintain a somewhat glassy, far-off expression—the result, perhaps, of being unable to take his eyes off the teleprompter—and an incessant smile that can be most generously described as unpersuasive. Mr. Stern performs so poorly on camera that one can only wonder why he was allowed to narrate the series. Didn't the producers—who are, after all, professionally concerned with such matters—recognize that they had failed utterly to come up with an American Kenneth Clark? In this respect, considered simply as an actor, Mr. Stern is far less compelling than many of his guests—than Jacquelin Robertson, for example, the dean of the architecture school at the University of Virginia, who joins Mr. Stern in the first episode at Monticello and whose mellifluous voice and dignified stage presence are in marked contrast to his host's efforts.

On the other hand, it must be said that Mr. Stern does not enjoy particularly good directing. For one thing, Murray Grigor, who directed and co-produced *Pride of Place* and whose film credits include *The Architecture of Frank Lloyd Wright* (1983), has what one might call a Mediterranean sense of pace. Things go *slowly* in *Pride of Place.* Throughout the series, but especially in the later episodes, there is an extraordinary quantity of tedious filler, little of it having anything to do with architecture. There are long, long pans across innumerable sunlit fields and endless façades, lingering shots of soldiers marching, of children playing in the grass, of Mr. Stern driving a red convertible along the highways and byways of America. Though much of this contributes to the series' moments of unintended comedy, it does not help to enliven Mr. Stern's performance. Nor does the glibly inept cinematography come to his aid. On the contrary, as often as not it undercuts or obscures the very points he tries to make, showing fragments of a building when the entire structure is called for, zooming in on irrelevant details, offering spectacular aerial views that tell us nothing about the buildings as experienced by the people who use them. It is a rare moment indeed when one can glean any sense of a building as an architectural whole. If Mr. Stern painstakingly describes the inviting sense of vertical flow that a grand staircase communicates, we can expect the camera to pan ever so slowly, ever so horizontally, across the middle of the stair. Architecture is notoriously difficult to present effectively on film, but it helps if the cinematographer makes some effort to follow the script.

The quality of the production and performances in any television series is always an important ingredient in its success, and the poor quality of both in *Pride of Place* is a serious handicap. But the real problem with *Pride of Place* is its failure as an exercise in architectural history. In part, this is simply a failure of communication. Each of the episodes contains references to a good many unexplained architectural terms and unidentified architectural figures. "Campanile" is one of Mr. Stern's favorite words—he uses it to refer not only to a bell tower but also to just about any slender vertical structure—but he never bothers to explain it, nor does he explain the score of other more or less technical terms that he and his guests use. Again, Mr. Stern gives us an elaborate account of who Ludwig Mies van der Rohe was—Mies is one of the series' arch-villains, so it is important that we know just who we are dealing with; but he leaves many lesser-known architects—Louis Kahn, for example, who figures prominently in his first episode—barely identified. One is reminded that public television, which was launched as "educational television," now seems to have abandoned any serious didactic aspiration whatsoever.

This is not to say that *Pride of Place* is too specialized or too full of architectural detail and the particulars of architectural history. Quite the contrary. While Mr. Stern displays and discusses innumerable buildings, we do not come away from the series having been instructed about architecture; rather, we feel that we've witnessed a particularly ambitious set of home movies or a travelogue. The book leaves one with an analogous feeling. I do not, for example, remember seeing a single architectural plan in the entire eight episodes. Nor does Mr. Stern take the trouble to discuss building types, architectural structure, or the relation of style to structure. Yet these are fundamental elements of architectural study, without which any discussion of the subject must lack intellectual substance.

Instead of architectural analysis, *Pride of Place* gives us a *House & Garden* version of American architecture. Everything is reduced to surface, façade, decoration, local color—the couture of architecture. Mr. Stern's discussion of Daniel Burnham's Flatiron Building (1902) at Twenty-third Street and Fifth Avenue in New York is a typical case. Noting that the windy open spaces north of the building's wedge-shaped front would "bare the ankles of the fashionable women on Fifth Avenue and Twenty-third Street," he points out that "The legend is that police called out 'twenty-three skidoo' to shoo away the male gawkers." In the television episode, we even get an animated short about the phrase. And this is about all we take away from *Pride of Place* about the Flatiron Building, one of the great early skyscrapers. All this has nothing to do with architecture, of course, but it is exactly the kind of trivia that pervades the series. Also characteristic is the disproportionate amount of time Mr. Stern spends wandering through the houses of the very rich: the "cottages" at Newport, Rhode Island, Hearst's San Simeon, James Deering's Vizcaya in Biscayne Bay, Florida, Isabella Stewart Gardner's Fenway Court, Boston, and so on. These are the places that have clearly captured Mr. Stern's imagination, not because they are of compelling architectural interest—in fact, they belong more to the history of conspicuous consumption than to the history of architecture—but because of their eccentricity, their aura of wealth and power, their snob appeal, and not least because of their campy extravagance, which gives Mr. Stern's penchant for coy irony full rein.

In order to understand what is really at stake in *Pride of Place,* however, it is necessary to look more closely at the "personal view" of American architecture that informs it. It is here that the series fails most conspicuously. At the center of that "personal view" is Mr. Stern's presumption that his approach to architecture constitutes a recovery of architectural tradition and history. His pose as a champion of history and tradition is suggested already in the title of his first, and in many respects his best, episode, "The Search for a Usable Past." Evoking the spirit of Van Wyck Brooks, whose notion of a "usable past" he appropriates, Mr. Stern here sets out the basic terms of his view of architecture and touches upon most of the themes that will occupy him in succeeding episodes.

According to Mr. Stern, the "crucial issue" facing American architecture today is its relationship to the past. Only if it retains a living bond with its past achievements can architecture hope to transcend its merely utilitarian tasks and "build a dream." Yet Mr. Stern points out that American architecture, lacking an indigenous tradition, had to fashion a tradition for itself out of a wide range of disparate elements; where Europe was born to its history and an architectural tradition, America in an important sense has always had to concoct its tradition, "inventing and reinventing" the past. Thus Mr. Stern calls for an architecture that blends "pragmatism and myth." Looking back to his youth in Brooklyn, he contrasts the fancifully ornamented skyscrapers of the Twenties and Thirties with the cooler, sparser modernist architecture of the Fifties and Sixties. For him, these later buildings betrayed the "dream" that promised to lift architecture from the realm of engineering to the realm of art; in reacting against historicism, modernist architecture showed itself to be enslaved to an ethic of functionality that "fiercely negated the past in favor of a single-minded orientation to the present." Modernism, according to Mr. Stern, abandoned the search for a usable past.

Somewhere in the midst of this tale of paradise lost, as Mr. Stern castigates the "insensitive, uniform boxes" of modernist architecture, the camera shifts abruptly from cheerful, long-distance shots of old New York skyscrapers and begins panning slowly across the glass façades of half a dozen modernist buildings. At the same time, the soundtrack, previously full of elevating arpeggios and trills, begins intoning a gloomy threnody. The entire sequence epitomizes the grossly manipulative quality of Mr. Stern's presentation. Moreover, Mr. Stern makes it clear that for him modernism's "fierceness" is not confined to its negative attitude toward the past; it also has dire consequence for one's social conscience. In one of his more extraordinary observations, he recalls his student days, when modernism was triumphant: "A new postwar world had dawned, I was reminded, and just as I must learn to love the bomb—or at least live with it—I must learn to love an architecture that exalted function and structural technique as the determinants of significant form." For Mr. Stern, it would seem, modernist architecture is not merely aesthetically displeasing, it has an insidious connection with instruments of death and destruction.

This, of course, is nonsense. There is no analogy between modernist architecture and atomic weapons whatsoever. Indeed, the chief interest of Mr. Stern's suggestion to the contrary is the cast of mind it betrays. And in this regard it may also be worth mentioning Mr. Stern's description of Mt. Vernon as "the Lenin's tomb of American architecture," a description that speaks volumes about Mr. Stern's sensitivity to history and tradition. This remark is noteworthy, too, because *Pride of Place* bills itself in part as a celebration of the American democratic tradition—a fact that no doubt explains why the State Department would have offered its premises for a screening and reception. Perhaps the best summary of Mr. Stern's thinking about these matters is to be found in his peroration. "The American dream has not been a blind leap into the future but a determined march," Mr. Stern rousingly concludes at the end of *Pride of Place*:

> at our best, our march forward has been directed by the lessons of what went before, and only when we have broken our contract with the past, with our best sense of what is noble and right, have we stumbled: we stumbled in the South Bronxes of our inner cities; we stumbled in Vietnam. When we stumble again, let us hope we do not fall down once and for all. Like Fitzgerald's Jay Gatsby, I believe "in the green light, the orgiastic future that year by year recedes before us." It eluded us at the dawn of our Republic, it eludes us now, "but that's no matter—to-morrow we will run faster, stretch out our arms farther . . . . And one fine morning—

> "So we beat on, boats against the current, borne back ceaselessly into the past."

Now we see that on top of everything else modernism is implicated in the decline of the South Bronx and in the Vietnam War. It is here, perhaps, in Mr. Stern's idolization of the pathetic figure of Fitzgerald's Gatsby—a character whose doomed pursuit of the "orgiastic future" rests upon a total fabrication of the past—that we have the real key to the conception of "history and tradition" as well as the motivating "dream" that informs *Pride of Place*.

But the main point of Mr. Stern's criticisms of modernism—the end to which the whole of *Pride of Place* strives—is to clear the way for the triumph of postmodernism. In short, his guiding theme is that modernist architecture was an aberration, an ahistorical rupture in American architectural history that is only now being repaired by the ascendancy of postmodernism. Finally, after the depredations of modernism, "the corporate world has come around again," Mr. Stern tells us; finally American architecture has found spokesmen for tradition and history in architects like Philip Johnson, Michael Graves, and Robert Venturi. Buildings like Johnson and Burgee's AT&T Building (described as the first New York skyscraper in forty years "to inhabit its height proudly") or PPG Place, Johnson and Burgee's "neo-Gothic" glass complex in Pittsburgh, are said by Mr. Stern to have "rekindled the confident spirit of the 1920s."

The ironies to be found in this "personal view" of the history of American architecture are no doubt endless. But the greatest irony is to be found in Mr. Stern's essentially campy posture as a champion of history and tradition. Throughout *Pride of Place,* he shows himself to be utterly incapable of distinguishing between real history and a superficial parody of history. Mr. Stern's romanticized version of history, like the versions of the past offered by the BBC in its dramatizations of novels and historical events, wraps the past in a glaze of nostalgia. Thus it turns out that Mr. Stern has a good reason for insisting that history and tradition in American architecture are "invented and reinvented," for his handling of history in *Pride of Place* shows that his real talents are in the realm of fantasy, not historical exposition. The picture of American architecture that he peddles in *Pride of Place* is woefully irresponsible when it comes to the historical record. The entire series rests on a systematic distortion of the character and achievements of modernist architecture. For while it is true that modernist architecture challenged the *ethos* of nineteenth-century historicism, to conclude that modernism is therefore anti-historical or anti-traditional is worse than simplistic; it is a blatant misrepresentation. As the German writer Wolf Tegethoff observes,

> Contrary to widespread opinion, in part deliberately promoted for purposes of propaganda, modern architecture did not make a break with history, but consciously adopted its achievements and sought to build upon them. Behind the presumed fundamentally new beginning that took place in the years just before and immediately after the First World War there ran uninterrupted strands of development that clearly exhibit this historical continuity.[2]

In this connection, one need think only of the deep and lasting influence of neo-classicism, especially of Karl Friedrich Schinkel, on modernism, an influence that Colin Rowe investigated in some detail as long ago as the late Forties.[3]

In fact, Mr. Stern's animus against modernism and its chief proponents completely undermines his analysis of its accomplishments. This is perhaps most amusingly evi-

---

2 *Mies van der Rohe: The Villas and Country Houses* (The Museum of Modern Art, 1985), p. 28.

3 See especially "The Mathematics of the Ideal Villa," "Mannerism and Modern Architecture," and "Neo-'Classicism' and Modern Architecture I," which have lately been collected in *The Mathematics of the Ideal Villa and Other Essays* (MIT, 1976).

dent in Mr. Stern's rhetoric and diction, which is not what one would call fastidious. Constrained to offer grudging praise for Mies's Seagram Building, because of the near universal admiration it has occasioned, Mr. Stern describes its design as "mordant." "Mordant," one wants to remind the Director of the Temple Hoyne Buell Center for the Study of American Architecture, means "bitingly sarcastic." What can it mean to describe the design of the Seagram Building—or any building, for that matter—as "mordant"? It means nothing at all, I'm afraid, though perhaps it does allow Mr. Stern to say one thing while suggesting its opposite. Whether he is conscious of this is hard to say, but he indulges in this sort of thing a lot, at times resorting to out-and-out contradiction. Thus, for example, he insists on one page that Mies "rejected history" and tradition but admits on another that "he struggled to create an order based on the steel I-beam that could compare with the traditional orders of Classicism." Often, in fact, Mr. Stern speaks truer than he means to, as when he lauds Robert Venturi's fanciful buildings at Princeton University, yet concludes by noting that "Venturi and his partners look at the past with a twisted smile," or when, in the midst of fulsome praise, he observes that the details at Michael Graves's new library at San Juan Capistrano constitute "an almost embarrassing climax of cuteness."

Furthermore, Mr. Stern's version of American architectural history is ludicrously anachronistic, interpreting every ornamental flourish from Colonial times on down as a prelude to postmodernism. Among the more irritating specimens of this tendency was Mr. Stern's description of Jefferson in terms that made him out to be, as it were, a postmodernist before his time. Jefferson, clearly one of Mr. Stern's heroes, was called upon to lend authority to all manner of folly. Thus Mr. Stern refers to Philip Johnson's famous Glass House as "a Modernist version of Jefferson's ideal," "an industrial age Monticello." In one of his many reflections about San Simeon, he writes that "Hearst's restless intelligence and obsessive nature resulted in an approach to building reminiscent of Jefferson's." One notes in passing that Philip Johnson's version of Miesian modernism is exempted from the criticism that Mr. Stern directs against Mies himself, perhaps because in Johnson's hands Mies's rigorous proportioning and use of materials have been abandoned for the sake of achieving a certain "look." But can Mr. Stern really believe that there is a Jeffersonian spirit animating the Glass House and San Simeon? Can there be any three buildings in all of American architectural history that have less in common than Monticello, the Glass House, and San Simeon?

The truth is that what we see throughout *Pride of Place* is the same arbitrary, deeply ahistorical approach to history and tradition that characterizes postmodernism itself. This approach is based on the belief that applying a Chippendale top or Egyptoid ornamentation to an essentially modernist skyscraper somehow represents a genuine recovery of history or tradition. History, from this point of view, is fundamentally a matter of packaging, decoration, and façade. Thus, after berating modernism, *Pride of Place* cuts without warning to Plimoth Plantation to give us a lecture in architecture as it should be. We watch as actors, in period costume, assemble the frame of a house. It is all very picturesque and romantic, especially the close-up shots of one of the men pounding the apparently hand-carved tenons into the mortises. The beams themselves, however, are awfully smooth—indeed, they are almost certainly machine-finished, a fact that gives the lie to the whole schmaltzy sequence and typifies the dishonest approach to tradition and history that Mr. Stern traffics in.

A similar pretense is at work in Mr. Stern's frequent invocation of "myth." He would have us believe that postmodernist architecture has helped put our culture back in touch with the dimension of myth, tradition, and "dreaming" that the rationalistic imperatives of modernism abjured. One hears such talk about "the recovery of myth" and the like a good deal these days, of course, though in truth it is rarely more than a rhetorical gesture. As Jacques Maritain has pointed out, myths in the sense Mr. Stern intends "have no force except through the faith man has in them. It is essential to them to be believed in."[4] But postmodernism's attachment to myth is purely superficial; it toys with myth the way it toys with historical ornamentation, arbitrarily appropriating first this, then that element or motif. At bottom, it remains as firmly rooted in the modern, technological world as the strictest Miesian, all the while refusing to acknowledge the implications of this contradiction. Never is there any question of belief, of authenticity; "myth" for postmodernism, like "history," is little more than a kind of costume, a kind of mask it dons in order to disguise its essentially modernist underpinnings and to achieve an aura of tradition.

Nevertheless, it is precisely postmodernism's talk of "history," of "tradition," of "myth" that gives it its great appeal at the present time. For though our culture is deeply shaped by science and technology and the essentially rationalized approach to the world that they imply, there remains a great nostalgia for something like a "mythic" view of the world. Postmodernism answers to that nostalgia, glibly dispensing the *illusion* of myth, the *appearance* of tradition, the *look* of history without bothering to involve itself in any of the fundamental commitments that genuine myth, tradition, or historical awareness would entail. Mr. Stern is only too happy to play this game, to speak grandly of recent architecture's resuscitation of history and mythic ambitions and, in the same vein, to import clichéd religious terminology in order to invest his discussion with an aura of spirituality and high purpose. Houses are "temples" for Mr. Stern, as are museums, as is even the Chrysler Building, and art is a sacred endeavor that consecrates our secular world. He goes on like this wherever possible, most egregiously, perhaps, in his discussion of the Pennsylvania Academy of Art and its "heavenly treasures." One can only wonder what terms Mr. Stern would use to describe a real temple or church—if indeed the distinction has any meaning for him.

A good deal of Mr. Stern's approach comes together in his discussion of resort architecture, "Resorts: Paradise Regained." He devotes an entire episode to the subject ostensibly because resorts have inspired significant architecture in this country, but really, or so it seems, because it gives him another opportunity to wallow in a world of fantasy underwritten by wealth, caprice, and eccentricity. It also allows him to offer us further extraordinary analogies, some of which are every bit as wonderful as his reference to the atomic bomb in the midst of his discussion of modernism. "Just as one can see normally buttoned-down men and women reveal their every physical and psychological nuance during a summer afternoon at the beach," Mr. Stern writes, "one can see national architecture preferences, free at last from so many economic and societal constraints, intensely expressed in resort architecture." But *do* men and women "reveal their every physical and psychological nuance during a summer afternoon at the beach"? Of course they don't. And can "national architectural preferences" really be said to express themselves in any important sense in resort architecture? Of course not.

Still, it is worth pausing over Mr. Stern's assessment of resort architecture; for while his discussion often borders on the absurd, it does provide a splendid example of the sensibility that characterizes *Pride of Place*. "The greatest American resorts have gone beyond conventional exercises in escape," writes Mr. Stern;

> resorts have functioned as stage sets upon which the nation has enacted a mythic version of its past . . . . Moreover, Americans have learned to live together in a community at their resorts. In a democracy where strict social traditions and codes of behavior do not apply, the resort has provided an image of

---

4 *Creative Intuition in Art and Poetry* (Meridian, 1974), p. 318.

> communitarian stability that the "real" world fails to provide. Whether at a grand hotel, a summer colony, or a theme village, Americans on holiday have dealt themselves strong lessons in social behavior, often under the benignly dictatorial hand of a hotelier or self-appointed tastemaker.

What are we to make of this passage? Leaving to one side the unexceptionable suggestion that American resorts have "gone beyond conventional exercises in escape," is there a single assertion here that can stand without qualification? We have already discussed Mr. Stern's invocation of the "mythic past." Here we can see that his notion of "community" is hardly more substantial. And the idea that the resort provides democracy with its ideal image of community is not simply false, it is obscene. At best, the resort can be seen as an ironic parody of a genuine community—though it is indicative of Mr. Stern's entire presentation that any distinction between an ideal and its caricature is lost. (Consider, in this regard, the arch quotation marks around the word "real" in the above passage—exactly what reality is Mr. Stern calling into question?)

At the center of Mr. Stern's discussion of resorts is the work of the Russian-born architect Morris Lapidus, whose best-known creation to date is probably the Hotel Fontainebleau (1954) on Miami Beach and whose genius for expensive kitsch allowed him, in Mr. Stern's words, to fashion "a new aesthetic identity for Miami." Mr. Stern is absolutely correct when he notes that "Lapidus invented a vision of an architectural past that never existed" and describes him as a "designer of permanent stage sets." But I hardly see that this makes his work "some of the most original and inventive architecture produced in this country," as Mr. Stern puts it. In fact, Mr. Lapidus's creations for Miami Beach, like most "resort architecture," are the trashiest concoctions, utterly without aesthetic or architectural merit. Their "elegance" is based on overblown, pseudo-historical pastiche combined with lots of lights and shiny surfaces. And the truth is that the works of Mr. Lapidus and his ilk are perfect for *Pride of Place* because they accord so completely with Mr. Stern's "personal view" of architectural history as a kind of "stage set" to be plundered in order to invest fundamentally modern structures with the patina of history and tradition.

The essential clue to the attitude behind this "new aesthetic identity" was aptly summed up by Mr. Lapidus himself when he observed:

> "People are looking for illusions; they don't want the world's realities . . . . Where are their tastes formulated? Do they study it in school? Do they go to museums? Do they travel in Europe? Only one place—the movies. They go to the movies. The hell with everything else."

"People are looking for illusions"—at bottom, that is the unacknowledged motto of postmodernism. Mr. Lapidus also displays great insight when he invokes the movies in this context. For it is the movies, not architecture, that provide Mr. Stern with his one stable cultural reference point throughout *Pride of Place.* He begins the series by telling us that New York in the Twenties was his "personal Oz," and there follow references to (and often clips from) all manner of movies and television shows: the main house in *Dallas* is adduced as an example of architecture inspired by Mt. Vernon; bits of *Citizen Kane* are shown during his discussion of San Simeon, *King Kong* when he discusses the Empire State Building; James Gamble Rogers is said to have "used architecture to provide Yale with a kind of WASP version of *Roots*"; and there are also references to *Goldfinger, Superman, High Noon, Bringing Up Baby, Christmas in Connecticut,* Fritz Lang's *Metropolis,* and on and on. Indeed, it seems at times that Mr. Stern can hardly make a point without bringing in a movie.

For example, Charlie Chaplin apparently provided Mr. Stern with a touchstone for understanding modernist architecture. "Mies willingly condemned architecture to an existential world without past or future," Mr. Stern tells us.

> But however rooted in the concrete and the practical, the technology that Mies deified was itself not an eternal truth but a variable, a constantly evolving standard. Mies's escape from the past into the technological present in time became subject to history as well, taking on, in less than half a century, a dreamlike, almost quaint quality, evoking the nostalgia for the machine age one now feels when watching Charlie Chaplin's 1936 film *Modern Times.*

Le Corbusier, too, reminds Mr. Stern of *Modern Times:*

> Le Corbusier sketched a world relentlessly locked into a shadowless present. His dream encased the bureaucrats of business and commerce in huge unornamented and uniform office blocks, which he dubbed "Cartesian" out of respect for the French logician. Le Corbusier's towers were to be reserved for the new managerial elite, who after their working day traveled high-speed roadways to be decanted into stacked duplexes around the edges of the park. Like his contemporary T. S. Eliot, Le Corbusier emulated this managerial elite, transforming himself into the bowler-hatted man in the black suit that Charlie Chaplin would parody.

But was Le Corbusier's world "locked into a shadowless present"? Was Descartes a "logician"? Is it fair to say that Le Corbusier's buildings were conceived for "the new managerial elite"? What about *Unité d'Habitation,* his widely admird apartment house in Marseilles? And T. S. Eliot—well, here Mr. Stern is once again indulging in the cheapest of cultural stereotypes.

After that initial screening of the first episode of *Pride of Place* in Washington, Herbert Schmertz, Mobil's vice-president for public affairs, stood up to assure us that what we had just witnessed was a serious exploration of cultural and architectural themes, not to be confused with such manipulative television drivel as *Lifestyles of the Rich and the Famous.* But the sad truth is that *Pride of Place* has virtually nothing to do with architecture or high culture and almost everything to do with "lifestyle." There is no attempt to come to terms with important architectural or aesthetic issues, or even to present an accurate and comprehensible picture of architectural history. Of critical judgment there is not a trace—Disneyland, San Simeon, Monticello, Newport: so long as its not modernist, it's all one to Robert Stern. Instead of a thoughtful, critically discriminating presentation of American architecture, we are given picture-postcard views of places and buildings—especially the houses and grounds of the rich and powerful—intermixed with Mr. Stern's cheerleading for postmodernism.

It seems entirely appropriate, then, that near the end of the last episode of *Pride of Place* we should see Mr. Stern and the utopian architect Leon Krier being driven around Williamsburg, Virginia, in a horse-drawn carriage and agreeing that in many respects the reconstructed Colonial village represents the best hope for the "future" of American architecture. Whatever virtues Williamsburg may have as an example of historic preservation, it has nothing to contribute to the central architectural problems of our time. But considered as an exercise in nostalgia, as a cosmetic rehabilitation of days gone by, it stands as a perfect symbol of Mr. Stern's postmodernist conception of history and tradition. "At Williamsburg," writes Mr. Stern, "one can simultaneously escape into history and escape from it." Williamsburg also stands as a perfect symbol for the cultural vision of public television in this country. Instead of the BBC's romantic tales of the British Raj, we get Professor Stern going around a reconstructed Colonial village in a horse-drawn carriage talking about the future of American architecture. If *Pride of Place* can be considered "educational" at all, it is only in a negative, admonitory sense. It is, alas, a cautionary tale.

(*May* 1986)

Pops in Portland
by Samuel Lipman

Artwise, as one might say, Portland, Oregon, is a special place. It is the home of a statewide symphony orchestra, its own opera company, a visual arts museum, a historical museum, various kinds of theater, and all the mutually supportive enterprises which go to make up what is locally called an Artquake. Even—or especially—the incoming Portland mayor has joined the parade: Bud Clark is none other than the sensitive soul who posed, backside to the camera and raincoat flung open before an art object, for that memorable poster captioned "Expose yourself to art." How's that for class?

At the present moment all the Portland artshearts are throbbing to the beat of a new space for symphony concerts. Dubbed the Arlene Schnitzer Concert Hall in honor of its major donor, this edifice is the old Paramount Theater, a movie house dating from the late 1920s, that halcyon era when plaster replicas of the interior of the Alhambra were just the thing for giving tone to the latest exploits of Rudolph Valentino and Douglas Fairbanks. Naturally the excitement over Schnitzer Hall is integrated into the whole Portland renaissance; even the signs on the temporary fences closing off construction areas outside the hall bear an injunction perhaps not unrelated to the mayor-elect's offering to art: "Flaunt Your Civic Pride," these signs urge those timid souls lacking in urban commitment.

So many caring instincts so bounteously displayed seemed to require (of at least this listener) a witness to what is going on in the erstwhile City of Roses. So on a Sunday evening late in October I found myself seated in the Arlene Schnitzer Concert Hall listening to the only musical offering taking place there during my three-day stay in Portland. The event was a "Merrill Lynch Pops" concert, one of the series of six events (each of them repeated twice) under the joint sponsorship of the famed brokerage giant and the Oregon Symphony Orchestra. To be fair, I don't suppose I would have chosen a Glenn Miller evening by which to judge either the hall or musicmaking in Portland, had I the choice: all the participants were heavily amplified, making acoustical judgment of the hall impossible, and a full menu of Glenn Miller and related arrangements seems (again to me) insupportable without convivial talk and a girl in tow. But arts-loving beggars can't be choosers, and I had just spent a lunch hearing Oregon's Governor, Victor Atiyeh, telling an audience of art-school deans that everything was art, from the souvenirs bought on the street to great paintings. So I went, and I sat through it all, two musty hours of nostalgia and reconstructed memories.

As is the case in most old movie palaces, the lobbies of Schnitzer Hall seem confined, doubtless because they were never meant to provide an audience with space in which to promenade before a performance and during intermission. Making matters worse, the available space was severely cramped by a profusion of wine bars, liquor bars, and snack and wine bars. Indeed, so many of those walking about before the concert and during the intermission were carrying full plastic tumblers that one could well understand how the arts function today as oases, if not from ugliness, at least from thirst.

While on the subject of Schnitzer Hall's public spaces, mention should be made of the Oregon Symphony Association curio cart just across the narrow lobby from the first wine bar as one walked in. There were the usual memorabilia on sale here, all doubtless bought from some novelty merchant who specializes in supplying shops in arts institutions. Here was a chance to buy an Oregon Symphony Wine Bag, T-shirts emblazoned "Jimmy" (in honor of the Oregon Symphony's music director, James DePreist), and an Oregon Symphony Appointment Calendar. My own favorite souvenir was a pair of notepads available at a modest price: the first pad had its pages wittily headed (in old-fashioned lettering) "Chekhov-Liszt"; the second pad was inscribed "Chopin-Liszt."

Because I too am tempted to engage in bad punning, I can honestly say that the concert itself was listless. There must be a lot of Miller fans and other aficionados of the big-band era; the concert I attended seemed just about sold out. Everything—upwards of twenty tunes performed by eighteen musicians and two vocalists—was received with decorous appreciation by an audience well in its sixties and older. The concert began and ended with "Moonlight Serenade," ploddingly played, as if the musicians onstage, most of them (except for the two blandly attractive vocalists) the same age as the audience, were going through the motions of old memories rather than playing anything fresh and exciting. The conductor was Norman Leyden, an accomplished band leader and conductor who has much experience in doing pops concerts in the northwest; in this capacity he does the pops for both the Oregon and the Seattle orchestras. Leyden beguiled and cajoled the audience, explaining, with many human touches, what was going to happen onstage—and then, when it happened, he led the audience in expressing its appreciation. It all was like Lawrence Welk live, an opening up of a time capsule stored in a retirement village.

What was missing, of coure, was the spirit of the music. One need not be a blind partisan of swing music to know that at its best it was tough, insistent, vital, and often even bitter in its suggestion of a world more opulent and glamorous than its musicians and listeners could ever themselves occupy. Tune after tune—the likes of "Tuxedo Junction," "Stairway to the Stars," and "A Nightingale Sang in Berkeley Square"—went by pointlessly, with the brass slides, the blue notes, and the rhythmic jabs losing all their corners in the general mood of tiredness. Fittingly, the lead saxophonist was given a solo to celebrate his retirement; these concerts, we were told, marked the end of his career.

But, disappointing as the musical lacks of the concert were, even more disturbing was a major question arising out of the whole sorry business: what was the Oregon Symphony Orchestra doing putting its name on the concert? One doubts that many of the orchestra's own musicians were involved in the performance; the repertory was not by the wildest stretch of the imagination a symphony orchestra repertory; altogether the evening had as much to do with the body of music which is a symphony orchestra's concern as Glenn Miller had to do with Arturo Toscanini. To say this is not to make value judgments or even—perish the thought—to be elitist. It is merely to make a necessary distinction in functions between properly separate kinds of musical activity.

Why, then, was this concert given? The answers are, it would seem, three. First, there can be no doubt that this Glenn Miller evening, and events like it (which in the case of the Oregon Symphony Orchestra include concerts titled "The Best of Broadway," "The Genius of George Shearing," "The Music of Richard Rodgers," "Frankie Laine at the Pops," and "Your Hit Parade"), make money; in so doing they not only swell the orchestra's coffers but convince potential corporation and foundation contributors that the enterprise is deserving of support because it is doing so much to pay its own way. Second, as with all cultural institutions today, much emphasis is put on service by orchestras to *all* the community, as if a hospital, to be doing its job, had to have its rooms occupied by everyone, not just the sick. And finally these concerts in Portland take place because Merrill Lynch construes its own interest as served by being seen to sponsor "the arts" when in fact the corporate endorsement is going to commercially viable popular culture.

What is so troubling about the Oregon Symphony Orchestra's willingness to appear before the public as an impresario of widely attractive entertainment is the message the organization is thus sending to its true present audience and to the future audience it must educate in the interest of its own survival. The message is that all musics are equally worthy of presentation, not just by someone somewhere, but by a symphony orchestra charged with the duty of promoting high culture through the performance of a "classical" music. It would be foolish, of course, to think that this duty is always to be discharged solely through the performance of the most difficult music; over many years in Boston, Arthur Fiedler proved that unsophisticated audiences could be musically interested in the classics by their lively presentation, with lighter stuff used at the end of the concert as a reward for staying the course.[1] In the case of the Portland concert I heard, no educational function was served, and the result can only have been confusion in the minds of well-meaning people about just what it is that a symphony orchestra does, or is supposed to do.

A word, too, must be said about Schnitzer Hall as a place to experience a cultural event. Sadly, totally lacking from Schnitzer Hall is anything of the true majesty and glitter of the era of great classical music and of the buildings which were coeval with this music; equally lacking is anything of the clean lines and structural audacity of the great architecture of our own century. Despite all the money that, through a patron's generosity, has been spent on remodeling this old Portland movie theater, the building remains today what it was at its birth: a dingy pleasure palace built to dupe a mass public with a cheaply built tinsel imitation of an "exotic" and dimly perceived original.

---

1 Indeed, the Oregon Symphony Orchestra does have such presentations, in this case called "Symphony Sundays"; significantly, though they are also performed in Schnitzer Hall, they are nowhere listed—though the pops concerts are—in "Portland Performs," the glossy brochure of downtown arts activity put out by the Association for Portland Progress and *Oregon* magazine. In any case the educational mission of these concerts is undercut by the rhetoric used to gull ticket buyers: "You'll love the greats of classical music! Favorite classical selections from *Grand Canyon Suite* to *Pines of Rome.*"

(*December* 1984)

"The Story of English" on PBS

by Bruce Bawer

This fall, television viewers in both America and Britain were presented with a nine-part series entitled *The Story of English,* co-produced by MacNeil-Lehrer Productions and the BBC. Though the series was purportedly a joint American-British endeavor, was hosted by the anchorman of an American news program, Robert MacNeil, and was funded principally by an American corporation (General Foods) and an American foundation (the Andrew W. Mellon Foundation), *The Story of English* had a decidedly British flavor. This should not be surprising, for it was conceived and co-written by an Englishman, Robert McCrum, the editorial director of Faber and Faber and a graduate of Cambridge University (the series' other writer of record was MacNeil, who is Canadian by birth), and was produced and directed by William Cran, an Oxford-educated journalist who has created documentaries for public television both here and in Britain. McCrum, Cran, and MacNeil are, furthermore, the authors of a companion book—also entitled *The Story of English*—which was published to coincide with the airing of the television show.[1]

The first episode of the series, entitled "An English-Speaking World," was less than promising. Its chief purpose seemed to be to tell us as many times as possible that English is "a language without frontiers," "the language of the global village of communication," "everybody's second language," "the indispensable language of progress for the Third World." MacNeil's cameras took us to Italy (where the multinational Iveco Corporation transacts all its business in English), to France (where the French-speaking countries, in general congress assembled, attempted to stem the tide of "Franglish" by coming up with French equivalents for *Walkman* and *compact disc*), to India (where young men want their brides to be fluent in English), to China (where the most popular television series is an English-language instructional program), to Japan, West Africa, Singapore, and so forth. This material started out by being fascinating and ended up by being very monotonous. The program dwelled in particular on California, whose "huge energy," MacNeil told us, "has overflowed into the language." He showed us surfers gabbing in "surf talk" ("check it out, dude"), Silicon Valley people using words like *on-line* and *high-tech,* and San Fernando Valley girls explaining "valley talk" (*grody, awesome*). An extremely unamusing homosexual comedian delivered a long routine that yielded exactly two examples of "gay slang" ("coming out of the closet," *queens*). Then, while we watched a group of women in sweatsuits practicing self-defense techniques, MacNeil rhapsodized about how "California has led the way in chopping sexism out of the language," and about how the

---

1 *The Story of English,* by Robert McCrum, William Cran, and Robert MacNeil. Elisabeth Sifton Books/Viking, 384 pages, $24.95.

elimination of words like *chairman* and *mankind* spells "the end of linguistic male chauvinism." Finally, MacNeil spoke ominously about "Pentagon language" ("predawn vertical insertion") and explained that it was the "ordinary fighting man" who had enriched military English, by coining words like *snafu.*

MacNeil explained, near the beginning of this first episode, that the series would speak of *varieties* of English, not *dialects,* for the latter "is often a loaded word." He said:

> Our story is not about the correct way to speak English but about all the different varieties and how they came to be. Why a MacNeil from Nova Scotia sounds different from a MacNeil here in Scotland or one in North Carolina or New Zealand . . . . In fact the idea of a correct or proper way to speak is surprisingly recent. There is such an idea, of course. It's often referred to as the Queen's English or BBC English or Oxford English or public-school English.

Whereupon *The Story of English* took us to Winchester, where a few high-toned teenage boys told us about the pressures public-school boys are under to speak the Queen's English. What's important here is that MacNeil, in pronouncing his refusal to endorse a "correct" brand of English, failed to distinguish between accent, on the one hand, and grammar and vocabulary on the other. To endorse one accent as correct would of course be out-and-out snobbery; to suggest that the grammatical rules of Standard English should be followed, and the received meanings of the words in its vocabulary respected, is something else again. *The Story of English,* for what its creators patently considered (in their ineffable Oxbridgean way) to be noble and egalitarian reasons, consistently blurred this fundamental distinction. Accordingly, MacNeil insisted at the conclusion of the first episode that, for all the scholars and writers and poets who have written memorably in English, "the making of English is not imposed from above. It bubbles up from below, from the speech of every man and every woman." Despite such ringing populistic declarations, however, the series had an unmistakable *de haut en bas* tone; though I didn't know when I saw this first episode precisely who had created the series, it was obvious from the program's strange preoccupation with public-school English (no matter what MacNeil actually happened to be saying about it), as well as from its desperately misguided stab at egalitarianism, that *The Story of English* was, in large part, the product of the Oxbridge mentality, with its perverse combination of snobbism and *nostalgie de la boue.*

Fortunately, the series was not as consistently offensive as the first episode suggested it would be. At its best, *The Story of English* presented a respectable simplified course in the history of the language. Episode Two ("The Mother Tongue"), for instance, effectively summarized the story of the language's beginnings. It covered the Indo-European background; the fifth-century invasion of Celtic Britain by the Anglo-Saxons, who brought with them their language, Old English, and borrowed relatively few words (*crag, tor, Avon*) from the Celts; the introduction of Christianity, with its Greek and Latin vocabulary (*angel, disciple, martyr, shrine*), in AD 597; the coming of the Vikings, with their Norse vocabulary, between the eighth and eleventh centuries (thanks to which speakers of English can either *rear* or *raise* a child, the former word arising from Old English, the latter from Old Norse); and the Norman invasion of 1066, which added a huge French vocabulary to the language (giving us a choice between the Anglo-Saxon *kingly* and the French *royal, regal,* and *sovereign*) and resulted in the development of Middle English. The episode took a deep bow in the direction of Chaucer, the language's first great writer, and of William Caxton, its first printer, who played a major role in establishing the language's spelling conventions; and it ended with an excerpt from the fifteenth-century play *Mankind,* whose language "is thoroughly and recognizably English."

The succeeding program, "A Muse of Fire," picked the story up from there, celebrating the English of the Renaissance, during which time between ten and twelve thousand new words were added to the language—words like *detail* (which was adapted from the French), *cupola* and *stucco* (Italian), *desperado* and *embargo* (Spanish), *smuggle* and *reef* (Dutch). From Latin, writers adapted words like *retrograde, reciprocal, defunct,* and *inflate,* which were widely regarded as pretentious and were known as "inkhorn terms." Sir Thomas More took the Latin word *communicare* and turned it into *communicate,* and Sir Philip Sidney combined the Greek words for "heat" and "measure" and created *thermometer.* The individual most responsible, however, for the enrichment of Renaissance English is Shakespeare, whose *Folio,* MacNeil told us, exerts a "direct influence on every one of us who speaks English today." Shakespeare, whose works contain a vocabulary of thirty-four thousand words (the greatest of any writer), "invented more words than anyone that ever lived," including *obscene* and *assassination*; a single line of *Macbeth* contains two new words, *multitudinous* and *incarnadine.* Shakespeare also made the language more flexible, using nouns for verbs (e.g., "grace me no grace"), and coined numerous phrases that have entered the language—which the program illustrated by a list of famous lines from *Hamlet* on the order of "Frailty, thy name is woman!" and "Alas poor Yorick." (The series' companion book does better by Shakespeare's phrase-making: it quotes a clever piece by Bernard Levin that is composed entirely of phrases originated by the Bard.) The program thereupon presented us with brief clips from the BBC's *Shakespeare Plays,* the purpose of which apparently was to remind us that Shakespeare wrote such lines as "Friends, Romans, countrymen, lend me your ears," and "The quality of mercy is not strained."

The episode moved on from Shakespeare to cover the King James Bible of 1611 (whose vocabulary consists of an austere eight thousand words) and the colonization of America—whose variety of English was founded, as MacNeil put it, upon the English of Shakespeare and the King James Bible. The majority of the settlers at Jamestown, we were informed, came from the West Country of England, whose stressed "r" sound, which is uncharacteristic of most English speech, became a notable characteristic of American English; the Puritan settlers of Massachusetts, on the other hand, came mostly from East Anglia (where one can find the original towns of Boston, Lincoln, Braintree, Cambridge, etc.), thus accounting for the fact that the New England accent, with its flat "a" and unstressed "r" (among other things), bears a strong resemblance to the East Midlands dialect. These accentual similarities were demonstrated—as such things were throughout the series—in longish sequences that took us into neighborhood pubs and shops on both sides of the Atlantic to listen to the natives chat each other up. In spite of the occasional inane detour, then, the second and third episodes of *The Story of English* were mostly fine, and one was able to imagine them being used profitably in conjunction with a high-school English course.

The same was true—but to a somewhat lesser extent—of Episode Four ("The Guid Scots Tongue"). When the Normans invaded England, they sent many Anglo-Saxons fleeing into Scotland, thus giving rise to the Scots dialect. Episode Four told us that the Scots—whose variety of English, but for the seventeenth-century union of the two kingdoms, might well have developed into a separate language—nonetheless have played an important role in the dissemination of English. (Incidentally, in one of the many discrepancies between the series and the companion book, the series told us that Scots—not to be confused with Scots Gaelic, the all-but-extinct Celtic language of the Highlands—might under different circumstances have become as distinct from English as Danish is from Swedish; the book tells us that Scots did indeed become as distinct from English as Danish is from Swedish.) Many Scots-Irish, MacNeil explained, emigrated to Philadelphia, and from there travelled westward through the Cumberland Gap, where their descendants speak the Appalachian dialect. That dialect's characteristic pronunciations (*bar* for *bear, cheer* for *here, hit* for *it*), in particular its open vowels, betray its Scottish origin. MacNeil maintained that not only the Appalachian accent, but the accents of the American Midwest and Southwest, all derive principally from Scots-Irish.

This episode—which was the first in the series to deal extensively with American English—had several notable failings. For one thing, like many of the episodes to follow, it sometimes fastened upon matters that seemed to have little or nothing to do with the topic at hand—truck drivers' CB-radio nicknames, for instance. More important, there was no mention that Charleston, South Carolina, received nearly as many Scots-Irish immigrants as did Philadelphia, and that the largest concentration of Americans of Scots-Irish ancestry is in the southern states. One expected to see this oversight repaired in a later episode, but it never was.

Indeed, the very next installment of the series compounded the confusion on this matter. This episode, interestingly enough, began in Charleston, but didn't so much as mention the Scots-Irish—or, for that matter, the French Huguenots, who also migrated in large numbers to Charleston and exerted a considerable influence upon the speech of white people in that part of the country. Entitled "Black on White," the segment was concerned rather with the influence of American blacks on world English. It was, one should add, probably the most disturbing episode of the series, the one that most plainly demonstrated the perverseness of many of the attitudes and assumptions upon which the entire series was constructed. "White American language and culture owe much to the blacks," MacNeil said by way of introduction. Whereupon he introduced us to an obnoxious pair of upper-class white Charlestonians—a pompous young man preparing for a game of polo, a snooty belle parading around in a crinoline dress suggestive of Scarlett O'Hara—whose English, MacNeil explained, was a direct descendant of the Plantation Creole once spoken by Southern slaves, which had in turn developed out of the makeshift English of the African slave coast. The implication was that the English of all white Southerners is strongly dependent upon Plantation Creole as is the English of Charleston; but the program failed to point out that the dialect of that city—the one-time center of the slave trade—is unique in the South, easily distinguishable from the English spoken in towns as close as fifty miles away.

This was not the episode's only peculiar omission. White Southern plantation children, we were told, learned to speak English from their black mammies, their black playmates, and their black house and field workers—who, significantly outnumbering the whites on the plantation, exerted a greater influence upon their language than did their parents. Well enough. But what of the great majority of white Southerners who were not plantation dwellers, outnumbered by their slaves? The program failed to take such people into account. (Those wealthy Charlestonians, with their aberrant accent and anachronistic way of life, were the only white Southerners featured in the whole series.) Nor, once again, did MacNeil distinguish between accent and grammar or vocabulary; certainly the grammar and vocabulary of most white Southerners were less influenced by Plantation Creole than were their accents.

MacNeil also introduced us to a community of blacks who live on the Sea Islands of South Carolina (and whose down-to-earth charm formed a distinct, and apparently intentional, contrast with the snootiness of the rich white Charlestonians). These blacks speak Gullah, a language peculiar to the Sea Islands, which is, in MacNeil's words, "one of the missing links between American and African civilization" and the "basis of black American English." From South Carolina, the program leapt across the ocean to the coast of West Africa where, two and three centuries ago, white and black slave traders communicated in West African pidgin English (a "pidgin" being a language with a simple grammar and limited vocabulary, and no native speakers, which is created so that people with different primary languages can talk to one another). This pidgin contained elements of a number of European and African languages (the pidgin word *pickaninny* derived from the diminutive of the Portuguese word *pequino,* "small"; *savvy* came from the French *savez-vous*). Because the captured slaves came from tribes that spoke a hundred and sixty different languages, pidgin English became their principal means of communication, not only with their captors but with one another; thus it developed, in time, into the English Creole of West Africa and the West Indies (a "creole" being a pidgin that has become the first language of a speech community) as well as into Plantation Creole—which, in turn, developed into Black English.

One aspect of Black English is "jive talk," which was spread to the white community by black musicians early in the twentieth century. Jive talk added an abundance of slang and colloquial words to the language —*uptight, jazz, groovy, lingo*—and gave new meanings to many old words, among them *cool, joint, square, chick, beat,* and *jam.* The program explored this phenomenon responsibly enough, but then wasted several minutes on "Mr. Spoons," a black Philadelphian shoeshine man who writes "poems" like this:

> Step up on the stand
> And get the best shine in the land.
> If you don't like your shine, you get your money back
> But if you don't pay, you get your head cracked.
> That's the business of the boot-black.

While Mr. Spoons recited "one of his finest poems," a less-than-impressive meditation on civil rights ("There just ain't no justice here for the Black man. / How then can that be but wrong. / You see they closed most of the schools to us down here, / And we pay taxes but afraid to vote."), we watched some Sixties-vintage film of white cops and dogs terrorizing black protesters. For a while, the supposed topic of the series got lost in the shuffle; the creators of *The Story of English* clearly felt obliged to remind us that (a) black people had a rough time in America for several centuries and (b) MacNeil, McCrum, and Cran felt just sick about it. So they took us on a little detour from the story of English and instead we got to see, for the hundredth time, the March on Washington and Martin Luther King's "I Have a Dream" speech, and got to hear MacNeil noting triumphantly that in the twenty years since that speech, "Blacks have gradually taken their rightful place in American life."

We then met one of the country's more successful blacks, Mayor Wilson Goode of Philadelphia, who, MacNeil informed us, once took a speech course in order to lose his North Carolina accent. In yet another of its habitual refusals to distinguish between differences in accent and differences in grammar and vocabulary, the program seemed to equate Mayor Goode's deliberate change of accent with the attempts of American educators to help black students learn Standard English. The program purported to take no sides in the controversy over Black English, but in actuality it came down strongly on the side of Black English, suggesting that one "variety" of language is as good as another, and even implying that the street kids who speak Black English are more vitally involved with language than are the English teachers who would have them adopt Standard English. After a black woman judge spoke eloquently against Black English, explaining that young black people need to master Standard English in order to compete equally in American society, MacNeil and company appeared to do their best to make her look like a reactionary, a traitor to her people and her culture. "Major changes in the language," MacNeil insisted, "don't happen because of educators and writers but on the street. The streets of the ghetto have been one of the great recent phrase- and word-factories of English."

And so MacNeil, in the last fifteen minutes or so of this episode, took us slumming on the ghetto streets, where "the traditions of Black English are alive and well." We met a gang of young blacks and listened to them converse with each other in their severely limited vocabulary (*funky fresh, wack, bad,* etc.) about a fight that one of them had almost gotten into with a dude from another gang; then we met a young street rapper named Perrey P who, MacNeil told us, has "made street talk into an art form all his own." Sample:

> Synthetics, genetics, command your soul,
> Trucks, tanks, laser beams
> Gus, blasts, submarines,
> Neutron, B-bomb, A-bomb, gas
> All that stuff will kill you fas'.

That their lack of fluency in Standard English all but guarantees that these street kids will grow into street adults seems not to have disturbed MacNeil, McCrum, and Cran; they displayed not the slightest hesitancy in celebrating the artfulness, the "vigor" and "zest," of these young people's language. One could not help but ask oneself: would MacNeil and company want their own children to talk this way, to be "artists" like Perrey P? Would William Cran hire a Perrey P to write one of his documentaries? Would MacNeil take him on as a reporter for *The MacNeil-Lehrer Newshour*? Would McCrum give him a Faber and Faber book contract? Of course not. There is no question but that the facile, modish praise of Perrey P and his brethren represented *The Story of English* at its most hypocritical, irresponsible, and condescending.

The next few segments of the series were considerably less worrisome. Episode Six ("Pioneers! O Pioneers!") covered the development of English in the American West, including the contributions of Mississippi riverboat gamblers ("up the ante," "deal me out"), the Forty-niners ("hit pay dirt"), the Indian pidgin ("no can do," "long time no see"), cowboy jargon (*lallapalooza, absquatulate,* "bite the dust," "hot under the collar"), frontier Spanish (*stampede, sombrero, loco*), and the railroads (*sidetrack, whistlestop,* "make the grade," "one-track mind"). The episode afforded MacNeil the opportunity to refer to the encounter between whites and Indians as a "tragic culture clash" and to deliver the following sentence, which was typical of the series at its most fatuously rhapsodic: "Railroads found a special place in America's heart, putting the country's energetic spirit on wheels, sweeping its people and their language to the remote corners of the Union, stirring the melting pot of American English." (This was almost as impressive as a sentence from the first episode, which made MacNeil, for a moment at least, sound strangely like *Star Trek*'s Captain Kirk: "In this series we will take an extraordinary journey from an obscure Germanic tribe to the ends of the universe . . . .") There was also an apparent contradiction with Episode Four, which had maintained that the Scots-Irish were mostly responsible for the middle-American accent; now, MacNeil told us that the accent of the Midwest resulted from a merging of the accents of the eastern states.

But no matter. At this point—with a bow toward Whitman, who "celebrated the pioneer spirit of America," and toward Mark Twain (whose achievement was summarized by that all-purpose transatlantic authority, the redoubtable Alistair Cooke)—the episode turned to the contributions of non-English-speaking immigrants of the post-Civil War period. While we viewed the requisite film of huddled masses at Ellis Island, MacNeil read some purple prose about "this melancholy gateway to the New World"; then the program cut to New York's skyscrapers (with, somewhat disconcertingly, Copland's *Appalachian Spring* serving as the background music). We watched a parade in New York's Little Italy while MacNeil explained that the Italian language gave us words like *spaghetti* and *manicotti*; we watched a Steuben Day parade while MacNeil saluted Germany for giving us *kin-*

dergarten, cookbook, and *delicatessen.* (At times, *The Story of English* made one downright hungry.) Finally MacNeil talked about how Jewish radio and television comedians spread Yiddish words (*chutzpah, schmaltz, kosher*) and phrases ("You should live so long," "Enough already") to the American public—apropos of which Leo Rosten, one of the many celebrated figures interviewed in the course of the series, offered a genuinely interesting observation about why Yiddish may well be (in MacNeil's words) "the most influential of immigrant languages." "Yiddish," he said, "lends itself to a remarkable range of psychological discriminations. It's steeped in sentiment and it's loosed with sarcasm. It knows that only paradox can do justice to the injustice of life. It adores irony because it knows that the only way Jews could retain their sanity was to view a dreadful world with ironic and astringent eyes."

But such moments of perceptiveness were few and far between in *The Story of English.* Episode Seven ("The Muvver Tongue") took a rather superficial, if diverting, look at the language of Cockneys and its influence upon Australian English (which also, the program informed us, preserves English localisms—Warwickshire's *larriken* for rowdy, rural Norfolk's *wowser* for killjoy—that are long since extinct in the Home Counties). Episode Eight ("The Loaded Weapon") was about Ireland and the Irish; it discussed the English language's borrowing of words like *smithereens, galore,* and *tantrum* from Irish Gaelic, the world's debt to Irish writers like Yeats and Joyce and Synge, and the Irish influence upon the New York accent in general and the coinage *yous* (as in "yous guys") in particular. Most of all, however, the episode seemed preoccupied with extremely familiar political matters—namely, with the centuries-old struggle between Ireland and England, in which the English language has of course played an important role. Accordingly, the program's final moments found MacNeil delivering an unsurprising conclusion to the effect that the Irish, their pipe dreams to the contrary, won't ever be able to shake off the English language and go back to Gaelic, but may yet "find in the accents of their English an escape from the prison of their history."

The series' closing installment, "The Empire Strikes Back," posed the question, "Will English, like Latin before it, gradually break up into separate languages?" MacNeil took us to Sierra Leone, Barbados, and Jamaica, where the natives speak English creoles. In Jamaica, activists expressed their desire to eliminate Standard English (which they look upon resentfully as "the language of authority") as the official state language, and to replace it with Jamaican Creole ("the language of the mass of the people"), so that street signs reading "No parking between signs," for instance, will be changed to read, "No paak betwiin dem sain ya." These activists—who referred to Jamaican Creole as the "nation language"—spoke of it in blatant political terms, encouraging its use not only on the island of Jamaica but among blacks, Jamaican and non-Jamaican alike, in Great Britain. Jamaican Creole, argued the Jamaican "dub" poet Desmond Johnson, is a unifying force among young blacks in London who "need to feel separate from a society that rejects them . . . . Caribbean patois gives them a language that's all theirs, and, when they imitate Jamaican Creole, a special sense of identity." MacNeil's contribution to all this, predictably enough, was to show us some Caribbean immigrant youngsters playing soccer in a London neighborhood and —apropos of their lively chatter, which was full of exotic soccer-related terms—to offer the observation that Jamaican Creole is "more expressive" than Standard English. (And what, one wondered, if these kids want to grow up to talk expressively about something other than soccer?) We watched snippets of a black riot in London while listening to a reggae protest song, then—as the song continued—saw a mural of a prone black man with a white man's foot pressing down upon his head. Ah, the joys of language!

MacNeil then took us to India, where, we learned, more and more words from the various Indian languages are creeping into

Indian English. "Local energies," he said, "are driving people away from Standard English." And apparently, as far as he was concerned, this was all just hunky-dory. "Our language thrives on change," MacNeil proclaimed, and quoted Anthony Burgess to the effect that English is "gloriously impure." Which indeed it is; but neither he nor the other creators of this series seem to have understood the real meaning of Burgess's observation. Indeed, the entire series appeared to be founded upon the principle that *every* sort of linguistic impurity is unquestionably glorious, that *any* change that takes place in a language is by definition a sign of "vitality." The series made no distinction between the changes in English introduced by Shakespeare, who broadened and deepened the language's expressive range, and those introduced by street kids, say, or surfers, whose jargon renders them incapable of discussing anything more subtle or complicated or abstract than a street fight or a good wave. That there can be both good changes in language (changes that make it more precise, majestic, and profound) and bad changes (those that make it more fuzzy and simpleminded) seems never to have occurred to MacNeil and company.

The *Story of English* companion book is so attractively designed, illustrated, and produced that one wishes it were more wisely and beautifully written. To be sure, it is, in many respects, superior to the television series. Though it covers essentially the same material, with each of its nine chapters corresponding to an episode of the series, it manages most of the time to be less tedious and pointless than the program. Whereas Episode Seven, for instance, paid inordinate attention to an Australian comedian named Barry Humphries, who likes to dress up as a woman, the coverage of Humphries in the corresponding chapter of the book is mercifully limited to a single photograph of him in drag. (Ah, the British sense of humor!) Likewise, one of the weaker aspects of the series was the excessive amount of time it devoted to interviews with quaint, aged speakers of archaic dialects (an unusual number of whom, as it happened, were fishermen); the reader of the book is spared all that. Yet, like the series, the book has its flaws. It is the sort of volume in which the authors offer, as testimony to the importance of English, the fact that it is "the official language of . . . the Miss Universe competition," and, twenty-three pages later, having somehow arrived back at the same topic, remind us that English is the language of the Miss World contest as well. Errors abound. In Chapter Three alone, the geographical areas indicated on two maps of the eastern United States don't jibe with their description in the captions; the territory covered by New Spain is misidentified; the English word *chocolate* is said to be derived from a South American or Caribbean Indian language, when in actuality it comes from the Aztec language, Nahuatl; and Puerto Rico is referred to as a "neighbor" of the United States.

The book's prose (most of which is, reportedly, the work of Mr. McCrum) is often quite awkward. Chapter Three tells us, for instance, that Tangier Island in Chesapeake Bay "forms one of the most vivid parts of the fossilized English language on the eastern seaboard of the United States." From Chapter Seven: "Unlike the Germans, the less-educated Italians made a more complete adoption of American English." And from Chapter Eight: Australian society "contrasts its classlessness with Britain's."

That the book is principally the work of an Englishman is especially clear, to an American anyway, in the passages dealing with the United States. McCrum and his colleagues write that "Thomas Jefferson, with his usual prescience, had seen that when the slave states of the South and the free states of the North competed to join the Union, there would be trouble." (Certainly the word *territories* would have served better than *states.*) The authors refer to Emerson, Thoreau, and Hawthorne—in contrast with Mark Twain—as "the men of the eastern districts." And, speaking of the European immigrants of more than a half-century ago, McCrum and company write that "in the schoolroom, and especially the playground, there were fierce pressures favoring the use of the American standard. The schools were the places where the immigrant children were rapidly Americanized by their playmates, and life was made intolerable, one imagines, for the child who had to use a foreign word rather than the English." On the contrary, most European immigrant children, living as they did in Jewish or Ukrainian or Italian ghettos, went to school with other European immigrant children; if they were rapidly Americanized nonetheless, it was because they and their parents *wanted* them to become Americans, to learn English and to make meaningful and productive lives for themselves in the New World. (In those days they didn't have Robert MacNeil to tell them, in his impeccable mid-Atlantic accent, how wonderful broken English could be; they didn't have Robert McCrum around, writing about "Americanization" as if it were some transatlantic counterpart of the Third Reich's Lebensborn program.)

The *Story of English* book manages to be at least as condescending as the television series. At the end of the "Black on White" chapter, for instance, the authors quote Walt Whitman to the effect that the English language has "its basis broad and low, close to the ground," and remark that "This is a sharp reminder that the best of English comes from a wide range of sources—Black and White." Pretty slick writing, that: the authors manage to praise black Americans and patronize them at the same time. (What's more, the sentence appears above two photographs of Martin Luther King and James Baldwin. Do the writers mean to suggest that King and Baldwin are in some way "low, close to the ground"?) In much the same vein, Chapter Eight tells us that "Italian Australians behave like Italians (promenading the street and ogling the girls)," while the book's epilogue, "Next Year's Words," describes Africans as "gifted linguists." (Are they also good tap dancers?)

Like the series, too, the book tends to wander into politics—and, when it does, tends not to find its way out for a good long time. Indeed, many of the political attitudes that are implicit in the television program are expressed more blatantly in the book. For example, McCrum and his colleagues mention with obvious dismay that "African governments, anxious in every other respect to throw off the shackles of imperialism, still show a genuine enthusiasm for speaking 'proper.'" The authors maintain that whereas the visits of Presidents Nixon and Reagan to Ireland were contrived for political purposes—with Nixon's visit, in particular, displaying "the element of chicanery so often associated with him"—President Kennedy's visit, by contrast, was "a genuine (though politically astute) pilgrimage, which drew huge crowds on a scale that his successors never matched." And the book complains that "gurus of grammar" like John Simon, William Safire, and Edwin Newman grouse too much about the possible dangers of English-Spanish bilingualism in America. The creators of *The Story of English,* naturally, don't worry about the consequences of American bilingualism. They've got it all figured out. "Black Power, Hispanic Rights, Feminism, Gay Liberation, anti-Americanism: these are some of the issues of our time, and the English language will always be used by conservatives as a stick with which to beat the opposition." According to *The Story of English,* it's as simple as that: the only problem connected with bilingualism, Black English, and so forth is that there are reactionary fuddy-duddies out there who persist in talking about these things as if they *were* problems. If your next-door neighbor tendered such a misguided opinion of Safire, Simon, and Newman—a group of writers whose principal offense, apparently, is to take a responsible attitude toward their language and their society—it would be ridiculous, nothing more. But for the creators of a high-profile property like this one to propagandize for such a point of view is nothing less than outrageous. In the end, this sneer at linguistic standards tells us all that we need to know, really, about the sensibility behind *The Story of English.*

(*December* 1986)

IV. Artists & Ideas

Copland's world
by Samuel Lipman

Once again the world of American music is celebrating Aaron Copland. In part, I suppose, all the attention now being given to the recent publication of the first volume of the composer's memoirs[1] comes about because music lovers seem to have so little else to celebrate. And yet to begin on such a rueful note is to ignore a simple fact: Copland is cherished as a serious composer because his music is loved by a serious audience which wants to hear many of his pieces over and over again. There are some, doubtless intellectuals educated beyond their intelligence, who will maintain that the same can be said of Frank Sinatra and other artifacts of our public culture. We ought to allow them their opinion—on the condition that they confine their attentions to those possibly attractive amusements which they, and most assuredly not we, truly love.

For those of us who, for better or worse, are stuck with (to use a term hardly popular these days) "classical" music, Aaron Copland has written a music of force and beauty which fascinates both musicians and laymen, which is often popular in appeal but always rich in musical and emotional resonance, and, most important, which occupies a special place in our national aural psyche as the way in which Americans hear themselves. And he is now eighty-four, an age at which he surely can look back on his career in music and find it good.

The life of a composer is in his music. Nothing which one reads in a book can alter the magnitude of an artist's achievement; in this respect autobiography, biography, and music criticism are all in the same leaky boat: words wither, but the music goes on—or doesn't, as the case may be. So it is in vain that we look in *Copland: 1900 through 1942* for any real insight into his music, or, for that matter, into the music of his many colleagues, colleagues whom he befriended and publicized.

But it is, after all, not *musical* insight which Copland's book is about. These memoirs are the best account we have had of the creative milieu out of which a viable American music can—and has—come. Now, when the prospects of serious music—not just of composition but even of performance—look ever bleaker as the funding hype waxes more eloquent, the social recollections of so major a figure as Copland provide an account of when art music was in the American mainstream, when it was part of the highest civilization, rather than taking part in an avant-garde *blague* or a world of plaster performing idols cherished for their spurious geniality.

Copland's creative milieu extended to the world in which he was born. Until the present book, he had always made his origins out to be a cultural and musical desert: indeed, his words about having been born

1 *Copland: 1900 through 1942,* by Aaron Copland and Vivian Perlis; St. Martin's Press, 402 pages, $24.95.

"on a street in Brooklyn that can only be described as drab . . . [where] no one ever talked music to me or took me to a concert . . . [and] music as an art was a discovery I made all by myself" have gone into American intellectual mythology as a proof of our national boorishness. The reality was instead that music—good music by any standards—was all around Copland as he grew up. His brother and sister could give a passable violin-and-piano performance of the Mendelssohn Violin Concerto; such an effort, viewed as a family accomplishment, now seems the height of elitist stuffiness. In addition, his sister took singing lessons at the Metropolitan Opera School. By his own testimony, he had gone with his mother to hear John McCormack at the old Hippodrome and Jascha Heifetz at Carnegie Hall; later, while still in his teens, he heard Walter Damrosch and the New York Symphony in Sunday afternoon concerts, and the Boston Symphony, who in those days "came to Brooklyn on Friday nights for a series of five concerts each year."

There were excellent teachers, too, to nourish the young Copland. His favorite piano teacher was the eminent Clarence Adler, a student of the great virtuoso Leopold Godowsky (himself an American resident since the outbreak of World War I); his composition teacher until his departure for France in 1921 was Rubin Goldmark, (a student in piano of the famous pianist Rafael Joseffy and of no less than the great composer Dvořák). Though Copland himself—horror of horrors—didn't go either to music school or to college, his closest friends were Aaron Schaffer, then studying French and French literature at Johns Hopkins, and his own distant relative Harold Clurman, then a student at Columbia and on his way to the Sorbonne. Nor should the influence of Copland's intensely Jewish background—suppressed by the composer until his decision to make the fascinating material contained in the present book available—be underestimated: reverence for learning and culture, the desire to see one's children rise in the world, and the particularly close relationship between Jews and music since the nineteenth century combined to make Copland and an entire generation of Jewish children attempt, many of them successfully, to become classical musicians of the first rank.

In France during the 1920s, Copland came face to face with Old World culture. Here was not just Nadia Boulanger, the teacher of Copland as of so many successful young American composers. Here was the still living Ravel and Saint Saëns, Diaghilev and the Russian Ballet, Stravinsky and the young *Les Six,* French food and wine, Paris and the countryside. Close by, in Germany and Austria there was a quite different kind of music from the French; here Arnold Schoenberg was lighting the torch of the twelve-tone system. But important as old Europe was in Copland's musical and cultural formation, at least as important were the relationships he made there with fellow American musicians of his own generation, among them Roger Sessions and Virgil Thomson. These relationships were to become important, even before the 1920s were over, in his development as a composer of not just music, but *American* music. Strangely enough, Copland (though he found France enchanting) was not beguiled into becoming an expatriate; like Sessions, he had to return to his homeland to flower as an artist. Indeed, his epistolary thoughts about home, even allowing for what he calls "not wanting the folks . . . to think I was getting too fancy," strike an authentic note of the pull back to the states:

> Don't think I've forgotten Washington Ave. [the street in Brooklyn where Copland was born]. I shall certainly think of you all eating those enormous dinners on Roshhashona and groan at the thought of missing the marvelous cakes after the fasting is over on Yom-kippur . . . .

Back at home, there was a receptive musical environment awaiting the aspiring composer. Serge Koussevitsky, the Russian-born, French-anointed conductor of the Boston

Symphony, offered Copland (at the behest of Boulanger) performances of a still-to-be-written *Organ Symphony*. The work, with Boulanger as soloist, was performed by both Koussevitsky in Boston and the already venerable Walter Damrosch in New York. Though Copland's symphony was more successful in Boston than in New York, what counted was not box office or even critical acclaim: the times were now ready to accept a native American classical music as worthy of serious attention.

It cannot be said that these moments of discovery of American music and composers were achieved without substantial efforts from famous musicians. Indeed, Koussevitsky was at this moment the chief force making for a proper appreciation of our native music. Hard as it is for us to appreciate, with our present plague of circuit-riding conductors from here, there, and everywhere (but never resident in the cities where they conduct and prosper), Koussevitsky made the Boston Symphony his life. Copland's memoirs make clear that this dedication didn't just mean the endless polishing of this week's hackneyed chestnuts; it meant Koussevitsky giving his full attention and commitment to the new music he had chosen:

> . . . if he liked a work, he liked it wholeheartedly, and thast meant a performance by the BSO, every young composer's dream.
>
> . . . Whatever the piece, no matter how the orchestra felt about it, Koussevitsky would demand the same attention as for a recognized masterpiece. He would say to the orchestra, "The next Beethoven vill from Colorado come!" He felt responsible, as musical leader of the community, for convincing both orchestra and public of the value of the new music which he accepted for performance.
>
> Koussevitsky's programs in Boston were planned so that the major portion of rehearsal time could be devoted to a new work, and when he invited composers to rehearsals, usually Thursday mornings, the orchestra members were on special guard—they knew the Maestro would be particularly demanding. He had the kind of authority over his men that no longer exists in American orchestras. One likes to think that it was his enthusiasm for the music that caught on to the players, but if not, his hold on them was so secure that we as composers felt supported by the entire BSO as well as its conductor. It is not by chance that during the twenty-five years of Koussevitsky's leadership, from 1924 to 1949, American symphonic music came of age.

As a composer, Copland was hardly content to push only his own music. As a writer about contemporary music, he early became a frequent contributor to Minna Lederman's invaluable quarterly *Modern Music.*[2] In the pages of this magazine, which was published from 1924 to 1946, he provided a calm, dispassionate, encouraging—though not uncritical—voice embracing the current scene. He was an entrepreneur too, collaborating with the musically very different Roger Sessions (though doing most of the work himself) on the Copland-Sessions concerts in New York from 1928 to 1931. These concerts provided a showcase for new music not just for musicians and the press, but also for a new class of patrons, including among them Alma Morgenthau Wertheim, the backers of the MacDowell Colony, and the Guggenheim Foundation. It was, all in all, a time when, in the words of *The New Grove Dictionary*'s article on Copland, "advanced New Yorkers [and, one might add, most sophisticated Americans interested in art] were hoping to outdo Diaghilev's Paris."

Though Copland's path-breaking *Piano Variations* of 1930 had propelled him to a kind of leadership of younger American composers, one vital element was still lacking to make his adjustment to his native environment complete. Interesting and important as the *Piano Variations* were, they were also hard, acerbic, and laconic; they spoke out of the compositional world of Arnold

---

2 A fascinating history of this brave venture, written by Minna Lederman, has just been published by the Institute for Studies in American Music at Brooklyn College under the title *The Life and Death of a Small Magazine*.

Schoenberg to a limited audience of cognoscenti. What was needed to fulfill Copland's career instincts were the large numbers of listeners which for a musician in a democratic society are the surest sign of success. Copland found the large audience he was seeking in a return to folk music less intellectually sublimated than the jazz he had mined in his early work. Now, in *El Salón México* (1936), he used folk tunes in the style of a Mexico City dance hall he had visited. Soon he returned to local American material itself, writing *Billy the Kid* (1938), *Rodeo* (1942), and *Appalachian Spring* (1944), all three ballets for the new serious American dance associated with Lincoln Kirstein and Agnes De Mille. In these enduring works he used such Americana as "Come wrangle yer bronco" and "'Tis the gift to be simple." He wrote movie music too, beginning with the scores for *Of Mice and Men* (1939) and *Our Town* (1940). And he even wrote, difficult as it is for us to understand in these days of ardently cultivated artistic alienation, *patriotic* music: the audiences, lasting until the present day, for the *Lincoln Portrait* and the *Fanfare for the Common Man* (both from 1942) are numerous and enthusiastic.

What can explain Copland's breakout, starting in the mid-1930s, from coterie composer to an American musical hero? Doubtless his ability to find a popular audience was always a part of his artistic talent. But for an artist, talent, though necessary, is never sufficient: the times must be right. The 1930s, economically a time of depression, of hunger and suffering, were nonetheless the seedtime of midcentury American power and prosperity. Recovery at home and participation in the world order made up our ambitious national agenda. It was a time of expansion in America's idea of how it saw itself, of a public vision of the nation as great *in* the world, not *apart* from it.

Nowhere was this development more marked than in art. The founding of museums—not least of them the Museum of Modern Art in 1929—and symphony orchestras all across the country was a symptom not just of a new awareness but of a new audience. Already at the beginning of the Depression, the American Communist Party had been quick to hold before artists' hungry mouths the appealing vision of a utopian society in which "workers by brain" would be more equal than anyone else. Copland soon became caught up in the endless round of consciousness-raising activities. Though never as involved in the movement as his friends composer Marc Blitzstein and playwright Clifford Odets, Copland became a "sympathetic" (the term used in the present memoirs by Copland's collaborator, Vivian Perlis) attendee at the Composers Collective, a group formed under the auspices of the Party-controlled Pierre Degeyter Club, a branch of the Workers Music League, which itself was under the discipline of "the Communist-backed International Music Bureau." Here the aims were, according to Blitzstein (the group's secretary), the writing of music ranging from mass songs "dealing with immediate social issues" to instrumental works carrying on "the best musical traditions of the past, now threatened by the collapse of bourgeois culture." Copland even had one of his songs published in material prepared by the Collective, along with songs by such undoubted Party types as Charles Seeger, Elie Siegmeister, Earl Robinson, and Hanns Eisler. And he reviewed some of this material, collected under the title *Workers Song Book No. 1,* in the Communist Party organ the *New Masses,*[3] calling it "the first adequate collection of revolutionary songs for American workers."

As the 1930s wore on, the Communist Party, responding to the new policies of its Soviet masters, was quick to introduce the Trojan Horse of the Popular Front as a means of harnessing the new homegrown

3 Interestingly, though Copland's writing for the *New Masses* is mentioned by Perlis in the body of the present book, the publication's name is omitted from the work's index.

creativity. Now an artist such as Copland was freed of any possible imperative that he submit to the dogmatic requirements of Party ideology; all that counted was that someone sympathetic to the Party might find a mass market for his artistic wares. Now the publicity apparatus of the Left was put at the service of Americanism, and except for the short period of the Hitler-Stalin rapprochement between 1939 and 1941, American artists were all together in the fight against the Nazis. Whatever the motives of the different players in the game, the atmosphere of patriotic consensus was good for the creation of a salable musical art, and Copland was the chief beneficiary of the era of good feeling. He delivered, and in delivering created, much of the music for which he today is justly being celebrated.

Perhaps the most interesting pages of the whole book of memoirs are those devoted to Copland's experiences after 1939, when he shared with Paul Hindemith the responsibilities of teaching composition at the newly established Berkshire Music Center of the Boston Symphony. Here was the unlikely conjunction of the very Jewish and very American Copland, himself at least partially a product of French influence, and the very, very German Paul Hindemith, perhaps the closest approximation to the immortal Johann Sebastian Bach we are likely to have in this century. The encounter was hardly without its frictions, but under the gentle guidance of the polyglot Koussevitsky it worked, and the student rosters of Copland and Hindemith read today like a who's who of American music.

World War II was not a wonderful time for writing serious music. Composers were either unavailable for composition at all or at best were tempted into the easy accents of unbuttoned patriotism. When peace came, it brought with it in music a desire to emulate European trends. American composers, instead of returning home and continuing their development of an American music, became outriders on the train first of European serialism and then of technological experimentation. Brought home and enshrined in the American academy, the result was a new music at once arid and footless, and eminently forgettable.

So massive was the failure of our native music in this period that the negative attitude toward it on the part of both performances and a sophisticated audience managed to extend itself to the earlier, and vastly more hopeful, production of the 1930s. Now that music too—except for the few spectacular pieces of Copland—seems under a kind of ban, with major works of such remarkable composers as Sessions, Walter Piston, and Roy Harris unheard in the concert hall and even largely unrecorded. Until recently it had seemed that this situation was irreversible, and that an American classical music, for all of Copland's heroic efforts, might once again have to start *ab ovo.*

But now, relatively suddenly, we seem to find ourselves in a new America, not just politically and socially, but culturally and perhaps even musically as well. There are plans afoot to record all the symphonies of Walter Piston and William Schuman in integral versions, played by American orchestras. The New York City Opera is talking of reviving distinguished American operas which managed to get written in the 1950s despite the surrounding academic desert. And serious composers like Ned Rorem and Hugo Weisgall, who managed to preserve their musical integrity and consistency despite the pressure around them to be bores and buffoons, are still writing valuable music; that music is being heard not just with respect but with something which appears very much like affection. Mention must be made too of the extraordinary new career of the veteran composer George Perle, who will be celebrating his seventieth birthday this spring. Renowned as the greatest living Alban Berg scholar, he had always been a composer; now his recent works, for example the beautifully crafted and immediately appealing *Serenade III,* as performed by pianist Richard Goode and conductor Gerard Schwarz in New York last spring, are suggesting that we may well have a new old master in our midst.

And so Aaron Copland's most recent memoirs may well have come along at just the right time. They speak to us of a world full of fresh creativity, of interesting people doing interesting things, of the living connection of new music to significant movements in culture and society. Invaluable as it is for us to learn about our neglected past in order to build a viable future, we still must remember that the past is there only as a teacher, not as a model to be slavishly imitated. What we can now learn from the life of Aaron Copland is that it once was possible to write music; with good will and hard work it doubtless is now possible to do so again.

(*January* 1985)

At the Picasso Museum

by Hilton Kramer

It was to be expected that the opening of the Musée Picasso in Paris would be a capital event, and so it has turned out to be. No secret had been made of the number and quality of the works of art which had come to the museum from the artist's estate. A blizzard of publicity had inevitably attended the deals that were made between Picasso's heirs and the French government in the aftermath of his death in 1973 at the age of ninety-one. Some of the more outstanding works which came to the museum as a result of those tax-settlement deals had already been exhibited in the historic Picasso exhibitions shown in Minneapolis and New York in 1980, and were much remarked on at that time. There was no question, then, that the museum would be an important repository of the master's work. Exactly what the full scope of the collection would be, however, remained something of a mystery. Picasso had long been known to be a hoarder of his own work, and in virtually every period of his long career he had, of course, been one of the most copious producers in the entire history of art. It was also known that as he grew older and commanded great wealth, Picasso had gone to some trouble to buy back, either through purchase or exchange, examples of his earlier work which remained in private hands and which he deemed especially important. The well-known masterworks permanently reposing in the collections of the Museum of Modern Art in New York, the Hermitage in Leningrad, and sundry other museums the world over were clearly beyond his reach, and it is doubtful, in any case, that he would have felt the need to alter their status even if it had been within his power to do so. They had, after all, been instrumental in spreading his fame and influence far and wide, and in certain cases—that of the Museum of Modern Art, for example—Picasso himself had at times played a role in shaping these important collections of his work. Yet in Paris, oddly enough, there was no comparable Picasso collection on permanent public view—a reflection of the fact that in the most crucial stages of the development of his work, the principal collectors of his art had tended to be foreigners. Thus, without the establishment of the Musée Picasso by agencies of the French government, there would have been no such public collection of his work in the city whose artistic life Picasso had dominated in the heyday of the School of Paris.

Now that the museum has opened and we have had our first look at its contents, there can be little question about its importance. The Musée Picasso contains the single most comprehensive collection of the artist's work to be found anywhere, and there is no possibility that it will ever be superseded in this respect. Even with *Les Demoiselles d'Avignon* in New York and *Guernica* in Madrid and other pivotal masterworks scattered throughout the great art museums of the world, the Musée Picasso is now the place where Picasso will have to be seen and studied if his work is to be fully comprehended. No other collection in the world gives us such a sustained and intimate account of his immense oeuvre. None affords us such unremitting access to the innermost recesses of his artistic thought. Only in certain loan exhibitions assembled from a wide range of public and private collections have we ever been offered anything like this detailed examination of the ways in which the artist worked when, upon taking possession of a new idea or a new experience—for Picasso, there was rarely any clear demarcation between the two—he developed it with an almost demonic speed and confidence until it had ceased to yield him a fresh inspiration.

In this regard, the only event in recent memory that invites comparison with the new museum is the mammoth Picasso retrospective organized by William Rubin at the Museum of Modern Art in New York in 1980. Yet as wonderful as that exhibition was in so many ways—it, too, will never be superseded in scale or quality—it was not only a temporary exhibition that can never be repeated but it was very much the work of a great scholar and connoisseur who inevitably imposed on the subject his own view of it. That it was, in my opinion, a very sound view and resulted in the greatest Picasso exhibition to be seen in our time does not alter the fact that it represented a curatorial gloss on the subject. It is not in the nature of things for such an exhibition, no matter how encompassing or informed, to represent with any exactitude the artist's view of his own oeuvre. That, we may be sure, is more likely to be shaped by a pattern of memories and associations, by strong feelings and unappeased obsessions and special affections, by prejudices both personal and artistic, than by the kind of "objective" criteria deemed appropriate to scholarly connoisseurship. At the Musée Picasso we are, so to speak, back in Picasso's court where it is the artist himself who largely determines what we see. This is so unusual in our experience of a great artist's work that the mind naturally goes in search of something comparable. But what is there? The Munchs in Oslo suggest themselves, but the period of real achievement in Munch's case is too circumscribed to constitute a persuasive comparison. Perhaps the Turner bequest in London might offer something similar if we ever get to see it in its entirety. For the most part, however, there is nothing comparable. In this matter, as in so many others, Picasso made certain that he would have no rivals. In the end he avenged himself on the collectors of his work, whom he needed and resented and manipulated all through his long career, by emerging triumphant as the single greatest collector of his own art.

What, then, does the museum collection actually consist of? The excellent inaugural catalogue[1]—the first volume in what will constitute a series—lists two hundred and three paintings, sixteen collages, twenty-nine reliefs, one hundred and sixty-two sculptures, and eighty-seven ceramics. It also lists over one hundred items from Picasso's private collection of other artists' works (Courbet, Renoir, Degas, Derain, Matisse, Miró, Balthus, et al., in addition to a great many primitive objects). Except for certain items in this collection of other artists' works, which will presumably be shown in the future, virtually everything in the catalogue—more than six hundred objects—is permanently on view. Then, too, there are the works on paper, which are said to number more than three thousand. These will no doubt be published in full in future volumes of the catalogue. Only a small portion of this material is now on view, however. Dominique Bozo, the founding director of the museum who has lately assumed the direc-

1 *Musée Picasso: Catalogue sommaire des collections.* Volume I. Introduction by Dominique Bozo. Catalogue by Marie-Laure Besnard-Bernadac, Michèle Richet, and Hélène Seckel. Biographical chronology by Laurence Marceillac. Published by the Ministère de la Culture, Éditions de la Réunion des musées nationaux. 316 pages. Paperback, 200 French francs.

torship of the Pompidou Center as well, proudly claims the drawing collection to be without parallel, and one can well believe it. For in addition to including a number of dazzling examples which are exhibited in appropriate contexts throughout this initial installation, the museum has also mounted as a special inaugural event a temporary exhibition focusing entirely on Cubist drawings. I doubt if there has ever before been an exhibition of Picasso's Cubist drawings to match this one. It not only shows the artist himself at the height of his powers, but constitutes in itself one of the supreme moments in the history of art in this century.

There is also, of course, a fair amount of documentation—photographs, manuscripts, letters, notebooks, exhibition catalogues and announcements, newspaper clippings, review articles, and other memorabilia—on view in the museum. This material is very intelligently selected, and the tact and discretion with which it is displayed cannot be too highly praised. Mr. Bozo obviously faced a difficult problem in relation to this documentary material. Picasso was the most highly publicized artist in modern times—perhaps the most highly publicized of all time. He was also the most autobiographical of artists. Certain aspects of his celebrity, moreover—especially those related to the women in his life—are not easily separated, if indeed they can be separated at all, from his purely artistic pursuits. The temptation to exploit this situation, to play to the crowd that knows (or thinks it knows) something about the artist's life but little or nothing about the true magnitude of his art, must surely have been great, and there is anything but a shortage of material available to abet this interest in gossip and scandal. I am happy to report that this temptation has been firmly resisted. So has the ghastly practice of imposing an excess of reading matter on our perusal of art objects. The documentary material is isolated in display cases at appropriate intervals in an installation arranged by periods determined by the subject's artistic development. The documents are readily accessible to those who want to study them, but they are at every point clearly distinguished from the art itself. And it is upon the art, first and last, that Mr. Bozo has focused our attention.

A similar sense of tact and taste has governed the handling of the museum building. It was a happy inspiration for the French government to acquire the Hôtel Salé, an elegant seventeenth-century house in the Third Arrondissement, for this museum. (The address is 5, rue de Thorigny, an easy walk from the Pompidou Center.) One can well imagine Picasso setting up his studio in a house of this sort, and the large airy rooms prove to be entirely sympathetic to the art which is now housed in them. Fortunately, no attempt has been made to provide a "period" setting—either of Picasso's time or that of the Hôtel Salé. And the one aesthetic addition to the premises—the chairs, benches, and chandeliers which Mr. Bozo commissioned from the late Diego Giacometti, who completed the work shortly before his death last year—has likewise proved to be an appropriate and delightful adornment. All in all, I think museum directors the world over—and not least, alas, in the United States—have much to learn from the way Mr. Bozo has carried this challenging project to a brilliant conclusion.

It helps, of course, to start out with a great collection, and this the Musée Picasso has in abundance. It is particularly rich in works from the early Cubist period—not only because of the drawings already mentioned, but also in the great number and variety of collages and relief-constructions, many of which (it is my impression, anyway) have not been exhibited before. In certain of these small painted constructions we rediscover the origins of all of modernist sculpture, and they also have the interest of showing the artist in one of his most inward and thoughtful, most apollonian periods. Never again, I think, does Picasso's art attain anything like the sense of harmony and disinterestedness which characterizes the work of the classical Cubist years. In the so-called Neo-Classic period, which is also strongly represented in the collection, he turns outward, to be sure, and produces much that is poignant and grave and beautiful, yet throughout this phase of his development one finds oneself waiting, a little nervously, for that detonation of rage and violence which, when at last they make themselves felt in all their shattering force, are scarcely ever again absent from his work right to the end of his life.

Our first glimpse of this impulse to untrammeled fury comes, indeed, in the midst of the calm usually associated with the Neo-Classic period, in the painting called *Les Amoureux* (1919). It is given a particularly intense and powerful statement in *Le Baiser* (1925), and remains an obsession in the pictures of his last years. It is this impulse to fury that dominates the paintings of the Thirties when for the first time a political element is mingled with and played off against the erotic, which nonetheless remains the artist's dominant obsession. Abetted by his interest in Surrealism, which aspired to precisely this identification of the political with the erotic, and much aggravated by political developments, especially in Spain, Picasso from the Thirties onward becomes, in a sense, another kind of artist—unappeasably *enragé* not only in relation to what was happening in Europe and the world but in relation to his own fate as a man. In tracing this downward course—downward, certainly, if we think of the Cubist years as marking the peak of his achievement—to an ever more dour and agonized old age, the collections of the Musée Picasso afford us an experience like no other I know. One does not, from the paintings of the Forties onward, always admire the works that one sees in this collection. (I remain, I am afraid, unashamedly unconverted to the paintings of the "late" Picasso, which have lately achieved an almost universal chic.) And there is no avoiding the grave issues of character and personality which are forced upon our attention by the artist's personal and political actions—the broken lives he left in his wake at every turn, for one thing, and his support of the Communist Party during one of the worst periods of Stalin's tyranny, for another. Yet, no matter what questions are raised or how repelled one may be by one or another aspect of the artist and the man, one leaves this museum in no doubt whatever that one has been witness to one of the central achievements of the age. One leaves, indeed, rather shaken, and not least by the thought that we are unlikely to see our civilization produce an artist of this magnitude very soon again.

Finally, I think we are lucky in having this museum available to us at this particular moment. In the years immediately ahead we are going to be treated to a great deal in the way of biographical revelation about Picasso, and my guess is that we are going to be in need of a strong stomach to get through it all. Before that deluge comes, therefore, it is well to be reminded of what the true glory of Picasso's art consists of, and to an appreciation of that glory the Musée Picasso makes an incomparable contribution.

(*January* 1986)

Killing moonlight: the Futurists in Venice

by W. S. Di Piero

One of the most unsettling images in the enormous exhibition of Futurist art now showing in Venice is Giacomo Balla's *The Mad Woman* (1905). The woman stands full length, framed by a doorway, her hair mussed and gnarled. The yellow springtime light shatters on the broad field behind her. Her body is a coil of wrecked nerves, her long form one pulled or stretched contortion, from her flyaway curls to the tensed flex of her foot. She waves a finger in front of her face at the world outside her disordered mind, in a gesture of negation or chastisement, as if to scold or correct us, while her other arm hangs stiffly at her side, hand cocked at an odd angle. In its present setting—in a show called "Futurism and Futurisms," which contains hundreds of paintings, drawings, sculptures, photographs, books, documents, and assorted paraphernalia from the Futurist movements in several countries[1]—Balla's picture has two quite different effects. Placed in the rooms designated "Towards Futurism," it helps to establish the formal matrix out of which the language of Futurist art was to evolve: the detonated coloring of Impressionism, the phosphorescences of Pointillism, and the tension between documentary fidelity to subject and the irresolutely colored images characteristic of the *macchiaioli* in the second half of the nineteenth century. But the young woman's look of bewildered chastisement also seems directed at the other pieces in the show, as if she were registering real dismay at the carefully scripted derangements soon to be staged by F. T. Marinetti and the Futurists as they assaulted the complacent rationalisms of the past.

Balla was, after Umberto Boccioni, the most gifted among Italian Futurist artists. Like other painters early in the century, he wanted to record on canvas the new industrial expansion that was carving out large pieces of the Old World's landscape and changing the sense of time experienced by workers. The two panels of Balla's *A Worker's Day* (1904) show laborers first on a building site then later returning home on a lamplit street at dusk. Each scene includes a house under construction, where the sign of the new age is the gridwork of woodrail scaffolding climbing high up the sides of buildings. By 1912, however, once committed to a Futurist program, as if by sheer willful self-conversion Balla ceased creating such moody realistic canvases and began to make a different sort of art. About halfway through the current show, one enters a room which I think of as "Balla's Speed Shop." On the walls are the famous series of paintings whose titles are miniature manifestos: *Speeding Car, Abstract Speed, Dynamic Expansion and Speed.* The dominant forms are repeti-

---

1 "Futurismo & Futurismi" is on view at the Palazzo Grassi in Venice until October 12, 1986. The catalogue for the exhibition was published by Bompiani, Milan (638 pages). It includes essays by Pontus Hulten, the organizer of the exhibition.

tive quarter moons, scythes, swallowtails, nautilus whorls—all abstract figures sliced across by triangulated planes with other echoing forms revolving and coiling inside. The pictures are from 1913, when Balla was seeking to accommodate the form of motion that was proliferating with spectacular quickness in Western industrial societies—the wheel, in all its manifestations: cars, trucks, trains; pulleys, casters, bearings; the figure traced by aeroplane propellers and locomotive cranks. Balla was the purest anatomist of velocity among the Futurists, analytical, precise, and objective. Some of his early work prepared him for this. The closed doors in his picture *Bankruptcy* (1902) are defaced with scribbled spirals and curves, prefiguring the general Futurist position that the past as a fund of wisdom and static forms was bankrupt, that the artist's only workshop and subject would be the present rocketing into the future. By the late Thirties, however, after a long association with Futurism (he signed two important early manifestos in 1910), Balla came out the other end, declaring that "pure art is to be found in absolute realism, without which one falls into decorative ornamental forms." The curse of the merely decorative was one that Futurism, as this show perhaps unintentionally demonstrates, could never escape.

If *The Mad Woman* was placed for its editorial effect, that would be in keeping with the self-conscious assertiveness of the entire exhibition, which fills the spacious three stories of the eighteenth-century Palazzo Grassi. The "Towards Futurism" section on the ground floor displays items by Edvard Munch, Picasso, Seurat, the Lumière brothers, Georges Méliès, and others who may have anticipated the various strains in Futurist art. The visitor has to infer this, however, and construct his own historical argument, since the catalogue limits its commentary to a brief introduction and a "Dictionary of Futurism." Above the dazzling marble foyer hang a monoplane and single-engine fighter, like profane versions of the Holy Spirit blessing the show and lending it the power of secular evangelism. Off the main foyer are two of the choicest objects in the show, an early model Fiat touring car with luxuriantly funereal black leather seats, and a Bugatti one-seater that looks more like a tin country mousetrap than a newfangled speed machine. Like Futurism, the exhibition is so full of its own energetic theatricality that it cannot quite control its range of reference, which becomes haphazard, and its ironic suggestiveness, which becomes confused and opaque. It is carefully programmed to allow for a generosity of reference and accommodation, to document what the curators obviously believe to be the omnipresent durable effects of Futurism. But like the movement itself, the show's infatuation with its own enthusiasm resolves into a very particular sort of modernist tedium.

The entire second floor is given over to Italian Futurism. While artists like Otto Dix, Mikhail Larionov, Duchamp, Gaudier-Brzeska, and Jacob Epstein might all be tagged as Futurists at some point in their careers, the most influential documents and "events" were produced by Marinetti, and no artist mentioned above can be treated so exclusively in Futurist terms as Boccioni, Carrà, Balla, and Severini. Venice is the ideally ironic setting for the show. In their manifesto "Against Passéist Venice" (1910), the Futurists called Venice the "great sewer of traditionalism," which ought to be purged of all its rotting leftover antiquities and turned into a military, industrial power. They wanted to burn the gondolas ("rocking chairs for idiots") and wrench Venice into a new age: "Let the reign of the divine Electric Light come at last, to free Venice from her venal hotel-room moonlight." The town was already a museum in Marinetti's time, the kind of historical "jewel" loathed by the Futurists because it represented the crippling presence of the past, old achievements enshrined (like Roman Catholicism) to oppress the contemporary imagination. The mastering idea behind Marinetti's pronouncements was that *passatismo* must be attacked and routed wherever it appeared, that the new century was so utterly new that art could no longer look presumptuously toward memory as a restorative, innovative power, that artists had to violently revolutionize their methods, choose new subjects, forge a new form-language, if they were to redeem themselves from the wasteful obedience to, and worship of, past forms. All the old poeticisms naturally came under attack. The most abrasive and rudely endearing Futurist manifesto is entitled "Let's Kill Moonlight." In place of the old cautious deliberations, the infinite refinements of sentiment, the laboriously arrived at nuances of representational realism, would come heroic speed, *dinamismo,* and quickened bright metallic facts. The failure of at least part of the Futurist program is bitterly apparent. Venice may be, for many, the island of eternally serene moonlight, but she is, first and always, Queen of Irony, cunning, indifferent, secretive, and greedy. She knows that her gondolas, most of them, are rocking chairs for idiots, but unlike the Futurists she does not care. More a museum than ever before and therefore more protective of her secret life, Venice has now coopted her most virulent critics and is charging admission to view them.

A new form of attention was, at any rate, necessary. The mechanical means of producing images of reality (and of reproducing copies of images of reality) induced a new self-consciousness of the moment's composition in time. In his "Animal Locomotion" series of 1887, excerpts of which are in the "Towards Futurism" section, Eadweard Muybridge used the photographic image to analyze motion by recording its serial instants. One of the images on display is of a nude woman descending steps. When, much later, the coppery turbine vanes of Duchamp's *Nude Descending a Staircase, no. 2* (1912) enact one Futurist obsession—that of registering the planes through which movement passes—the historical arc is neatly closed. Artists therefore needed to review and revise their awareness of the process of motion and of civilization's new life-altering products. Marinetti—poet, prosewriter, and man of independent means—was the most tireless and best-organized advocate of accommodation. In order to reach the largest audience as quickly as possible, he spread the call by publishing his manifestos in newspapers. He was a resourceful promoter whose tone was unapologetically explosive, peevish, insulting, and belligerently ecstatic. His position as the most conspicuous representative of Italian Futurism was adversarial, subversive, and intolerantly democratic. The events of the Twenties and Thirties, however, were such that what began as an earnest, and in many respects necessary, program for global, pan-cultural change became nearly indistinguishable from totalitarian ideology. The rigor of the Futurists' denunciations and their energetic, petulant enthusiasm for the new, gave much of their work a strange double valence, at once blissfully liberating and punishingly authoritarian.

The double valence is shockingly apparent in the first image one confronts at the top of the staircase. Boccioni's *Unique Form of Continuity in Space* (1913) is probably the best known Futurist icon. We recognize at once the formal principles that he explored so brilliantly in his Futurist years, from 1910 to his early death in 1916. The tall striding figure, with its monumental streaking-bronze effect in space, realizes Boccioni's desire to obtain what he called a "simultaneity" of duration and stasis, "a synthesis between what is remembered and what is seen." From his teacher Balla he had learned the new stress on dynamism, but against the more schematic representation of velocity in Balla's work Boccioni wanted time's quick stream seen and felt in the rhythm of its flowing. The statue is a stunning articulation of matter in motion. Installed in its niche, however, surrounded by tall black enamel panels, that human image with its abstract title is also the most powerful martial icon of the century. Up from the bronze platform, out of the thick bronze pedestals, toils a monstrously sinewy, invulnerable man-machine, a pure urgency of will untrammeled by meditative delay. Small wings, reminiscent of Balla's swallow forms, flare from the heels and calves like instruments of flight, but also like spurs, or scythes—the entire lower body looks like an unstoppable harvesting machine. The torso, all curvilinear flanks and planes, is expressive at once of the continuities of the human form moving through space and of that form armored in thick bronze folds that overlap like wings. In "Man Multiplied and the Reign of Machinery," Marinetti announced: "We believe in the possibility of an incalculable number of human transformations, and we declare without a smile that wings slumber within the flesh of man. When man is able to externalize his will so that it extends beyond him like an enormous arm, dream and desire, which today are vain words, will reign supreme in vanquished space and time." The Futurists believed that units of force composed the essence of objects, and that these could be externalized in "force lines," the tensed vectors and radiating blades and gills so evident in their images. The force lines in Boccioni's statue describe, and celebrate, the exercise of Marinetti's transformational will.

Boccioni, however, is too complex an artist to be treated as a mere exemplar or implementer of Futurist ideas. This much is obvious from the selection of his pre-Futurist work in another show, "Boccioni in Venice," at the Chiesa di San Stae. The early portraits are particularly interesting because they dramatize a tense truce between the flesh of the subject and the thing-world surrounding it. The cross-hatched inner structure they both share, especially evident in the pastels, is always faintly visible as the common ground of reality. The flesh has to resist the necessity of surrounding matter. In a portrait of his mother from 1906, in grays and half-whites, the subject's inertia is flustered by the flyaway strands of gray hair that pick up the oscillating rhythms of the background. Although the sitter is heavily *there,* dynamism is yet tightly coiled within her form. Even this early in his career, Boccioni is painting a study in movement, but the dynamism waits to be set free as an independent force from the figurative conventions of portraiture. In another *la madre,* from 1907, the action of the thing-world is more fused to the figure; both are heavily scored by that under-form, that hatchwork (which in Boccioni's early house-under-construction scenes becomes fully externalized in the scaffoldings). The background in the 1907 portrait is now more tightly knit—the colors are becalmed blacks, grays, and smokey whites—to the life of the flesh. Again, wisps of hair float behind the mother's head. In *The Sick Mother* of 1908 the subject reclines on snowy linen streaked with green highlights, as if the quickened vegetable world were ceding to the candor of mortality. Only the smudged gray and powdery orange tints of the mother's face preserve her from being taken over by the geological scorings of the background. These early canvases are important, I think, because even while working within the conventions of portraiture, with all its tremendous stillness, Boccioni is developing a vision of the action of matter which will lead him quite naturally toward the extreme kineticism of Futurism.

Boccioni held certain Futurist convictions as early as 1907, three years before he met Marinetti, when he wrote in a letter that Italians were living "*in un sogno storico*"—that is, in a reverie of history that induced torpor and useless nostalgia. With his turn away from meditative portraiture, away from the endless and enervating inflections of historical reflectiveness, came an apposite change in his work. Around 1910, the year of his first one-man show at Ca' Pesaro in Venice (introduced by Marinetti), Boccioni began to change the essential style of his drawing. He declared in 1910 that *The City Rises,* a large canvas completed that year, was "*un lavoro di trasizione e credo degli ultimi.*" It was indeed among the last, for in its surging tidal forms of men and beasts heaving a city into existence, the force holding the elements together is centripetal. When he became a Futurist, he said that "the figure has to become the center from which plastic directions depart into space." The new force is centrifugal: the stress lines of matter radiate from the figure, they do not converge upon it. In 1912, he painted two more portraits of his mother, though now she is called *Horizontal Construction* and *Materia*. The finely tissued webwork of the early portraits has been transformed into steely, sheeted, intersecting facets and angles. Boccioni's subject is no longer the flesh struggling in an object-world, but rather the action of an energy in the life of forms.

Much of what he and other Futurist painters had to say about their practice focused on draughtsmanship. In *The Salon of 1846* Baudelaire wrote that "pure draughtsmen [as opposed to colorists] are naturalists, endowed with one excellent sense; but their drawing is a rationalist enterprise, whereas that of the colorists is a matter of feeling, an almost unconscious process." Boccioni was, in Baudelaire's terms, a pure draughtsman. And the great strength of Futurist art, from the antic angular caricatures of Depero to the moody social documentary of Carlo Carrà, is largely in its draughtsmanship. A colorist depends too much on precisely the sort of irrational feeling and instinct for movement that artists with a program need to avoid, for fear of sabotaging the program. Moreover, the traditions of the great colorists—the *macchiaioli* were the most recent in Italy, though their influence on the Futurists goes entirely unremarked in the catalogue—run counter to the anti-sentimental purpose of the Futurists. At its most debased, coloring for the Futurists was merely a sort of sensational violence exercised upon inventive draughtsmanship.

The Futurist program went beyond art. It meant to change people's hearts and minds. "Anarchists are satisfied to assault the political, judicial, and economic branches of the social tree," Marinetti declared, "whereas we want much more . . . . We want to tear up and burn that tree's deepest roots." Those roots were nourished by "cowardly quietism, love of the old and ancient, of what's sick and corrupt, the horror of the new, contempt for youth, the veneration of time, of the accumulated years, of the dead and the dying." Marinetti singles out his targets, but each one represents a general condition; taken all together they are so manifold that the Futurist attack must be waged on a broad global front. Consequently, most of the manifesto literature produced by the movement has both a particularized aphoristic force (the force of tables of law) *and* the intimidating hysteria of wild machine-gun bursts. The exhibition catalogue, in keeping with the Futurist spirit, suffers from the same overparticularized but blurred purpose. Its encyclopedic format offers a blizzard of facts, while obscuring long clear views. Since it is crucial to the show's public success that Futurism be shown to be the most influential and relevant "ism" of the early century, all sorts of names are enlisted under its banner. Nietzsche, Sorel, Munch, Apollinaire, John Marin, Ungaretti, Charles Demuth, Dino Campana—all become, in the catalogue's retelling, near or distant figures in the Futurist story. What neither the show nor the catalogue offers is lucid historical analysis (and because of the hundreds of documents on display, the exhibition had a real opportunity to do so) or a coherent argument. The curators offer instead more of what the Futurists themselves provided in abundance—self-glorifying publicity.

The most prickly issue, and the one most thoroughly botched in the catalogue, is the relationship between Futurism and fascism. An essay by Antonello Trombadori in a recent special number of *Nuovi Argomenti* argues that when Marinetti and the members of the Futurist Political Party broke from fascism in 1920, after their initial participation in the *Fasci di combattimento,* it was not because they felt that fascism had turned too sharply to the Right, but because they themselves held to an "ultrafascism." Official fascism did not go far enough. The Futurist position was even more nationalistic, anti-monarchical, and anti-clerical than the fascist line. In Trombadori's analysis, the Futurists were, at that time, more single-mindedly intolerant of any divergence from their program to level the past and dissolve the fogs of "historical consciousness." Trombadori's argument is directed against those apologists who present the Futurists as leftist dissenters and early opponents of the regime. In 1923, at any rate, Marinetti publicly realigned himself with fascism; in 1929 he was elected to the Academy of Italy, and as late as 1935 was a vocal advocate of a fascist future.

The catalogue entry on "Ideology" by Renzo De Felice refuses to draw any equation between Futurism and fascism. To accomplish this, he has to insist that Futurism had no ideology, only "artistic attitudes" and strategies: "On the whole Futurism had no ideology, nor did it want one. If to some extent it is possible to construct an ideology after the fact, this assumes contradictory, changing forms which vary according to the groups composing the movement, so it cannot be forced into the narrow limits of an abstract lowest common denominator." To explain Marinetti's announcements in the 1909 manifesto, "We will glorify war—the world's only hygiene—militarism, patriotism, the destructive gesture of freedom-bringers, beautiful ideas worth dying for, and contempt for women," De Felice concocts the proposition that "war" be taken metaphorically, "as fullness of life and even as rejoicing, essentially as an individual and artistic fact, which became collective for the Italians in 1911 and more particularly in 1915-18 because it took on the value of a 'revelation' of the 'true Italian powers,' that is, of the triumph of 'futurism' over '*passatismo.*'" Those quotation marks are little nooses choking off the oxygen that might clarify De Felice's ideas. The hygienic purpose of war, as he reconstructs it, is to restore life—festively—individually and socially. But not "real" war. Marinetti could not possibly have meant real war, since that is a tragic business, and Marinetti did not believe in tragedy. (He looted Nietzsche's vocabulary of will and power but dismissed Nietzsche as a retrograde classicist who believed in tragedy.) What De Felice refuses to acknowledge is the strain of giddy nihilism in Futurist thinking.

The torturous ambivalence of De Felice's explanation imitates what I think was Marinetti's own fiery confusion. He wanted two things at once: the artist as holy noisemaker, announcing and creating the future, answerable only to his responsibilities as a Futurist, not obliged by norms that apply to established social and political orders; but also the artist as inciter, as provocateur promulgating the new program to the masses, shaping their lives with his vision and his products (the Futurists made clothing and furniture, designed advertising campaigns for Campari, wrote a cookbook, etc.). The artist would therefore have actual power over the life of the crowd, but because of his holy noisemaker status he was also morally autonomous. The artist was thus a pure performer, intent on changing the lives of his audience but feeling no sense of consequence for that power. Many of Marinetti's pronouncements are performances in that sense: his ideas are italicized by their manner of presentation, and their exhilarating inconsistencies become grotesque but unignorable. In the first famous manifesto published in *Le Figaro* on February 20, 1909, he announced: "Except in struggle, there is no more beauty. No work without an aggressive character can be a masterpiece. Poetry must be conceived as a violent attack on the unknown forces, to induce them to prostrate themselves before man." That beauty results from strife is, though Marinetti pretends not to know it, a Romantic article of faith. That poetry is above all an "attack," offensive and assaultive, rather than a receiving or contemplative activity, is a more stringent (and attention-getting) assertion. To believe that poetry is essentially imperialistic, conquistadorial, and that its purpose is to subdue and subjugate those coyly unidentified "unknown forces," is to model the purpose of poetry so closely on the forms of political power that it may more readily and "innocently" become an instrument of state power, of state "knowledge," of ideology. The tone here and in other Futurist documents (even in Valentine de Saint-Point's *Manifesto of the Futurist Woman,* written in 1912 to oppose what Germano Celant calls Marinetti's "masculine hysteria") is unremittingly aggressive and proclamatory. Even if we allow for Marinetti's occasionally sly, bad-boy humor, the martial tone dominates: "Art, in fact, can be nothing but violence, cruelty, and injustice." The anti-sentimental impulse in Futurism became obsessional avoidance, and its emotional range was narrowed accordingly. The sort of world the Futurists called for was an emotionally impoverished and over-legislated one. They were not, all things considered, masters of the finer tones, not even Boccioni. As ideology and practice, Futurism was in too violent a hurry to bother with nuance and discrimination.

The Futurists were driven by the need to pursue what Marinetti called "the implications of new facts," which had to be absorbed and transformed by artists. In their early paintings of workers and houses under construction, Boccioni and Balla were already coping with the implications of new facts. But later Futurist pronouncements, along with the stabbing, overexcited vitalism of their canvases, suggest an even deeper anxiety: that the artist was being made more and more marginal by the new facts and by the velocity with which those facts came and went (or reproduced themselves). The artist had not only to keep pace, he also had to define (or improvise) his own position along the way. The Futurist strategy was to adopt the manners of competing technologies—to be quick, aggressive, efficient, explicitly manipulative, unsentimental, and intrusive. Here, too, their methods were helplessly equivocal insofar as they were adversarial in contesting the new "marginalization" of the artist, but conciliatory and imitative in their accommodations.

The attention to new facts, along with the importance they attached to *dinamismo,* led Futurist artists to investigate the nature of their materials. "Instead of *humanizing* animals, vegetables, and minerals (an outmoded system) we will be able to animalize, vegetalize, mineralize, electrify or liquify our style, making it live the life of matter." Marinetti is speaking here about Futurist poetry, but his intent to "destroy the canals of syntax" and rid poetry of its sentimental and historical excrescences had its equivalents in the practice of Futurist painters. Gino Severini's *Armoured Train,* with its slashed multiple perspectives, discloses a file of infantry firing from what looks like a rolling steel-plated trench, a mounted artillery piece blasting away from the front end. Embedded in sulphurous scissors and triangles of green and yellow light, the train looks encased in its own velocity as it cuts a swath through the teeming air. New martial facts are the painting's subject, but more importantly for Severini the Futurist, the life of matter is being enacted in paint. In keeping with Futurist predilections, however, the scene is empty of sentimental content. The faceless infantrymen in blue capes, like so many cowled anonymous monks at prayer, are presented by the artist's imagination as *matter equivalent to* the knobby rivet-heads efficiently distributed around the train and cannonplates. The soldiers are thus nothing more than elements in a scheme of new formal facts. Like the vehicle they occupy, they have been made over into senseless instruments of a will not their own. The transformational activity Marinetti called for is indeed apparent here, as elsewhere in Futurist art, but the discriminating faculty has been sacrificed to the enthusiasm for likenesses.

Contrived, programmatic excitement leads to terminal weariness. The Futurists' relentless brassy optimism, combined with all that elated moonlight-killing, in an exhibition of this size leads almost inevitably to the sepulchral tedium and quaintness one feels in a wax museum. The "Futurisms" of Russia, Latin America, Japan, Germany, France, and other countries, which occupy the third floor galleries, hammer Futurist mannerisms into different shapes, with varying degrees of wit and anger (and, in the special case of Maiakovsky, with different political import). But the surprise comes near the end, in the room devoted to British Futurism, and especially in the work of Christopher Nevinson and Wyndham Lewis.

Two large canvases by Nevinson, *Returning to the Trenches* (1914-15) and *Troops*

Resting (1916), exploit the formal resources of Futurism. (His ties with the Futurist movement, loose as they were, lasted until 1919). *Returning to the Trenches* is nearly overloaded with the dynamism of soldiers scrambling for safety, ranks tilted and hurtling back towards cover, legs flashing through the serial "moments" familiar in Futurist images. The panic, however, is palpable. The image is a design of mortal fear. It accommodates a world of new facts, but the quickness in the draughtsmanship and coloring enacts the quick of feeling. Unlike in Severini's *Armoured Train,* here we can distinguish human from mineral fact. In *Troops Resting,* the angular planes of Futurist drawing enact the exhaustion of troops slumped on a railway embankment. Each face has a singular character. Over all their heads runs the telegraph line, hovering like an instrument of execution. In *A Battery Shelled* (1914-18), Wyndham Lewis paints a world in which nearly everything is or will soon become war debris. The stiff forms of the artillerymen imitate the bristling groups of stacked shells which look like monstrous vegetables, whereas the soldiers' bodies (not those of the officers, who look on calmly from a distance) seem reptilian, armor-plated. Mineral ordnance assumes the look of vegetable abundance; the human is being transformed into mineral matter. The metallic folds of the human forms mock the shape of the landscape, the crudely terraced earthworks colored a sickened blue-green. Here, too, we have a chronicle of new transformations, but they are calibrated by a discriminating intelligence. Lewis's painting is febrile, angry, and accusatory; the passion is enacted in a recognizably Futurist vocabulary of forms. But Lewis plays off the cool angularity and centrifugal movement of Futurism against the brittle dread being lived out through those forms.

Marinetti and his group loathed what they called the professorial past. As one arrives at the British room, however, the polemical program of the Futurists and its expression in the painting have begun to smell of the lecture hall. For all their clamorous enthusiasm and announcements of passion, the art the Futurists made is eerily lacking in temperament—which seems somehow to have been edited out of their program—and this deficiency turns much of their work into academicism. The British room is, on the contrary, practically overripe with temperament; it is, in any case, stretching the issue to identify Nevinson, Lewis, Jacob Epstein, and Gaudier-Brzeska as Futurists. The four were also associated with Vorticism, which for a brief time had points of contact with Futurism. The Vorticists, too, prized energy, action, and force, and insisted on claiming the world of facts. But the new motion valued by the Vorticists did not exclude the velocities of the past; it welcomed, insisted on, all past "vectors" of knowledge as part of the vortex that revolved around the individual artist. A genuinely new work of art, for Gaudier-Brzeska and his friend and advocate Ezra Pound, was inevitably worked on, shaped, by the action of the vortex. Art was an emergence *from* and *out of.* The Futurists, on the other hand, had only the initiating ego. In his catalogue entry on "Philosophy" Massimo Carrà says that "The Futurist ego, or 'I,' is its own act; it acts itself and is nothing without this acting." It acted, moreover, according to a program. The result was to bleed its art of temperament and mood, and to turn it into a new set of idealizations. Any quest for the sort of purity sought by the Futurists has to suppress, eliminate, or reduce to academic exercise the expression of passion for the human. After 1910, in Boccioni's work there is no longer any contest between the flesh and its surroundings because the sense of the carnal is entirely gone.

The British artists were also trying to reckon with world war, and when necessary they tried to enlarge the confines of older narrative conventions in order to accommodate the new efficiencies for creating what Elias Canetti calls "the heaps of the dead." I've already suggested that Futurist optimism was a cultivated ignorance, but that is obvious enough and perhaps simplistic. Behind that optimism was, I think, a neurotic fear of reflectiveness and moral consequence. The loud, belligerent generosity that runs through the Futurists' art and writings is also self-righteous protectiveness. They cared abundantly about what artists never ought to care about. They cared about being right. Marinetti called for the expression of a new consciousness, but he and many of his fellows were too impatient, and too performance-obsessed, to do the deeper work—to brood on the nature of that consciousness.

(*September* 1986)

The outrageous Mr. Wu

by Joseph Epstein

In his inevitably charming essay "Quia Imperfectum," Max Beerbohm proposed a museum composed of incomplete masterpieces, which would include among other items Penelope's web, the original drawings for the Tower of Babel, the manuscripts of *Edwin Drood* and "Kubla Kahn," the fragments from Racine's "Iphigénie," and the blank spaces and bare pedestals for the paintings and statues that Michelangelo planned but never completed for the Baptistery of San Lorenzo. I wonder if I might suggest yet another item for inclusion, that of the quite scrappy notes for an essay that George Orwell had hoped to write about Evelyn Waugh before death, the ultimate deadline, arrived to rescind all others in Orwell's active journalistic career. Like the other items in Beerbohm's museum dedicated to enshrinement of the incomplete, a full-blown George Orwell essay on Evelyn Waugh does seem deliciously promising. One imagines that essay to have been a lengthy piece of work, on the model of Orwell's essays on Dickens or Kipling, pellucid, shimmering with good sense, and slicing to the core of Waugh's art as no other writer has thus far been able to do. "Sorry," as certain rather sadistic practitioners of the science of librarianship have been known exuberantly to exclaim, "but that work is not available."

A very great deal has been written about the art of Evelyn Waugh: the recently published *Evelyn Waugh: The Critical Heritage* runs to over five hundred pages[1]; Christopher Sykes's friendly but not uncritical biography of Waugh has long been in print; and a weighty volume of Waugh's letters, an even weightier one of his diaries, and now *The Essays, Articles and Reviews of Evelyn Waugh*[2] have all appeared. One nonetheless feels that, even though all the pieces are now on the board, no one has quite succeeded in assembling the puzzle presented by this extraordinary writer and his enchanting art. Strip away what one takes to be his mask and one discovers another under it and then yet another under that one. So much seems to interpose itself between his literary career and our understanding of it, not least the preposterous persona he sedulously erected for himself. Yet this much can be said at the outset: A man afflicted by boredom his life long, he unfailingly avoided passing boredom on to his readers. If there is a serious writer in this century who has given more pleasure to his readers than Evelyn Waugh, I cannot think of his name.

One doesn't think of modern literature as strenuously devoted to purveying pleasure. Complexity, yes; seriousness, often; a certain jokiness, occasionally. But pleasure of the kind available in the art of Evelyn Waugh

---

1 *Evelyn Waugh: The Critical Heritage,* edited by Martin Stannard: Routledge & Kegan Paul, 537 pages, $36.

2 *The Essays, Articles and Reviews of Evelyn Waugh,* edited by Donat Gallagher: Little, Brown; 672 pages, $40.

is very rare. I do not mean to imply that aesthetic pleasure of the highest order isn't abundantly available in such modern writers as Joyce and Proust, T. S. Eliot and Wallace Stevens; obviously, it is. But in the work of Evelyn Waugh high aesthetic pleasure—he was a consummate artist, the masculine elegance of whose prose is unrivaled in our time—is combined with pleasure such as only a comic genius can provide. Evelyn Waugh's comedy has had many followers—such British group efforts as "Beyond the Fringe," "That Was the Week That Was," and, on a cruder level, "Monty Python's Flying Circus" are quite unthinkable without the precedent of Waugh—but no successful imitators. There are two reasons why there has never been a convincing parody of Evelyn Waugh: first, no one else is quite that funny, and second, no one else can write quite that well.

Evelyn Waugh's friend John Sutro coined the word "Wavian"—on the model of Shavian for George Bernard Shaw—to apply to the distinctive comedy of Evelyn Waugh. It is comedy that cannot be explained but only displayed. Samples available without request: On our first encountering Waugh's bounder-hero Basil Seal, nearly a third of the way into the novel *Black Mischief,* he is coming awake the morning after a great binge on the sofa of what is to him a totally strange flat. Waugh notes:

> There was a gramophone playing. A lady in a dressing jacket sat in an armchair by the gas fire, eating sardines from the tin with a shoe horn . . .

Stop the cameras here. That lady eating sardines from the tin with a shoehorn is a pure Wavian touch. So, too, is the following sentence from the first and only installment of Waugh's autobiography, *A Little Learning,* which appears in the chapter in which the author recounts his days at Lancing, his public school: "Apart from general malevolence and particular cruelty, we were not vicious." Finally, from the thesaurus of Wavian anecdotes, Christopher Sykes, in his biography, reports visiting Waugh in the hospital, where he found him grumbling in great pain in the aftermath of an operation for piles. Attempting to solace his friend, Sykes remarked that he assumed the operation, painful though it might seem now, was in any case necessary.

"No," Waugh replied," the operation was not necessary, but might conceivably have become so later on."

"Not necessary?" said Sykes. "Then why did you have it done?"

"Perfectionism."

Sacha Guitry said that a successful joke requires three people: the person who tells it, the person who appreciates it, and the person who doesn't get it. In its whimsy, in its obliquity, sometimes in its cruelty, Evelyn Waugh's comedy is not for everyone. But those who do appreciate it, appreciate it hugely—can scarcely, in fact, get enough of it. Waugh was a man with a ferocious appetite for the ridiculous, and, with his observant eye, he never went hungry for long. In his writing, if not always in his life, he possessed the gift of viewing everything as if from a great distance, *sub specie aeternitatis*—under the aspect, that is, of eternity, from which aspect nearly everything humankind does is of course ridiculous, absurd, comical.

But the comedy of Evelyn Waugh would not have been possible if not dressed out in his carefully measured prose. That prose is the straight face from behind which the smashing punch lines are delivered. There is nothing flashy or idiosyncratic about Waugh's prose style. It has a precision and a delicacy of syntax that elides into an elegance of its own—the elegance of absolute correctness. He commanded a concision that, combined with his towering contempt for cliché, permitted him to write with dead-on directness. He had an interesting though not flamboyant vocabulary, which he was able to assemble in charming juxtapositions (writing of the "desperate levity" of his youth) and unexpected locutions (college bills at this time of desperate levity "engorged his allowance") that gave it a continual freshness. Like his friend Ronald

Knox, he was said to have known the exact meaning and derivation of every word he used; perhaps it was this that lent his language its weight and authority. As a writer he thought of himself as a craftsman, and he enjoyed bringing to book those who practiced shoddily the craft he revered. Of a sloppily written book by Harold Laski, Waugh noted that Laski was "so set on preaching the dignity of labour that he shirks his own work." Of another slapdash prose writer, Stephen Spender, Waugh writes: "to see him fumbling with our rich and delicate language is to experience all the horror of seeing a Sèvres vase in the hands of a chimpanzee."

In *A Little Learning* Waugh wrote that he remembered no Greek and read no Latin for pleasure, yet claimed a great debt to his youthful classical studies for such skill as he had as a prose writer: "only by them can a boy fully understand that a sentence is a logical construction and that words have basic inalienable meanings, departure from which is either conscious metaphor or inexcusable vulgarity." But more than a grounding in classical studies is required to make an Evelyn Waugh; there were also his fastidiousness and his devilish (I use this word with some forethought) powers of comic formulation. Who but Evelyn Waugh could have devised, as a euphemism for Harold Acton's homosexuality, the phrasing, he "did not fret for female society"? Who but he, in one of his travel books, *Remote People,* could describe two young Germans encountered in Aden as speaking "English, one rather better than the other, but both very fluently, loudly, and unintelligibly." "Proper words in proper places," as Swift famously said, "make the true definition of a style." Waugh knew the proper words and he knew their proper places; he also knew that style, which he thought derived from the conflation of lucidity, elegance, and individuality, was the great preservative of literary art—that which allowed it to live beyond its time.

But then neither Evelyn Waugh's comic genius nor the high quality of his prose has ever been in serious dispute. What is disputed is the use he made of his gifts. There is, to begin with, very little agreement about which are Waugh's best books, why his literary career took the shape it did, or what in summation his nearly forty years of literary effort come to. Edmund Wilson, for example, a great admirer of Waugh's early novels, bailed out on him with the publication of *Brideshead Revisited.* Claiming that this novel "has been a bitter blow to this critic," Wilson, himself always a bit of the village atheist, could neither understand nor endure the Catholicism at the center of the novel. George Orwell, who reviewed, briefly, Waugh's slender novel *Scott-King's Modern Europe,* though properly appreciative of Waugh's skill, was troubled by his politics, and ended his review by suggesting that the author "occasionally turn aside to read a sixpenny pamphlet on Marxism." Christopher Sykes thought *Unconditional Surrender,* the third volume of Waugh's World War II trilogy, *Sword of Honor,* his great masterpiece, while the full trilogy for Kingsley Amis finally neither coheres nor convinces. Martin Green is keenest on Waugh's early novels (excepting *A Handful of Dust* and *The Loved One*), while V. S. Pritchett, an admirer of Waugh's early novels, nonetheless felt that his later novels, particularly *Sword of Honor,* marked an "advance toward a compassionate study of human nature." Clearly, Evelyn Waugh's is not a case in which one can accuse the critics of being in collusion.

Such a critical dissensus has its own interesting implications. It implies, for one thing, that Evelyn Waugh's literary reputation, even now, is far from settled; it implies, for another, that Waugh's work is of a kind that critics feel they can pick and choose from: accepting the Waugh they approve and setting aside the Waugh they disapprove. Perhaps we all do that with authors whom we wish to admire in spite of their holding to ideas that we find uncongenial. (Supposing literature to be a luncheonette, my order is for Dostoevsky, hold the anti-Semitism and Russian Orthodox Christianity.) But with Evelyn Waugh this isn't so easy. It tends to be standard practice to admire the early Waugh while deploring the later, attributing his falling off to his conversion to Catholicism and his deepened reactionaryism. In this reading one admires Waugh's prose style and comic high jinks and leaves the ideas that propel them aside. "It is the business of literature," Desmond MacCarthy once said, "to turn facts into ideas." But Waugh's critics usually either ignore his ideas or set out to attack them for the stirring reason that they disagree with their own. Others choose not to confront those ideas.

The first fact to recognize—a fact wrapped in an idea—is that Evelyn Waugh was a true reactionary. "A reactionary," according to a sprightly definition by Kenneth Minogue, "is someone with a clear and comprehensive vision of an ideal world we have lost." Reactionaryism obviously has a political component, but its politics, in an artist, need not be primary. In her book, *Evelyn Waugh, Portrait of a Country Neighbor,* Frances Donaldson remarks that "Evelyn suffered permanently and terribly from nostalgia," and recalls him once telling her, apropos of his not voting in general elections, "The Conservative Party has never put back the clock a single second." He adored the architecture of every century but his own. An essay he wrote in 1955 entitled "The Death of Painting" begins: "'From today painting is dead,' cried Paul Delaroche in 1839, when first shown a daguerreotype. He spoke too soon." He also wrote: "I think it is time we made up our minds that poetry is one of the arts which has died in the last eighty years." Nothing seemed more absurd to Waugh than whoring after modernity. "There is an unhappy man in Paris called M. Cocteau whose whole life is occupied in trying to be modern," he wrote in 1930, when he was himself only twenty-seven.

Scratch a reactionary and you will find a right-winger—as Christopher Sykes says, Waugh had an "instinctual aversion to all social progress"—but scratch him a little harder and you will find a romantic. It is well to recall that Evelyn Waugh's first published book was a study of Rossetti. The archetypical Waugh hero, from Paul Pennyfeather of *Decline and Fall* through Tony Last of *A Handful of Dust* to the eponymous hero of *The Ordeal of Gilbert Pinfold* is a romantic—and a romantic who, not to put too fine a point on it, gets it in the neck. Not much of a century for romanticism, the twentieth, or so Evelyn Waugh, in his novels, kept pointing out.

This knowledge did not make Waugh any less a romantic; it did, however, make him an extremely interesting one. A romantic is drawn to the heroic, which Waugh was. But he, Waugh, was even more powerfully drawn to the ridiculous. One does not regularly think of the romantic and the ridiculous commingling in the work of a single writer. In Waugh it did. His sense of the ridiculous was nearly all-pervading; to it he owed much of the delight and penetration of his art. Even critics who despised all that he seemed to stand for allowed that he was a greatly gifted man. This did not stop critics from attacking him personally. In 1947, in a letter to Nancy Mitford, Waugh wrote that most of the reviews of his novel *Scott-King's Modern Europe* "instead of being about the book, have been about me, saying I am ill-tempered and self-infatuated . . . . Would you say I was a very ill-tempered and self-infatuated man? It hurts."

Having recently read through Christopher Sykes's biography and Waugh's own *Letters* and *Diaries,* I should say that he was not at all self-infatuated but very ill-tempered indeed. He obviously knew this to be the case. Gilbert Pinfold asks, "Why does everyone except me find it so easy to be nice?"; and the narrator of the brilliant but unfinished novel entitled *Work Suspended* remarks, "I am afraid you greatly overrate my good nature," a thing not many people who knew him were ever likely to do to Evelyn Waugh. He suffered fools not at all, yet boredom frequently—and excruciatingly. Boredom to Waugh was, like a disease, palpable in its effects. In *Work Suspended* he has his narrator say of another character that he was "still smarting with the ruthless boredom of my last two or three meetings with him." *Ruthless boredom*—that is a juxtaposition only an acute sufferer could contrive. Off in Yugoslavia during World War II, Waugh could—and did—scold his second wife for the dullness of her letters:

> Darling Laura, sweet whiskers, do try to write me better letters. Your last, dated 19 December received today, so eagerly expected, was a bitter disappointment. Do realize that a letter need not be a bald chronicle of events; I know you lead a dull life now, my heart bleeds for it, though I believe you could make it more interesting if you had the will. But that is no reason to make your letters as dull as your life. I simply am not interested in Bridget's children. Do grasp that. A letter should be a form of conversation; write as though you were talking to me.

To the ardent boredom that always loomed on his horizon Waugh joined a bullying streak, an oddly detached strain of motiveless cruelty that remained with him all his life. Cecil Beaton, who attended the same preparatory school as Waugh, recalled the boyish Evelyn Waugh as "a tiny but fierce" ringleader of bullies. (Waugh, in his own autobiography, recalling Beaton, remarked coolly of his and his friends' treatment of Beaton: "Our persecution went no further than sticking pins into him and we were solidly beaten for doing so.") Beaton also noted that, when he ran into him later in life, Waugh had a knack for making even compliments sound suspicious. Beaton retells an anecdote heard from Lady Diana Cooper about Waugh one day giving quite precise instructions to a stranger who asked the whereabouts of a railway station. When Lady Diana afterwards remarked, "How clever of you to know where the station is," Waugh replied, "I don't. I always give people the wrong directions." Once, when he had behaved with particular rudeness to a young French intellectual at a dinner party in Paris at the home of Nancy Mitford, Miss Mitford, angry at his social brutality, asked him how he could behave so meanly and yet consider himself a believing and practicing Catholic. "You have no idea," Waugh returned, "how much nastier I would be if I was not a Catholic. Without supernatural aid I would hardly be a human being." Was he joking?

The more one learns about the life of Evelyn Waugh, the less one is inclined to think it a joke at all. In his biography, Christopher Sykes reports Waugh's strong aversion to Dylan Thomas, who used to appear from time to time at evenings at Cyril Connolly's house. Waugh asked Connolly, in fact, never to invite him when he knew that Dylan Thomas was to be there. The reason, as Sykes explains, is that in Thomas—who dressed in checked suits resembling Waugh's, whose language was like Waugh's made up of parody and fantasy, who like Waugh again was small and portly, and who like Waugh still again was often drunk (though Waugh was not, like Thomas, a boisterous drunk)—in Thomas Evelyn Waugh saw a caricature of himself. "He's exactly what I would have been," Waugh told Sykes, "if I had not become a Catholic."

There can be no greater impropriety than questioning the quality of another person's religious faith. As Evelyn Waugh himself wrote, "Every soul in his traffic with God has his own secrets." But in Waugh's case it happens that we do know the motives behind his conversion, in 1930 (at the age of twenty-seven), to Roman Catholicism, for the good reason that Waugh has described them in an essay entitled "Converted to Rome." In this essay he makes plain that he converted to Catholicism not because *"The Jesuits have got hold of him,"* or *"He is captivated by the ritual,"* or *"He wants to have his mind made up for him,"* but because he saw the present phase of European history as one in which "the essential issue" was "between Christianity and Chaos." In this issue he came down on the side of Christianity, and he chose Roman Catholicism because he thought Christianity more universal, better disciplined, and existing "in its most complete and vital form in the Roman Catholic Church." Waugh closed this essay by noting what was for him a crucial distinction in the churchgoing attitudes of Protestants and Catholics: "The Protestant attitude seems often to be, 'I am good; therefore I go to church,' while the Catholic's is, 'I am very far from good; therefore I go to church.'"

Such a document as this essay says less about how clearly Evelyn Waugh perceived God than about how vividly he felt the encroachments of chaos. What had his keen sense of chaos, what had his conversion to Catholicism, to do with his first wife's deserting him for another man in 1929 cannot be known with assurance, but certainly this event can only have contributed to both in no small way. Like so many of the characters in his novels, in his brief first marriage Evelyn Waugh had been a victim. How devastating this must have been to the young man of twenty-six who until now had strode through life without knowing serious setbacks: comfortably upper-middle class, adored by his parents, befriended by all whom he wished to befriend, gifted as both an artist and a writer, already celebrated as a dazzling comic novelist—only to end up as a dupe and a cuckold through the agency of a woman who now claimed to have married him without ever having loved him. He was shattered and humiliated. (Of Basil Seal, the character who in some respects functions as Waugh's alter-id, Waugh, in *Put Out More Flags,* writes: "He rejoiced, always, in the spectacle of women at a disadvantage.") After the breakup of his first marriage, some of Waugh's friends, according to Christopher Sykes, saw in him "a new hardness and bitterness and an utter disillusion which showed itself in cruelty."

The breakup of his marriage may also have confirmed Evelyn Waugh in his sense of his own unworthiness. Far from being self-infatuated, he was apparently always self-reproachful—friends with a penchant for psychologizing thought him self-hating—always the first to spot flaws in himself. Later in life, now long a Catholic, he chalked this up to a heightened sense of sin; hell, it was said, was his favorite Church dogma. Certainly he tended to feature his own vices. Waugh's diaries are filled with chronicles of his drinking and drugging (he took a drug called chloral for the insomnia that he suffered all his adult life). Reading his diaries one wonders when, between boozing bouts ("Monday 1 August 1955 . . . Uneatable dinner but plenty of champagne"), he was able to get any writing done. In fact, he turned out a great deal of work, scarcely ever missing a journalistic deadline, and needed his literary earnings to keep his large family afloat. But he preferred to emphasize, even if only to himself, how wicked he was. Recall, please, the line about the Catholic's attitude to churchgoing: "I am very far from good; therefore I go to church."

Evelyn Waugh was not the first connoisseur of chaos to sight his earliest specimens of chaos in the laboratory of his own heart. Having found chaos first by looking inward does not mean that chaos does not truly exist outwardly as well. One of the many hallucinations Gilbert Pinfold suffers is overhearing a voice say, "He doesn't really *believe* in his religion, you know. He just pretends to because he thinks it aristocratic. It goes with being Lord of the Manor." Cool and impersonal though Waugh makes his conversion to Catholicism sound, there is no reason to doubt its authenticity nor to doubt his religion's use to him as a barrier to the chaos he found both in his soul and in the world around him. It is also well to remember that, with the exception of his youthful book on Rossetti and *Decline and Fall* (1928), all of Evelyn Waugh's books were written while he was a Catholic. Waugh did not like being pigeon-holed as a Catholic writer; and it is not true to say of him, as he once said of J. F. Powers, that his whole art "is everywhere infused and directed by his Faith." Still, it can be said that a fierce sense of chaos looms over all that Evelyn Waugh wrote after his conversion. Not that he made the least pretense to being able to subdue the chaos that haunted him all his days; through his art, though, he was able to wrest a great deal of laughter from it.

As a Catholic Evelyn Waugh was very legalistic, even pedantic, knowledgable about minor points of doctrine and observant of all scraps of ritual. His Catholicism fit snugly into the formality of character he had created in his life. He early set himself up as a back number. He was very keen for old-world courtesy—for, that is, receiving it. (Giving it was something else.) He lived amid heavy Victorian furniture; he became something of a specialist in Victorian painting. He played the lord of the manor, all right, but, it must be added, he usually played it for laughs. He was the curmudgeonly little squire in the thick checkered suits who affixed before his house in the Gloucestershire Cotswolds a notice reading "No Admittance on Business." He refused to use the telephone. He called the day on which *The New Statesman* arrived "Black Friday"; he regularly read that journal as an act of self-provocation. When his hearing began to fail, he took to toting around an ear trumpet; he is usually described as "brandishing" this ear trumpet, which is not imprecise, for he used it as a social weapon to make other people uncomfortable. Once, at a dinner in his honor, when Malcolm Muggeridge rose to deliver a eulogy to him, Waugh, seated at a dais, deliberately set his ear trumpet away from him, to make clear to all in the room that nothing Muggeridge was about to say could possibly be worth hearing. He only gave this ear trumpet up when, at a dinner party given by his friend Ann Fleming, after using his trumpet to cause the maximum awkwardness all round, his hostess, having had all she could bear of his shenanigans, soundly thwacked the trumpet with a spoon while it was in his ear, causing, as Waugh later allowed, a sensation akin to that of having had a pistol fired in one's ear.

What lay behind this extraordinary act? Whimsy, for one thing, quite wild whimsy. But it was also very carefully calculated. Evelyn Waugh set out deliberately to outrage. Like his own Mr. Pinfold, he created "a front of pomposity mitigated by indiscretion." Spiritually and intellectually he was at odds with his age—and dressed and acted the part. (Interesting that George Orwell, the other writer of Waugh's generation who is greatly valued, also dressed and acted a part—that of a member of the working class.) Reviewing a book of contemporary etiquette, Waugh wrote: "The need now is for order." Reviewing a recently issued volume of the *Dictionary of National Biography,* he wrote: "This is not the age of reformation but of defence, when every man of goodwill should devote all his powers to preserving the few good things left to us from our grandfathers."

The pose of being perpetually outraged and the ploy of consistently outraging was for Evelyn Waugh a clever and useful gambit. Stripped down to his fundamental views, and devoid of his high gifts, Waugh might have seemed quite as drab and grumpy a figure as any other crotchety conservative gremlin. Outrageous though Waugh could be, he outraged with charm. He was never stupid, for, as Donat Gallagher, the editor of *The Essays, Articles and Reviews of Evelyn Waugh* rightly says, his "flourishing extravagances always cling to a solid core of talent and intelligence."

In time people expected the outrageous from Evelyn Waugh, and he usually could be counted upon to deliver. As a young man, he played the radical to conservative friends and the conservative to radicals. Once he sensed which way the wind was blowing, he headed straight into it. Apart from his second wife and a few very close friends, no one knew quite how to take him. In his *Diaries* Chips Channon, recounting a lunch in London in 1934, notes:

> Also Evelyn Waugh, alias Mr. Wu. I never know . . . is he good trying to be wicked? Or just wicked trying to be nice? He looks like a ventriloquist's doll, with his shiny nose; I feel his ideals are measured by publishers' royalties. He told me today that he thought that anyone could write a novel given six weeks, pen, paper and no telephone or wife.

Serving as a liaison officer in Yugoslavia in World War II, Waugh spread the rumor that Tito was a woman, a lesbian in fact, which supposedly got back to Tito. (Waugh was not precisely an ideal liaison officer, or officer of any kind; at one point he had to be removed from his command because it was feared that, in combat, his own men might shoot him.) He began a review of Randolph Churchill's book about a libel suit by writing: "No one who knows Mr. Randolph Churchill and wishes to express distaste for him should ever be at a loss for words which would be both opprobrious and apt." In the same review he makes the point that the journalists found guilty of libel are not sufficiently punished, for their wealthy newspapers pick up the costs when they are found guilty, so he concludes: "The time, I think, is ripe for the restoration of the pillory."

I believe I have established that Evelyn Waugh could be, as they used to note in folders in the personnel departments, "a difficult personality." Was he a snob into the bargain? Snobbery was of course part of his subject as a novelist. He was endlessly interested and amused by the intricacies of the English class system, which was beginning to come apart as he came to maturity. For him the joke was that no one seemed too lowly to look down upon someone else. In *A Handful of Dust,* Tony Last has gone off to a hotel in the countryside with a prostitute to establish his infidelity so that his wife can divorce him. At the hotel, as visitors come swinging through the doors of the dining room, Waugh writes: "'Yids,' explained Milly [the prostitute] superfluously. 'Still it's nice to get a change from the club once in a while.'" (The cruel art in that line of dialogue falls on the word "superfluously.") As for his own social tastes, "Evelyn," Frances Donaldson notes, "liked the smarter of the intellectuals, the more intellectual of the smart—and no one else." About the age of the common man, Waugh, a most uncommon man, had his qualms, and that is putting it very gently. When someone accused him of not caring for the Man in the Street, he replied that there was no Man in the Street—only men and streets. Upon publication of *Brideshead Revisited* he came in for heavy criticism not only for his often idealized treatment of that novel's aristocratic characters but for his rough portrayal of the young lower-middle-class character he called Lieutenant Hooper. Hooper is a man without the least shred of romanticism or interest in heroism, who accepts his induction into the army "like the measles," who is bereft of the least scintilla of culture, who has "an overmastering regard for efficiency" without the least aptitude for it, and who for Evelyn Waugh represents the grey crushing wave of the future. *Brideshead Revisited* was written while Waugh was on leave from the British Army in 1944. With the victory of the first Labour government in the general election after the War, for Waugh the Age of Hooper had arrived in earnest.

In a review of Edgar Johnson's biography of Charles Dickens, Waugh wrote: "Faults which would be excusable in other men become odious in the light of Dickens's writing." Something like the reverse applies to the life of Evelyn Waugh. Given the coolness of his art and the ferocity of his public mask, one is always surprised to discover him not acting perfectly monstrously. Of Gilbert Pinfold, he wrote: "He was not what is generally meant by the appellation a 'philanthropic' man; he totally lacked what was now called a 'social conscience.' But apart from his love of family and friends he had a certain basic kindliness to those who refrained from active annoyance." Waugh was a faithful husband; at home he played the Victorian paterfamilias, and none of his six children has ever written about him except in a kindly manner. To his small circle of close friends—Nancy Mitford, Diana Cooper, Ann Fleming, Christopher Sykes—he was a devoted if sometimes difficult (and socially dangerous) companion. Along with being modest about his own accomplishments, Waugh never displayed the least jealousy toward writers who were his contemporaries, and with the two among them who might have been considered his greatest rivals, Graham Greene and Anthony Powell, he never wrote nor spoke in other than an appreciative way. He came to the aid of a number of friends whom he found in illness or sore financial condition. And of course when he chose he could be utterly charming.

Studying the arc described by Evelyn Waugh's literary career, one discovers nearly at its middle an uncompleted novel entitled *Work Suspended.* Waugh began the book in 1939 and published it, in its incomplete form, in 1942. It is a brilliant piece of unfinished business, one fully worthy of a place in Max Beerbohm's museum. Waugh makes only two references to it in his *Diary*: one noting that, "I have rewritten the first chapter of the novel about six times and at last got it into tolerable shape"; the other, four years later, noting that Desmond MacCarthy was full of praise for it. What went wrong? Why, after only a hundred pages, did Waugh decide to throw in his pen?

One cannot know with any real precision, but in *Work Suspended* Waugh does offer a few clues. The novel's protagonist, who is a writer, comes into an inheritance that relieves him of the need to work for a few years, which causes him to remark that "it was a matter of pure athletics to go on doing something merely because one did it well." Does it seem pushing things to read into this sentiment Evelyn Waugh's own artistic boredom at continuing in the line of madcap comedy at which he was by now a pastmaster? The protagonist-narrator also remarks, about his father, who is the most splendidly comic of the many comic fathers in Waugh's work—he has strong views on the Jews being responsible for the vogue of French impressionist painting—that, "I had not then learned to appreciate the massive defences of what people call the 'border-line of sanity.'" I find this a haunting line, and one that puts one not only in mind of Waugh's own later bout of insanity (recounted in *The Ordeal of Gilbert Pinfold*) but of what seems to me the most penetrating single sentence in all the criticism I have read of Waugh's work; it is a sentence written by V. S. Pritchett that reads: "His early books spring from the liberating notion that human beings are mad; the war trilogy [*Sword of Honor*], a work of maturity, draws on the meatier notion that the horrible thing about human beings is that they are sane."

World War II doubtless played a strong role in turning Evelyn Waugh away from his old sure-fire mode of comic creation. "The Great Bore War" he called it. His was the generation that came to maturity between the Wars. Virginia Woolf may have said that "human nature changed in 1910," but the Bright Young People who comprised Waugh's social set could still find spacious margins of leisure and luxury in which to gambol: lunches at the Savoy, bouts of giglous champagne drunkenness, a ready supply of servants to clean up the mess. But World War II put paid to that kind of life, and no one knew it better than Waugh. Long though he might for the old life, a man as unillusioned as he could scarcely convince himself it was any longer attainable. *Brideshead Revisited,* the first novel he completed after his failure with *Work Suspended,* is easily Evelyn Waugh's most nostalgia-laden book, and sings a threnody to a lavish style of life now quite dead.

After the War the comedy in Waugh's work is still there but now much subdued. Waugh's killing off Major Apthorpe in *Men at Arms,* the first of the novels in *Sword of Honor,* is strong evidence of this. Apthorpe, it will be recalled, is the extraordinary character who never travelled without his preposterous kit, which included a portable thunder-box, or water-closet, made by the firm of Connolly Chemical Closets. (Whimsical even in his depressions, Waugh loved to drag Cyril Connolly's name into his novels: the ridiculous British military figure in *Black Mischief* is General Connolly; Connolly is the name given to the monstrous children in *Put Out More Flags*; and a cruel portrait of Cyril Connolly himself under the name of Everard Spruce, the editor of a wartime journal entitled *Survival,* appears in the last novel of the trilogy, *Unconditional Sur-*

render.) Perhaps Waugh killed off Apthorpe for fear that his marvelous comic blandness would take over his trilogy; at any rate, in the second volume of *Sword of Honor* he is replaced by Major Hound, a greatly less delightful figure who, as Waugh has another character note of him, "seems strangely lacking in the Death-Wish." *Sword of Honor* is not barren of comedy—"Guy, how are you?," asks a character of Guy Crouchback, the trilogy's rather drab hero. "Forty," he replies—but the comedy now has a certain edge that it didn't have in the past. Wavian comedy was always cool, and sometimes cruel, yet invariably it had a lovely gaiety about it; now it begins to take on a less attractive asperity. *Sword of Honor* is more ambitious, more mature, than the earlier of Waugh's novels. No one can accuse this work of not being in pursuit of the largest questions: what is honor, how to achieve personal salvation, is there a will to war propelled by an international death wish, are among the questions raised by the trilogy. Yet Evelyn Waugh in quest of the answers, even though his own earnestness is completely convincing, is now aesthetically less than satisfying.

Is it possible that Evelyn Waugh's was a naturally destructive talent? This sounds a degradation, a put-down, but it is not intended to be. The fact—I see it as a fact—is that Waugh was at his triumphant best on the attack. Think of the subjects that, in his early novels, he had taken on, and how absolutely on target he was in dealing with them—as those of us who have lived beyond his day have reason to know. In *Decline and Fall* he took on the joke of English education; in *Vile Bodies,* the emptiness of gossip-column high life; in *Scoop,* the inanity and insanity of modern journalism ("Look at it this way. News is what a chap who doesn't care much about anything wants to read. And it's only news until he's read it. After that it's dead."); in *Black Mischief,* what is now called the Third World (read today, that novel reads like V. S. Naipaul played for laughs); in *A Handful of Dust,* the toll exacted from family and tradition by attempting to live the smart life; in *Scott-King's Modern Europe,* the swindle of modern Communism in Europe. (Forgive me if I neglect *The Loved One,* my least favorite of Waugh's novels, because its target, the nuttiness of California funerary rites, seems to me too easy to knock off.) Evelyn Waugh did not really know how to write an unreadable novel; but these early novels of his, judged by their craftsmanship, their comic radiance, their intellectual brilliance, are quite without peer.

Writing about his friend Ronald Knox, Waugh noted: "The more learned and philosophic the man, the less likely he is to be 'contemporary,' for he will know that most 'new' ideas are restatements of very old ones, and that the latest events are in all essentials repititions of what has happened before." This remark is not without its applications to Evelyn Waugh himself, who was both attracted to the contemporary and repelled by it. As an artist, he was very much a modernist: a master of irony, of decisive reticences, of abrupt juxtapositions of material that today seem cinematic yet derive from Ronald Firbank, whom Waugh acknowledged as one of his chief artistic influences. As a man, Waugh came more and more to hate modernity. But then so many modernist artists have come out against modernity. T. S. Eliot wrote, "I will show you fear in a handful of dust"; I believe Evelyn Waugh—who used part of that line for the title of one of his novels—truly saw the fear Eliot speaks about.

The hallucinating Gilbert Pinfold believes he overhears yet another disturbing conversation, in which one party asks another: "Were his books ever any good?" "Never *good.* His earliest ones weren't quite as bad as his latest. He's written out." Not only is this an hallucination; it's poor criticism into the bargain. But it was not half bad as prophesy. After *The Ordeal of Gilbert Pinfold* (1957), Waugh produced only one more novel, *Unconditional Surrender* (1961). Still under the lash of having to earn a living for his large family, he continued to produce a goodly amount of very high-quality literary journalism. His last years seem to have been terribly unhappy ones. Plagued by insomnia, bothered as always by boredom, he attempted to fight off the first by stronger drugs, the second by retreating into an alcoholic haze. In a photograph of Evelyn Waugh taken in 1963—three years before his death by heart attack—among the members of an old group of friends from Oxford days known as the Railway Club, poor Waugh looks like a figure one might meet along the boulevards of hell: porcine, plastered, pathetically done in by life. In his last years he apparently felt his life was over, and wished it soon would be; an aphorism he composed around this time runs: "All fates are 'worse than death.'"

Apropos of Chesterton, a writer for whom he had qualified admiration, Waugh wrote:

> Humility is not a virtue propitious to the artist. It is often pride, emulation, avarice, malice—all the odious qualities—which drive a man to complete, elaborate, refine, destroy, renew, his work until he has made something that gratifies his pride and envy and greed. And in doing so he enriches the world more than the generous and good, though he may lose his own soul in the process. That is the paradox of artistic achievement.

It is a profound paradox, and one that is poignantly illustrated if in no way resolved in the life and career of Evelyn Waugh. All we know is that out of this gifted man's pain and terror has come a great deal of joy and laughter for his readers. It isn't much to know, but a lot for which to be grateful.

(*April* 1985)

The obsessions of Marguerite Duras

by Fernanda Eberstadt

After the Second World War, a succession of French novelists—most famously Alain Robbe-Grillet, Nathalie Sarraute, and Michel Butor—developed a kind of fiction which, though influenced by American writers like Ernest Hemingway, nonetheless took on qualities distinctly its own. The features which characterize what came to be known as the "nouveau roman" include, in the words of one (amazingly) sympathetic literary historian, "plotless stories from which motivation, the stock property of the traditional novel, is absent; nameless hero-narrators; banalities expressed by disarming clichés; absence of psychological verisimilitude." Much of this fiction is addressed to the reader in the second person singular and takes place in the present tense; what action there is transpires in cinematic, non-chronological quick-takes; the thought, often tinged with Marxist ideology, tends toward an inscrutable abstraction, a tricky relativism, a fretwork of paradox, in which life is found to be a death sentence, or silence a more telling form of speech. In the work of writers like Maurice Blanchot, Georges Bataille, or Marguerite Duras, the deliberate banality of tone and obliqueness of narrative are used to describe bloodcurdling violence and extremes of sexuality.

The impassive surface and affectless protagonists that marked the French novel of the Fifties, Sixties, and Seventies held a special social significance: they were intended to mimic the doomed mediocrity of modern life, and in particular, to signal the bankruptcy of bourgeois society. It is no accident that some of these French novelists were members of the Communist Party, although being littérateurs, they inclined more toward nihilism than toward political activism. Thus, the nouveau roman—which has been called by some the "anti-novel"—served after the War as an eminently appropriate literary form for a demoralized nation.

In recent years, however, while its Marxist cousins in the field of critical theory have gained popularity abroad, the nouveau roman has fallen on hard times. Indeed, in the last several years, such pioneers as Nathalie Sarraute have turned instead to triumphantly readable semi-autobiographical blockbusters. Of those French intellectuals who have long been associated with the nouveau roman but who have emerged—at least intermittently—from its cryptic toils into a new accessibility and forthrightness of narrative, none is more famous than Marguerite Duras, today the leading lady of French letters, whose latest novel, *The Lover* (1984), won her the Prix Goncourt and became a best-seller both in Europe and in the United States.

Marguerite Duras was born in 1914 in Indochina, the daughter of two French schoolteachers. Her colonial upbringing provides inspiration for the sinister and exotic images that trail through her books—it also forms the subject both of an early novel, *The Sea Wall* (1950) and of its recent and more celebrated reworking, *The Lover.* Duras came to Paris in 1931 and obtained a law degree four years later. She worked as a secretary in the Department of Colonies—a post she left when the Germans occupied France in 1940, at which time Duras joined the Resistance. This experience is described in a recently published diary, *The War* (1986). She was also for a decade a member of the French Communist Party, about which she writes today with laconic contempt. Duras has led a full career both in print journalism and in television—she gained renown for her investigation of the Ben Barka affair of 1965, in which an exiled Moroccan leader was kidnapped and murdered in Paris, possibly with Gaullist complicity. Until recently, however, she has been best known abroad for her screenplays, of which the most celebrated is the 1961 *Hiroshima, Mon Amour,* directed by Alain Resnais.

Duras is at once a prolific and a parsimonious writer. She is the author of some fifteen novels, most of which are as brief as short stories and many of which she has converted into movies, plays, or other novels. Characters, place-names, lines of dialogue, incidents, and situations persistently recur throughout Duras's work, creating an atmosphere of claustrophobic self-referentiality. Thus, at the beginning of *The Lover,* when the teenaged heroine meets a Chinese millionaire in a black limousine, the author interjects, "Yes, it's the big funereal car that's in my books. It's a Morris Léon Bollée. The black Lancia at the French embassy in Calcutta hasn't yet made its entrance on the literary scene." In this manner, like a hostess who won't let her guests talk among themselves, Duras continually dins upon the reader the reminder that this is not life but fiction (in the more derogatory sense of something "made up") and, what's more, *her* fiction. This feeling of characters and events not experienced or truly believed but only fantasized infects even—or perhaps especially—those works which are the most "autobiographical."

Duras's novels in essence are meditations on the theme of an erotic love that leads to enslavement or death. Though there is much violence in her work, it is a violence of which her characters are not agents but rather complicit observers. In her first novel, *Les Impudents (*1943), the heroine covers up her brother's probable murder of his girlfriend. In her second novel, it is his murder of an uncle that she conceals. (The boy then kills himself.) In a skilled and energetic novella, *10.30 on a Summer Night* (1962), a woman on vacation in Spain engineers the escape of an unknown local who has just murdered his wife and her lover. The heroine dreams of starting a new life with the stranger and is offended when he repays her solicitude by committing suicide.

In contrast to the Gothic explosiveness of the subject matter, the atmosphere that pervades Duras's work is one of alcoholic lassitude, sloth, hypnotic passivity, boredom, and self-pity—or, conversely, the *dolce far niente* that comes from feeling one has nothing left to lose. It is no coincidence that most of the action in these novels takes place while their protagonists are on (extended) vacation. Duras's men and women sleep, drink, and wish they were dead: they are lackluster dolls who exercise no control over their destinies, and thus prime candidates for manipulation by a bossy author with much to say (though never directly) on the subjects of death, solitude, and nothingness.

In place of action is sensation in Duras's novels: the twin passions are narcissism and a longing to suffer. This longing frequently is sated by sexual voyeurism: the typical Duras heroine prods her boyfriend or husband into seducing her best friend so she can watch—a theme whose raciness may help to explain why Duras's work should have reached an audience wider than that usually attracted by experimental French fiction.

The absence of action, plot, or character development in Duras's fiction is not accidental but programmatic. Though her heroes are awash in capricious impulses and dull discontents, they are nonetheless not individual men and women at all, but rather generalized and allegorical stand-ins for concepts or psychological states. Thus, the French actress and Japanese architect who star in *Hiroshima, Mon Amour*—two characters who seem continually to be shivering on the brink of an intense and genuine individuality—are constrained by their symbolic functions as the "reprieved" witnesses of man's inhumanity to man, here represented by the American atom bomb dropped on Hiroshima. "Hi-ro-shi-ma. That's your name." "That's my name. Yes. Your name is Nevers. Ne-vers-in France." These, the couple's parting words at the end of the film, permanently relegate character to geography.

Marguerite Duras is frequently commended for her beautiful prose style. The literary manner of these slender and oblique tales of heat, languor, and betrayal is simple. The sentences are short, dialogue is reduced to an exchange of obsessively repetitive soliloquies, scenes are brief and surreal. At its best, her prose achieves an incantatory insistence and a precison of incidental detail that can be arresting. (French readers have complained, however, about her involuted syntax and her shaky hold on grammar.) She is adept at summoning up locale and custom: a summer night's downpour in a Spanish village, underwater fishing in an Italian river, Chinese family photographs as a form of ancestor worship, or "the frightful loneliness of serving in outposts upcountry, stranded amid checkered stretches of rice, fear, madness, fever, and oblivion." In her finest pieces, moreover, Duras displays a certain gay tenacity which stands in defiant contrast to the haplessness of her characters, to the cryptic mumbo jumbo they utter, to the lack of narrative momentum, and indeed, to the portentousness of the authorial message: that only through a criminal "love unto death" can one escape from the truly fatal banality of human life.

This gay tenacity, which keeps her best books afloat, is evident, for instance, in an early novel, *The Sailor from Gibraltar. The Sailor* tells of a menial employee in the Department of Colonies who abandons job and mistress to sail the seas on the yacht of a rich woman in search of a seafaring murderer she once met. This book manages to cover in three hundred pages most of Duras's perennial themes: obsession, masochism, alcoholism, tropical torpor, sexual betrayal, sympathy for the murderer as the ultimate innocent. But for all its potential darkness of theme and lack of narrative purposiveness, in its second half *The Sailor from Gibraltar* winds up a tale of fantastic travels, which is as cheerful and absurd as a chapter from *The Adventures of Doctor Doolittle.*

The Sailor from Gibraltar was published in 1952. Since that time, Duras has mostly abandoned its note of high spirits and occupied herself with flat, stark narratives after the existentialist manner, such as the highly praised *The Square* (1955), in which two strangers on a park bench reveal the futility of their lives in sixty pages of poker-faced monologue. In this vein, too, is the execrable *Malady of Death* (1982), which has just appeared in English[1]—a short story about a doomed autistic stranger buying sex from another stranger eked out to sixty pages of elephantine print and addressed to the reader in the second person, subjective mood.

The Lover, which was published in France in 1984, heralds a return to more purposeful storytelling.[2] Though short on suspense and long on self-pity, it has the makings of a penny dreadful. Narrated in the first person and advertised as "semi-autobiographical," this novel tells of an impoverished French family—a widow schoolteacher and her three children—living in desperate gentility in upcountry Indochina in the late 1920s. The fifteen-year-old daughter, a fragile and precocious child, takes up with a Chinese millionaire, a misalliance which scandalizes the colony but one which the daughter pursues in order to save her mother from destitution. The Lover's black limousine picks up the little girl from school every day and brings her back to his seedy Saigon apart-

1 *The Malady of Death,* translated by Barbara Bray; Grove Press, 60 pages, $9.95.

2 *The Lover,* translated by Barbara Bray; Pantheon, 117 pages, $11.95.

ment, where he ravishes her with feminine delicacy. The Lover—as he is referred to throughout—worships the child hopelessly and ruinously; he wants to take her away with him, but his father "won't let his son marry the little white whore." Nor does the heroine herself care for the Lover: rather, she joins with her family to exploit the wealth of this patsy of inferior race. Toward the end, the heroine sails for Paris, leaving the Lover a weeping and emasculated wreck. Back in France, she hears of his marriage to a Chinese girl of suitable family, and fantasizes that he will be unable to consummate the union for love of the little white whore. Years later, when the heroine has become a famous French author and intellectual, the Lover telephones her and confirms in a trembling voice that indeed "it was as before, that he still loved her, he could never stop loving her, that he'd love her until death." End of novel.

The Lover is the most elegantly written of Duras's works, and it has been well-served by its translator, Barbara Bray. Its prose is crisp and delicate. Moreover, the manic-depressive mother—a particularly French type of woman, at once hard-boiled and utterly impractical in her schemes—is portrayed at times with a rueful compassion which is markedly absent from Duras's previous work. But for all the novel's felicities of style, there is something essential that is very wrong with *The Lover*. Although it has been hailed by many critics as a work of eroticism and even grand passion, *The Lover* on the contrary is eroticism's very antithesis: a monument of brutal, blind, and unremitting feminine narcissism. The author is adept at capturing a lonely fifteen-year-old's rapt self-absorption: her yen for vampish clothing, her fondness for being lusted after by strange men, her hunger to test her sexual powers, and above all her desire to make an older man (preferably of inferior station) her love-slave, to incapacitate and destroy him for life. What is astonishing is that the author, fifty-five years after the "semi-autobiographical" events described, should record these deliciously self-gratifying dreams of conquest without distance, without qualm, without a hint of irony or self-knowledge. Astonishing, too, is that such a work should have been greeted by American reviewers—all female—as a true portrayal of (in the words of one of these) "the confounding nature of passion." (Some of the book's more sympathetic French critics have suggested gallantly that although the story of the affair with a Chinese millionaire must surely be imaginary, nonetheless it has validity as an allegory or as a Freudian fantasy.)

Nineteen eighty-six saw the American publication of *The War,* which appeared in France last year under the more accurate and revealing title *La Douleur.*[3] This is a collection of disparate sketches, some fictional, some detailing Duras's experiences in a Resistance network headed by François Mitterand. Of the "texts" that make up this volume, Duras instructs us: "Learn to read them properly: they are sacred."

Sacred or not, the most compelling is the title story, a 1944 diary which Duras tells us she recently discovered in a cupboard. The diary records Duras's weeks of waiting to find out if her husband has survived a Nazi concentration camp where he had been a political prisoner; it records her watching his slow recovery from hell, and her informing this silent stranger that their marriage is over and that she has left him for his best friend. This tale of sleepless nights, of rationing, of waiting, and of nursing "Robert L." back to life is delivered in a somnambulist's voice that muffles all distinctions between the trivial and the monumental. Much space and attention are devoted to analyzing every fluctuation and varying shade of the author's apathy, her headaches like malignant tumors, her wishing she were dead. Although at times the diary is electrifying in its cold precision, its self-dramatization expresses perfectly what one might call the tyrannical insensitivity of the neurasthenic. "No-one can know my struggle against visions of the black ditch," a typical

3 *The War: A Memoir,* translated by Barbara Bray; Pantheon, 183 pages, $13.95.

passage runs. Another: "I feel very close to the death I wished for. It's a matter of indifference to me. I don't even think about it's being a matter of indifference. My identity is gone . . . . Sometimes I'm amazed I don't die." When her boyfriend reprimands her for self-indulgence, the author breaks into the "diary" to express parenthetically her enduring amazement at his insensitivity. Such passages alternate with descriptions of the husband that are at once tender and clinical, including a day-by-day catalogue of his bowel movements, detailed with an exhaustiveness worthy of the most fastidious anthropologist—a catalogue which surely exceeds a self-respecting man's worst nightmare of what his ex-wife the novelist might do to him in print.

The War, along with *Hiroshima, Mon Amour* and, to a lesser degree, *The Lover,* contains the most explicit declarations of Duras's political vision, which might best be described as a kind of aristocratic and aestheticized misanthropy: an attitude which in an earlier age would likely have attached itself to right-wing politics, but which in our own day is often to be found on the Left. As mentioned earlier, Duras was a member of the French Communist Party for some ten years. Her writing about the war and about politics—though littered with references to class consciousness, collectivism, racism, and "the people"—betrays the curious intellectual dodginess, the unwillingness to call things by their proper names, the reliance on opaque universalities, that mark the imagination of the fellow traveller. One of the most interesting features of Duras's writings on World War II, for instance, is her reticence on the subject of Germans and Nazism. As it happens, *The War* treats French collaborators with sympathy and tact; it is also blistering in its denunciation of De Gaulle, whom Duras excoriates for toadying to the United States by publicly mourning Roosevelt's death, and for his reluctance "to credit the people's suffering with a share in the victory." But the book is almost silent on the subject of the enemy against whom the war was fought (or, in France's case, not fought). The exception is an account of her role as the "girlfriend" of a Gestapo officer, later executed—an account which Duras tells us in her introduction she had suppressed for forty years out of consideration for the man's family, and that she was persuaded by friends to publish only for its utility in illustrating "the illusion that a person may exist solely as a dispenser of reward and punishment." (A high-sounding phrase which universalizes this particular member of the Nazi secret police out of existence.)

This same reticence is most apparent in Duras's screenplay, *Hiroshima, Mon Amour.* The film follows a twenty-four-hour love affair between a Japanese architect and a French actress who is working on a peace film in Hiroshima. Its theme is the banality of evil, as illustrated in flashbacks to World War II—but Duras's twin symbols of that war's barbarity are willfully selective: the American bombing of Hiroshima and the shaving of the heroine's head when she was a young girl for sleeping with a German soldier. Just in case the audience does not understand Duras's purpose here, she spells it out in *The War:* "If Nazi crime is not seen in world terms, if it isn't understood collectively, then that man in the concentration camp at Belsen who died alone but with the same collective soul and class awareness . . . has been betrayed. If you give a German and not a collective interpretation to the Nazi horror, you reduce the man in Belsen to regional dimensions. The only possible answer to this crime is to turn it into a crime committed by everyone. To share it. Just like the idea of equality and fraternity."

Duras's world outlook over the last forty years has changed remarkably little. Although today she writes of the Communist Party with scorn, it is a scorn consistent with the notion of a collective guilt which frees the individual—in this case, her—from responsibility for his beliefs and actions. In *The Lover,* Duras describes a charming and urbane couple she knew during the war who collaborated with the Nazis. "And I, two years after the war, I was a member of the Communist Party. The parallel is complete and absolute. The two things are the same, the same pity, the same call for help, the same lack of judgment, the same superstition, if you like, that consists in believing in a political solution to the personal problem." Duras is quite right in seeing an identity between French Communists and French collaborators: both were accomplices to a murderous foreign power. But in reducing this complicity to its psychological causes or to appealingly waif-like motives, Duras once again skirts the duty of an artist and an intellectual to answer for his ideas and what comes of them. To this picture of an artist-intellectual as a cuckoo hatching young that others must cope with, one might usefully compare that of a Czechoslovakian novelist raised under Communism. In *The Unbearable Lightness of Being,* Milan Kundera reminds us through his hero that Oedipus Rex, on learning that he had unwittingly killed his own father and slept with his mother, put out his own eyes and became a wandering beggar. A similar demand of consciousness, writes Kundera, is placed upon an intellectual who from whatever noble or sympathetic motives has wished upon his country a murderous and tyrannical political system and lives to see what he has done. This fidelity to consciousness, one of the hallmarks of the serious artist, contrasts dismally with those twin demons of narcissism and self-ignorance that dance attendance on even the most elegant of Duras's fiction, and leave her a purveyor of pretentious and empty fancies.

(*September* 1986)

The fictive music of Wallace Stevens

by Bruce Bawer

Thirty-one years after his death, more people than ever are reading the sublime poetry of Wallace Stevens, and his critical reputation—which has grown steadily since 1950, the year he was awarded the Bollingen Prize—has never been greater. But even today, in the minds of many readers who feel perfectly at home with his contemporaries Eliot, Yeats, and Williams, the name of Stevens is, beyond all else, synonymous with enigmatic symbolism and abstruse epistemology. To a dismayingly large number of people, indeed, the most interesting thing about him is not his poetry but the fact that he wrote most of it while serving as vice president in charge of surety claims for the Hartford Accident and Indemnity Company.

The more consideration one gives to this disaffection for Stevens's work among certain types of readers, the more firmly one believes that their problem is not with its difficulty but with Stevens's monolithic impersonality—an impersonality that makes a good deal of Eliot's poetry look, by comparison, positively diaristic—and his devotion to abstraction. In an age when celebrated poets tend to glory either in simpleminded self-celebration or purposeless physical description, these unreceptive readers doubtless find the sort of poetry that Wallace Stevens wrote far from easy to digest.

Two recent books—one an oral portrait, the other a work of academic criticism—seem specifically designed to make the impersonal, intellectual Stevens more congenial to this sort of contemporary reader. The first book is Peter Brazeau's *Parts of a World: Wallace Stevens Remembered* (1983), which has just been reissued by North Point Press, and which is based on interviews with dozens of Stevens's surviving friends, relatives, and co-workers.[1] I say "oral portrait" and not "oral biography" because, unlike any number of other recent life studies that are constructed of a series of excerpts from interview transcripts, *Parts of a World* (whose title is taken from that of Stevens's fourth collection of verse) does not, strictly speaking, tell a story. Instead, Brazeau offers us a numbingly monotonous and generally unrevealing series of sepia-toned snapshots, as it were, of Stevens the business executive, Stevens the poet, Stevens the family man. In part, this monotony is unavoidable. Stevens, born in 1879 to a upper-middle-class family in Reading, Pennsylvania, went on to live a life that, on the surface, was extraordinarily uneventful. After attending Harvard College and New York Law School, he married a hometown girl, Elsie Kachel, and spent the remainder of his life married to her and working in insurance. He never travelled to Europe, made virtually no intimate friends, probably never had an affair, and lived one day pretty much the same way as the next. But Brazeau's "oral portrait" format

1 *Parts of a World: Wallace Stevens Remembered,* by Peter Brazeau. North Point Press; 330 pages, $12.50.

makes this book even more static and colorless than it had to be. Not only do his interviewees tell us precious little of value about Stevens; they almost invariably tell us every banal detail a dozen times.

The first of the book's three sections, for instance, which is devoted to Stevens the insurance man, consists largely of testimony wherein his former colleagues at the Hartford describe how "gentlemanly" he was (or—take your pick—"urbane," "charming," "courtly," "gracious," "civilized," "distinguished," "polished," "dignified," and "impressive," most of which crop up at least twice); what a "first-class" insurance lawyer he was considered to be (perhaps the best surety-claims man in the country—though one is not quite sure, for a while, precisely what a surety-claims man is); how wonderfully sarcastic (and, to those who misunderstood him, arrogant and insulting) his deadpan humor could be; how lucid, concise and beautifully written were his business letters, how illegible his handwriting, how marvelous his vocabulary; what integrity he displayed in all business matters; and how much he loved imported tea, fresh fruit, good cigars, and cinnamon buns (of which he partook frequently at his desk).

Certainly, some of this material is of real interest. But Brazeau never seems to realize when he's reached the saturation point. For example, when his interviewees explain, one after the other, that they never really got to know Stevens (who believed in all work and no play at the office), Brazeau insists upon giving us every deathless word:

> I didn't see much of Stevens. He was generally tucked away somewhere in connection with his work. He wasn't the kind of fellow, "Well, I'm Wallace Stevens!" He wasn't the blustery type. He just went quietly about his business and did what was necessary.

> [Stevens] was a rather aloof person [who liked to] hold people at arm's length . . . . Most executives, whenever they're free to do so, love to sit around and relax, unwind, lollygag. Stevens was not that kind of person. He was not receptive . . . . He was always, to most people who didn't understand him, formidably busy.

> He had difficulty relating to people . . . . He was sort of a loner . . . . He was not what I call a hail-fellow-well-met person.

> He was hard to get acquainted with.

> I always had the feeling that here was a man you just didn't get to know too well. He was always somewhat of a stranger, in the sense that most of the company men that I met I became very friendly with. We had many things that we exchanged, personal things. But you didn't do that with Wallace Stevens. He was always aloof and pretty much his own man.

> He was not a warm personality as far as those in the office went. He wanted his privacy and respected the privacy of others.

Not, mind you, that Stevens was a perpetual sobersides. If he steadfastly avoided chummy behavior at the office, he was equally adamant in his refusal to discuss business after hours. Indeed, at parties, and at his beloved Canoe Club (which, one gathers, was the sort of place where George Babbitt would have gone for a good time), he was, with a couple of drinks in him, "one of the boys"—a cutup, a teller of smoking-car jokes, the very picture of "Harvard-Yale football-game levity," who, upon arrival at a nightclub, would tell the orchestra leader to play "Did You Ever See a Dream Walking?" That such words as "playful," "jovial," and "jolly" recur as frequently in the interviews as "austere," "aloof," and "somber" simply affirms that Stevens's life was, as *Hudson Review* editor Frederick Morgan tells Brazeau, "neatly compartmentalized."

And compartmentalized it was, right down the line. Stevens kept his insurance work separate from his home life, and his poetry separate from both. Rarely did he so much as breathe his wife's name at the office; never did he take her to business functions; and only two or three times, in his thirty-nine years at the Hartford, did he invite a colleague over to the house for dinner. "It was a standing matter of astonishment at the office," recalls one colleague, "that no one ever got to see his family." Nor, unless they took the trouble to hunt down one of his collections at the local bookstore, did more than a few of them get to see his poetry either. True, once he had published a couple of volumes, it was no secret at the Hartford that there was a poet on the premises. Far from it: he regularly sent his underlings to the Oxford English Dictionary to check the meanings of recondite words that he planned to use in his poetry, and on rare occasions even read poems in progress aloud to associates, asking their opinions. But most of the time he nipped in the bud any attempt on the part of a colleague to engage him in a discussion of poetry, or to persuade him to explicate a given poem.

In the second and third sections of the book, "The Man of Letters" and "The Family Man," Brazeau attempts to open up to us those areas of Stevens's life that he kept to himself at the office. Unfortunately, most of the people interviewed in Part Two—among them such familiar literary names as Richard Wilbur, Harry Levin, Cleanth Brooks, and Léonie Adams—knew Stevens no better than did the folks at work. One problem here is that most of the writers and editors with whom Stevens had extended relationships (William Carlos Williams, for example, and Harriet Monroe) are no longer with us; another problem is that Stevens had, it appears, only two really close literary-type friends in his entire life, neither of them a well-known writer, both of them now deceased: Henry Church (a denizen of an artsy New York clique of which Stevens was, for a time, a sort of associate member) and Judge Arthur Gray Powell of Atlanta (whose colorful conversation inspired the titles and some of the details of several of his poems, among them "A High-Toned Old Christian Woman" and "Decorations in a Nigger Cemetery"). We do learn, in Part Two, that Stevens loved Braque, Klee, Stravinsky, Berlioz, and Greta Garbo, that he highly esteemed Delmore Schwartz (whose work represented, to him, a hope for twentieth-century poetry), and that he disliked Hemingway, Cummings, and Frost (who, for his part, thought of Stevens as a "swell from Harvard"). On the admirable side, Stevens consistently refused to accept payment for lectures, readings, or magazine publication of his poems; on the unadmirable side, he was, alas, as full of the prejudices of his time as anyone else, criticizing a restaurant for catering to Jews and referring to Gwendolyn Brooks as a "coon."

It is not until the last (and briefest) section of the book that Brazeau covers what one feels should have come first—Stevens's parents, his upbringing, his life as husband and father. Since Elsie is dead and his only child, Holly, isn't one of Brazeau's interviewees, the picture of the poet as family man is based solely on the testimony of nieces, neighbors, and the like, who were vouchsafed only occasional glimpses of the Stevenses. Though vague, the picture they paint is a decidedly somber one. There was, unsurprisingly, "not much communication" in the Stevens home—no fighting, just silence at the dinner table and closed bedroom doors. Elsie is variously described as sweet and cruel, pathetic and strict, a naïve homebody, a willing serf; all witnesses agree that she was an excellent cook and an obsessive homemaker, and that neither she nor Stevens was a particularly affectionate parent.

It is in the description of the poet's father, Garrett Barcalow Stevens, that *Parts of a World* comes closest to suggesting an explanation for all this. Garrett Stevens was, as Brazeau explains, a corporate lawyer and amateur versifier who, by every account, was distant, domineering, and emotionally undemonstrative, not to mention highly conscious of his family's "respectability"—all characteristics for which Wallace Stevens would be noted. When young Wallace announced that he wanted to marry Elsie, an undereducated girl both literally and figuratively from "the other side of the tracks," Garrett objected and, when Wallace married her anyway, didn't speak to his son for years.

A generation later, the pattern repeated itself almost exactly; Holly decided to marry, and Stevens objected on the grounds that the boy she had in mind, whom Stevens called a "Polack," was simply "not her equal." Holly married him anyway, and she and Stevens were, as a result, estranged for several years.

What is one to make of this? Why did Stevens, in so many ways, become a tintype of his father? Why was such an enlightened modern poet weighted down, psychologically, with so much philistine freight? It almost seems as if, in some sense, Stevens was paying his father *hommage*—or, perhaps, penance. If he admired Delmore Schwartz so fervently, surely this admiration had a good deal to do with Schwartz's endless contemplation, in his poetry, of the theme of parents, children, and fate, and of the strong but subtle ties—of guilt and resentment, love and hatred—that bind sons inescapably to their fathers. In this connection, Stevens writes in "Esthétique du Mal" that

> It may be that one life is a punishment
> For another, as the son's life for the father's.

He speaks to the same theme, but takes an utterly different tone, in "Recitation after Dinner," a poem he read at a meeting of the Saint Nicholas Society (whose members all trace their lineage back to the early Dutch settlers). The poem—in which he borrows Virgil's image of Aeneas carrying his father Anchises on his back (an image Stevens used more than once)—helps to account for the keen interest in genealogy that Stevens developed in middle age; in it, he speaks of tradition as

> . . . a clear, a single, a solid form,
> That of the son who bears upon his back
> The father that he loves, and bears him
> from
> The ruins of the past, out of nothing left,
> Made noble by the honor he receives,
> As if in a golden cloud. The son restores
> The father . . . .

Here, then, Stevens sees the father—and, by extension, all the generations preceding him, and the entire past—not as a dreadful burden but as something marvelous and ennobling. There must be an illuminating story behind all of this. But it is not a story that any of Brazeau's interviewees is able to tell us.

Indeed, what *Parts of a World: Wallace Stevens Remembered* demonstrates more persuasively than anything else is the weakness of the composite oral portrait as a form of biography—or, at least, literary biography. With a relatively uncomplicated subject like Andy Warhol's starlet Edie Sedgwick, whose life provided the material for Jean Stein's book *Edie,* this weakness was not critical. With a more substantial subject, though, the oral form is less defensible, its fundamental superficiality far more manifest. If a book like Peter Manso's *Mailer* nonetheless succeeds to a considerable extent, it is because Mailer is a colorful personality who has led an unsettled and combative life, and because he wears his id on his sleeve. But applied to a man like Wallace Stevens—the turbulence of whose soul rarely, if ever, roiled his smooth surface, and who had nothing but contempt for the Hemingway or Mailer type of writer, who gives the impression that he has to throw himself into life in order to write about it—the oral form fails to provide either insight or entertainment in enough abundance to justify the endeavor.

It would be wrong to mention Ernest Hemingway without taking note, in passing, of Stevens's most dramatic—and out-of-character—literary encounter. So strong was Stevens's antipathy for Hemingwayesque prose that, in February of 1936, the insulting remarks that Stevens made at a cocktail party in Key West provoked the novelist to engage him in a fistfight, which Stevens lost and Hemingway magnanimously agreed to keep quiet about. The tussle is symbolic of the utter contrast between the two writers' approaches to their art. If Hemingway strained, in the best Conradian manner, to *present* objective phenomena rather than explicitly render his subjective reactions to them, Stevens considered the "mere rendering of an object or scene . . . an imaginative failure." So observes Milton J. Bates in *Wallace Stevens: A Mythology of Self,* our second recent book under consideration.[2]

The relationship between reality and the imagination, of course, is at the thematic center of Stevens's poetry, and is the subject of most of the lectures collected in his sole volume of prose, *The Necessary Angel: Essays on Reality and the Imagination* (1951). Of the seven pieces in this volume, it is the earliest, "The Noble Rider and the Sound of Words," in which Stevens most fully and coherently explains his aesthetic theory. Poetry, he writes, is a phenomenon characterized by "the interdependence of the imagination and reality as equals." It is not a sedate interdependence but an active, even an agitated, one: for the mind, wherein the imagination resides, "is a violence from within that protects us from a violence without. It is the imagination pressing back against the pressure of reality." Yet Stevens does not mean to suggest that, during the writing of poetry, these two entities are at war with one another; on the contrary, the creation of poetry is, to his mind, "not a choice of one over the other and not a decision that divides them, but something subtler, a recognition that here, too, as between these poles, the universal interdependence exists . . . they are equal and inseparable." The measure of a poet is "the measure of his power to abstract himself, and to withdraw with him into his abstraction the reality on which the lovers of truth insist. He must be able to abstract himself and also to abstract reality, which he does by placing it in his imagination." (For instance, a poet may write about creativity, "the maker's rage to order words," by writing about a woman singing on the beach at Key West.)

If twentieth-century poetry is not all that it could be, Stevens suggests, it is because not only poetry but all of the arts have suffered, in modern times, from the "pressure of reality." Reality, in other words, has gained the upper hand over imagination. Why? Because the modern world, as Stevens sees it, is a world no longer able to maintain its belief in its chief imaginary construct (i.e., God), and therefore no longer able to wield the imaginative powers it once commanded. The things of the imagination, as a result, have become weakened, watered down, debased; "the idea of nobility"—to Stevens, a crucial element in poetry, and "imaginary" because it would not exist without a human mind to conceive of it—"exists in art today only in degenerate forms or in a much diminished state."

That Stevens does not consider such an abstract entity as nobility to be "real" does not mean that it is unimportant to him; without such "fictions" as nobility, it is clear, life would be meaningless. And this, in fact, is to him the essential function of poetry in the modern world: to provide us all with a "supreme fiction," a grand, subsuming illusion to take the place of God, and thereby to restore to life its meaning, or, rather, its semblance of meaning—which amounts, in his philosophy, to precisely the same thing. As he says at the end of "The Noble Rider," poetry seems "to have something to do with our self-preservation; and that, no doubt, is why the expression of it, the sound of its words, helps us to live our lives." Or, in the words of "The Man with the Blue Guitar,"

> The earth, for us, is flat and bare.
> There are no shadows. Poetry
>
> Exceeding music must take the place
> Of empty heaven and its hymns,
>
> Ourselves in poetry must take their place . . . .

I have used the word "philosophy," but Stevens, though he has been described as a philosophical poet, was no philosopher—at least not in the sense that the term is usually understood. His realm was that not of logic

---

2 *Wallace Stevens: A Mythology of Self,* by Milton J. Bates. University of California Press; 319 pages, $24.95.

but of intuition; as the title of one of his essays, "The Irrational Element in Poetry," suggests, he saw poetry as a discipline that transcends the boundaries of reason. When, in a late poem called "The Sail of Ulysses," he writes of knowledge—the sort of knowledge, naturally, that poets deal in—he distinguishes it unambiguously from reason:

> . . . knowing
> And being are one: the right to know
> And the right to be are one. We come
> To knowledge when we come to life.
> Yet always there is another life,
> A life beyond this present knowing,
> A life lighter than this present splendor,
> Brighter, perfected and distant away,
> Not to be reached but to be known,
> Not an attainment of the will
> But something illogically received,
> A divination . . . .

In his preoccupation with the imagination, Stevens recalls Coleridge, who (along with the other English Romantic poets) was an important influence upon his conception of poetry. In an essay entitled "The Figure of the Youth as Virile Poet," Stevens describes Coleridge as "defining poetry all his life"; and the fact is that Stevens, in both his prose and his verse, was continually doing the same thing. But he did not do so in the manner of a professional philosopher: like Coleridge, he was both brilliant and unsystematic, at times inconsistent in his terminology, never proceeding from theory but always from feeling.

Coleridge is hardly the only poet or critic who helped to shape Stevens's literary theory and practice. Indeed, *Wallace Stevens: A Mythology of Self* is largely concerned with identifying the ways in which various writers influenced him. Among these influences are Walter Pater and the Aesthetes, who were all the rage at Harvard when Stevens was an undergraduate there. Though Stevens patently had more regard for everyday reality than did the Aesthetes, he believed, with them, that the poet does not have a "social obligation" to anyone, that poetry's purpose is not to "say something" about life but to attain the nonreferential purity of music, and that the creation of a poem is no less important than any other human activity. The Aesthetes, moreover, must be given much of the credit for Stevens's often récherché diction, bizarre wit, and sumptuous imagery, as well as his Wildean affinity for paradox. The central idea of his *oeuvre*—that modern man must believe in something he knows to be a fiction—is, needless to say, paradoxical, and a number of his poems, like many of Wilde's epigrams, derive their effectiveness largely from the device of saying that X is not X, or X is the opposite of X:

> A. A violent order is a disorder; and
> B. A great disorder is an order . . . .
> —"Connoisseur of Chaos"

> This is form gulping after formlessness . . . .
> —"The Auroras of Autumn"

> We do not prove the existence of the poem.
> It is something seen and known in lesser
> poems.
> It is the huge, high harmony that sounds
> A little and a little, suddenly,
> By means of a separate sense. It is and it
> Is not and, therefore, is . . . .
> —"A Primitive Like an Orb"

> It is possible that to seem—it is to be,
> As the sun is something seeming and it is.
>
> • • •
>
> It is a world of words to the end of it,
> In which nothing solid is its solid self.
> —"Description without Place"

> It must be visible or invisible,
> Invisible or visible or both:
> A seeming and unseeming in the eye.
>
> • • •
>
> There was a myth before the myth began . . . .
> —"Notes toward a Supreme Fiction"

> A sunny day's complete Poussiniana
> Divide it from itself. It is this or that
> And it is not.
> —"Poem Written at Morning"

Along with the Aesthetic influence, of course, went that of the French Symbolists. From them Stevens, like most modern poets, learned a number of lessons, among them the value of mystery and ambiguity in poetry. Mallarmé's remarks on this subject, as quoted by Bates, might well have been written by Stevens himself, so well do they describe the way his poetry operates:

> The Parnassians take something in its entirety and simply exhibit it; in so doing, they fall short of mystery; they fail to give our minds that exquisite joy which consists of believing that we are creating something. To *name* an object is largely to destroy poetic enjoyment, which comes from gradual divination. The ideal is to *suggest* the object. It is the perfect use of the mystery which constitutes symbol. An object must be gradually evoked in order to show a state of soul; or else, choose an object and from it elicit a state of soul by means of a series of decodings.

By taking the Symbolist path in this regard, Stevens was, as Bates observes, rejecting not only the Genteel Tradition that had governed American poetry in his youth, but the Imagist revolution as well, whose principal criteria for effectiveness in poetry were simplicity and directness.

Stevens was never one to rush into print, and his first collection, *Harmonium,* did not appear till 1923, when he was forty-four. The book is distinguished by an air of modernist gloom, as exemplified by the final lines of its outstanding poem, "Sunday Morning":

> We live in an old chaos of the sun,
> Or old dependency of day and night,
> Or island solitude, unsponsored, free,
> Of that wide water, inescapable.
> Deer walk upon our mountains, and the quail
> Whistle about us their spontaneous cries;
> Sweet berries ripen in the wilderness;
> And, in the isolation of the sky,
> At evening, casual flocks of pigeons make
> Ambiguous undulations as they sink,
> Downward to darkness, on extended wings.

This anguish about the godlessness of the universe, however, is supplanted in succeeding volumes by the conviction that poetry can and must take the place of God as a principle of order and virtue. "I desire my poem," Stevens once wrote in a letter, referring to "The Man with the Blue Guitar," "to mean as much, and as deeply, as a missal." This determination is evident in one poem after another—in "The Idea of Order at Key West," for instance, wherein the woman singing creates a world:

> She was the single artificer of the world
> In which she sang. And when she sang, the sea,
> Whatever self it had, became the self
> That was her song, for she was the maker.
>   Then we,
> As we beheld her striding there alone,
> Knew that there never was a world for her
> Except the one she sang and, singing, made.

In developing the notions that are implicit in this poem, Stevens was in many respects a student of Nietzsche, who recognized the social and psychological benefit of the illusion of God and who said, as Bates reminds us, that "Art is with us in order that we may not perish through truth." Like Nietzsche, Stevens worried that the twentieth century's loss of faith in God would mean, eventually, the loss of faith in the virtues that God represented; thus, like Nietzsche, he was taken with the notion of an imaginary hero, whom Nietzsche called *Übermensch* and Stevens called "major man," who would embody the paramount virtues of the race. The idea of "major man" was introduced in Stevens's single longest poem, "Notes toward a Supreme Fiction," but is elaborated upon in other poems, including "Paisant Chronicle," wherein Stevens writes that the major men

>   . . . are characters beyond
> Reality, composed thereof. They are
> The fictive man created out of men.
> They are men but artificial men. They are
> Nothing in which it is not possible
> To believe . . . .

To the influence of Nietzsche, we must add that of two philosophers closer to home: William James and George Santayana. Both were professors at Harvard when Stevens was a student there; James published his book *The Will to Believe* less than a year before Stevens entered Harvard, and Santayana published *Interpretations of Poetry and Religion* the year Stevens left. In a letter explaining the attitude that informs the book *Notes toward a Supreme Fiction,* Stevens invokes the title of James's book:

> Underlying it is the idea that, in the various predicaments of belief, it might be possible to yield, or to try to yield, ourselves to a declared fiction.
>
> This is the same thing as saying that it might be possible for us to believe in something that we know to be untrue. Of course, we do that every day, but we don't make the most of the fact that we do it out of the need to believe, what in your day, and mine, in Cambridge was called the will to believe.

Yet, as Bates observes, Stevens goes beyond James. The philosopher of pragmatism had declared that it is sensible to believe in something that is not known for certain to be true, but which might, indeed, be true; Stevens declared that it is a good idea to believe in something one knows to be false. In taking this position, he was less in line with James than with Santayana, who saw both poetry and religion as fictions of human manufacture—worthwhile, to be sure, but fictions nonetheless.

It was in the Thirties that the convictions Stevens had forged out of these influences—and the poetry that he, in turn, had forged out of these convictions—had the roughest time of it. During the Depression years, Marxist critics habitually condemned Stevens as an elitist, even a fascist, for his refusal to join the vanguard of Socialist Realism by writing poems about enchained workers and bloated capitalist bosses. In *Owl's Clover* (1936), he succumbed to this pressure, in a sense, by attempting, as he put it, "to make poetry out of commonplaces: the day's news"—or, as he explained in a letter to a reviewer of the book, "to dip aspects of the contemporaneous in the poetic." Aesthetically speaking, the results of this experiment were not conspicuously successful; most of the poems in *Owl's Clover* fell far beneath Stevens's usual standard, and did not merit reprinting in *The Palm at the End of the Mind,* the definitive selection from his poetic *oeuvre.*

Rather than regard these poems, however, with the majority of Stevens's critics, as an unfortunate temporary descent into the maelstrom, Bates, while recognizing their literary weaknesses, nonetheless appears to perceive them as a major step in Stevens's development. His extensive discussion of *Owl's Clover,* furthermore, is accompanied by a scholarly disquisition upon the subject of Stevens's attitude toward Marxists—whom Stevens despised not because they were idealists but because they were not his *type* of idealists. Stevens saw himself as a visionary idealist, proceeding "by fits of visionary insight rather than calculation." Marxists, on the contrary, were bound by theory, by their own brand of logic, and claimed to know what they were headed toward: a perfect Communist state, as laid out in the *Manifesto.* Stevens found this sort of programmatic certainty to be at odds with reality as he knew it, not to mention at odds with his convictions regarding the proper function of the imagination. Yet at times, paradoxically, he seems to have seen his Marxist contemporaries as being far more in touch with reality and logic than he. Bates, in discussing these matters, sometimes appears disturbingly willing to accept this characterization of Thirties Marxism, seeing Stevens as the unrealistic, pure poet and the Marxists as the keen-eyed viewers of reality. One manifestation of this tendency is that Stanley Burnshaw—whose fatuous critique of Stevens "inspired" *Owl's Clover* in the first place, and provoked the contemplation of Marxism entitled "Mr. Burnshaw and the Statue"—is described by Bates as practicing "intelligent criticism." (In fairness it should be noted that Burnshaw, in later years, repudiated the views he held in the Thirties.)

These are not the only problems in Bates's book. He seems to look upon Stevens's poetic theory as being more rigidly and elaborately thought out than it really was, and to regard his poetic practice as having undergone a progressive development from one volume to the next in a fashion that—in one reader's opinion—is a bit too tidy to be thoroughly convincing. There are other flaws: Bates includes a substantial amount of biographical information but does very little with it; he goes on far too long about such matters as the history of leftist poetry in the early part of the century and the journalistic career of Richard Harding Davis (who he feels must have influenced Stevens's brief youthful foray into reporting); and he writes a plodding academic prose that makes reading this potentially absorbing study a wearisome chore. But these misgivings having been registered, it must be said that *Wallace Stevens: A Mythology of Self* does succeed, in many respects, in explaining how Stevens came to be the sort of poet that he was.

And what sort of poet, in the final analysis, was he? Decades ago, Yvor Winters labeled Stevens a "hedonist"—the idea being that Stevens's verse was solipsistic, that he was interested merely in his own sensations. Randall Jarrell, for his part, complained that Stevens had his head too far up in the heavens and not even one foot on the ground. But it is difficult for this critic, at least, to discover any justification for such complaints. Far from being preoccupied, in his poetry, either with himself or with dehumanized abstractions, Stevens is, rather, concerned throughout his work with celebrating the miracle of the human mind—its ability to create its own order, to conceive of beauty, to make moral discriminations, to take dominion over the things of earth—the genius of the sea, the slovenly wilderness. His is not the undisciplined joy-seeking of the hedonist or of the wielder of disconnected abstractions, but, on the contrary, the joy of the artist in his own ability to discipline the physical world around him in a comprehensible whole, to find—as Stevens writes in "The Sail of Ulysses"—"meaning in design / Wrenched out of chaos."

(*February* 1986)

Henri Rousseau and the idea of the naïve

by Rackstraw Downes

Eumaeus, Homer's swineherd, is surely the only person in the *Odyssey* who is totally without guile. Respectful, loyal, hospitable, conscientious, he lives in the hills in a hut he built for himself adjoining his pigsties; he avoids the town and considers the influence of the court as corrupting. His character indicates that culture's wistful love affair with what it called nature, the idea of the natural, must be very old, no doubt as old as culture itself.

This idea supposes a condition which existed before culture, and continues to exist outside of it and in contrast to it; the love of the natural also includes the thought, if it does not originate with it, that something may easily go wrong with what is too deliberately cultivated. Far from being merely the product of romanticism, this is expressed in the structure of language; from "art" derives "artificial," from "craft" "crafty," and Eumaeus first appears, no doubt with intention, right after that very worldly moment where Athena, simultaneously shocked and tickled to discover that Odysseus is telling her an elaborate lie, notes with pleasure that in terms of their talents for tactical deception he and she are a match for each other. Homer later reveals that this swineherd was a king's son, stolen when "so high" and sold into slavery. Was this elaboration of his character motivated by doubts as to whether such a person could really exist without breeding, the way some sceptics refuse to believe that Shakespeare wrote Shakespeare?

This seems likely, because in fact, as soon as it gets past a mere hypothetical yearning after nature, culture invariably reveals hesitations, ambivalencies, scruples. Like a dynasty, culture sometimes welcomes energy from outside itself, but it is also concerned to refine and protect itself. Roughly, the nineteenth century, with its taste for the exotic as well as the natural, was involved with the former, and the eighteenth century with the latter. C. S. Lewis remarked of the Tory writers like Pope and Swift that "the number of things they did not want to hear about is enormous." The Whig Addison, on the other hand, "wants to hear about everything." Still, his is a carefully defended inquisitiveness. When he writes about the old Border ballad *Chevy Chase,* product not of his own neo-classical culture but of a popular oral tradition, he does not praise it for enlarging the scope of his own taste at all; on the contrary, he defends it precisely by demonstrating that it passes all the tests of classical criticism. Thoreau, on the other hand, uses the contrivance of good writing to urge an uncontrived way of life, perhaps as an exit from, and certainly as a critique of, his own culture. In *Walden* he has an experience with an odd reflexive irony to it. This writer who wants to try a life divested of culture, meets in the process "a true Homeric or Paphlagonian man" whose own culture is so rudimentary as to be effectively nonexistent. Thoreau is intrigued, and becomes fiercely observant of this Canadian wood chopper. He is a discovery. One senses Thoreau's admiration, but it is underlain by mystification: "To a stranger he appeared to know nothing of things in general, yet I sometimes saw in him a man whom I had not seen before, and I did not know whether he was as wise as Shakespeare or as simply ignorant as a child, whether to suspect him of a fine poetic consciousness or of stupidity." It is as though Thoreau, meeting someone from the very country he himself is headed for, is perplexed as to whether he has found anything of value or not. He goes on: "A townsman told me that when he met him sauntering through the village in his small close-fitting cap and whistling to himself he reminded him of a prince in disguise." Here is the same image Homer used. Thoreau, trying to put his finger on nature itself, finds himself accounting for it as a clandestine form of culture. This implies that nature subjected to analysis is impenetrable, or it evaporates.

Schiller in his essay "Naïve and Sentimental Poetry" accepts this impenetrability as a given. This essay, which Thomas Mann called "the greatest of all German essays," divides all of poetry into two kinds over this issue of culture's fascination with the natural. Poets who live in a healthy, youthful society think and feel naturally, they themselves *are* nature; while poets who live in an artificial society *seek* the natural. The first are naïve, the second sentimental. Schiller's opening paragraphs constitute a searching inquiry into the phenomenon of the naïve. Nature itself Schiller leaves alone; he discusses it in terms of its affect, of the particular kind of emotion it produces in us, and the conditions under which the emotion is provoked. This approach seems inevitable: since nature consists precisely in what is not contrived, it cannot be aware of itself, nor does it define itself in ways that are perceptible to culture. "Nature," says Schiller, "considered in this wise, is for us nothing but the voluntary presence, the subsistence of things on their own, their existence in accordance with their own immutable laws." He goes on to make these points:

1) The appeal of the natural in objects or in human behavior is not aesthetic but moral. To demonstrate this he borrows an image from Kant; if we are enjoying the song of a nightingale and discover that it is actually only an imitation, our enjoyment, and the emotion Schiller is defining, would disappear. The natural appeals to us because of an idea it represents, not because of—and often in spite of—the form it takes.

2) The idea represented in natural objects—"the serene spontaneity of their activity"—is both an image of our own lost childhood and, as it reveals to us the unnatural in ourselves, an ideal toward which we aspire. Yet the perfection of these objects "is not to their credit because it is not the product of their choice. They accord us then the quite unique delight of being our example without putting us to shame."

3) When the love of the natural is occasioned by the presence of children and childlike folk we look upward, from the awareness of what has become actual in ourselves, at the potential that is in them. "In the child *disposition* and *determination* are represented; in us that *fulfilment* that forever remains far short of those."

4) When what we take to be naturalness makes us feel the restraint or artificiality—the invalidity—of culture, this indicates the presence of the naïve. This presence provokes

> those mixed feelings which the *naïve* mode of thought excites in us. It connects *childlike* simplicity with the *childish*; through the latter it exposes its weakness to the understanding and causes that smile by which we betray our (theoretical) superiority. But as soon as we have cause to believe that childish simplicity is at the same time childlike, that in consequence not of lack of understanding, not incapacity, but rather a higher strength, a heart full of innocence and truth, is the source of that which out of its inner greatness scorns the aid of art, then that triumph of the understanding is set aside, and mockery of ingenuousness yields to admiration of simplicity. We feel ourselves obliged to respect the object at which we formerly smiled, and since we at the same

time cast our glance upon ourselves, bemoan the fact that we are not likewise endowed. Thus arises the entirely unique phenomenon of a feeling in which joyous mockery, respect, and melancholy are compounded.

The twentieth-century taste for naïve art is a twist in the long story of this ancient antithesis of culture and nature, and what Schiller had to say about the naïve in 1795 is apropos today. The naïve in naïve art is not there by virtue of what the picture represents, since a naïve action or sentiment could just as well be depicted in a sophisticated painting. Rather, an equation is made between an unknowing technique and a pure heart. Thus, Philippe Soupault: "In order to paint Rousseau dipped his brush in his heart." If one can ignore the saccharine content in this metaphor, there is a point being made—the opposite of the one George Orwell was making about Salvador Dalí when he spoke of "a dexterity that goes no higher than the elbow." Rousseau bypasses the artifice in the arm.

In naïve art, then, style is a fixed moral issue; therefore it must be made clear that the unknowingness of the technique is not counterfeit, that it did not come about through laziness, incompetence, or contempt for the culture of painting, but through a true lack of awareness of what the culture is and how to acquire it. Much of the writing about naïve art consists of anecdotes about the artist's way of life and his distance from any cultural milieu, whether it be Wilhelm Uhde picking his way through some working-class Parisian *quartier* in search of the postman Vivin, or Elizabeth Bishop on some seedy block in Key West finding her first Gregorio Valdes in a barbershop window. The point is to establish the existence of an unbridgeable gap between the sources of culture and the place and frame of mind in which these artists work. The writer draws back the curtain to reveal that the nightingale—the nightingale of Schiller's example—is not an imitation. The seemingly discursive, picturesque writing confers on the artist exactly the opposite of an art school diploma or a fine arts degree, and it puts us in a frame of mind to enjoy the work, as Schiller puts it, "not because it gratifies our senses, nor yet because it satisfies our understanding or taste (the very opposite can occur in both instances), rather, simply *because it is nature.*"

Apart from the circumstantial evidence, though, it will be those moments in a naïve painting that proclaim the artist's ignorance—moments which might be taken in a sophisticated painting merely to reveal the artist's defects—that aver his genuine naïveté. This makes the question of what constitutes quality in naïve art quite problematic. Nevertheless, the artist's resourcefulness at such moments might be inspired, and will in any event give the painting its character. Also at issue is the question of intention. If naïveté consists in ignorance of the culture and isolation from it, how can naïve art demonstrate any definite character in relation to it? The naïve artist cannot intend his work as progressive, conservative, romantic, provincial, or whatever without understanding the layout of the existing culture—at which point he is no longer naïve.

There has always been ample confusion about the quality and intention—the character—of the work of Henri Rousseau, subject of an important retrospective exhibition at the Museum of Modern Art.[1] In his own day many Paris critics took him for a joke, while certain avant-garde artists and intellectuals were fascinated by him. Was he a naïve? Was he a Salon artist manqué? Was it that he "instinctively painted in the manner of four hundred years earlier?" Or is it that his style is only "apparently naïve" and that the

1 "Henri Rousseau," which originated at the Grand Palais in Paris, will be on view at the Museum of Modern Art until June 4. Carolyn Lanchner and William Rubin, of MOMA's Department of Painting and Sculpture, developed the exhibition, together with Michel Hoog of the Musee de l'Orangerie in Paris. The exhibition's catalogue, *Henri Rousseau,* was published by MOMA: 280 pages, $40 hardbound, $15 paper.

character of his work "clearly places him within the Post-Impressionist, Symbolist orbit?"[2]

Rousseau was an autodidact, he got no painting culture from any formal training. But this in itself does not make him a real nightingale. The British painter Francis Bacon is self-taught, but there is no question of his having failed to absorb the culture, nor of his painting lacking a definite character in relation to it. But the radically different opinions about the fundamental nature of Rousseau's art indicate that it has not found itself a clear-cut place. The definition of his art remains contested and contestable.

On entering the Rousseau show after looking at the work of his contemporaries what is immediately striking is the effect of brittleness everywhere. His forms acquire little weight in the middle or thickness at the edge. The earliest paintings, from the late 1880s, are three medium-sized woodland scenes, the execution of which is meticulous; one is a winter nocturne and it especially aspires to a degree of finish one associates with Salon painting. The woods take the form of a flat plane of trees, their branches or sparse foliage fanning out against the sky; quite small figures are placed flatly against these trees near their foot so that problems of spatial construction or the depiction of volumes are kept to a minimum. But there are awkwardnesses about the little figures, and the faces especially tend toward the simplistic. They are fancifully dressed; in one painting, the heads of a couple kiss in a diamond-shaped area which is framed by twigs and lit more brightly than the rest of the picture. These pictures, in their invariably clear-cut contours, the enumeration of each stereotyped leaf, the stylized swellings and undulating curves of the limbs of trees, and in the distinct feeling of *displacement,* as though one is not sure where one is—watching in memory some melodrama in a small-town theater, perhaps, where the conventions are all familiar but the lighting unnatural—emphasize decoration, costume, sentiment. In this, they distinguish themselves totally from any avant-garde nineteenth-century French painting that represents the outdoors; lacking the skills of the Salon, they reveal a taste one might call popular. Though more modest, more fastidious, and more graceful in a conventional way than the bulk of Rousseau's work, they are an indicative prelude to it.

Myself, Portrait-Landscape (1890) is Rousseau's first large, assertive painting. It is a picture of contradictions, and of stops and starts. The figure of the artist himself, as has often been pointed out, floats in front of the landscape in a quite different scale so that, in spite of the number of recognizable details, we are not in a world of realism. Nor, in spite of the artist's black suit, painted flat and with much attention to contour, are we in a congruous, connected world of flatness such as Gauguin had already developed. Elements that belong to the two different scales of the painting are not linked as the saints, donors, interiors, and landscapes all in different scales are linked—with sophisticated virtuosity—by a fifteenth-century "primitive." Nor are they contrasted to any telling effect, either in terms of form or imagery; in fact, there is enough indefiniteness about this conjunction that even those who wish it were deliberate can only describe it as "almost surely" so. The size of the figure has been drastically reduced, shortened from top down and bottom up, and narrowed from both sides. Was this done to reduce the disparity of scale between figure and landscape? In any event, in making his corrections, Rousseau did not bring the new sky color with which he narrowed the suit area down between the chimneys on the left of it or behind the trees on the right of it; he stopped short of those objects, leaving them against the original lighter sky. This is odd in a painting with much careful workman-

2 These points of view have been, or are, held by respectively: Wilhelm Uhde, a contemporary art dealer and writer who befriended Rousseau; Dora Vallier, author of a Rousseau *catalogue raisonné*; Kenneth Clark; and Carolyn Lanchner and William Rubin, authors of "Rousseau and Modernism," an essay in the catalogue to the present show.

ship in it, but it indicates that for Rousseau contiguity is no more a leading concern than congruity. Nor is proximity; does the shape of the beret resemble that of the cloud right next to it to any purpose? What can be said for certain is this: each has its own peculiar character as an isolated thing.

Here we meet the underlying assumption of Rousseau's mind, and the source of that brittleness that distinguishes his work. Things are not brought to an end, they stop dead at the contour; they do not positively attract or repel what is in front, behind, or next to them. Although they are not really heading anywhere, they bump into one another—because they live in a world of one-thing-at-a-time. Things in this picture are no more subject to modification by nature than they are by a firm idea of art. Space, volume, light, movement, wind, gravity, density, air mostly have no pronounced effect on Rousseau's objects; if they do it is an erratic, piecemeal one. His things are all on display in some sort of final form, logos of their own identities, insignia of themselves. Each one contributes its own bit of information. Rousseau's palette does not rest on his arm as it would when he works, it is tilted parallel to the picture's surface, so the names of his first and second wives can be clearly read. All the flags on the ship extend neatly out in a nonexistent wind, like the flags on the ships of John and James Bard, so they too can be clearly read. Rousseau's eyes and eyebrows are not attached to any imagined form of the skull, they stare out from the surface with mesmeric ferocity. In other pictures one sees that a red sun or a white moon is a fact not a force, it has no effect on anything. And in the one picture where the wind does blow, *Surprise!* (1891), it creates no confusion, but bends each leaf, branch, and blade of grass separately; nothing moves, and rain appears not as something that wets these objects, but as a separate sign of itself, in parallel strokes of dark varnish added after everything else.

If Rousseau paints each object with attention to its separate nature, so in choosing his imagery he selects things that have their own preexistent meaning, in the popular culture for instance, or the established facts of his own biography: the artist's beret, stereotypical sign of his profession—what other painter of the time showed himself wearing this stage prop?—or the Eiffel Tower, latest engineering wonder. He poses himself on one of the *quais* which he knew from patrolling them as a toll collector. His picture is an inventory of fixed symbols. What he paints is not what he discovers for himself in the continuum of life, which he then imbues with personal meaning, but what is already posing for him, and he accepts the face it puts on. His landscapes, as Tristan Tzara pointed out, are "souvenir landscapes"; they record some local landmark, some neighborhood spot. His mind is thoroughly exoteric, he paints what everyone knows—the regimental portrait, the latest fad in sports. His imagery, by the time of his self-portrait, has already divided itself into the realistic and the poetic; reality is a matter of pre-selected, accepted signs. Poetry—and this is also a conventional idea—is what is exceptional and someplace else; it comes in costume in the woods, and later on it will find its way to the jungle or the desert. Underlying the eccentric appearance of his paintings, Rousseau's imagery expresses the mind of an ordinary man with his daydreams.

The literalism of Rousseau's rain is found throughout his paintings in different, inconsistent forms. The connection between the real object and the flat canvas is a direct one; it bypasses the metaphor of any encompassing form. Leaves in the jungle, instead of turning their backs to the sun, turn them parallel to the canvas; flowers are seen in exact profile or from overhead, each bloom distinct. Trees which are too far away to allow their individual leaves to be represented turn into a kind of clogged texture, which often contrasts with the weightlessly flat surfaces of nearby buildings. When there are many things repeated like the windows in *Myself,* or the artists in *Liberty,* they get onto the canvas by a rubber-stamp procedure; there is no concept of such a thing as summary. But the literal flatness of the canvas has an opposite effect on volumetric forms; it creates bits of isolated metaphor without a context, and these account for some of Rousseau's most astonishing and fascinating successes: the provocative shapes of black dogs, striped cats, or striped football players, the black snake charmer, the horse in *War*, or the puffed-up shoulders of a lady at a wedding, and the bride's outrageous veil. These ungainly and aggressive things can be repellent, laughable, and wonderful at the same time. They are not only to be found in Rousseau, though. The larger of the two standing portraits of women is reminiscent of the colonial American portraitist Pieter Vanderlyn. Both artists deploy the huge flat fixed-contour shapes of their model's dresses in a similar way, fitting them on the canvas as a carpenter uses a board, wasting little. This shape they contrast with the decorative patterning of small flowers or floral patterns; and in both the faces are finished, with emphatic calligraphic elegance and barely any modeling, into an immobile certainty. The meaning of the resemblance can hardly be mistaken. We are looking at painting which uses only a primary vocabulary, with hardly any sense of metaphor. Anyone who has ever taught painting to a class of absolute beginners will recognize the symptoms. However, the comparison also shows Rousseau's extraordinary power: his imagination, his facility, his wit, his ambition, his panache compared to Vanderlyn's thin, stiff charm.

But it is impossible to mistake Rousseau for a deliberate master who preferred to work with this limited vocabulary, for he does not extrapolate from his successes. At the very end of his life in *The Dream* (1910) he paints a sonorously deep green cardboard jungle whose animal population is contained by a meshwork of foliage and flowers. To this he adds the unforeseen invention of Yadwigha on her couch floating in from stage-right like a diva on a gondola. But the nude itself is disappointing; ugly in the extremities, she has been subjected to poor and feeble modeling. One longs for some Modigliani to bring a released sensuousness to this figure without destroying her flatness. But if one were to start tampering with the nude, what is one to do with the storybook lions or the paper parrot? The picture lives by benefit of the accord between its naïve vision and its naïve technique, clues which leave us realizing that we cannot be any better satisfied than by its unrealization and its unreality.

It is interesting to follow Rousseau as a painter of landscapes. Given his predilection for literalism, and for flattening volumes into shapes, the depiction of the horizontal foreground planes of landscape will be a test of his inventiveness, and of how aware he was of the consequences of his style. *House on the Outskirts of Paris* is a good example. On the left of the painting Rousseau conceals much of his ground plane behind a low wall of short vegetation and three trees, and all the planes on this side read vertical. On the right he describes a road which runs straight ahead into the picture as though he were looking at it from well up in the air; it reads like a steep incline, spliced not too obtrusively to the side of a house in the middle of the picture. The side-by-side contrast of these two different approaches to space gives the pleasurable jolt of an unexpected solution. But it needs to be compared to, say, de Chirico's use of a rather similar construction in *Gare Montparnasse (The Melancholy of Departure)* (1914), where it becomes an element in the hands of a virtuoso whose architectonics are the source of his disturbing poetry. The Rousseau is dated c. 1902. In two landscapes of 1908, however, Rousseau has not explored any consequences of his idea. In *The Quai of Ivry* and its companion *The Fisherman and the Biplane*, the water and its embankment rise up disturbingly in front of the houses like the town walls of Lucca. And while the dirigible in the first picture floats beautifully through the air in perfect tonal pitch, the biplane in the second is a pasted-on catastrophe. In yet other landscapes like *River Bank* (1890) and *Flamingos* (1907), Rousseau bypasses construction by reducing the composition to a set of more or less parallel horizontal bands. *River Bank* has a shy, antique look, but in *Flamingos* Rousseau's imagination is liberated by his maneuver; painting four independent groups of signs with a mythopoeic simplicity, he gets a preposterous, tall-story effect. This is travel for the untravelled, travel as in childhood we thought it ought to be, fantastic travel as in Mandeville.

In his landscape constructions, then, Rousseau oscillates between the inventive, the defective, and the circumventive, without building on his discoveries, without making progress. In delighting in his successes one could say with Schiller that "their perfection is not to their credit because it is not the product of their choice."

In his jungle pictures which began around 1904-05, Rousseau reverts to the vertically oriented solution of his early woodland scenes, though often on a vast, commanding scale and with an entirely new flamboyance to the imagery. The whole canvas is covered with vegetation. In his catalogue essay "Rousseau in his Time," Michel Hoog compares these paintings to the completely covered canvasses of Monet's waterlillies or Cézanne's woods pictures of the park at Château Noir. But such a comparison draws attention to the fundamental differences. In Monet and Cézanne the surface of the canvas is a metaphor for space, a space which is envisaged as a preexistent, pliant whole; it can be infinitely modified and inflected in any place at any moment. Monet's stroke grazes imagined veils, varying their density, transparency, or luminosity. Cézanne turns and turns his edges so they thicken to an insistent palpability and weight. With both these artists imagery and space are simultaneous functions of one another. In Rousseau's jungles there is no vision of any space like that; space is a wall which remains scarcely modified as the ivy of his imagery spreads all over, unit by added unit, pressing flat against it. It is the natural solution for an artist to whom construction is an onus and who is, unlike the impassioned observers Monet and Cézanne, an armchair traveller whose imaginary voyages are set in motion by leafing through the *National Geographic*; it gives Rousseau full license to let fantasy and decoration take over. Rousseau's jungles are best when they are most flat and frontal as in *The Hungry Lion* with the red sun now looming behind the foliage, *The Merry Jesters* or *The Snake Charmer*.

In the catalogue essay by Carolyn Lanchner and William Rubin, "Rousseau and Modernism," Rousseau's work is placed "within the Post-Impressionist, Symbolist orbit." To get it there, comparisons are made to Seurat and Gauguin. But the resemblances drawn are superficial and fortuitous; they are not the resemblances of genus or species. The Post-Impressionists all severally invented a grammar of the whole painting; this grammar modified all the forms in their pictures. Equally, insofar as these forms can be considered as modifications of a naturalistic vision, they all help define the character of this grammar of the whole. This is not the case with Rousseau. His most unified pictures, his jungles, are not governed by any whole metaphor of space and form; they are held together by exclusion of any kind of form that might violate their inflexible frontality, and by the repeated piled-up overlappings of homogenous units of vegetation. Lanchner and Rubin also argue that Rousseau was a deliberate stylist who cultivated his naïve manner on purpose (in his life they allow him to have been really naïve). In framing their argument they attach great significance to Rousseau's little landscape sketches which they call "competent, even expert, impressionistic works," and which they take as proof that Rousseau could have worked in a different style had he wanted to. I seriously doubt this. In the first place, their description of these sketches is inaccurate. The sketches show no assimilation of Impressionism, being extremely dark, and exhibiting no concept of cast light or broken color. Rousseau does, however, generalize and summarize a bit within the different areas and leave their edges ragged and sometimes blur them, things he does nowhere else in his work. But these are nothing more than the natural, if not inevitable, results of working rapidly on a very small scale on projects which are only preparatory. If there were similar, more developed works on a larger scale one could, if one needed to, contend that Rousseau entertained the alternative of working either in a loose or a tidy manner, but no such works seem to exist. All the larger paintings that derive from the sketches are in fact organized into tidy, separated forms as a result of the equation Rousseau makes—typical of naïve painters—between the distinctness of each part and the finish of the whole. Lanchner and Rubin's argument is forced; their account of the work of this artist whom Dora Vallier called "an intruder" has an altogether Addisonian flavor to it; in effect they are saying "If Rousseau is interesting it must be possible to demonstrate that he is not a naïf but really a modernist."

The sophisticated artist who made an encompassing style out of the same characteristic that forms the basis of Rousseau's art was Miró. His series of paintings, beginning about 1918, of which *The Farm* (1922-24) is the best known, are made out of separately individualized units like Rousseau's. But Miró's compositions have none of the uncertainty about space that Rousseau exhibits when obliged to construct. Miró takes the implication of a device such as Rousseau used in *House on the Outskirts of Paris* and develops it into a principle of style: each thing is presented so as best to display its ultimate personality, whether that means looking at it in profile, or from slightly above or below, or from due overhead. In such a context any "wrong" perspective will look clearly deliberate, lending character, not uncertainty, to the whole. As Al Held once remarked of *The Farm,* "every object is in its own space." Miró admired Rousseau's work, and these paintings make a profound comment on its essential character as well as being a criticism of its indefiniteness. This relationship between these two artists might be taken to parallel the one Schiller perceives between the *disposition* of a child and the *fulfillment* of an adult.

Surely one of the first and best aestheticians of naïve art was Shakespeare. Many of his best-loved low-life characters, like Dogberry and Verges or "bully Bottom," show how inadvertent inventiveness may spring from ignorance and ineptitude. In the naïve play of "Pyramus and Thisbe" from *A Midsummer Night's Dream* the personifications of Wall and Moonshine are examples of this, and surely they would have appealed to Alfred Jarry much as Rousseau's *War* did. The Angel of Liberty and the Lion of Courage in *Liberty Inviting Artists to Take Part in the Twenty-second Exhibition of the Société des Artistes Indépendants* (1906), or the Muse in *The Muse Inspiring the Poet* (1909) are the somewhat schooled cousins of Moonshine and Wall. They introduce a level of humor into two pictures which might easily have become creaking contraptions of pompous attic allegory. But at the same time we must also remember that Shakespeare was not Peter Quince. In Shakespeare's (as opposed to Quince's) play the necessary clues are all in place for an audience to have a shared feeling about the overall tone. Such controls are not operating in the *Muse* or *Liberty* of Rousseau. No doubt Rousseau, whose whole life's ambition depended on the unjuried shows of the Indépendants for any sort of fulfillment, meant his *Liberty* sincerely. No doubt also that we appreciate not only the comic effect of the lion and the angel but the irony of all these independent painters dressed in uniform and each carrying a canvas of identical size. It is a satire on artists out of *The New Yorker.* The picture we actually see is mock-heroic, and because of that the pomposity inherent in Rousseau's presentation of his sentiment is dissipated and the picture carried by his brilliant patterns and decorative flair. It is one of his most sophisticated performances, comparable in its literary tone to the Restoration heroic plays which succeed, as William Empson pointed out, because "they are so close to their parodies." However, the literary sophistication of this picture cannot be considered intentional, because the appearance of some of the animals and figures in Rousseau's jungle scenes, which also derives from ineptitude, produces only a crippling effect of bathos.

In *War* there is no such problem. The *genre* of this wonderful picture is the grotesque, therefore any awkwardness or ugliness contributes to its effect. It belongs to a clan of images that includes Breughel's *Dulle Griet* and Posada's *Calavera de Don Quixote.* It makes one regret that Rousseau resorted more and more to the repetitious *horror vacui* of his walls of jungle vegetation and the concomitant stasis of their fauna. Here the marvelous horse, its underside skating along the horizon, is stretched right out across the canvas all striving head and legs and trailing tail, moving against an opposing pattern of tilted verticals, the sky filled with Bellona's smoking firebrand and the red clouds of horror, so much more intense than the cliché suns and moons—one, alas, with a face in it—of Rousseau's "exotics." This is the zenith of his mythopoeia. Below it, the blue sky of his wedding, the white sails of his boats, his regiment, his flamingoes, and his dream, form a galaxy of images whose categorical conceptions make available to us again the emotions of childhood; not, as Schiller would have said, sentimentally by depicting them, but actually, by embodying them in the form of the painting.

It is a pity in a way that Jarry commissioned Rousseau himself to make the lithograph of *War* for his and de Gourmont's magazine *L'Ymagier,* for the result was rather tame. One wonders what Posada would have made of it. The thought raises some interesting questions. Posada's art is much more secure than Rousseau's in technique, in artistic conception and in its social meaning. It is not naïve art but folk art, that is to say, for the people as well as by the people. These two categories have recently been lumped together, an Edward Hicks classed with a John Kane. Hicks, like Posada, was an assured artist, he had a workshop training in decorative painting (carriage doors, inn signs) and his work expressed a clear-cut Quaker ideology. There is probably a Durkheimian principle to be invoked here; artist and audience understood each other in one another's terms. Rousseau's world was nothing like so clearly defined. As Dora Vallier pointed out, his artistic ambitions split him off from his own working-class world, but he did not belong either in the artistic milieu to which his work had introduced him. Rousseau is often depicted as a man who painted only for the love of painting, another Ryder, but something else emerges from the facts of his biography which have been coming to light plentifully over the last twenty years. He may or may not have been, as Gertrude Stein put it, "a little small colourless frenchman with a little beard like any number of frenchman one saw everywhere," but he was certainly a man with enormous dreams, not just of tropical forests—that was the least of it—but of a glorious artistic career. There is only the meagerest record of any painting activity on Rousseau's part until the Prix de Rome winner and former director of the School of Fine Arts in Lyon, Felix Clément, moved to the house next door to Rousseau. The same year Rousseau painted a battle scene over a tracing taken from an engraved magazine illustration; two years later Clément helped to get Rousseau a copyist's card for the Louvre, something that would otherwise not have been so easy to come by. From his very first showing at the Indépendants he subscribed to a press-clipping service and pasted every notice of his work, however insulting, in a copy book. When the service sent him an announcement that a different Henri Rousseau, a Salon painter, had been awarded the Silver Medal, Rousseau had this title printed on his card. He had the vision of himself as a complete artist. He volunteered to teach at the Philotechnic Association, (where his pupils were mostly working men); there was the writing and publishing of a waltz, the writing and attempt to publish two plays, the *soirées* with their formal invitations, the letters to the state requesting a subsidy or the purchase of his exhibited works; and the explanations that, had his parents perceived his talent and educated him properly, he would be one of the foremost artists in the nation.

The contrast between Rousseau's "Salon-struck" ambition and his preparation, his equipment for the career he desired, is one of the fascinating things about him; the contrast holds in terms of what he really managed to assimilate from the painting culture as opposed to what he attempted in his work; the huge scale, the elaborateness, the variety in his imagery and his undertakings not only totally distinguish him from any other naïve, but they make him something of a trapeze artist without a net, a risk-taker, in comparison with whom a Hicks or a Posada is altogether convention-bound. So that, without deliberately striving for any revolutionary goals like the artists of the avant-garde, it gives him a certain chance spiritual affiliation with them. But the nature of his work and what it came to mean to these artists are two different things. (The latter is explored in great detail by Lanchner and Rubin.) The little twin portraits of Rousseau and his wife that Picasso owned, and always kept by him, have less artistry than the worst recent "Bad Painting." They have none of the cause and effect of a deliberate style, they bypass form-making, they are as indefinite as the conjunction of figure and landscape in *Myself.* They exist outside art, outside the painting culture, not as *art* but as a *challenge* to art. This is not what Rousseau meant but it is what Rousseau meant to the next generation. It took Picasso many years and some pretty drastic measures of breaking up and reassembling not just the grammar of painting but the grammar of the human face before he achieved through form-making a blatant, strident presence equivalent to these. Picasso's use of these paintings exemplifies precisely something Schiller said of naïve objects: "They accord us then the quite unique delight of being our example without putting us to shame."

At the time of the Galerie Charpentier's fiftieth anniversary Rousseau retrospective in 1961, Janet Flanner reported in *The New Yorker* on the state of Rousseau interpretation in Paris: "It is now supposed that the famous Montmartre banquet of honor given him by Picasso and Appollinaire at the Bateau-Lavoir was only an elaborate vinous farce. Since they so wonderfully built up his painting reputation as a joke, it is further deduced that once he was dead and they had the legend of his innocent genius laid at their door, like an exotic wreath, they had to revivify it out of shame and loyalty." Now it is certainly true that there is often some humbug in Rousseau criticism, that it has a way of turning into Rousseau veneration. Apollinaire, for example, is usually cited as a Rousseau champion, but actually during Rousseau's lifetime he wrote some of the best-aimed barbs against him to appear in print. His famous eulogy, which appeared four years after Rousseau died, is written with only half an eye on the paintings and one and a half on the pathos of the old man who made them. Flanner's explanation seems unnecessarily ingenious though. Rousseau's art and his career in art cannot help but provoke a braided reaction, just as much in us now as it did in the young artists during Rousseau's lifetime; among the elements that compose that braid might well be cheerful mockery at its childishness, admiration for its simplicity, and regret for our own lost innocence.

(*May* 1985)

The case of Roy Campbell

by Robert Richman

Of many selves we all possess
My meanest has the most persisted . . .

A shifty and insidious ghost,
Of all my selves he is the one,
Though it's with him I meet the most,
I'd go the longest way to shun . . . .

Within his heart, so chilled and squamous,
He knows I've but to sell my pride
To make him safe, and rich, and famous;
And he would fatten if I died.
—Roy Campbell, in "Reflections"

For the biographer or critic, there can be few tasks less appealing than the rehabilitation of a universally despised writer. At the very least there is always the risk that the odium heaped upon the writer in his lifetime will rub off on the author of anything written in his defense after his death. In the case of the South African poet Roy Campbell, who forged an uneasy place for himself on the London literary scene between the two World Wars, any reconsideration is made all the more difficult by the atrociousness of the poet's beliefs, the waywardness of his actions, the general disarray of his life, and the perversity of his character. It was all this and more that prompted Stephen Spender—Campbell's foremost literary and political enemy—to denounce him categorically in 1946, when the antagonisms of the prewar years were once again being revived with a new intensity. In a private letter to Campbell, written in June of that year, Spender spoke of him as an "infamous slander[er] . . . a liar . . . an empty-headed boaster, a coward, a bully and a Fascist."[1]

A few days later Spender's review of Campbell's *Talking Bronco* in the weekly *Time and Tide* pronounced a similar judgment: ". . . with Mr. Campbell," Spender wrote, "we are face to face with something that puzzles us everywhere—a mixture of pretentiousness, violence, glamour, cruelty and ignobleness." The immediate cause of Spender's outburst was the poem that gave *Talking Bronco* its title. In this poem, Campbell created a figure called MacSpaunday. This was clearly an acronym for the circle of left-wing writers—MacNeice, Spender, Auden, and C. Day Lewis—that had dominated the literary scene in the Thirties, all of whom Campbell accused of having written Communist propaganda for financial gain. Spender's response to this attack was not merely an expression of personal rancor, however—though there was plenty of rancor in it. His words also expressed nearly twenty years of literary London's collective hatred of Roy Campbell.

But if Roy Campbell has passed into liter-

1 The letter is quoted in Peter Alexander's *Roy Campbell: A Critical Biography,* Oxford University Press, 277 pages, $27.95. Peter Alexander is also the editor of *The Selected Poems of Roy Campbell,* Oxford University Press, 131 pages, $19.95.

ary history as a villain, it is not due solely to the prejudices of his enemies on the Left. He himself played the largest part in his downfall. He was, after all, an active supporter of fascist causes, an outspoken racist, and a sworn enemy of democracy. His hatred of blacks, Jews, and "Bolshies" had disfigured much of his poetry and his two prose autobiographies, *Broken Record* and *Light on a Dark Horse.* Like Hemingway he was an aficionado of bullfighting, soldiering, and guns ("the smell of cordite, next to that of carnations," he wrote, "is the most exciting perfume in the world"), and he combined these tastes with a showy masculinity that, again like Hemingway, was often the mask of an uncertain virility. Stalking London in a toreador's cap and cloak, as he did in his later years, and boasting, in *Broken Record,* of writing only in red ink, Campbell often behaved as if he were little more than a figure in a disagreeable literary farce.

The question that needs to be asked about Campbell is not whether he was in many respects a repugnant and repulsive character. Of this there can be little doubt. The question is whether there is anything left in the wreckage of his career worth saving. In the twenty-five years since his death in a car crash in Portugal, his work has been very little read. Indeed, if Campbell is remembered at all today, it is for his translations of Baudelaire and St. John of the Cross. The publication of Peter Alexander's two books marks the first attempt in many years to revive interest in his life and work. Alexander, a South African scholar now living in New Zealand, has clearly set out to rehabilitate this most notorious of his literary countrymen. It must be said that he does not really succeed in this endeavor. But the story he tells is an interesting one, despite his special pleading on Campbell's behalf. Along the way he reminds us of what it was that constituted Roy Campbell's appeal in the first place. Whether this will spark a revival of interest in Campbell's poetry remains to be seen. The obstacles, after all, are formidable.

"My ancestors," Campbell wrote in *Broken Record,* "cleared out of Britain at the first whiff of the nineteenth and twentieth centuries." Campbell believed it was to his distance from what he considered the poisonous progressive culture of modern Europe that he owed his happy childhood. He certainly did not loathe his parents in the manner so familiar to us in the lives of the Englishmen of his generation. His mother seems never to have failed him, and his father, a wealthy Durban doctor, "spoiled" his young son by the remarkable device of establishing an open account for him at the local bookshop. Though Campbell did not do well in school, he took to drawing and poetry at an early age. He was not the accomplished athlete he boasted of being in his memoirs. (He was not many of the things he boasted of being.) He was more aesthete than athlete in fact. But already idealizing the life of action, he tried, at sixteen, to run off to war. His mother caught him before he could board the train.

Two years later Campbell left Durban for Oxford, hoping to pass Responsions (the first of three examinations required for the B.A. degree) in Greek and enter the university. He failed, and took the blow badly. He did not fail, however, to adopt the fashionable tastes of the day, among them heavy drinking, floppy hats, homosexuality, left-wing politics, and *Wheels,* the literary magazine of the Sitwells. In a letter at the time, he grandly declared:

> We have passed the ages of Romanticism, Parnassianism and Symbolism. We have come to the age of Psycho-Analysis—futurism.

Though nearly all of these tastes—except for drinking and homosexuality—would be modified or abandoned, Campbell's attraction to Oxford's bohemian life was not simply another passing phase. It was consistent with his idea of himself as a superior outsider. Campbell professed to detest mediocrity and was therefore thoroughly at home with the bohemians' scorn for the mundane values of the middle class. Once Campbell realized that the bohemians merely substituted their own brand of mediocrity for that of the middle class, he turned on them too. Recalling, in *Broken Record,* a trip to Paris in 1919, Campbell observed that "[e]verybody was his own genius," and that he

> had the impression of a vast communal conspiracy to dirty and destroy all that is vertical, clear, or distinguished in human or artistic values [and] qualities that were within everybody's reach, naïveté, skittishness, naughtiness, and affectation were exalted, as faith, enthusiasm, and reverence were debased.

Such sentiments did not prevent Campbell from acquiring a taste for the poetry of the French decadents, however, and, more importantly, the poetry of Paul Valéry, whose *Charmes* provided him with a model for his later lyric poems.

In 1922, Campbell married Mary Garman, who was to remain his wife until his death. Mary, a beautiful, masculine, and strong-willed woman, picked up Campbell in a London restaurant; and it was she who, for the rest of their lives together, directed the household, paid the bills, and had most of the affairs—in her case, lesbian affairs. Peter Alexander writes that in "the early stages of their married life Campbell suffered a good deal from jealousy" over Mary's past "friendships" with women, and Campbell made his wife suffer too. On one occasion he held her out of a window in his arms, threatening to let her drop three stories to the ground. Campbell's jealous rages notwithstanding, Mary's sexual character must have somehow appealed to Campbell's own sexual uncertainties. In an unpublished section of *Light on a Dark Horse,* he spoke frankly of "my awful physical shyness of girls, which has been the bugbear of my existence."

In a converted cowshed the Campbells called home, located three miles outside the Welsh village of Aberdaron, Campbell composed *The Flaming Terrapin* (1924), the long, book-length poem that established his fame. He was only twenty-three.

> The Ark is launched; cupped by the streaming
>   breeze,
> The stiff sails tug the long reluctant keel,
> And Noah, spattered by the rising seas,
> Stands with his great fist fastened to the wheel.
> Like driven clouds, the waves went rustling by,
> Feathered and fanned across their liquid sky,
> And, like those waves, the clouds in silver bars
> Creamed on the scattered shingle of the
>   stars . . .

The poem uses the Noah legend as the basis for a tale of the earth's regeneration after a great disaster. Its extraordinary exuberance and linguistic richness brought its young author considerable acclaim. The Irish poet AE wrote that he knew of no other writer who had mastered "such a savage splendour of epithet or could marry the wild word with the wild thought." Edward Garnett and other reviewers praised it in similar terms. Desmond MacCarthy also admired it. The book had been published by the prestigious firm of Jonathan Cape at the suggestion of Augustus John and T. E. Lawrence. (Campbell had sat for John when the poet was nineteen; a reproduction of the portrait adorns the jacket of Peter Alexander's biography.)

The poem was not without flaws, of course. Its governing idea is only loosely integrated with the poem's verbal felicities. Metaphor functions strictly as a medium of speed and rhythm, and Campbell's alertness to color and sound is similarly divorced from the poem's intellectual substance. Most important, the poem is overburdened by the weight of its legend-theme; its relevance to the modern world seems questionable at best. But readers of the time responded to the poem's direct—indeed, almost unmediated—expression of Campbell's electric personality. The South African poet's lush world, galvanized by a distinctive and exotic vitality, seemed, as one critic put it, a breath of fresh air for a demoralized postwar England. "The Terrapin," wrote Campbell in a letter to his parents, "is the symbol of masculine energy." There were apparently readers enough who agreed.

Following the success of *The Flaming Terrapin,* Campbell returned to South Africa a celebrity. One of the first things he was asked to do was give a speech to the home folk. Campbell agreed, and proceeded to praise Wilfred Owen, Siegfried Sassoon, and D. H. Lawrence. He dismissed the war as a piece of "sentimental hysteria," and he called the province of Natal a "grocer's paradise." His imprudent tongue deeply shocked his conservative audience. Scarcely a week went by without one scandal or another. When Campbell founded the literary review *Voorslag* ("Whiplash") with William Plomer, they promised to "sting with satire the mental hindquarters of the bovine citizenry of the Union." Campbell kept the promise. He relentlessly chided the South Africans for everything from the "fetish that rules the country—colour prejudice," to their literary criticism, which was said to be "either in its infancy or in its dotage." Campbell resigned after just three issues, following squabbles with the furious backers as well as with Plomer, whom Campbell accused of wanting to start a colonial outpost of Bloomsbury. (He probably wasn't wrong about that.) "The Freudianised Boer," said Campbell apropos his break with Plomer, "is a dismal figure." Campbell left South Africa, licking his wounds, in December 1926, only two and a half years after his return there.

In the final days before his departure Campbell penned his parting shot at South Africa, a satire called "The Wayzgoose" that successfully combines arrogance and good humor about his disenchantment with his native land.

> Attend my fable if your ears be clean,
> In fair Banana Land we lay our scene—
> South Africa, renowned both far and wide
> For politics and little else beside.

In England once again, Campbell settled into what would become a fixed habit—reversing his opinions on everything. In London, blacks were now transformed from oppressed, mistreated heroes to hypochondriacal, servile, demanding crybabies. South Africa was no longer a boorish, culturally philistine hellhole but a beautiful, sane, and sorely missed paradise. Campbell's systematic alienation from wherever he happened to be at the moment enabled him to see himself as a perpetual victim. This in turn prompted him to adopt whatever attitudes he felt were necessary to the combative self-defense of the outsider. Plomer understood this bizarre psychology when he wrote: "It was as if he felt he had to make enemies in order to see himself as a victim and at the same time a hero—or almost as a martyr and a saint."

The volume *Adamastor,* published in 1930, contained many of the poems Campbell wrote while still in South Africa. "To a Pet Cobra," written in 1926, is one of his first serious experiments with the theme of self-martyrdom and self-glorification.

> There is no joy like theirs who fight alone,
> Whom lust or gluttony have never tied,
> Who in their purity have built a throne,
> And in their solitude a tower of pride.

A month later Campbell wrote "Tristan da Cunha," which explores the same subject with admirable self-restraint and with a greater command of poetic artifice.

> Exiled like you and severed from my race
> By the cold ocean of my own disdain,
> Do I not freeze in such a wintry space,
> Do I not travel through a storm as vast
> And rise at times, victorious from the main,
> To fly the sunrise at my shattered mast? . . .
>
> We shall not meet again; over the wave
> Our ways divide, and yours is straight and endless,
> But mine is short and crooked to the grave:
> Yet what of these dark crowds amid whose flow
> I battle like a rock, aloof and friendless,
> Are not their generations vague and endless
> The waves, the strides, the feet on which I go?

When the poem was first published in the

New Statesman, T. S. Eliot wrote a letter to the magazine (published on October 22, 1927) praising Campbell for his "remarkable mastery of meter and language." Thus began an important friendship for Campbell, the immediate result of which was the publication of *Adamastor* under Eliot's Faber imprint. The book, certainly one of Campbell's best, contained many of the "African" poems that would eventually find their way into W. B. Yeats's *Oxford Book of Modern Verse* and Philip Larkin's *Oxford Book of Twentieth Century English Verse.* Even though Campbell already had a reputation as an obnoxious show-off and gadfly, the book was generally praised. Desmond MacCarthy called it a book destined to be famous. Arnold Bennett hailed Campbell as a "master of words." In America, Allen Tate declared it "a distinguished book."

Campbell's return to England, alas, was not as happy as the reviews that greeted *Adamastor.* In August 1927, the Campbells, having been befriended by Harold Nicolson, were offered the gardener's cottage at Long Barn, the Nicolson residence, free of rent. It was, according to James Lees-Milne, Nicolson's biographer, "a disastrous move," for the Campbells "would bring them much distress . . . repay their hospitality with hostility and . . . give unwelcome publicity to their sexual predilections." In a matter of weeks Mary Campbell and Vita Sackville-West (Nicolson's wife) began a protracted affair that, according to both Peter Alexander and James Lees-Milne, devastated Campbell. After some ugly scenes, Mary (who by this time had already borne two daughters) finally returned to Campbell, although she would harbor strong romantic feelings toward Vita for some years afterward and write her imploring, explicit letters. It is hard to believe that Campbell was entirely surprised by this affair, however. That the Nicolsons were both homosexuals was well known to their literary friends, and only a dullard could have construed an invitation to Long Barn as a gesture of disinterested generosity toward a bright young poet. Peter Alexander reminds us that Campbell and his wife were "a strikingly handsome pair." Nicolson, to begin with, did not feel let down. After listening to Campbell's account of his life he proclaimed him "another Rimbaud." At any rate, Campbell, as his biographer writes, "had to adjust to the idea of a wife who was no longer wholly his . . . [and] Mary had to adjust to the idea of a husband who needed her more than she needed him." "It is hardly coincidental," Alexander adds, "that Campbell in several poems referring to the period calls Mary his 'sister.'"

Campbell's revenge and public martyrdom over the Sackville-West affair once again took the form of a poem, this time a dismal satire called "The Georgiad." Like "The Wayzgoose," it is an attempt to cause pain to his enemies. Yet because Campbell felt genuinely desperate about Mary, and somehow inferior to his reviled subjects, the satire fizzles.

> It was a voice of 1930 model
> And in Bloomsbury accent it could yodel
> Between its tonsils drawling out long O's
> Along its draughty, supercilious nose:
> Or coo in satire gentle and polite
> To fill the soul of Humbert with delight . . .
> His voice thus tried, our hero turns about
> And in the mirror, with a joyful shout,
> Seeing his new physique, decides to patènt
> The whole machine, in which, so far from
>   latent,
> Both sexes rampantly dispute the field
> And at alternate moments gain or yield.
> This was no neuter of a doubtful gender,
> But both in him attained their fullest
>   splendour,
> Unlike our modern homos, who are neither,
> He could be homosexual with either
> And heterosexual with either, too—
> A damn sight more than you or I could do!

By reversing himself about his own homosexuality, the poem becomes an act of self-denial; by ill-using his poetic gifts (Campbell himself later called the poem "coarse, swinging doggerel") Campbell made his poem an act of self-destruction as well. Predictably, Campbell's enemies were delighted by its failure.

In the spring of 1928, publicly humiliated by Mary's betrayal of him, Campbell was once again off and running, this time to Martigues in Provence. Campbell wrote pathetic letters begging Mary to join him. Much to his surprise, she did, arriving in the small port town in May with the couple's two daughters. But Mary's return scarcely represented an affirmation of their love. She returned only because Vita Sackville-West's interest in her had fallen away. Along with pursuing a literary career, Sackville-West was at the time carrying on no less than five other affairs.

Whatever the underlying reality, Mary did return, and the period of calm that ensued enabled Campbell to write some of his most serene and technically accomplished poems. In many of them, the exotic element is replaced by the first hints of his growing interest in Christianity. Like T. S. Eliot's entry into the Anglican Church a year earlier, Campbell's turn toward Christianity was an attempt to escape, through religious faith, what he deemed to be the harsh realities of the modern world. And again, like Eliot, it was also an attempt to transcend a disastrous marriage. The religious imagery in the exquisite sonnet "Mass at Dawn" (written in 1929 and included in *Adamastor*) suggests that Campbell was abandoning his earlier stance of fierce and proud isolation for the "cool planes" where the possibility of companionship exists:

> I dropped my sail and dried my dripping
>   seines
> Where the white quay is chequered by cool
>   planes
> In whose great branches, always out of sight,
> The nightingales are singing day and night.
> Though all was grey beneath the moon's grey
>   beam,
> My boat in her new paint shone like a bride,
> And silver in my baskets shone the bream:
> My arms were tired and I was heavy-eyed,
> But when with food and drink, at morning-
>   light,
> The children met me at the water-side,
> Never was wine so red or bread so white.

During this period Campbell also returned to the theme of isolation, but the terms and tone are much more temperate and lucid than they had ever been. This development may well derive from the new peace he had forged with Mary, whose calm, often impassive, image appears again and again in the sonnets written in Provence.

> When gathering vapours climb in storm
> The steep sierras of delight,
> Wings of your hair I love to form
> And on its perfume soar from sight.
> For in those great black plumes unfurled
> The darkest condor of my thought
> May stretch his aching sinews taut
> And fling his shadow on the world.
> When sick of self my moods rebel,
> The demon from his secret hell,
> The eagle from his cage of brass,
> They have been lent such scented wings
> Over the wreck of earthly things
> In silence with the sun to pass.

The sharp and pure language of "Wings" is representative of the entire volume *Flowering Reeds*, published in 1933. It is Campbell's best book. Not only is the poet's mastery of language at its peak in this collection; he also displays a wider emotional scale. The sureness and self-reliance of tone that Campbell had perfected in *Adamastor* is contrasted in many of the poems of *Flowering Reeds* by new doubts and hesitations. With an unexpected and disturbing self-awareness, Campbell begins to elaborate in verse the truth of his own deeply divided nature.

Before tracing the way this divided nature expresses itself in *Flowering Reeds*, however, we must first look at the other book Campbell published in the same year: his first prose autobiography, *Broken Record*. In it, Campbell gives free rein to his deepest and darkest prejudices. The result is some fairly repellent reading.

> Whoever invented the word 'rights,' especially conjugal 'rights,' should have been passed through the Inquisition, which after all had its beneficial uses . . . it has no meaning at all, but only a vague, infectious, hypnotic effect on Saxons, Jews and Quakers, who would sooner fight for their 'rights' than for a living idea, or a person, or a King . . . .
>
> I am all on the side of the natural human relationship of slave and master. No colour feeling ever existed until slavery was abolished. . . .
>
> I disagree with Plomer's ideas about Rhodes, as I have always disagreed with him about the criminality of the whites. If one wants to make sensations about that sort of thing, Saxon America is the place to go, with its lynchings, etc. . . .
>
> The clinical attitude penetrates into every branch of thought. From the amount of advertisements dealing with dyspepsia, bad-breath, smelly arm-pits, flat feet, blenorrhoea, piles, obesity, constipation, varicose veins, etc., one's first idea of London is as an enormous hospital ward; and the idea of illness and disease as the normal state becomes patent in everything from quack medicines to literature. The idea is generally spread by Jews or Quakers who accept the idea of original sin, and uncleanness, physically, morally, and intellectually, as far as it concerns the white man. The biggest anti-white alarmist bureau in London is run by a well-meaning Jew and a crowd of Quakers. Passionately negrophile and misanthropic at the same time, it publishes anything that would dirty the reputation of the white man, whether it comes from the side of fanatical over-domesticated bourgeois or from the far more powerful Jewish submarine torpedoes. I am no pogromite myself. One can forgive the Jews anything for the beauty of their women, which makes up for the ugliness of their men. But I fail to see how a man like Hitler makes any "mistake" in expelling a race that is intellectually subversive as far as we are concerned: that has none of our visual sense, but a wonderful dim-sighted instinct for dissolving, softening, undermining, and vulgarising.

"Dissolving, softening, undermining, and vulgarising" were, Campbell goes on to say, the hateful products of the twentieth century's two characteristic forms of government: Communism and democracy. Campbell made little distinction between the two. Both, he felt, were based on the corrupting ideas of egalitarianism and moral relativism, and both encouraged the mediocrity he so detested. The "tragic symbol of the Decline of the West," Campbell wrote in *Broken Record,* was—astonishingly—Charlie Chaplin, who "sneaked into the most august and sacred places, and stood picking his nose in the middle of Western culture." For Campbell, Chaplin represented Western civilization's death wish. He derided power, authority, and faith, and he embodied all the "poisonous" intellectual trends of the modern era, from Freud's legitimization of the son's wish to usurp the father to the democratic idea that all men—Jew, black, and white—are created equal.

It is worth recalling, in this context, that around the time that Campbell was giving the world these reflections, T. S. Eliot was expressing some very similar views on liberal democracy and its culture in the lectures he was delivering at the University of Virginia under the title *After Strange Gods.* (These were published in 1934, and never reprinted.) It may be that in an observation Eliot offers us in this work we shall find a key to the contradictions that divided Campbell in his work of this period, and probably through his entire career. Eliot is commenting on the differences (as he then saw them) between poetry and prose:

> I should say that in one's prose reflexions one may be legitimately occupied with ideals, whereas in the writing of verse one can only deal with actuality.

Nothing could better state the distinction between the hateful "ideals" that are upheld in *Broken Record* and the actuality that is reflected in *Flowering Reeds.* Indeed, in Campbell's case the difference between the two kinds of expression is so great that he often seems hopelessly at odds with himself.

What makes this split literary personality even more curious is Campbell's complete awareness of it in *Flowering Reeds* and complete suppression of it in *Broken Record*. In a poem called "The Gum Trees" from *Flowering Reeds,* Campbell uses the image of an avenue lined on opposite sides by trees that initially seem to merge in the distance.

> Far on the sky, with crests aflame,
> The tapering avenues unite,
> And to a single target aim
> The keen velocities of sight . . .

But the "impetus their beauty breeds" towards the blissful peace of "some less transitory world" is only fleeting. By stanza thirteen we read:

> But as the gloom around them fades,
> The old hallucination flees,
> They swiften through the rushing shades
> Their endless marathon of trees;
>
> The winds they wrestled with are thrown,
> The miles they trekked are spurned and dead,
> But there before the blazing throne
> They blacken into shapes of dread,
>
> And on and on without control
> Still in the same direction tread:
> They, too, have dreamed they sought a goal
> When merely from themselves they fled!

By the end of the poem, with early hope now revealed as an "hallucination," the poet blithely accepts his fate.

> Their giant skeletons of shade
> Are blackly charred upon the eye,
> In motley rags of gloom arrayed
> They wear the scorn of earth and sky.
>
> The dusty winds begin to sweep,
> The distance stretched before them lies,
> Antaeus-like from caves of sleep
> Their old antagonists arise.

The somber sonnet "The Secret Muse" also deals with Campbell's painfully divided self.

> Between the midnight and the morn,
> To share my watches late and lonely,
> There dawns a presence such as only
> Of perfect silence can be born.

If anything forced Campbell's muse into hiding, it was the bitter foe within himself.

Broken Record also focuses on Campbell's abiding hatred of poets and literary men. His aversion became so profound that Campbell claimed it as the reason he fled to Provence. Not only was the region bereft of writers, but Campbell himself would not gain glory there as one. Instead, he would be loved, he writes in *Broken Record,* "due entirely to my prowess with horses and cattle. . . ." In later poems Campbell would complain often of what he called the "rabies of the brain" and—the title of one of his poems—"The Virus of Literacy." This is the man who spent so many hours of his youth in the Durban bookstore.

But Campbell's greatest attack on his literary side in *Broken Record* takes the form of ruthless excision: nearly all of it is left out. Instead, we are treated to Campbell's feats of strength, his running with bulls, battling with pythons, shooting buck, and so on, all carefully, often beautifully, rendered. At one point in *Broken Record* he interrupts a disquisition on shooting to ask: "What has all this got to do with my progression as a poet?" He answers:

> Everything. My eye, even shooting an antelope at five hundred yards, ordered the sinew in my arm and finger to see, to design, to trigger, to fire, to kill: and it ordered my other members too . . . . If I like Cervantes and Camoens apart from other poets [it is because] they are both soldiers and their images are not literary . . . . There is nothing, no difference at all, between a verb and an act.

Clearly, Campbell's "prose" side cannot talk about poetry—indeed, anything—without resorting to the rhetoric of action and violence; all is reflexes, muscles, killing. There is no difference between a verb and an act.

When Campbell and his wife and two daughters moved to Spain in 1933 he was more estranged from the literary community than ever. He was also without money, and without prospects for getting any. All he possessed was an extremely fragile marriage. The political confrontation that was brewing in his newly adopted country offered him yet another cause. When Campbell and his wife converted to Catholicism in 1934—a move, one would think, in the direction of serenity—it turned out to solidify Campbell's growing political commitment. To be a Catholic in these circumstances was to be political.[2] Perhaps Campbell knew this. At any rate, it came home to him quickly enough when in 1936 his confessor was shot dead on the street and he himself was severely beaten by left-wing Assault Guards. However justified Campbell's fury about these incidents was, it had an adverse effect on the poems he wrote during this period, which were published in a volume called *Mithraic Emblems* (1936).

> I never felt such glory
> As handcuffs on my wrists.
> My body stunned and gory
> With toothmarks on my fists . . . .
>
> And four of those Red bastards
> To hold one wounded man
> To all the staring rabble
> Proclaiming thus my clan.
> ("In Memoriam of 'Mosquito'")

These lines are actually some of the better ones in the book. Most of the poems suffer from an obscure religious symbolism that seems oddly disconnected from the feelings the poems contend with. Yet others—"Christ in Uniform," "Hot Rifles," "Junction of Rails—Voice of the Steel"—show a brutal realism, in which "holy excaliburs" will cleanse Spain of Communists.

Campbell's mixture of militarism and Catholicism appears again, at interminable length, in "Flowering Rifle," the epic-length poem about Spain published in 1939. Campbell is no longer content, as he says in another poem from this period, to "go stark: and let my meanings show." But this does not mean that he will state his faith, or even assert it; he wishes to impose it, along with a number of other things, and the result is a mania of purification that is truly terrifying.

> The hatred of the Cross is their Disaster,
> Than the great flood, a cataclysm vaster:
> Thinking to tear it down they tore the Sky,
> A rain of blood, and lightning from on high,
> And the great thunder, headlong and terrific,
> When Abel stretched his length to the Pacific,
> The land a murder, and the wind a cry:—
> And hence a War *for* War, to the last breath,
> The Sword he came to bring, the Sword of
> Death!
> No "War-to-end-War" (and beget ten more!)
> To "fight for Peace," the Babylonian Whore,
> The turtle-winged Sow that comes to farrow
> Blood baths for which the ocean is too narrow;
> A war for eagles—not for turtle-doves
> Henpecked to bleeding corpses by their loves!
> A war for warriors, not for pacifists
> To tear the living womb with gory fists
> Who rape, castrate, and torture, and deplore
> With uplifted hands the very name of War!
> And well may they abominate the Sword,
> The bared and naked vengeance of the Lord—
> And curse the Soldier, his, the human brand,
> That came to lop the sacrilegious Hand,
> The root of godless vermin from the land.

This is a writer out of control. In Campbell's five-thousand-word poem not one of his obsessions is omitted.

---

2 It was also a release from the couple's tormented sexual lives. In his memoir *As I Walked Out One Midsummer Morning,* the British poet Laurie Lee gives this vivid description of the newly converted Mary Campbell: "And in her, for the first time, I saw the banked up voluptuousness of a young and beautiful convert, holding to this single passion in which all hungers were answered and all doubts quietly put away. Here, romantic love was kept on ice, sealed by an unfaltering spiritual flame, and accompanied by a vocabulary of torment, physical denial and ecstasy which promised an eternity of sensuous reward . . . ."

> But the old world is "braver" than the "new."
> Can use it as its foot-stool or its shoe:
> Or when it rots as it's begun to do,
> As a sharp knife can cut that Stilton through,
> Cough though the scientist or squirm the Jew,
> Or stink, abjectly dead, the poets too.

None of these lines, by the way, is included in Peter Alexander's excerpt of the poem in the new *Selected Poems,* yet they are essential to our understanding of it. Alexander's fifty-five-line excerpt is perhaps the only sustained passsage in the entire poem that is somehow inoffensive, and it leaves the reader with the impression that Campbell had written nothing more than a rather bland version of *The Flaming Terrapin.* But Alexander omits the offending lines for good reason: for the reader who is unable to share any of Campbell's perversity, the rhyming couplets fall into a dreary hum. Gone is Campbell's exacting attention to the shape of lines and sound of words, the hallmarks of *Adamastor* and *Flowering Reeds.* In place of the vitality that characterized *The Flaming Terrapin* and the "African" poems is a blatant litany of revenge, a fervor to destroy the objects of the poet's hatred. And replacing a vigorous satire on the follies of contemporary literary and political life is a fantasy that envisions its subjugation and death. In "Flowering Rifle" the "tapering" avenues of the prose writer and poet in Campbell do indeed unite—and the prose sensibility wins out. The result is pure nihilism.

By mid-1939, with war imminent, Campbell's fascist beliefs were abruptly put aside when he joined the British Army. In a matter of months, he disavowed his view that fascism was the sole upholder of the spiritual values he cherished. It is Peter Alexander's view that the Hitler-Stalin pact caused Campbell to reverse himself once again. Although it may have been the only intelligent political decision Campbell ever made, let us not forget the real reason for it: Hitler, by selling out to the Russians, was not enough of a fascist for him. But like his counterparts on the Left who also reversed themselves as a result of the pact, the decision allowed Campbell the opportunity—or at least the hope—of beginning the postwar years on a new footing.

In 1941, Campbell declared that the English people are "greater, nobler, and better than ever before in history," their nation "the healthiest . . . alive!" But his literary enemies remained unforgiving. "A member of the Axis, I believe," said Augustus John upon meeting Campbell again, and Robert Nichols called him "that horrid fascist." No one seemed to care that Campbell was now a proud soldier in the Royal Welch Fusiliers. He wrote at the time:

> And if the dreadful hour should chime
> For British blood, and steel as grim,
> My clock will wake, and tick the time,
> And slope his arms and march—and I'm
> The one to fall in step with him.
>
> ("The Clock in Spain")

Campbell here shifts into a contemplative mode, as he does in "Heartbreak Camp," a haunting, desolate ballad which suggests the grief of a man in need of yet another ballast, but unwilling to entrust himself to one.

> Red as the guardroom lamp
> The moon inspects the trees:
> High over Heartbreak Camp,
> Orion stands at ease:
>
> With buttons lit, for Sentry,
> He challenges who's there
> Acceding all the entry
> Whose passport is Despair. . . .

And in "Rhapsody of the Man in Hospital Blues," Campbell's gentle self-mockery about his increasing age barely covers his deep misgivings about the fate he has been assigned—or that he has assigned himself.

> From Notting Hill to Prince's Gate
> I'd started breaking-in my stick
> And of my new, three-legged gait
> Acquired the quaint arithmetic . . . .

That though he seemed a drunken lout,
Less of a comrade than a weight,
I had no further choice or doubt
But to accept him as my fate . . . .

Gone was the thunder of great herds,
Lost was the lilt of marching men,
And void the bandolier of words
That feeds the rifle of my pen . . . .

We must be silent when men mutter,
We must keep calm when tempers rise,
And when we're shoved into the gutter
It's we who must apologise.

To have one's Cross laid on inside
Abates no ardour in the strife
Though something in us might have died
Yet something more had come to life.

For all the poignancy of these lines, the something that "had come to life" was not original poetry, for Campbell all but renounced it in his last decade. Peter Alexander provides us with no adequate clues about this decision (the biography on the whole contains very little material about Campbell's last decade), but it certainly seems as if Campbell himself had finally given up on all attempts to speak in his own poetic voice. In 1951 a second autobiographical volume called *Light on a Dark Horse* appeared. It is not as vitriolic and vengeful as *Broken Record,* but it sheds scarcely any light on its subject either. Its digressive, artless narrative consists almost entirely of embroidered or wholly fabricated accounts of travel adventures and personal exploits. Once again the poet and the poetry are, for the most part, censored out.

Campbell's actions at this time became as trivial as his words. When the aging poet bloodied Spender's nose at a reading sponsored by the Poetry Society in April, 1949, and when he supposedly slapped Geoffrey Grigson in the BBC canteen because of Grigson's attack on Desmond MacCarthy (to whom Campbell owed his job), the furors that erupted were tinged with pathos. Interestingly, it was the Grigson fray that won for Campbell the admiration of Edith Sitwell, who had had a long-standing feud with Grigson. Concerned at this stage of her life with little more than settling old scores, Sitwell adopted Campbell as her noble knight-errant—or dupe—whom she would send out to fight her petty literary squabbles. Sitwell returned the favor by writing a preface to the third volume of Campbell's *Collected Poems* (published by The Bodley Head in 1957) in which she called him "one of the very few great poets of our time."

Campbell devoted himself in the years after the war to translations, primarily of Baudelaire and St. John of the Cross. His translations of St. John of the Cross were published in 1951 to wide acclaim. The literary world embraced Campbell for the first time in nearly twenty years. Significantly, it was for poems that were *not* written directly out of Campbell's own experience.

There is, however, a distinctly personal element in certain of these translations. The St. John poems, for example, can be seen as the most important gloss on Campbell's fight against the hysteria of his earlier life. With their seemingly effortless and breathtaking clarity and devotional purity, they embody Campbell's final, willed effort to remove himself from the material and political world that had nearly destroyed him, as the following excerpts indicate.

To chase a quarry so divine,
I had to soar so high and fine
That soon I lost myself from view . . . .

Nor keep me bound and struggling here
Within the bonds of living breath . . . .

The man who truly there has come
Of his own self must shed the guise;
Of all he knew before the sum
Seems far beneath that wondrous prize . . . .

The best known poem in the collection is "Upon a Gloomy Night," printed here in its entirety.

Upon a gloomy night,
With all my cares to loving ardours flushed,
(O venture of delight!)
With nobody in sight
I went abroad when all my house was hushed.

In safety, in disguise,
In darkness up the secret stair I crept,
(O happy enterprise!)
Concealed from other eyes
When all my house at length in silence slept.

Upon that lucky night
In secrecy, inscrutable to sight,
I went without discerning
And with no other light
Except for that which in my heart was burning.

It lit and led me through
More certain than the light of noonday clear
To where One waited near
Whose presence well I knew,
There where no other presence might appear.

Oh night that was my guide!
Oh darkness dearer than the morning's pride,
Oh night that joined the lover
To the beloved bride
Transfiguring them each into the other.

Within my flowering breast
Which only for himself entire I save
He sank into his rest
And all my gifts I gave
Lulled by the airs with which the cedars wave.

Over the ramparts fanned
While the fresh wind was fluttering his tresses,
With his serenest hand
My neck he wounded, and
Suspended every sense with its caresses.

Lost to myself I stayed
My face upon my lover having laid
From all endeavour ceasing;
And all my cares releasing
Threw them amongst the lilies there to fade.

How far Campbell is from the image-clogged lines of *The Flaming Terrapin,* the obscure symbolism of *Mithraic Emblems,* and the political squalor of "Flowering Rifle," and from what he called, in 1933, the "human lineaments" of fascism. Campbell wrote like a man released from the burdens of earthly experience. He finds no occasion for venom and revenge. These translations—begun at the age of thirty-nine and completed at fifty—are Campbell's best work, the work that now seems most likely to survive.

Given the complex and divided nature of Campbell's life, it is no wonder that he proves such a formidable challenge to the writers and critics who have attempted to write about him. Nearly everyone who has accepted this challenge has had some stake in his beliefs and actions, even when those beliefs and actions were the objects of attack. From Sitwell to Spender, no one has been able to separate the judgment of the poet from that of the man.

Unfortunately, Peter Alexander suffers from much the same handicap. He is guilty of special pleading for his literary compatriot. This special pleading takes the form of sweeping aside the more repugnant aspects of Campbell's personality by claiming that they were merely a pose. Thus, a lifetime of beliefs, politics, and action is said to be nothing more than a "realistic mask" which "must be torn aside before an attempt is made to see Campbell as he really was becomes possible."

This view often prompts Mr. Alexander to misrepresent his material. For example, in the two paragraphs he devotes to *Broken Record,* he dismisses Campbell's Hitlerism as a "mildly approving reference to the dictator." Regarding the reception of *Broken Record,* Alexander writes that

> the bourgeois-shockers (and nearly everyone else) believe[d] Campbell when he claimed to be in favour of Mussolini, and against nearly everything from machinery to Charlie Chaplin.

Alexander begins his chapter on 1933, the year of *Broken Record,* this way:

> Campbell began 1933, the year Hitler came to power, with a sense of deep foreboding. In January the poet wrote presciently to C. J. Sibbett, 'the year nineteen thirty-three promises to be the dirtiest since the war—the Europeans are becoming barbarians again, I fear, and rapidly, too.'

This leads the reader unfamiliar with *Broken Record* (one, that is, who has only read Alexander's sparse quotation from it) to believe that Campbell felt 1933 to be the "dirtiest [year] since the war" because of Hitler's coming to power. This is manifestly untrue.

Campbell's purification fantasies of the late Thirties are described by Alexander in these terms.

> He longed for a simpler world, with a Romantic longing that is reminiscent of D. H. Lawrence's constant dreams of a 'colony of escape.'. . . It seems clear that Campbell expected the approaching conflict to culminate in an all-destroying Armageddon, and that the triumph he hoped and longed for would be the triumph of Resurrection. . . . After the holocaust, Campbell liked to believe, there would be left the green world of cowboys and ploughboys and poets.

According to Mr. Alexander, Campbell only rarely made decisions, especially political ones. Most often, people and events acted upon him: ". . . the battle lines were being drawn," "the cause had sought him out," and so on. "In Altea in late 1934," he says at one point, "the issues were more academic than real," but even if they were real "[t]he Campbells read no papers and owned no radio [and the] mail was unreliable at best."

Of Campbell's trip to Italy in the fall of 1938 (embarking on Mussolini's proud new ocean liner, the *Rex*), Mr. Alexander remarks that

> Campbell had always had a deep love of Latin literature and for all things Roman; he immensely enjoyed being a tourist in the city of his new faith.

This suggests that Campbell was at heart really something other than the sought-after celebrity-author of "Flowering Rifle," an avowedly ideological guest who remained in fascist Italy until March 1939. It does not surprise us, then, when Mr. Alexander remarks that the extremism of "Flowering Rifle" is evidence only of "the simplicity of [Campbell's] belief that [the poem] would aid Franco's cause."

Nor does Mr. Alexander adequately come to terms with Campbell's very uneven *oeuvre*. Alexander's selective quotations do little, in fact, to aid us in understanding Campbell's life and work, and very often they mislead the uninformed reader. For a judgment of Campbell's poetic accomplishments, at any rate, we would do better to turn to Mr. Alexander's edition of Campbell's *Selected Poems*.

The editing of a volume of selected poems need not be governed by the question of how adequately it represents the poet's entire *oeuvre,* but rather by the criterion of excellence alone. And in this Mr. Alexander has done a splendid job. His selection contains all of Campbell's best lyrics and even the choice excerpts from the longer poems is generally the right one. (Though his book might have contained a wider selection of Campbell's translations, especially those of *St. John.*) Poems like "Mass at Dawn," "The Gum Trees," "A Jug of Water," and the "Mary" sonnets represent the superb core of what is indisputably a fine collection by a genuine poet.

Peter Alexander's discrimination in assembling this *Selected Poems* has made possible, for the first time perhaps, the kind of disinterested judgment of Campbell's poetry that it has so desperately needed for a very long time. The *Selected Poems* increases the stature of a poet whose immense technical skill and vibrant, exotic eye will no doubt surprise and inspire a generation of readers and poets for whom he is, if not altogether obscure, at least shrouded in mystery and myth.

In "The Olive Tree I" Campbell wrote that "The enemy who shaped his thews/ . . .

is inherent to his will." The poet's continual reversing of his opinions, the debauching and degrading of the noble ideals of his youth—heroism and nobility—by dragging them through the mud of fascism, and the violent attacks of the "prose" Campbell on the poet, all undermined Campbell's reputation in the way no left-wing conspiracy ever could. Campbell was not, as his wife Mary suggested in her preface to the Penguin edition of the St. John poems (1960), tyrannized by the modern world. He was tyrannized by himself. It seems to have been Campbell's bizarre wish that he become not just a famous poet, but a famous ruined poet. Only now, perhaps, are we in a position to determine the extent to which he succeeded in this ambition.

(*September* 1983)

"I am alone": Le Corbusier, bathrooms, and airplanes

by William H. Jordy

A suitcase found in a closet in Le Corbusier's Paris apartment at 24 rue Nungesser-et-Coli after his death contained seventy-three sketchbooks neatly ordered. They include a mélange of sketches and notes: on designs in progress (not only for architecture, but for paintings and sculpture as well), travel observations, rough drafts or outlines for writings or talks, diagrammatic plans for exhibitions, vituperations against those who crossed him, and philosophical musings—all mixed with the jottings of daily routine: telephone numbers, appointments, things to be bought, things to be done. He referred to the sketchbooks as "une chose active." They are a fascinating record of the day-to-day actions and thoughts of genius on the run, often telegraphic and fragmentary in brusque memoranda and scribbled notation; they also show Le Corbusier grasping a moment free of pressure for rumination and for making elaborate drawings of things seen or imagined.

The handsome four-volume publication of these pocket sketchbooks, the joint enterprise of the Fondation Le Corbusier, which owns them, and the Architectural History Foundation, reproduces each one of the four thousand and thirty-nine pages on which there is so much as a single word or tentative sketch.[1] Those in color appear in color. Printed captions in French beside each page make Le Corbusier's scrawl legible. These are, in turn, supplemented by English translations at the front of each volume, and by admirably terse but informative introductions to the contents and context of each of the sketchbooks by Françoise de Franclieu.

At last, we are privileged to participate in this *chose active* which, although often visible to Le Corbusier's collaborators on the site, he tended to keep pretty much to himself during his lifetime. As early as 1952, however, there is a reference in one of the sketchbooks to the possibility of publishing them. Some time later, with an assistant, he began ordering them chronologically. To his handwritten labeling of the cover of each sketchbook with its date and principle contents (not always completely accurate, because he sometimes returned to sketchbooks partially filled) he added more imperious cataloging by stamping each with the kind of bold stenciled font used on shipping crates. He favored such stenciled letters for identification, doubtless for their ambiguity as items both read and also intensely experienced as objects-in-themselves. For undiscernable reasons the letters A to T organize the sketchbooks in a sequence of series of various lengths. Numbers beneath run continuously from "A-1" to "[T]-70" (the last

---

1 *Le Corbusier Sketchbooks,* preface André Wogenscky, introduction Maurice Besset, notes Françoise de Franclieu. The Architectural History Foundation with the MIT Press in collaboration with the Fondation Le Corbusier, 1981-1982, 4 vols., approx. 2,000 pp., 4,039 illus., many in color, $500

actually only showing a "70" scratched in pen in a crude approximation of stenciling). Three more sketchbooks, initially overlooked, but inserted into the grand scheme with "bis" numbers, bring the total to 73. There are gaps. The volumes open with a sketchbook for 1914, although Le Corbusier presumably began to use such pocket notebooks as early as 1907. Moreover, none exist for the important years 1919-1929 or 1936-1945. Two, which were with Le Corbusier in his cabin at Cap Martin overlooking the Mediterranean when he went for his fatal swim in 1965, were filched. Others may be missing. But fragmentary as the record is, the rows of sketchbooks from his suitcase nevertheless illuminate the interplay between daily incident and creative act in Le Corbusier's career and with an immediacy that is unparalleled for any other major twentieth-century architect.

Le Corbusier would have approved of the way in which the image of each sketchbook, photographed to actual size, provides its own laconic introduction. The series of battered artifacts appears as though lifted one by one from the suitcase—abraded, foxed, creased, bent to the body. Laconic fact was always Le Corbusier's starting point. The first sketchbooks are covered with cardboard, a cloth spine and perforated pages. In 1930, the initial spiral binding appears and soon thereafter takes over. With his enthusiasm for the machined entity, he must have welcomed the metallic spiral and the literalism of this kind of sketchpad, which is quite bluntly asserted as a pile of drawing paper protected by cardboard covers.

Browsing through the sketchbooks calls forth a spectrum of themes, any one of which ramifies in unexpected ways. Consider, for example, a subject so important to Le Corbusier's theory as modern technology. It was Le Corbusier who attacked traditional eclectic architecture of the 1920s by asserting that the modern house, properly considered, should be "a machine for living in." He put forward this idea in articles in *L'Esprit Nouveau* (which he edited with the Purist painter Amedée Ozenfant in the early Twenties) and popularized it in the bundling of these articles in *Vers une architecture* (1922), which was destined to become the single most influential volume on architectural theory in the twentieth century. He dismissed as having "eyes that do not see" those whose interest fixed on columns, pilasters, metopes, swags, and the rest of what he regarded as the irrelevant baggage of traditional architecture, instead of such "modern" artifacts as ocean liners, automobiles, and airplanes. He dotted his staccato text with images of current transportation machinery, so that glazed eyes might begin to see.

From such an enthusiast one might expect to find many allusions to this aspect of modernity in the sketchbooks. But it does not appear in the way that one anticipates. Although the period of Le Corbusier's greatest exhilaration with the machine is missing from the sketchbooks, the years from 1919 to 1929, one expects more. True, he is impressed with the flock of dock cranes in Rotterdam during a visit in 1931: "to our Dutch friends," he writes in a sketchbook, "put your school of architecture in the harbor on an old steamer." Harbors and steamships are endlessly fascinating to him. Skyscrapers attract both praise and blame. As might be expected, he is least kind toward what he regarded as the desecration of his design for the United Nations Secretariat (his preliminary scheme was turned over to the American Wallace Harrison for development): "the morguish light behind the blue glazing of the UN skyscraper; air-conditioned in the middle of August. [The] artificial everywhere, away from the conditions of nature." He occasionally notices what used to be called "good design" in such items as modern outdoor lighting standards. He wants to export them to Chandigarh, the new capital of Punjab in northern India that he is building. The Bhakra Dam is one of his design projects at Chandigarh, but, traveling in Spain in 1931, he voices his concern: "Watch out for Electricity—progress: destroyers of a people who are in a state of sublime equilibrium unique in the world today." His regard for modern technology is only occasionally evident throughout the sketchbooks, and when it does appear it is edged with skepticism.

For one who is often vulgarly understood as wedded to a standardized, mechanized world, Le Corbusier can more frequently be found in the sketchbooks taking the opposite tack. "Oh sociologists of minimal housing," he asks, "why don't you study the stages of the minimum heart?" Following a lecture in Sweden, he recalls his response to a question from the audience: "'Funktionelle!' Here it is, Messieurs . . . . OK, sure, sure! But what do you want to tell me? About laundry-lists, or about the heart?" On an early trip to the Netherlands, he had been impressed by the "total harmony" evident in the use of its land, but returning in 1958 it seems depressingly "Funktionelle . . . . constipated, finished. There is nothing left to do but die . . . . paradise (of imbeciles): we'll be happy (we're not going to have a lot of fun! we'll sing psalms, with our tits sagging to our knees) Amen!" It is the United States that really draws his wrath for its "disproportion" in everything. It "floods the world with its stupidity and *human mediocrity.*" None too happy anyway at having been held in New York overnight because of plane trouble, he looks from the bus carrying him to the airport in the glum "morning twilight, at the gloominess of the idiotic skyscrapers, then the *modern* ones, the 'post-UN' ones, smooth, sharp, sad, stupid, enormous, a gigantic and multiplied texture, void of spirit. These people *feel* nothing. They live '*modern,*' a brutalizing life."

So Le Corbusier's attitude toward the standardized, mechanized aspects of modern life is far from one of automatic approval. But then the careful reader of *Vers une architecture* knows as much. If, in the Twenties, Le Corbusier rated the work of the modern engineer over that of the common architect, it was because the engineer showed the way to the "new spirit." It was the architect imbued with this spirit who would ultimately "touch the heart." Two aspects of the modern world, however, do engage him repeatedly in the sketchbooks: bathrooms (along with other tiny spaces that are elaborately equipped) and airplanes.

In a *wagon-lit* in 1928 he drew a quick sketch plan of the compartment, using his sketchbook to measure its length: "8 times this sketchbook . . . . All the hardware is superb." On another occasion, "Sleeping-cars 'Train bleu' July 19, 1956," he measures adjacent doors of sleeping compartments for the kinds of clearances they provide to the passageway, and to one another. In Bogotá he measures a room in the Hilton-Sheraton sort of hotel, together with its furnishings. He is pleased by it efficient compactness. He measures as well the Hotel Janpath in New Delhi, designed by an American, and the Hotel Khayam in Baghdad. Aboard the *Vernon S. Hood* he draws the stateroom fittings and toilet; aboard the *Etoile de Mer,* the stateroom and its wall lamps, which impress him for their neat fit and flexibility. He sketches a toilet and bathtub at the Hotel Plaza in Brussels. "Constellation October 27, 1951/the toilet + sink are astonishingly comfortable with their small dimensions + lighting/the sink basins of stainless steel . . . I must at all costs get drawings of this equipment." In a similar vein: "Delhi–Bombay plane at 10:15-10:30 in the morning/We are flying over very beautiful country . . . Write to Bhabha Tata who supplies *hardware* for Air India planes (WC lock/hooks/aluminum/lamps etc." At "16 nov 57 Luynes [Touraine] chez Martin" he sketches all the modern bathroom equipment at the house where he is staying. And again, staying with José Luis Sert in Cambridge at the start of his work on the Carpenter Visual Center at Harvard, he sketches and measures the bathroom. Visiting Pierre Jeanneret's quarters in India, where Jeanneret was assisting his cousin at Chandigarh, he draws the stand-up WC with footprints on its oval orifice, and the sitz-bath tub with an enclosure so high as to make it something of a seat in a tiny cell.

As fascinated as Le Corbusier was with bathrooms, one might expect that he would have been quite as concerned with the kitchen, that other domestic room which was so rapidly undergoing mechanization and modernization during the period. But not at all: no kitchen attracts his ruler, nor does any kitchen equipment call up the sketches so often inspired by the anatomical implications of bathroom equipment. Not only did the anatomical overtones of the bathroom attract Le Corbusier, but also its implications of solitude and contemplation. The kitchen makes no such appeal.

If the sketchbooks show his rapt examination of the modern cell, with its elaborate services shoehorned to fit, they also show his continuous interest in the subsistence cell. He recalls his youthful tour of Italy in 1907, when he was enamoured of the visual distinctness of the monks' cells ranged around three sides of a court at the Monastery of Ema (Charterhouse of Galluzzo) near Certosa. These cells were to have a profound effect on his work. There is the ovoid cell for meditation and study in the Ozenfant studio of the early Twenties, hung up in a corner of the studio and reached by a metal ladder-stair similar to those used for servicing machinery (the place for action complemented by the place for contemplation). There are the images of airplane cockpits in *Vers une architecture.* There is the furniture-like apartment building in Marseilles, his Unité d'Habitation, standing on squat legs and receiving the apartment units as (in his own images) drawers pushed into a dresser or bottles into a rack. And, to come full circle, there is his Monastery of La Tourette at Evreux, near Lyon, with its cornice of monks' cells.

In the sketchbooks the cell that receives his principal attention is his own cabin for retreat at Cap Martin. The project as a whole consists of a series of small cabin-like living units climbing a precipitous rise out of the Mediterranean on the Côte d'Azur—an Unité tilted, so to speak, to let the drawers fall out in a terraced rectangle. (They would be "condominiums" today; in fact, this densely packed community, where each cell is separately expressed, as in Le Corbusier's ideal monastery, is the prototypical condominium.) Above this sloping and stepped field of densely packed units he built a cabin for himself. It was close by but in a superior position, and alone. A number of pages in the sketchbooks are devoted to this cell of wood and rough stone, and to studies of its spartan, built-in cupboards, wall lamps, and furniture meticulously Modulored, according to his patented scheme of harmonic measurements, to the limited space. He twists the WC on a forty-five-degree angle, with its reservoir hung on the exterior wall of the house outside the bathroom, the better to make compact the arrangement inside. He asks his builder to find him a wall-hanging hospital basin, "small model."

"I am a loner desiring silence, a great worker. I am seen nowhere." So he confides at one point. Even when the occasion is one of mingling, as when he received an honorary degree at Cambridge in 1959, he shows himself isolated. "CAROLUM EDUARDUM LE CORBUSIER" introduces the occasion, and below this simply "(!)," then ground plans of the winding procession and of the platform, with Le Corbusier's seat indicated by a fat dot in relation to the Chancellor's, and two views of the procession. One of these shows the mace-bearers and Chancellor striding before him, all others receiving honorary degrees behind in a bunch led by Henry Moore. He marches alone and centered—positioned like the cabin at Cap Martin. From a window above the procession, a figure pops out, arms akimbo, crying "à bas l'Académie!!"

The second pervasive theme of modernity in the sketchbooks is even more emphatically centered in modern technology: the airplane. Here again technology leads him to search for the ways in which the machine can be integrated into human experience, an integration out of which, he believes, the only authentic modern culture can come.

Le Corbusier seems never to have lost

that initial sense of the romance of the airplane. "Beirut January 6, 1959, airport," Le Corbusier writes, ". . . the planes =*shining* aluminum *silvery* colors (= bright, luminous, optimistic) the flags and signs are painted in full strength: Blue white red Holland / Green white-orange Indian." There is real passion in his enthusiasm for the airport, and an odd exuberance, considering the date. He goes on to speculate about the use of "gleaming aluminum finely riveted" and "bold coloring" for the Bhakra dam and powerhouse. At Palim airport in New Delhi in the spring he notes, "The airplanes in the flowers." Why not an airport with flowers? "The total runway / the flowers / the impeccable airplanes / the macadam / the sea / the flowers." The terse oscillation in Le Corbusier's thought here, between the poetics of nature and those of the machine, is characteristic. He is more hard-headed in another airport: "*Nice* July 24, 1954. How about proposing to Air France to let Corbu outfit an airplane." On several occasions he sketches the clip-on interiors of the planes in which he is flying, and he studies the compactness and refinements of their hardware and bathrooms.

In fact, the themes of cell and sky are intimately linked. The cabin for solitude and meditation that he most frequently mentions in the sketchbooks is his seat in the plane. He is on one of his many trips to Chandigarh, with other stops along the way. "[By] Plane 2½ hours Paris Rome / 4½ Rome Cairo / 9 Cairo Bombay / 3¾ Bombay Delhi . . . I am arriving in Delhi." Most would feel wilted; not Le Corbusier. "I have never been so relaxed and so alone, engrossed in the poetry of things (nature) and poetry pure and simple (Apollinaire's *Alcools* and Gide's *Anthologie*) and meditation." "*Airplane 6:15 PM* Paris *time* . . . these first six hours in Flight have been a paradise. I am *alone* (with myself) *free* . . . . I read, I think, they offer me whiskey: one, then two. I am free, no one nor any thing is bugging me." The mood is momentarily broken when he fishes from his luggage an article critical of Chandigarh written by "cretins," but the mood returns as he watches the sun set and stars begin to appear. "I am on the Paris Bombay plane, 8 o'clock in the evening, having left Paris at 2:00 PM." How he marks the time! "I am in a state of perfect equilibrium, perfect serenity, almost elation . . . And here I am in Paradise, in the air like a bird . . . ." On a flight from Paris to Geneva, he is immersed in the "calm sea Heaven! limpidity, Fluid Simplicity. Immanence! Below, down there? Filthiness, conflicts, disputes, hatred, antagonism." But there is an hour to go, time to read Gide's *Thesée,* "to change atmospheres. To be young again!!" All too soon it is over. He has landed, once more, "down below." On an Ahmedabad to Bombay flight, he muses wryly, "Corbu is all over the world, traveling, his dirty raincoat on his arm, his leather satchel stuffed with business papers, with razor and toothbrush, brilliantine for a few hairs, and his suit from Paris, a temperate place, which clothes him here in Tokyo or in Ahmedabad (without the vest) . . . Arriving at night, at dawn or at noon . . . and guys [waiting for me] at the airport—my helpers . . . but having seen and contemplated things from on high." On a Paris to Delhi flight in 1955 he whiles away part of the time by listing all the cities he has known. At the bottom "= 110."

While in the solitude of flight, he not only organizes correspondence and schedules but also outlines books and plans exhibitions. He reads widely in the classics—especially his constant companions, Cervantes and Rabelais. "My travel readings always begin with Don Quixote . . . I open to any page and I'm bitten, I'm hooked . . . And it always ends with this darned Rabelais . . . What a stomach, what an intestine. He evacuates everything. He is always like a dog who just crapped: he is happy, he gallops . . . the body, the soul and the gut of man." While he flies he occasionally peers out at the land below and the sky around. He is astonished and dismayed at how little his fellow travelers look out. They keep "their nose[s] in magazines and detective novels" throughout the flight, rarely if ever looking through the porthole at what most enthralls him.

Looking down, he is of course interested in panoramas of various sorts. The quickly sketched air view begins for him back in the Twenties when he discovers the airplane. But what may be the most prevalent object of his attention from this vantage point, certainly the one on which he lavishes most comment and thought in the sketchbooks, comes as something of a surprise. It is estuaries and deltas. How astonishing it is that Le Corbusier, who was so devoted to clear forms, who complained that "the almost-but-not-quite is everywhere. Nothing exact, definite . . ." should find the amorphous windings of watercourses, bearing the silt that causes the shifting meanders, so fascinating.

The estuaries attract as his native Alps repel. Repeatedly flying over the Alps on his way to or from Paris, he is reminded of his father's presidency of the Alpine Club; but he no longer finds these mountains exhilarating. On the contrary, they are "sublime and repellent." "November 28, 1951/I saw the Alps this morning . . . all naked! . . . (9:40 AM GMT) I prefer the setting sun on the Arabian sea [which he had just experienced]. The Alps are anything but inviting = the anti-man! It's horrible! Good for Freudianism! They convey an image of inextricability." And later, during yet another flight over the mountains, point-blank, "I hate the Alps."

Not so his aerial views of deltas and estuaries, which could have been quite as daunting if experienced on the ground. "Bombay Delhi Plane November 13, 1953—5 PM/ The estuaries of the sea, the deltas are in scale with the Himalayas. Just as inaccessible to man: silt, amazing pools, effects of tide far into the interior, danger[ous] probably." On another occasion: "I again see this endless delta from Karachi to Ahmedabad . . . gradient of waters, erosion, the patient ebb of the sea, molecular then by streams, and great arms of meanders calmed by their undulating progress. One cannot draw [it], the pencil fails. Because it is a question of the most delicately shaded values, the most tenuous ramifications, of impeccable [color] gradations . . . . the immensity . . . ." Or: "everything comes to the sea/13h 13 nov 55," and he sketches the mini-tributaries, half mud, half water, that join the bigger flows. As the flow widens to the mouth of the river, he quickly outlines the estuary with a lead pencil, and scribbles in the muddy shores and shoals with two shades of brown pencil. At the mouth, he stretches his word "immense" with opposed arrows to indicate that no mere sketchpad could encompass such vastness. He is entranced by the color of the delta near Karachi: "February 27, 1954 . . . perfectly smooth red violet-shaded meander (and with cobalt blue) pattern of an intense acuity . . . Cut with a razor—very pale blue: 5%." The low tide at Bombay leaves behind "decalcomania" of black sand. Near Bombay, on another flight, the undulations of river and rivulets in the delta call up recollections of "Knossos [Crete] pottery" and "Modern Style 1900." The glints of a lake-dotted, river-wound landscape near the Gath Mountains bring Leonardo's labyrinthian landscapes to mind. Between Basrah and Bombay, he notes "a formidable 'branched' delta—like the boughs of gigantic oaks," with pools depended from the meander like leaves; between Chandigarh and Cairo he sees another delta, this time of dried salt marshes, which appear in the sketchbook as withered foliage.

What accounts for this fascination with primeval landscape, more intensely absorbing for Le Corbusier, it would seem, than comparable views of the configurations made by human actions on the earth? Obviously one can make a connection between the colossal windings of the dominant meanders and his projects for the immense wind of highway-scaled buildings around the harbors of Algiers and Rio, or his subsequent conception of the linear regional development of urbanism in Western Europe, where major center connects major center in river-like windings following the principle routes of transport, with open space (as he hoped) left in the interstices of the webbing. And the graduated quality of movement within the delta—from percolations in the sand, to rivulets, to streams, to river meanders—are surely analogous to his ideal hierarchy of traffic movement along the "7-Vs" (Voies), graduated from footpath to superhighway. Yet the meaning for the delta must go deeper.

A clue appears perhaps in a scribbled comment written while he looked down on an estuary in Cuba: "the law of the meander (1929) meanders 1947 etc./erosion, the law of rhythm and equilibrium at any moment, the relationships of measuring out = proportion."

This enigmatic entry refers to a lecture in a series he gave in South America in 1929, in one of which (entitled "A Man = A Cell/From Cells = A City") he spoke of the "law of the meander." *Précisions,* the book that resulted from this lecture tour, reproduces it. The "law of the meander" illustrates the manner in which nature corrects developments toward excessive complexity and elaboration. It serves as an analogy for understanding the cause and correction of problems occurring in the modern urban situation. A river following a relatively straight course is deflected by an obstacle on its left bank. Water currents are deflected toward the right bank. Erosion occurs. With time, the scoop of this erosion deflects the current back toward the left bank. Now erosion occurs on the left bank, and the current swings back to the right bank again. So the river increasingly winds. As the oscillating erosion continues, the windings become labyrinthian, taking the form of deep curves, eventually assuming near figure-eight configurations. But as the barrier of silt between each of these turnings is lessened, the river finally breaks through the fragile barriers. It returns to its original direct course, ready for the slow process to begin anew.

Involved in the analogy are four actions, all significant for Le Corbusier's ideas on healthy physical and social planning: a natural and dynamic process; a state of continuous, but changing, equilibrium; an inevitable increase in complication over time; and a radical breakthrough to correct too much complexity, without which both the dynamic process and its sequential states of equilibrium would be destroyed. A dense and ambiguous metaphor, then: for urban planning it implies the need for such heroic breakthrough measures as super-buildings, whether towers or viaducts, which Le Corbusier tends to favor early in his career; it implies as well the need to attend to the slow workings of natural processes, which Le Corbusier increasingly appreciated later in his career, especially after his contact with less developed societies.

Significantly, on the very next page of the sketchbook, where he muses over the "law of the meander" (with its "law of rhythm and equilibrium at any moment, the relationships of measuring out=proportion"), his thoughts shift back to India. He recalls "the essential joys of the Hindu principle: brotherhood, relationship between the cosmos and living things: Stars, nature, sacred animals, birds, monkeys, and cows, and in the village children, adults, and old people, the pond and the mango trees, everything is present and . . . poor but *proportioned.*" He is moved by the chaos of primal stuff, in continuous, organic flux, but always in equilibrium—"proportioned" perhaps in the combination of its equilibrium and in the elemental nature of its composition. He believes that the airplane has opened the ways of Asia to the Western world, and sees this inversion of the technological as the silting counter-element, so to speak, to the delta of future civilization, checking the swift flow of modernization.

In Cairo, he is attracted by a park in which paths wind every which way in squiggles around trees and clumps of foliage, made by the mesh of people moving in all directions across it. In Chandigarh, across the skewed rectangular grid of the street system he creates a winding counter-grid of paths for pedestrians. In the center of each super-block these crossing pedestrian rivulets expand to irregular communal pools as meeting- and marketplaces, like the bend of the swamp-bound river seen from the air in

Bogotá, fed by a series of pools of varied sizes along its course. Chandigarh, he proclaims, will be, above all, a pedestrian city, the walkers' warp woven into the automobiles' weft. Looking at the movement of people in the streets of Asia, he generalizes the situation for the future of human culture: "Let us overlook our kind of street, we knew it in our childhood. But the street of the Indians, the Egyptians, the Chinese it's a huge thing in full ferment and possible bloom."

The delta, and that other immense, amorphous environment—the sky—obsesses him as he soars in "peace" and "solitude" between the calls of his career. Cosmic slime and cosmic heavens are the extremes that meet in his view of nature, which is less that of the farmer, like Frank Lloyd Wright's, and more that of the aviator, the sea captain, and the motorist at full throttle. Repeatedly Le Corbusier confronts the changing skies in his sketchbook and records the impossibility of taking it all in, let alone taking it down. The usual results are garish notations in colored pencil accompanied by astute written comment, or, better perhaps, pencil sketches with the colors simply noted. On a flight to Karachi over the Indian Ocean ("10 nov 55") he fills a page with a Rothko-like series of color bands: a narrow band of bright yellow edged with vivid green and orange at the center; rising from it, brilliant red flaring horizontals; below, a quiet blue shading off into pale lavender. Beside the page in color he draws a diagram: "the intensity [is in the central band] the force [is in the red] the density [is in the lower zone] the depth [is in the whole]." He devotes a number of pages to skies. Some, especially evocative, show cloud columns rising through cloud banks toward the clear sky of the high-flying plane. But one more must suffice. Again he makes his color sketch, a looser series of somber bands this time, layered with views through to puffy clouds below; immediately ahead a deep blue, out of which red and yellow flare up to (and he writes this at the top of the page because there is no more room to include it) pale green overhead with the spectral appearance of a high white moon. As before, on the next page he comments, "1. *in the east*: the violet bite out of the horizon of fire and light, on a base of gray-violet clouds lit from behind/ 2. in *the west* . . . the ineffable, gentle attenu*ated* values/one could play the 2 effects in succession and rise to the contrasting crescendo . . . ."

He was working at the time on the Phillips Pavilion, to house a display for this major European electrical company at the Brussels Exposition. The sketchbook shows a number of crude diagrams of the multimedia effects that were to engulf the visitors to Le Corbusier's tilted aluminum tent (originally more in the shape of the cannon skylights on the roofs of his chapels for the Monastery of La Tourette). There are pages of scenario for the mixed environment of sound, color, picture, and didactics that would envelope the visitor's consciousness.

Another page of the sketchbooks shows in the quickest of crude diagrams the museum which he would have liked for Chandigarh—a variant, and reduction, of which was eventually completed after Le Corbusier's death. His ideal museum would be housed in three separate buildings. There is a large building for permanent display of artifacts from the history spiral that Le Corbusier had originated in his Mundaneum project of 1929: one entered by way of an underground passage to the core gallery, with the rectangular spiral of galleries growing from this center and extending as needed. Beside this is an open pavilion with a gently gabled roof abutting another with the gable inverted, like two gazebos pushed together. Le Corbusier had projected the idea originally for the "Porte Maillot" display in Paris in 1950 and toward the end of his life resurrected the scheme for the Centre Le Corbusier in Zurich. In contrast to the permanent exhibition in the spiral box, the open, less monumental pavilion structure would feature temporary shows. Finally, beside this, is the third component—what he terms the Miracle Box. He does not precisely define its function; but he intends it as a place of performance. In it he envisions something of a cross between the stylized theater of the Noh drama, which had impressed him in Japan as being adaptable to some sort of ritualistic pageant based on local folk tradition, and a multi-media electronic program comparable to that which he finally realized for Phillips. What he has in mind, however, is not "electronic vaudeville," or some other kind of show with superficial technological tricks to grip the audience. He wants what he terms "electronic effects"—by which he seems to mean effects endowed with the same magical and transcendent presence as signs in folklore and ritual, signs distilled from everyday experience, and signs of the cosmos, like the skies into which he sailed in his travels.

A Miracle Box! But the true Miracle Box was there in the closet at 24 rue Nungesser-et-Coli, the valise crammed with its neat rows of sketchbooks.

It is some time on 22 November 1951. He seems again to be in the midst of flight, somewhere in the peace of the sky between New Delhi and Bombay, lost to blessed aloneness and meditation. He is reading (or perhaps merely remembering) Mallarmé, and writes in the sketchbook at hand:

Car j'installe, par la science
l'hymne des coeurs spirituels
En l'oeuvre de ma patience

(*April* 1983)

Metrical illiteracy

by Brad Leithauser

American verse is probably passing through a peculiar period when the word *disturbing* can, unadorned, serve as commendation on a dust jacket. The willing reader, or at least the willing reader of advertisements and blurbs for books of contemporary poetry, is offered *disturbing collections* and *disturbing new voices* and *disturbing sensibilities.*

To this particular reader of poetry, the word seems ironically appropriate. For while the books themselves are apt to prove not so much *disturbing* in any tonic, regenerative sense as simply *dismaying,* the state of contemporary verse as a whole does seem disturbing in the prime, portentous connotations of the word—worrisome, unsettling, even destructive.

Anyone generalizing about contemporary American poetry must first acknowledge that given its diffuse, factionalized condition any conclusions must be presented with hesitation. For diffusion more than any unifying trait defines its fundamental nature, and indeed at once provides the generalizer with one impregnably safe generalization: American poetry has never passed through such a scattered era. This diffusion may be a result of the deaths in the last few decades of so many of its ablest practitioners and guides (Eliot, Frost, Roethke, Bishop, Berryman—and these but begin the unhappy list), or perhaps it is tied to the larger directionlessness that seems presently to haunt so many of the arts.

Hesitantly, then, I would suggest that a second generalization might safely be tendered: there is a widespread perception that we are not living in a golden age of poetry, and that mediocrity prevails in the periodicals and on the bookstore shelves. It is this near-unanimous consensus that is of interest here rather than the mediocrity itself, for mediocre poems have always preponderated in the periodicals and on the bookstore shelves, and always will. In many of the anthologies of ten and twenty years ago one met boisterous assertions that American poetry was passing through a great age (a greatness variously led, depending on the anthologist's predilections, by the Beats or the New York School or the Whomevers). This is a claim less frequently or easily made now, I suspect, when our *vitality* rather than our *greatness* will likely be cited. Of course this consensus concerning the mediocrity of contemporary poetry is superficial and fragile. On closer examination, one would find little agreement about which constitute the few good, needle-bright poems, and which the haystack of bad ones. Still, this consensus offers its revealing and rather humorous picture—that of hundreds and hundreds of bad poets saying, "There are hundreds and hundreds of bad poets out there."

A third generalization is that very few young writers have worked diligently in poetic form. Such a commonplace is this that it's apt to obscure a rather remarkable fact. Never before in the long line of English verse have we seen the ascendancy of generations of poets who have at no time in their careers worked seriously with form. There are sometimes compelling artistic reasons for abandoning form, a few of which I will touch on, but most lying outside the focus of this article. Nonetheless, this abandonment represents a fundamental schism, something far more significantly divisive than any mere shift in formal fads or tastes. Throughout history, traditional forms and conventions have of course suffered their eclipses; the search for new methods and the impatience with tired ones (what Keats called "dead leaves in the bay wreath crown") have generated much of the brilliance and excitement of English literature. Take for example that robust Italian music box the sonnet (from "sonnetto," little song or sound). After displaying an overtaking brilliance under Shakespeare, Donne, Milton, Herbert, it was essentially set aside for more than a century; was born again, singing new melodies, with Wordsworth and the Romantics; underwent a great many freshening changes only to find itself, with Cummings and Pound a hundred years later, successfully sporting *thee*'s and *hath*'s and other locutions that Wordsworth himself on a good day probably would have eschewed as old-fashioned. A sonnet in the level, colloquial voice of Elizabeth Bishop may seem hundreds of years advanced over the rounded, often florid intonings of Edna St. Vincent Millay (though both women's working lives overlapped), and the former's work may even be seen as something of a repudiation of the latter's. Yet this process of repudiation, the fertile ferment of quiet revolution, is all taking place within the larger domain of English formal poetry. Two poets working in form, whatever the distaste they harbor for each other's verse, will probably share a kinship which a formal poet and an exclusively free-form poet will not know.

A fourth and final generalization is that while the poetry market in this era of blockbuster books is pitifully small, and a hardcover printing may run less than a thousand copies for even a prize-winning poet of some "fame" (a word that usually trumpets with bombastic humor when applied to any inhabitant of the contemporary American poetry scene), there are far more poets out there, and far more poems being produced, than ever before. One hears that an open manuscript competition like that for the Yale or Whitman Prize may draw a couple of thousand submissions—more submissions than the winning manuscript will sell books. More colleges are teaching poetry writing than ever before; more students are graduating from such classes and colleges in treadmill search of other such classes to teach.

Obviously these four conditions—diffusion, perceived mediocrity, the eschewal of form by the young, and an ever expanding number of poets—will greatly overlap. Take for example the last of these, poetry's burgeoning population. In a mock-scholarly way, one might even chart (much as an ecologist charts the population of birds or fish based on data about weather, predators, etc.) how the first three conditions might affect the number of people who choose to write poetry. For example, we would expect diffusion and population to exist in direct correlation: the more poets we have, the less we can logically expect unanimity or the hegemony of a single poetic school; conversely, the more diffusion, the greater the chance that new people will encounter some inspiring style or subject matter that nudges them into writing verse. The perception of mediocrity, too, can lead to rising numbers; for while great art can spark that liberating love which says *I want to create,* mediocre art may foster an equally propulsive *I can do that just as well.* Mediocrity often betokens opportunity. Similarly, once most of the demands of form have been scuttled by the young—once the notion is lost that poetry is a craft which, like carpentry, requires a long apprenticeship merely to assimilate its tools—there's no reason for anyone experiencing a potent joy or grievance, the stirrings of a cry from the heart, to feel excluded from Parnassus.

Actually, the rising number of poets, while

it may create headaches for the poetry editors of magazines receiving perhaps a thousand submissions a week, would seem a healthy phenomenon for at least three reasons. First, it may help us regain some of the ground poetry has lost within the popular culture and thereby offer poets a re-burnished self-esteem, so that even if as civic beings they do not, with Shelley, believe themselves the unacknowledged legislators of the world, they might fancy themselves a small but clarion-voiced group of lobbyists (like the Audubon Society). A second benefit is that mediocre or even bad poetry can have a salutary effect on very young (especially precollege) potential poets, a group for whom the sort of poetry they're exposed to may be less important than the mere fact of their being exposed to poetry at all. This is a group in whom one cannot reasonably hope to instill a discerning love of what's good, but one can perhaps engender an embracing excitement about poetry that will in time lead to critical refinement. Third, a larger number of poets would seem to increase the likelihood (as in that familiar, though here perhaps unflattering, image favored by students of statistics: monkeys pecking randomly at typewriters) of durable, rewarding poems being written.

The diffusion of poetry, too, presents theoretical advantages. It would seem to increase the chance of a poet's finding useful models and a natural voice. A dominant poetic form or group of forms (rhymed pentameter, say) can squelch a great many poets not temperamentally suited to such strictures. One might reply that genius finds its own forms and surmounts the obstacles of pervading fashion—one might even erect a plausible definition of genius on such a premise—but surely not all great poems are written by geniuses and many great poems will be lost when a charmingly wayward muse is hitched up (by a sort of arranged marriage) to an autocratic prosody. Diffusion would seem to offer a utopian community where everyone practices what he or she does best.

In any case, diffusion would appear to be an inevitable and a lasting condition of the American poetry scene. Fashions will rise and fall, but it's extremely difficult to picture all of our wildly disparate schools and tastes again converging. It is as if after the big bang of modernism and its aftereffects the drifting bodies have finally moved too far apart, lack sufficient mass and centripetal gravity, ever to re-gather again around the core of a ruling orthodoxy.

Diffusion also seems inevitable for a second, extremely cynical, reason. A great many well-known poets simply have not worked in form and could not successfully if they tried. Ungainliness—a simple lack of professionalism—would immediately show itself. Formlessness (ostensibly an avant-garde impulse) may, then, actually be kept alive by conservatism in its most basic sense—conservation of the self, the preservation of one's reputation in the poetry scene.

What is so surprising about this diffusion, whether viewed as ultimately benign or merely inevitable, is how narrow on examination it turns out to be, especially as manifested in our college writing programs. Rarely is it Chaucer or Milton or Pope or Dickinson or Tennyson to whom such classes turn, but almost always a host of mediocrities risen since World War II, most of them theoretically progeny of William Carlos Williams (insofar as he can be read, falsely, as an endorser of plain-spoken disorder). While diffusion ideally ensures individuality, we find instead dozens and dozens of interchangeable tenured Blakes, visionaries without vision, who, having set up campus satraps, are continually venturing forth for drearily unproductive workshops, symposia, conferences. So goes the business of teaching poetry . . .

Admittedly, the poetry teacher occupies a problematic position, for the writing of poetry, despite the exploding population of poets, represents an increasingly "unnatural" practice. There was a time when poets might naturally, as a part of their culture, be steeped in verse, a time when anonymous ballads could flourish and perhaps even help a society find and define itself. In recent years, a number of poets and critics (notably Randall Jarrell, Richard Wilbur, W. H. Auden, George Steiner) have written fine, elegiac pieces about this decline, whose implications are enormous, minatory, and obscure. It is clear, however, that today, when that steeping process is no longer naturally imposed, young people who wish not merely to read but actually to absorb someone like Pope, so that lines will volley unexpectedly to mind, must perform an arduous, solitary task. According to a romantic view of poets (and when poets are thought of at all it is usually romantically), this task will be accomplished almost effortlessly, as the young poet, driven by a voracious love of poesy, engorges every stanza and line he can put his hands upon. It probably *is* love, as much as anything, that motivates the apprentice poet, but the romantic view fails to consider that an elementary mastery of this particular craft requires work of a decidedly onerous variety. The young poet who has spent an afternoon seriously grappling for the first time with, say, the cruxes and quibbles of the Shakespeare sonnets is apt to wind up feeling that, like his counterpart the apprentice carpenter, he has splinters in his fingers and sawdust in his lungs.

Ours is a clangorous and increasingly violent age, and the art of poetry, in all its subtleties and near-fatal unsexiness, is easily lost in the din and jostle. It will take years for any young poet who has spent his share of time at the movies, where knifings and garrotings and chain-saw eviscerations are served up with such ferociously unblinking exactitude, or at rock concerts where the very walls are set to shuddering, to appreciate the delicate but prodigious violence packed into a sonnet like Milton's "On the Late Massacre in Piedmont," with that central image of horror: ". . . and in their ancient fold/Slain by the bloody Piemontese, that rolled/Mother with infant down the rocks." (Palgrave in his *Golden Treasury* called this "the most mighty Sonnet in any language known to the Editor.") And years to understand how a sonnet like Frost's "Design" is both presenting a wittily terrifying view of destiny and prosodically raising the stakes, doing Milton one better, by not only meeting all the rigid constrictions of the Miltonic sonnet form but imposing a further obstacle, the use of one of the same rhyme-sounds ("ite") in both the sestet and octet:

> I found a dimpled spider, fat and white,
> On a white heal-all, holding up a moth
> Like a white piece of rigid satin cloth—
> Assorted characters of death and blight
> Mixed ready to begin the morning right,
> Like the ingredients of a witches' broth—
> A snow-drop spider, a flower like froth,
> And dead wings carried like a paper kite.
>
> What had that flower to do with being white,
> The wayside blue and innocent heal-all?
> What brought the kindred spider to that height,
> Then steered the white moth thither in the night?
> What but design of darkness to appall?—
> If design govern in a thing so small.

With a lucid, colloquial diction ("plain American which cats and dogs can read," in Marianne Moore's phrase), Frost has gone fourteen lines with hardly a break in the pentameter and with the employment of but three rhyme-sounds. Actually, at one point Frost contemplated writing this much-revised sonnet with even fewer rhyme-sounds. Given his awesome technical proficiency, he probably could have accomplished this, but perhaps to the detriment of the poem's music and emotional impact. Here is another fruitful tension—that between visceral force which ever seeks to loosen formal constraints and the technician's perverse urge to tighten them—whose appreciation requires years of study.

Even if the culture itself does not steep the young poet in poetry, he or she may be fortunate enough to grow to poetic adulthood in an era when form flourishes. Perhaps one of the reasons why so much accomplishment has come from American poets born in the 1920s (Anthony Hecht, Donald Justice, James Merrill, W. D. Snodgrass, Richard Wilbur, the late James Wright—and again this but begins the list) is that they had the good fortune to begin their careers during the Forties and Fifties, when an orthodoxy of formal verse obtained. This period is often criticized as sterile, and doubtless in some of their work formalism has stunted the soul of a potentially fine lyric, but surely it was advantageous for them to train in the same basic tools as the titans of English verse. These are a generation of poets who have "gone to school." One cannot read a poem like Richard Wilbur's "'A World Without Objects Is a Sensible Emptiness,'" written while he was still some years short of thirty, without reflecting that here is someone who purely in terms of craftsmanship has mastered a great deal. In twenty-eight lines he manages articulately to state a philosophical position on the dilemma of the spirit/body conflict; to enlist in support the prose of Thomas Traherne, the seventeenth century poet and theologian from whose *Centuries of Meditation* he draws the title; to cast a fresh and lively language into the matrix of one of the hoariest poetic forms in English verse, the ABAB quatrain. In the first fourteen lines he portrays the spirit's inclination toward the deserts of ascetic withdrawal; at the midpoint, the fifteenth line, the tone shifts from description to exhortation, the verbs from declaratives to imperatives; and in the closing eleven he openly urges the spirit to "turn back," to enter the world fully:

Turn, O turn
From the fine sleights of the sand, from the long empty oven
Where flames in flamings burn

Back to the trees arrayed
In bursts of glare, to the halo-dialing run
Of the country creeks, and the hills' bracken tiaras made
Gold in the sunken sun,

Wisely watch for the sight
Of the supernova burgeoning over the barn,
Lampshine blurred in the steam of beasts, the spirit's right
Oasis, light incarnate.

Note how the form is jerked deftly awry by the swallowed final rhyme of "barn"/"incarnate." How the cool scientific nuances of "supernova" brilliantly contrast with the hinted reference to that ancient image of the star over Bethlehem; how directly yet subtly "Wisely" evokes the Three Wise Men; how the reference to Christ's birth—the Incarnation that is our most potent and poignant image of the Spirit's embrace of the Material—at once broadens the poem's argument and concords so sweetly with the philosophy of Traherne himself. Wilbur has not only gone to school, he has proven himself a star pupil, and this training gives his work an amplitude very few living poets can match. (One might lightly, affectionately note that while the slight misquoting of Traherne in Wilbur's title is probably an act of poetic license, it may show that at that school which he attended Wilbur did not study transcription.)

Yet the poet who has not gone to school suffers more than a narrowing of the breadth of his own verse. His critical faculties are truncated. A crucial understanding of the past is lost. Under normal circumstances, the poet can offer a unique critical vantage. He is apt to understand better even than a far more erudite scholar a poem's *construction.* The poet empathetically senses which line in a wobbly heroic couplet has engendered the other; understands why a particular stanzaic pattern may have been selected, and even which stanza might have been the germ whence the pattern grew; knows firsthand how the paucity of English rhymes (especially for such much-used words as "self," "God," "truth") may unwittingly bend the flow and sense of a lyric; distinguishes between cases where "cheating" on formal requirements derives from felt necessity, and where from a deliberate, fine rebelliousness. Of course the poet has this special insight only if he has worked with these forms himself. Poets tend to resent, often rightfully, being reviewed by non-poet critics, who may not fully compass the actual ways a poem is constructed; but having once sacrificed a first-hand knowledge of poetic form, these poets themselves are, when passing judgment on the formal masters of the past, in precisely the same position as the non-poet critics they resent. The poet has lost that craftsman-to-craftsman affinity which is his special contribution to the ongoing evaluation and reappraisal of English-language verse. This loss seems especially grave when considered against the much diminished role verse now plays in the lives of the general populace, whose poetic tastes and sympathies might once have been expected to perform a preserving, archival function. If today poets themselves do not maintain an intimacy with formal technique, who can we expect will do so?

The exploding population of poets, the dizzying diffusion, the sense of open opportunities—clearly these conditions will little profit us so long as a belief persists that a person who is not a decent prosodist can be a decent poet. Or so long as we fail to recognize that metrical illiteracy is, for the poet, functional illiteracy. To write a competent Miltonic sonnet—not even a good one, but merely one which satisfies formal requirements without relying on padding or wrenched syntax or archaic inversions—is a surprisingly difficult undertaking. Surely all poets ought to know this, even if not all critics do.

(*January* 1983)

V. Figures of History

American literary radicalism in the Twenties

by James W. Tuttleton

Writing in the current issue of *Dissent* (Winter, 1985), David Bromwich—associate professor of English at Princeton and author of a recent study of William Hazlitt—reflected on the phenomenon of "Literary Radicalism in America" as a means of ascertaining the effect of American literary avant-gardes on the politics and art of this country. In the course of his essay, he adverts to *The New Criterion* and to its writers as being engaged in the effort to "invent cultural conservatism in America," a task he evidently finds lacking in high seriousness, if not vain. I should not have said that this was the general aim of the journal, since cultural conservatism has been a constant fact of American life and is reflected in our jurisprudence and law, in aspects of our politics and religion, in the human sciences, in social and intellectual history, and in our art and criticism. It therefore cannot be invented, although cultural conservatism can provide a perspective from which to interrogate the conditions of American culture.

Bromwich is clearly right to suggest that the conservative wishes "to guard" at least some of "the values already in place" in American society. But his reduction of conservative thought to a set of judgments dictated by "a sequence of implicit equations: taste = inherited opinions = rules = norms (= social norms)" is so breathtaking an oversimplification of any serious conservative critique of American culture that the mind can do nothing with it. But I know of no serious conservative who is unwilling to scrutinize the problems of taste, inherited opinions, rules, and norms. In the long run, the conservative will likely conclude that there is some valuable wisdom to be gained from the past and he will want to affirm and defend that. In fact, the conservative meditation on the cultural forms by which wisdom is transmitted from the past is far more intellectually flexible and alive than Mr. Bromwich's equational reductionism.

In any case, the burden of Mr. Bromwich's essay is somewhat different—to hold out for our consideration two radical avant-garde groups who have deeply affected the course of American literature and to meditate on their suggestiveness for the future. These two groups are: 1) Emerson and the circle connected to him at *The Dial* in the 1840s (only Margaret Fuller is mentioned); and 2) "their successors," whom Bromwich lists as William James, Van Wyck Brooks, Randolph Bourne, and John Dewey—"those social critics whose work began in earnest about 1915." The intent of his essay would appear to be expressed in his statement that "The legacy of Emerson, Fuller, James, Dewey, Bourne, and Brooks is what we still have to build on."

Now the politics of dissent can sometimes make strange bedfellows, so nothing will seem odder than this collection of disparate minds brought into unnatural intercourse under the cover of "literary radicalism." What is, after all, the common bond between the Emerson, whose essential genius was to commend consciousness over against society (which he called "a conspiracy against the manhood of every one of its members"), and Brooks, who espoused a redistributive socialism more revolutionary than that of Howells, a Christian Socialist, and other progressive-era "men of good hope"?

What is the link between Emerson and Bourne, who had little to say about Emerson but who acclaimed the cultural determinism espoused in Edward Thorndike's *Individuality* (1911) and who—in "The Next Revolution"—commended "the three cardinal propositions of Marx—the economic interpretation of history, the class struggle, and the exploitation of the workers by capitalistic private ownership of the means of production"? Bourne had at the end of his life, incidentally, no use for Dewey's instrumentalism, which he saw as a tool for justifying America's entry into World War I. And Brooks likewise found in pragmatism's emphasis on "social efficiency" a lack of idealistic vision. Brooks is inescapably clear, in *Letters and Leadership* (1918), that James and Dewey "failed us," and not merely failed us but "traduced us" by their devotion to the given, to the "existing fact," that is, by their acceptance of the socioeconomic status quo. For Brooks, who took his cue from Bourne, pragmatism was "the dog in the manger of the creative life."

Emerson found the revolutionary agenda by which the status quo was to be transformed as distasteful as the organized party politics by which American political life, in his time, expressed itself. "Hence," he observed in "Politics,"

> the less government we have the better,—the fewer laws, and the less confided power. The antidote to this abuse of formal government is the influence of private character, the growth of the Individual; the appearance of the principal to supersede the proxy; the appearance of the wise man; of whom the existing government is, it must be owned, a shabby imitation. That which all things tend to educe; which freedom, cultivation, intercourse, revolutions, go to form and deliver, is character; that is the end of Nature, to reach unto this coronation of her king. To educate the wise man the State exists, and with the appearance of the wise man the State expires. The appearance of character makes the State unnecessary. The wise man is the State.

Bromwich observes that "Since Emerson, the project of literary radicalism has never been isolable from an ambition to reform our social arrangements." But as Emerson's remarks make plain, this reform will arise only as a consequence of the moral reform of single individuals who aspire to wisdom and character, not as a consequence of socialistic movements which subordinate the individual to the state. Emerson would in fact have been appalled at the veneration of the state in twentieth-century radical politics of the Left. In this his thought has a conservative cast, which will make it irreconcilable with statist ideologies.

The socialists at Brook Farm, according to Emerson, had a noble intent in wishing to institute a Fourierist phalanx at West Roxbury, Massachusetts, in 1841. But the intent was based on a misunderstanding of human reality in its social and sexual character, and its productive commodity constituted a mere competition with that of the surrounding farmers. In "Historic Notes of Life and Letters in New England," Emerson praised the noble intentions of the reformers who tried to induce him to join their commune, but he accounted for his refusal in observing that

> in spite of the assurances of its friends that it was new and widely discriminated from all other plans for the regeneration of society, we could not exempt it from the criticism which we apply to so many projects for reform with which the brain of the age teems. Our feeling was that Fourier had skipped no fact but one, namely Life. He treats man as a plastic thing, something that may be put up or down, ripened or retarded, moulded, polished, made into solid or fluid or gas, at the will of the

leader; or perhaps as a vegetable, from which, though now a poor crab, a very good peach can by manure and exposure be in time produced,—but skips the faculty of life, which spawns and scorns system and system-makers; which eludes all conditions; which makes or supplants a thousand phalanxes and New Harmonies with each pulsation.

For Emerson, in practical terms, Brook Farm failed because there was "no head," because "intellectual sans-culottism" and impulse ruled. But the condition of failure was implicit in the plan. And what he said about the vision of the Brook Farm reformers might be said of any such socialist utopian scheme: "The mistake is that this particular order and series is to be imposed, by force or preaching and votes, on all men, and carried into rigid execution."

Emerson's idea of politics, then, is indeed radical, but it is radical in its aversion to the very concept of political organization; and it is grounded epistemologically on the priority of the unarguable moral intuition as an affirmation of the Divine Will. Such a view presents its problems for the conservative as well, who will not have a perfectibilitarian view of human possibility, or a belief in the direct apprehension of divine reality through transcendental intuition. But the conservative will assent to Emerson's emphasis on the individual, his critique of statism, and his disbelief in impractical utopianism. In retrospect, Emerson was right to call the Brook Farm experiment "a perpetual picnic, a French Revolution in small, an Age of Reason in a patty-pan." Consequently, Emerson does not well serve the radicalism of Brooks and Bourne, for whom a collectivist mentality led them in the direction of a vague undoctrinaire socialism expressed in *The New Republic, Seven Arts, The Freeman,* and in other journals of the Teens and Twenties. And, finally, Emerson's politics will not well serve the purposes of *Dissent.* For his emphasis is always on the priority of mind, of consciousness, and of individual self-reformation as the instrument of the amelioration of social ills.

To present Emerson as the radical predecessor of socialist critics of the 1920s, like Bourne and Brooks, is also to ignore the whole history of developing socialist thought in the 1880s and '90s, evident in both party politics and in literary works by Howells, Bellamy, London, and others. These are of course lesser figures than Emerson; thus there is always a tendency to co-opt the best major figure of the past as the spiritual father of whatever may be the current movement. But the progressives I have named are the real American forebears of Brooks and Bourne, Floyd Dell and John Reed, Waldo Frank and Max Eastman—even as George Ripley, C. A. Dana, Warren Burton and William Henry Channing at Brook Farm are the American predecessors of the *fin-de-siècle* "men of good hope."

In fact, none of the major artists of the American Renaissance, as F. O. Matthiessen called it—not Emerson, Thoreau, Dickinson, Melville, Hawthorne, or even Whitman—will serve as an adequate foundation, in political and economic terms, for the socialist reconstitution of America called for by literary radicals in the 1920s, although since these are the memorable figures, one or another of them is recurrently hailed as the significant predecessor.

Much of Van Wyck Brooks's conception of the American experience and American literature is, in retrospect, hardly adequate—even, I should imagine, for literary radicals. The reason for this is plain: in respect to our significant writers, it is widely understood that Brooks manipulated the facts of our literary past in order to prove a thesis about the inadequacy of American culture as nutriment for the writer. I am particularly speaking here of Van Wyck Brooks before 1930, not of the later author of the comprehensive "Makers and Finders" series. That impressive multi-volume literary history is not marked by the socialist extravagances of Brooks's youth; it deals with our past more in historical and literary than in ideological and political terms. But in his youth Brooks's cultural disgust with America overwhelmed his perception of the literature before him. I need not go into his fantastic arguments about Twain's genius being thwarted by the frontier experience, which Bernard De Voto demolished years ago, nor his dubious interpretation of Henry James's expatriation, which biographers and critics have long ago corrected. Nor, finally, can one commend his understanding of Emerson, who provoked in him "a persistent spleen."

Yet in one respect Brooks was right about Emerson: he intuited that Emerson's individualism could be translated into the *laissez-faire* capitalist's advocacy of commodity and power. As Brooks conceded in *America's Coming-of-Age* (1915), "if the logical result of a thorough-going, self-reliant individualism in the world of the spirit is to become a saint, it is no less true that the logical result of a thorough-going, self-reliant individualism in the world of the flesh is to become a millionaire." In consequence, Emerson's views were never "inconveniently inconsistent with the facts and requirements of business life." They therefore served to support the economic status quo. Bromwich disagrees with this reading of Emerson by Brooks, for he wishes to salvage Emerson for the tradition of radical Left politics. But as John Gerber demonstrated some years ago, in "Emerson and the Political Economists" (*New England Quarterly,* 1949), Emerson's economic views tried to "combine socialistic ends with capitalistic means" and thus proved incompatible with communistic experiments.

Brooks was highly critical of Emerson and his Transcendental circle for what might be called the absence in them of rigorous intellectual discrimination. He complained of them as "that queer miasmatical group of lunar phenomena, in which philosophy, self-culture, politics, art, social reform and religion were all mixed up and all felt to be, in some vague way, the same thing." This is a highly perceptive insight. But I wish to extend it in order to suggest that it is true of many American avant-garde literary groups. It was manifestly true of the generation of Brooks and Bourne, although living in it, and aflame with their passions and enthusiasms, they were not prepared to see that such an objection might be raised against themselves. But let me extend this yet one step further.

To co-opt Emerson and William James for the purposes of Left political radicalism is of a piece with the intellectual muddlement evident in the *Partisan Review* circle of the 1930s and '40s, who attempted forcibly to yoke together Trotskyist politics and Eliotic artistic modernism. That project revealed a bizarre misunderstanding of both philosophical horizons. Although it constitutes a minor scandal in recent American critical thought about the relation of politics and literature, Bromwich is disposed to gloss over the contradiction implicit in the *Partisan Review* position and even to celebrate it as constituting "a new conception of intellectual freedom," as being an instance of a "style of cultural tolerance."

Whatever may be the virtues of cultural tolerance and intellectual freedom, and they are many, they are purchased, in this case, at the cost of intellectual consistency. In the Twenties, amongst the more lucid radicals of the time, these things were understood more clearly. V. F. Calverton, writing in "American Literary Radicalism" (*Modern Quarterly,* September-December, 1926), acknowledged that many literary modernists were radical in literary technique while conservative in socio-political ideology. He took no comfort in this; nor did he see this contradiction as a means of effecting the Revolution. Max Eastman, as editor of *The Masses,* claimed to be hospitable to intellectual diversity, but in some remote part of his mind he understood that some of his contributors praised modernist literary radicalism without understanding its contradiction to a "correct" politics. Writers like Bourne and Brooks wanted to give intellectual "leadership" to the Revolution; but Eastman made it perfectly plain in *The Liberator* in 1921 that writers and critics, the young intellectuals, would need "guidance and careful watching by the practical and theoretical workers of the movement." This point of view came to full fruition in the Thirties, when the Stalinist theoreticians made it plain to Leftist writers and intellectuals that even the truth would have to be sacrificed for "the greater social good." This was more than even Eastman could stomach. But looking back on the immediate postwar years, Eastman told Ely Estorick in 1931, as reported in Calverton's *The Liberation of American Literature,* "I suppose that the most unique and important feature of the old *Masses* . . . was that while maintaining an editorial policy essentially Marxian it drew into its pages the works of wide circles of the intelligentzia who had revolutionary feeling, but *no understanding of such a policy and very little conception of what it was all about*" (italics added).

I am not sure that Bromwich knows what it was all about. And certainly Brooks and Bourne lacked the foresight and insight to know what it was all about, to know what was being asked of them by Eastman, John Reed, and the political radicals just before and after World War I. The *Masses* and *Liberator* group knew what it was all about: they knew what they wanted, and what they wanted was an American revolution along the Soviet line. What it was all about the events themselves, as they unfolded in the Thirties, made plain. The Stalinist agenda, like the Fourierist, was to impose its regimen, "by force or preaching and votes, on all men," to carry it "into rigid execution." Brooks, Bourne, and the young intelligentsia hadn't the wit to foresee the enormity of such a social engineering scheme. They wanted to ventilate a moral contempt for big business, puritanism, Comstockery, prohibition, and the older generation.

Especially the older generation. "The Apostolic 'Student Movement,' or, the Priests of Young America" is how Daniel Aaron, in *Writers on the Left* (1961), has rightly characterized the "League of Youth" clustered around Bourne and Brooks—Lewis Mumford, Waldo Frank, James Oppenheim, Paul Rosenfeld, and, to some extent, Walter Lippmann. We should make a distinction here between the political radicals of the Twenties and the literary radicals I have just named. Yet the latter largely gave themselves to the idea of political revolution.

Bourne advised Brooks that the liberalism of *The New Republic* (Croly, Lippmann, Dewey) was lacking in "youthful violence" and was too "priggish." In "The State," Bourne annexed Marx to Charles Beard's economic determinism (in *An Economic Interpretation of the Constitution* [1913]) in order to equate, as Lenin had done, capitalism and imperialism with war. Not for nothing did *The New Masses* create, after his death in 1918, the Randolph Bourne Memorial Award. They wanted to honor a radical who, at the end, said that he felt "very much out of touch with my times, except perhaps with the Bolsheviki." Perhaps it was Lewis Mumford who most clearly spoke their faith: they wished, he said in *The Forum* in 1930, for "an uprising on the part of the downtrodden, who would overthrow the master class and bring about a regime of equality and brotherhood." Mumford, like Brooks, of course outlived Bourne, who died in the influenza epidemic, and both outlived their radical ideas. But it is important to remember them as they were in the Teens and Twenties. Speaking of the clarion call to youth in *Letters and Leadership,* Bourne told Brooks that "There is a certain superb youthful arrogance in your implication that it is we and our friends who are to be masters," to be directors, that is, of America's revolutionary coming-of-age. Of course they thought they were equal to the task.

With their repudiation of the past and their emphasis on youth, Brooks and Bourne created the conditions under which Floyd Dell, in all seriousness, could dismiss the nineteenth century and all that it meant: "We can now discount almost to worthlessness—for our own purposes—the greater part of what New England took the trouble to say," he intoned in *Intellectual Vagabondage* (1926). For this young coterie of literary and political radicals, "We had our own lives to live—and all these classical utterances of the nineteenth century literature had no relation to our lives." So much for the utility of Emerson and his circle at *The Dial.*

About the most that can be said for Van Wyck Brooks and the members of the Apostolic Student Movement of the period 1915-1930—and I fix the time precisely, since a number of its members outgrew their youthful views—is that they were young, brash, estranged from their own culture, sentimentally utopian but without an understanding of the political consequences of their ideas, and without political foresight. However noble may be the goals of equality, brotherhood, and spiritually fulfilling labor, the Brooks-Bourne tradition through 1930 (which, by the way, refused itself connection with the Emerson, James, Dewey line) serves mostly as a cautionary instance—like the counterculture movement of the 1960s—of the effects on idealism of passionate incompetence.

I go into these matters because two recent publications—Gorham Munson's *The Awakening Twenties: A Memoir-History of a Literary Period*[1] and Bruce Clayton's *Forgotten Prophet: The Life of Randolph Bourne*[2]—raise anew the question of literary radicalism in the era of Bourne and Brooks. Clayton's biography is generally a sensible work in that it characterizes Bourne's life and work fully and fairly and submits it to judgment. It is original in its research into unpublished materials and is informed by the erudition of a professional historian. But while there is much to commend in the book—the tactful and judicious use of Erikson's theories of personality development, the sympathetic yet critical portrait of Bourne and his friends—readers will be dismayed at Clayton's uncritical approval of Bourne's unjustified argument that war is the health of the (capitalist) state. There is much to commend in Bourne: his right-minded cultural pluralism, his claims on behalf of intelligence and art, his triumph over his personal handicap. But his conception of state capitalism and war reveals a grotesque Leninist distortion that appears to have seduced not only ideologue historians of liberalism like Charles Forcey and Robert Wiebe but Clayton as well. It is well worth remembering, and emphasizing, that Bourne's antiwar rhetoric was wildly Anglophobic, that his admiration for German *Kultur* was never far below the surface, and that many articulate socialists disagreed with Bourne and approved the war as a just response to the German barbarities in France and Belgium.

Munson's memoir-history subjects the Twenties to a critique by one who was deeply involved in the Brooks-Bourne milieu. Munson died in 1969, but he had completed a nearly finished draft of the book, which has now been polished by his widow Elizabeth Delza and the press editors. It is not a compelling book on the level of mind; nor is its style worth commending. Certain chapters seem choppy, and the book is backbroken by the irreconcilable double intention signified by its subtitle. But it is not without its interest in relation to the problematic of literary radicalism in America.

We have had many such books in the past half century: Malcolm Cowley's *Exile's Return,* Matthew Josephson's *Life Among the Surrealists,* Harold Loeb's *The Way It Was,* Hemingway's *A Moveable Feast,* and Brooks's *Days of the Phoenix.* What does Munson have to add? First, another perspective on personal interrelations amongst writers and artists, editors and publishers whom he knew well: Hart Crane, Carl Van Vechten, John Reed, Floyd Dell, Waldo Frank, Alfred Stieglitz, Robert Frost, William Carlos Williams, Bourne and Brooks, Margaret Anderson, Jane Heap, Mable Dodge, Emma Goldman, Herbert Croly, Eugene O'Neill, George Bellows, William Sommer, Marsden Hartley, Man Ray, and others. Second, he tries to see these figures as composing a generation of the avant-garde in the arts. He is not so much inter-

1 *The Awakening Twenties: A Memoir-History of a Literary Period,* by Gorham Munson: Louisiana State University Press, 384 pages, $19.95.

2 *Forgotten Prophet: The Life of Randolph Bourne,* by Bruce Clayton: Louisiana State University Press, 320 pages, $25.

ested in politics as he is in describing what Pound had called for in "Patria Mia" (1913), an "American Risorgimento," or "intellectual awakening," in which the arts would lead the way.

In his essay on "Advance-Guard Writing in America: 1900-1950," Paul Goodman has argued that "An artist does not know that he is advance-guard, he must be told so or learn it from the reaction of the audience." But as we have seen, most of these figures claimed themselves to be an avant-garde almost before they had written a line. If they called themselves *les jeunes,* it was, thanks to Bourne and Brooks, without a trace of irony. Munson describes himself and his friends as flushed with "the opportunity to rebel and fulfill themselves." For them, every manifestation of the new art and letters was a "revival of the national spirit," an occasion for enthusiasm—largely, one might add, an undiscriminating enthusiasm. Munson details in near rhapsodic terms what life in the bohemia of Greenwich Village meant, what enthusiasm was generated, at the Washington Square Book Shop, by each new issue of *The Little Review, The New Republic, The Nation, The Dial, Vanity Fair, The Smart Set, Seven Arts,* and *Secession*—the last of which Munson edited with Matthew Josephson and Kenneth Burke. (He conspicuously omits *The Masses* and *Liberator.*)

As befitting his historical intent, Munson introduces our time to the editors of these and other then-popular magazines, reprints their manifestos, and summarizes their typical content. He offers extended discussion of the publishers of the avant-garde in the 1920s—Alfred Knopf, Boni and Liveright, B.W. Huebsch, Charles Scribner, and Harcourt, Brace, and Howe. Munson recreates the art world of the Armory Show of 1913 and the Woodstock colony of painters and writers then flourishing, as well as the evenings of animated talk at Mabel Dodge's salon or the studio of Rosetta O'Neill. All of this adds up to intellectual and artistic ferment of an intense order. But what was it grounded on, for Munson, and what were its fruits?

With respect to its politics, insofar as Munson and his circle had an identifiable politics, we have already noted how Bourne and Brooks, together with Charles Beard and others, had predisposed *les jeunes* toward a perpetual revolution that would somehow lead to socialism. Bourne, who had been a member of the Intercollegiate Socialist Society at Columbia ("the brainchild," according to Clayton, "of Jack London and Upton Sinclair"), electrified Munson with arguments such as this, from "For Radicals": in America, wrote Bourne, "the very food we eat, the clothes we wear, the simplest necessities of life . . . have their roots somewhere, somehow, in exploitation and injustice. It is a cardinal necessity of the social system under which we live that this should be so, where the bulk of the work of the world is done, not for human use and happiness, but primarily and directly for the profits of masters and owners." Munson and the others thrilled to Bourne's invocation of the Wobblies as the true "revolutionary Socialists." Clayton correctly sees how much of Bourne's youthful Marxism was "schoolboy rhetoric." But other schoolboys, like Munson, whatever their age, were electrified by the daring of such pronouncements.

One can see this in Munson's enchantment with Waldo Frank's *Our America* (1919), which intoned the socialist denunciation of America. "Our America," for *les jeunes,* was "the America of cultural radicals and social radicals, 'the men who listen to Stieglitz, and have not quite joined him in their mind with the example of Bill Haywood.'" For *les jeunes,* the America of the Founding Fathers was "Their America," whereas "Our America began with Thoreau, Lincoln, and Whitman." This was heady stuff to young Munson, and it led him to write *Waldo Frank: A Study* (1923), in which Frank's genius and the new faith were stoutly proclaimed.

But Munson obviously could not reconcile his literary interests and the political radicalism of his contemporaries. He perhaps changed more rapidly than any of them. Particularly, he could not reconcile his growing belief in Jeffersonianism ("that government is best which governs least") with the statism of Marx, Shaw, Wells, Eastman, Gold, and the rest. Thereupon ensued what Munson called his period of "philosophic anarchism," which was stimulated by the contributors to *The Freeman*. An amalgam of vague notions proclaimed by Albert Jay Nock, Francis Neilson, Emma Goldman, and Margaret Anderson, this anarchism of Munson's led him to abandon electoral politics "on principle," to attack the liberalism of *The Nation* and *The New Republic,* which he had formerly espoused, and to regard the state as "fundamentally anti-social." The task at hand, said *The Freeman,* was to improve the state "off the face of the earth, not by blowing up office-holders, as Mr. [A. Mitchell] Palmer appears to suppose, but by the historical processes of strengthening, consolidating and enlightening economic organization." When we recollect that the enlightenment of the economic organization proposed by these anarchists rested upon the ideas of Henry George (the unearned increment, the single tax), the absurdity of the position becomes manifest. Munson himself eventually came to realize the untenability of his situation:

> Having been in rapid succession a liberal, a socialist, a supporter of the Soviets, I had called myself for a couple of years a philosophical anarchist . . . . Anarchism was an emotional choice; I waved the question of practicality. The vision of Kropotkin would prove practical in the washing, I told myself . . . . Looking back, it seems I had an ambition without a clear goal and a vague sense of dissatisfaction with current American writing without a fixed viewpoint to give meaning to my dissatisfaction.

This is a remarkable admission. It expresses the impulse, fitfully evident in the book, to reconstitute the Twenties as a time of diversely energetic enterprises, in art and social thought, yet one lacking principle, lacking a clear understanding of what America was all about, of what philosophically and historically was meant by the notion of the individual and the state, and of what the role of literature and criticism might be within the state. Being young geniuses together, then, had produced a Twenties version of the intellectual follies. Although Munson tries to remain as impersonal as possible, truth breaks in with all her matter-of-fact in this extraordinary assessment of the time:

> But taking a retrospective view of those days . . . , I will venture the remark that if the word for the Yellow Nineties is pretty *infantilism,* the word for the Twenties is *arrogant juvenility.* Perhaps that is why I cannot, in the manner of several chroniclers of the early jazz age, review my immersion in it with romantic regret over time's passing. The period was something to be outgrown.

One appreciates the candor and self-criticism of this remark. It is an older and perhaps wiser man's reflection on the excesses and confusions of his youth. It witnesses to a truth that has been obscured by the self-serving memoirs of its survivors who have romanticized their intellectual, artistic, and political muddlement under the banner of liberal values.

Perhaps the central issue is thought, meditation, reflection on principles, and the consequences of abandoning reason to feeling. For Bourne, "too much rationality makes a man mercenary and calculating," as he observed in "The Experimental Life." Bourne preferred the monitions of the heart as "usually better than the logic of the head, and the consistency of sympathy is superior as a rule for life to the consistency of the intellect." This represents a perilous anti-intellectualism for youths who aspire to criticize culture and is implicitly dismissive of historical understanding. Jefferson, Madison, Hamilton, Franklin, and the others had already worked out the logic of our constitutional democracy, established the essential arguments for our system of political, economic, and civil rights, had already considered and rejected the alternative that seemed a novelty in the Twenties to *les jeunes.* The formulation of the Framers was not yet perfect, as they understood, but it was susceptible to rational change, based on an electoral consensus. Especially they understood what Emerson was later to call, in "Politics," the "law for man" and the "law for property," each of which will always assert its claim, both together making up our life in society. But *les jeunes* were impatient with rationality and accumulated experience; they were deficient in historical understanding, insufficiently educated in polity. Their critique of property rights in the name of economic redistribution, based on admirable enough humanitarian feeling, produced in the Twenties both a longing to overthrow the system—through labor violence, if need be, as Big Bill Haywood proposed—and the reactionary excesses of state authority in the form of Attorney General A. Mitchell Palmer. Between perpetual revolution and reactionary repression the American people were somehow supposed to make a choice. It is not a matter of luck that neither type of extremism succeeded in carrying the day. The constitutional safeguards to American liberty and legal provisions for social order contained, despite much testing and some failures, both the kind of violence Haywood propounded and the repressive intolerance of the embattled authorities.

Munson's Twenties is not, then, after all, the Twenties of socialist revolutionism. Nor is it the Twenties of the Jazz Age, the Lost Generation, the Waste Land cult of cynicism, the era of Flaming Youth, Bohemianism, and indiscriminate debunking. Pretty much, for Munson, the immediate excitations of Freudianism, Jungianism, Constructivism, Futurism, Imagism, Vorticism, Cubism, Skyscraperism, and Dadaism were versions of an energy without a clear principle or objective, a manifestation of the confusion of the times. In retrospect, Munson cannot see what he once saw in Waldo Frank, and he is certain that Irving Babbitt's New Humanism offered more than its critics would allow. An instance of the speed with which Munson was growing out of the jejune romanticism of the Twenties is his book *Robert Frost: A Study in Sensibility and Good Sense* (1927), which found Frost's conservative "classicism" an antidote to the anarchy of the times.

Anarchy may seem an exaggerated term, but Munson's account of Malcolm Cowley's Dadaist phase will perhaps clarify a period which, for sheer literary inanity, is matched only by the 1960s. Munson describes how Cowley was taken over by the excesses of Louis Aragon and André Breton, who repudiated rationality in favor of nonsense manifestos and "significant gestures" of violence intended as a "shock treatment for a crazed humanity." Cowley's punching of the proprietor of the Rotonde in Paris is invoked by Munson as an instance of what Cowley's Dadaist principles apparently "required" him to do. But perhaps a more significant gesture of revolt against reason was the episode, at Cowley's home in Giverny, marked by a book-burning and micturating party. There Cowley was said to have burned a number of books (including perhaps a set of Racine, on whom he was writing his thesis) in a gesture of revolt against rationality and "book fetishism." Accounts of this episode vary, but Cowley was described by Harold Loeb as roaring "Too much *merde,* too much junk. Words aren't enough," while "the soft night smelled of urine and burning paper." Ah, *les jeunes.* Horace Gregory was later to ask: "What group of young Americans today would set fire to books written by their betters in an open fireplace?" He could hardly have guessed, in 1959, that within a few years whole libraries would be trashed and some, like the library at University College of New York University, would be set aflame.

It is very likely that Cowley, Loeb, and others at the book-burning party were drunk. And Cowley has minimized the incident as involving only some execrable French reviews and old textbooks. But in fact this Dadaist repudiation of the literary tradition enacted at Giverny, with Cowley speechifying, commending his books to the flames, and peeing on them, is not different from that wonderful satirical scene, in Chapter Forty-one of Maugham's *Of Human Bondage* (1915), where Maugham describes the young literary radicals of the *fin de siècle* in Paris. They sound breathtakingly like Cowley and *les jeunes* of the New York literary scene in the Twenties:

"Great art can't exist without a moral element."

"Oh God!" cried Lawson furiously. "I knew it was that. He wants morality." He joined his hands and held them towards heaven in supplication. "Oh, Christopher Columbus, Christopher Columbus, what did you do when you discovered America?"

"Ruskin says . . ."

"Gentlemen," he said in a stern voice, and his huge nose positively wrinkled with passion, "a name has been mentioned which I never thought to hear again in decent society. Freedom of speech is all very well, but we must observe the limits of common propriety. You may talk of Bouguereau if you will; there is a cheerful disgustingness in the sound which excites laughter; but let us not sully our chaste lips with the names of J. Ruskin, G. F. Watts, or E. B. Jones."

"Who was Ruskin anyway?" asked Flanagan.

"He was one of the great Victorians. He was a master of English style."

"Ruskin's style—a thing of shreds and purple patches," said Lawson. "Besides, damn the Great Victorians. Whenever I open a paper and see Death of a Great Victorian, I thank Heaven there's one more of them gone. Their only talent was longevity, and no artist should be allowed to live after he's forty; by then a man has done his best work, all he does after that is repetition. Don't you think it was the greatest luck in the world for them that Keats, Shelley, Bonington, and Byron died early? What a genius we should think Swinburne if he had perished on the day the first series of *Poems and Ballads* was published!"

The suggestion pleased, for no one at the table was more than twenty-four, and they threw themselves upon it with gusto. They were unanimous for once. They elaborated. Someone proposed a vast bonfire made out of the works of the Forty Academicians into which the Great Victorians might be hurled on their fortieth birthday. The idea was received with acclamation. Carlyle and Ruskin, Tennyson, Browning, G. F. Watts, E. B. Jones, Dickens, Thackeray, they were hurried into the flames; Mr. Gladstone, John Bright, and Cobden; there was a moment's discussion about George Meredith, but Matthew Arnold and Emerson were given up cheerfully. At last came Walter Pater.

"Not Walter Pater," murmured Philip.

Lawson stared at him for a moment with his green eyes and then nodded.

"You're quite right . . . ."

In the case of these youth, an exception for Pater could be made in the name of aestheticism. But whatever the Victorian past might have meant in terms of social values and moral ideas, these—insofar as they were embodied in the work of the great Victorians—counted for naught. All young artists of course commend themselves on the ground of the purity of their art. Yet one invariably finds in such instances of youthful literary radicalism little understanding of the relation between the aesthetic and the social or historical; in fact, there is an evident inclination to deny the relationship.

In "The Idea of Order at Key West," Wallace Stevens meditated on the creative process as a "rage for order," with the implication that art is constructive and constitutive of reality. And so it is. Art orders reality by ordering perception and understanding. Painting and music, literature and architecture, these and the other arts, together with those social institutions that, by their very survival, testify to their necessity for us as social beings—these make up the indispensable elements of civilization that the conservative would guard; they are values already in place, but continually in question, and the destruction of them would be an impoverishment of our lives.

But another argument could be and has been made that art is a rage for disorder, for the destruction of form, with the implication that such "beautiful murderings of reality" (to use E. E. Cummings's description of Picasso's art) are necessary to destroy our encrusted perceptual habits, our tendency to passive, thoughtless, surrender to the culturally given. There is merit in this view. Whenever original genius reconstitutes our perception of reality in beautiful forms we are individually enriched; and culture in its historical configuration becomes a more valuable gift to the young coming into it. But the burden on the young of the culturally given can never justify their periodic tendency to want to destroy it; nor can the conservative wish them to have the social power to realize their aims. Was there anything exaggerated in Edith Wharton's satire, in *Hudson River Bracketed* (1929), on the Parisian radicals' wish to "break the old moulds" and "demolish the old landmarks"? As her character Lorry Spear puts it: "Who ever consulted you and me when the Pyramids were built—or Versailles? Why should we be saddled with all that old dead masonry? Ruins are what we want—more ruins!" This is merely a fictive way of saying what Aragon, Breton, Antonin Artaud, Paul Eluard and twenty-four other artistic radicals said in their "Open Letter to M. Paul Claudel, French Ambassador to Japan" (1925): "We are not concerned with creation. We fervently hope that wars and colonial insurrections will annihilate this Western civilization whose vermin you protect in the East, and we appeal to this destruction as the state of affairs least inacceptable to the mind."

This is No, in Thunder. This is cultural alienation in the extremity of its crisis, a self-loathing and a self-destructiveness that would bring down the temple of civilization on everyone else too, a death kit for what is seen as only a charnel house of horrors. The Twenties had no monopoly on Life As a Nightmare, on the desire for Apocalypse Now. Twain wanted to wipe out nineteenth-century civilization in The Battle of the Sand Belt in *A Connecticut Yankee,* Captain Ahab revenged himself by destroying the *Pequod* crew, West's *The Day of the Locust* hankered for "The Burning of Los Angeles," and Pynchon's *Gravity's Rainbow* concludes in a nuclear catastrophe. If God repented himself for having created mankind and wished to destroy his civilization in a universal flood, we should not be surprised that novelists and critics sometimes succumb to the apocalyptic madness. It arises out of cultural disappointment, desire unfulfilled, out of the discrepancy between a personal fantasy of possible perfection and the hard, intractable order of reality, of life, which, as Emerson observed, cares little for systems and system-makers, whether they be utopian social engineers or makers of aesthetic systems.

What should be the relationship between the modern artist and his culture? In "The Fate of the Avant Garde" (*Partisan Review,* Summer 1957), Richard Chase commended the view espoused by William Phillips, who saw the avant-garde artist as a "suspended man" who "keeps the balance of opposing forces," who is situated "between tradition and revolt, nationalism and internationalism, the aesthetic and the civic, and between belonging and alienation." There is something to be said for this formulation. But this was not a position adequately allowed to the avant-garde artist by the critics of the radical Left, who demanded political alienation. Even literary radicals like Brooks and V. L. Parrington posed literary issues in terms of sociological categories, as in fact mutually exclusive extremes: liberals and reactionaries; highbrows and lowbrows; and, more recently, palefaces and redskins. The center ground in the Twenties was the joke of middlebrowism, with all the negative implications of a bourgeois conservatism ascribed to it. This middle ground was thus no ground at all for the writers of what Chase calls "the insurgent movement in this country which defended 'modernism'—that is, the aesthetic experimentalism and social protest of the period between 1912 and 1950."

The reduction, by Brooks and others, of America's rich cultural complexity and diversity to such oversimplified sociological categories thus left many artists in the 1920s with nowhere to stand. Fortunately, the best artists stood for their art. How did the radical Left receive them? A good test case is the reception of *The Waste Land* and *Ulysses,* both published in 1922, both cornerstones of the modernist avant-garde. As literary editor of *The Freeman,* Van Wyck Brooks had nothing worthwhile to say about them. To have acclaimed them would have entrapped him, he understood, in a political contradiction that he—unlike the later *Partisan Review* group—could not tolerate.

But if Chase did not accurately perceive the dilemma of the experimental artist who was being told that socialist alienation was his only response to American life, he did grasp the ways in which the irreconcilable motives of insurgency in art and politics disoriented Brooks, once he came to understand them:

> Brooks abdicated from modern culture about 1925, drawing back in horror from the genie whose bottle his early polemics had helped to unstopper. For behold! among the great writers who really spoke for the present and the future were Eliot, Joyce, Proust, Gide, Hemingway, and Pound, and they all seemed to Brooks culturally dangerous—they were, he said, undemocratic, highbrow, coterie writers.

Of course it is improbable to think that Eliot, Joyce, Proust, Gide, and the rest would have been bottled up, and uncreative, had not Brooks's polemics unstoppered them. Brooks's influence was America-oriented, and essentially important to writers of the second order. The conclusion is thus inescapable that the really great artistic modernists of the Teens and Twenties managed to realize their genius by ignoring, or resolutely rejecting, the alienated insurgent politics demanded of them by the literary sociologists of the Left. In declining what "the age demanded," they sometimes appeared to be more undemocratic than, in fact, they were—the Pound of the Thirties always, of course, excepted.

But what of avant-garde writers who could not find themselves, or find that ideal middle ground within American culture that Phillips hypothesized? Here, both Hart Crane and Gorham Munson are exemplary. Close friends during Crane's best years (1919-1925), they both were wracked by the cultural incoherence of the time. It is with great sorrow that Munson recounts the story of Crane's collapse into alcoholism, compulsive homosexuality, artistic paralysis, and eventual suicide. Crane is held forth to us as an instance of the cost to genius of the intellectual deracination and spiritual alienation so pervasive in the Twenties.

Munson himself, as we have seen, did not fare too well in the period up to about 1924, for the demand upon him, as well as upon others, to be insurgent in socio-political thought as well as in art immersed him in such a welter of competing political, social, and literary movements that, without a principle with which to interrogate the concept of insurgency itself, he was at sea. In reaction to Brooks's tendency to reduce literature to an instrument of class analysis and social change, Munson eventually came to call for a deeper aesthetic understanding which would see the work of art in its own right, and not as a datum of "sociological criticism." In his *Dial* essay of January 1925, "Van Wyck Brooks," Munson's pre-New Criticism search for a ground upon which the work of art could regain an intrinsic aesthetic autonomy is evident. This search became more obvious in his book on Frost, which commended such principles as restraint, order, and the "law of decorum or measure or proportion." Such a view smacked of the New Humanism, which had tried to reintroduce the faculty of reason into these issues; but with this, of course, radical insurgency could have no traffic.

Yet it would be a mistake to keep the focus on these literary matters. For the dominant intent of *The Awakening Twenties* is not to offer a private correction of our literary history in aesthetic terms. When we ask how Munson escaped the chaos of rootless insurgent intellectualism in his time, the answer does not lie in a more precise understanding of the character of art or its social function. Munson escaped, it must be immediately said, through spiritualism. Introduced to P. D. Ouspensky's *Tertium Organum* by Hart Crane and thence to the bizarre mysticism of G. I. Gurdjieff and his English apostle A. R. Orage, Munson surrendered himself to the esoteric regimen by which, his masters alleged, one could ascend to the highest level of cosmic consciousness. This does not get us much beyond Whitman and his disciple Richard Maurice Bucke, and is of a piece with it. But Gurdjieff claimed to have rediscovered the technique, lost in antiquity, by which the Egyptians, Buddhists, Pythagoreans, and Gnostics attained unto "The Fourth Way." In private meetings in New York salons and at Gurdjieff's Château du Prieuré, where Gurdjieff had founded his Institute for the Harmonious Development of Man, Munson and his wife submitted themselves to the discipline, which involved sacred gymnastics or exotic dancing, the repression or denial of the ego, and humiliating manual labor (like breaking up stones on the guru's estate), all intended to produce the new illumination.

Gurdjieff was a quack and a charlatan or a spiritual genius, depending on one's point of view. For Waldo Frank, who went to Prieuré seeking the Light, Gurdjieff was a devil; Munson thought otherwise, and there is no use quarreling with him. What seems evident is that in the intellectual, social, and moral disorder of the Twenties—in what Crane called "the spiritual disintegration of the period"—rootless artists and intellectuals were predisposed to search for absolutist remedies that conferred, at least for a while, some meaning on life. Some took the route of political radicalism. Others found it in Theosophy, Anthroposophy, Coué-ism, or Moral Rearmament, in the Society for Psychical Research, Freudianism, Anglo-Catholicism and Royalism, in Aimee Semple McPhersonism, in the esoteric doctrines of highly touted swamis, and in the California nut cults that Nathanael West satirized in *Miss Lonelyhearts.*

Something of the ridiculous side of Twenties spiritualism is inadvertently revealed in Munson's fond descriptions of the meetings of the Orage group in New York City—at Muriel Draper's, Rosetta O'Neill's, and Margaret Anderson's—where Gurdjieff's mysticism was commended to what Munson calls the *intelligentsia,* "the public that in 1924 read the *Dial* and the *New Republic* and *Vanity Fair,* listened to Stravinsky and Schoenberg, looked at Picasso and Matisse, discussed psychoanalysis and the progressive education of John Dewey, and inclined toward socialism." If this was the pastime of the intelligentsia, it sounds suspiciously like the *soirées* that enchanted Carol Kennicott in Sinclair Lewis's *Main Street.* But as Mencken remarked, Lewis's identification of this with culture was bogus. Yet we find in Munson's account the record of those who came to Orage's presentations—some to scoff, some to pray: Brooks, Padraic Colum, Edna Kenton, Mable Dodge Luhan, Boardman Robinson, T. S. Matthews, Herbert Croly, Melville Cane, Jean Toomer, Hart Crane, Margaret Naumberg, Frank and Helen Westley. Toomer, like Katherine Mansfield, seems to have been a total convert, but Crane was turned off by those who had "rushed into the portals of the famous Gurdjieff institute and have put themselves through all sorts of Hindu antics, songs, dances, incantations, psychic sessions, etc."

Munson's conversion in 1924 to the Ouspensky-Gurdjieff work of spiritual self-development may have brought him serenity, even cosmic consciousness, although Munson is modest about this. But it was not a good preparation for writing a personal memoir, much less a literary history of those turbulent years. For the resultant prose is flat and affectless. It lacks personality: after all, Gurdjieff had taught his disciples to regard themselves as "non-entities." Hence, Munson found it "very difficult," in writing this book so many years later, "to feel oneself back in 1921." Not even the hijacking of his magazine *Secession* by Malcolm Cowley and John Brooks Wheelwright provokes much more indignation than "Ah, yewth,

yewth! We fledgling writers were more adept in sizing up books than in sizing up people." And his account of his fistfight with Matthew Josephson—whom he had called an intellectual faker before the assembled American Dadaists in a Prince Street speakeasy—is downplayed as mere boyish high spirits.

That time may soften old enmities and reconcile literary antagonists, especially if one has been converted to the Higher Way, is perhaps understandable. But what does not ring true to the biographical record is Munson's account of the decline of the poet in "The Untold Story of Hart Crane." Stripped to its essentials, Munson argues here that Crane was well on his way to a true understanding of Ouspensky's view that "Art in its highest manifestation is a path to cosmic consciousness." But when Orage came to America to elaborate on Ouspenskyian-Gurdjieffian mysticism, Crane was unwilling to submit himself to the discipline of the "C" influence, which is "exercised only by direct contact of master with disciple." Crane recoiled from Gurdjieff, "as though shocked by a high-voltage current," in consequence of which his "magnetic center" dissolved, he became creatively paralyzed, failed to finish *The Bridge,* and presumably was fated for suicide. One would have to be one of the mystic's disciples to accept this reading of Crane's tragic decline, which in fact expressed a poignant instability of self lacking, in that chaotic time, the support that a coherent culture may provide.

What necessary effect, if any, does an imperative of political insurgency have upon a literary avant-garde moved by idealistic social longings? In the case of Munson's *les jeunes,* we can see that the legacy of Bourne and Brooks was a legacy of cultural criticism on a wobbly base, with the effect that, along with other forces, it served to unsettle their politics, to subvert, at least implicitly, the principles of constitutional democracy as envisioned by the Founding Fathers, and to render somehow plausible the more explicit and chilling Communist Party agenda of the 1930s. If Munson escaped into spiritualism and sacred gymnastics, something of the same moral history can be seen in some of the insurgent youth of the 1960s who were swept up into New Left radicalism, fomented social disorder, got a good look into the Abyss, became disillusioned, withdrew to Tibet, submitted to one or another popular guru, worshipped one or another Rock group, wrote Wichita Vortex Sutras, or took up the saffron robes and tambourines of the Hari Krishnas. Such avenues of escape from the alienation of self in a time of social disorder are a perennial fact of American cultural experience. They are of a piece with the Millerites withdrawing in white sheets, on October 22, 1844, to await the Second Coming. But most of us are fated to live in the real world, the world of work and love, of getting and spending, of thinking and feeling, and of integrating our experience into a sense of the continuity of our culture, aware of the finitude of our private being.

In such a world the vitality of particular works of art and the utility of the critical tradition must invariably engage the mind. In respect to criticism, we note that Clayton calls Bourne a "forgotten prophet," and it may be true that he is of value only when war seems imminent. Perhaps Clayton is also right in remarking that "Only historians and a few older professors of English take Brooks seriously today." Clearly the best art of the period from 1915-1930 was not amenable to the sociological reductions of critics like Brooks and Bourne. Eliot, Pound, Frost, Hemingway, Faulkner, and Stevens—as instances of literary modernism—created works of art that still claim our attention. Their continuing command upon us is inextricably connected to their rejection of a pragmatic or functionalist view of art as the instrument of social change. This does not mean that they are without social effect, for they transformed consciousness then and they still do today.

We need the kind of imaginative experimentalism, the kind of *literary* radicalism their work represents. For the reconstitution of aesthetic forms is by no means unassimilable with the conservation of worthwhile values in American culture. Much of aesthetic experimentalism may lead down blind alleys toward dead ends. But we can never predict what elements of form, sedimented in our culture or lost to feeling in a neglected work from the past, will somehow be revitalized and renovated, suddenly foregrounded in a new work of genius. Culture is immediately enriched by the recognition of such works. Human perception is clarified, taste is corrected, unseen intellectual relations are discovered, and standards of judgment are more nearly perfected. And the relation of these matters to the regulative and normative conditions of our public being, as a democratic society under the rule of a law hospitable to individual genius, is made plain to consciousness. When we think about *The Waste Land,* the *Cantos, The Sound and the Fury,* and like works, they bring into focus questions about taste and judgment, politics and culture, tradition and the individual talent, in a way that the works of Floyd Dell and Waldo Frank, of Max Eastman and Upton Sinclair, of Sinclair Lewis and Mike Gold—the stalwarts of literary radicalism—can never do.

(*March* 1985)

Who was Josephine Herbst?

by Hilton Kramer

Condemn the fault and not the actor of it?
—Measure for Measure

There is a passage in an essay by Henry James—it occurs in the obituary article he wrote on "Dumas the Younger" in 1895—which defines very exactly the feeling we are likely to experience when, at a certain age, we see the people we have known and who have meant a good deal to us pass away and become in death something very different from what they were in life, both in their own lives and in ours.

> One of the things that most bring home his time of life to a man of fifty [James wrote] is the increase of the rate at which he loses his friends. Some one dies every week, some one dies every day, and if the rate be high among his coevals it is higher still in the generation that, on awakening to spectatorship, he found in possession of the stage. He begins to feel his own world, the world of his most vivid impressions, gradually become historical. He is present, and closely present, at the process by which legend grows up.

For the past year or so I have had reason to ponder this passage a good deal as I have read—first in manuscript, then in galleys, and finally in its published form—the biography which Elinor Langer has devoted to my old friend Josephine Herbst.[1] When Josie Herbst died in 1969, I wasn't yet, to be sure, a man of fifty. I was almost ten years younger than that. Nevertheless, both her death and its aftermath gave me for the first time and to an extent unequaled by the passing of any other writer or artist I have known precisely the perspective, with all of its attendant nuances, that James spoke of. They gave me, that is, my first experience of seeing "the world of [my] most vivid impressions, gradually become historical." And now, with the publication of Elinor Langer's book these fifteen years later, I have the distinct feeling of finding myself "present, and closely present, at the process by which legend grows up." For if I read the signs correctly, Josie Herbst is about to be readmitted—and with a certain fanfare, too—to the public arena of literature and politics where, before her fall, she had passed so much of her adult life. It will not be primarily as an admired author, however, that she will now be rediscovered. Almost all of her writings have long been out of print, and few of the enthusiasts who are now eagerly preparing to assist in her elevation to stardom can be expected to have read them. This time it will not be as a novelist or journalist or memoirist that Josie Herbst will be welcomed into the company of the elect—not yet, anyway—but as a radical heroine and martyr of the feminist movement. Which, if this should come to pass, would

1 *Josephine Herbst* by Elinor Langer. Atlantic Monthly Press/Little, Brown; 374 pages, $19.95.

tell us—as all such acts of canonization do—a good deal more about the strange times in which we are now living than it would about the tormented life and the failed work of the woman herself.

To the world that presides over canonizations of this sort—the world where reputations are made, influence wielded, and significant sums of money dispensed—Josie Herbst had become a ghostly figure in the years that I knew her, the last dozen years of her long life. Although recognized by name in the councils of the literary establishment, she was nonetheless shunned and "forgotten"—a writer who, though she might still be expected at some future date to make a comeback, was pretty much left to make it on her own. Except to a small circle of (mostly younger) friends and admirers and an even smaller circle of survivors from her own generation, she had dropped out of sight. Whether this constituted a withdrawal on her part (which to some degree it was) or an outright rejection by her contemporaries (which in part it also was) is a matter likely to be a subject of debate and speculation now that her life and career are up for re-examination. For all practical purposes, however, she was in the years that I knew her an "unknown" figure. She was ignored, she was unread, and she was very poor—living, as a matter of fact, largely on handouts from her friends, a few of whom had some money but most of whom were, like myself, just getting by on modest salaries and makeshift incomes. More often than not in those days she was reduced to wearing hand-me-down clothes, and she spent much of her time, especially in winter, since her house in Pennsylvania had neither central heating nor indoor plumbing, residing in one borrowed apartment after another. She was not only broke, she was broken—shattered by the vicissitudes of an unhappy life that she was desperately attempting to come to terms with and never quite succeeding.

That she was also in those years a woman of tremendous vitality and spirit, a sparkling talker and articulate storyteller possessed of a vivid personality, an appealing sense of humor, and a genius for making herself interesting and even endearing; a woman, moreover, for whom the glamour and the hardship of the old literary life had never lost their magical spell—all of this only added to the high drama of her situation and the terrible poignancy of her shattered hopes. For make no mistake about it, it was as a failure and as a peculiarly significant failure—as a failed writer and as a failed woman—that some of us knew her in those last years. Call her, if you like, a heroine and a martyr—that, certainly, will be the approach of those now bent on enlisting Josie Herbst in their various causes—but to do so is, among much else, to sentimentalize a tragedy. It was, in any case, as an example of a certain kind of failure that we knew her, and as a failure, oddly enough, that she made her claim upon us.

In the biography that Elinor Langer has now given us—the first to be devoted to Josephine Herbst—no attempt has been made to soften this sense of failure or to shift responsibility for it onto others. Miss Langer understands very well that, whatever else may have been involved, the principal cause of Josie Herbst's undoing was Josie Herbst herself, and she doesn't flinch from disclosing a good deal of ugly detail—much of which will be a revelation even to those few who think they know the subject well—in the course of telling her absorbing story. There are villains in the book, and some surprising ones, too, and no shortage of mean-spirited and even horrific actions, all meticulously recounted. But it is one of the virtues of this book that its author never attempts to disguise or to mitigate the role played by Josie herself in some of the most terrible episodes of her life. Miss Langer is an unsparing writer, and a very gifted one, too, and it is a mark of her candor that the tale that is told in *Josephine Herbst* is almost unrelievedly grim. She not only has a keen grasp of the wretchedness that dominated so much of Josie Herbst's life, but she has had the skill to so arrange the narrative that many of the most horrifying events are told in Josie Herbst's own words—though not, of course, from her point of view alone. Miss Langer maintains her own authorial voice throughout, and while her sympathy for Josie Herbst is openly stated and deeply felt, in biographical matters it does not blind her —except in one outstanding regard—to her subject's more egregious failings.

On only one issue—but one that is absolutely central to the life of Josephine Herbst —can Miss Langer be said to have failed, and failed utterly, to take hold of her subject with the requisite tough-mindedness and deal frankly with its implications. That issue is politics, about which Miss Langer appears to share so many of the illusions that disfigured Josie Herbst's life and work that she can no more bring herself to deal with them than Josie herself could. As a result, Miss Langer is obliged to lapse into a kind of silence or else take refuge in a kind of innocence or insouciance about the one phenomenon which, more than any other, caused the woman she is writing about to become a casualty of her time. That phenomenon, of course, is Stalinism in all of its many manifestations, political and cultural. About the role of Stalinism, then, both in Josie Herbst's life and in Elinor Langer's book, there is much to be said, and I shall address that issue here in its appropriate place. Astonishingly, Miss Langer leaves the subject untouched. Yet the life of Josephine Herbst cannot really be understood in isolation from the Stalinist ethos that shaped so crucial a part of it.

In writing about Elinor Langer's *Josephine Herbst,* however, I cannot pretend to speak as a disinterested observer. I must declare my interest, which, both in relation to Josie Herbst and in regard to Miss Langer's book, has been a very close and somewhat paradoxical one. It is not only that I knew Josie Herbst and spent a great many hours in conversation with her over a period of years, or even that I felt—despite our many differences—a deep affection for her. There is more to it than that. Shortly before her death, Josie Herbst made an arrangement with Yale University for the sale of her papers, and as a result an extensive Josephine Herbst archive was established at Yale's Beinecke Library. At the time she made this arrangement, Josie asked me to serve as the executor of her estate in the event of her death. This I agreed to do. When she died, I therefore found myself with the sole responsibility for granting access to her papers. This meant, among other things, that no serious biography of Josephine Herbst could be written without my cooperation. Perhaps I should add that restrictions had to be placed on the papers in the interest of protecting the privacy of many living persons. All her life Josie had been a tireless correspondent. Often, especially in her later years, she made copies of her letters. In some cases her letters were later returned to her en bloc. Her correspondence with certain writers she had known—Katherine Anne Porter, for example—was copious. Friends frequently confided their innermost secrets to her; perhaps at times they even invented some for her benefit. It was not unusual for casual acquaintances, people she hardly knew but upon whom she had made an emphatic impression, to bare their souls when writing to her—especially in response to her own letters, which were often marvelous. In addition to the letters there are also notebooks. Some of these, too, deal with intimate affairs, her own and others'. Josie appears to have kept everything. The papers are voluminous. Obviously some sort of limit had to be placed on access to them, and I made certain that this would be done. I have never myself read through the entire archive; as far as I know, Miss Langer is the only person to have done so. But in the period immediately following Josie's death I read just enough in these papers to acquire a pretty good notion of what their potential might be for causing pain, embarrassment, or worse to a great many people. I took it as part of my task as executor to ensure that this would not happen.

Exactly why Josie Herbst selected me for this task is not a question to which I can give a definitive answer. I frankly don't know for certain. She had several friends with whom she shared political confidences (I now realize) she never shared with me; and there were others she was closer to in other ways. She certainly knew there were many political issues about which we disagreed categorically, and she was well aware, too, that there were many aspects of her life about which she had been less than candid with me. The painful truth is, she lied much and she concealed much. (But this, of course, I did not discover until after her death.) I can only assume that about the things that mattered most to her at that time she trusted my judgment, and that in any case she wanted an executor who would allow the truth to be told about her life when the time came to tell it. I think it was important to her, too, to know that her literary affairs would not fall into the hands of an academic. She had a very low opinion of the way the professors of literature were coming to deal with the writers of her generation. (Carlos Baker's biography of Hemingway, whom she had known well in earlier years, was a particular object of scorn; she could rail about it for hours. And some of the interpretations then being made of the work of her friend Nathanael West prompted similar outbursts.) About all that, anyway, we were agreed; it was a subject we discussed many times. That she was also fond of me I knew, and that no doubt contributed to her decision. Perhaps, being childless, she had come to think of my relation to her as somehow filial. (She was thirty-six years my senior—roughly the same age as my mother. Her first novel, *Nothing Is Sacred,* was published the year I was born.) As far as I know, moreover, she never spoke ill of me. This, alas, was unusual with Josie. She had a volatile temper, and was not always in control of it. She also had a nasty habit of saying—and writing—terrible things about her friends, not only those she had for some reason broken with but even some who remained close and who were important to her survival. Some of this was mere gossip and banter, but some of it was designed to cause pain and it did. Whatever the reason, I appear to have been among those exempted from this disagreeable practice. We never quarreled.

Very soon after her death I faced the first test of the trust she had placed in me. Obliged to go through the things she had left in the little stone house in Bucks County that had been her home since the Twenties—but which she had never owned—I discovered, buried under a pile of old clothes at the bottom of an ancient steamer trunk in the attic, a parcel of papers neatly wrapped in brown paper. On the outside was written, unmistakably in Josie's own hand, the word "Destroy." It frankly never occurred to me for a moment that I should follow this injunction, or indeed was meant to. Josie had lived in that house for forty years with a wood-burning stove in the living room, and she had ample opportunity to consign to its flames whatever papers she wished to destroy. I assumed—and Miss Langer's biography seems to confirm—that Josie could not bring herself either to destroy or to take responsibility for preserving what this parcel contained. What it contained, as it turned out, were the letters, which had been returned to her, that chronicle one of the key episodes of her life. This was the love affair with another woman, Marion Greenwood, that led directly to the breakup of Josie's marriage to John Herrmann—an event that had caused her the deepest unhappiness of her life, and from which in fact she never recovered.

These letters proved to be important in another respect. For they did much, though far from everything, to explain one of the mysteries of Josie's later years: why it was that, despite years of work on what she well understood was the best writing she had ever done in her life and the strong and repeated encouragement of her friends—Saul Bellow and Alfred Kazin, among them—Josie could never bring her own volume of memoirs to completion. She had a publisher ready to produce the book, and everyone who read the completed portions of it expected it to be a masterpiece—her first, by the way. Yet it was never finished, and I now realize that there was never any possibility of its being finished. For Josie could never deal with either the sexual or the political events that had destroyed her life, and neither could she deny them. But on this matter, too, I shall have more to say here in the appropriate place. Like so much else in Josie Herbst's life, it brings us back to the ugly issue of Stalinism, which came to play an important role in her marriage, in its breakup, and in the life she lived thereafter.[2]

She was born in Sioux City, Iowa, on March 5, 1892. (The year is worth noting, for beginning in the Twenties Josie gave 1897 as the date of her birth.) Her parents were poor, respectable, small-town people who had migrated to Iowa from their native Pennsylvania with two baby daughters. Josie's father, who had a farm implement business that failed, was amiable but unambitious. Her mother, whom Josie adored, was a more spirited character, interested in reading and an avid storyteller herself, and never quite reconciled to life in the Iowa provinces. It was from the stories that she told of her family and its travails that Josie drew much of the material for her fiction.

Josie was the first of the Herbst daughters to be born in Iowa. Her younger sister Helen followed three years later, and they both grew up sharing their mother's contempt for Iowa and its benighted ways. Like a good many American writers of her generation who came out of the Middle West, Josie had determined from an early age to leave it. But this was not a mission easily accomplished. Lacking money, she was in and out of college for eight years, working at one small-town job or another to pay for her education, and desperately lonely and unhappy the whole time. She first attended Morningside College while living at home, then the University of Iowa and the University of Washington until, at the age of twenty-five, she made it to Berkeley, where she graduated from the University of California in 1918.

She seems always to have wanted to be a writer, and it was at Berkeley that she was first encouraged in that ambition by one of her professors. It was there, too, that for the first time she found a radical milieu hospitable to her own rebellious spirit. "I always knew," Josie wrote her mother at this time, "that somewhere in the world were people who could talk about the things I wanted to talk about and do the things I wanted to do and in some measure at least I have found them."

> Nothing Josie did with her friends in San Francisco [writes Miss Langer] seems very remarkable now. They listened to speeches and climbed Mount Tamalpais and shared festive bohemian dinners . . . or just sat around . . . arguing about the war and capitalism and wondering what was going to happen next.

All the same, it marked the real beginning—a late, hard-won beginning—of Josie's adult life, and not only because of what it contributed to her political or literary outlook. "For the first time in her life," writes Miss Langer, "she was comfortable with men."

Despite this initiation into radical bohemia, however, Josie had still never had a real love affair when she arrived in New York in the fall of 1919, and it was never her fate to be lucky in love. When she did have her first affair, she was twenty-eight years old, and it ended badly. Her lover was Maxwell Anderson, who was later to achieve renown as a playwright but who was then an editorial writer for the *Globe,* a New York newspaper. The problem was, he was married. It was through his wife, in fact, that Josie had met him soon after arriving in New York. For him the affair was a diversion and he soon ended it, but for Josie it was love. When, after the breakup, she discovered she was pregnant, she wanted to have the baby, but Anderson opposed it and persuaded her to have an abortion. It was a decision she bitterly regretted.

2 The three published sections of the memoirs are: "The Starched Blue Sky of Spain" (*The Noble Savage,* Number 1, 1960), "A Year of Disgrace" (*The Noble Savage,* Number 3, 1961), and "Yesterday's Road" (*New American Review,* Number 3, 1968).

The novel that Josie afterwards wrote about this experience—it was never published, or indeed publishable—was pretty grim, a tale in the Dreiserian mode, but the real life story had an epilogue that even Dreiser might have hesitated to write. As she was recovering from the abortion, Josie was suddenly bombarded with appeals from her beloved younger sister. Like Josie, Helen had been determined to get out of Sioux City, but she hadn't yet made it. She had married her Sioux City boyfriend, who shared her worldly ambitions—he was later to have a distinguished career as a newspaper editor—and they had been desperately saving money to make their getaway. But now she found she was pregnant and she didn't want to have the baby. It would ruin their lives, she thought. Josie thought so, too, and so without ever disclosing to her sister (or to almost anyone else) the nature of the ordeal she had just been through herself, she encouraged Helen to have an abortion. Helen did, and she died as a result.

Overcome by guilt and remorse, Josie suffered something of a breakdown in the aftermath of her sister's death, and while she eventually pulled herself together it was an event that had a permanent—and damaging—effect on her life. Miss Langer is right, I think, in observing that "when [Josie] lost Helen she lost part of herself and the most important relationships of the rest of her life were attempts in one way or another to bring her sister back." But there is more to it than that. For what this whole episode revealed was a fundamental fissure in Josie Herbst's character—a refusal of honesty and responsibility that turned out to be one of the deepest things about her. This was the hardest thing for Josie's friends to come to terms with after her death. It was certainly the hardest for me, especially since her whole personal style—both in private conversation and in her extraordinary letters—gave the impression of achieving a degree of candor and self-revelation that was both unusual and exemplary. The mask—or what Miss Langer calls the "performance"—was so appealing that many of her friends have to this day refused to abandon their belief in it, preferring the fiction to the reality. And so great is their need to believe in that mask—for it is now theirs as well—that I doubt if even the revelations of Miss Langer's biography will do much to modify it.

Despite the ordeals that Josie suffered in New York in the early Twenties, it was there that her literary career began in earnest, and there too that she became an active participant in the literary-radical-bohemian world which remained her spiritual home for the rest of her life. In 1920 she landed a job with H. L. Mencken and George Jean Nathan—not, by the way, on the *Smart Set,* but working on some of the "sleazier publications," as Miss Langer correctly calls them, which they were also producing at that time. This led to the publication of her fiction in the *Smart Set,* and won her Mencken's support when she later tried to find a publisher for her novel about the Anderson affair. Her friends in this period included Genevieve Taggard, Mike Gold, Joseph Freeman, Floyd Dell, Jessica Smith, Alex Gumberg, Max Eastman, and Albert Rhys Williams, all of whom were already ardent and active supporters of the Bolshevik Revolution. When she went to Europe in the spring of 1922, having saved enough money for the trip, she spent the summer traveling with Eastman and Williams, who then went on to Moscow while Josie herself settled in Berlin. There she remained for the better part of two years, working on the novel that she hadn't quite finished when she went off to Paris and met John Herrmann—"a young and beautiful boy," as she described him to Genevieve Taggard—with whom she instantly fell in love.

Herrmann was twenty-three; Josie was thirty-two, but passing for twenty-seven. He was extremely good-looking; she had never been beautiful. Like herself, he had just spent two years in Germany—in his case, Munich, where he had gone to study art history but where he had devoted himself instead to working on a novel. They were both Midwesterners. He was from Lansing, Michigan, the son of a prosperous, straight-laced businessman with whom he could not get along and not quite get along without. John was weak, and Josie was strong. He was also already an alcoholic. On the day she was introduced to him at the Café du Dome in Montparnasse, he was suffering from a severe hangover. "Everything that was true when they parted," Miss Langer writes, "was true when they met. Josie was ambitious and John was not ambitious, he preferred the company of the cafés and she preferred the solitude of the typewriter, he had confidence in his charm but not in his book and she had confidence in her book but not in her charm. But what became difficult oppositions when things were dissolving between them were magnetizing complements at the time they began."

In France their whirlwind romance had been an idyll of sorts, but when they returned to the United States, which they promptly did, there was trouble, of course. John was still dependent on his despised parents. He was also an incorrigible womanizer—he seems never to have been faithful to Josie for very long. What Josie wanted most was for them to live in rural Connecticut, near writer-friends of hers, where they would live simply and work on their books. She was nothing if not determined to have her way. The only obstacle was money, and she solved that problem by blackmailing Maxwell Anderson, whose love letters she had kept. Miss Langer doesn't use that ugly word, but that is what it came to—and John knew all about it. It was not, perhaps, the soundest basis for a serene relationship.

Off they went, then, to a small farmhouse in New Preston, Connecticut, in the fall of 1925. Josie afterwards called this period "The Hour of Counterfeit Bliss," and it was undoubtedly the happiest time in her life. But it was soon over. John's mother got wind of the fact that her son was living in sin, and she hired a private detective to investigate. As a result, since John could not resist the pressures of his family and there was always the hope of getting some money out of them, he was forced into marrying Josie. This was not what they had planned on doing. Josie always spoke of it, with varying degrees of humor, resentment, or sarcasm, as her "shotgun marriage"—though in truth, she wanted very much to be married to John Herrmann. And the hope of getting some money out of it was not unfounded—though, like everything else, this, too, didn't turn out as they had hoped. John's parents were persuaded to put up twenty-five hundred dollars for the old stone house in Bucks County that Josie wanted to buy—she had found it, as Miss Langer writes, in "the eastern Pennsylvania countryside she had been hearing about from her mother all her life"—but John's father kept the deed in his own name. That house was to be the only home Josie had for the rest of her life, but it was never her house, and she had to fight hard to remain in it after the marriage had dissolved.

Still, they were together and they were living the literary life they wanted. In 1927, just before they moved to Pennsylvania, John's novel, *What Happens,* was published by Robert McAlmon in Paris, and it was refused entry into the United States on grounds of obscenity. (Morris Ernst took the case, and lost.) Josie's first published novel, *Nothing Is Sacred,* followed in 1928. Hemingway and Ring Lardner provided the blurbs, and Ford Madox Ford and Katherine Anne Porter reviewed it favorably. Josie and John were both publishing in the magazines, too, though she more than he, and among the visitors they welcomed to Pennsylvania were Malcolm Cowley and Kenneth Burke. They spent some time with Hemingway in Key West.

By that time, however, they were being drawn into the political movement that came to play a dominant role in their lives. In 1930, at the suggestion of Mike Gold, they went to Russia to attend the International Congress of Revolutionary Writers in Kharkov. Miss Langer describes this trip as "More of a lark than a pilgrimage," but "lark" doesn't strike one as quite the *mot juste* for it. In any case, John emerged from the experience a complete convert to Communism and a dedicated supporter of the Soviet Union. Josie, though she expressed private doubts (as she always would), was also enthusiastic. "Perhaps as early as 1931 he joined the Communist Party," writes Miss Langer. "It was something that Josie never did."

She was still primarily a writer; John was now less interested in literature than in political action. Josie's response to the political atmosphere was to re-interpret the story of her family's history in Marxist terms, and this is what she did in the trilogy of novels that was her main work of the Thirties—*Pity Is Not Enough* (1933), *The Executioner Waits* (1934), and *Rope of Gold* (1939). John's response, in the beginning at least, was to become a public speaker for Communist Party causes, but before long he was drawn into the Communist underground where, if the word of his widow Ruth Herrmann is to be believed, he achieved the historic distinction of being the man who introduced Whittaker Chambers to Alger Hiss.

Before that fateful drama was enacted, however, another, more personal crisis had intervened to shatter what remained of their disintegrating marriage. Josie met Marion Greenwood. In the summer of 1932 Josie was at the Yaddo colony in Saratoga Springs by herself. John had taken her there, and then gone on to Michigan for the summer. Marion Greenwood, a young painter, very talented and very beautiful, arrived at the colony soon after Josie, and Josie fell madly in love with her. Josie had had romantic attachments to other women, but nothing like this. The affair that ensued quite swept her off her feet, and she was tenacious about keeping it going. And as it progressed she still harbored the illusion that she could keep her marriage going too. Toward this end she contrived to bring John into the affair after her term at Yaddo was over. The three of them went off to Mexico together where Josie and John took turns, as it were, as Marion's lovers. It couldn't last, and it didn't. As sexually susceptible and as weak-willed as John was, he was clearly humiliated by the whole sordid experience, and he took off. In a panic, Josie chose her husband over her lover. She still couldn't believe her marriage was coming to an end—that, in fact, it was over. She clung to John as long as she could, but it was soon over, anyway.

Politically, the issue that most excited them in this period was the effort of the Communist Party to organize the farmers—to organize them, it is worth remembering, against the policies of the New Deal. John was much involved in this effort, and Josie wrote about it for the *New Masses*. "For Josie," Miss Langer writes, "it was not only her moment of greatest identification with the farmers but of consonance with the Communist Party 'line.'" For John, it proved to be his ticket to the Communist underground. In 1934 he was summoned to Washington by Hal Ware, who presided over the special underground operation which Chambers, among others, was already serving. When Josie followed John to Washington, still hoping for a reconciliation, she lived in his apartment, and was thus in a position to know something—if not everything—about the secret Party work that John was engaged in. She knew Hal Ware, she knew Whittaker Chambers, and she knew at least enough about what they were doing to disapprove of it and ridicule it. Which was not, to say the least, the way to John's heart at that moment, but she did it anyway—and not because she disagreed with Party policy, but ostensibly because she considered the work ineffective (or so Miss Langer suggests). I think the real reason she disapproved was that she feared that she was losing John to his new involvement in the Party underground—which she was, and in more than one sense. For the woman John married after he finally broke with Josie and with whom he was already involved was his confidante in Party activities. (It was she, forty years later, who told Elinor Langer that John had introduced Chambers to Hiss over a lunch in Washington in 1934.) One of the things that Josie knew, too—it may have been the only important thing she ever knew about the whole operation—was that Alger Hiss was somehow involved.

It was this knowledge that placed Josie, at the time of the Hiss case, in a position to change the course of history by revealing what she knew, but she never did. Out of her loyalty to the Left and out of her loyalty to John—with the passage of time, these became virtually identical in her mind—she not only didn't speak up, but she offered her services to the Hiss defense lawyers. (She also lied a good deal to the FBI, and sent word to John, who had fled to Mexico, about what she had said.) Being a true believer in the ideals of the Left, she proved to be something of an embarrassment to Hiss's lawyers, however. She urged them to encourage Hiss to speak up in court by defending his political beliefs, which she knew to be Communist. But this, of course, would have identified Hiss as a Communist, and it was the whole point of the Hiss defense to deny that he had ever been one.[3] Yet she went along with that, too, and kept her silence—and at considerable personal cost to herself, for Chambers had already given her name, as well as John's, to the FBI, and she was frequently interrogated on the matter. This was no doubt one of the things that led to the denial of a passport when she applied for one in the Fifties.

There is much more to Josie Herbst's story, of course—the trips to Cuba, Germany, and Spain in the Thirties; the job she took with the Government in Washington after the United States entered the Second World War, and the reason she was fired from it; the breakup of her long friendship with Katherine Anne Porter, and the reasons for that; and the affair with the poet Jean Garrigue that was even more disastrous and far more protracted than the affair with Marion Greenwood—and Miss Langer has told it all very vividly. Yet there is a sense in which it can truly be said that Josie Herbst's life came to an end when John Herrmann walked out of it for the last time, and that what remained in all her later years was a half-life of shadows and chimeras, of concealments and denials and lost hopes, which, though she no longer had the power, for the most part, to turn them into effective literary fictions, she became more and more adept at transforming into a fictional personality for herself, the dazzling mask that enchanted so many of her friends. Only once, in my own acquaintance with Josie, was I ever given a glimpse of the ravaged spirit that the mask so effectively concealed. I had been spending the weekend at the house in Pennsylvania, ostensibly to talk over the manuscript of the memoirs on which she was working. It was clear to me that she was stymied—I thought, of course, temporarily—and she talked about some of the reasons why she was having so much trouble writing this book. Lack of money, lack of time, problems with the house, distractions of every kind—as the litany continued, I could see that even she wasn't convinced by what she was saying, though her life was anything but comfortable or serene. Just before I left—we were standing in the doorway, about to walk down to the car—I said to her: "Josie, you must finish it. Why can't you finish it?" To my astonishment, she cried out: "It's *John,* I can't deal with John!" And she was so overcome with fits of sobbing that it took some time, and some drinks, before she could pull herself together. All I knew about John then was that he had left her for another woman. I knew nothing about his involvement with Hiss and Chambers and Hal Ware—or Josie's, for that matter. I knew nothing about Marion Greenwood. But from that moment on I was never as confident as I had been that the memoirs would ever be finished.

What few of Josie's friends in her later years understood, I think—and it may be that Miss Langer doesn't quite grasp it, either, though she provides ample evidence for it—is the degree to which Josie's experience as a woman, especially the experiences that she initiated, together with the passions and dishonesties that marked her political life, and the effort involved in concealing, for so much of the time, the true nature of

3 Allen Weinstein's *Perjury: The Hiss-Chambers Case* (Alfred A. Knopf, 1978) was the first work to provide a detailed account of Josie's role in the case.

both, had the effect of brutalizing her personality. There was a streak of sheer ruthlessness and brute callousness in her personality that is as observable in her personal relations, especially in her relations with her lovers, as it is in her politics, and it would be a mistake to think that politics was responsible for what finally must be regarded as a defect of character. Politics does not account for her role in Helen's death, for the blackmailing of Maxwell Anderson, or for the way she corrupted—there is no other word for it—her own beloved husband in the Marion Greenwood affair. All her life she was drawn to weak, vulnerable, romantic men and women, whose lives she hoped to overwhelm and control, and she could never quite understand why it was that in the end they always fled.

Yet, if politics does not explain Josie Herbst's character, it nonetheless contributed much to the brutalization I speak of. Which brings us to the question of Stalinism, and its role in Josie's life. It is in the nature of Stalinism for its adherents to make a certain kind of lying—and not only to others, but first of all to themselves—a fundamental part of their lives. It is always a mistake to assume that Stalinists do not know the truth about the political reality they espouse. If they don't know the truth (or all of it) one day, they know it the next, and it makes absolutely no difference to them politically. For their loyalty is to something other than the truth. And no historical enormity is so great, no personal humiliation or betrayal so extreme, no crime so heinous, that it cannot be assimilated into the "ideals" that govern the true Stalinist mind, which is impervious alike to documentary evidence and moral discrimination.

Was Josie Herbst a true Stalinist? Despite all the reservations and criticisms she voiced in private and despite her many disagreements with the Communist Party and its policies, I think it must be said that for the most part she was. That wasn't all she was, of course, but in a large part of her mind for an important part of her life she was, all the same. The slaughter of the peasants in Stalin's collectivization campaign, the Moscow trials, the Great Terror and the Hitler-Stalin pact, not to mention a great many later developments in the post-World War II period—however much she may have suffered over them, she nonetheless swallowed them. There was a lot she choked on, but in the end she swallowed it all. Which is why she remained "loyal" in the Hiss case, and in many lesser causes as well. Whatever she disapproved or regretted or even disavowed—Miss Langer cites many instances, and I could describe others—was always done privately, and never where it would make any difference, and always subsumed under the comforting and exonerating rubric of "What went wrong?" There was never an acknowledgement—even privately, as far as I know—that it was the whole political outlook that was wrong. There was no conception of how evil it all was.

It was the process of brutalization that resulted from all this, I believe, that first confused and then immobilized her as a writer once the audience ready to embrace radical certainties evaporated from the literary scene in the Forties. When she started to write again in the Fifties, it was in a very different mode—a mode of Proustian reminiscence in which the old certainties were dissolved in an evocation of cherished experience. In the memoirs even the most painful memories of the past are, so to speak, aesthetized in a style that Josie would have been incapable of commanding in the heyday of her radical involvement and personal rebellion. Upon this whole later phase of her literary work there is to be found, I believe, the influence of Jean Garrigue—the poet she met (again at Yaddo) in the winter of 1949-50, and with whom she promptly fell in love—and the influence of Jean Garrigue's literary tastes. Jean Garrigue had no interest in politics, no interest in social issues, no interest in anything having to do with the radical movement that had shaped Josie's adult life. She was a romantic aesthete, a lyrical poet of considerable delicacy and nuance whose interests were mainly confined to artistic and amatory experience. In all personal matters she was completely irresponsible, and she and Josie managed to cause each other a great deal of pain over the long course of their stormy attachment, but in literary matters Jean's influence proved, I think, to be decisive in the way Josie now conceived of writing her reminiscences. It is precisely their "aesthetic" character that sets them apart from all her earlier writing.

Yet there were some experiences that resisted this new mode of Proustian reminiscence, and they turned out to be the most crucial. The central emotional crisis of Josie Herbst's life was so intimately connected with its central political loyalty that there was no way of separating them. In the end, the late-blooming aesthetic writer of the memoirs lost out to the vanquished, silent survivor of the Thirties.

Josie Herbst's death in January 1969 came at a moment when events in the world of both politics and culture were swiftly bringing in their wake a significant change in attitude toward the radical movement of the Thirties. The emergence of the New Left in response to the Vietnam war and the accompanying eruption of a vigorous anti-government, anti-middle-class counterculture had the effect of casting even the most extreme Stalinist positions of Thirties radicalism in a new and more favorable light. Actions and beliefs which had long been regarded as morally repugnant because of their abject subservience to the interests of the Soviet Union and which, as we know, in some notable cases had led to spying and espionage, began to enjoy the benefit of a sweeping revisionism. Liberals who had once known better, or seemed to, now either tempered or abandoned their opposition to radical militancy, as liberals generally do when the tide is running in favor of the radical position. Even in the ranks of the most stalwart anti-Stalinist intellectuals there were some notable defections—such as Dwight Macdonald's and Philip Rahv's—to this revival of the radical dream. All of this made it possible for Stalinists who had survived the debacle of the Thirties and the investigations of the Fifties to come forward once again to bask in the rosy glow of yet another (promised) red dawn. As the call to revolution beckoned the young and the revivified romance of the Left renewed the celebrity of aging radicals, a kind of sainthood began to be conferred upon almost anyone who had once been identified with Stalinist causes and had not at any time publically repudiated them.

Josie Herbst died just a little too soon to reap the full benefit of this historic reversal in her lifetime. By the late Sixties, when the new revisionism was beginning to acquire some real momentum and influence, she was too ill, too weak, too demoralized, and too scattered in her efforts to do much more than act as an interested but ineffectual witness to its development. That she welcomed it there can be no doubt. But at the time she was extremely discreet, if not actually devious, in what she said about it and to whom. To friends like myself, whom she knew to be unsympathetic to the radical cause, she often voiced skeptical and even critical views of its conduct. Without exactly denying her loyalty to the radical position—something she would never bring herself to do—she could nonetheless be quite vehement in her criticism of the actions and attitudes it was then engendering. Yet in speaking or writing to dedicated radicals or those she hoped to convert to the radical cause, she was even more vehement and a lot less guarded in her expressions of support. It is possible, of course, that this zigzag course reflected a genuinely divided attitude on her part, but I doubt if that was really the case. Elinor Langer's biography leaves little room for doubt in this matter.

Josie had been dead a very short time when I began receiving inquiries about the Yale archive. Given the political temper of the time, I naturally expected that any new interest in Josie would focus on whatever reputation she had as a radical and, more specifically, on her contribution to the so-called "proletarian" novel in the Thirties. But at the outset this was not usually the case. Most of the inquiries came from graduate students who had little or no acquaintance with the novels Josie had published between 1928 and 1947. Often these students did not even know what she had written. Some may have read an installment or two of the published memoirs. Others, to my astonishment, had read nothing by her. They had simply been given her name as a possible subject for research by faculty advisors who themselves knew little more about her than that she had once been associated with some famous writers—Hemingway, Dos Passos, et al.—in the Twenties and Thirties. Unembarrassed by their ignorance, most of these students were frankly fishing for "original" documents—letters, manuscripts, etc.—that might be turned into thesis material, and they weren't going to do any unnecessary reading until they knew what they had. They seemed to have no larger literary or intellectual interests, or indeed to have read anything that had not been assigned to them in a course. As kindly as I could, I told them that they would first have to read Josie's published work, which included short stories, essays, and a good deal of journalism in addition to the books, and then come back with more specific requests. The majority of them were never heard from again. It was all a ghastly confirmation of Josie's worst fears about the fate of literature in the academy.

Of the people who contacted me about Josie Herbst in the years immediately following her death, the most serious were the young women—there were never more than a few of them—who had come to their interest in her through an involvement in and partial disenchantment with the radical movement of the Sixties, an experience that had somehow led to a rediscovery of her novels. It was very much as a woman and as a radical that Josie interested them. This was the first indication I was given that Josie's posthumous reputation, if she was to have one, would owe something—I had no idea then how much—to the feminist movement, and specifically to that branch of it in which the residue of Sixties radicalism was quickly finding a home. (For what it is worth, the unserious applicants were all men.) Obviously these young women had been moved—in a way, it must be said, that I had never been—by the portrayal of female experience in the novels and by the sensibility of the female radical who had written them. This response inevitably prompted an interest in Josie herself, for virtually all of her fiction is transparently autobiographical in one degree or another. It didn't take long, moreover, to discover that Josie had herself been a far more compelling character than any she created in her fiction, and this, in turn, led to expressions of interest in writing her biography.

This, more or less, is how Elinor Langer came to write the biography that has now been published nearly a dozen years after she first contacted me, and how I came to play a role of sorts in its preparation. Miss Langer gives an account of how she came to the subject in the very first chapter of the book:

> In 1973, when I first heard of Josephine Herbst, I was living by myself in a small town in Vermont and teaching at a small college . . . yet what I appeared to be doing and what I was doing were two different things because, like so many people I knew then, I was in retreat from the radical movement of the 1960s, and in reality I was spending most of my time mulling over what had happened to the movement, and to myself, and why . . . . [T]o the extent that it was possible in my immediate circumstances I included in my brooding and my browsing as much of the literature of the 1930s as I was able to find—something I had always done, more or less, because the 1930s had felt like family history to me even before the "New Left" was born, but which I now pursued with a greater urgency than ever before. On a visit to Chicago, in a secondhand bookstore, on a shelf labeled "Marxism," I found a collection of essays by participants in the events of the 1930s called *As We Saw the Thirties,* and I bought it as a matter of course. The essay on literature had been written by Granville Hicks, and in it . . . was a small, inviting reference to a trilogy by Josephine

> Herbst. Not much . . . but it was enough to send me to the university library the following morning and home with the novels [*Pity Is Not Enough, The Executioner Waits,* and *Rope of Gold*] that very day.
>
> My notes from my first reading of the trilogy are a cross between a sigh of relief and a shout of joy: as if I were a traveler who had somehow gotten detached from my party, and Josephine Herbst were the rescuer sent out to bring me home . . . . The decades between when the trilogy was written and when I was reading it simply fell away from me as I held it in my hands and I felt as if a conversation brusquely terminated with the turn of the 1970s had suddenly been renewed . . . . Of my literary reactions I was far less certain.

Whatever her disappointments with the radical movement of the Sixties may have been, Miss Langer emerged from the experience with a good many of her radical pieties intact, and it was clearly in the interest of vindicating them, as well as of attempting to gain a greater understanding of them, that she was drawn to the subject of Josephine Herbst in the first place. In this respect, as in others, her book is very much a product of the cultural ethos of the Seventies. For one of the least examined aspects of the political and cultural history of the Seventies may be found in the widespread effort that began to be made in that decade to justify the spirit of the radical movement of the Sixties, its failures no less than its successes, by rewriting the history of the Thirties. In attributing all manner of innocence and idealism to Thirties radicalism, even in its most blatantly Stalinist manifestations, and by minimizing, if not actually obliterating, all trace of its evil consequences, this revisionist historiography succeeded in exonerating Sixties radicalism, too, of its worst elements. This impulse certainly plays a large role in the book that Elinor Langer has spent a decade writing, and there can be no doubt that her book belongs to this literature of exoneration.

That it has also turned out to be something more than that is a tribute to Miss Langer's honesty about and understanding of Josie Herbst's character and the nature of her personal tragedy. A radical feminist herself, at least when she began to work on this book, Miss Langer had clearly intended to cast Josie in the role of a radical feminist heroine, but it couldn't be done. All the evidence—mostly, of course, Josie's own evidence—defeated the idea, and Miss Langer found herself obliged to portray a very different figure. This will not prevent others from drafting Josie Herbst's life into the service of feminist causes, now that the life itself has been so meticulously documented. Ideology, when sufficiently motivated, has a way of overlooking obstructive truths. But Miss Langer, anyway, has escaped most, if not quite all, of the temptations to give ideology priority over truth in this matter.

The same, alas, cannot be said about Miss Langer's handling, or mishandling, of the role of Stalinism in Josie Herbst's life and work. In this matter *Josephine Herbst* does indeed belong to the literature of exoneration. To the whole question of Stalinism and its place in Josie's life Miss Langer devotes exactly one footnote and little more. The footnote (on page 199) reads as follows:

> I have frequently been asked during the course of this work whether or not Josie was a "Stalinist" and there are those who believe, primarily on the basis of her connection with the Communist Party during this period, that she was. If her relationship to the American Communist Party and in turn its relationship to the Soviet Union automatically makes her a Stalinist, so be it, but for her long record of independent thought and action—albeit in association with the Communist Party—for my part I find "Stalinism" not only a meaningless, but, indeed, a misleading description.

One could write a lengthy dissertation on the implications of this footnote, and it would begin with an examination of exactly what is meant by its reference to Josie's "long record of independent thought and action—albeit in association with the Communist Party." *Albeit,* indeed. As if the Communist Party had ever, in Josie Herbst's lifetime, accorded a place for independent thought and action in its programs or policies or in the use it made of writers like Josie! There were, as I have noted, many instances in which Josie criticized the Party and opposed its course of action. But when she was overruled and told, in effect, to shut up, she shut up and she stayed shut up, however much she may have suffered in the process. One wonders if Miss Langer really understands what the word "independent" means in this context.

The sad truth is that Miss Langer cannot deal with the issue of Stalinism and the history that lies behind it. Even on the question of Alger Hiss's guilt, though the evidence—especially Ruth Herrmann's revelation of John Herrmann's role in introducing Hiss to Chambers in 1934—has obliged her to agree that Hiss was indeed lying and that he *was* working for the Communist underground, just as Chambers claimed, she still cannot quite face the basic truth of the matter. Hiss even lied to *her* about John Herrmann, as she candidly reports in her book, and yet she goes on to write about the case as follows:

> The Hiss case is one of the greatest miasmas of American politics . . . . There are no arguments which have not been shaken, there is no evidence which has not been obfuscated, there have been no sentences either uttered or written that have not been parsed into nonsense.

Now this is simply not true. Despite massive and protracted legal attempts to have Hiss's conviction for perjury reversed, the verdict has stuck because the evidence could not—despite Hiss's best efforts—be obfuscated. It has withstood every challenge. To write about the Hiss case in this manner is not an attempt to deal with the historical truth—never mind the moral truth—but an attempt to escape it.

And this, finally, is what Elinor Langer attempts to do with the whole question of Stalinism, both in Josie Herbst's life and in itself—escape it. To have faced it, I suppose, would have meant facing something in her own radical past that she has not yet come to terms with. And so, in yet another generation of disenchanted but nonetheless loyal radicals, the posture of innocence is invoked as a screen against the political realities of our time. It is sad to see this perpetuated in a new generation of writers—and especially in a writer as good as Elinor Langer—but that too, I am afraid, must be counted as an important part of the legacy that Josephine Herbst's silence has bequeathed us.

(*September* 1984)

Cyril Connolly and the groans of success

by Cynthia Ozick

I first came on a paperback reprint of Cyril Connolly's *Enemies of Promise* when I was already in my despairing middle thirties. Though I had been writing steadily and obsessively since the age of twenty-two, I was still mainly unpublished: a handful of poems, a couple of short stories, a single essay, and all in quirky little magazines printed, it seemed, in invisible ink. Connolly's stringent dissertation on the anatomy of failure had a morbid attraction for me: it was like looking up one's disease in the Merck Manual—I knew the symptoms, and it was a wound I was interested in. One day I urgently pressed my copy of Connolly on another failed writer a whole decade younger than myself; we were both teaching freshman composition at the time. He promised to read it; instead he hurried off into analysis and gay pride. I never saw the book again. My ex-colleague has, so far, never published. *Enemies of Promise* went out of print.

After that, I remembered it chiefly as a dictionary of low spirits, even as a secret autobiography. Over the years one of its interior titles—"The Charlock's Shade"—stayed with me, a mysterious phrase giving off old mournful fumes: the marsh gas writers inhale when they are not getting published, when they begin to accept themselves as having been passed by, when envy's pinch is constant and certain, when the lurch of humiliation learns to precede the predictable rebuff. Writers who publish early and regularly are not only spared these hollow desolations, but acquire habits of strength and self-confidence. Henry James, George Sand, Balzac, Mann: these amazingly prolific presences achieved as much as they did not simply because they began young, but because they were permitted to begin young. James in America started off with book reviews; so, in London, did Virginia Woolf.

But in my despairing thirties it was hardly these colossi of literary history I was fixed on. All around me writers five years older and five years younger were having their second and third novels published, establishing their idiosyncratic and intractable voices, and flourishing, sometimes with the left hand, this and that indomitable essay: Mailer's "The White Negro," Sontag's "Notes on Camp," Roth's "Writing American Fiction," Baldwin's "The Fire Next Time," Styron's reply to the critics of *Nat Turner,* and so on. John Updike, the paramount American instance of early publication, conquered *The New Yorker* in his twenties, undertaking even then the body of reviewing that nowadays rivals the amplitude and weight and attentiveness of Edmund Wilson's. At about the same time, in the New Rochelle Public Library, I pulled down from a high shelf of the new-books section a first volume of stories called *By the North Gate.* The author was an unknown writer ten years my junior; not long afterward, the name Joyce Carol Oates accelerated into a ubiquitous force. A good while before that, in college, I had known someone who knew Truman Capote; and Capote had published in magazines before he was twenty.

In short, these were the Famous of my generation, and could be read, and read about, and mulled over, and discussed. They were—or anyhow they embodied, they were shot through with—the Issues; and meanwhile I was a suffering onlooker, shut out. I could not even say that I was being ignored—to be ignored you have first to be published. A hundred periodicals, both renowned and "little," sent me packing. An editor who later went to Hollywood to write *Superman* led me into his *Esquire* office to turn back a piece of fiction with the hard-hearted charm of indifference; he looked like someone's baby brother. Another day I stood on the threshold of the office of *The New York Review of Books,* a diffident inquirer of thirty-five, and was shooed away by a word thrown out from a distant desk; I had come to ask for a review to write. *Partisan, Kenyon, Sewanee, American Scholar, Quarterly Review, Furioso,* dozens of others, declined my submissions. An editor of a small Michigan periodical, a poet, wrote to remark that I "had yet to find a voice." In New York, a respected reader at a well-known publishing house, having in hand three-quarters of my novel, said it wouldn't do, and rocked me into a paralysis of hopelessness lasting nearly a year. And all the while I was getting older and older. Envy of the published ate at me; so did the shame of so much nibbling defeat. Twenty years of print-lust, muscular ambition, driving inquisitiveness, and all the rest, were lost in the hurt crawl away from the locked door. I wrote, and read, and filled volumes of Woolworth diaries with the outcry of failure—the failure to enter the gates of one's own literary generation, the anguish of exclusion from its argument and tone, its experience and evolution. It wasn't that I altogether doubted my "powers" (though often enough I did, profoundly, stung by disgrace); I saw them, whatever they were, scorned, disparaged, set outside the pale of welcome. I was ashamed of my life, and I lived only to read and write. I lived for nothing else; I had no other "goals," "motivations," "interests"—these shallownesses pointing to what the babblers of the hour call psychological health. Nor was it raw Fame I was after; I was not deluded that publishing a first novel at twenty-five, as Mann had done, would guarantee a *Buddenbrooks.*

What I wanted was access to the narrowest possibilities of my own time and prime; I wanted to bore a chink. I wanted a sliver of the apron of a literary platform. I wanted to use what I was, to be what I was born to be—not to have a "career," but to be that straightforward obvious unmistakable animal, a writer. I was a haunted punctuator, possessed stylist, sorter of ideas, burrower into history, philosophy, criticism; I wrote midnight poetry into the morning light; I burnished the sentences of my prose so that each might stand, I said (with the arrogance of the desperately humiliated), for twenty years. And no one would publish me.

For this predicament, it was clear, I needed not an anodyne, but salt—merciless salt. Connolly not only supplied the salt, he opened the wounds, gave names to their mouths, and rubbed in the salt. He analyzed—or so it appeared—all the venoms of failure. He spoke, in a kind of metaphoric delirium borrowed from Crabbe, of "the blighted rye," "the slimy mallow," "the wither'd ears"—all those hideous signs of poison and decomposition from which the suffocated writer, kept from the oxygen of the age, deprived of print, slowly dies. There was no victory crow to be had from reading Connolly. If he provoked any sound at all, it was the dry cough that comes with panic at the dawn's early light.

This, at least, is how, all these years, I have kept *Enemies of Promise* in my head: as a mop and sop for the long, long bleeding, the intellectual slights, the disgraced imagination, the locked doors, the enervating growths of the literary swamp, the dry cough of abandonment. The rest I seem to have forgotten, or never to have noticed at all, and now that the book is once again on the scene, and again in paperback,[1] I observe that it is a tripartite volume, and that, distracted by what I believed to be its diagnostic powers, I missed two-thirds of its substance. What I once saw as a pillar of salt turns out to be, in fact, a puff of spun sugar. And this is not because I have "gotten over" the pounding of denigration and rejection; I have never properly recuperated from them, and on their account resent the white hairs of middle age with a spitefulness and absurdity appropriate only to the hungry young.

"*Enemies of Promise* was first published in 1938," Cyril Connolly's 1948 Introduction begins, "as a didactic enquiry into the problem of how to write a book which lasts ten years." Yet the question of literary longevity is raised and almost instantly dropped; that this particular book has now "lasted" more than four decades is hardly the answer. And I am not sure it *has* lasted, at least in the form it claims, that is, as an essay about certain ideas. It hangs on instead as a curiosity, which does not mean it is wholly obsolete; it is only peculiar. Even in organization there is peculiarity: a trinity that does not immediately cohere. The first section divides prose style into Mandarin (a term Connolly takes credit for coining in this context) and vernacular; surely this issue is with us as bemusedly as ever. The second section—"The Charlock's Shade," which so fed my gripes and twinges—now looks to be not so much about failure as about success and its distractions. The third part, finally, is a memoir of Connolly's childhood in a boarding school for the rich called St. Wulfric's, and afterward at Eton. In my zealously partial reading long ago, though I was attracted by Connolly's definitions of Mandarin and vernacular diction, it appears I never took in the autobiographical segment at all; and what drew me to "The Charlock's Shade" (or so it now strikes me) was three lone sentences, as follows:

> Promise is like the mediaeval hangman who after settling the noose, pushed his victim off the platform and jumped on his back, his weight acting as a drop while his jockeying arms prevented the unfortunate from loosening the rope.
>
> Sloth in writers is always a symptom of an acute inner conflict, especially that laziness which renders them incapable of doing the thing which they are most looking forward to.
>
> Perfectionists are notoriously lazy and all true artistic indolence is deeply neurotic; a pain not a pleasure.

Here, and only here, was the poisonous wisdom that served my travail. All the rest supposed a sophistication and advancement that meant nothing to a writer who had barely begun, and Connolly's classifications of dangers hardly applied. To succeed as a writer, he admonished, beware of journalism, politics, "escapism," sex, and success itself. Journalism: never write "a review that cannot be reprinted, i.e. that is not of some length and on a subject of permanent value." Politics: once the writer "has a moment of conviction that his future is bound up with the working classes . . . his behaviour will inevitably alter"—in other words, he will be much improved. Escapism: drink, drugs, talk, daydreaming, religion, sloth. Sex: hazards of homosexuality, domesticity, babies, wives. And, aha, success: here the peril lies in getting taken up by the upper crust, according to E. M. Forster's dictum as cited by Connolly: "To be aristocratic in Art one must avoid polite society." But how could any of these cautionary alarms have mattered to a writer who had for years gone altogether unnoticed? Speaking for myself: I never thought about politics. Journalism was something less than a snare, since no one would offer me so much as a five-hundred-word review. I was in no danger of becoming a fad or a celebrity. I didn't drink or shoot up. I confined religion to philosophical reading, and daydreaming to a diary. I had no baby and no wife. (Connolly, though he mentions Virginia Woolf among

1 Persea Books, 265 pages, $6.95

the Mandarins, has an ineradicable difficulty in positing a writer who is not male. This is a pity, because the writer's husband is a worthy, perplexing, and often tragic subject.) Even talk was no drain; what went up into air for others, I mainly put down in letters to literary friends—letters, those vessels of calculated permanence. Then what in Connolly could possibly appeal to the untried and the buried? In his infinite catalogues of "promise" and its risks, only the terrors of perfectionism and the pain of sure decline had the least psychological concurrence. For the sake of this pins-in-the-ribs pair, Connolly stuck.

He begins now to unstick. "It was Edmund Wilson who remarked that [*Enemies of Promise*] was not a very well-written book," Connolly confesses. Wilson was right. Connolly is a ragged writer, unraveling his rags behind him as he goes, and capable of awful sentences. If Wilson recoiled from some of them, it might have been in part on account of Connolly's description of Wilson's own *Axel's Castle,* which, we are reminded, "includes essays on Yeats, Valéry, Eliot, Proust, Joyce and Gertrude Stein. His summing up," Connolly continues in a typically unpunctuated long breath, "is against them, in so far as it is against their cult of the individual which he feels they have carried to such lengths as to exhaust it for a long time to come but it is a summing up which also states everything that can be said in their favour when allowance for what I have termed 'inflation' is made." (Observe that the style is neither Mandarin nor vernacular, but Rattling Boxcars.)

Patches of this sort might unglue any essayist, but there is something beyond mere prose at stake. Did Connolly notice that his so-called enemies of promise were in reality the appurtenances of certain already-achieved successes? The warning that journalism threatens art applies, after all, only to fairly established writers long familiar with the practice of getting paid for writing. "He is apt to have a private income, he renews himself by travel," Connolly says of the homosexual writer, assuming long-standing privilege and money. A successful wife, he remarks, is not only "intelligent and unselfish enough to understand and respect the working of the unfriendly cycle of the creative imagination," but "will recognize that there is no more sombre enemy of good art than the pram in the hall." And of course: "Of all the enemies of literature, success is the most insidious."

Does failure ever appear at all in *Enemies of Promise*—the word or the idea? Once. "Failure is a poison like success. Where a choice is offered, prefer the alkaline," and that is all. Such sentiments burn rather than salve. And even while cautioning against the "especial intimacies" of the fashionable, Connolly has a good word for them: "It must be remembered that in fashionable society can be found warmhearted people of delicate sensibility who form permanent friendships with artists which afford them ease and encouragement for the rest of their lives and provide them with sanctuary." And in defense of the seductions of wealth not one's own: "It is because we envy [social success] more than other success that we denounce it so often," Connolly explains. He himself does not denounce the ingratiation of writers with the rich so much as their ingratiation with one another:

> There is a kind of behaviour which is particularly dangerous on the moving staircase—the attempt to ascend it in groups of four or five who lend a hand to each other and dislodge other climbers from the steps. It is natural that writers should make friends with their contemporaries of talent and express a mutual admiration but it leads inevitably to a succession of services rendered and however much the writers who help each other may deserve it, if they too frequently proclaim their gratitude they will arouse the envy of those who stand on their own feet, who succeed without collaboration. Words like "log-rolling" and "back-scratching" are soon whispered and the death-watch ticks the louder.

The death-watch? If there is any warning being rattled in all this, surely it must compete with the complicit wink of the sound counselor. A denunciation, one might say, that has the look of a paragraph in a handbook on the wherewithal of success. And a wherewithal that, at a particular rung of society, is affable enough: the comfortable network of class and school associations.

It is the moment for bluntness. *Enemies of Promise* is an essay—according to the usual English conventions of the early part of the twentieth century—about class and modishness. It has almost no other subject important to Connolly. There are digressions on, say, age, that are nearly worthwhile—more worthwhile when the aperçu is not Connolly's own (though the syntax is): "Butler said an author should write only for people between twenty and thirty as nobody read or changed their opinions after that." There is much recognizable humanity in this, whereas Connolly, attempting to generalize in his own voice, manages mainly a self-indulgent turn: "The shock, for an intelligent writer, of discovering for the first time that there are people younger than himself who think him stupid is severe." Or: "It would seem that genius is of two kinds, one of which blazes up in youth and dies down, while the other matures, like Milton's or Goethe's . . . . The artist has to decide on the nature of his own or he may find himself exhausted by the sprint of youth and unfitted for the marathon of middle age." As if one could choose to be Milton or Goethe merely by deciding, as Connolly advises, to "become a stayer." Modishness dominates: the notion of likely styles of intent, the short-length will and the longer-range.

Modishness rules especially in the politics. Writing in 1948 (the famous year of Orwell's *Nineteen Eighty-Four*), Connolly suggests that he has "retained all the engagingly simple left-wing militancy [of 1938] since it breathes the air of the period." True enough: ten years after its composition, Connolly is offering us *Enemies of Promise* frankly as a period piece. But the point of the exercise, we are bound to remember, is that ten years after its composition he is also offering it as a successful instance of "how to write a book which lasts ten years." Are we to conclude, then, that the more a book is dated, the longer its chances of survival? A remarkable hypothesis. No, it won't wash, this period-piece candor: Connolly had no wish to revise or update or tone down the "left-wing militancy" (less "engaging," forty-five years later, and in an age of left-linked terrorism, than he might have supposed); perhaps it was only "artistic indolence." Or perhaps it was because of an intuition about his own character and its style: a certain seamlessness, the absence of self-contradiction. Connolly is always on the side of his own class, never more so than in his expression of "left-wing militancy." It is not that Connolly, in 1938, is mistaken when he declares that "today the forces of life and progress are ranging on one side, those of reaction and death on the other," or that "fascism is the enemy of art," or that "we are not dealing with an Augustus who will discover his Horace and his Virgil, but with Attila or Hulaku, destroyers of European culture whose poets can contribute only battle-cries and sentimental drinking songs." He means Hitler: but the very next year, in 1939, the year of the Hitler-Stalin pact, would he have been willing to mean Stalin too? "The poet is a chemist and there is more pure revolutionary propaganda in a line of Blake than in all *The Rights of Man,*" he asserts: a sophistry that can only be the flower of an elitist education. In 1938 what literary intellectual was not moved by the word "revolutionary"?

Nothing, in fact, is less dated than the combination of Connolly's elitism and his attraction to revolutionary militancy. Any superficial excursion into universities in Western Europe and the United States currently bears this out, nowhere more vividly than in American elitist departments, history, literature, and political science especially. All this is a cliché of our predicament as it was of Connolly's. "The atmosphere of orthodoxy is always damaging to prose," Orwell wrote in *Inside the Whale,* and here is Connolly as prooftext: "Often [solidarity with the working classes] will be recognized only by external symptoms, a disinclination to wear a hat or a stiff collar, an inability to be rude to waiters or taxi-drivers or to be polite to young men of his own age with rolled umbrellas, bowler hats and 'Mayfair men' moustaches or to tolerate the repressive measures of his class." This wizened sentence may be worth the belly laugh due anachronism, but its undigested spirit lingers on. For "disinclination to wear a hat" substitute an earnest inclination to wear Ché boots. And "the repressive measures of his class" is as bruisingly trite and vacuous as any bright young Ivy League graduate's assault on the American bourgeoisie, of which he or she is the consummate product.

The consummate product of his class. Should Connolly be blamed for this? Probably. Orwell went to the same schools at the same time, Eton preceded by St. Cyprian's (St. Wulfric's in Connolly's genial account, Crossgates in Orwell's lugubrious one), and saw straight through what Connolly thrived on. Orwell despised the tyrant-goddess who ruled over St. Cyprian's; Connolly maneuvered to get on her good side. And of Eton Connolly writes (in the ardently arrested parochial tone of one of the "bloody-minded people at the top"), "My last two years of Eton . . . were among the most interesting and rewarding of my whole life and I do not believe they could have been so at any other public school or in any other house than College." The allusion is to school elections; Connolly was, we learn, an ecstatic member of the exclusive "Pop," which he counts, along with romantic homoerotic adolescence, among those "experiences undergone by boys at the great public schools . . . so intense as to dominate their lives." Orwell, reviewing *Enemies of Promise* soon after its appearance, hoots: "He means it!" And sums up the politics of those cosseted few who, between 1910 and 1920, after "five years in a lukewarm bath of snobbery," have fabricated sympathies they have no way of feeling: "Hunger, hardship, solitude, exile, war, prison, persecution, manual labor—hardly even words. No wonder," Orwell charges, "that the huge tribe known as 'the right left people' found it so easy to condone the purge-and-Ogpu side of the Russian régime and the horrors of the First Five Year Plan. They were so gloriously incapable of understanding what it all meant."

Nothing in his brief 1948 introductory note to *Enemies of Promise* tells us whether Connolly did or did not remain one of the right left people a decade later. "We grow up among theories and illusions common to our class, our race, our time," Connolly opens his school-days memoir, but only as a frame for the apology that follows: "I have to refer to something which I find intolerable, the early aura of large houses, fallen fortunes and county families common to so many English autobiographies." He ends by fretting over whether "the reader can stomach this." What is even harder to stomach is a self-repudiation that is indistinguishable from self-congratulation. The memoir itself, with its luxuriant pleasure in "our class, our race, our time," its prideful delight in British Platonism, "popping up in sermons and Sunday questions . . . at the headmaster's dinner-parties or in my tutor's pupil-room," its insurmountable glorying in the stringent achievements of an English classical education—the memoir itself repudiates nothing, least of all the narrator's background, character, or capacities. To preface such an account of high social and intellectual privilege with the hope that it can be "stomached," and then to proceed with so much lip-smacking delectation, is, as Orwell saw, to understand nothing, and to stop at words.

Words, it turns out, are what deserve to last in *Enemies of Promise*—not Connolly's own sentences, which puff and gasp and occasionally strangle themselves, but the subject of his observations about styles of prose. Critical currencies have altered in the extreme since Connolly first set down his categories of Mandarin and vernacular, and unless one reminds oneself that these terms once had some originality of perspective (they are not so facile as they sound), they drop into the hackneyed posture they now permanently evoke. It is true that the New Criticism, which had the assurance of looking both omnipotent and immortal, has come and gone, and that the universal semiotics shock even now hints at softening, if not receding (though only slightly, and then out of factionalism). And other volumes of this kind, siblings or perhaps descendants of *Enemies of Promise,* have ventured to record the politics and history of the writer's predicament—among them critical summaries by Malcolm Cowley, Van Wyck Brooks, John Aldridge, Alfred Kazin, Tony Tanner, Tillie Olsen. The post-Connolly landscape is cluttered with new literary structures of every variety. All the same, Connolly's report on the increasing ascendancy of journalistic style over the life of contemporary fiction—language stripped of interpretive complexity, language stripped even of "language," that is, of the resources of the lyrical or intellectual imagination—remains urgent. The Mandarin "dialect," as Connolly intelligently calls it (and he is wary in his praise of it, especially when it decays into dandyism, "the ability to spin cocoons of language out of nothing"), has now given way to a sort of minimalist data-prose, in which sympathies and deductive acuities are altogether eliminated. In poetry, the minimalists (whether, in all their determined phalanxes, they know it or not) are by now played out, moribund, ready for a turning; only the other day I heard a leading subjectivist, a lineal heir of William Carlos Williams, yearn aloud to sink into a long Miltonic sequence. But among fiction writers, the fossilized Hemingway legacy hangs on, after all this time, strangely and uselessly prestigious. (I attribute this not to the devoted reading of Hemingway but to the decline of reading in general.)

Connolly's distinctions and his exposition of them, however, address the adherents of both "dialects." "From the Mandarins," he exhorts, the writer

> must borrow art and patience, the striving for perfection, the horror of clichés, the creative delight in the material [a phrase that itself arouses horror], in the possibilities of the long sentence and the splendour and subtlety of the composed phrase.
>
> From the Mandarins . . . the new writer will take warning not to capitalise indolence and egotism nor to burden a sober and delicate language with exhibitionism. There will be no false hesitation and woolly profundities, no mystifying, no Proustian onanism.

From the "talkie-novelists," he continues—that is, from the laconic anti-stylists influenced by film—the new writer can acquire the "cursive style, the agreeable manners, the precise and poetical impact of Forster's diction, the lucidity of Maugham, last of the great professional writers, the timing of Hemingway, the smooth cutting edge of Isherwood, the indignation of Lawrence, the honesty of Orwell," as well as the gift of construction. (It is notable that in nearly fifty years not one of these names, not excluding Maugham and Isherwood, has lost its high familiarity, and Orwell, at least, has increased in prestige.) The defects of realist or colloquial style Connolly lists as the consequence of "flatness"—"the homogeneity of outlook, the fear of eccentricity, the reporter's horror of distinction, the distrust of beauty, the cult of violence and starkness that is masochistic." Nowadays we might add the conviction of existential nihilism. "It is no more a question of taking sides about one way or another of writing, but a question of timing," Connolly sensibly concludes. All these are good and salubrious particulars—though it is worth recalling that, in prose at least, and wherever we find ourselves in the cycle of reaction, there are no stripped-down Conrads or Joyces; and that modernism never turned its back on plenitude.

As for my own disappointment in encountering *Enemies of Promise* after so long a hiatus: it was never Connolly's fault that I made up a book that wasn't there. I wanted to brood over failure. Connolly presides over the groans of success. He knows no real enemies—unless you count the threat to revolution ambushed in Mayfair moustaches.

(*March* 1984)

Michel Foucault

by David Gress

Michel Foucault, the French thinker, historian, and epistemologist, died in 1984 at the age of fifty-seven. In recent years his reputation has grown rapidly in American academic life. Professor Frederick Crews of the University of California, writing in *The American Scholar,* speaks of "an exodus from the camp of Marx to that of the late Michel Foucault, who is also the clear favorite of a new academic generation that cares little for the tortuous history of Marxist apologetics." Crews adds:

> It is a nice question . . . whether Foucauldian analysis arose in order to thwart Marxism or, rather, to save its debunking spirit from its doomed propositional content. Foucault himself, significantly, began as a Marxist and a student of Althusser's; they were both Party members in the dreary Lysenko period . . . . [T]he ever-shifting, self-ironic, and brilliantly original style of analysis that Foucault eventually developed can also be regarded in part as a solipsistic Nietzschean travesty of Marxism . . . . In Foucault, perhaps, we are looking at the Marxist to end all Marxists.

As regards the way Foucault has been received in the American academy, especially certain departments of English, history, and art, Crews is on the mark. Nevertheless, the use of Foucault in support of a Marxist stance is a dubious enterprise. One of the major impulses behind Foucault's work was a rejection of the political "games of truth" which he knew firsthand in France in the Fifties, when Party ideology dictated what Communist academics were supposed to study and how. Foucault derived from this experience, and from the use of terror in the name of social health in the Soviet Union, the idea that definitions of sanity, health, and normality were not universal but dependent on changing power relations. He added to it the view of Friedrich Nietzsche that modern rationalism itself was no more reliable a guide to truth than premodern forms of thought. This Nietzschean position—which is neutral toward modern rationalism in all its forms, including Marxism—is incompatible with the attitude of bourgeois academic Marxists, who certainly believe that their own stance of opposition to the Western political system is based on superior insight. Read selectively, Foucault can indeed be used to rescue Western Marxism from decay. Read properly, and with an understanding of motive and context, his ideas and propositions are no more appropriate to that purpose than those of Nietzsche himself.

Foucault's outer life appears to have been quite uneventful. He was born 1926 in Poitiers in central France, the son of a doctor. He studied the history and philosophy of science in Paris in the 1950s under Gaston Bachelard and Louis Althusser, whose writings inspired the structuralist version of Marxist determinism that swept Paris in the 1960s. Foucault's dissertation was published in 1954 under the title *Mental Illness and Psychology,* inaugurating the first of the three major phases of his published work, that of the investigation of health, illness, and madness, and the borders and definitions among them, in the early modern period, primarily the seventeenth and eighteenth centuries. This phase, referred to by some commentators as Foucault's "archaeological" phase, continued at least through the publication of *The Archaeology of Knowledge* (1969), in which Foucault investigated the foundations of the modern social and behavioral sciences. In 1960, he left Paris, unwillingly one suspects, to take up his first permanent post at the University of Clermont-Ferrand, where he remained until 1968, when he returned to Paris, first to the new campus of the University of Paris at Vincennes (1968-70), then to the Collège de France, where he became professor of "the history of systems of thought." The appointment to the Collège was an extraordinary honor for a man as relatively young as Foucault still was at the time. (He was forty-four.) He could with confidence have looked forward to over a quarter century of independent research and teaching. The great advantage of the Collège over ordinary institutions of higher learning is that the faculty design their own courses in complete freedom. They are not required to repeat courses, nor is there any basic curriculum. By common consent the professors at the Collège represent the very elite of France's academic and intellectual life.

About the time of his appointment, Foucault began publishing the works of his second phase or area of interest, namely the "genealogy" and triumph of what he called "bio-power," the practices by which we, the inhabitants of modernity, survey and control each other. Foucault regarded this type of power as peculiar to the modern world, which is characterized by a belief in technology and the methods of natural science and by the irresistible spread of democratic and egalitarian ideas. A crucial aspect of modernity for both Nietzsche and Foucault was the rise of humanitarianism, that is, the belief that the purpose of society and the state is the improvement of life, both material and psychological.

In *The Genealogy of Morals,* Nietzsche traced this humanitarianism to its roots in bourgeois notions of propriety, guilt, public morality, and common sense. Since Nietzsche's style and method broke with the common standards of philosophical and historical argument, it is often overlooked that his critique of humanitarianism was not entirely original, but formed a crucial part of the cultural criticism of leading Western social thinkers such as Tocqueville, Burckhardt, and Max Weber. Foucault was profoundly influenced by Nietzsche's aphoristic, elliptical, yet assertive style; he believed that the resulting opacity and obscurity of argument was a necessary part of Nietzsche's message rather than an obstacle to understanding. Foucault's own main work of this phase was *Discipline and Punish* (1975). Here he sought the origins of modern "bio-power" in the physical drills and corporal training of eighteenth-century armies, which were regarded as miniature images of social organization, and in the universal surveillance of the modern prison. For Foucault, the modern prison—based on the idea of rehabilitation through punishment—was the prime example of humanitarianism as coercive power. Before the eighteenth century, he pointed out, imprisonment was highly unusual; the standard types of punishment for criminal behavior were fines, flogging, banishment, or execution.

The period around 1970 was politically dramatic in France as elsewhere, and despite an often stated distaste for politics, Foucault found himself unavoidably involved in debates and discussions on the events of the day. In the 1970s, Foucault gave interviews rejecting the Communism of his youth and the persistence of radical utopianism; these statements led many to categorize him as a neoconservative. While it is true that he hailed the "new philosophers"—a loose grouping of former radicals who had rejected Marxism in the late Seventies—this label fits Foucault as badly as any other. Those of his writings that do have a topical concern are frequently as ambiguous in their recommendations as his academic work was unclear in its implications.

Fixed conclusions were nevertheless drawn from Foucault's writings, especially by the academic Left in America, where Foucault enjoyed his greatest and most uncritical popularity in the Seventies and after. This was ironic, since his dissection of humanitarianism and of Marxist truth-claims ought logically to have prevented it. The explanation is that his admirers on the American academic Left chose what they wanted from Foucault according to their own agenda, while ignoring the context and deeper intent of his arguments. The reason they could do this was, as Frederick Crews noted, that Foucault's wildly generalizing style lent itself to selective use. After absorbing a few chapters of one or the other of Foucault's books, it is fatally easy to generate Foucauldian critiques of any institution, practice, or attitude one happens not to like. Conversely, Foucault's rejection of the standard canons of scholarship means that one cannot object to selective readings in the name of such canons without risking the accusation that one is simply incapable of understanding how to read and use his work.

Even though much of the use made of Foucault in America has arguably been in violation of his own purposes, it must be admitted that his general "debunking spirit," to use Crews's phrase, is well suited to the leftist temperament. Foucault constantly claimed to be unmasking, in a manner unattainable by normal methods, the coercive character of social institutions ordinarily considered to have generally benevolent purposes, like hospitals, armies, or prisons. This posture was directly borrowed from Nietzsche, who frequently used the metaphor of the mask as the true picture of a reality that is never what it seems and always conceals more than it reveals. In Nietzsche, and even to some extent in Foucault, the act of unmasking is directed with complete objectivity against all social idols, those of the Left as much as those of the Right. Foucault's American followers, however, have happily appropriated the posture of unmasking while discarding the cool objectivity that is its necessary complement. In a recent book on Foucault and Marxism, for example, Mark Poster, a historian at the University of California, Irvine, defines Marxism not as an economic theory but as "a critical view of domination which as historical materialism takes all social practices as transitory and all intellectual formations as indissociably connected with power and social relations." He can then argue, with evident satisfaction and relief, that "Foucault is continuing the work of the Western Marxists by other means."[1]

Thus Foucault's debunking posture easily lends itself to political exploitation by American Leftists, for whom capitalist freedom is a hoax and America, especially under Reagan, is a morally inferior regime that threatens the rest of the world with oppression and war. Foucault was at bottom a kind of anarchist; he did not want to distinguish between degrees of coercion. His institutional critiques left little room for the assertion of any real difference between various types of institutions—say, between a Nazi or Soviet concentration camp on the one hand and a Western prison on the other. Likewise, his debunking of humanitarianism as coercion hardly allowed for judging the relative merits of liberal democratic procedures and the significance of legal rights

---

1 The title of Poster's book is *Foucault, Marxism and History: Mode of Production versus Mode of Information*; Polity Press (Cambridge, England), 174 pages. As the title suggests, Poster argues that Foucault is doing for our modern society—where the control of knowledge and information is said to be as important as the control of material resources—what Marx did for the nineteenth century. In other words, Foucault is saving what Sidney Hook called "existential Marxism" from collapse. Poster's claim of superior insight into "domination," however, is itself an assertion of power—the irresponsible will to power of the tenured intellectual over the society that, by ignoring or resisting his analysis, supposedly demonstrates its moral inadequacy.

as against the arbitrary actions of despotic regimes. This refusal to acknowledge any real distinction between the intentions and the uses of power in different political systems made his arsenal of arguments very attractive to those of his American academic admirers who were less interested in the history of knowledge and power than in undermining the moral legitimacy of the democratic system.

The third phase of Foucault's work became public in 1976 when he published the first volume of his *History of Sexuality.* In this book he argued against the modern idea that Western sexuality had undergone a repression in the nineteenth century from which it was only now emerging. Instead, he saw sexuality in general, both before, during, and after the Victorian era, as part of a continuous Western view of the self and its proper development and care. In volumes two, three, and four of the *History* he returned to classical Antiquity in order to uncover the origins of this Western idea of the self, particularly as it was expressed in ideas about sex.[2]

This enterprise was ended by his unexpected death in Paris in May 1984. Foucault had been spending the winter before at Berkeley, the last of his many visits to American campuses. He had been chronically ill; and on his return to Paris he went into hospital, where certain discoveries were made. According to James Harkness, the translator of some of his works, it is "almost certain that the so-called 'disease of the nervous system' that killed him was made possible by the breakdown of his immune system as a result of having contracted AIDS."[3] Foucault was indeed a homosexual, but for most of his life he had been of the old-fashioned kind who do not regard it as the essence of their being and hence do not need to flaunt it at every turn, insisting that others recognize its superiority. His attitude changed somewhat during the era of his American success, perhaps because homosexuality on American campuses had by then become almost inevitably blatant and political. At New York University, for example, where Foucault taught in the early Eighties, he did not resist being publicly associated with homosexual activism.

Foucault was concerned with definitions of truth, self, and power, and with the uses made of these factors of human existence at various times, especially during the period that marked the breakdown of the classical *episteme* and the construction of modernity. The notion of *episteme* recurs often in Foucault's writings. The original Greek meaning of the word is "knowledge" or "understanding." Foucault used it to mean a combination of world view, form of knowledge, and the entire body of methods and outlooks used to apprehend and analyze phenomena. Thus, he referred to the "classical *episteme,*" by which he meant the ideas, sensibilities, and philosophical orientations of Western Europe that prevailed until the late eighteenth century, and to the "modern *episteme,*" which arose in the revolutionary era of 1770-1800. The modern *episteme* included the extension of power from overt coercion and discipline to the hidden coercion of modern institutions and practices; in fact, Foucault argued that this new use of power was the defining characteristic of modernity. The beginnings of the classical *episteme* were uncertain. In the *History of Sexuality* Foucault appeared to be arguing that its origins were to be sought in classical antiquity.

Foucault's concerns were posed as such by the philosophy that above all others defined the terms of modernity, that of Hegel. Foucault inherited his concerns from those who challenged the consequences of Hegel's system, notably from Nietzsche, but also from the French tradition of Hegelianism, a tradition that, through the work and personality

2 The second volume of Foucault's *History of Sexuality* has just been published in English translation by Pantheon, under the title *The Use of Pleasure*; 293 pages, $17.95. The first volume, *The History of Sexuality: Volume I, An Introduction,* was published by Pantheon in 1981.

3 *The American Spectator,* December 1985, page 39.

of Alexandre Kojève, was intimately connected with French Communism. In the Thirties, Kojève gave a widely influential series of lectures on Hegel's *Phenomenology of Spirit,* attended by Sartre among others, the gist of which was that Hegel had reconciled freedom and necessity and that free human action was no longer possible because history had come to an end. This end of history was said to be concretely exemplified in Stalin's Russia, which therefore represented the inevitable fate toward which all modern industrial societies must move. After the war, Kojève, as a senior civil servant, devoted his career to the development of the European Economic Community, without finding this to be in conflict with his earlier determinism. Since he is also supposed to have believed that the superior man is never obliged to reveal his true opinions on anything, it remains uncertain whether his Stalinism was a mask or a genuine conviction. However that may be, it was as an apologist for Soviet totalitarianism that Kojève influenced a generation of French Communist and fellow-travelling intellectuals.

Foucault himself rejected the Stalinist tenor of Kojève's teachings in favor of those of another, and greater, French Hegelian, Jean Hyppolite, concerning whom he wrote one of his most important articles, "Nietzsche, Genealogy, History." The philosophical and political strands of Foucault's heritage cannot be clearly separated, nor can his cultural descent, which ran from Nietzsche through the French Surrealists and their supporters, especially Georges Bataille. Nevertheless, for purposes of exposition, it must be done, and I would start with a recursion to Hegel himself. Hegel laid down the terms even for those, like Nietzsche, Bataille, and Foucault, who rejected modernity—or, rather, who decided that the premises of modernity were unsustainable.

Classical Western philosophy had three branches: ontology, epistemology, and ethics, corresponding to the questions of being, knowledge, and action. Plato and Hegel, at the beginning and end of the classical tradition, proposed systems that included all three branches. The crucial difference between the two was in the status of the knowing subject. Plato's subject reached enlightenment by discovering what already existed in reality; Hegel's subject reached enlightenment by changes of consciousness. These changes led to a discovery of the actions and the meaning of objective Spirit, but the process was dialectical; in some real sense the objective Spirit itself was a creation of the enlightened consciousness. It is in this sense that Hegel's system, and the modern thought that builds on (or against) it, can be said to be the ultimate subjectivity. This notion of subjectivity was, as we shall see, crucial to Nietzsche as well as to Bataille.

Hegel produced the first and last complete attempt to reconcile reason and reality. What we would call true objective understanding was for Hegel an ultimate stage of subjectivity, the realization of the harmony that existed between the self and the world. In Hegel's political philosophy, the paternalistic and bureaucratic state was the ideal and proper form of human social existence, the highest manifestation of objective Spirit.

Hegel's system gave rise to disputes which have not changed their basic terms since the 1840s. The German political philosopher and leftist thinker Jürgen Habermas, with whom Foucault is often compared, defines the entire "discourse of modernity" as essentially derived from the fight over Hegel's heritage. Since that discourse has been primarily political, all serious political argument on the European Continent since 1840 has been to some extent part of this fight.

Crudely put, the basic notion common to all who appealed to Hegel in the nineteenth century was that reality should be ruled by reason. For the Hegelians of the Left the problem with the rule of reason was that it was the rule of *bourgeois* reason. Hence the task was to liberate the potentialities of reason and to overcome the one-sided rationalism of the bourgeois world. Marx himself essayed this project. (And, in our own day, Georg Lukacs, the Western Marxists of the

Frankfurt School, and lately Habermas as well.) Hegelians of the Right, on the other hand, emphasized the need to have faith in the reasonableness of prevailing reality. They tended to regard the revolutionary tendencies of their Left cousins as subjective error, and to regard the socialist belief in the need and the logic of political change as romantic folly engendered by an exaggerated belief in their own rationality.

Nietzsche, finally, criticized the basis of both forms of rationality, the revolutionary as well as the conservative. For him, reason itself was nothing other than an expression of the will to power, which was the fundamental constant of human history and civilization. In all societies everywhere there are those who control and those who are controlled. Nevertheless, the means by which control is exercised differ. In premodern times, Christianity performed the function of denying the ubiquity of the will to power and of sublimating it; religion became the vehicle by which a certain type of person exercised power over society by moral injunction, exhortation, and guilt. In modern times, Nietzsche continued, we believe less in Christianity and more in science, technology, and social progress; therefore, the will to power can be seen in the use of scientific claims and political arguments. This, as I have indicated, was Foucault's view exactly. The more advanced the society, the less power is exercised as naked force and overt coercion. Instead, people internalize the will to power, and power becomes not an emanation of the state but an aspect of the most intimate relations. The distinction between the wielders and the objects of power disappears. All are at one and the same time both wielders *and* objects of power. This is the paradox of modern humanitarianism. It began in opposition to older forms of power, but once established as the chief principle of modern societies it could not avoid becoming the newest vehicle of the will to power, which is permanent and ubiquitous.

Foucault shared with Nietzsche the belief that the will to power was permanent and that conflict was the essential feature of human society. Foucault was fond of saying that politics is war carried on by other means. Since power is exercised through reason, moreover, he tended to argue, again in Nietzschean fashion, that all attempts at grasping reality involve power. In his work, the discourse of modernity in the Hegelian sense—that is, the attempt to bring reality in line with reason (whether revolutionary or conservative)—is turned on itself and shown to be merely another manifestation of the permanent will to power. Thus he almost never referred to the institutional or political changes of modern times as progress, but emphasized always their paradoxical, power-enhancing effects. He exemplified this in his studies of hospitals, armies, and prisons, and in his analysis of the systems of thought that in each period determined the purpose of such institutions. The most important of these studies are *Discipline and Punish* and other writings of the Seventies collected in English in the volume entitled *Power/Knowledge.*[4]

From Nietzsche came also the method that Foucault declared to be most appropriate to his task. This was "genealogy," as opposed to the linear evolutionary schemes of conventional historians. Foucault describes genealogy as a discovery of origins which "will never neglect as inaccessible the vicissitudes of history. On the contrary, it will cultivate the details and accidents that accompany every beginning." Genealogy is the opposite of comprehensive analysis. The genealogist does not seek a complete explanation. Complete explanations, in Foucault's world, are rejected precisely because they are judged to be examples of the hidden power he is concerned to unmask. The secret revealed by genealogy is that things "have no essence or that their essence was fabricated in piecemeal fashion from alien forms." To Foucault, finality and essences are elements of a form of domination far more comprehensive and insidious than the coercive

4 *Power/Knowledge,* edited by C. Gordon, was published by Pantheon in 1981.

power of political authority normally studied by historians and political scientists, which includes orthodox socialism and Marxism, with their strong beliefs in historical purpose and in a certain form of political rationalism. (Thus, Foucault felt liberated by the student rebellion of 1968 to the extent that it was not a traditional socialist movement, but rather, as he thought, an expression of the refusal to participate in traditional politics.)

Nietzsche's thought undermined the Hegelian claims to realism and rationality as much by its style, which was aphoristic and pointillistic, as by its arguments. The inspiration found by Foucault in Nietzsche was thus both cultural and philosophical, and it was expanded by Foucault's fascination with Georges Bataille.[5] Bataille's writings cover an extraordinary range, from erotic (some would say pornographic) stories to serious essays in economics and political and social anthropology. Politically he was close to the Communist Party in the Thirties and studied Kojève, but after World War II he moved away from the Stalinist Party line. In a manner probably only possible in France, he combined his dissenting Communism with a belief in the regenerative importance of liminal experiences, that is, experiences that crossed the boundaries accepted in the world of "normal life." The following passage is crucial evidence of Bataille's position, which came to mean so much to Foucault:

> The life of man, distinct from legal existence and as it takes place in fact on an isolated planet in the heavens, from day to night, from one country to the next, the life of man can in no way be limited to the closed systems assigned to it by rationalist conceptions. We can express the immense, turbulent labor of everflowing abandon that constitutes it by saying that it only begins where those systems fail; whatever order and reserve it allows only has meaning from the point where the forces that are ordered and reserved free themselves and lose themselves for ends which cannot be made subject to anything capable of rational accounting. It is only by virtue of such insubordination, however miserable, that the human race ceases to be isolated in the unconditional splendor of material things.[6]

Foucault took from Bataille the idea that human life is richer than any possible description of it, that its very essence is not, as orthodox economists say, scarcity, but rather excess and abandon. This idea was reflected throughout Foucault's work in two ways. First, in his constant insistence that all facets of culture, all elements in and changes of the *episteme,* had unforeseen and paradoxical consequences (paradoxical, that is, in terms of traditional rationality). For example, hospitals, founded ostensibly to cure people by virtue of a particular theory of illness, became institutions of coercion and normalization. This led directly to Foucault's most important claim, namely that in modernity, the traditional legal and political forms of power are being replaced by an even more intrusive kind of power, exercised "from below." It was to this new form of power that he gave the name "bio-power," since it was primarily wielded over the human body in the name of mental and physical health. The locus of power is thus no longer the "objective" rules of public authorities but the practices that define health, illness, and well-being.

The other way in which Bataille's notion

5 Foucault's article, "Preface à la transgression," in the issue of *Critique* devoted to Bataille after his death (August-September, 1963), is an interesting early version of his theory of sexuality. The essay appears in English in *Language, Counter-Memory, Practice,* edited by D. F. Bouchard (Pantheon, 1977). On the Surrealists in general, Foucault contributed an early book, *Raymond Roussel* (1963), and an article on Magritte, Klee, and Kandinsky, *Ceci n'est pas un pipe,* which was published as a book, with illustrations by Magritte, in 1973. (The English translation, *This is Not a Pipe,* was published by the University of California Press in 1983.)

6 From "La notion de dépense," quoted by Jean Piel in *Critique* (August-September, 1963).

of excess was reflected in Foucault's work was in Foucault's deeply personal conviction that simple, positive description of any fact, idea, or institution is not only inadequate, but somehow immoral: "As for those for whom to take pains, to begin over and over again, to make mistakes, to start from scratch, and still to find reason to hesitate; as for those for whom, in short, to work in tentative apprehension is tantamount to failure, well, all I can say is that we clearly do not inhabit the same planet." In other words, finality is constricting and bad; discourse must be open-ended, vague, and general if it is not to be coercive. For the same reason—the belief that any simple label is unfair to its object—he distinguished between "discussion" and "polemics," praising the former while rejecting the latter: "Has anyone ever seen a new idea come out of a polemic? And how could it be otherwise, given that the interlocutors are incited, not to advance, not to take more and more risks in what they say, but to fall back continually on the rights that they claim, on their legitimacy . . . ." Apart from echoing Bataille and his vision of the richness of life, Foucault was here rejecting the Party procedures familiar to him from his youth in France. But even as he rejected the Communist Party, Foucault seems to have retained the belief that Party procedures were archetypal expressions of political power—no matter what the outward character of the regime. This belief may explain Foucault's zeal to unmask what he believed were secret coercions hidden in apparently innocuous modern social and political practices. Since the Party model is not the quintessential model of modern power, however, Foucault's debunking approach is clearly not equipped to deal with the pluralism of democratic procedures.

The effect of Bataille's erotic writings of the Thirties and Forties was to glorify liminality, which he also called heterogeneity, in opposition to the homogeneity of the bourgeois world. The concept, as Jürgen Habermas says, "condensed the basic experience of the Surrealists, who set for themselves the task of mobilizing as shockingly as possible the ecstatic forces of intoxication, dreams, and sexual drive against the imperatives of the useful, the normal, and the sober." According to Habermas, Bataille's concern, like Foucault's, was to "break out of the prison-house of modernity, out of the closed universe of the world-historically victorious reason of the West. Both wanted to overcome the subjectivism that covers the world with its reifying power and causes it to coagulate into a totality of technically available and economically definable objects."[7] The opposition to a world in which all objects, including people, are "technically available" echoes the later Heidegger, who was another influence on Foucault, although much less important than either Nietzsche or Bataille. Bataille's Communism, which came to resemble Kojève's, sits oddly with this opposition, of course. In a world-state ruled according to Stalinist principles all men and all objects would be available for manipulation by the will of the sovereign. As we have seen, this perspective repelled Foucault. And his rejection of Kojève's teachings extended to their interpretation by Sartre and Merleau-Ponty. (In *Humanisme et terreur* [1946], for example, Merleau-Ponty defended the Soviet regime, arguing that true humanism and true terror were mutually necessary.)

Although Foucault rejected the political servility of Merleau, he did borrow important elements from him, particularly the notion of the human body (*le corps vécu*) as the stage on which power is enacted. "The body," Foucault would write, "is the inscribed surface of events (traced by language and dissolved by ideas), the locus of a dissociated self (adopting the illusion of a substantial unity), and a volume in perpetual disintegration."

7 These remarks appear in *Der philosophische Diskurs der Moderne* (Suhrkamp Verlag, 1985). An English version of this book, in my opinion the most interesting of all Habermas's work (based on lectures given at the Collège de France and at Cornell), is forthcoming from MIT Press.

Foucault's work in the Fifties and early Sixties—on the development of modern practices of health and on the rise of the modern understanding of physical and mental illness—turned out to have an immediate political dimension. Foucault's membership in the Party ended when the suppression of dissent in genetics and linguistics in the USSR by decree, and the terror exercised against dissenters, shocked him by what he saw as its analogies to what he was studying. In view of Soviet practices which were not then as notorious as they have since become —but which were still something "it was better not to talk about"—the history of madness and health was not a subject likely to be popular with the politburo of the French Communist Party. Consequently, as Foucault later drily remarked, "what I tried to do in this domain was met with a great silence among the French intellectual left."

Foucault used the word "archeology" in the titles of his three major works of the Sixties, all of which ultimately grew out of his early work on medical history: *The Birth of the Clinic* (1963), subtitled in French *Une archéologie du régard médical* (which means "an archeology of medical observation," and not "medical perception," as the translation has it); *The Order of Things* (1966), subtitled *An Archaeology of the Human Sciences,* and finally *The Archaeology of Knowledge* (1969).[8] In a recent study of Foucault, Hubert L. Dreyfus and Paul Rabinow define the archeological method as one in which "the archeologist performs on all discourse and knowledge, especially our own, the same sort of distanciation of truth and meaning [i.e., by not allowing modern meanings to influence interpretation of old ones] which we naturally bring to the medical accounts and other theories of the Classical Age . . . . Once we treat the language and practices of a discipline from another age as mere meaningless objects, we can gain access to a level of description which shows that what remains incomprehensible is not without its own systematic order."[9]

The connoisseur of Continental fashions will immediately recognize the resemblance of Foucauldian "archeology" to the *structuralisme* that was marching to victory in Paris around 1960. Like Foucault, the structuralists saw human action and society as determined by their structures, which had their own autonomous existence. The pre-archeological Foucault of *Madness and Civilization* (1961) had been a prisoner, as he might put it, to an epistemology that promised true insight (valid for something beyond the discovery of past discursive practices themselves) based on "exegesis," which was his term for the interpretive method of Husserl and the early Heideger. After *Madness and Civilization,* Foucault realized that, because it relied on an external standard, exegesis was the last refuge of the tradition of humanistic scholarship. Humanism as a scholarly ethos implies, first, that there is a single standard of human reason that can explain human actions, and second, that there is genuine progress of insight and enlightenment in scholarship as well as life generally. By his "archeological" phase, Foucault had already rejected both claims.

In the introduction to *The Order of Things,* he summarized the nature and purpose of his "archeology" with untypical clarity—untypical because, as we have seen, deliberate ambiguity was regarded as a virtual moral necessity by Foucault. The investigation, he said, "will not describe the progress of knowledge toward an objective standard recognizable by our sciences of today; the purpose is rather to bring to light the . . . *episteme* within which forms of knowledge, without regard to any criterion of rational value or objective form, display their positivity and thus manifest a history which is not that of an increasing perfection, but rather that of their conditions of possibility. What

8 *The Birth of the Clinic* was published by Pantheon in 1973, *The Archaeology of Knowledge* in 1982. *The Order of Things* was published by Vintage in 1971.

9 *Michel Foucault: Beyond Structuralism and Hermeneutics* by Hubert L. Dreyfus and Paul Rabinow; University of Chicago Press, 1982 (second edition, 1983).

I hope will appear in this account is the configurations that . . . have given rise to the various forms of empirical knowledge." The focus of interest was the mentality and entire system of perception and understanding of the classical era, seen in its own right and not merely as different from—or less adequate than—modern science.

The result of these archeological investigations was the assertion of "two great discontinuities in the *episteme* of Western culture." The *ancien régime* believed in natural history, based on the notion of the Great Chain of Being, in universal grammar, based on the notion of an original language underlying all spoken languages, and in mercantilism, based on the idea that wealth is fixed and must be hoarded. Modernity believes, by contrast, in biology, comparative grammar, and economic growth. Foucault's structuralist method is to elucidate the inner functions of the older period, which he called the Age of Representation, while denying any superior merit to modern science. He concluded by arguing that the idea of man as a rational entity with a mind and a body functioning in certain predictable ways was an illusion destined, though he does not say why, to fade like an image in the sand erased by the rising tide.

The Order of Things is in many ways a thrilling book. But the idea that past cultures, including the past of our own culture, had different standards of truth which are not *per se* inferior to our own is, of course, not original with Foucault; it was a commonplace of the historical school of the nineteenth century. The writings of Foucault's archeological period display to an irritating degree the all-too-frequent parochialism of certain Gallic writers, who with great apparatus and fanfare produce deep-sounding statements about facts or methods that have been perfectly well known for decades, if not centuries. No reader of Arthur Lovejoy in America or of Frederic Maitland in England would have the least trouble taking past systems of thought on their own terms or understanding such systems from within, according to their own code (as the structuralists say). As Frederick Crews has pointed out, however, the matter is tangled up with politics and temperament. No with-it professor of English or history in this country, even if he had heard of Lovejoy and Maitland, is going to admit to reading (much less admiring) *them* when Foucault, with his mantle of radicalism and his unmasking posture, is available to replace the blunted Marx in the great class(room) struggle.

Though much of Foucault is often as overvalued as *The Order of Things,* his writings on the subjects of power and self are useful for an understanding of modern forms of power that, like the concealed power-drive in the humanitarian impulse to improve life, are both "intentional and non-subjective." In this later period Foucault began to write and speak more openly of power in modern politics. Since his criticism of power included the intellectual power dear to the Left, he lost much of his reputation in France, at least until the turn away from Marxism took hold after 1975. By the same token, Foucault is partly responsible for the victory in much of French political culture of a critique of power that included intellectual as well as overtly political power. It remains to be seen how much of *this* Foucault is received in America, given the fact that the people in question are precisely those American Marxist and quasi-Marxist academics who assert the right to power of their own ideology. Unlike him, they completely lose their vaunted critical faculties when the question of their own interests arises. Whatever one can say of Foucault, such convenient blindness was never one of his faults.

Around 1968, Foucault returned to Nietzsche for the concept of genealogy. Foucault's discussion of forms of power in his genealogical phase often displays a curious paradox. He seems on the one hand interested simply in uncovering domination in unexpected places and presenting it for observation; on the other hand, in scattered remarks, he takes it for granted that power of any kind requires resistance. To encourage resistance, or to imply that domination is immoral, seems, on the face of it, to be evidence precisely of that humanitarianism which, according to Nietzsche and Foucault, is itself a particularly insidious form of power masquerading as benevolence and emancipation.

Foucault took from Nietzsche the notion of the rise, throughout modernity, of a form of domination based on claims to superior knowledge and on the ability to set standards of knowledge and truth, as opposed to domination based on specific legal and political claims. In Germany, this notion descended from Nietzsche to Max Weber and from him to a disparate group of social theorists critical of the arrogant claims of their colleagues and of the intellectual "producers of meaning" in general. These thinkers—Arnold Gehlen, Helmut Schelsky, and Friedrich Tenbruck are the most important—stood far to the right of the center in postwar West German intellectual culture. Their main argument was that the distinguishing characteristic of modern societies is the existence of an intellectual elite, a knowledge class of rulers who legitimize their own control in the shape of theories about society. Those who were close to the left-liberal and neo-Marxist center of West German culture, like Habermas, denounced these thinkers as neoconservative reactionaries. This was harder to do in Foucault's case, given his political antecedents. Also, he clothed his analysis of intellectual power in a language and style wholly different from the tradition of Weberian sociology.

Foucault arrived at the nexus of knowledge, rationality, and power from his studies in the history of medicine and the treatment of disease, both of which he saw as coercive. "Take the example of philanthropy in the early nineteenth century: people appear who make it their business to involve themselves in other people's lives, health, nutrition, housing; then, out of this confused set of functions there emerge certain personages, institutions, forms of knowledge: public hygiene, inspectors, social workers, psychologists . . . . Naturally it's medicine which has played the basic role as the common demoninator." In conventional sociological analysis we are used to seeing the great change coming about when, in the welfare state of the Thirties and after, the public sector eclipsed private philanthropy. For Foucault, this shift from charity as an individual social obligation to charity as a function of the bureaucratic welfare state is part of a broader process. The process was described in an essay on Foucault by the Canadian political philosopher Charles Taylor, known as a Hegel scholar and as a defender of a mildly socialist and egalitarian position:

> The picture is drawn . . . of a constellation combining modern humanitarianism, the new social sciences, and the new disciplines which develop in armies, schools, and hospitals in the eighteenth century, all seen as the formation of new modes of domination . . . . Humanitarianism itself seems to be understood as a kind of stratagem of the new growing mode of control. The new forms of knowledge serve this end. People are measured, classed, examined in various ways, and thus made the better subject to a control which tends to normalization . . . . Far from explaining the rise of this new technology of control in terms of the modern identity of man as an individual, Foucault wants to explain the modern notion of individuality as one of its products . . . . What is wielded through the modern technologies of control is . . . not concerned with law but with normalization . . . with bringing about a certain result, defined as health or good function.[10]

Here we see in part the legacy of Merleau-Ponty's *corps vécu*; the focus on the body as a locus of the exercise of power makes it a secondary matter whether therapeutic power originates in the dominant sentiments of a culture or in the welfare legislation of a modern government.

The role of government in modern social development appears at a different stage in Foucault's analysis, namely in the shape of

10 *Philosophy and the Human Sciences,* by Charles Taylor (Cambridge University Press, 1985): pages 157-58.

the "well-ordered police states" of the eighteenth century. Since he was not speaking to historians, Foucault explained that the modern meaning of *police* was only about a hundred and fifty years old; before then, "'police' is the ensemble of mechanisms serving to ensure order, the properly channelled growth of wealth and the conditions of preservation of health in general." In the sixteenth century, the words "policy" and "police" were often not distinguished from one another; gradually, "policy" came to take on meanings similar to those of today. "Police," on the other hand, came to mean "a program of government rationality . . . a project to create a system of regulation of the general conduct of individuals whereby everything would be controlled to the point of self-sustenance, without the need for intervention." When the point of self-sustenance was reached, government could be restricted without sacrificing social control. The ideology of modern liberalism (in its European sense) defended this restriction of government on the grounds that people were better at managing their own affairs in society than a ruler was. Foucault argued that this ideology represented a ruse; in fact, the social control remained, but it was now automatic: the old-fashioned "police state" was no longer needed.

As in the case of *The Order of Things,* I cannot help thinking that Foucault displays more than a little historical naïveté, or at least a certain parochialism, in his discussions of the early modern "police states." He seems to fall prey to a simple nominalism, confusing a dislike or distrust of police, in the contemporary sense of the word, with the character of police in its *ancien régime* sense. As historians know, in the eighteenth century "police" was an administrative term, not an element of law enforcement. This sort of confusion of contemporary connotations of a word with its meaning at an earlier stage of the *episteme* (as it were) is of course absolutely incompatible with Foucault's emphasis on distance and on the equal validity of classical and modern forms of knowledge (and power).

Foucault has not been the only scholar to argue that the paternalistic governments of the Prussian and French "police states" entailed new forms of power, forms not easily captured in works of the older schools of legal and institutional history. In *The Well-Ordered Police State,* for example, the historian Marc Raeff argues that the social order aimed at by eighteenth-century governments was possible only because the rulers succeeded in inculcating certain values and norms that, after a certain point, no longer required positive enforcement. Though Raeff does not use the word "power," he is talking about exactly the same process that is described by Foucault in *Discipline and Punish* and elsewhere. In a different vein, Michael Oakeshott, the conservative English philosopher, has maintained that rationalist politics are a dangerous form of power precisely because in such politics the power claims are concealed by pretentions of philanthropy and benevolence. He devoted a third of *On Human Conduct* to the ways in which the administration of power over people grew in early modern states, and to the psychological attitudes and dispositions underlying choices of power.

The generalizing, pointillistic style and the air of revelation of long-kept secrets with which Foucault displayed ideas well known to professional scholars obscures the force of his description of modern power. The central element of that description is his insistence on the Nietzschean position that "there can be no such thing as a truth independent of its regime, unless it be that of another," expressed in an interview on "Truth and Power" given in 1977.

> Truth isn't outside power, or lacking in power . . . . truth isn't the reward of free spirits . . . nor the privilege of those who have succeeded in liberating themselves. Truth is a thing of this world: it is produced only by virtue of multiple forms of constraint. And it induces regular effects of power. Each society has its regime of truth, its "general politics" of truth: that is, the types of discourse which it accepts and makes function as true; the

> mechanisms and instances which enable one to distinguish true and false statements, the means by which each is sanctioned; the techniques and procedures accorded value in the acquisition of truth; the status of those who are charged with saying what counts as true.
>
> In societies like ours, the "political economy" of truth is characterized by five important traits. "Truth" is centered on the form of scientific discourse and the institutions which produce it; it is subject to constant economic and political incitement (the demand for truth, as much for economic production as for political power); it is the object, under diverse forms, of immense diffusion and consumption . . . ; it is produced and transmitted under the control, dominant if not exclusive, of a few great political and economic apparatuses . . . lastly, it is the issue of a whole political debate and social confrontation . . . .
>
> It is necessary to think of the political problems of intellectuals not in terms of "science" and "ideology," but in terms of "truth" and "power."

Though it is clear how the Foucault who argued this way was quite welcome to some of the revolutionaries of 1968, particularly those who wanted to destroy the university, it is equally clear that they could not be really comfortable with him for long. Foucault's strength, which is also his weakness, is that he was never able to contemplate an example of rationality or a triumph of reason without simultaneously seeing its potential for danger—danger to the very liberation or progress which it had just helped to achieve. "How can we exist as rational beings, fortunately committed to practicing a rationality that is unfortunately crisscrossed by intrinsic dangers?" This question could almost be Foucault's life motto.

The tendency to view power as a moral problem rather than a fact with moral effects is, of course, a common trait of the modern temper, particularly of the leftist temper, as it was once defined by the Catholic existentialist Jacques Maritain. Maritain distinguished a physiological (as he called it) from a political meaning of Left and Right. The first meaning was the more important, since it circumscribed unchangeable types of temperament. "The pure man of the Left," wrote Maritain, "despises Being, always preferring in principle, as Rousseau put it, *that which is not* to *that which is*; the pure man of the Right hates justice and charity, always preferring in principle, as Goethe put it . . . *injustice* to *disorder.*"[11] Nietzsche well illustrates the difference between Maritain's physiological and political senses of Right and Left. He was certainly by temperament an almost pure example of the Right, yet politically he despised conservatives, especially the German nationalists who engineered the process of German political unification in 1866-71. Foucault, his modern admirer, to some extent illustrated the opposite condition. His critique of the politics of truth in modern societies, and of therapeutic domination—that is, social control in the name of health, order, or universal betterment—put at least that part of him close to the "new philosophers" and to some neoconservatives. On the other hand, his Bataille-inspired conviction that any system is limiting, and that full life begins where the systems end, was closer to Maritain's temperament of the Left. "The questions I am trying to ask are not determined by a pre-established political outlook . . . . I am attempting, on the contrary, apart from any *totalization*—which would be at once *abstract* and *limiting*—to *open up* problems . . . that approach politics from behind and cut across societies on the diagonal."

Following *Discipline and Punish,* Foucault turned to what became his last major project, the *History of Sexuality.* It was originally planned to be a six-volume study of modern subjectivity as expressed in ideas of sex-

11 From *Lettre sur l'indépendance* (1935), which appears in the sixth volume of *Oeuvres complètes,* by Jacques and Raissa Maritain (Paris: Editions Saint-Paul, 1984). There is much else of interest in this passage, including the remark that "the most terrible rev›lutions are revolutions of the Left made by temperaments of the Right," such as Lenin.

uality. In his by now standard manner, Foucault proposed to show that this idea was a constituent of the modern *episteme.* The notion of sexuality as something repressed in modern bourgeois society and hence deserving of liberation was, he claimed, itself imposed by a certain epistemology and psychology. "The self experience whereby we have a sexual nature which is held down or confined by rules and tabus is itself a creation of the new kind of power / control. In going for liberation, we see ourselves as escaping a power understood on the old model. But in fact we live under a power of the new kind." (Namely, the "bio-power" of mutual domination.) After volume one, which unmasked Freudian and other theories of sexual health as forms of power, Foucault changed course. The three volumes he subsequently wrote concern not the modern end of the Western *episteme,* but its distant origins in the ancient and early Christian "care of self." He explained the shift and its dependence on his earlier work as follows:

> The idea was to investigate how individuals were led to practice, on themselves and others, a hermeneutics of desire . . . . In order to understand how the modern individual could experience himself as the subject of a "sexuality," it was necessary first to extricate the way in which Western man throughout the centuries came to recognize himself as a subject of desire.
>
> A theoretical shift had seemed necessary to analyze what was often called the advance of learning; it had led me to ask questions concerning the types of discursive practice that articulated knowledge [i.e., *The Archaeology of Knowledge*]. A theoretical shift had also been needed to analyze what is often called the manifestations of "power"; it had led me rather to ask questions on the multiple relations, the overt strategies and rational techniques that articulated the exercise of power [i.e., *Discipline and Punish*]. It now seemed necessary to undertake a third shift, to analyze what is called "the subject"; it seemed appropriate to find out what were the forms and means of the relation to self by which the individual constitutes and recognizes himself as a subject . . . . I had to choose: either to maintain the original plan and adding to it a brief historical sketch of this theme of desire, or to reorganize the entire study around the gradual formation in Antiquity of a hermeneutics of self. I chose the latter option, reflecting that after all for many years I have adhered to the project of disentangling some of the elements that might serve for a history of truth.

The next three volumes, which Foucault lived to complete (the fourth volume of the work is being prepared for publication in 1986), describe Greek and Roman attitudes to sexuality and point out how many of them survived into Christianity and hence into our Western *episteme.* The main difference was that the Greek care of self was focused on self-mastery for the sake of civic life. James Harkness describes Foucault's view of the Greeks this way: "Embodied in 'techniques of the self' and an 'art of living,' the usage of pleasures imposed shapeliness on sensitive, highly charged areas of life, an order independent of intrusive legal or political enforcement." In Christianity, on the other hand, self-restraint was commanded by religion, and the care of self came to include the care of others through the Church. This care of others gradually built up, or was built up by, a system of "pastoral power," which was occasionally contested by medieval heretical sects and later, more successfully, in the Protestant Reformation. But Protestantism continued pastoral power in other forms, one of them being the "police state" of eighteenth-century Prussia, another being the intrusive philanthropy of the Protestant Victorians. Thus Foucault (for volume four of the *History* stops with the earliest Christians) produced yet another turn back to his concern with forms of power.

As James Harkness points out, the *History of Sexuality,* especially volumes two and three, "will be widely regarded as works of 'gay liberation,' aimed at historically legitimating homosexual eroticism and life-styles," because Foucault devoted considerable space to Greek homoeroticism. Foucault, however, had no interest in presenting a brief for homosexuality; such an essentially polemical procedure was alien to his principles. On the contrary, he found in the Greeks' thought on homosexuality precisely the point at which

> they formulated the need for the most rigorous austerities . . . and the principle of "indefinite abstention". . . . We see, in Greek culture and in relation to the love of boys, the formation of some of the major elements of sexual ethics that would reject it precisely on account of this principle: the need for symmetry and reciprocity in relations of love, [and] the need for a difficult and laborious struggle with oneself . . . . The fact is that the demand of total abstention and the privilege granted to the question of desire introduced elements that were not easy to accommodate within the search for the usage of pleasures.

Foucault, in the end, is perhaps less ambiguous than some of his admirers will make him. He maintained a Nietzschean neutrality toward the claims of modern doctrines, including Marxism and the vague rationalist liberalism on which the political consensus of most Western countries seems to rest. His intellectual and political anarchism, however, also led him, as we have seen, to claim that his posture of unmasking and of discovering coercive elements in every single habit, institution, and idea of human society was the only responsible one. Yet his revelations were accompanied by a personal stance that was open to abuse by persons with political agendas that, according to his own principles, ought to be rejected. His political gestures were eclectic: he was in favor of the student rebels of 1968, the New York homosexuals in the Seventies, the "new philosophers" in 1977-79, and against Soviet repression in Poland in 1982-84. Such eclecticism allows for the selective use of his ideas for political purposes. We should probably expect the Foucault boom on the American academic Left to continue. Its object is not the disinterested study of past ideas but the "unmasking" of contemporary American society as illegitimate. The fact that Foucault's analysis applies equally well to that leftist ideology itself will not be recognized, partly because Foucault's own anarchism was, finally, inadequate as an instrument of political analysis of the challenges of our time.

(*April* 1986)

Edgar Wind as man and thinker

by Creighton Gilbert

Edgar Wind (1900-1971) became a celebrity of sorts at the age of sixty, with a series of BBC talks called "Art and Anarchy." The book that followed was eventually translated into six languages, and individual talks even appeared in *L'Oeil* and *The Saturday Evening Post.* Wind never enjoyed the kind of fame that Kenneth Clark or Jacob Bronowski achieved with their later series; Wind's talks were on the radio, not television, and they could not convey that pleasant extension-course feeling of being helped to a big piece of culture. But they had more bite. Although too intricate to follow with ease, they did seem to present an Oxford don with a middle European accent, yet with a graceful English style, endorsing the view that modern art was decadent.

In Wind's own world of art-historical scholarship he had of course long been a presence. Rudolf Wittkower, his closest colleague in the Thirties, once said that Wind was "the one true genius of his acquaintance." Lectures were Wind's medium. The series of lectures that he gave in the Forties at colleges throughout the United States, about Raphael and Michelangelo, were recently remembered by a listener as "magic." They were never written down. Asking us to consider works of art as precipitates of religious, mythological, and intellectual forces, Wind seemed to make us see what in Renaissance culture had conditioned the art of these masters, what had made their art what it was visually. Wind was following the interdisciplinary approach to scholarship that took seed and flourished at the Warburg Institute.

Today the Warburg method is known by the tag name of iconology and Erwin Panofsky is rightly called its key exponent. But its creator was Aby Warburg, who now seems almost as much a myth as the themes he loved. With money from his family's banking fortune, he devoted himself to building a library in Hamburg, Germany, a library which even in its classification system urged that attention be paid to the interaction of segments of culture over long epochs, with special emphasis on classical antiquity and the Renaissance. By the 1920s, the Warburg Library had become a gathering place for young scholars, like Panofsky, who were affected by Warburg's intellectual outlook. The Library became in effect a research institute. In the Thirties it moved to London, where it remains today.

Over the years the Warburg Institute has generated much fresh thinking on largely overlooked connections. Frances Yates's inquiry into systems for remembering and Michael Baxandall's study of painting through the clichés of gesture and rhetoric are two recent examples. It has sometimes seemed to exist in a state of interdisciplinary balance, but at other times art historians have seemed to run it and to let other subjects simply assist. This is probably the natural result of the fact that all the people associated with the Institute belong to some specialty and of these only art history has been able to bring the others inside one fold. Warburg studies—such as Panofsky's studies of proportion through the ages, or of tombs, or of images of time—are hardly different from social anthropology done through material culture, except that anthropology's otherwise universal "study of man" tends to exclude man in Western history, concentrating instead on either the contemporary or the primitive. The rest has been left to Warburg and to the scholars in his tradition, like Edgar Wind.

The announcement that a book of Wind's selected essays on the Renaissance was to be published made one hope that finally his Michelangelo lectures would appear in print. But instead the volume, entitled *The Eloquence of Symbols,*[1] reprints a dozen mostly very short pieces, mainly written in the 1930s, averaging eight pages of big type. The omission of even the published studies of Michelangelo was a "necessity," the editor explains, because Wind never finished his big book on Michelangelo. The decision seems to carry homage very far, but it certainly follows Wind's wish; in the 1940s he declined to review the major Michelangelo studies by Tolnay, which would have entailed giving signals about his own views. There is to be a second volume of essays by Wind on the eighteenth century. Since his writings in this first volume add up only to some one hundred and ten pages, this too has the air of a bow to genius. But again it follows precedent: Wind's first art-history book, on Bellini, has less than sixty pages of big type, and his *Giorgione* even fewer, which cannot but make any author envious. These books are in effect lectures, just as his two larger books, *Art and Anarchy* and *Pagan Mysteries in the Renaissance* (1958), are sets of lectures.

The longest section of *The Eloquence of Symbols* is a memoir of Wind by a distinguished colleague at Oxford, Hugh Lloyd-Jones. Understandably, it is benign, glancing only occasionally at the difficult Wind whom others remember. It might be defined as the kind of memoir in which the subject's first wife is not mentioned. Among other things, it shows that Wind became identifiable as an art historian surprisingly late. Although he ended up being the first professor of art history at Oxford, where he spent his last sixteen years, much of his teaching until then had been of philosophy. Indeed, the study of philosophy played the major part in the early intellectual development of this young German—not, as the chronology of Lloyd-Jones's memoir suggests, a discipleship with Aby Warburg. In fact, Warburg was not in Hamburg during Wind's student years.

Wind's thesis, completed in 1922, compared the aesthetician's and the art historian's approaches to an object. Lloyd-Jones writes that, according to a letter Wind wrote at the end of his life, the thesis was supervised by Panofsky, but "by a private arrangement," since Panofsky himself had not yet passed the relevant academic hurdle. Ernst Cassirer, the senior professor of philosophy, also "helped supervise." So Wind was, in Lloyd-Jones's words, "Panofsky's first pupil." This interesting image does not fit other accounts, however. According to Herbert von Einem's obituary essay on Panofsky, Panofsky had passed that academic hurdle in 1920. Moreover, Panofsky's own amused account of that time tells of how, because there was no senior person in the new art-history department, he had "the unusual privilege of accepting and examining candidates for the doctorate" while he was still a *Privatdozent,* in 1921. Such supervision being authorized, Wind's description of his arrangement with Panofsky being "private" doesn't seem plausible, and prompts the thought that its not having been on the books was because Panofsky wasn't in charge: Cassirer was.

Cassirer is remembered today only by specialists. As the title of his major work of the Twenties—*The Philosophy of Symbolic Forms*—

1 *The Eloquence of Symbols,* by Edgar Wind; edited by Jaynie Anderson. Oxford University Press, 133 pages, $39.

might suggest, he was a philosopher in whom Aby Warburg could happily find backing for his own concerns with the meanings of images, although the two men meant very different things by symbolism. Conversely, Cassirer resembled Warburg to the extent of exploring the application of his philosophy of symbolic representation on cultural history, especially the Renaissance and following centuries. His work obviously had some influence on Panofsky's classic "Perspective as Symbolic Form," but Panofsky's work is Warburgian while Cassirer's is not. Typically, Panofsky in these early Hamburg years collaborated with Fritz Saxl—Aby Warburg's librarian and successor, and a splendid scholar—in teaching seminars and in the writing of a book on Dürer's engraving, *Melancholy,* that traces the evolution of this psychological concept and its images through the ages.

Presumably because the inflation of the period offered no jobs, Wind left Hamburg in 1924 to live in New York with a cousin. He worked as a substitute high-school teacher for a year, a classic profile of the poor, educated immigrant. During this time he was able to publish, in American philosophy magazines, spin-offs of his thesis and a report on current German philosophy. The report is indeed a "general account" of German philosophy, as Lloyd-Jones's memoir notes, but it also contains, surprisingly, an attack on Cassirer. According to Wind, Cassirer's effort to combine the construction of a system with a view of how thought evolves in history seemed "deliberately to disregard" the inevitable "historical limitations" in his own system. It seems odd that Wind omitted here one of his favorite procedures, the resolving of apparent contradictions with witty paradox. He would later argue, for instance, in *Pagan Mysteries in the Renaissance,* that the same Renaissance symbolic figure signified love and death. (This in turn led to the criticism that Wind's procedure allowed him to identify the meaning of a symbol any way he wished.)

Where the criticism of Cassirer does prefigure the later Wind is in the vividness of its putdown. One sample, which can be analyzed more briefly than most, comes from his contribution to a volume honoring Panofsky, which is reprinted in *The Eloquence of Symbols.* The neo-Platonist philosopher Ficino, Wind writes, was justified in asserting his own conformity with Plato on a particular point; Ficino "did not indulge, as has been claimed, in empty declamation." Wind duly attaches a footnote purporting to document this charge of emptiness, but the quotation only shows a scholar saying that Ficino's assertion was "in alleged reference to Plato." Wind obviously had no wish to misrepresent the other scholar; he included a direct quotation, after all. So when he turned the man's cautious "alleged" into an accusation by the scholar that Ficino was a fraud, he evidently thought the passage had been meant to convey that notion by hinting, and that his readers would agree. Apparently, such slight evidence was, for Wind, sufficient. It should be pointed out that Wind's own argument here, that Ficino conforms to a text in Plato, is shaky, and the tough treatment of another opinion undergirds it. Indeed, exasperated complaints about Wind's method from less scintillating professors appeared in reviews throughout his career, and Wind's mocking replies play an unusually large part in his bibliography.

In 1925 Wind left his substitute teaching in high schools to accept one of two postdoctoral fellowships in philosophy that were available at the University of North Carolina at Chapel Hill. The fellowships existed because a family of rich alumni, who in 1927 also gave the university a football stadium, had fallen under the spell of North Carolina's legendary philosophy teacher, Horace Williams. Williams constantly invoked Hegel and the *Begriff,* but was really a cracker-barrel spellbinder. He appears as Virgil Weldon in Thomas Wolfe's *Of Time and the River.* (Wolfe was in the class of 1920.) Wind also taught philosophy, as one of two instructors. The other instructor was the remarkable Paul Green, class of 1921, whose main energies were already directed toward playwriting. In 1927, at the age of thirty, Green won a Pulitzer Prize for his tragedy of black farm life, *In Abraham's Bosom,* and in 1931 another of his plays, *The House of Connelly,* was the Group Theatre's first production. He and Wolfe were the two star pupils of another Chapel Hill professor, who counseled aspiring writers to tell of their own regions. The other post-doctoral fellow was Katherine Gilbert, my mother, whose book on modern aesthetic theorists appeared in 1927. Green and Wind were the two people she asked to read the book in manuscript. The Wind-Gilbert contact continued for some fifteen years, while Wind was in Hamburg, London, and New York.

The early American years also saw Wind's brief first marriage. But in 1928, Wind was able to return to Hamburg and get on a proper career ladder. While working as an unpaid *Privatdozent* in philosophy at the university, he earned money arranging philosophy books at the Warburg Library and attending to various bibliographic projects. He now got to know Aby Warburg, in his last days, and certainly felt his powerful influence. When a congress on aesthetics held its annual meeting in Hamburg, Wind gave a talk—reprinted in the present volume—explaining how the Library worked. He exalted Aby Warburg by contrasting his method—studying meanings and seeing how "contradictions are reconciled"—with that of art historians like Wölfflin and Riegl, who emphasized style and who "declined to deal with major questions." This view is in sharp contrast to that of Panofsky, who once told a colleague that his own work was in the traditions of both Warburg and Riegl, and a little of Wölfflin too.

But most of Wind's intellectual energy would seem to have gone into his nonpaying post in the philosophy department, which Cassirer still headed. Wind's inaugural lecture on Plato's idea of art was followed by a short book typical of German academic philosophizing, a variation of Kant's explanation of knowledge. At this time Wind also wrote his first art-history article, on Gainsborough and Reynolds, in which he argued that the philosophers of the eighteenth century—Hume, for example—were the key to understanding the work of these painters. The Warburg bulletin published the essay, although it was still far from a typical Warburgian theme. Indeed, the article is closer to the work of Cassirer, who often branched out from his base in philosophy to cultural history, and even wrote on English philosophy.

All of this was cut off by Hitler. The saga of the Library's flight to London is told here by Lloyd-Jones entirely in terms of Wind's efforts, which are certainly worth recalling: the standard account of the move, written by Warburg's nephew, gives all the credit to Saxl and has nothing to say of Wind's role. In London, Wind became deputy director of the Warburg Institute, which was only logical, since Saxl and he were the only men who had come over from Hamburg. Panofsky and others had scattered to different places, while the Institute's new members, like Wittkower and E. H. Gombrich, now arrived from elsewhere.

In 1937, Wittkower and Wind started the Warburg journal, which brilliantly made Warburg's kind of scholarship known to English-speaking students. In the journal, the Library's resources and Wind's brilliance in English fused with dazzling results. Even today, some of Wind's contributions of a page or two—several of which are reprinted in *The Eloquence of Symbols*—remain valid and memorable.

Around this time, the American dancer Agnes De Mille was in London, a little-known avant-garde figure. When she first met Wind, in 1933, she had found him impressive, but they had no further contact for more than a year. Then, after two of her concerts in London, great bouquets came to her with an "ardent and disturbing" card, and Wind's name. He arranged to be free for three days. "A man of position, of stature, of achievement, was courting me," she later wrote in her memoirs, *Speak to Me, Dance with Me.* "I was infatuated." "His kiss held peace and promise." She had to leave on a trip to America; in his letters to her there, "he said he truly loved me," but she was disquieted: "I'd seen him four times." When she returned, Wind met her at the boat and took her in his arms: "it was magic with happiness." "Two days later I received a letter from him stating that he had thought it all over carefully and that he could never see me again. No explanation." When she did see him, he told her of another woman whom he didn't love but to whom he had obligations. Another time he said that he was having a breakdown. There were a few stolen meetings, but then Wind "shut all the doors." De Mille "went down as though poleaxed."

She could not have known of the belief Wind expressed in his inaugural lecture in Hamburg. There he attempts to answer the puzzle of why Plato banished art from the state. Art in Greece was not simply a pleasant background decoration, Wind argued, but something with magic powers that could destroy the logic and morality of society. Modern man, he went on to say, has lost Plato's understanding. Thus, we should renounce art, but not without some experience of it; when young, we should practice especially "poetical expression and dance movements," in order to know what to fear and where to draw the line. Significantly, Wind had been drawn to De Mille because she was a dancer. When she worried whether he really loved her, he answered: "Yes I do. I've seen your work. I know you. You have genius and I love you." So when he cut her off, he was being true to his theory and to his belief that art is not separate from life.

Coming to America to lecture in 1939, Wind was preceded by the excitement his magazine and articles had aroused. He was invited to speak at colleges everywhere and even to give six lectures at the Museum of Modern Art, certainly the only historian of older art to do so. These lectures fall between the essay on Plato and the later BBC series. They deplore art's departure from the central place it once had in human concerns, especially in ritual, and they cite Picasso's *Crucifixion* as an example of the failure of modern efforts to get back to the traditional center. When Wind lectured at the Morgan Library soon after, on Michelangelo, the Surrealist painter Tchelitchew came, brought by Agnes Rindge Claflin, the Vassar professor of modern art history. Clearly, Wind was in fashion. But some people had their doubts. After one of these talks, Meyer Schapiro gave a spontaneous counter-lecture, complete with bibliography, in a nearby coffee shop. Others asked whether what Wind said could be relied upon.

The war naturally kept Wind in America. After just two years as an adjunct professor at New York University's Institute of Fine Arts, he transferred to the University of Chicago. A "permanent appointment" was better, as Lloyd-Jones reasonably says, but this is hardly explanation enough. The NYU Institute at that time was the art historian's Mecca, and if Wind left by preference he was unique. At Chicago, it turned out, he was "not happy," and in two more years he accepted an invitation from the president of Smith College to occupy its best appointment, the one-year Neilson Professorship. When the president of Smith renewed the appointment for three more years, some very distinguished permanent faculty grumbled. Among other things, Wind had light duties and a salary far above their maximum. Eventually, he dropped down to the rank of professor and was given only half a slot in the art department, the other half of his responsibilities being in philosophy.

There were other disappointments. He produced his first art-history book, the little book on Bellini, but it was generally not well received. Wind wrote a rebuttal to his critics in *The Art Bulletin* longer than most of his own pieces, with elegantly sharp rhetoric. He did the same two years later to defend his ideas on Michelangelo and the Sistine Chapel. In 1951, in a form for *Who's Who,* he reported that a book on myth would appear that year, by him and the distinguished scholar Douglas Bush, but it never did. Perhaps most important, his relationship with the Warburg Institute, which had officially continued through these years, now ended, after a "week of talks" with Saxl. Wind's doubts about Saxl's scholarly projects, mentioned by Lloyd-Jones in his memoir essay, are surely an insufficient explanation for Wind's resignation. It is hard to imagine that he did not dream of being a principal member at the Institute. It was thus no doubt a wonderful change, if not a vindication, when Oxford invited Wind to start its art-history department. He ended up producing three books during his sixteen years there, as against only one during the preceding twenty.

Just before Wind died, his thoughts returned to Aby Warburg, in a book review for *The Times Literary Supplement*. The book under review was a biography of Warburg by E. H. Gombrich, the director of the Warburg Institute and the man who had to an extent succeeded Panofsky as the quintessential Warburgian. Wind's piece is filled with strictures about the "depressing tone" of Gombrich's book, with its "pullulating swarm" of notes, all of which falsify the image of Warburg and present him as a "tormented mollusc." The piece was greeted with astonishment, and, for once, did not persuade; Gombrich's book was in fact praised on virtually all sides. Wind's criticisms did not seem substantive, and the different image of Warburg he offered did not seem right. Warburg's lectures used to go on for hours, but Wind calls his style "compact," "economical," "aphoristic," "astringent." This sounds much more like an ideal picture of Wind's own style and reinforces one's feeling that the review is really a final cry to be recognized as Warburg's rightful heir, rather than the intruder Gombrich.

Wind never got that recognition. He is known for his combination of abstruse erudition and scintillating talk, but the big Michelangelo book he was already preparing thirty years before his death was never done. It does not seem likely that Wind feared his critics, or let the hope of finding one more source impede his writing—the usual reasons for a scholar's sterility. Possibly a long, sustained work was not in him. What makes Wind extraordinary is that he so richly articulated the achievement he desired, making its manqué status uniquely glaring. It was a classic, even a heroic, tragedy—scholar division.

(*October* 1984)

Balthus: the curious case of the Count de Rola

by James Lord

When the English art critic John Russell was preparing an important retrospective exhibition of works by Balthus for the Tate Gallery, London, in 1968, he was instructed by the artist to state in the catalogue, "Balthus is a painter of whom *nothing is known.*" This extreme craving for privacy seems peculiar, especially on the part of an artist, an individual, after all, whose overriding purpose in life is to secure public appreciation of endeavors which inevitably reflect the innermost aspects of his being. It is an odd fact, though, that many artists have been secretive. Perhaps they have feared that the overt quest for admiration was already revealing too much, betraying secrets which had best be kept from the world, and even from themselves. The very willingness to exhibit creations produced in circumstances which are the ne plus ultra of privacy presupposes a certain tendency toward exhibitionism, an inclination akin to that which impels children to seek adult approval of make-believe playthings and imaginary dwelling places. Children, too, are secretive, of course, but they seldom advertise it and tend to avoid situations whereby their fantasies run the risk of grown-up consequences. An artist who seeks to make a mystery of himself seems to be playing at blind man's buff with the far greater mystery which it is his professional purpose to unmask. Creation goes hand in hand with revelation, and the fullest measure of the former comes from a candid profusion of the latter, while common sense advises that the creator's personal life is paltry stuff compared with the great existence expected of his work. Having created it, moreover, the very best he can do by it is to die.

Michel Balthazar Klossowski was born in Paris on the twenty-ninth of February, 1908. That accident in the date of birth—assuming that any occurrence in the enactment of a calling can be accidental—has allowed the artist to regard his maturity somewhat as a prolonged childhood and adolescence, because the number of his actual birthdays has till now been only eighteen. All during his early manhood he delighted in calling attention to this natal singularity, suggesting that it did, indeed, guarantee enduring access to the pristine enchantments of youth. More recently, though, he has grown chary of such intimations, the fewness of birthdays having not diminished the accumulation of years, and he has resented revelation of the date, however singular. If, as Baudelaire remarked, "Genius is childhood recaptured at will," the conquest becomes increasingly tricky as the decades grind on, because great purity of spirit and tenderness of heart are needed by an old man looking for triumph through the visual innocence of a child.

The little boy, nicknamed Baltus by his parents, was their second and last offspring, an older brother named Pierre having been born in 1905. The father, Erich, came of a Polish family of minor but "immemorial" nobility, and his forebears had fled abroad in the mid-nineteenth century to escape the partitions of their homeland by its neighbors. He was a highly cultivated man, wrote a monograph on Daumier, and had aspirations, though little talent, as a painter. The mother, née Elisabeth Spiro, was also Polish, though not by birth an aristocrat, being Jewish, daughter of a cantor from Wroclaw. She, too, painted, and with considerably greater talent than her husband, signing her works Baladine. The Klossowskis were at home in intellectual, artistic circles. Among their friends were Bonnard, Vuillard, Valéry, and Rilke. An involuntary tribute to Baladine's creative competence was paid one day by Bonnard when he came to visit, saw a recent picture by her hanging on the wall, and said, "Hmm, when did I paint that?"

The family moved to Switzerland, first to Bern, then to Geneva, while the boys were still young, and it was there that Baltus grew up. Precocious, imaginative, given to reverie, he was coddled and made much of by his parents and their distinguished friends. In later life he used to say, "When I was young, I always felt like a little prince." So the disposition to conceive an aristocratic image of himself seems to have been ingrained almost from the beginning. It became more and more pronounced and productive as time passed. Rilke was one of those most impressed by the boy's precocity. "One can't imagine where he gets all his assured knowledge of Chinese Imperial and artistic dynasties," he said, and volunteered to write the preface for a little booklet of reproductions of drawings of cats executed by the thirteen-year-old artist: *Mitsou,* 40 drawings by Baltusz 3, preface by R.M. Rilke (Rotapfel Verlag, Zurich, 1921). The "z" appears to have been put on solely for the sake of this publication, as it did not stick, and it does add a livelier zing to the nickname, along with the suggestion that subtle adjustments of identity might be all to the good in the interests of art. The budding artist later painted a self-portrait inscribed "A Portrait of H. M. The King of the Cats Painted by Himself." Royal reverie was mingled with symbolic premeditation, for cats appear repeatedly in the works of the grown man, adding the suggestiveness of their own sphinx-like secrecy to scenes already enigmatic and sometimes menacing.

Well before their twentieth birthdays both Klossowski boys were back in Paris, Pierre determined to make a career in literature, arriving with an introduction to André Gide from Rilke, and Baltus resolved to follow in his parents' footsteps as a painter. He needed no introduction to the reigning artists of the older generation, having acquired entrée to the most exalted milieu by right of birth. Of the illustrious elders who counted for much in the outlook and career of the young newcomer the most important by far was André Derain. Although he had been an authentic member of the avant-garde in the first years of the century, one of the wildest of the Fauves, Derain's ferocity had faded fast: while his confreres increasingly abandoned all notion of a viable rapport with traditional aesthetic values in their stampede toward uncharted territory, he beat a strategic retreat to the rear area of proven precepts and consecrated virtues. It took some courage, plus a good deal of egotism, for Derain to do that, because it was so defiant of the contemporary trend, and left him with little to show for his strategy save a display of tactical skill, which went without saying anyway. But Derain was phenomenally persuasive about stating his case. A brilliant conversationalist and ingenious dialectician, he had the personal authority to make his professional stand seem unassailable. He presumed to be the sole champion in his generation of the continuing relevance and vitality of the grand tradition represented at its best by Titian, Rubens, and Renoir. From 1920 onward he produced myriad works in a manner clearly derived from this commitment to the conservative principle. His industry, however, brought forth not masterpieces but chic portraits, wooden nudes, slick landscapes, and static still lifes. The amazing thing is that for a long time nobody questioned either the validity of his claim or the value of the works. Even so fanatic a disparager of all things bourgeois as André Breton, the panjandrum of Surrealist anarchy, who categorically shat upon the art of the past, was very slow to see the fatal error of Derain's strategy: what he stood for was not the sustaining grandeur of tradition but the profitless triviality of convention. This, to be sure, was by no means obvious half a century ago, especially in the commanding presence of the artist. It is perfectly understandable that Derain might have seemed, to a newcomer in his early twenties, an admirable contemporary likeness of the great masters of the past. That is how Baltus appears to have seen him, and a profound impression was plainly made.

The youthful painter seems to have decided from the beginning to retain as the adult appellation of his artistic career the nickname he had been given as a child, signing his early works "Baltus." The "h" was added a few years later, and it is, of course, a great addition, evoking more explicitly the homage of the wise man to a miraculous child. By signing his childhood name to grown-up works of art Balthus was making a point which presumably could not be made in any other way, a point somewhat similar to the one made by the fewness of birthdays, but more insistent and telling, because an artist's signature represents a commitment no man can take lightly, binding him beyond the extent of his own lifetime to the prospective perpetuation of his good name. The means by which Balthus set out to affirm the integrity of that bond had much to do with nomenclature, and in due time he once more made the point by insisting on his entitlement to a name not his own but which again suggests a childlike fixation on the make-believe. As to the aesthetic course and creative aims he was destined to pursue, the untried artist seems never to have entertained an instant's doubt. His work was to be resolutely, and one might well say defiantly, figurative from start to finish. Though he sometimes questioned his power to attain fulfillment according to the exalted standards he had set for himself, he disdainfully dismissed the relevance of any others. His were those which had stood the test of time and guaranteed the eminence of masterpieces of the past. He revered Piero della Francesca, Velásquez, Seurat, and above all Gustave Courbet. He traveled to Italy especially to copy works by Piero on the spot, and while in Paris he so devoted himself to study of the masters he admired that their vision became almost second nature to him. Such infatuation with the past is all very well so long as it inspires a creative passion capable of self-transfiguration in the future.

Lacking in technical virtuosity, yet Balthus's youthful paintings show an instinctive grasp of spatial and structural relationships, and reveal the artist's haughty inclination to make his work reflect the world within him more vividly than the world around him. It is, in fact, almost uncanny to see how early, how positively, and how permanently Balthus's creative demiurge took control of his talents and turned them to compelling account. He obviously worked as hard at his craft as he looked at the prototypes meant to consecrate it. The lesson of the masters was learned the hard way, self-taught, by the sternest discipline and command of self, though the imperious pupil made lavish provision for the dictates of self-expression. Balthus never crossed the threshold of an École des Beaux-Arts. If he were to become a master, it would be entirely by his own doing and on his own terms. Aged nineteen, he was a beginner, and less than ten years later he had already painted a number of the pictures upon which his future reputation will stand or fall. He had developed a highly personal style and adapted it to the exploration of subject matter even more personal. Neither subject matter nor style were to evolve very much during the half century to come, as if to demonstrate yet again that Balthus had found both himself and his art once and for all in the experience and vision of youth. It is a peculiarly intimate vision but at the same time strangely aloof in its attitude toward the experience. Pubescent young girls became the painter's preferred subjects, portrayed with obsessive diligence and frequency, often nude, daydreaming or asleep, with cats alongside them, and sometimes in situations of overt eroticism from which an element of the sadistic is not absent. Their poses, their very expressions, frequently refer back directly to identifiable works by the masters he most admired. The dream of youth is a haunting nostalgia for the noble certainties of long ago. An aristocratic reverie pervades Balthus's paintings. However effete, however irrelevant may have seemed the criteria of the past to his contemporaries, to Balthus they remained incorruptible and sublime, it seems, precisely insofar as he could prove himself worthy of them and live up to the proud vindication of their legacy. That, as it turned out, would take some doing. Noblesse oblige.

What saved Balthus from becoming a mere pasticheur of the past, however great his talents and high his standards, was the very down-to-earth integrity of his obsession with his subject matter. It took precedence over the display of painterly skills for their own sake. It presided over the creation of the never-never land in which girls, boys, and cats, even landscapes, vases of flowers, and bowls of fruit hover outside time, outside everyday reality, bathed in an aura of ambiguous tranquillity, motionless, speechless, and yet aquiver with the vital certainty that they will dwell forever in a realm secure from the rude intrusion of common mortals. The very otherworldliness of Balthus's world, and the arrogance, the downright hauteur, with which he pictured its configurations and inhabitants were what saved him from seeming passé and drew the attention of his contemporaries. He deigned to accept it, as it was merely the most prestigious then obtainable, bringing the offer of a one-man exhibition from Pierre Loeb, the favored dealer of the young avant-garde, a man who had already made a market, and a packet, off his carefully nurtured reputation for aesthetic clairvoyance. The first one-man exhibition of paintings by Balthus took place at the Galérie Pierre in the spring of 1934, when the artist was just twenty-six years old. Though sales were not many in that period of financial crisis, people of discernment were impressed. They wondered what sort of man had created these works so hauntingly evocative of the past and yet so powerfully present in their overt depiction of fantasy and malaise.

Balthus was a loner. A self-made artist, he felt free to devise whatever inventions seemed essential to the making of his name and to invest them with the passions most profoundly relevant to himself. That was his contemporary side, promptly and appreciatively noticed by the Surrealists, committed as they were to unbridled indulgence of the unconscious. They would have been glad to welcome Balthus to their group, and it went without saying that they believed no young artist could aspire to greater distinction. Balthus didn't think so. He was disposed to accept their homage but clearly could not be bothered to participate in any of their "nonsense," and would never have submitted to the aesthetic dictates of another man, be he even so commanding a personality as André Breton. Besides, the Surrealists were very mixed up in politics, they talked revolution, preached Marx, and were on speaking terms with the Communists. That, to be sure, was the *dernier cri* for young intellectuals in the mid-Thirties. From the imperturbable vantage point of his devotion to the ideals of other times, however, Balthus viewed all this brouhaha with unmistakable distaste. As for the moral challenge inherent in the social issues of his day, he seems to have deemed it simply too vulgar for notice. His idol, Courbet, had mistakenly identified aesthetic revolution with political revolution, had left his studio and taken to the streets, whereupon he paid for his errors by a stint in prison and death in exile. No such misjudgment ever suggested itself to Balthus. He had a lordly, romantic view of his calling, and thought of the artist as an heroic, mythic figure, one still prepared to dedicate himself to a noble ideal in an age which made a mockery of chivalry, a man with the spiritual fortitude to pursue a lonely, lofty path rather than mingle in the lamentable plodding of the masses. His view was, in a word, Byronic. He had read *Don Juan* in its entirety in the original when only twenty and had been profoundly influenced by the lyrical, cynical masterpiece of an aristocrat too proud to bow before public opinions he despised. The Byronic view, moreover, was nicely self-sustaining, as luck would have it, since Balthus maintained that by some far-fetched familial coincidence he was related to the English lord. Affinity of spirit, in any case, was quite authentic enough to transcend the prosaic happenstance of genealogy. Unfortunately, however, the Parisian painter had no title, no fortune, and no fame. By dint of indefatigable diligence he would eventually contrive to gain all three.

The artist-hero in the image of Lord Byron was not the only source of inspiration vital to Balthus in the genesis of his persona. There was another, also literary and also English: the masterpiece of somber beauty and passionate imagination by Emily Brontë, *Wuthering Heights.* Heathcliff, its protagonist, is a romantic, almost demonic character, proud and moody. A waif, he is encouraged to frame high notions of his birth in order to compensate for its obscurity. For a time he attains the height of joy by sharing with the adolescent daughter of the man who has saved him from the gutter a wild fantasy of everlasting bliss, only to have it shattered when he overhears her saying that she would feel it degrading to be wed to one so lowly, whereupon he flees the scene, eliminating himself from the eventuality of further humiliation. Balthus was fascinated by *Wuthering Heights.* The obsessive, overwrought, almost perverse relationship between Heathcliff and Cathy struck a chord of primal feeling that reverberates throughout the artist's life and work. Once again the commanding vision of creativity comes from the past. Balthus clearly identified himself with Heathcliff, for in 1933 he made an extraordinary series of pen-and-ink drawings illustrating various scenes from the novel and gave his own features to the brooding hero. The identification, moreover, goes beyond these particular works, extending into the future as a source of emotional and thematic revelation, Balthus and Brontë bound forever, as it were, in the idealistic dream of two young people romantically out of touch with reality. The *Wuthering Heights* drawings set the style, and established the very schema and poses, for painting that would not be executed until many years later. It has been noted that only the first third or half of the novel, concluding with Heathcliff's frustrated love and disappearance, engaged the artist's attention. The latter portion, when the onetime foundling reappears miraculously transformed into a wealthy gentleman of fashion, if not a genuine aristocrat, obviously did not possess the same passionate potential for identification. Or possessed it, perhaps, too much.

Balthus fortunately had the right physique for the role of the romantic artist-hero. Slender, almost gaunt, with angular features, dark eyes, and intent gaze, he was handsome. Even his good looks, though, were those of another era, and his few self-portrait drawings seem to call for the accessories and attire of a more formal time. They are the best and most accurate images of him that we have, because he has always fought shy of the camera, as of so many things contemporary, distrusting its mechanical "eye." The handsome, sensitive, moody young artist aroused passions. He was greatly appealing to women, but the passions he aroused seem to have been wanting in some essential ingredient needed for mutual satisfaction. Maybe the prospects appeared a bit too easy, and that viewpoint, too, might have stemmed from a nostalgia for the traditional notion of love as an impossible longing for an unattainable ideal. However it may have been, until the age of twenty-five no decisive emotional attachment had come between the artist and his valiant devotion to his craft.

Aristocratic by character as well as by the concept of his vocation, Balthus felt drawn to seek the company of those who were aristocratic by birth. His own, of course, might have seemed so, from the father's side, at least, but the paternal antecedents were remote and obscure, lacking in self-evident grandeur, while the maternal origins were definitely not made to gratify a class-conscious temperament. Despite her charm, her intellect, her talent, and perhaps in part because of all that his own endowments owed to her, Balthus felt ashamed of his mother. To be sure, it was not easy for the grandson of a cantor from Wroclaw to assume that he was the social equal of a direct descendant of a noble house dating back in an unbroken line of high rank to the Middle Ages. But he did, and if that was naïve, even silly, it also took a kind of grand, reckless purity of spirit to fancy that he would be, or need be, up to the game. And a game, indeed, is what it surely was, a further incursion into the sphere of the make-believe.

The artist regularly returned to Switzerland, revisiting the scenes of his childhood, as to a source of essential refreshment and renewal, and there in Bern in 1933 he made the acquaintance of a young woman of twenty-one named Antoinette de Watteville. Now, of the few ancient, aristocratic families which for six or seven centuries had lorded it over the canton of Bern, none was more grand or more proud of its past than the Wattevilles. Their ancestral mansion, built in a style splendidly reminiscent of Versailles, was, and remains, one of the finest buildings in the city, a symbol of power, prestige, and privilege. Antoinette was blonde, beautiful, wide-eyed, voluptuous, serene in the self-assurance of her physical and social distinction. Balthus fell madly in love with her. The Wattevilles received the intense, romantic—and penniless—young painter with painstaking politesse. He pressed his suit as best he could, pretending all the while to be entirely familiar with the way of life of people like the Wattevilles, a person to whom every little reflex of aristocratic savoir vivre was second nature. It didn't work. Even he was unconvinced, and he was the one who most seriously needed convincing. In the *Wuthering Heights* drawings, where he is represented as the morose but idealistic Heathcliff, the features of Cathy are unmistakably those of Antoinette. The Wattevilles may have been polite, but they were condescending. They smirked behind the artist's back, and he was far too sensitive and vulnerable not to sense it. The experience was desperately humiliating for a youth whose instincts and intelligence told him that the nobility of his calling far outclassed the lineage of these people who looked askance because he couldn't ride horseback like a gentleman. But his passion for Antoinette drove him to struggle against all odds to overmaster a situation in which the very odds against him were of his own making. That, perhaps, is the inevitable course for an artist. Antoinette, however, didn't care two straws whether her suitor was an artist or not. She found him unacceptable and after a while sent him packing.

This rejection had a shattering effect. It came, ironically enough, in the same year as the artist's first one-man exhibition, but there seems to have been no consolation in the prospect that his name might presently bring honor in the province of art. Fleeing from Bern in a rage of romantic agony, Balthus went back to his poor studio in Paris and there undertook to assert the supreme sovereignty of the creative personality by doing away with himself. It was only a gesture, necessary no doubt but essentially artistic, as a response to the shattering effect. The would-be suicide was discovered in plenty of time by his friend Antonin Artaud, the semi-demented, near-genius actor and writer, and the doctor said that the dose of poison swallowed had not been nearly lethal.

To an artist prepared to fly straight in the face of contemporary taste, ready to flaunt his disregard for the aesthetic temper of his times, a sentimental and social setback, however shattering at the moment, is unlikely to seem insurmountable. In fact, it may provide grist for his creative mill, and that seems to have been just what happened with Balthus. Antoinette did not disappear either from his life or from his work. In 1935 she came to Paris, where he was better able to press his suit personally and artistically. Meanwhile, in both realms he was making significant strides. He executed striking portraits of his friend Derain and his colleague Miró, and in 1936 an important breakthrough came when he was commissioned to paint the Viscountess de Noailles, an imposing patroness of the arts and herself a person of exceptional endowments. The portrait, too, is imposing. Though unmistakably a work of its era, it also has the timeless quality so characteristic of Balthus, and there are the familiar reminiscences of past masters—not so much Courbet this time as Velásquez—which make no secret of the artist's ambition to paint masterpieces. The viscountess was delighted, especially since the painter had made her look a bit like one of his little girls, and she introduced Balthus to her fashionable friends. In the next year he painted a picture, entitled *The Children,* based directly on a sketch of Heathcliff and Cathy, which was acquired by no less a connoisseur and celebrity than Pablo Picasso, with whom the young painter also became friendly.

His closest friend among other artists was a man seven years older than he who had already achieved some reputation as a Surrealist sculptor. Their friendship, which survived numerous contradictions and quirks for thirty years, had begun in the late winter of '34, just before the Pierre Loeb exhibition, when André Breton and Paul Eluard came to call one day at Balthus's studio, bringing with them Alberto Giacometti. The painter showed a selection of his recent works, all much admired by the visitors with the exception of one small painting which the sculptor criticized insistently, saying that he found the tonal relationships all wrong. The criticism brought a coolness, and when the callers had come out into the street again, Breton said to Giacometti, "Well, you've just made an enemy." The following summer, having traveled to Bern to make the acquaintance of Paul Klee, Giacometti went beforehand to visit the famous bearpits, where the municipal mascots spend hours on their hind legs waiting for visitors to toss them carrots. And who should he find also rapt in contemplation of the bears' ungainly acrobatics but Balthus? It was at the time of his frustrating courtship of Antoinette. So the two artists fell into conversation and though Alberto was in a hurry because of his appointment with Klee, they went to have a drink together on the terrace of the Kursaal. The conversation grew heated, calling for close attention and careful thought, since both men were exceptional conversationalists—the one self-conscious and precise, like his painting, the other visionary and impulsive, like his sculpture—and as it evolved the two found that they were in agreement about almost nothing. With most men that would have seemed good reason for leaving acquaintance slight, but with artists of the caliber of Giacometti and Balthus, who were searching for compatible relations entirely in terms of a personal vision, the challenge of a peer was irresistibly exhilarating. By the time they finished talking that summer day it was 7 P.M., Alberto had forgotten all about his appointment with Klee, and an historic encounter was missed. A dialogue was begun, however, which by its strange, almost perverse polarity gave each artist occasion to take stock of himself from a point of view profoundly concordant, though almost opposite.

Alberto was interested in the art of the past as a means of seeking his way to the future, and this was just the period when he was abandoning Surrealist fantasy in order to devote himself entirely to rigorous representation of what he saw before him. Balthus was interested in the past as a means of reaffirming past values. Alberto was preeminently a man of his own time, responsive to its philosophical, political, and cultural climate, while Balthus had little use for the present. Alberto was the frankest of men and made candor the cornerstone of his ethical concept of human relationships. Balthus loved make-believe and secrecy. Alberto revered his mother. Balthus was ashamed of Baladine. Alberto lived like a pauper because he knew that riches and possessions can rob one of life's greatest luxury: spiritual freedom. Balthus yearned for grandeur, pomp, and things that money can buy. An enumeration of differences could be made much longer. But the two were united in their uncompromising commitment to representational art and to the indispensable continuity of a tradition which many believed extinct. They never saw eye to eye about the best means of continuing it, and if the truth were known, which it is, they didn't much admire each other's work. The more severe was the elder, the less critical the younger. They were bound together by their passionate care, if not for one another, then for what they both represented—perhaps, too, by a community of interest in somewhat perverse erotic adventure—and by an awareness, which must have been almost as clear to them as it is to us, that they were to represent the final flowering of the School of Paris.

In 1937 Balthus completed an enormous painting, eight feet by twelve, in which half a dozen figures are shown in various poses amidst a landscape of jutting and precipitous mountain peaks. The evocation of Courbet is overt, insistent, serving notice once again that for this artist, as for his nineteenth-century forebear, the concern with painting well was incidental to a dogged resolve to paint masterpieces. Indeed, it is difficult to think of any other painter of our era whose guiding preoccupation has so clearly been the periodic production of a work conceived precisely to define itself as a masterpiece, and in this, as in so much else, Balthus proudly stands apart from his time. *The Mountain,* whether masterpiece or not, is a stunning achievement for a man of twenty-nine. The haunting, otherworldly Balthusian world is conjured up in the golden clarity and unearthly stillness of high mountain air, and right in the center of the picture, the largest, brightest figure present, her arms upraised in a gesture both ambiguous and fetching, stands Antoinette de Watteville. However he may have worked his wiles upon her, whether as a suitor or as an artist, charming both the woman and the aristocrat, Balthus and Antoinette were married in 1937. Seen in the perspective of previous humiliation, it must have appeared the definitive realization of the youthful dream. In fact, it was only the beginning.

The couple had two sons. The father kept on painting, while his work found an appreciative, and prodigiously long-suffering, dealer in New York in the person of Pierre Matisse, who held an exhibition in 1938. Little sold. War came, but Balthus was demobilized before the fighting became serious. He took refuge first in a small village in Savoy called Champrovent, then in Switzerland at Fribourg, and in both places peacefully went on painting pictures into which not the slightest hint of contemporary turmoil or anguish was permitted to intrude. When the hostilities were finished, and life in France had been revived in a style tolerably approximate to normalcy, Balthus returned to Paris. The postwar trend in taste was less than ever favorable to figurative art, but nothing so deplorably transitory could have altered the way in which Balthus saw things, and he went right on painting as before. A change, however, had come over him. It began to manifest itself in a rather peculiar way. Balthus, of course, was anything but commonplace, and prepared to go to considerable lengths to prove it.

Marriage to an accredited noblewoman had not, it seems, turned out to be as thrillingly aristocratic as the imaginative young artist had expected. The grand luster, to be sure, of Antoinette's maiden name had been sacrificed at the altar, and the husband on his own account had little to offer by way of prestigious compensation. This was galling. There was his art, yes, but that didn't seem to promise anything very opulent or even impressive for the time being. Resources were low because Pierre Loeb conformed to the contemporary taste, leaving Balthus dealerless in Paris, while Pierre Matisse, though prepared to buy pictures that did not sell, paid accordingly. Then there was another problem, which might have been foreseen, considering prospects from the outset, by anyone but those concerned. Nobody was growing any younger. Madame Klossowski was a married woman well past thirty, the mother of two not-so-little boys. Balthus, though, by the still-beguiling arithmetic of birthdays, was barely more than a child, and he seems to have felt an overpowering need to find a real person with whom he could enter into the kind of fantasy relationship that he entertained with himself by means of his paintings, through their subject matter, their technical and conceptual references to a vanished world, and their haughty disdain for the opinion of anyone but the artist. Just such a person was provided at just the right moment by one of those miracles which the creative temperament ruthlessly conjures up and then proceeds to consider as commonplace as the morning sun. This person was the teenage daughter of a well-known writer, a longtime friend of Balthus's, whose work included much musing on matters of erotic mystique, and of a beautiful actress who had recently taken as her second husband a celebrated psychoanalyst, himself a man of highly esoteric disposition. These adults thought it fine for the artist to take an interest in the young girl, for her to pose for him, and they presumably also felt that whatever else might transpire between them would be all to the benefit of posterity. Besides, Antoinette did not seem to mind, and she presently returned to Switzerland to a life of luxury befitting her station. As for the young girl, the benefit to her of these arrangements got rather lost in the shuffle, though the loss itself will remain resentfully present as long as she does. Of course, it was merely the loss of innocence, which remained but an image in the superb portraits Balthus made of her.

Nor was all this all the change that had come over Balthus as he approached the statistical age of forty. Very tentatively at first, almost jokingly, casually, as if the truth were embarrassingly self-evident anyway, he started putting it about that, being of noble birth, he was privileged to use the title of count. Oh, he just let the revelation slip out. His rightful name, he said, was Count Balthazar Klossowski de Rola. He didn't insist on it in the beginning, he merely seemed to suggest that the aristocratic fact might, after all, be allowed to speak, if not to whisper, for itself. To those who were listening, however, the utterance sounded strident beyond belief, and they happened to include Derain, Giacometti, Picasso, Artaud, Albert Camus, the Viscount and Viscountess de Noailles, Princess Caetani, et al. Some laughed, some sneered, some smiled indulgently, and everyone took it for granted that the artist had no legitimate claim whatsoever to a title. In that, at least, everyone was right. Titles in historic Poland were nonexistent before the partitions save for the handful of princes descended from sovereign houses of the Grand Duchy of Lithuania and counts originally designated by the Holy Roman Emperor in the sixteenth century. After the partitions a few titles were accepted, or bought, from the Austrian emperor or the Russian czar. There was, however, a genuine aristocracy, defined by relationship to senatorial office, and its members had often assumed titles suited to their style of life while traveling abroad in the nineteenth century, a time when titles still designated economic, social and, one might almost say, spiritual realities. But that time and that practice were far in the past in the wake of the Second World War, which only made Balthus's presumption seem more fantastical. As for the name Rola, it was an heraldic appellation applicable to families other than the Klossowskis, like a clan name in Scotland, and it rather insisted on the modesty of provincial origins, as in Polish the word refers to arable land. It conferred no title whatsoever. To this fact members of the artist's own family were embarrassingly ready to testify, and as if that were not enough, documentary evidence was, and remains, readily available.[1] In view of all this one might have thought that Balthus would drop his ongoing dalliance with the make-believe.

He did nothing of the kind. He began ever so slightly to dwell on it. His self-depre-

1 *Herbarz Polski* by Adam Boniecki, Gebethner and Wolff, Warsaw, 1907, Volume 10, page 185; *O Heraldyce I "Heraldycznym" Snobizmie,* by Simon Konarski (a work dealing specifically with pretenders to nonexistent Polish titles); Ksiegarnia Polska, Paris, 1967, page 43.

cating smile and mocking drawl when mentioning it began to harden, so that those who heard him were given fair warning of serious intentions and of potential consequences equally serious. Many were appalled, denouncing the affectation as a lamentable lapse into the crudest kind of snobbery. Derain wanted to break off relations with his disciple, but his mistress tactfully recalled him to reality, which in his case now represented a drastic tarnish of his reputation, and told him that the only artist friends of consequence he had left, he who had known them all, were Giacometti and Balthus, so he relented. Balthus didn't. He kept on allowing it to be understood that he was a count. If people laughed behind his back, he could not be bothered to notice. Besides, he had always been proud. People did laugh, and they said that the painter was an unconscionable snob whose noble pretensions made him look like a fool. Had they looked more closely, they might have seen that neither foolishness nor snobbery could account for an idiosyncrasy so overt on the part of an artist as secretive, subtle, and refined as Balthus.

The issue of the title per se was in a strange way beside the point, though it pointed precisely to what was central, because every artist's responsibility as well as his license is to create a self capable of creating the art necessary for the sustenance of that self. In Balthus's case the aristocratic pose did not signify a vulgarity of spirit. On the contrary. Aristocracy clearly represented for him a distinction of personal bearing that reflected the integrity of his commitment to standards and values which had prevailed when titles still meant something. Moreover, it was a way of emphasizing not only his detachment from the aesthetic fashions of the day but his positive loathing for them. And further, it was a way of asserting that childhood dreams can come true, since the man who painted the portrait of the Viscountess de Noailles knew very well that by doing so he had made a more vital contribution to the spirit and tradition of aristocracy than ever that lady did by bearing her title and name.

But even all this was neither all nor enough. Balthus had already before the war secured as a studio in Paris a couple of splendid rooms in a grand old building that had once been part of the residence of Diane de Poitiers, mistress to Henry II, King of France. He wearied of it. He wearied, in fact, of the bustle of Paris, where it became increasingly difficult after 1950—even in the ancient neighborhoods Balthus favored—to sustain a credible and fruitful identification with the past. He wearied also, it must be said, of the young girl, who showed disconcerting signs of having grown up, and had herself become weary of serving as model for fantasy visions of eternal youth. The artist felt due for a change, while the nobleman hungered for it. What was wanted was a castle, a place both secure and imposing, where Balthus could live in peace with all the dreams and ambitions—both obvious and obscure—befitting his vocation. If, as it has been said, the hallmark of a true aristocrat is to have grand aspirations, Balthus had them to burn, and he made no bones about it. He roundly asserted, "I have a greater need for a château than a laborer for a loaf of bread." It was a *bon mot,* of course, but most people thought it in pretty bad taste. Besides, it was not a joke. And who are common mortals, after all, to evaluate the legitimate needs of the creator? So the Count de Rola traveled around the provinces, searching for a suitable residence. Châteaux in those days were a dime a dozen. There was one called Meyrargues, a superb fortress perched above a valley near Aix-en-Provence, but the price was also high, and a new roof was needed. It later became a hotel. Dora Maar, Picasso's recently repudiated paramour, proposed a handsome alternative in the village where she spent her summers, adding, in the hope of making it more attractive, that the property traditionally brought with it a title. Balthus said, "Oh, titles? I've got a surplus of those." The place was subsequently purchased by another painter, one who also bore a prestigious name: Nicholas de Staël, who never laid claim to any nobility other than that of his métier, which, alas, he did not find sufficiently uplifting to keep him from suicide a few years later.

The search for the château was made difficult by two things: the searcher didn't have a dime to his name, and the genuine artist had requirements just as exacting as the make-believe count. Everything considered, and in fair view of the muchness which everything entailed, the place that Balthus finally found seemed nearly ideal. Art made it so, in any case. As châteaux go, Chassy didn't amount to much. Standing on the down slope of a small hill, overlooking a perfectly ordinary little valley on a back road halfway between Paris and Lyon, it was merely a very large house, with round towers at each corner, in a quite mediocre state of repair. But it was for rent, not sale, and the rate was low. There was no garden, no park, not a single fountain, urn, or stately vista, and the approach was marred by an utterly vulgar farm. At least, however, the peasants consented to address the newcomer to the château as "Monsieur le Comte." The interior was unfurnished and unheated. Breezes whistled under loose-fitting doors. The roof leaked. There was no telephone. The nearest village, a hamlet called Blismes, was several miles distant. To settle for Chassy took exceptional force of character and an inflexible determination to make the workaday routine of life obey dictates of high imaginative purpose. Amenities meant nothing viewed in the perspective of a dedication which dismissed mere happiness as an uncouth irrelevance insofar as it had any bearing at all on the pursuit of man's noblest fulfillment. That pursuit took Balthus to Chassy, and some people said that the itinerary was absurdly circuitous, but nobody could say it failed to take into account the potential grandeur of the destination. What Chassy had to offer was space, both actual and ideal. There were vast, high-ceilinged, well-lighted rooms, in which it was possible to see and to conceive works of art free from the constraint of twentieth-century confusions and preconceptions. Balthus believed that he was richly entitled to such space by virtue of his resolve to make good in his own time standards which nobody else had the stamina or distinction to save from present-day frivolity, mediocrity, and anarchy. On the basis of evidence put forward by this view to secure its own vindication, the judgment of hindsight seems to be very much on the side of the artist.

In the meantime, given an inclination to seek romantic parallels in unexpected settings, the Château de Chassy could easily have been taken for a Gallic version of Wuthering Heights. The first winters there were quite as bleak as any imagined by the melancholy Ellis Bell. (The childlike propensity of the Brontë sisters for make-believe also included a fondness for made-up names.) Someone was needed, though, to play the part of Cathy, not an easy role to fill as Heathcliff grew older and more finicky. Though she proved to be only a stand-in, someone was brought onto the scene by Alberto Giacometti, which was rather peculiar, as he was often heard to grumble, "We're fed up with Balthus and his little girls." This one, to be sure, was a bit old for him, being already in her mid-twenties, and maybe Alberto fancied there would be no drama. She was the daughter of farmers, but unconventional ones, freethinkers, if not Communists, and she wanted to make a mark in life. Having met Alberto in a café, it came out that she wanted to make her mark as a poet, although she unfortunately had to do something about earning a living. Balthus was just then setting himself up at Chassy, where his station and the size of the house called for servants. But he had little money. Alberto suggested that the poetess might do as a housekeeper. Then she could write while Balthus painted. It was an exceptionally bad idea, and everybody concerned thought it grand. For a time, indeed, the handsome, haughty artist and the sensitive idealistic poetess seem to have found life in the gloomy, uncomfortable château perfectly congenial. He painted some splendid pictures, one of them one of his most persuasive assertions in the bid to create a masterpiece, an enormous canvas called *Le Passage du Commerce Saint-André,* a view of a Parisian back alley where neither Courbet nor Baudelaire would have noticed anything incongruous. It is interesting to consider that in order to bring it off the painter was compelled to set up shop at a far remove from the present-day scene. The poetess, who also did a bit of cooking and dusting, wrote a collection of verse, sadly—because so inappropriately—entitled *Unvanquished Poems.* Balthus once asked her what historical person she might have liked to be. "Trotsky," she said. He tartly rejoined, "You might have chosen Lenin. He, at least, succeeded."

The artist himself, however, was for the moment far from successful. Sales were rare, prices low, collectors still the happy few, and the fastidious far between. He subsisted with some difficulty and much resentment on the dole provided by a consortium of half a dozen dealers and connoisseurs, who were willing to take a modest flyer on the chance that a nostalgia for masterpieces might one day produce some. In exchange for a monthly stipend they expected to receive the painter's entire output. But Balthus worked very slowly. It's true that he always seemed to have all the time in the world, and never appeared to doubt for a moment that posterity would make time for him. Meanwhile the château needed to be filled with suitable furniture and appointments, for which works of art had to be offered in exchange, and some members of the consortium were aggrieved to learn that canvases were being traded for curtains and couches. The painter's Parisian dealer, a woman who had once worked as secretary to Pierre Loeb, made representations. Balthus sneered, said that she was a hyena, and showed her the door. All this was most unbecoming. Nor, as time passed, did the poetess help matters by growing quite noticeably old as she approached thirty. Then the artist recalled that the wife of his older brother had a very pretty teenage daughter by a previous marriage named Frédérique, in whom he had already taken a somewhat more than avuncular interest, and it seemed to him that she might do beautifully to preside over the Château de Chassy. And by another of those convenient miracles that ease the creative life, all parties found the plan quite pleasing. Except one. The count was unconcerned for the opinion of his housekeeper. There were scenes. The poetess made an effort to end her suffering by ending her life; it was unsuccessful, for an ambulance was summoned in good time to take her to the hospital in Nevers, and the keen eye of the artist observed with sardonic merriment as the vehicle departed that the name of its proprietor painted on the door was Sépulchre.

The Château de Chassy brought out the best in Balthus, especially after the arrival of his "niece," whose girlish charm and commendable adaptability lent the place an aura of enchantment it would never otherwise have attained. Of course, an artist's vision was required to make all this believable. During his years at Chassy—less than ten, unfortunately—Balthus reached the climax of his career, painted many of his finest works, and executed scores of superb drawings. He made numerous portraits of Frédérique, who considerately remained an adolescent in pigtails till long after her twenty-first birthday. Of the ordinary little valley where the château stood, and of the vulgar farmyard in front of it, he created a remarkable series of radiant images. The Count de Rola had felt that a castle was required to house his self-esteem, and Balthus that it was the least he owed to the invaluable continuity of artistic tradition. Together they did very well at Chassy, and by it. The nobelman, the painter, the artist, and the château, not to mention Frédérique, made a beautifully composed and perfectly congruous *tableau vivant.* To be sure, it was not everybody's cup of tea, but precious few were invited to frame an opinion. It's a pity that things couldn't have gone on forever as they were then, in a state of exquisite equilibrium between artistry and aristocracy.

The public had gradually begun to notice that a painter of extraordinary powers was hidden away in that oddly nondescript neck of the woods. People started buying. The Museum of Modern Art in New York put on a retrospective exhibition in 1956, though Balthus couldn't be bothered to cross the ocean to see it. Creative trends on the other side of the Atlantic were, in any event, so far from congenial as to be virtually repellent, and what interested Balthus most about America was that one of his earliest and most ardent collectors there happened to be an eccentric clergyman from Los Angeles, California, where languorous nymphets may have looked right at home on the walls of the manse. Critics and collectors began arriving at Chassy to pay their respects and, if possible, purchase a picture or two. They were greeted by an Italian majordomo in a white jacket with gold braid who told them that the count was in his studio and could under no circumstances be disturbed. Fine furniture now filled the rooms and oriental carpets lay on the floors. The Baron Alain de Rothschild presented his compliments and said he would be very pleased should the count consent to paint a portrait of his wife, Mary. Balthus agreed. Ingres, after all, had painted the baron's great-grandmother. The portrait, when completed, was appropriately large and impressive, though the baroness looked rather like a gamine—like a Balthus, in short. The Rothschilds were delighted. A sumptuous reception celebrated the installation of the finished work in their mansion, where it was kept company by a couple of Rembrandts and a clutch of other masterpieces. The reception was attended by many of the noblest, most fashionable people in Paris, but few artists were present.

Then Balthus was given a boost by one of his old cronies, André Malraux, a creator also dedicated to concepts of personal glory and exalted spiritual purpose which many deemed passé, and some, in fact, outré. But in his own time he had become an almost legendary figure and was now enjoying a kind of mythic consecration as Minister of State for Culture, the favorite of General Charles de Gaulle, to whom the idea of grandeur was the stuff of life itself. Malraux believed that art exists virtually as an autonomous reality, and is thus more an outgrowth of past art than a response to contemporary stimuli. He and Balthus were made for discriminating mutual esteem. In 1961 Malraux appointed his friend director of the French Academy in Rome, an institution established by Louis XIV in the seventeenth century when the Roman sojourn and initiation had been a prestigious sine qua non for any artist who hoped to make a name for himself. The Prix de Rome was coveted as an evidence of outstanding promise until, at least, the mid-nineteenth century, and happily accepted by great and mediocre alike. Ingres was a promising winner at age twenty-one, later spending many contented and industrious years as director of the Academy. So the post came in the gratifying context of glorious antecedents and precedents. These, it's true, may not have looked like much when considered from the viewpoint of young artists overseas who regarded Picasso as effete and elevated to the rank of contemporary icon the clumsy and garish portrait of Marilyn Monroe. But such a viewpoint was precisely what Balthus considered beneath his notice, and a better refuge for his abhorrence could hardly have been found than the French Academy. Besides, Chassy had begun to seem a bit cramped. The count complained that he had barely space enough in which to contemplate with decent impartiality his achievements. He cannot, however, have failed to observe that his "niece" had definitely reached marriageable age. Removal to Rome must have appeared to offer the best of imaginable worlds, and to the Count de Rola it indubitably did. Balthus, on the other hand, forfeited a significant degree of distinction.

Standing at the brow of the Pincian Hill, the French Academy is housed in the Villa Medici, one of the noblest landmarks of the Eternal City, erected in the sixteenth century with a helping hand, so it's said, from Michelangelo himself. Its public rooms are of awe-inspiring dimension, and the private apartments hardly less palatial. But when the new director arrived in 1961, he found that the villa had fallen on hard times and showed distressingly little evidence of erstwhile splendor, though it was not in the least like Wuthering Heights. The overwhelming relevance of that novel, in any event, was by this time evidently a closed chapter. To restore the Villa Medici to a viable degree of magnificence, and make it into a fitting residence for one who did not balk at the dictates of nobility, became the new director's first priority, one which he pursued in person with exemplary elegance and attention to detail. He even found time to take a passing interest in the young winners of the Prix de Rome, whose aesthetic fortunes were temporarily entrusted to his supervision, though none of them gave signs of great promise and only a couple had the good taste to paint pictures that resembled his. As for his own pictures, very few were produced during these years, because the director was too busy looking after palatial appointments to paint, while the count had a very crowded schedule of official and social engagements. He also had a countess to pay attention to. A year or two after taking up residence at the villa, Balthus traveled to the Far East and in Japan made acquaintance with a young woman named Setsuko. She accompanied him back to Rome, becoming bride and countess all at once.

The craving for grandeur and nostalgia for the standards and style of a bygone age got all the satisfaction at the Villa Medici that anybody could have dreamt of, and more. Princes and princesses, cardinals, ambassadors dined at the count's table, where exquisite foods and wines were served on plates and in goblets emblazoned with golden crowns. If the count had been cautious, almost apologetic, about using his title in Paris, and even during the early years at Chassy, no circumspection prevailed in Rome. Protocol was the inflexible rule. Invitations to official functions at the villa were sent out in the names of the Count and Countess Klossowski de Rola. The French ambassador was made to understand that the director of the French Academy and his wife were unlikely to appear at receptions and dinners in the Palazzo Farnese should they fail to be received, presented, and seated with all the deference due their rank, which made things a bit ticklish for the diplomat, because there were plenty of noblemen in Rome whose ancestors had for a millennium or so been keeping an implacable eye on their places in relation to the salt. Still, the Rolas were much in demand, a great social success in Rome. Balthus was suave, witty, sardonic, an excellent teller of entertaining stories, trenchant in his judgments of art, literature, music, and manners. Setsuko was exquisitely gracious, attired in gorgeous kimonos of silk so heavy and richly embroidered that they looked as though they would stand up by themselves. The guests and friends were not all nobility, diplomats, and churchmen, either. There were also a few artists and writers, congenial spirits, and one of the closest of these, in fact, was a latter-day virtuoso of personal fantasy and erotic make-believe named Federico Fellini.

If anybody wondered what was going on in the artist's secluded studio in the villa's gardens while the count and countess were busy being sociable and aristocratic, the curiosity was neither well-received nor well-rewarded. Visitors were greeted with impeccable politesse, but even the painter's dealer, now compelled to advance enormous sums against the promise of pictures that existed only in the artist's imagination, even Pierre Matisse, frequently found the studio door denied him. It was Balthus, and Balthus only, it seems, who was in the artist's own view entitled to any reward. He had awaited it with unbending determination for forty long years, and he was resolved to have it on his own terms, since it was on those terms entirely that he seems from the beginning to have staked his belief that the reward due to great achievement must be but another aspect of the deference due to great aspiration. And certainly no one could contend that Balthus was undeserving of high esteem. But somehow or other in Rome the fragile equilibrium between aspiration and achievement went awry. Perhaps it was because while there Balthus at last came completely into his own as a self-creation commensurate with his ambition to personify and perpetuate traditions of an erstwhile order. The Count de Rola had become a real person, not a fiction, not a storybook character, and in the process he had somehow lost the old power to create a convincing world for the obsessive inhabitants of his imagination. Compared with the pictures painted at Chassy, the few executed in Rome look stilted and artificial. They are works of exceptional formal skill and refinement, needless to say—Balthus has never known how to be vulgar—but the onetime passions and life-giving fantasies are gone, leaving behind only self-indulgent, decorative reminders of a simpler day, signed with the same name though not by the same man.

Balthus lingered on in Rome. The original term of his appointment expired, but he managed to get it renewed. The villa hadn't yet been restored entirely to his taste. And then there were the gardens, too, which were grandly entitled to attention. Hadn't Velásquez painted there? So the count lingered on. Something about the Eternal City held him. Maybe it was in part the memory of one of his ancestors, Jacob Maximilian Klossowski, sent by King Ladislaus IV in 1643 to administer the Polish Church of Santo Stanislav, a charge he tenaciously held despite havoc at home until his death thirty years later. Rome is the city in the western world richest and most imposing in a continuous accumulation of art and history, of cultural, intellectual, and spiritual associations. The artist and the nobleman felt comfortably at one with it and with each other in it. The time would fatally come, however, when directorship of the Academy must pass into other, less illustrious hands, and against the anomaly of that day Balthus looked around for an alternate residence. He found something north of Rome, not far from Viterbo. Called the Castello di Montecalvello, it was a very large, ancient, and patrician pile, more in need of repairs and appointments than Chassy had ever been. This time, though, there was no want of money. At the very moment when the artist's powers had begun to flag, the prices of his works took a leap and have never since ceased climbing. The old consortium had long since been disbanded, but their flyer had turned out to be really meteoric. When at last a new director was named to the Villa Medici, Balthus blandly informed him that the place couldn't be vacated overnight, owing to urgent creative commitments already undertaken. This urgency lasted a couple of years or so, while the count and countess kept on entertaining and the artist painted a few more pictures and made a lot of drawings that looked like things done long before by Balthus. Even the countess got to work with brushes and paints, and her things, too, looked wonderfully like Balthuses. So the dominion of the make-believe made itself in its own image. And then the couple had a child. A little girl. That, perhaps, was all that was needed to close the magic circle within which Balthus had lived since his own childhood anyway.

The infrequency of birthdays, however conducive to visions of youth, had failed to avert the audit of years, and one day the Count de Rola found that he was well past retirement age. After a decade and a half he was compelled to relinquish the Villa Medici. A sense of deprivation seems to have ensued, and the alternate castle didn't prove satisfying as a substitute for the grandeur of the Eternal City. Moreover, with old age staring him in the face, the artist found that he might yet want to take his chances on the advent of a masterpiece or two by getting down to some hard work. To the surprise of all except those who knew him intimately he went back to Switzerland. It was in Switzerland that he had spent the better part of his childhood, and his first great infatuation with the aristocratic principle had taken place in Switzerland. And there was even a creative association, for his most important artist friend, though unlike him in almost every way, had nonetheless been Swiss, and while director of the Villa Medici he had been able to pay homage to the memory of that friendship by organizing in 1970 a retrospective exhibition of works by Alberto Giacometti. So the final return to Switzerland was in many ways a reaffirmation. Balthus had long ago created an otherworldly world, and now the Count de Rola retreated into it and reigned over it, closing off the frontiers to others and insisting upon prerogatives that nobody had ever wanted to argue about in the first place. He established himself, wife, and daughter in an immense eighteenth-century chalet, reputed to be the largest in Switzerland, at Rossinière in the Canton of Vaud. It was very grand, but the atmosphere was said to be rather cheerless and lonely. Exhibitions of his work were organized, but the artist, as usual, loftily declined to appear, leaving the workaday arrangements of fame and honor to others, brusquely rebuffing the solicitations of journalists and the inquiries of art historians. In 1977, when Pierre Matisse held a large exhibition in New York, the catalogue preface was penned by the count's Roman colleague, Federico Fellini, who concluded his panegyric with the assertion that to understand Balthus is to understand the times we live in; the lesson is made plainer, he says, quoting Michelangelo, "if at the end of the day, we look inside ourselves so that we can finally distinguish the only reality possible from all that seemed real to us—invented reality." Maybe yes, maybe no.

Then the curators of the French National Museums and of the Metropolitan Museum of Art in New York decided jointly to mount a great retrospective exhibition intended to establish and consecrate once and for all Bathus's stature as a modern master descended directly and legitimately from those great predecessors chosen long ago by the aspiring youth as his rightful forebears. Such an exhibition requires painstaking, lengthy preparations, but for once the artist surprisingly and uncharacteristically intervened to urge the greatest practical dispatch, and the schedule was brought forward as much as possible.[2] It will be interesting to see whether on this occasion Balthus may deign to appear in person, allowing for the surmise that aristocrat and artist have always had in common a secret hankering for the inelegant commotion of popular apotheosis. In the meantime, the count remains remote in Switzerland, receiving select visitors with courtly decorum. His status as a living legend has recently received the public sanction of his elder son, Stanislas, who has gone the count several times better by calling himself the Prince de Rola, and who composed the preface for a glossy volume of reproductions. Having nothing original or illuminating to say about his father's work, the arrogant offspring saw fit to introduce his lack of insight by recalling the paternal admonition that "Balthus is a painter of whom *nothing is known.*" If the artist really expects us to accept that description, then he seems to be demanding that we submit, as he has, to the self-deluding supremacy of the make-believe. Illusion is essential to art, of course. The very concept of beauty deals in criteria elusive and changeful. But the heart of the matter, as Keats saw, lies in individual dedication to truth.

An artist who stands haughtily aloof from his own time, basing his whole aesthetic posture upon that stance, is exposing himself to the danger that the future may pass him by. The history of art is pitiless, more pitiless even than the rest of history, because the kind of immortality it offers is the truest kind, and the offer is for all or for nothing. Great creators have usually looked into the future for the prospect of great fulfillment, seldom into the past, for the past proposes mainly the ground of criteria which are, after all, fruitless to cultivate, having been harvested already, and duplication, where possible, is by definition pointless. Looking to the future, though, is a daunting business, which does not sit well with an appetite for emulation, anachronistic honors, and titles. The most, and least, an artist can do for posterity is to acknowledge that his personal demise will differ in no way from that of a billion other men, and prove that he has been able to take great creative account of that grim, miraculous fact. If he can do that, then maybe his creations will

2 "Balthus" will be shown at the Centre National d'Art et Culture Georges Pompidou in Paris from November 4, 1983 to January 23, 1984, and at the Metropolitan Museum of Art from February 29, 1984 to May 13.

live up to the one dream which appears to set man apart from other creatures on earth, and by doing so provide his fellow men with a few noble instants of surcease from the contemplation of their own nonentity. This, perhaps, is too somber and idealistic a view of the artist's option, in which case it would leave ample room for the possibility that the future may do well by a bid for its attention put forward by one who shows little confidence in its discrimination. Admirers of Balthus will hope so, and it is true that their hopes are not based on bluff. The nobleman may have been bogus, though indispensable, but the artist was real. His reality was even greater than his identity, and he was bound to an involvement with it so passionate that the outcome went beyond the personal. Greatness always starts that way. How far it can go, time, and death, will tell.

(*December* 1983)

Enclosures: Barbara Pym
by Hortense Calisher

Everybody knows how cozy certain English novels can be. Like those foggy walks on the Downs which envelop the human figure in mildly mythic illumination and a gently courted sense of disaster, they almost always bring one home safe for tea. Often they belong to the genre of the series-novel, in which a continuing environs or reappearing characters can bring us that sense of familial enclosure which is one of the great precincts of the novel, and one we all crave. In effect, that is what any novel is, whether sliced near and parochial or projected abysmally far. Those enclosures which become great of themselves are inhabited by creatures who bear terrifying or encouraging resemblances to ourselves, no matter their station in life or ours. After that, these novels take their tone from how daringly their creator will violate the safety of the enclosure to show us the raw facts outside. Trollope's cynicism will do that. Jane Austen stays within—though so trippingly that her novels, if not strictly related as in the true genre, from a distance appear to be. Later, in France, Balzac's gargantuan appetite would attempt to make all human character his enclosure, and still later Proust, burrowing from within, would make his sequence all one book. Indeed, one measure of a novelist seems to be how we do or do not succumb to the ever-present temptation to serialize what we see.

There the English have often been specialists, brought to it by the continuities of class difference and the permanences of provincial life, in which during the later nineteenth century all the literate would seem to have been subscribers to Mudie's Library, lender par excellence to the long stretches of middle-class time. So the sought-for genre scene of life high or low could flourish on. If Mrs. Gaskell's Cheshire proved too modest you could exert your snobberies in Barchester, although, staying with either, you would ultimately find yourself moving on from *Cranford* to *Mary Barton* and working women in an industrial town, or from a cathedral close to the raunchy idlers of *The Way We Live Now* and on to Parliament with Phineas Finn.

Meanwhile, comfortingly localized place and domestic character would persist in the crannies of all the major novelists, either per se or enlarged, and often in strange mixture. Think of those marvelously *echt* curates and textbook-saint village women in Charlotte Brontë's *Shirley,* so curiously static, almost like period pieces, even as the novel is moving on into the world of the Luddite labor riots. It is George Eliot who will most have the courage for the world scene, yet it is her earlier evangelistically moral novels of village life which will provide the grounding for that most modern-sounding of Victorian novels, *Middlemarch.* Dickens will go farthest into the abyss of human misery, but with that strange alternation which will keep the great interlocking scenes of outer London separate from his lesser gallery of comic turns and fixed types, some of which may go back to those early Mystery plays in which accounts of English village life begin. While his women of course remain impossible. They are Mudie readers second-class and beyond, down to those kitchen-maid penny-dreadfuls they would have had to procure at the stationer's. I suspect even Little Dorrit of it. Even Little Nell.

All the while that other stream of the more stringently enclosed novel has persisted in one or another variation, as it always will. There would be Disraeli's friend Ada Leverson's sassy novels of titled manners, sexually explicit in all but language and antecedent of both Mitford and Wodehouse. In the early 1930s Angela Thirkell initiated her series of light novels of country-house life set in a borrowed Barsetshire with *High Rising,* succeeded by such titles as *Pomfret Towers, Before Lunch,* and *Cheerfulness Breaks In.* Intellectuals proclaimed themselves unable to read them, and it was said that her son Colin MacInnes, the distinguished author of *City of Spades* and other novels of West Indians in London, could not bear mention of them. Yet beginning in the 1920s there had been a series much tolerated, even cherished, as more by one of the intellectuals' own. These were the "Lucia" novels of E.F. Benson, son of the Archbishop of Canterbury and biographer of, among others, Edward VII. Recently I reread them. They recount the infuriating progress and satisfying defeats of an impossibly arrogant and enchantingly self-willed country-town social arbiter as surrounded by the not always compliant gossip-on-the-green antics of her coterie, characters farcical enough in themselves. One sinks guiltily in their coy charms, grudging each book's end, grateful for its encore, and meanwhile swaddled away from one's own bothers by this dottily appealing contredanse, for it's a round-the-clock read in which continuity is the real sugarplum. Feydeau bouts of time-off fun for the brainy, cloyingly too delicious by far, they are ridiculous *in toto,* savorable in all their parts, from which one exits at last with a vast "pouf." Only later does one notice how the surface moralities of a decade have been proffered us in ironic bouquet.

It is such books, if not these precisely then the whole secondary stream of them—and not the divine Jane, as is the current analogy—that are the antecedents of Barbara Pym. Perhaps in this lies the reason why, after issuing six of her books during the 1950s, her publisher rejected her next, bringing on a silence lasting until 1977, when with *Quartet in Autumn* her reputation was revived. She died in 1980. I recall encountering her at the Booker Awards dinner in 1977. If she knew she was dying she may have had thoughts on those belated tributes which are so often the lot of the artist crippled or moribund, for that same evening a prize to Paul Scott for his *Raj Quartet* was accepted by his daughter, since he was then on his deathbed. We often do the same, only a little later, for our suicides. Thereafter one must take care to assess the work, not the discovering fans. It is possible to love Jane and still flee the Jane-ites. In the case of Pym I find myself somewhere between.

One must of course never trust English life not still to contain those quiet corners which once symbolized it. The heroine of *Excellent Women* (1952), an ecclesiastical spinster who clocks her life by the Lent Service at St. Ermin's or by a "I was formally introduced to Mrs. Gray at the jumble sale," decides that "love is a terrible thing" and "not quite my cup of tea." Tea is the strongest drink—or metaphor—in all of Pym, and the coda of all crises. We also meet Everard Bone, anthropologist yet passionate convert. They are in a shabby corner of London the wrong side of Victoria, meeting at church, Learned Society do's, antique shops, and front doors, some thirty years ago. Passing there now one might see punks of both sexes packing a car just as possibly for a picnic as for an orgy, though their hair may be waxed in magenta porcupine quills. Yet only last month, in the cathedral town of St. Alban's, my hostess shyly showed me some vignettes of local life she had been writing, and very well too, for the church magazine, these and its other announcements quite appropriate to the Pym paperback I had read en route. Or as the punks might have been, if Pym had got around to them, for it is her disarming habit to modulate to the contemporary surface while she keeps her own vantage.

In *Less than Angels* (1958) we are still in a covey of anthropologists—so often Pym's rather transparent cover for life-study—who here put Floradora on the player-piano and ask each other, "I hope you eat the meat of brownfleshed birds" (duckling in this case, venison having been served the day before). Catherine, the young writer, wears "the fashions of the day" when "women of thirty could dress like girls of twenty, their hair apparently cut with nail-scissors." What one eats, drinks, wears—and what one quotes from a collectively known poetry index—will be important to all these novels, linked as they are by recurring preoccupations as much as by characters, and by the floating minutiae of daily living never treated as trivia, to which these mild psyches are wittily but exhaustively attached. Of Paris cafés, where, it is said, "if you sat long enough everybody you had ever known or loved would pass by," Catherine thinks: "Surely it couldn't be quite *everyone,* that would be far too emotionally exhausting." Pym is fondest of the heroine of limited appreciations, and for our pleasure is not above patronizing them, as with Wilmet, the sub-adulterous young matron in *A Glass of Blessings* (1958): "We were to learn the subjunctive and I found myself wondering whether I could take so kindly to the Portuguese now that I realized how often they used it." There is often some such slippage of irony between the character's own irony and what the author herself cannot contain, and it is then that one wishes for some heavier sword to poke through this fine arras of wit always interposed. Or perhaps it is that, in novels so based on the perfect dig and—one must say it—on ticking people off, the steady small rain of apperception finally palls. Still one is grateful for the glass always offered, of intelligent amusement from an ever-observant mind which only boundaries appear to excite.

The sexual is merely grazed even when it is the subject. Middle-aged women fall in love with homosexuals, or, like Leonora, the narcissist of *The Sweet Dove Died* (1978), with young men like James, who feels after making love with a younger woman that "while he was not particularly anxious to repeat the experience he liked to think that he could if he wanted to." Emma of Pym's last novel, *A Few Green Leaves* (1980)—the name-parallel with Austen's *Emma* going not unmentioned—thinks of a man with whom she had once had a brief love affair: "To say that he had been her lover was altogether too grand, for there had not been that much love about it, no more than proximity and a mild affection." When he comes to sleep occasionally at her cottage, "Sometimes he would have to be content with her company only, her conversation, and whatever else he might be prepared to ask and she to give." So do Pym readers have to be, the author not saying what that "else" is, or indeed what is meant by "company." One can end up feeling that not all the reticence in these books comes from art.

Pym enjoys people who have not quite had passion. As the gentle insights come on, poking fun more wellbred than the wellbred, it's like having a sly friend, gifted at protracted gossip and with a special eye for those whose timid energies have almost been expunged. You may feel superior to her people for the circumscription of their lives, from which so much is absent, in the main children, often marriage, or a love not arrived at from languid motives or over-spiritual ones. Yet, as with any world watched in wax and wane, people take on dignity with their own finiteness.

In Pym's last book, Emma's friend Ianthe, now in love with a "gay" (the word still being made much of), was once the young librarian of *An Unsuitable Attachment,* the book whose rejection had silenced its author. Destiny, or applied psychology, has rounded out Ianthe —always the serial temptation. Looking back, one might see how that book's deceptively limp cat-lovers and people-fanciers might have appeared during the rise of the Beatles, the welfare state, and the Labour

Party, and the concomitant decline of the Kensington drawl on the BBC. An audience was changing. People were wanting to read about new-class energies. Partisanship verging on propaganda was required of a writer's stance on the people written about, and Pym's perfectly adjusted harmonics could leave one in doubt. Did she love her characters too much, or not very? Kinship is not part of her spectrum—except to ordinary events, the squashed ones. The kind of hurt which could emanate from Stevie Smith, in her work as in her presence, that winning empathy of the minor for the minor, evades Pym. She is rather a finely ticking ear, with a taste for those who are squelched.

Further, the female audience for the serious novel was not quite as it had been. George Eliot's audience, and that of even later writers, had not been so sexually divided; non-literary men of that era read novels without qualm. The kitchen-maiders would be ever with us, Tauchnitz to Harlequin. Now there was a new middle group. Pym is very good on the comfort women take in each other, but there was Lessing now. There would also be those novels of popular or sociological family concerns which raised the intelligence ante perhaps, yet gave the feminine reader a workout in her own domestic world which refreshed exactly as exercise does in a salon.

Meanwhile, Drabble would soon be re-identifying the university couple and the in-crowd of liberal opinion. Angus Wilson's homosexuals were coming in from an altogether sharper world. Above all the language had changed, violently. While the language of a class society is always referential, and indeed one of England's prides, the references had changed; once again the vowels had bent. Pym's cadence could sound coy. Most of all, the enclosures of the serial novel itself had shifted. Joyce Cary had his Irish eye on the netherworld of art, C.P. Snow was issuing his scoops on the politics of ambition, and Anthony Powell's *Music of Time* was making its annual serio-comic grumble of disquiet over all the losses. The world of the *conversazione,* which Pym's essentially is, was a beleaguered world, even where it existed. Such a reality was in some disgrace.

Equally one can see why the time for its resurrection has come. As with some of the "period" television shows on both sides of the Atlantic, Pym's gently acerb serial makes it intellectually possible to escape into a postwar period many in England can remember and some over here can be charmed by, while the pleasures of participatory fandom—remember Tolkien?—can be as stylish as transatlantic chess. Yet novels like these have a residue, persuading us that our own lives, where quiet, are not valueless, especially when wit, like lemon to tea, can be added. Even the fan-dom which a run-on novel so often evokes is a kind of piety toward the novel form. Yet when the comparisons run wild, then one does have to remark that the size of the target inevitably defines the stature of the satirist. In Pym's work itself there is no indication that we are to take its devotion to the smallish as aspersion on the real extravagance.

The enclosed novel doesn't have to take place in the drawing room. It can be a "No Exit" of metaphor. Or it can exist, as the Ivy Compton-Burnett novels did, on superficiality, in one of the more elegant drawing rooms of hell. What one asks of the great enclosures (and gets) is an assurance that the sequestration is natural within the life of the times, and within human nature as well. In Austen one receives both. One has no wish to see her travel abroad. The measure of what we get from her is marked by a certain relief that she never did. One is brought into all the parlors of the world. Yet in that modern apostrophe to dailiness, Tanizaki's *The Makioka Sisters,* one is never allowed to forget the implied world outside. Perhaps that points to why, for us now, the enduringly poignant enclosures are those which are broached, as when, in the parlor exchanges of Prince Myshkin, the poorfolk alleyways suddenly intrude. Or when, embosomed in the Cheerybles, we remember the vast, interlocking streets of the miserable child. When tea will not do, when safety is not intended, somehow that is where we best find it.

(*September* 1982)

Paris possessed: Eugène Atget
by Dan Hofstadter

Something remarkable happened to Eugène Atget whenever he came near to the river Marne: he found himself able to draw an almost baptismal joy from the landscape. This, at least, is what you sense in his photographs. There's one in particular I'm thinking of. The air in this picture is holy; the water is holy; the lone angler is a veritable saint of "atmosphere." The myriad reflections of trees and boats stretch away in stillness to a pair of Lombardy poplars mounting sentry against the sky. Everything here is perfect: it's all so neatly locked together that if you rocked a skiff in the foreground the trees in the distance would shudder. One reach of water imprisons in its burnished pavement the essence of the Île-de-France.

The area around Paris is known for its Gothic towers, but Atget seems never to have climbed to the top of any one of them with his camera. The unfolding green design of the market gardens, the racing cloud shadows, the inevitable approaching rainstorm—these things were not for him. He preferred to head down toward the nearest river, to wander—judging by the angle of his views—along the ancient towing paths, which even in his day were probably overgrown with stinging nettles and St. John's wort, and already separated by trees from the water. More often—you can see it from the shots—he is tramping along a dirt road. Rainwater gleams in a rut. He spies a thatched cottage with its windows tucked under its eaves, and he plants his camera right beside it so it will fill his ground glass. Or he stops in a village street and composes his picture with a few yards of cobblestones and eight or ten houses. It is not light and shadow which particularly tell here—sunshine in the Île-de-France is fickle anyway—but the local textures of things, the speckled aggregates and knobby surfaces, the mottled, the grooved, the veined. The relative amounts of these textures are as important as they are in cookery. You take three parts of roughcast masonry, two of paving stones, a sprig of wisteria, and so on and so forth, and *voilà*—terrine of village.

The taste for Atget's photographs, once rare, has by now become nearly universal. One sign of this is the mass diffusion of his pictures. The best collection of these is the luxurious new four-volume set entitled *The Work of Atget,*[1] which was issued by the Museum of Modern Art and the New York Graphic Society to coincide with a major show held earlier this year. It features good to excellent sepia reproductions, together with thoughtfully written essays and notes by Maria Morris Hambourg and John Szarkowski. Though there are plenty of good Atget photos that do not appear in these four books,

---

1 The four volumes of *The Work of Atget,* published between 1981 and 1985 by the Museum of Modern Art and the New York Graphic Society, are: *Old France* (180 pages, $40); *The Art of Old Paris* (192 pages, $40); *The Ancien Régime* (192 pages, $40); and *Modern Times* (192 pages, $45).

they still offer the fullest overview of his images to appear in print thus far.

From about 1891 to his death in 1927, Atget took over seven thousand photographs of the hamlets of the Île-de-France, the architecture, decoration, and street life of Paris, and the suburban parks of Versailles, Saint-Cloud, and Sceaux. These prints went into his commercial image bank, and could be borrowed, for a fee, by illustrators, artists, and researchers. The primary value of *The Work of Atget*, then, is that it enables the viewer to sense the overall structure and purpose of Atget's archive. But it is also a treasure trove of hitherto rarely seen pictures that will enrich and may alter our view of his work. Chief among these are the many photos of rural France that appear in Volume One, for it turns out that the most urban of all photographers adored the country. We learn that he favored the villages south of Paris for his excursions; unlike the northern suburbs, they retained their rusticity well into this century, and were easily reached from the Gare Montparnasse or the railway station at Denfert-Rochereau. Atget lived at 17 bis rue Campagne-Première, an old street in Montparnasse where hundreds of artists and artisans lived. Rimbaud had dwelt there; Modigliani would do so too; the Douanier Rousseau, to whom Atget has often been likened, worked, until his death in 1910, not far away, in the rue Vercingétorix. Montparnasse in those days was a little universe of solfège teachers, sign painters, painter-decorators, scribblers, and other well-trained foot soldiers of the arts. Atget was one of their number, a skilled craftsman who made two-dimensional equivalents of what the *mouleurs d'art,* the manufacturers of plaster casts, had been making for centuries in the shadow of the Faculté de Médecine. Nonetheless, he must have looked, as he ventured forth on one of his outings, clad in his long overcoat and bent under the weight of his rucksack of glass plates, like one of those exotic itinerant types who so often figure in his pictures.

In his first years as a photographer of the countryside Atget tended to concentrate on studies of semi-isolated subjects: a few lilies, an arch of pleached pear trees, a constellation of rambler roses. What he was doing wasn't really landscape photography: there are no broad sweeps here, no receding copses or harmonious stands of trees. Instead he singled out particular plants as if for salvation, for membership in a botanical elect. He seemed to desire fellowship and the personal note. Presented as successive plates in a book, these photos gain thematic weight. You can feel Atget's tread along the country lanes, and you can vaguely sense that his outings are akin to some of the other rhapsodic excursions of the period: some of Ravel's music, perhaps, or parts of Proust's huge novel. Atget's suburban albums—what he called the "Old France" series—held over a thousand prints. As he grew more fascinated by rustic architecture he began to weave in and out of the same half dozen villages, catching the same stone structures under different effects of light, returning to the same blessed spots after a few hours or a few years. There's a whiff of spring about his pictures: orchards in blossom, freshly tilled fields, a profusion of timothy and wild oats and blurry wildflowers. Though one may legitimately talk about Atget's love of nature, there is little nature here in the North American sense of primitive, virginal growth. There is only "culture," which to the French connotes the cultivation of plant strains as well as of minds. The gnarled, wild-looking willows in Atget's photos have in fact been carefully pollarded for the osier-weavers; and I suspect that even the occasional ancient oak or beech has been deliberately spared to hold the soil against the ruin of time, or to serve as a witness-tree. It has often been said, correctly I think, that Atget's lifework is itself a species of testimonial. He documents a symbiosis, a rare wisdom in the matter of what goes with what. *A boire sur fruits de mer . . . sur pâtés . . . sur viandes blanches,* counsel the wine columns in the French newspapers about this or that vintage. Atget too is gesturing toward exemplary affinities: "This sundial in this little court . . ."

Atget's tight shots of village architecture remind me of old "tupenny-ha'penny" cardboard stage settings for finger puppets. The world is seen as in a shoe box. There's a foreground and a middleground but no distance. Short streets curve rapidly out of sight; prospects are screened by masonry or a dense trained vine. It's not that you feel lonely here—a white-haired *p'tit pépère* with a cockerel under his arm could come round the bend at any moment—but there's a sense that the rectangle of vision is a sealed chamber somewhat analogous to the camera itself. Rarely is a glimpse of the surrounding landscape afforded, and even the sky is largely blocked, which is a boon, because Atget's old-fashioned negatives had no receptivity, it seems, to the tonal nuances of clouds. His camera also lacked any provision for "movements," which meant that he couldn't align rectangular structures with the edges of his viewing screen. Things cant and sway, like jolly elderly uncles. Studying these country images, you sense after a while that Atget simply treated himself to whatever might claim—by extending the circumference of his affection—to be an authentic part of his life. "Intimizing" the outdoors, he often showed a charming insouciance, as when he brought back, from a visit to a château, a negative of the poultry yard. Such wafer-thin pictorial slices he called "picturesque corners," using the word "corner" not only in its metaphorical connotation of "neighborhood" but also, as one gradually discovers, in its strictly physical sense as well. For most of his corners fall into two quite concrete types. One is the corner as wedge, the projecting house- or streetcorner. The other is its complement, the inside angle that is formed where one wall of a courtyard meets another. Courtyards are really a species of outdoor room, and though Atget made quite a few negatives of courtyards outside Paris, it was in the city itself, rich in such shadowy cavities, that he would one day turn this sort of picture into a veritable genre.

Nowadays we tend to be bothered by the idea of an artist letting his work be influenced by non-artistic considerations. Yet Atget was such an artist: his photographs have preservationist undertones, the subjects almost pleading to be left as they are. His selection of sites also reveals pronounced architectural preferences. He didn't photograph the Eiffel Tower or any of the great steel-and-glass railway stations. He got up early to avoid having motorcars in his pictures. He was uninterested in the Madeleine and the Bourse and the newly opened Ritz, though I doubt that he failed to notice that all three of them—the seats respectively of religion and capital and ostentation—had somewhat similar temple façades. By sticking largely to quaint stone or brick houses fronting on narrow streets he was, consciously or unconsciously, reflecting the populist bias of the artisan class under the Third Republic.

Though Atget photographed the vanishing order of things, his handling of space and composition sometimes anticipates the modern camera work that followed him. The question of his ambiguous relation to modernism is treated with tact and perspicuity by Maria Morris Hambourg and John Szarkowski in their commentaries to the present volume. Many people perform contortions nowadays trying to prove that what they like is part of the modernist mainstream. It's as if a chef were to slaughter a pig at your table to show that your chop is fresh. Mrs. Hambourg and Mr. Szarkowski are merciful enough to leave the pig behind at the farm; if there are "virtues of omission" they will surely get into heaven for omitting to discuss, except very briefly, the "aesthetics of photography." It has often been observed that many of Atget's photographs are far from technically perfect—"blocked" in the highlights or black in the shadows, often too harshly "contrasty"—and that he accorded all his prints, whether good, bad, or indifferent, a single page in the multivolume portfolio he was creating. Mr. Szarkowski deals subtly and concisely with the problem of whether Atget's vast uneven archive is really a product of art. "We could point out," he writes, that he worked both for others and for himself and that the work he did for himself was better, because it served a more demanding master. Or we could say that it was Atget's goal to explain in visual terms an issue of great richness and complexity—the spirit of his own culture—and that in service to this goal he was willing to accept the results of his best efforts, even when they did not rise above the role of simple records . . . . On practical grounds, the idea of artistic service to an artistically extraneous cause does have much to recommend it, for it invites the artist to confront interesting questions to which there are no known artistic answers . . . . He may make new mistakes, produce original failures, some of which will define new opportunities. It is possible that Atget's habit of revisiting a given motif began with the need to correct such failures.

Mr. Szarkowski also tracks the emergence of an "elegiac tone" in the botanical and architectural pictures. Much of this imagery does indeed acquire a veil of pathos, perhaps summoned up by the depredations of the 1914-1918 war; Atget photographed the Marne, for example, when that river was still a symbol of national resistance. Yet even before the war he had discovered in himself a great sympathy for the lights and shadows of timeworn things. He was after "the texture, not the text" of the past, as Mrs. Hambourg puts it. Gazing at his views of gutted Paris houses, or at his many portraits of cankered and contorted trees, their roots gripping the earth like the claws of some gigantic turkey-cock, you may begin to feel that a certain melancholy is native to this terrain. But Paris is not known as a morose place, and in fact Atget's work embraces many moods and draws upon many compositional expedients, none of which sums him up. The camera is an easy instrument with which to try out new ideas, and Atget had so liberal a view of his craft that he could pursue, at one and the same time, entirely dissimilar projects.

His most surprising affection was surely the one he conceived for three of the great estates outside Paris—Versailles, Saint-Cloud, and Sceaux. In the decade before his death in 1927, he devoted several hundred negatives to these domains, rather in the fashion of a cook who, after a lifetime interpreting bourgeois cooking, tackles *haute cuisine*. Mrs. Hambourg and Mr. Szarkowski devote a whole volume (they call it *The Ancien Régime*) to these photographs, an allotment of space which roughly reflects the great store he set by them. In those days Versailles had a special aura which it has since lost. In 1918 and 1919 it was the venue of a peace conference in which France, after decades of humiliation, reasserted her traditional role as the dominant Continental power. As the result of a gift in 1924 from John D. Rockefeller, Jr., the palace and gardens, forsaken during the Revolution and largely passed over by the regimes of the nineteenth century, were on their way to being restored to something like their original splendor. Here, then, as elsewhere, Atget's enterprise, never an errand into the wilderness, built upon work undertaken by others, and his selection of this subject at this time had mild, and by no means unsympathetic, cultural-nationalist overtones.

The gardens at Versailles were designed in the 1650s by André Le Nôtre, a man trained as a painter. I believe it is correct to say that Le Nôtre's chief aim was to reconcile the effect of absolute order with that of multiplicity or variety, and on this score, at least, any visitor can attest to his success. Viewed from the house, the impression of axial order in the layout of parterres, manicured broderies, and framing shrubberies entirely dominates; yet a walk into the depth of the gardens affords ever-changing novelties of vision. Gesticulating statues, reflected in pools of water, appear to move against a background of moving clouds, and a few clever asymmetries forbid the stroller from ever composing a mental map of his surroundings. Soon he is half-lost in a living metaphor for France herself, a place at once firmly governed and full of spontaneous enchantments. Nonetheless, the common judgment of the park is that the sensation of government is rather *too* firm: many people find it severe, even heartless. One might think that Atget, with his love of the higgledy-piggledy, would have subscribed to this view, and steered clear of Versailles altogether. Instead he tried to make something of it.

In his pictorial stroll through this emblematic acreage Atget soon seems to stray—if I may enlist a horticultural metaphor—into the herbaceous borders. He drifts into the margins of Le Nôtre's architectural manner, his eye burrowing narrowly and obliquely through vast verdant formalities. He is at cross-purposes with the original designs. Now he slices into a story-telling sculpture group, now he digresses along a forest-skirt till it fades out of sight. You feel that he would be altogether more at ease if an English park had billowed into existence here for the Sun King; and happily for him the trees at least have obliged, having grown, during a century of desuetude, into the sort of tall, full-crowned affairs that you find in Hampstead Heath.

What Atget does here is to cut on the bias through another man's dream. This is, all told, a pretty shrewd approach when one cannot, in the nature of things, make one's own dream out of whole cloth. Atget queers Versailles, turning its classical gardens into something exceedingly Romantic. During the eighteenth century, some people (including, I believe, the great comic playwright Marivaux) started complaining that Le Nôtre's ideas had been old-fashioned from the start. They felt that he had merely blown the old Italianate garden scheme out of scale, as if Poussin had never painted; yet, as they saw it, Poussin had achieved the ideal equipoise of dressed stone and well-tended sylvan vegetation in his more Titian-influenced pictures. One suspects that Atget would have agreed; in his photos Le Nôtre's gardens are made to feel like bits out of Poussin, especially when he homes in on dramatic sculptures before a screen of dark foliage. Of course there is nothing false or distasteful in letting the camera isolate one sun-dappled statue out of a narrative group, or in letting it portray a little bosquet as a virtual forest. The problem is that such devices are all too easy, and the results correspondingly conventional. They show what your average English gentlewoman, at any time in the last two hundred years, would have wished Versailles to be, which is to say cozier in parts and wilder in parts, and tending, here and there, to ruin. The motif of great trees mirrored in the water, like that of a single statue imparting (rather empty) drama to an artificial glade, was already hackneyed in Atget's day.

It would be easy to cavil at these pictures, to complain of brutal exposures and a certain lack of tenderness in the rendition of foliage tones. I suspect that Atget's non-panchromatic plates were none too sensitive to the color green, and that some of his starker compositions simply made a virtue of necessity. In the long shots, where objects in perspective required to be played off precisely against one another, he did not, I feel, spin his vision to a fine enough thread. Only a superb dereliction, encountered in another estate, would put him on his mettle. Prowling amid stone fragments and piles of autumn leaves, he wandered across the border of classicism into poetically uncharted latitudes. Nominally he was now in the domain of Sceaux—where Colbert's country house had once stood—but the park had wholly gone to seed by the Twenties. Mr. Szarkowski's intriguing selection of photographs reveals a place of sun-bewitched tree-boles and fungus-spotted statuary, of half-dead branches and riotous columbine. This landscape, festooned as it is with the tokens of its own continuous decay, meets the eye as pure imagination: the imagination of perpetual relinquishment. Here Atget rediscovered the fellowship of perishable things. Here, too, he could fix his gaze, not on the formal, rigid past, or the pitiless present, but on the instant of forfeiture between the two.

Though there is much to enjoy in the record of Atget's suburban outings, it is for his photographs of Paris that he first became known to the world. Parisian archivists who saw his prints were intrigued by his feeling for the urban condition. In 1907 the city public library asked him to make, for twice his usual fee, a topographical survey of several sections of Old Paris; in 1910 he received a commission at a similar rate of pay from the Bibliothèque Nationale to make an extensive series of pictures of Parisian life. Even after he had completed these assignments he continued to take pictures of the city and its people.

The theme of Parisian life has received a whole volume in the new four-volume set. It is called *Modern Times*. Curiously enough, the remoteness of this title from the material in the book affords a measure of how much the Paris that Atget loved was already hostage to "progress." In image after image he concentrates on the most frail or vestigial aspects of street life. Tinkers and buskers, old-fashioned brothels, crumbling bistros, quaint outlying *pavillons*—all combine to proclaim the Paris of the dawning century. Yet they are just the sort of curiosities whose disappearance anyone with an ounce of prescience could have foreseen at the time. Since they are not counterbalanced by many modern things—taxis, trucks, cranes, buses—they have a bittersweet, valedictory air.

I wonder, apropos of these pictures, how much Atget's concerns reflected the culture around him. Until recently, the French haven't been terribly interested in his work; it was, after all, an American photographer, his great friend and helper Berenice Abbott, who saved most of his negatives and prints for posterity. Yet only someone who knows French culture from the inside could explore the connections (if any) between Atget's photographs and, for instance, Arséne Houssaye's journals, or Jules Vallès's *La Rue,* or the novels of Joris-Karl Huysmans, or the poetry of Paul Fort, or Émile Verhaerens's *Les Villes tentaculaires*—all of which reveal a vivid city-sense, a flair for "the spirit of the spot." One writer who obviously did have a big influence on Atget was the man whom the French have taken to calling, on the centennial of his death, "Big Victor"—the same whom generations of wretched readers referred to as "Victor Hugo, alas." Just as whole districts of medieval Paris were being demolished, Hugo raised the old city anew in the never-never land of Romantic myth. In his writings and drawings he constructed a glamorous Gothic townscape as a home for his recurrent protagonist, The People. This Romantic daydream worked so powerfully upon the public conscience that it eventually spawned a preservationist movement which managed, among other things, to prevent the complete destruction of the Quartier de Notre-Dame on the Île de la Cité, one of Hugo's chief settings and later a major Atget motif. The photographer reportedly read every word the poet ever wrote; I cannot imagine that there was no tincture of bitterness in his feelings about urban modernization.

The wrecking ball was not the only threat to the French architectural patrimony. A new enemy, German militarism, appeared in the 1870s. By the end of the Franco-Prussian War one particular deed stood out in the French mind as emblematic of the attitude of Prussian military circles toward material French culture: the shelling of Rheims Cathedral by German troops in 1870. Rheims is far from Paris of course, it is the capital of Champagne, but its cathedral is as symbolically important to the French as Westminster is to the English: it is the church where the French kings were traditionally crowned. This attack awakened a national dread that was as lurid as it eventually proved well-founded: by Armistice Day in 1918 German troops had burned much of Rheims again and had destroyed scores of French monuments, including the Cathedral of St. Étienne in Metz, the Church of St. Wolfram in Abbeville, and most of the Abbey of Saint-Médard in Soissons, along with hundreds of ancient towns and villages. This grievous record is part of the background against which Atget's encyclopedic labor of documentation was carried forward.

The visual evidence suggests that Atget fitted so neatly into his cultural habitat that most of his photos must really be considered collaborations. He was as little the sole author of his architectural pictures as a theater director is the sole originator of a new production. Most of the time he was creating not with raw materials but with the products of conscious design, the finished work of master-masons, shopfitters, sign painters, couturiers. His charming shots of the carousel at the 1926 Fête de Vaugirard, for instance, would not have been possible without the unwitting aid of the creator of the revolving figures, who was none other than Paul Poiret, the great fashion designer.

One particular panoramic view clearly reveals Atget's debt to other artists. Standing on the quai aux Fleurs in the Île de la Cité, he registered with two exposures the entire sweep formed below him by the meeting of the rue des Ursins and the rue des Chantres. Together the two negatives covered a 90° angle of vision, and he pasted the resultant prints side by side in one of the albums he showed to prospective customers. On the right-hand side we look down the rue des Ursins, which meanders picturesquely into the distance; the rows of medieval or medieval-type houses on both sides form a clear and beautifully lighted enfilade. Directly across from us is the Hôtel des Deux Lions with its ground-floor café and its name spelled out along the wall in what I take to be tin or cast-iron letters in a variant of the old-fashioned "Egyptienne" type face. On its left-hand side the inn sports about six signs, including a sans-serif advertisement for hire-barrows which has left trails of rust on the building, a little projecting oval ("vins, hôtel"), an ad for the Pigier correspondence school, and so forth. Way down beyond the blind end of the rue des Chantres, inserted in a narrow slot of sky, the splendid spire of Notre-Dame looms in the early morning mist. The panorama is a representative (almost an exhaustive) picture of the tiny triangular neighborhood once known as the Quartier de l'Ancien Cloître. You might think that it was one of the last purely medieval sights in Paris, and that that was why Atget selected it. Yet a quick consultation of any good Paris guidebook would reveal this conclusion to be inexact. Spared by Baron Haussmann, the quarter had been partially restored by the time Atget arrived on the scene. Even the tower hanging in the distant air was actually a recent addition. It is the spire above the transept of Notre-Dame, erected (according to twelfth-century plans) by the great restorer Eugène Emmanuel Viollet-le-Duc in the mid-nineteenth century. One might even say, by way of self-instructive exaggeration, that much of what Atget was looking at was in the nature of a modern mirage, an inspired piece of Romantic scenography. It had been deliberately refashioned as a focus for educated sightseeing, and its author was, in a more than figurative sense, "Big Victor," for it was the publication of *The Hunchback of Notre Dame* in 1841 which had sparked the restorations on the Île de la Cité. In 1845, Viollet-le-Duc (who at the age of twenty-six had already been appointed to restore Vézelay by Hugo's friend Prosper Merimée, then commissioner of public monuments) commenced work on the cathedral. It was to take him twenty-one years to bring it to its final perfection, and to tart up the interior of the nearby Sainte-Chapelle until it became the psychedelic chocolate box that we see today. I find the question of Atget's debt to Viollet-le-Duc an interesting one; the problem with trying to elucidate it is simply that there were so many Viollet-le-Ducs. The man was, it seems to me, a fine draughtsman yet a poor designer, a brilliant theoretician yet a nearly unreadable writer. His restoration of the cathedral church at Vézelay is surely one of the great architectural masterpieces of the last century, bringing a visionary conception of the Middle Ages to life before our very eyes. But what is one to make of the Château de Pierrefonds, for example, with its mix-and-match "Gothic" interior, full of sculpted salamanders, eagles, storks, and cats? Most educated French people used to hold Viollet-le-Duc in contempt; now they are not so sure. Was he a historicist vandal or a "post-modernist" *avant la lettre* whose flamboyant piles stand directly athwart the architectural mainstream, somewhere between Strawberry

Hill and the Disneyland Castle? One doesn't know quite what one feels, which makes it all the harder to guess how Atget felt. He didn't (to our knowledge) own copies of Viollet-le-Duc's two treatises, but he did photograph a lot of the man's work, along with the collections (now in the Cluny Museum) of his colleague Alexandre du Sommerard. What seems to me incontrovertible is that Atget's taste was in some ways close to Viollet-le-Duc's. There is a populist and romantic-nationalist strain in both men's affection for pre-Renaissance French architecture. Many of Atget's rustic and even urban views could be used to illustrate Viollet-le-Duc's conception of the primeval Gallic house, which is quite like your basic Monopoly hotel, blown up to a modest scale and executed in stone. Both men doted on gabled cottages and Romanesque and Gothic churches. As Viollet-le-Duc had restored the French picturesque, so Atget documented it, though his documentation was by far the purer expression of attachment.

Atget's two-part panorama of the Quartier de l'Ancien Cloître wouldn't be interesting if it only acknowledged his cultural debts. It also acquits them by parlaying them into a unique contribution. The American painter and critic Fairfield Porter used to say that one should look for the abstraction in realist pictures and ask what abstract pictures tell us about the world. Though it doesn't help to regard photographs as one does paintings, this two-print panorama can, I think, be compared to a piece of graphic design, like, say, a magazine spread with type, which is surely an abstract sort of visual presentation. One notes the dextrous placement of scores of tiny squares, the delicate apportionment of sepia tones. The profusion of printed, stamped, and stenciled type brings the whole piece up to a machine-cut pitch of perfection. Gorgeous and various in itself, the type also pins down the image on the page, balances it on its own axes. Atget, like many Frenchmen of his generation, had an excellent eye for letterforms; following him through the streets of Paris sometimes reminds me of what it's like to window-shop there with an observant commercial designer, someone who at every step points out how smartly that show card goes with that blouse, or how daintily that poster makes its pitch for that brand of aperitif. It is all a beguiling demonstration of how the picturesque may be mated with the everyday and even with the vulgar. By marrying photography to printed type Atget not only registers this accommodation but also embodies it; stooping under his focusing cloth on the quai des Fleurs, he too becomes a part of the big picture, a living lesson in what "goes" with what.

It might seem a willful vagary to speak of Atget as an exponent of the picturesque, for he is usually portrayed as a classicizing and a modern photographer. Yet over and over, it is the patently picturesque that he singles out to record—boats along the Seine, queer old tavern-signs, the ghostly residence of André Chénier, the great poet who was guillotined during the Terror. When confronted with classical symmetry and pomp he throws himself upon the mercy of the trees in the boulevard, or the chimney pots on high, or even the weather—whatever will screen or half-hide the vexing grandiosities in question. If it is not utterly perverse of him he will decline to inspect a façade head-on but will sidle rather to the left or to the right, to secure two elevations, front and side, of his subject—his famous love of "corners" once again. He will place his camera so that blocks of houses appear laterally askew and the eye is forced to zigzag along the build-up of two-point perspective. For the commoner brand of stateliness he hasn't a care: when he crouches in the public gardens to line up the Luxembourg Palace behind a droopy pinnacle of bellflowers, you almost forget that it is the senate house of a great republic which he is snapping.

One reason that Atget may not usually be thought of as a photographer of the picturesque is that the word is so hard to define. The expression "picturesque architecture" brings different effects to the minds of different people, and no single effect seems essential to everyone. Such qualities as I have just described in regard to Atget's imagery may well enter one's mind; others are randomness, novelty, strong contrasts of light and shade, sculptural depth of relief, and richness of edges, especially those which tell against the sky. But the one attribute which almost anyone would associate with the picturesque is age. Fine architecture is meant—in Ruskin's famous phrase—to last "for ages"; it "connects forgotten and following ages with each other, and half constitutes the identity, as it concentrates the sympathy, of nations." So the English critic informs us in "The Lamp of Memory," an essay which, in its concern for the monumental and commemorative aspects of the urban environment, bears directly upon Atget. Ruskin claims that there is a loveliness in the effects of time which nothing else can replace, and which we naturally tend to desire. The marks of age may be regarded as evidence of resistance to ruin, or as so many prophecies of ultimate doom; but however we see them, they embody what he calls "an actual beauty"—that is, as I take it, an indwelling or inherent one. This "actual beauty" is very close to what we commonly call "texture" when scrutinizing Atget's images; and thinking of texture in this way, we begin to surmise why it can sometimes compel an almost silly devotion in which our whole being consents.

To pore over Atget's photos of Old Paris is to promenade your gaze through the choicest precincts of shared memory. A national identity is recaptured, while a sympathy widely transnational—the recognition of aesthetic fellow-citizenship—clots around cherished monuments. At the same time, Atget's perceptions reach into the personal realm. Often enough you are left in the street with only the vapor of your emotions for company. The little courtyards in which you so often find yourself are not only "picturesque corners," they are also condensation chambers for misty, indistinct feelings. To contemplate, from the *porte-cochère,* the forecourt of the townhouse at 1 rue de la Perle, at the edge of the Marais—the former residence of Libéral Bruant, architect of the Invalides—is to surrender to a reverie of secluded elegance. From the moiré of the cobblestones to the roof tiles rising behind the garlanded pediment, everything is in keeping with everything else. Even the recessed concierge's bell at your right hand prettily echoes the shape of the five oculi in Bruant's façade. It is all so jammily stained and freckled and foxed that you're set at once to move in. The centuries have been doing it up for you; you've been fondly remembered by people long dead at your birth.

Atget has framed this scene to suggest a secret chamber, a stone bower for an antiquarian taste. It is penetrated by a single shaft of light. Though this sunbeam is adequately rendered, Atget has "exposed" primarily for local patina, not stark lighting effects. Wanting the richest variegation of local tones compatible with clarity and simplicity, he keys his picture, in effect, to texture, to Ruskin's "actual beauty." In so doing he seizes upon an affinity of medium and motif. Photography can capture patina with far greater ease than can painting or drawing, where the very attempt easily declines into a cramped fussiness. Atget handily achieves the tonal effects, for example, that Piranesi had to strain for. Like Atget, the Italian was drawn to subtle shifts of tone on the surface of weathered antiquities; but in attempting to describe them with an etcher's needle he often muddied up his light-struck planes, so that some of his pages look oddly blotchy or smeared. In photography, only the grossest underexposure of negatives will allow this to happen. Old masonry, like signs on walls, seems to call for the camera as its natural instrument of representation.

A view into the courtyard at 28 rue Bonaparte, off Saint-Germain-des-Prés, excites emotions quite different from those raised by the image of Bruant's mansion. We are positioned parallel to a dank stone stairway which leads up four steps to a landing, then divides. One side winds into a broad, inky proscenium where only an occasional baluster, standing out against a patch of faint light, reassures us that the stairway ascends. On a sort of flying arch over this stagey stairwell is inscribed, in huge letters, the legend LIBRAIRIE. Two hunched doors lead down into the presumed cellar of this gloomy establishment; they seem reserved respectively for Quasimodo and Fantômas. The whole place is like a Piranesian *carcere,* or prison, an evocative, proto-expressionist stage-setting—architecture spiced by fear. Here the picturesque, turned inside out, summons up only morbid or horrifying fantasies.

I am in doubt how the sensibility exemplified by this and some six or eight other photos should be characterized; perhaps as a Romantic delight in the grotto-like, the "grotesque." The whole mode, as embodied in dark courts and blind alleys and grim industrial canals, rings a mild if unexpected change on an ancient fascination. The Egyptians were fond of such blank, fearful rigor; during the Cinquecento Giulio Romano used it effectively, and Palladio toyed with it in his wonderful, unfinished Villa Serego, which is all massive ashlar opening up into cavernous voids. After the excavation of Pompeii and Herculaneum in the mid-eighteenth century, the taste for vast glooms and stairs leading nowhere—for grottoes, tombs, and excavations, for viaducts, sewers, and catacombs, for derelict factories and blasted fortresses—led to a whole new architectural wave which prefigured the modern taste for strong geometrical shapes. Piranesi drew his *carceri* and his chilling *antichità*; Diderot included in his *Encyclopedia* many plates of perplexing machines in punitive-looking workshops; Ledoux designed the somber saltworks called "Salines de Chaux"; and Delafosse speculated, chalk in hand, as to how "the ideal jail" should look. That human beings must have some strange penchant for "obscurity" and "privation" was a notion to which Edmund Burke devoted considerable thought, little suspecting that the twentieth-century metropolis would become the theater of these two categories. It's hardly surprising that Atget absorbed this eighteenth-century sensibility of the visually misanthropic; after all, the so-called Egyptian Taste was being revived in his day. In so doing, however, he took the most exciting trend in pre-Revolutionary French design and made of it something all his own. What he never really succeeded in doing in his Versailles pictures—capturing the antique in the prism of the new—he brought off with aplomb in his shots of bleak courtyards in the Latin Quarter or the Bourse district. It is in reference to these strict rectilinear compositions that one can really begin to talk of an Atget who is alive to modernity.

As the photographer trains his camera on such instances of obscurity and privation as may be found within the modern city, his imagination grows. His work becomes less an act of sensibility and more a freewheeling exertion of creativity. Ragpickers' shantytowns and gypsy encampments afford material not only for documentation but for expression as well. These are peopled, even overpeopled, places; the people give focus to their surroundings. Atget's interest in the gypsies, a picturesque folk par excellence, is of course characteristic; his fascination with street types is of much the same order. In those days the street trades were usually plied by immigrants: Savoyards peddled bric-a-brac, Auvergnats purveyed spirits, Alsatian Jews hawked cheap clothes, Italians laid paving stones and mended shoes, and the Breton lilt could be heard a little everywhere, as it still can today. Many of these people were literally *paysans de Paris,* villagers and small-townsfolk from agricultural areas who had moved to the French capital to find employment. Atget himself was from Bordeaux; one of his problems during his early years as an actor had been his refusal to abandon his Bordelais twang. He was an outsider pursuing a marginal way of life that no wealthy bourgeois in the Faubourg Saint-Honoré would for a moment have regarded as a profession, much less a career. Like the hurdy-gurdy man and the little songstress whom he recorded so tenderly in a famous photo, he was an errant oddball with a box of titillating apparatus; all three would have been quite at home among the personnel of Apollinaire's *Alcools.* Atget's extraordinary "merchant of lampshades," a sort of walking château bristling with conical turrets, is as much a challenge to the prosaic as Rousseau's sleeping gypsy.

Atget does not meet modernity so much as he confronts it. At some point he realizes that by recording the fashion in dress—a certain purely contemporary ruche, say, or bandeau or décolleté—he can subvert modernity, squeeze it into the past. No sort of subject matter grows so rapidly old. Fads in dress go out of date so soon that to catch one in a picture is virtually to subject the present to artificial aging—as one might a cheese. In the shopwindow with its manikins Atget hits upon an especially fertile source of pictures. Patrolling the rue de Rivoli, the Boulevard du Port-Royal, and the periphery of the Bon Marché, he is dealt, over and over, the occasion for a minor masterpiece; for every time he snaps an extravagant window dressing behind a plate of reflective glass he is directing his gaze into one of the swifter rapids of the river of time. It might even be said that the unfurling ribbon of the Paris shopwindows, their surfaces aglitter with the colors of passing motorcars and kaleidoscopic with shards of sky and cloud and the slivered sheen of other windows, is his most beloved river, before even the Seine and the Marne. The collision of reflections and apparel across the surface plane is curiously aquatic, reminiscent of Monet's cloud-and-water-lily friezes. Such visual counterpoint hints at what may be the great submerged theme of Atget and other turn-of-the-century French creators: the suspension of one experience in another. The days live suspended in memory, as the past lives suspended in the stream of days. It is a matter of current and undercurrent, of direction and indirection, of what turn-of-the-century thinkers liked to call "perceived time" *(la durée).* That this theme should be elaborated within the context of fashion is of course typically—and wittily—Parisian.

The shop-front motif already had a long history. In *Gersaint's Shopsign* by Watteau, some people of fashion are shown looking over an art dealer's stock. It is anyone's guess why one lady *en tenue de ville* is portrayed inspecting her appearance in a glass presented by a shop assistant; yet the question as to what this may have to do with the purchase of pictures would give no pause whatever to your average chic Parisienne. The art dealer's pictures, she would doubtless argue, were really nothing but rococo decor; what smart young woman (or man, for that matter, for a man too is portrayed gazing at his image) would buy one for her salon without first holding up a mirror to inspect the figure that she cuts against it? This interpretation is a bit perverse, but it does serve to remind us of the delicate irony implicit in Watteau's scene—that art comes and goes, but fashion is forever. Every sea change in taste whirls about a core of personal vanity. That is why window dressings are the paramount still lifes of our civilization; they show what is to be had, and how (for a season) we shall look. Yet if Atget inherits this visual trope from Watteau and others, he also bequeathes it, much enriched, to posterity. In their own way his photos further extend the notion of the shopwindow as the shrine of a comic *beau idéal.*

An extension of a familiar theme: the same might also be said of the dozen photos of certain rouged personages that Atget took in 1921, almost all in La Villette and Versailles. The finest of these shows a *fille de joie* sitting and waiting by her doorway. Here Atget seems to have used a long lens: the woman looks compressed, in a highly modern way, by her surroundings. She also quickly dispels any idea you may have of prostitutes being feral creatures, or of prostitution itself being a preserve of wildness. This gal, tricked out in one of those vaguely nautical numbers so popular at the time, is really an accomplished fact of culture—even, one might say, of agriculture. Her sow-like embonpoint is as snug in its surround of stucco and stone as a *saucisson* is in its *croûte.* Tame as can be, she looks for all the world like a product of animal husbandry. In the end we can only smile at her transformation of the ritual of self-advertisement into something like the observance of a propriety.

There is a passage in Proust's novel in which the young narrator visits a prostitute in a nearby village. He is seeking to confirm his virility. No sooner does he enter her lodgings, though, when he discovers to his horror that her sitting room is chock-a-block with his aunt's old furniture, which the whore has acquired at a sale. This anecdote suggests what is likely to befall any attempt to recover, within the confines of French civilization, the savage state; one feels that Proust would have been much amused by Atget's pictures of brothels and whores. They are not the only Atget photos to put viewers in mind of his writing, however, for a general similarity has long been observed. Proust's most creative period was very nearly coeval with Atget's; their worlds to a degree coincided; both spent their later lives on one huge project; both rummaged in "lost time" and sounded the elegiac note.

The delights and the difficulties of "illustrating" the work of the faded social butterfly with that of the rough-and-ready artisan are well demonstrated in a book published some twenty years ago called *A Vision of Paris: The Photographs of Eugène Atget, The Words of Marcel Proust.* Arthur D. Trottenberg, its editor, matched charming quotations from Scott Moncrieff's translation with equally charming pictures from Berenice Abbott's collection; yet the pairing is often perverse. A passage about Louis Quinze furniture is coupled with a picture showing Louis Seize chairs; another passage, from the famous jumbo pun on the names of churches (". . . Quim*perlé* among the rivulets with which it babbled, threading their *pearls* . . ."), faces the image of a village street partially fronted by a dark chunk of Romanesque basilica, thereby showing that Proust and Atget both liked old churches. Other juxtapositions are richly suggestive, however. "From my darkened room," runs one Proust quote, "with a power of evocation equal to that of former days but capable now of evoking only pain, I felt that outside, in the heaviness of the atmosphere, the setting sun was plastering the vertical fronts of houses and churches with a tawny distemper"; and facing this passage is the photo of a house on whose surface the declining sun projects the tremulous wintry shadow of an unseen tree. It is just Proust's "power of evocation," I suspect, that really makes him seem similar to Atget. He too wishes to apprehend life through the patina, the integument of things; even more than Atget he is sensible of how much of the past seeps up into the present.

The first of Proust's architectural meditations—the "Ruskinian Pilgrimages in France" —appeared in *Le Figaro* for February 13, 1900, three weeks after the English critic's death and thirteen years before the publication of *Du Côté de chez Swann.* More articles followed. Engrossed in Ruskin's purple rhetoric, Proust journeys to Amiens, Abbeville, Dijon, Avallon; he reads Viollet-le-Duc and visits the Vézelay restoration. He is at Senlis with the Prince Bibesco, in Venice with Reynaldo Hahn; he tries to jot down, amid the same sort of scenery that Atget was beginning to record, the meanderings of his deepest thoughts. He translates into French (without knowing English!) Ruskin's *The Bible of Amiens*; and years afterward, when he starts his long novel, he has the rhythms of *Praeterita* still running in his head. The Latin title of Ruskin's autobiography ("things past") becomes, in a slight metamorphosis, *le temps perdu.*

Much later Proust offers a picture of his younger self on one of his "Ruskinian pilgrimages." It is in *A l'Ombre des jeunes filles en fleurs.* The novel's narrator is to catch the 1:22 from the Gare du Nord to "Balbec" to see its famous church; his grandmother will accompany him partway. He is already afflicted with his chronic ailment, and to ease his frazzled nerves ("Is *this* the enchanted voyager whom Ruskin wrote about?") he downs a few potent drinks in the bar coach. Returning to his compartment he finds his grandmother deep in the memoirs of Mme de Beausergent, and as he sits down she offers him the other book with which she always travels, Mme de Sévigné's letters. He reads; after a few hours he leaves his grandmother off with a friend, and reboards another night train alone. He falls asleep to the rhythm of the wheels clicking over the cross ties. At dawn, he awakens; the train is winding into a Norman hamlet nestled between two steep hills. And then he sees the girl. As the train comes to a halt she is climbing up to the station from the rushing stream below, as roseate in the light of the rising sun as a marble saint beneath a stained glass window, tall, graceful, carrying a pitcher of hot milk for the passengers' morning coffee. Everything about her is perfect; she fills him with a desire to live, whets his appetite for happiness. He calls to her, she throws him a piercing glance, but already the railway men are slamming the carriage doors; the train lurches forward.

> Whether my exaltation had been produced by this girl, or, on the contrary, had itself caused most of the pleasure that I felt at being near her, it was, in any case, so much a part of that pleasure that my desire to see her again was, above all else, the moral need not to allow this state of excitement to perish altogether—not to be separated forever from the creature who, all unknown to herself, had participated in it . . . . This beautiful girl, whom I could still make out as the train gathered speed, was like part of a life other than the one I knew, separated from it by a gap, and in which the sensations awakened by objects were no longer what I expected; and to forsake this new life now would be like dying unto myself.

The narrator did not, as we know, "die unto himself," that is, grow numb to his experiences and feelings. This passage encapsulates not real but imaginary alternatives to actual circumstances. The French prose is almost all in the subjunctive; in telling us what might or ought to have been, it catches, like a camera, a unique instant when a poetically intelligible world becomes fleetingly real or plausible. There is a way in which Proust is always folding his phrases back into themselves, like a baker kneading dough. I wouldn't care to overstress the similarity between Proust and Atget, but as I study the latter's photographs I feel, more and more, the same sort of folding taking place. In the midst of pressing home a point about the spirit of his culture, Atget begins to create a sort of pictorial space that is metaphorical in itself—a space in which the scattered elements are lovingly blended together. This coalescence creates an inner figure, or pattern, different from the objects in the picture but apprehended by degrees as their mystical sum. When Atget feels an outleap of interest toward the things he is looking at, he identifies himself with them; then it seems that his imagination is actually moving in the scene before us, disguised as a tree, or a painted lady, or a sundial in a little court. That is why his claim to a vast territory (so like Proust's annexation of a long stretch of time) was essential to his art: he shifted his position so as to shed his self, leaving it outside him in the shape of seven thousand negatives. That too is why, when he sat down one day in November of 1920, at the age of sixty-three, to pen a letter to the Minister of Fine Arts in which he asserted his rightful ownership of all that his lens had remembered for the greater glory of his city, he felt wholly at peace and assured of his entitlement: "Today this enormous artistic and documentary collection is finished; I can say that I possess all of Old Paris."

(*December* 1985)

The career of Gaston Gallimard

by Frederick Brown

During the past decade, more and more attention has been paid to the role that certain publishers played in French literary life of the nineteenth and twentieth centuries. Books about Louis Hachette, Georges Charpentier, Bernard Grasset, and now Gaston Gallimard—the subject of a new biography by Pierre Assouline[1]—illuminate the peculiar conditions defining a business that has always been held to transcend mere business, in which men who could rightfully account themselves captains of the industry they helped to create also figured as soldiers of intellect and promoters of cultural reform. Such men have become almost legendary. The imprints with which each one marked his age no longer bespeak a personal temperament, style, or adventure but survive, where they do survive, as ornaments that lend moral prestige to bland, corporate entities.

Born in 1881, Gaston Gallimard grew up on the Right Bank, in the social environment immortalized by Marcel Proust. Indeed, his father had much in common with Charles Swann, being a bourgeois scion who set himself a leisurely course that saw him progress downward through life from youthful aestheticism to middle-age dissipation. What Gallimards before him had earned in commerce Paul Gallimard spent on *objets d'art* and the woman he married at age thirty brought a dowry sufficient to let him pursue his hobbies without restraint. "In the idiotic world of bibliophiles, in the world of people slavishly devoted to old printed matter, this fellow Gallimard, who will spend three thousand francs for a private, deluxe editon of a modern work like *Germinie Lacerteux,* stands alone," Edmond de Goncourt observed in 1889. Books of this kind lined his shelves, but it was the art on his walls that attested most persuasively to his flair for recognizing modern genius and investing in it. Beside Corots and Delacroix hung works by Courbet, Manet, Monet, Degas, Boudin, Cassatt, Toulouse-Lautrec, Cézanne, Sisley, and especially Renoir.

With the last he enjoyed a close friendship. During the 1890s they regularly travelled abroad together and Gallimard's country estate near Deauville in Normandy was one of those preserves to which Renoir paid impromptu visits, toting all his paraphernalia, whenever the urge came upon him. Gallimard, in turn, often appeared at the Renoir household. "He always brought in with him the magic atmosphere of Parisian life," wrote Renoir's son, Jean. "He reflected the glory of the brilliant performances which took place in his theater, the Variétés. My father often used to repeat passages from *Orpheus in the Underworld* to us, asking Abel Faivre to sit at the piano and play him

---

1 *Gaston Gallimard: Un demi-siècle d'édition française* by Pierre Assouline; Editions Balland, 493 pages. Harcourt Brace Jovanovich will be publishing an English translation of the book in 1987.

some of the Offenbach airs that he especially liked. Consequently I developed the greatest admiration for this visitor who was on such intimate terms with Jupiter, Cupid and La Belle Hélène." Renoir himself called him "a real eighteenth-century Frenchman."

No doubt Renoir had in mind the rakish side of eighteenth-century France, for Paul Gallimard, possessed by the *démon du midi,* began to collect women rather than art when he reached fifty. Buying an important theater was like lowering a net into the fishing ground of demimondaines, and these fast swimmers, whom Dumas *fils,* among others, had decried as a threat to the bourgeois order, accomplished Gallimard's estrangement from his family. "[He] now spends all his evenings at the Variétés, sporting a boutonnière, amid the hetaerae of his establishment . . . and loudly declares that artists, who were until now his boon companions, are melancholy, sad, bothersome creatures and that he wishes henceforth to surround himself with gaiety," noted Goncourt. One by one, his paintings joined him in a townhouse he bought on the rue de Clichy, where day generally began after nightfall. His sons—Gaston, Raymond, and Jacques—stayed behind. It was as if they, and the memory of hours spent with Claude Monet at Giverny, belonged to another life.

Time would tell how deeply this example affected Gaston. The adolescent portrayed by those who knew him well seemed bent on making amends for it. As quiet and even prudish as Paul Gallimard was flamboyant, he cut an unremarkable figure, betraying no inclination to shine or seduce, to question the pieties of his class or stray from the path of duty. Lawyers, notaries, and stockbrokers were much in evidence when the clan assembled at dinner on Mondays, and this ritual gathering, though painfully incomplete without father, provided a counterweight to his absence. There was also school. At Condorcet, the neighborhood lycée where Mallarmé taught English and Proust had been awakened to modern philosophy, Gaston met young men (notably Roger Martin du Gard) with whom he formed friendships that later stood him in good stead.

Duty relaxed its grip on him before he took the *baccalauréat* examination, however. He dropped out of school and, succumbing to what Pierre Assouline describes as his constitutional "nonchalance," became a Right Bank dandy—a *boulevardier.* "He was elegant in his carriage, his attitudes, his gestures . . . . He abhorred errors in taste and exhibitionism and played the esthete's casual air off against the stiffness of phoney dukes." Café society led him on a constant round from plays to salons to balls to concerts by way of visits to his tailor. Later in life, he would declare that contempt was all he had ever felt for Paul Gallimard, but this social agenda, which could easily have brought them face-to-face on any evening at the Café Weber or the Pré Catelan, implies a more ambivalent relationship. Like his father, Gaston loved everything that made *fin-de-siècle* Paris the hedonist's Promised Land.

Like his father, he loved in particular the excitement generated by the Boulevard, with its ornate theaters, its beautiful women, its gastronomic ingenuity, its odor of perfumed rot. When a fashionable playwright named Robert de Flers, who had been Proust's schoolmate at Condorcet, needed an assistant to help him monitor rival playwrights, he chose Gaston as someone well suited for such espionage, and Gaston came through. The by-product of their collaboration was a newspaper column about life behind the scenes, which appeared unsigned. It did not redound to young Gallimard's credit at home. Nor did it suggest that a man so obviously absorbed in idle gossip could even imagine crossing over to the Left Bank and joining with the solemn, high-minded literati, led by André Gide, who had founded the *Nouvelle Revue Française.* Yet this is what happened at the beginning of 1911.

The ground on which the NRF established itself and the staunchness it showed in defending its values inspired antagonists to characterize it as "Protestant." Protest it did.

Where Anatole France reigned, Gide's companions saw mediocrity triumphant. Romanticism having degenerated into a widely shared taste for the overstuffed and overstated, and Classicism having become another name for the xenophobia of militant reactionaries affiliated with *L'Action française,* they felt trapped between Scylla and Charybdis. Patriotic self-infatuation, religious bigotry unleashed during the Dreyfus Affair, commercialism, facile rhetoric were the evils that held literature in thrall, and this Left Bank group took it upon itself to improve matters by setting an example of critical stringency. With no *parti pris* except the belief that their countrymen could profit from foreign influence, they recognized not only Europe outside France but a France that the custodians of French culture had seen fit to disinherit. "France dried up and prissy, curious about itself and itself alone, huddled over its past as over a wizard's book of spells, intent on understanding itself from one angle, on mutilating its historical glory" was how Gide assailed rabid nationalists in whose lexicon words like "hybridization," "deracination," "transplantation" meant danger. "It is noteworthy that our greatest artists have most often been the products of hybridization and the result of deracination—transplantation I mean," he sneered. Hospitality to the foreigner extended above all to banished creatures of the mind. The loftiness of the NRF did not keep it from extolling artists who ventured underground, who exploited "the incomparable material found in the lower, wild, feverish, uncleaned regions." Along these lines, Jacques Rivière wrote a piece entitled "Metaphysics of Dream," while Gide himself expounded on Dostoevsky.

After two years of existence, the *Nouvelle Revue Française* had acquired a sufficient readership to justify the idea of enlarging its sphere of influence and publishing books under its imprint. An informal search began in 1910 for someone who could direct this enterprise yet bend to Gide's will, who would help finance it and not expect immediate dividends, who had the acumen of a businessman and the taste of a literary mandarin. No candidate was found to embody such paradoxical virtues, but Gallimard's name recurred more often than any other, despite the onus he bore of coming from a milieu scorned by his future confrères. What may have been discernible even before he started work was a gift that proved as useful to them as his fortune. "At twenty-five, without being highly cultivated, he possessed an infallible instinct that led him straight to works of distinction, not for reasons he could articulate logically but out of a kind of gluttony," wrote Jean Schlumberger, who stood just below Gide at the NRF.

Operating in cramped quarters, soliciting manuscripts in his own hand, and relying on the prestige of the NRF to command attention, Gallimard improvised valiantly. The pleasure he found in serving a worthwhile cause mitigated the pain of being treated as a dapper subordinate whose opinions were contaminated by his worldliness. It was some time before the dynamo pent up inside the former playboy overcame this prejudice. Days did not have hours enough to satisfy his appetite for work and when, in 1913, the NRF's first editor in chief, Jacques Copeau, founded the Théâtre du Vieux-Colombier—a repertory theater which stood opposite the Boulevard in every sense—Gallimard took on the additional burden of administering it. Only war could slow him down. Exempted from military service, he followed Copeau to New York, where the French government had the Vieux-Colombier play for Franco-American solidarity, but otherwise he languished in a void, until his nerves gave out. "Your health is what counts, it's one of the bases of everything I hold dear—the common enterprise no less than our friendship," wrote Roger Martin du Gard, an NRF author (and future Nobel laureate), who was serving at the Front. "We must ardently cling to it and make all necessary sacrifices."

This common enterprise had in fact never been free of dissension between Gallimard and Gide, and during the war, which afforded them the leisure to cultivate their differences, an open rift developed. Gide could not pardon Gallimard for having grown in stature, while Gallimard felt increasingly unhappy with constraints placed upon him by Gide. The issue of financial solvency brought them smack against each other. Much as he desired it, Gide was fearful that expansion would ruin the occult milieu in which he functioned best and thus work to Gallimard's advantage. For in Gallimard he saw not only the bogeyman of commercialism but someone even more sinister, namely, the conqueror or paterfamilias whose boldness made him shrink. Two such egos needed separate quarters, which is what Gide proposed in a note apparently expurgated from the Pléiade edition of his journal. "In order to avoid being held responsible for attitudes and acts I would publicly disavow if friendship did not restrain me, I'd rather the imprint of the house were changed," he wrote. "I agree with Copeau that Gallimard alone should decide policy, but in that case it behooves him, and him alone, to sign his decisions . . . ." Immediately after the war, in 1919, matters were set right when the "Librairie de la NRF" became the "Librairie Gallimard."

Though Gaston now ruled, his brother Raymond serving as chief administrative officer, in other respects past practice held sway. The mercurial Gide flitted in and out, writers blessed by the review could expect consecration from the publisher, and an atmosphere of "we the happy few," which had always pervaded the NRF, continued to make itself felt. While every hopeful author knew that at, say, Editions Bernard Grasset he would plead before a jury of one, at Gallimard verdicts emerged anonymously from a Readers Committee meeting every week in secret session. "The Readers Committee is an institution typical of Gallimard," notes Assouline. "In the early twenties it acquired an aura of mystery and prestige which it deliberately cultivated." The hush that fell over Librairie Gallimard whenever this episcopal body convened became habitual, and employees tended to speak among themselves *sotto voce.* A satirist searching for a quip could not have done better than the wag who once dubbed Copeau's Théâtre du Vieux-Colombier "The Calvin Follies."

Furthermore, Gaston Gallimard's first great victory consummated maneuvres that had taken place under the old regime. In 1912, Marcel Proust, whom he knew slightly, broached the idea of submitting a novel. Given some encouragement, Proust sent along fourteen hundred typed pages, which were skimmed by Gallimard's fellow editors and, at their regular Thursday afternoon conference, discarded as the work of an effete snob chummy with the wrong people. "Not for us, it's full of duchesses. And besides, it's dedicated to Calmette, director of *Figaro,*" Gide is reported to have said. No sooner did Grasset publish *Du côté de chez Swann* in 1917 (at the author's expense) than remorse swept the NRF. Gallimard undertook to woo Proust back and, after a courtship byzantine in its legal ramifications, succeeded in doing so. The unsold stock of *Du côte de chez Swann* travelled by pushcart from Grasset to the NRF's establishment on rue Madame, where Gallimard had it put between new covers. Two years later, in 1919, its sequel, *A l'ombre des jeunes filles en fleur,* won Proust and Gallimard a Goncourt prize.

This was destined to be the first of many prizes Gallimard wrested from Grasset as these archrivals fought tooth and nail for literary gold in the aftermath of a war that had made a number of venerable old publishing houses go bankrupt. Success begot success and every year his editorial prospectors—Jean Paulhan, Brice Parain, Robert Aron, Bernard Groethuysen, Benjamin Crémieux, André Malraux, among others—came up with fresh talent, they themselves being writers whose work added to the firm's luster. "Gaston Gallimard left no stone unturned: the idea that someone else might capture a book or writer of consequence gave him fits," Assouline observes. The passion for collecting expressed itself more generously, to nobler ends, and on a grander scale in Gaston's life than in Paul Gallimard's, but his father nonetheless shadowed him and may have been bound up in his mind with the rival from whom he stole one author after another. "For the most part, authors are not men," he told a confidant. "They are females, whores whose services one buys in the knowledge that they are always ready to offer themselves elsewhere." This filial resemblance grew stronger during the 1930s, when he achieved preeminence as a publisher. In 1930, on the verge of his fiftieth birthday, he left the woman he had married eighteen years earlier to take a second wife, who could not have entered holy matrimony without realizing that she would be, at best, *prima inter pares.* Surrounded by female admirers, Gallimard denied himself nothing, least of all the companionship of Valentine Tessier, an actress from Copeau's troupe. It was for her that he tried his hand at producing films and especially a film based on *Madame Bovary,* in which the Gallimard family saga came full circle: Tessier played the titular role under Jean Renoir's direction.

With multilingual editors each of whom was the firm's proconsul in a foreign literature, Gallimard, true to yet another NRF tradition, had them bring home exotic goods and stood behind their enthusiasm for Faulkner, Joyce, and Kafka. He also made the most of France's patrimony by acquiring, through André Gide, the "Bibliothèque de la Pléiade." This beautifully designed library was the brainchild of a Russian-Jewish immigrant named Jacques Schiffrin, who found that with bible paper he could force sprawling classics into modest volumes. The economic crisis spelled disaster for him, but Gide importuned Gallimard to salvage the collection and after several years, in 1933, overcame his misgivings. What Gallimard halfheartedly bought would all by itself have assured him fame and fortune. More scholarly now than in its original incarnation, the collection has continued to grow, proliferating even beyond France in the Pléiade-inspired Library of America.

Between the wars, hardly a year passed that did not see Gallimard adopt or father a collection, a review, a newspaper. By means of such dependent organs (*Les Nouvelles littéraires, La Revue du cinéma, La Revue musicale, La Revue juive, Voilà, Marianne,* etc.) he found it possible to advertise gratis, to run novels serially, to employ down-at-heel authors, to balance the losses he took on poetry. But they reflected as well his imperial will to reach every public, and nowhere was this made more evident than in the creation of a weekly tabloid called *Détective,* which specialized in *faits divers,* or lurid reports about criminal mischief. "In the austere publishing house . . . the paper was viewed as a bastard of noble descent," writes Assouline. "It wasn't hidden, for there would have been no way to conceal the bond between Gallimard and *Détective* . . . but neither was it mentioned." Like turn-of-the-century aristocrats who staged masquerades at which they impersonated characters from Zola's *L'Assommoir* and who, for occasional Saturday-night entertainment, sauntered through the dangerous slum known as "Apache territory," Gallimard had no trouble descending beneath himself, or recognizing a Gallimard in his uncouth child. On the contrary, this hugely profitable venture, which inspired several equally profitable series of detective novels, gave him as much satisfaction as his legitimate offspring. "On Tuesdays, when it was put to bed, Gaston often dropped by with Raymond and Valentine Tessier, before the staff capped off the evening at a working-class restaurant in La Villette. 'Let's go see the circus!' he would say to them." The esoteric crowd at Librairie Gallimard stifled him (especially Jean Paulhan, who carried furtiveness so far as to write editorial notes in Malagasy), while lower down, among barkers fluent in the language of the vulgus, he felt free. Camaraderie on that level became increasingly important during the 1930s, when his upper house was torn by ideological strife. A reconciler rather than a militant, a collector whose principle of discrimination did not operate between Right and Left (any more than it had between

Right Bank and Left Bank), Gallimard saw himself transcending all parties. "I forbid you to make me face my own contradictions," he once thundered at the firm's commercial director and what this implied —a contempt for inner boundary lines— extended to dogma in general.

Ignoring boundary lines was a habit one could not indulge with impunity under Nazi rule, however. In June 1940, Gallimard joined the horde of civilians who fled southward when Hitler's army overran Northern France and for five months—months spent mainly on the Côte d'Azur—debated whether to wait out the storm in America or to resume his entrepreneurial life in the occupied zone. To do the latter involved one significant condition of which informants up north made him aware, which was that he accept as the NRF's new editor in chief a fascist writer named Pierre-Eugène Drieu La Rochelle. Galled by this arrangement but no less galled by the prospect of relinquishing his literary treasure trove, of marking time somewhere beyond the pale, and of losing out to Bernard Grasset, who was already currying favor with the Pétain government at Vichy, he found Paris irresistible. "It's in Paris that one must be," he told Gide in December 1940.

Several months earlier, the Union of French Publishers had signed a "censure agreement" that established policy in accordance with rules laid down by Germany's ambassador, Otto Abetz, after whom was named the "Otto list" of banned books. "Implementing the censure agreement, German authorities are about to publish a first list . . . of works withdrawn from the market either at their behest or on the initiative of publishers," a Union circular warned in September.

> Other lists may follow, inspired by the spirit of the agreement. An impartial examination of the Otto list reveals the large number of foreign authors who had found refuge on our French soil and whose works had come to clutter our domain. French thought has risen to such heights in world history that we need entertain no fears. Thus disencumbered, it will express itself in all its fullness and radiate as brilliantly as before . . . . Every French publisher is wholly responsible for his own stock. He must see to it that what he publishes (a) neither overtly nor in some disguised form undermine German prestige and interests (b) not be the work of any author whose works are banned in Germany . . . .

The *Propagandastaffel* dinned the message that France's fall had been engineered not by Germany but by alien residents masquerading as Frenchmen, whom the French were advised to purge of their own accord and for their own salvation. Germany would help France recover her "true" identity. "The international spirit formerly presiding over literary exchanges—mainly of Jewish origin, as Bernard Grasset has noted" was how one Nazi publisher denounced their common enemy, and collaborators availed themselves of this line to point an accusatory finger at Gallimard in particular. "A gang of malefactors functioned in French literature from 1909 until 1939 under the orders of a leader: Gallimard," wrote Jean Mamy in the collaborationist paper *Au pilori*. "Thirty years of abject and underhanded propaganda in favor of anarchy, of revolutionaries of every stripe, of the 'antis': antifascists, anti-nationalists, anti-anything-at-all. Thirty years of literary, spiritual, human nihilism! . . . Gallimard wishes to return and already the negroes, negroids, and gallimardic negrophiles have gathered at the Deux Magots for their thirty pieces of silver!"

Such gusts of hatred would often rock him during the next four years as he steered through the Occupation trimming his sails to the wind yet doing what could be done to stay on course. Unlike Jacques Copeau, whose brief, inglorious administration at the Comédie-Française in 1940-41 left him shattered, Gallimard was made of pragmatic stuff, and experience had taught him how to sleep with the compromises necessary for survival in a morally equivocal world. Since survival depended on paper, and the acquisition of paper on evidence that one did not spurn German literature, he published Goethe (Goethe having been officially Aryanized) and two novels by Ernst Jünger, which he might have bought under any circumstances. The same imperative prompted him to attend functions at the German Institute, where Parisian literary folk hobnobbed with Nazi brass. These were not seen to be merely venial sins on Judgment Day, but Gallimard, who also sheltered *résistants,* could argue in his own defense that, by and large, fellow publishers behaved worse than he. As one journalist noted in 1941, "It seems that French publishing, through the voice of its directors, has adopted the motto of the Head of State—'Work, Family, Fatherland'—and has loyally set out . . . to publish books that drive this motto home." The Occupation did wonders for trade, and if paper had been abundant, publishers would have known even greater prosperity flogging three-decker novels to an imprisoned people who sought refuge in fiction from hunger, boredom, and moral distress. "As far as the book trade is concerned, these are euphoric times," observed Albin Michel's literary director, and euphoria sustained itself with arguments that made a virtue of business-as-usual. "Nowadays we have more clients than we want, or, rather, more than we can satisfy. However, as long as we aren't halted by material obstacles we shall work with faith and the certitude that it is our one way of 'serving' at this moment."

It was not easy to thwart a foe shrewd enough to exploit the spiritual wealth of captive nations. At times, distinguished writing served the Reich even more effectively than arrant propaganda, as Gallimard learned when he bought yet another magazine, *Comoedia,* and transformed it into a classy journal that numbered among its contributors Paul Valéry, Jean-Paul Sartre, Arthur Honegger, Jean Cocteau, Henri de Montherlant, and Jean Giraudoux. The tribute exacted by Gallimard's overlord amounted to a single page in each issue where Nazi-sponsored cultural events (the Bayreuth Festival, Mozart week) or books translated from German received special mention. But the hidden price paid for this weekly symposium went beyond such reckoning. The magazine's quality was made to speak against those in the outside world who accused Nazis of ruthless barbarism. "*Comoedia* lent credence to the image of occupied France being propagated abroad by the Nazis . . .: a country whose brilliant culture had not been stifled, but, on the contrary, [allowed to flourish]," writes Assouline.

In the aftermath of liberation, when tribunals sprang up everywhere, harsher punishment was meted out to writers who had aided and abetted the enemy than to publishers who published them. A "purification committee" looked hard at Gallimard, but the case made against him by Vercors crumbled under the weight of favorable testimony offered by Malraux, Aragon, Sartre, Camus (a house reader), Salacrou, Paulhan, and Eluard. Only one man might have discredited their assertion that Gallimard had held the plague-stricken NRF in strict quarantine and he, Drieu La Rochelle, killed himself shortly before he stood trial, leaving, as virtually his last words: "I read and I wait. I will die sooner or later. I don't believe in literature and I think the time of literature is gone." The wrath of a jury that could neither hang Drieu nor blame Gallimard fell on the NRF itself, which it sentenced to death.[2]

With this burdensome past liquidated, Gallimard began filling gaps in his collection, and it tells us something about France's postwar leap from scapegoat justice to general amnesty that the authors he openly courted in 1950 had been marked men in 1945. First came Henri de Montherlant, who deserted Bernard Grasset after twenty-eight years of marriage. Gallimard then set his cap for Louis-Ferdinand Céline, an outspoken anti-Semite whose novels the French government banned until 1951. "I would be so happy to be able to publish Céline," Céline's agent remembers Gallimard saying. "I have brought to my house the greatest

---

2 It was subsequently revived under the title *La Nouvelle Nouvelle Revue Française.*

names in literature: Gide, Claudel, Faulkner, Valéry . . . . Everyone! And the only one I've bungled is Céline. I let him slip through my fingers, which was a mistake . . . ." Gallimard corrected his mistake. The abuse to which Céline took pleasure in subjecting him was the price he gladly paid for a trophy that furthered his monopolistic designs on twentieth-century French literature.

This monopoly, or the will to preserve it, is what saw Gallimard reach eighty and then ninety with his wits very much intact. Absorbing other firms, riding through dynastic quarrels that seriously divided the house, and meanwhile spurning all official honors, he became a law unto himself. To be sure, old age did not spare him moments of bleak summing up. "I bungled my life . . . and from the time I became a businessman lost my real friends," he confided to the novelist, Louis Guilloux. "You know, I don't sleep. The other night I composed a whole book . . . . You're lucky because you have your vocation. Not me. All I have is money and money does me no good. At bottom I like only men who fail. The greatest always commit suicide." But when he died at ninety-four, the phrase that had gained currency in Paris—*Hors Gallimard, point de littérature* (outside Gallimard, there is no literature)—could have been inscribed on his stone without doing serious violence to the truth.

Pierre Assouline has used rich material to dubious effect. His work is not so much a biography as it is a journalistic hodgepodge that leaves important questions unanswered and significant details unexamined. One doesn't learn from it what went into Gallimard's lifelong passion for theater, why Sartre exercised such influence over him, who the women were he married, how he groomed his sons, etc. It conveys neither the pith of a culture nor the inner workings of a complex individual. Dwelling on the Occupation years, which take up about a quarter of the book, Assouline skews Gallimard's character while pursuing an argument clearly intended to demonstrate his lack of character. Still, issues of moment are raised, and foremost among them that of Vichy casting its long shadow on present-day France. The amnesia encouraged by Charles de Gaulle, who saw self-scrutiny as an obstacle to national resurgence, has, forty years later, inspired prosecutorial histories. What one generation buried, another exhumes almost vengefully, which calls to mind Freud's dictum that "no mortal can keep a secret. If his lips are silent, he chatters with his fingertips." So it is here. The trial Gallimard never endured takes place in the chatter of Assouline's narrative.

(*February* 1986)

Putting the Sixties to bed

by Jed Perl

"Definitive Statements" is a show about American art between 1964 and 1966 that Kermit Champa, who teaches at Brown University, organized in collaboration with a group of graduate students there. The exhibition and the accompanying catalogue set out to demonstrate how postwar American art reached a high tide of achievement in the Minimalism, Color-field, and Pop Art of the mid-1960s. Paintings and sculptures by LeWitt, Marisol, Oldenburg, Olitski, Stella, Warhol, and twenty-six others are presented as works of established, unquestioned value. Both the show, which was elegantly installed at the List Art Center at Brown in March, and the catalogue, with its scholarly apparatus all in place, bespeak a serene confidence in the significance of everything that's under consideration.[1]

In a preface to the catalogue, Champa explains that "The challenge in *Definitive Statements* was to attempt an essay—both in the exhibition itself and in the accompanying catalogue—in art history of the most recent sort." Champa thinks that "American art of the 1964-1966 period has become, in spite of its recentness, historical rather than any longer contemporary." He sees the period as "a kind of sealed aesthetic unit containing both major work and major criticism" that is "positively ripe for scholarly review." There's a touch of glee in Champa's preface: the professor here finds himself sending his students off to study not Paris in 1860 or 1910, but a past he actually lived through and in which, as he tells us, he "played a 'bit' part." It must be fun to have your students write about the period you yourself participated in as a critic. In the bibliography we find Champa on Bannard (in 1968), on Frankenthaler (in 1972), on Olitski (in 1967), and on Poons (in 1968). Now, fifteen years later, Champa is looking at it all again from the perspective of the academy, with his students struggling through the bound volumes of the art magazines in the stacks. Champa found the work interesting when it was produced and he still likes it today: this continuity of taste is normal and altogether to be applauded. What's peculiar is Champa's willingness to let something he found urgent and vital twenty years ago slide—or even be pushed—into a closed past.

Why is there this haste to transform the contemporary into the historical? Champa insisted that his students, whenever possible, "avoid increasingly unreliable verbal

---

1 "Definitive Statements" was on view at Brown University's List Art Center, in Providence, Rhode Island, from March 1 to March 30. It will be on view at the Parrish Art Museum in Southampton, Long Island, from May 3 to June 21. The catalogue of the exhibition, published by Brown University ($10, 181 pages), includes a preface by Kermit Champa and essays by Michael Plante, Christopher Campbell, Megan Fox, Mitchell F. Merling, Jennifer Wells, and Ima Ebong, the graduate students who organized the show.

history." He told them not to consult "the artistic and critical 'characters' of the period"—himself included—because these could be "unreliable." (Curiously, two dealers—André Emmerich and Leo Castelli—were interviewed by one of the graduate students: are dealers less biased than artists or critics?) It's as if the chief actors—most of whom are still alive and active—are being wished dead, so the messy weight of experience can be reduced to whatever record remains and the sorting and categorizing can begin. Champa believes that by relying on "the considerable written record" (Champa's articles included) "something like 'real' history has been served." Those quotation marks around real are really something. "Real" history is, apparently, history in a book, where everything has been neatly processed to fit into a single perspective—the perspective of the historian. The confidence of "Definitive Statements"—reflected in that very final-sounding title—is a bit unbelievable. Perhaps the self-assurance masks some sort of anxiety: a feeling that the art one believed in when one was young no longer looks the same. This urgency about getting the preserving fluid into the body of Sixties art and the body comfortably ensconced in the mausoleum—could it be based on a fear that the whole mix of elements in the work of some twenty years ago remains all too alive, and subject to drastic alterations by experience, changes of perspective, the ravages of time?

When the art of the 1960s is shown in New York it never feels merely "historical." Pop, Minimalism, and Color-field are living issues—alive in the art of those who continue to work out of these ideas, and alive in the enormous impact they've had on everything that's come after. Warhol can't be separated from Salle; Judd can't be separated from Serra. Today's art world, with its trend setters and fashion forecasters, has its origins in the consensus-thinking that Pop, Minimalism, and Color-field laid on top of the old-fashioned heterogeneity of the art world of the 1940s and 1950s. (Back then they didn't even call it an "art world"—it was too small.)

"Definitive Statements" makes the Sixties look squeaky-clean; it's the mid-Sixties as a Yuppie success story. Clement Greenberg is Chief Executive Officer, Minimalism represents Heavy Industry, and Pop takes care of the mass-market end of things. Nowhere in the catalogue is it even suggested that anyone ever questioned—either during the 1960s or later—the whole gestalt of mainstream Sixties aesthetics. In the amazingly homogeneous installation at the List Art Center at Brown, one got the feeling the mid-Sixties were a kind of Parnassus of High Art, with poets and a few muses living in perfect harmony. No one else need apply.

The work gathered here is characterized pretty much without exception by its imperturbable, seamless surfaces. Aside from the poured forms of Frankenthaler (which really belong to an earlier moment), there's a near total absence of the autographic touch, and this makes a connection between the Color-field paintings of Olitski and Poons, the Pop of Warhol and Wesselmann, and the Minimalism of Judd and Andre. For the organizers of the show the up-frontness of the work—its rejection of literal depth or the sensation of depth—is the culmination of painting's long march, since the mid-nineteenth century, toward the surface. We can all probably agree that in modern art pictorial space is less and less a matter of fictive depth; with Cubism pictorial space does in fact move forward from the picture plane—into the viewer's space. But at "Definitive Statements" it's as if the space has closed up completely, and what drama remains isn't a drama within the painting so much as a drama that takes place around the work. The defenders of Color-field will probably say this is the case with Minimalism but not with Color-field—Greenberg has said something along these lines. But all this work puts the viewer in the position of looking *at* something rather than looking *into* it. And this is a distinction that seems to me fatal to the health of painting and sculpture.

John McCracken's luridly colored *Violet Block in Two Parts*—it's made of plywood sprayed with some thirty coats of paint to look as shiny as enameled metal—might be a kind of emblem for the entire show. Though the McCracken—which was made in Los Angeles—has a particularly Southern Californian ethos, the lion's share of the works in "Definitive Statements" reflect a related fondness for technological perfection as a utopian ideal. At "Definitive Statements" one is carried back to the New Age Sixties sensibility. It was a time when computers were just beginning to be talked about, and a lot of people believed technology was going to create a Global Village—a high-tech Family of Man. "Definitive Statements" also includes—in Marisol's oversized doll and in Bontecou's multi-layered iron construction—a bit of the artsy-craftsy underside of the Sixties sensibility. But most of the art in the show has the gleaming colors and easy-clean surfaces of suburban America in the penultimate days of its postwar dream. The materials—formica, neon, plexiglass, sprayed paint—are the stuff of shopping centers and fast-food chains. The unnaturalness of the colors—the brilliant reds and greens, violets and magentas—suggest a conquest of messy nature.

The homogeneity of this mid-Sixties art made it possible for the organizers of "Definitive Statements" to put together one of the niftiest pieces of installation I've ever seen. So perfect was the juxtaposition of colors and forms that it was easy to believe the various loans had been engineered with a precise installation plan in mind. This was exhibition installation as interior decor. There was a black, white, and gray corner, where a LeWitt, a Morris, a Martin, an Oldenburg, and a Bontecou resided in happy harmony. An Olitski with circles of deep red and blue was set next to an Andy Warhol *Brillo* box, decorated in almost exactly the same colors. Artschwager's *Telephone Directory,* in greenish-gray formica, was next to Stella's greenish-gray *Abajo.* Caro's *Kasser,* with two flat purple "arms" angling into the air, was next to Noland's *Off,* in which the stripes, though of different colors, were exactly the same width as the elements in the Caro. Poons's colored ovals (in *Sagre de Christo*) made a neat decorative backdrop for Marisol's *Baby Boy* (you could also see Poons's spots nicely reflected in Larry Bell's untitled glass box). And in perhaps the cleverest juxtaposition in the whole show, di Suvero's wood and iron *Departure 2001* was set next to a Wesselmann still life, so that the rough hunk of wood projecting off of a tilted piece of steel in the di Suvero looked amazingly like the big piece of crumpled aluminum foil held in the hand of a woman in the Wesselmann. Despite the cramped quarters in which "Definitive Statements" was mounted, the show flowed beautifully.

It was fun to get in tune with this curatorial matching game. Once you realized every single juxtaposition was carefully thought through, you could begin to play along, figuring out why a piece was in a particular place, as if you were doing a visual crossword puzzle. What made it all work was the odd, silent complicity of the art, which rarely asserted anything beyond the prettiness of its colors or the handsomeness of its forms. The most interesting pictorial effects one encountered in "Definitive Statements" were a certain shimmering of the surface (Olitski) or a flexing of the plane, which gave a sense of space as made up of several hinged units (Noland, Stella, Caro). Otherwise, the images were somnolent, items in a decor. The whole ensemble sat together so neatly, so pertly, you had to smile.

"Definitive Statements" looked like a high-art version of the 1960-1975 section of the "High Styles" design show which was at the Whitney Museum this past winter. One had at "Definitive Statements" all the essential elements of Sixties taste: the sleek surfaces, the high-tech materials (some of which by now look rather low tech), the romance of misty colors, and the elevation of pop images to icon status. "Definitive Statements" should have included a little decorative-arts coda, like the one at the Boucher show at the Metropolitan: all you needed was an inflatable vinyl couch, a Fillmore poster with art nouveau lettering, and a big violet plastic coffee cup.

At the deepest level, what joins all the art in "Definitive Statements" is a spirit of grasping, voracious ambition. In these works one feels an eagerness to be done with the messy nonsense of producing works of art—a desire to get on with what the artists obviously believe is the real business of art, the business of taking one's place in history. The Minimalists, the Pop Artists, and the Color-field painters have different views of the history of modern art; but they have all defined themselves, almost from the beginnings of their careers, through their desire to enter the history books. They're not interested in the Romantic idea of the artist as an individual creator; they want to be validated in the cavalcade of current events, which they believe leads straight to immortality. This is probably why their art fits so neatly into the scheme of an art-historical show like Kermit Champa's at Brown: the art lies down and plays dead for the historians because that's what it's always really wanted to do. The various disagreements between the Color-field people, the Minimal people, and the Pop people make the would-be historian's job all the easier, because the history is self-dramatizing in a clear, unequivocal way. Since one isn't ever pulled very far into the paintings or sculptures as distinct, irreducible experiences, it's easy to categorize them. They were made to be placed; one might almost say they were placed before they were made.

Everything in this show feeds off a jingoistic, provincial insistence on the myth of the great moment of American art—which is Abstract Expressionism. This confidence is evoked in the very first line of Michael Plante's catalogue essay on "The Fifties Legacy: Toward a New Aesthetic." "The period from 1964 to 1966 represented the culmination of a twenty-five year development in which Amerian art—particularly that produced in New York City—reached the zenith of avant-garde production in terms of originality and quality." Heady words: zenith, originality, quality. Art history is here a glorious, unimpeded climb from (to quote Christopher Campbell in "The Art of the Sixties: Soliloquies and Conversations") "formalist reductionism" to "profoundly new experiences." The whole period from the end of World War II to the middle of the 1960s is seen as instant history, with works of art taking their places in some definitive art-historical chronology practically while the paint is still wet on the canvases in the studio (and don't forget how fast acrylic dries). In writing about Olitski's paintings "from 1965 forward" Campbell says that "they continue the historical precedent of Pollock's gravitationally driven line, Louis' sluice of liquid paint, Stella's hand-painted imprecision, and Noland's spreading color stain." That expression "historical precedent" is extraordinary. Paintings created one, two, five, ten, at most fifteen years before are seen as "historical precedents"—as fixed points in a completed past. Some of us aren't as sure about Rembrandt and Raphael as Kermit Champa and company are about Stella and Noland: this assurance is a kind of oppression, a deadening of experience.

The yearning for conclusions that haunts "Definitive Statements" keeps bringing the authors of the catalogue essays back to Clement Greenberg. Though Greenberg doesn't like between half and two-thirds of the work in the show, his certainty, his assertion of the importance of the moment, is a benefit to everyone involved. He's quoted insistently, and the Sixties begin to look like a great Greenbergian pure water river out of which and toward which other smaller streams flow. Even when he's not quoted, his obsessions—with the collapse of color and line into a unified, all-over surface, with the end of chiaroscuro—are repeated like a cult follower's mantra. Here is Michael Plante on Louis: "Louis poured and flooded his canvas, negating drawing, working against shape, and avoiding light and dark contrasts." Ideas about postwar art which have an urgency when encountered in Greenberg's work are turned into conventional thoughts in the "Definitive Statements" catalogue. The picture of Greenberg presented here is a typical contemporary view.

We get no sense of the grand, clear prose style of *Art and Culture,* of the critic who insists on the direct experience of the work of art, or of the few, trenchant insights he garnered from Hofmann and the other artists in the faraway days on Eighth Street. One has in "Definitive Statements" none of the sense of discovery that floods through Greenberg's beautiful essay on "The Late Thirties in New York." (There are, in that essay and elsewhere in Greenberg, insights about personalities and motivations which suggest the gifts of a great autobiographer.) No: at Brown we get the other side of Greenberg. Here Greenberg is the author of a science of art criticism; he lays waste to the entire history of postwar art in order to clear a highway for the fortunate few. Quality, that great Greenbergian word, becomes in "Definitive Statements" something fixed and dead. The benign prettiness of every single object in this show is dangerously close to—is, finally, indistinguishable from—quality in fashion. Taste is a reduction from some known standard of the past. To add anything fundamental to the brew would be to call first principles into question—and this must never be done.

The attraction of this art-critical position most likely rests in its immunity to doubt. This line of thought makes it possible to avoid those moments in front of works of art when we don't know exactly what we're looking for or if we've found it. The theory we encounter in "Definitive Statements" has such cachet because it explains the passage of time and gives ultimate value to the mad, chaotic headlong rush of events. Those of us who don't buy this partitioning of the 1960s into categories with titles which sound like name brands—Color-field, Pop, Minimal, Op (though Op isn't regarded by the Brown crowd as quite respectable)—have nothing so neat to offer in response. Other critics who have written about the period—Fairfield Porter, Hilton Kramer—look disheveled in the variety of their interests, the variousness of their enthusiasms. The 1960s of a Porter or a Kramer would be too much for the grad students: too many movements, figures, no main line. Yet it must be said that Clement Greenberg is a critic who prompts something like rage in many painters and critics who were active during the 1950s and 1960s. Probably precisely because many of Greenberg's contemporaries feel somewhere deep in him the genuine love of art, Greenberg's denial of a variety of values—his rejection even in his beloved Abstract Expressionists of what he calls Whitmanesque longings—seems a terrible monopolizing and homogenizing of experience. But in mentioning what some of Greenberg's contemporaries say about him I've broken Kermit Champa's rule to "avoid . . . verbal history." Better to accept what's in the final chapters of Janson's and Gardner's histories of art. "Real" history.

So tight is the clutch of Greenbergian formalism around "Definitive Statements" that we hardly get any sense of the social history of the Sixties. Art has no obligation to respond to the times, but one imagines, when Pop is under discussion, that the social scene will loom larger than it does in Ima Ebong's gingerly essay on "The New Visual Culture." Ebong proposes to step into the heady delirium of the Sixties sensibility, but she takes with her only Greenberg (of course) and, as a kind of counterbalance, the biggest gun of Sixties mass-culture literature, Marshall McLuhan. In her Greenberg/McLuhan polarity (she also mentions Harold Rosenberg), Ebong achieves a nicely formalized, sanitized version of a decade that brought forth a great, rich outpouring of thought. The essay has no texture. Where is Dwight Macdonald, whose *Against the American Grain: Essays on the Effects of Mass Culture* was published in 1962? How about Pauline Kael, who brought out her first collection, *I Lost It at the Movies,* in 1965, and whose seminal essay, "Trash, Art and the Movies," appeared in *Harper's* in 1969? And where is the Susan Sontag of "Notes on Camp" (1964) and "One Culture and the New Sensibility" (1965), both collected in 1965 in *Against Interpretation*? Perhaps all this might get us lost along too many diverse avenues.

Only once at the exhibition do the 1960s as a time we all lived through seem to rear their head. This is on a little wall where a small version of Robert Indiana's *Love* is hung above one of Andy Warhol's *Race Riot* silkscreens. Seeing these legendary images at firsthand is an odd experience; they look pale and recessive, not a bit as zingy as when we first saw them in the color pages of *Time* and *Newsweek.* Looking at the "originals" makes one think of Lincoln's remark when he first met Harriet Beecher Stowe: "So this is the little woman who started this big war." There's still a little surprise in the phenomenon of something so diminutive and unimposing setting off the attack of Pop. At Brown, Pop turns academic and authoritative and grand. The show could have been called "Reductive Statements."

It was interesting to go through the paintings and sculptures in "Definitive Statements" with an eye for the little evidences of physical decay. One could note the peeling off of pieces of tape on Stella's *Sunapee IV*; the dirty surfaces of Olitski's *Half Chinese Patutsky* (has anyone ever written an essay on Sixties titles?); the doll's face cracking and peeling on Marisol's *Baby Boy.* The issues of Sixties art are still very much alive; but for these particular works the slow slide into oblivion has begun. This scholarly show was an Ivy League version of the pop music stations' walks down memory lane. The Sixties had been put to bed.

Displayed on a pedestal at "Definitive Statements"—a bit gray with the dust of twenty years—was Oldenburg's plaster wedge of wedding cake. This piece has to it a sweet story. In 1966, Oldenburg made a plaster cake for the wedding of two collectors, and slices were given out to the guests as party favors. This sculpture is a souvenir of the Sixties—of the noisy, electric Innocence and Experience of those Blakean years when it seemed one's personal growth (forgotten word) was part of a larger, oceanic growth —a surge in the cosmos. One can imagine that Sixties wedding—an event probably no more or less amusing than many in Surrealist Paris or 1920s New York. Apocalypse, of a pleasant, purplish variety, was in the air. The Oldenburg cake—this was a wonderful conceit. It gave a self-consciously artistic aura to the whole affair. What fun to take home a piece of Pop by a real Pop artist. The wedding became a send-up of weddings, and at least a few guests probably left with the knowledge that they had in hand "An Oldenburg." A work of *value.*

(*June* 1986)

William Empson: a tribute

by Cleanth Brooks

William Empson first swam into my ken in 1930-31 while I was reading for honors in the English School at Oxford. I cannot remember how I first heard of him: perhaps through his association with I. A. Richards, whose work I had discovered on my arrival at Oxford in the autumn of 1929.

I devoured Richards's *Principles of Literary Criticism* and his *Practical Criticism.* I was fascinated with what he had to say about the workings of language, and though I did not like his positivism and his psychologistic vocabulary I had to admit that he was telling me more about the inner workings of poetry than I had ever heard anyone tell before.

In the excellently selected open-shelf English literature room in the Bodleian Library, I easily located Empson's *Seven Types of Ambiguity* and sat down to read it. But I made the mistake of starting at the first page to read the book through. I quickly became bogged down in Empson's attempt to differentiate between his various kinds of ambiguity and put the book aside.

I did not read it through until 1938. In the meantime I had come home, had begun to teach at the Louisiana State University in 1932, and in 1934 had been joined there by Robert Penn Warren. In 1936 we issued our first textbook, *An Approach to Literature,* in which we offered analyses and discussions of poems, stories, plays, and essays. In 1938 we published *Understanding Poetry,* which employed the methods used in the poetry section of the earlier book.

In the meantime, Warren and I had heard enough about Empson to want to read his *Seven Types of Ambiguity.* By then, however, it was out of print; but I managed to get for us a couple of copies from a second-hand bookseller in London.

This time, I was bowled over by what I found. Here was a critic working along lines original to himself but recognizably parallel to our own, who had a dazzling imagination and a wonderfully deft hand at dealing with the ways in which words worked together to achieve rich and delicate shadings of meaning. If I remember correctly, *Understanding Poetry* was by this time already in galley proof, but fortunately there was sufficient time to include a quotation from *Seven Types of Ambiguity.*

As for Empson's seven types, I could still make little of them. His distinctions among them were vague and wavering, and depended more on the reader's reaction to the poem than to qualities in the poem's structure. But what did it matter? The analyses of actual lines, phrases, and metaphors counted for a great deal. They were always brilliant and usually convincing.

The word *ambiguity,* I concluded, was not happily chosen. It was a term derived from expository prose and suggested a flaw—a muddle to be cleared up. A better term might be *multiple implication* or even Philip Wheelwright's jaw-breaking term, *plurisignification.*

As will be seen, the "methods," if they

can be called that, which were used in *Understanding Poetry* were not derived from Empson but represented a parallel development. Speaking for myself, I had been much influenced by Richards. Warren may also have been, but I suspect that the Fugitives' discussions of their poems and the poems of others in their meetings in the early 1920s also had their influence on Warren, and through him, on me.

Richards was Empson's supervisor of the first part of the English tripos at Cambridge, and his books undoubtedly left their mark on his pupil. In *Seven Types of Ambiguity* Empson handsomely expresses his debt to Richards, but he goes on to write: "And I derive the method I am using from Mr. Robert Graves' analysis of a Shakespeare Sonnet, in *A Survey of Modernist Poetry.*"

After Richards took up his post at Harvard, we met for the first time and soon came to know each other. On one occasion Richards filled out for me Empson's account of how he came to write *Seven Types of Ambiguity.* Empson, having just read *A Survey of Modernist Poetry* by Laura Riding and Robert Graves, came up to Richards and said that what Riding and Graves had done with Shakespeare's Sonnet Ninety-four he could do with any other poem. Since thus far Empson had shown himself as no more than a rather aimless and lackadaisical student, Richards replied rather testily: "Then why don't you do that?" To his utter amazement, in a week or so Empson returned with a bulky manuscript, the fruits of his application of the method to a whole cluster of lyric poems. The manuscript was the core of what was to become *Seven Types of Ambiguity.*

From that moment, Empson was a made man in Richards's eyes—as indeed he should have been. As a mere *tour de force, Seven Types of Ambiguity* was a dazzling achievement. But it was much more than that, for its exemplification of techniques for exploring the verbal makeup of poems and the penetrating comments on the poems themselves constituted a permanent contribution to literary criticism.

By sheer coincidence, *A Survey of Modernist Poetry* came into my hands for review in 1929. I read it with great interest. But the book did not evoke from me the response that it set off in Empson. I was then primarily concerned with what the authors had to say about modernist poetry as such. In the early 1920s Robert Graves had become very interested in John Crowe Ransom's poetry, and there was much friendly correspondence between them. In 1926 Laura Riding, another member of the Fugitive group—the only woman member—went to England and was soon collaborating with Graves, not only in the *Survey,* but in several other books on poetry.

Were these relationships consequential? Do they constitute linkages between the British "close readers" of poetry and their American counterparts? Frankly, I don't know. Perhaps some day a Ph.D. candidate, hungry for an untouched dissertation topic, may want to inquire. I wish him success, but doubt that he can find any decisive evidence. I expect that in addition to a few specific acknowledged influences, such as that of Richards on myself, the answer may be as simple as this: after a long season of inquiry into sources, cultural influences, and biography, the times were ripe for a renewed (though much intensified) attention to the verbal content of literary works.

At this point I should point out that Empson (like many of the rest of us) had interests that took him beyond the inner detail of a literary work. Such interests appear even in *Seven Types of Ambiguity.* For example, Gray's "Elegy in a Country Churchyard" provokes Empson to comment on the fact that "eighteenth-century England had no scholarship system or *carrière overtes aux talents.*" There is no explicit reference to this in the poem, and it is far from certain that Gray gave it a thought: he probably simply accepted this situation as the normal order of things. But this is just my point: Empson is constantly moving outside the poem.

In *Some Versions of Pastoral* (1935), published in this country as *English Pastoral Poetry,* his concern for cultural and historical issues becomes paramount. For instance, he firmly sets *Alice in Wonderland* in its Victorian context, and the oddly assorted creatures that, along with Alice, make their way out of the pool of tears suggest to Empson a muffled allusion to Darwin's theories of evolution.

The connections are daringly speculative, but usually ingenious and often convincingly pertinent. *Some Versions of Pastoral* is my favorite of Empson's books. But I must not imply that his interests in the cultural bearings of literary works had by this time supplanted his interest in literary theory. The very title of the book refutes any such supposition, for in using the term *pastoral,* Empson gives it a new and precise meaning. He discards the traditional trappings, sheep and shepherd's pipes and crooks, in favor of a genre definition that goes to the heart of the matter. In pastoral, the writer uses a character less complex than himself or than his typical reader. He does this in order to give a view of our complex world from a fresh and often illuminating perspective. Thus, his chapter on *Alice in Wonderland* is titled "The Child as Swain." The child's uninhibited gaze illumines and often unmasks the pretenses of the adult world. It is an extremely useful definition. In the light of this definition we may regard *Huckleberry Finn* as a pastoral.

Empson's *The Structure of Complex Words* (1951) is of all his books the most elaborately thought out and worked out. But the very diversity of Empson's interests, which gives vitality and body to *English Pastoral Poetry* seems to me to beget confusion in *Complex Words.* As W.K. Wimsatt and I put it in *Literary Criticism: A Short History,* "Empson's inveterate psychologism constantly makes him put such questions as these: Why would a reader of such and such a kind find this ambiguous? What historical circumstances make the 16th-century reader, say, prone to take this rather than that as the primary reading? . . . Empson's interest sometimes seems to be merely a curiosity as to what could be made of a particular passage if he simply gave his mind to the search for puzzles." In this regard he seems to anticipate some of our current literary theorists—those, for example, who specialize in reader-oriented criticism.

Yet finally Wimsatt and I had to agree that in Empson's work the cognitive principle is never completely overwhelmed. What Empson regarded as "valuable ambiguity" adds richness and complexity to the meaning rather than throwing the meaning into doubt. Perhaps I should say that the limitations I find in *Complex Words* do no more than reveal my own limitations.

In 1940 Warren and I succeeded in securing an article by Empson for *The Southern Review,* which we were then editing. It was entitled "Honest Man." It is a brilliant study of the chameleon-like tonal colorations of the only apparently forthright word "honest," as it is moved out of one contextual field into another. We would cheerfully have used more of his work in the *Review* had we been able to come by it.

While we were negotiating for the essay, Empson was in China, and I tried to persuade him to travel from China to New York by a southern route so that we might have a visit from him, but Baton Rouge was too far off the beaten track. Thus I did not meet Empson until the summer of 1948, when we were both on the faculty of John Ransom's newly founded School of Letters at Kenyon College.

We were given rooms in close proximity in one of the older buildings. There were thus opportunities for talk, and we did have some conversations during those eight weeks. But I found him a very difficult man to know. He was not only shy, but, like many of the young Englishmen that I remember from my Oxford days, inhibited, bottled up inside himself. Often only a long acquaintance would open up these reticent Englishmen or, in the proper hour, enough alcohol. I had heard that Empson went in for drinking, but I never saw any evidence of it; and though we got to be on amicable terms, at Kenyon I never felt that I knew him.

He was a poet, and I would like to comment on his poetry, but I find that I have little to say. His poetry had character. It wasn't like anybody else's. The phrasing was often brilliant. Contrary to what one might have expected from his carefully analytic prose, the poetry seemed bardic and rhapsodic. This was one of the oddities of this fascinating man. But for some reason—probably my fault—I must regretfully own that his poetry never really spoke to me.

I return to Empson's contradictions and oddities. He was a compendium of them. I'm told that he was of a solid, even staid, Yorkshire family. Yet he was quietly but firmly rebellious. He wrote a book in praise of Milton but deploring what he held to be Milton's demonic God. His politics were distinctly leftish. He admired China and what the revolutionaries were preparing to make of it. Though he greatly admired Richards as his old friend and master, he had no compunction in pointing out where the master had gone astray. In sum, he was the independent, very much his own man, even to a whimsical degree. I see him as a worthy member of that noble band of eccentrics that England has produced through the last two and a half centuries.

I take it that his work is at the moment out of fashion. But then, the literary world is notoriously given to fads and fashions. What is of importance is the very solid achievement that he has left it. If the generations to come neglect that, they have impoverished none but themselves.

(*September* 1984)

Philip Larkin 1922-1985

by Donald Hall

Unless there is a cache of poems secreted somewhere in Hull, which we may doubt, the poet Philip Larkin died before the man. As far as I know, his last poem was "Aubade," published in the *Times Literary Supplement* almost a decade ago. It begins:

> I work all day, and get half drunk at night.
> Waking at four to soundless dark, I stare.
> In time the curtain-edges will grow light.
> Till then I see what's really always there:
> Unresting death, a whole day nearer now,
> Making all thought impossible but how
> And where and when I shall myself die.

The fear of dying, daily companion of many, found its Homer, Dante, and Milton in Philip Larkin. His post-religious, almost Roman skepticism looks forward only to "total emptiness for ever, / The sure extinction that we travel to." As in his early "Church Going," his language acknowledges religious feeling without diluting skepticism, sentimentalizing loss, or asking for pity. Larkin is resolute, forthright, witty, and gloomy. This is the man who famously said that deprivation was for him what daffodils were for Wordsworth. Yet surely the results of this life, in the shape of his poems, are gifts, not deprivations.

The Less Deceived announced Philip Larkin in 1955. As a young man he had published *The North Ship,* poems lyrical and Yeatsian and not yet Larkinesque. The early work resembled other young Englishmen: neo-Romantic, even a bit *wet* . . . By the time I found him he had acquired Philip Larkin's voice. I heard him first on John Wain's BBC program, "New Soundings," in 1953—where I also first heard Kingsley Amis telling about *Lucky Jim.*

Larkin's quality was clear; it was also clear that something new was happening. Although *The Less Deceived* was a small-press book—published by George Hartley who ran the Marvell Press and edited *Listen,* the best literary magazine of its time—it was published with a list of subscribers which included almost all English poets under forty: Amis, Bergonzi, Boyars, Brownjohn, Conquest, Davie, Enright, Hamburger, Hill, Jennings, MacBeth, Murphy, Thwaite, Tomlinson, Wain. (Thom Gunn was in California; Ted Hughes was not yet Ted Hughes.) And there were dons: Bateson, Dobree, Dodsworth, Fraser, Kermode, Leishmann.

It was not long before Larkin became a popular poet in England, second only to Betjeman in public affection. When a good poet becomes popular there is always some silly reason as well as recognition of excellence. Dylan Thomas became a bestseller in this country—surely the obscurest poet ever to sell ten thousand copies—because tales of drunkenness and irreverence sold copies. With Robert Frost, the carefully cultivated rural manner—gussied up by the Luce publications until he resembled Scattergood Baines—sold copies and had little to do with the real man.

With Larkin and his English readers, the silliness which helped to make him popular was his genuine, uncultivated, sincere philistinism. In his prose he wrote disparagingly of painters who put two noses on one face and sculptors who carved holes through bodies; he lectured us on the *ugliness* of modernism, most especially the three P's: Pound, Picasso, and (Charlie) Parker. In the United States the terrorists of modernism have frightened the semi-educated middle class into accepting anything that carries the Avant-garde Seal of Approval. In England the middle classes are not so gullible; many remain secure in the conviction that Picasso is a fake, and that good painters can be defined as the ones who make horses that look like horses. When he made an anthology, Larkin's *Oxford Book of Twentieth Century English Verse* was a monument to modesty and amateurism: Sir John Squire and yards of doggerel. Doubtless it is the *worst* anthology of modern poetry, with the possible exception of Yeats's . . .

Larkin's poetry of course is another matter. There is nothing modest or amateur about "The Whitsun Weddings" or "Aubade." *The Less Deceived* was a superb volume, with three or four of Larkin's best poems and two dozen fine ones. Some are corny but splendidly achieved: "At Grass" is the best horse picture ever painted. Back in the mid-Fifties, the jocular and tough-minded "Toads" stood out. Gradually, the softer and more ruminative "Church Going" seems more to represent Larkin's best. In his second volume, *The Whitsun Weddings,* the title poem may be the finest moment in all his work. Characteristic in the place it is spoken from—a little to the side of life, watching, commenting—it is both empathetic and aloof, both superior and wistful. It ends:

> I thought of London spread out in the sun,
> Its postal districts packed like squares of wheat:
>
> There we were aimed. And as we raced across
>   Bright knots of rail
> Past standing Pullmans, walls of blackened
>   moss
> Came close, and it was nearly done, this frail
> Travelling coincidence; and what it held
> Stood ready to be loosed with all the power
> That being changed can give. We slowed
>   again,
> And as the tightened brakes took hold, there
>   swelled
> A sense of falling, like an arrow-shower
> Sent out of sight, somewhere becoming rain.

Look at the way sentences curl down the page. Who else among us has made such motions?

The answer, I think, is Robert Frost, but I do not suggest direct influence. If there is influence, Frost to Larkin, it comes by way of Edward Thomas, whom Frost instructed. Although Thomas Hardy is Larkin's master—the only earlier twentieth-century poet clearly superior (and Geoffrey Hill the only contemporary)—the comparison with Frost remains useful. Frost loved to play the English sentence across the English line, usually pausing to rhyme on the way, mimicking what he called "sentence sounds." These sentence sounds show themselves by phrase-pitch and perform a sophistication of syntax. At the end of "Mr. Bleaney," from *Whitsun Weddings,* we can see Larkin using the imitative gesture of syntax as well as Frost did it.

> But if he stood and watched the frigid wind
> Tousling the clouds, lay on the fusty bed
> Telling himself that this was home, and
>   grinned,
> And shivered, without shaking off the dread
>
> That how we live measures our own nature,
> And at his age having no more to show
> Than one hired box should make him pretty
>   sure
> He warranted no better, I don't know.

This awkward, difficult-to-say sentence mimics the reluctance of the mind to reach conclusion about its own worth or lack of worth. The muscular gestures of its hesitation express, by form and mimickry of grammar, the state of mind that the language describes. In this coincidence of manner and matter is a good portion of Larkin's genius.

But not only here. In an interview Larkin spoke about his reputation as a melancholy man, and protested that he thought he was rather funny, actually. True enough: "Sexual intercourse began / In nineteen-sixty-three / (Which was rather late for me)— / Between the end of the *Chatterly* ban / And the Beatles' first LP." But something besides humor redeems the gloom of Philip Larkin. His poetry is beautiful, which gives us deep and abiding pleasure, however melancholy a paraphrase may be. At the end of "Aubade," Larkin makes a metaphor, appropriately sinister, in a gorgeous pentameter line:

Meanwhile telephones crouch, getting ready
 to ring
In locked-up offices, and all the uncaring
Intricate rented world begins to rouse.
The sky is white as clay, with no sun.
Work has to be done.
Postmen like doctors go from house to house.

Doubtless the poem is *deprived* enough . . . but if you don't walk out of the theater humming the tune, you don't read poetry.

(*February* 1986)

Max Beerbohm and the law of levity

by Joseph Epstein

Max Beerbohm once claimed that there were fifteen hundred readers in England and another thousand in America who knew what he was about. Small enough numbers, one would have thought, but he claimed them with a faint air of boastfulness. When S. N. Behrman first visited Max Beerbohm at his home in Rapallo in the early 1950s, Beerbohm showed him a publisher's statement from the firm of Alfred A. Knopf, which had recently reissued a book of his essays. On the right-hand side of the statement was an unbroken column of zeros. "*There's* a publisher's statement!" he announced ("carolled" is the word Behrman uses). As a frequent sojourner in used-book shops, I can testify that Behrman's own book, *A Portrait of Max,* handsomely printed and lavishly illustrated though it is, and charmingly written into the bargain, is an almost inevitable inmate upon the dusty shelves in these shops. Beerbohm would doubtless have been cheered by this, too—evidence that both the life and work were quite unsaleable.

In the closing paragraph of a 1947 essay in celebration of Max Beerbohm's seventy-fifth birthday, Louis Kronenberger remarked, "How big Max's audience will be a generation, or a century, hence is something else again." A generation has now passed, and I think I know how big his audience is: fourteen hundred in England and eleven hundred in America. As for the size of his audience in 2047, my guess is that he will have thirteen hundred readers in England and twelve hundred in America—cultural progress in this colony is slow but steady. Yet all of these readers, I have no doubt, will be devoted. The taste for the writing of Max Beerbohm is a minority taste but a strong one.

If there were a job description for a Max Beerbohm reader, it would, I fear, be severely delimiting. To begin with, the Max Beerbohm reader must be a fairly bookish person, someone who knows a certain amount of literary history and has an appetite for the literary life, for Max Beerbohm, though not an omnivorous reader, was himself literary from his pate down to his spats. The Max Beerbohm reader must have an affection for language and be pleased at witnessing it on exhibit with an always playful but ultimately serious precision, for Beerbohm was, to use one of his own words, a "precisian." Along with having an affection for language, he must enjoy seeing it artfully deployed—he must, that is, adore style, for Beerbohm was one of those writers for whom, without style, there is no message or indeed much of anything else. The Beerbohm reader must take pleasure in irony, for irony, the art of saying one thing and meaning another, was at the center of much that Beerbohm wrote. Delicate, whimsical, sly, his was irony of a kind quick readers are likely to miss. (Test sentence: "To give an accurate account of that period," he wrote in an essay entitled "1880," "would need a far less brilliant pen than mine.") Finally, the

Max Beerbohm reader must share the comic view, which means that he can see the prospect for laughter in all but the most dire of human commerce, and especially not fail to see it in himself, for to take oneself altogether seriously, Beerbohm once averred, is to court insanity.

How might one best describe Max Beerbohm to someone who knows nothing about him? Well, for a start, one might imagine D. H. Lawrence. Picture the shagginess of Lawrence, his thick beard, his rough-cut clothes, his disdain for all the social and physical niceties. Recall his passionateness—his passion, so to say, for passion itself—his darkness, his gloom. Think back to his appeal to the primary instincts, his personal messianism, his refusal to deal with anything smaller than capital "D" Destiny. Do not neglect his humorlessness, his distaste for all that otherwise passed for being civilized, his blood theories and manifold roiling hatreds. Have you, then, D. H. Lawrence firmly in mind? Splendid. Now reverse all Lawrence's qualities and you will have a fair beginning notion of Max Beerbohm, who, after allowing that Lawrence was a man "of unquestionable genius," felt it necessary to add, "he never realized, don't you know—he never suspected that to be stark, staring mad is somewhat of a handicap to a writer."

To think of Max Beerbohm as D. H. Lawrence in reverse is a start but a start merely. He really was *sui generis.* George Bernard Shaw was on to something when, on May 2, 1898, in his last column as drama critic for the English *Saturday Review,* before turning the column over to Beerbohm, he wrote: "The younger generation is knocking at the door, and as I open it there steps sprightly in the incomparable Max." Beerbohm had to live with this epithet all his days, and once, writing to his first biographer, John Bohun Lynch, he mildly protested against it:

> Years ago, G.B.S., in a light-hearted moment, called me "the incomparable." Note that I am *not* incomparable. Compare me. Compare me as essayist (for instance) with other essayists. Point out how much less human I am than Lamb, how much less intellectual than Hazlitt, and what an ignoramous beside Belloc; and how Chesterton's high spirits and abundance shame me . . . . Apply the comparative method to me also as a caricaturist.

In this same letter Beerbohm, who was chary of having a biography written about him, especially while he still lived, added:

> My gifts are small. I've used them very well and discreetly, never straining them; and the result is that I've made a charming little reputation. But that reputation is a frail plant. Don't over-attend to it, gardener Lynch! Don't drench and deluge it! The contents of a quite *small* watering-can will be quite enough.

A point to be made about both these passages is that each is quite accurate. As an essayist, Beerbohm is less human than Lamb, less intellectual than Hazlitt, and so forth. He never did strain his gifts; he did use them well and discreetly; he had in his lifetime, as he has now, precisely a charming little reputation. Frail plant though his reputation may be, the same cannot be said of his talent; it was a delicate flower, no doubt, yet a hardy one. But let us turn now to examine it at its seedling stage.

Max Beerbohm's father was a man born in Memel, in Baltic Germany, of Dutch and German and Lithuanian extraction, who had settled in London at the age of twenty-three and had married an English woman with whom he had three sons and a daughter. He made a modest success as a grain merchant. When his first wife died, he married her sister, with whom he had three more children, two daughters and a final child, a son, Max. His father was sixty-one when Max was born, his mother in her forties. The Beerbohms' was by all accounts a happy household and a comfortable one—so comfortable for Max that he never left it until his marriage, in his late thirties, to the American actress Florence Kahn. As one would expect from a man with a subtle sense of humor, Max Beerbohm had a strong antipathy to the clichés of conventional psychology, and, given the fact that he adored his parents and his brothers and sisters, he wondered if he would one day be thought victim of an Oedipus complex. After mentioning this to S. N. Behrman, he paused, then said: "They were a tense and peculiar family, the Oedipuses, weren't they?"

Max was in awe of his two half brothers, Herbert and Julius. Herbert was an actor and theatrical manager, and was known professionally as Herbert Beerbohm Tree. He was large, red-haired, and robust, with a madcap sense of humor. (Once, when a man walked past him groaning under a grandfather clock he was carting on his back, Herbert announced, "My good fellow, why not carry a watch?") Julius was an unflappable dandy, a gambler with a taste for disastrous financial schemes, whom Max remembered once polishing a translation from Heine while downstairs in his house mover's men were taking away his furniture. Of his brothers Beerbohm wrote: "Herbert was (then and always) a hero to me. But, let me add, Julius was a god."

His older brothers were adult and long out of the house when Max Beerbohm was a boy. The household he grew up in was consequently a feminine one. In it the young Max, a precocious and precise child, was the cynosure. In his biography, *Max,* David Cecil makes the interesting point that Max was not a mother's boy but what "can be described as a sister's boy." Not a bad thing to be, a sister's boy, for it gives one a certain ease in dealing with females; a receptivity to the gentler aspects of culture, over which women have traditionally presided; and a corresponding distance from the brutishness of a steady fare of youthful male companionship. In Max Beerbohm's instance, the sister in question was Dora, who was five years older than he and a child with a talent for drawing and decorative art and a sweet selflessness that later led her to become a postulant of the Anglican Order of Sisters of Mercy. It was in large part from Dora, and within the walls of his family home, that Max Beerbohm learned the rudiments of the art of pleasing—an art that, as he grew older, he would eventually buff to a high sheen of perfection.

So adept was Max Beerbohm at this art of pleasing that he is perhaps the only writer of the past hundred years to go through the English school system without being spiritually scathed. Accounts of his school days present no tales of his being bullied, as was E. M. Forster at the Tonbridge School, or of him as the victim of a totalitarian monstrosity in miniature, as Orwell makes out the school he calls St. Cyprians to be. As a schoolboy, Beerbohm loved Latin and was clever at drawing and had no interest in games. Charterhouse, the public school to which he was sent at age thirteen, was not much to his taste, but he survived it by reading Thackeray, drawing charming caricatures of the masters, and when necessary withdrawing into himself. At Charterhouse he learned, as he later put it, "the knack of understanding my fellow-creatures, of living in amity with them and not being rubbed the wrong way by their faults, and not rubbing them the wrong way with mine." There was never a trace of the rebel in him; even as a young boy he was too detached for rebellion or even for serious participation in school activities. He was an onlooker, more comfortable on the sidelines, someone who finds the spectacle of life rather more interesting than life itself. He was, in two words, "an artist."

Along with his other gifts, Max Beerbohm had the gift of an equanimous temperament. He was one of those lucky people to whom life never seemed to present itself as a struggle. He appears never to have felt the need to dominate; envy was an emotion unknown to him. It was said that he never had an adolescence but instead went directly from childhood to young manhood. When he arrived, at nineteen, at Merton College, Oxford, he seems to have been fully formed. He was self-contained, self-controlled, self-sufficient. His career at the university was of the kind Evelyn Waugh wished he had had: effortless, elegant, quietly dazzling.

Shortly after arriving at Oxford, at Ryman's to purchase some engravings for his room, the young Beerbohm saw Walter Pater—"a small rock-faced man, whose top-hat and gloves of *bright* dog-skin struck one of the many discords in that little city of learning or laughter"—and judged him to be coarse. While an undergraduate he published caricatures in some of London's smartest journals. He placed an essay, a *succès de scandale* entitled "In Defense of Cosmetics," in the first issue of that smartest of all smart literary magazines, *The Yellow Book.* Oscar Wilde announced that he had a prose style "like a silver dagger." A self-declared dandy, Beerbohm was famous for his clothes, his wit, his sangfroid. When the artist Will Rothenstein, who was to become his lifelong friend, arrived at Oxford to execute portraits of the leading figures at the university, Beerbohm was among his choice of subjects. He did not complete his last year at Oxford, for the life of literature and art beckoned too seductively for him to remain a student. He needed a degree about as much as the Pope needs a bowling trophy.

Whom the gods would destroy, they first grant early success. Max Beerbohm, however, was able to elude the gods. He did so through precise knowledge of his own limitations and a sense of humor about himself. At twenty-four he published his first book, a slender volume of seven essays—with a bibliography appended that included a letter to the editor of the school paper at Charterhouse and a schoolboy Latin exercise—which he entitled *The Works of Max Beerbohm.* (His next two volumes of essays he entitled *More* and *Yet Again.*) In the essays of this first little book his entire artistic program was adumbrated. In "Dandies and Dandies" he set out the aesthetic that was to govern his own creation. Ostensibly writing about Beau Brummell, he noted: "All delicate spirits, to whatever art they turn, even if they turn to no art, assume an oblique attitude toward life." Of Brummell specifically, but of himself more generally, he wrote: "Like the single-minded artist that he was, he turned full and square towards his art and looked life straight in the face out of the corners of his eyes," which is as exact a formulation of the method of the ironist as one is likely to find. From the figure of the dandy, too, may be extrapolated Beerbohm's own yearning, in his art, for perfection in detail in all things. Like Brummell yet again (and Beerbohm with him), the dandy is "ever most economical, most scrupulous of means." There remains only to add that the dandy, like the artist, strives to please chiefly himself. What we have here is the full prescription for Max Beerbohm's art, both as a prose writer and as a caricaturist.

In an essay entitled "Diminuendo," written when Beerbohm was all of twenty-three, he predicted his own early retirement from the hugger-mugger of London for the life of contemplation. (Was this prediction meant to be ironic? "I wish," he once wrote, "I could cure myself of the habit of speaking ironically; I should so like to express myself in a quite straightforward manner.") "What uproar!" he announces in this essay. "Surely I could have no part in modern life." Here he avers that the life of action has no charm for him. It is instead only "the things one has not done, the faces or places one has not seen, or seen but darkly, that have charm." He imagines his retirement spent in some backwater English village, where he will borrow his neighbor's copy of *The Times.* He declares himself already a back number. "I belong to the Beardsley period," he writes, which was of course riding its crest at the very moment he indited the sentence. He claims he will stop writing; he is ready to stand aside without regret. The essay closes on the following absolutely accurate predictive sentences: "For to be outmoded is to be a classic, if one has written well. I have acceded to the hierarchy of good scribes and rather like my niche."

Although he lived six decades beyond the 1890s, although all of his best work was done much later than the Nineties, Max Beerbohm became—and seemed to wish to become—indissolubly linked to that decade. "I am," he once remarked, "what is known as 'an interesting link to the past.'" But then he himself forged that link and rather insisted upon it. The Nineties was the period of his artistic formation, the period of Oscar Wilde and Aubrey Beardsley, Henry James and Walter Sickert, a time when Meredith was still walking the earth and Thomas Hardy and Whistler and Shaw. It was the era of the aesthete—and an aesthete Max Beerbohm ever was. In later life he returned to draw figures from the Nineties over and over; his literary tastes were rooted in the decade as well, causing him to overrate some writers for their stylishness (Lytton Strachey, in my opinion, for one) and to be antipathetic to all art not grounded in the beautiful. One of his many complaints against Shaw was the latter's blindness to beauty. Of Shaw's panning *The Importance of Being Earnest,* Beerbohm once remarked, "Perhaps while the play was going on he was improving his theory of rent."

If Max Beerbohm was an aesthete, he was an aesthete with a serious difference. The difference was that, unlike almost every other aesthete, from Flaubert to Pater to Pound, his aestheticism was never permitted to override his common sense. S. N. Behrman well says that "the animating spirit of all Max's criticism—as, indeed, of all his writing—is a cultivated common sense." The emphasis needs to be placed on the adjective "cultivated," for his common sense was informed by a true artistic sensibility. He once said of Trollope that he "reminds us that sanity need not be philistine." Of him it can be said that he reminds us that one's adoration of art need not extend to lunacy.

It was during the Nineties, which was his own twenties, that Max Beerbohm began to build his reputation. His was the reputation of a charmer, a literary and artistic lapidarian. He worked small and took pride in doing so. "How many charming talents have been spoiled," he wrote, "by the instilled desire to do 'important' work! Some people are born to lift heavy weights. Some are born to juggle with golden balls." Max Beerbohm was, obviously, among the jugglers.

The golden balls he kept in the air were those of the essayist, comic draughtsman, and elegant young man about town. His friends were Aubrey Beardsley, Will Rothenstein, and Reggie Turner. Turner, whom Beerbohm knew from undergraduate days at Merton College, was the wealthy illegitimate son of Lord Burnham, the press lord; he was a homosexual, a failed novelist, and was said by Somerset Maugham to be the most amusing man he had ever known. Of his own novels Turner once said: "Other people's first editions are rare. With me it's the second editions that are rare; in fact they don't exist." Max Beerbohm simultaneously kept up a vigorous social round in the highest reaches of English society; as a charming and socially presentable young man, he frequently dined among the Balfours and Asquiths and Churchills, where he would on occasion meet Henry James, whom he described as looking "like a Russian Grand Duke of the better type." James was nearly thirty years older than he, but paid him the compliment of treating him as an equal. David Cecil tells the story of James and Beerbohm standing together at one such dinner party when a woman came up to declare that they looked very distinguished. "We *are* distinguished," Henry James replied. "But you need not look so terribly so," she responded. "We are shameless, shameless!" said Henry James.

Living at home, earning a few pounds for an essay here, a caricature there, Max Beerbohm never held a serious job until 1898, when he was asked to become drama critic of the *Saturday Review.* He jumped at the opportunity—backwards. He had the gravest doubts about it, but agreed to take it chiefly because, his father having died, he thought the additional money would be useful at home. But he began on a note of disclaimer: his first column was entitled, "Why I Ought Not to Have Become a Dramatic Critic." He was not, as he noted in that column, stagestruck. He was happy among pictures, had an unenlightened but real love for music, cared about literature most of all and could talk about it intelligently. Having grown up as the brother of Herbert Beerbohm Tree, he explains, he has never been able to associate the theater with glamour but instead only with "the conclusion to a dinner or the prelude to a supper." He has little interest in branching off, as his predecessor G. B. S. did, into "discussions of ethical, theological or political questions," about which he claims to be "singularly ill-informed." Worse, his is a satiric temperament, which makes him amusing when laughing at any one but deadly dull when praising. He is sure that having to write this column is "quite likely to spoil and exhaust such talent as I might otherwise be exercising in literary art." His one advantage is that, having written these columns, at least he will not be compelled to read them. Talk about blowing one's own trumpet. Has anyone ever organized for himself a more extraordinary fanfarade?

His disclaimers were not made in false modesty; they were, once again, quite accurate. Although Max Beerbohm stayed on as drama critic for the *Saturday Review* for fully twelve years, he is not among that very small group of very special drama critics, a group that includes Hazlitt, Shaw, James Agate, and, in our own day, the young Kenneth Tynan. He was not sufficiently febrile; the missionary spirit did not exist in him; he was temperamentally too cool. He asked that a play be entertaining, convincingly coherent, and intelligent—and in the theater, then as now, that was way too much to ask. As might be expected, he was good at deflation: amusing about the hypocrisy of English audiences, imprisoned in linguistic ignorance, watching Signora Duse play *Hedda Gabler* in Italian; riotously funny about the mad unreality of Sarah Bernhardt's memoirs; penetrating on Shaw "using art merely as a means of making people listen to him." None of his reviews is inept; most have felicitous touches, charming asides, digressions from which one wishes he would never return to the business at hand. But for the vast most part his drama criticisms grow boring when he begins to discuss the play under review—which is another way of saying that Max Beerbohm was an essayist and not a critic.

Which, in turn, is another way of saying that Max Beerbohm was above all else an artist. In a tribute to the music hall comedian Dan Leno, he wrote: "In every art personality is the paramount thing, and without it artistry goes for little." He went on to say that especially was this so in the art of acting, but I would assert that it is no less so in the art of the essay. Think of a significant essayist and you think of the personality he conveys: the gentle Charles Lamb, the passionate William Hazlitt, the gloomy George Orwell. Max Beerbohm's artistic personality is not so readily captured in a lone epithet. It is complex and elusive, yet distinct for all that. It is the personality of the slightly world-weary spectator, sitting along the sideline, a cigarette in hand, a man far from indifferent to worldly things but not quite caught up in them either; a man of considerable sophistication who has yet retained a certain oddly childish mischievousness; charming but not hotly intimate; ready to admit his own flaws but too exquisitely tactful to point out yours; yet for all his charm, his admitted naïveté, his penchant for fun, decidedly not someone over whose eyes you can ever for a moment hope to pull the wool (make that, in Beerbohm's case, cashmere).

Max Beerbohm was too much the conscious artist not to be aware of the impression his own work conveyed, or of the difficulties that personality in art could make. Cyril Connolly, for example, regarded Max Beerbohm as "a psychological case, a supreme egotist masquerading as a detached observer." Beerbohm once put his case in a letter to his wife:

> I am not thinking that "I am I" and must be interesting to everyone else. I am nothing more than I—a detached and puzzled spectator—detached, yet knowing more about myself than any other subject, and offering myself humbly for the inspection of others. I think there is a difference between this and egotism.

Was this personality a fake, a fraud, a made thing? Beerbohm was of the generation of Wilde and Yeats, a generation that believed in masks. He wrote a longish fairy tale, *The Happy Hypocrite,* about the subject of masks. In it a Regency rake named Lord George Hell sets out to seduce the pure Miss Jenny Mere. In aid of this conquest he wears a mask—an actual mask—that lends him a look of goodness and virtue. So long does he wear the mask, so long does he try to live up to it, that at the book's close, when he is inevitably unmasked, his real face has changed, and "line for line, feature for feature," his own true face becomes the saintly face of the mask he had been wearing. The tale's final paragraph reads:

> So he took her in his arms, as though she had been a little child, and kissed her with his own lips. She put her arms around his neck, and he was happier than he had ever been. They were alone in the garden now. Nor lay the mask any longer upon the lawn, for the sun had melted it.

The moral is not in the least murky: the mask, worn long enough, becomes the man. I suppose it can be said that Max Beerbohm created his own mask. Unlike so many others, he set to work on it young and perfected it early. Most of us would like to create a mask of our own, which would represent us at our own highest self-valuation. The modern invocation to "be oneself" implies one's having a suitable self to be. Many of us, not finding that self suitable, try masks but cannot quite bring them off: the eyebrows won't stay straight, the mustache keeps lapsing into the mouth, the nose permits no breath. It is a botch, which Beerbohm's never was. In him the mask became the man, and the man and mask became, as he signed his caricatures and as devoted readers tend to think of him, Max. It is as Max that I should like to refer to him for the remainder of this essay.

The year 1910 was the turning point in Max's life. It was the year he quit his job as drama critic for the *Saturday Review,* which he had long before found onerous in the extreme. As a prose writer he was a perfectionist—he had always discovered writing to be much more difficult for him than drawing—and his weekly deadlines did not permit of the polish perfection requires. He wrote his weekly *Saturday Review* piece on Thursdays; even decades later he would wake on a Thursday morning with a clutch at his heart in momentary fear about having to set aside the day to write his criticism. If the pressure of these deadlines was hell, dispensing with them altogether was nearly heaven. That same year, at thirty-eight, he married the actress Florence Kahn, and made his plan to move, permanently, to Rapallo.

A man's marriage is perhaps the appropriate place to put to rest the question of whether or not he was a homosexual. The question only arises because Malcolm Muggeridge raised it some years ago in an essay entitled "The Legend of Max." Not that Muggeridge questioned it; in his essay he asserted it: "Beerbohm, it seems to me to emerge, was in panic flight through most of his life from two things—his Jewishness and his homosexuality." It emerges *for* Muggeridge, though no evidence for either assertion emerges *from* Muggeridge. Even from the old Mugger himself, this is pretty wild stuff.

As for the claim that Max was Jewish, Muggeridge contends he once heard this from a man who once heard it from Herbert Beerbohm Tree. Yet odd, does it not seem, that Max, a man supposedly ashamed of being Jewish, would take to wife a woman, Florence Kahn, who was herself Jewish? The claim for Max's homosexuality is made on even shakier grounds; it is based wholly on association—specifically, on Max's connection with the Wilde-Beardsley circle in the Nineties. That Max while an undergraduate had an infatuation with a music hall performer named Cissy Loftus is not allowed to stand in the way. Nor is the fact that he was later engaged to an actress in his brother's theatrical company, and after that had a love affair with yet another actress. Odd, too, that a man in panic flight from his homosexuality would choose to flee with a wife in tow. Does Malcolm Muggeridge, now that he is an earnest Christian, still believe what he wrote about Max? If he does, I hope Saint Peter will one day ask him to supply more serious evidence for his assertions—will make such evidence, in fact, an unwaivable requirement for his entrance to heaven.

In the event, Max's departure from London for Rapallo proved a most cunning move. "When a man is tired of London, he is tired of life," Samuel Johnson wrote, "for there is in London all that life can afford." But Max was not a man to be put off by a Dr. Johnson quotation; nor, as we shall see, a man to be overly impressed even by Dr. Johnson. Besides, a Londoner born, he really had had all that London could afford in the way of fame, sociability, urbane pleasures. Italy was then so much less expensive than London and would allow him to work at his art at the leisurely pace it required. The Beerbohms acquired a small house in the town of Rapallo, long a haunt of English Italophiles; the house overlooked the Gulf of Genoa and was called the Villino Chiaro. In this small house, working in a small study on the terrace, Max produced some of his best work: the fantasy novel *Zuleika Dobson,*[1] the stories of *Seven Men,* the essays in *And Even Now* and other books, and drawings too numerous to catalogue.

What is of especial interest is how little Max seemed to need the outside world. Living frugally, alone with his wife and a single servant, each day he would suit up, pop a straw boater upon his exceedingly round head, and repair to his terrace overlooking the Gulf of Genoa. From the terraces of nearby villas he was occasionally sighted, alone, laughing, doubtless at some superior joke, or twist of language, or human oddity that occurred to him in his endless ruminations upon the past. He never bothered to learn Italian; he rarely went into the town of Rapallo; he had no interest in touring Italy. In time he became an object of intellectual tourism himself, receiving guests who had just come from visiting Bernard Berenson at I Tatti and would afterward call upon Somerset Maugham at Villa Mauresque. He returned to London from time to time to help mount exhibitions of his drawings (he took a serious interest in all the details having to do with his own work), and he and his wife returned to live in England during the two world wars. But for the rest, from 1910 to 1956, he lived for all intents and purposes imprisoned in Villino Chiaro and utterly free in his own imagination.

Standing on that terrace for the better part of forty years, the sun above, the blue Gulf of Genoa before him, of what did he think? Of the past, doubtless, but the past, one imagines, in very small pieces: the chin of Kipling, the back of Shaw's neck, the beard of Rossetti. From there perhaps he strode to his study on the terrace and redrew these figures from his own past that he had drawn so many times before. "I can draw caricatures at any moment," he once wrote to his wife, "and how I rejoice in them. *They* are what I was put into the world to do." A great many others have rejoiced in them as well, except perhaps those who were their subjects. Edmund Gosse, in a letter to Logan Pearsall Smith, noted that Max had done a caricature of him and, as with most of Max's subjects, he was not likely to appreciate it. "We don't like it, and you won't like it, but must pretend, as we all do, that you like it. You can console yourself, at any rate, with the thought that it will give enormous pleasure to your friends."

Charming Max's caricatures are, but harmless fun they aren't. He claimed he was a Jekyll as a writer but as a caricaturist a true Hyde, and once referred to himself as "a ruthless monstrifier of men." His own elegant definition of a caricature cannot be improved upon: "The most perfect caricature is that which, on a small surface, with the simplest means, most accurately exaggerates, to the highest point, the peculi-

1 Yale University Press has just brought out a new edition of *Zuleika Dobson* featuring Beerbohm's own illustrations: *The Illustrated Zuleika Dobson,* 350 pages, $19.95.

arities of a human being, at his most characteristic moment, in the most beautiful manner." Yet a Max caricature is never a delineation of physical peculiarities merely, but instead uses these peculiarities to penetrate his subject's personality. The personality caught will be found to be comic in its pretensions, or vulgarity, or stupidity, or obtuseness. He loved, too, to play with comic incongruity. My own favorite of his caricatures in this line comes from the book *Rossetti and His Circle* and is entitled "Mr. Morley of Blackburn, on An Afternoon in The Spring of '69, Introduces Mr. John Stuart Mill." In this drawing a willowy and bloodless John Stuart Mill, hat in one hand, a little leather bag containing galley proofs in the other, looks off into the distance as a small, sharp-nosed John Morley is speaking to a highly dubious looking Rossetti, who fingers his goatee; in the background hangs a Rossetti portrait of an extremely sensual pre-Raphaelite woman. The lengthy and perfect caption reads:

> "It has recently," he says, "occurred to Mr. Mill that in his lifelong endeavor to catch and keep the ear of the nation he has been hampered by a certain deficiency in—well, in warmth, in colour, in rich charm. I have told him that this deficiency (I do not regard it as a defect) might possibly be remedied by *you*. Mr. Mill has in the press, at this moment, a new work, entitled 'The Subjection of Women.' From my slight acquaintance with you, and from all that I have seen and heard of your work, I gather that women greatly interest you, and I have no doubt that you are incensed at their subjection. Mr. Mill has brought his proof-sheets with him. He will read them to you. I believe, and he takes my word for it, that a series of illustrative paintings by you would," etc. etc.

Max's caricatures were always prettily done. Although he drew them easily, even rapturously, he nonetheless took great pains in perfecting them. What makes them special is that in his drawings he joined caricature and cartoon. Not only are his drawings salient but so are the situations in which he places his subjects. As John Felstiner has remarked: "Beerbohm's innovation, one that only he was capable of making, was to bring the dynamics of parody into caricature." This invests his caricatures with not only the broad truth of satire but the more delicate truth of irony. It also frees them from the charge to which caricature is most liable, that of crudity, and lends them a weight in insight to which no other caricaturist can lay claim. "It is this immediate clarity of insight, free from all malice or prejudice, which makes Max superior to most caricaturists, even to Daumier," W. H. Auden wrote. "Even his most devasting portraits never strike one as unjust; one never feels that for personal or ideological reasons he had decided to uglify his victim before he looked at him."

Although Max never ceased to draw, later in life his caricatures seemed to lose their merry malice. "I seem to have lost my gift for dispraise," he told S. N. Behrman. "Pity crept in." But not everywhere. Max never lost his distaste for pretension, and for no one did he feel this distaste more sharply than for those men whom the world regarded as geniuses. Something there was about extravagantly large talent that set Max off, that made him wish to find its weakness, to diminish it, to bring it down to size. Perhaps it was the narcissism of genius; perhaps its confidence in its own primacy; perhaps its disregard for everything smaller than itself. Whatever it was, no genius ever quite passed muster with Max.

E. M. Forster once remarked that Goethe was the only genius who wasn't stupid. Max would probably have assented, if Forster would agree to remove Goethe from his generalization. In his essay "Quia Imperfectum" Max ponders why an obscure painter named Wilhelm Tischbein never completed a portrait of Goethe that he worked sedulously to persuade Goethe to sit for. Later in the essay, he conjectures that Tischbein was infatuated with an English woman in Naples, which caused him to break off a number of meetings with Goethe, thus permanently delaying completion of the portrait. Earlier, though, he suggests that Goethe may have "irked" Tischbein. But it is obvious that it is Max whom Goethe irks. It is Goethe's perfection that gets to him, all-embracing Goethe, who, as Max writes, "was never injudicious, never lazy, always in his best form—and always in love with some lady or another just so much as was good for the development of his soul and his art, but never by more than that by a tittle." Or, as he puts it earlier, "a man whose career was glorious without intermission, decade after decade, does sorely try our patience." He certainly tries Max's patience, and throughout this essay Max subtly but relentlessly chips away at the marmoreal German genius.

It is the self-importance of geniuses, their absolute confidence in their own value, that Max cannot abide. It is the chinks in their personality that he prefers to emphasize and, in so emphasizing, to magnify. In his essay "Hosts and Guests," he mentions what a miserable guest Dante was in exile, forever complaining about the conditions he met with in the houses in which he stayed; and Max adds that Dante would probably have been a worse host "had it ever occurred to him to entertain any one or anything except a deep regard for Beatrice." His animus extends even to that most congenial of geniuses, Samuel Johnson. In a brief essay entitled "'A Clergyman,'" Max recounts a brief but definitive put-down of an obscure fellow whom Boswell, in his *Life of Johnson,* refers to only as "a clergyman." The scene for this little devastation is set just before dinner at Thrale Hall. Boswell, interrogatory as ever, is questioning Johnson about the great sermonizers of the day, when the following exchange ensues:

> A CLERGYMAN, whose name I do not recollect: Were not Dodd's sermons addressed to the passions? JOHNSON: They were nothing, Sir, be they addressed to what they may.

Slam! That is it: The clergyman has popped up and been shot down by the cannon of Johnson's confidence. He is never heard from again; his name isn't even recollected; he is target practice for genius. Max writes: "My heart goes out to the poor dear clergyman exclusively." Max then goes on to recount how, as he imagines it, the clergyman never recovers from this blow, the paw of a lion flicking a mouse, and that, as a result of it, he dies young, never to have known a pleasing moment for the remainder of his days. "I like to think," Max ends the essay, "that he died forgiving Dr. Johnson."

Max himself was a good deal less forgiving of the geniuses of his own day. Something in strength there was that made him search out its weakness. He was appalled by the bullyboy in Kipling and detested the violence in his writing. He recognized that Ibsen was a genius but could never forgive him his humorlessness. Of William Morris he wrote: "Of course he was a wonderful all-round man but the act of walking round him has always tired me." He ridiculed the wildness and wooliness of the Russian writers, who were then being translated into English by the Garnetts, in his comic piece "Kolniyatsch," a name deriving from the English lunatic asylum Colney Hatch. Antipathy was the strongest emotion he felt toward Yeats: "Geniuses are generally asinine," he noted, "but his particular asinineness bores me and antagonizes me . . . ." As for Bertrand Russell, of him Max remarked: "It is Bertrand Russell's saving grace that he isn't a woman. As a woman he would have been intolerable." Apropos of T. E. Lawrence's wretched translation of *The Odyssey,* he said: "I would rather *not* have been that translator than have driven the Turks out of Arabia." It was the absence of subtlety he deplored in Shaw—"the best brain in England but no beauty except that of an engine"—and his unwavering self-confidence that caused him to be a bad influence "even on himself." When his secretary told Max that he would have liked meeting Sir Isaac Newton, he replied, "I would have taught him the Law of Levity."

The one genius of his time for whom Max retained reverence was Henry James. Not that this reverence was unmixed with comedy. He saw the humor both in and about Henry James. He drew at least six caricatures of James. In one James is doubled over, as if in great pain, and the caption reads, "Mr. Henry James in the act of parturiating a sentence." In another James, his all-seeing eyes bulging beneath his domed forehead, is kneeling outside a hotel room door, outside of which are a pair of male and a pair of female shoes, his ear to the keyhole. The caricature carries no caption, but if it did it would clearly read, "Mr. Henry James learns about sex." (Max waited to publish this caricature until after James's death.) And of course his parody of James, "The Mote in the Middle Distance," is unsurpassed—so good that even James delighted in it.

But the comedy that James occasioned in Max did not lessen his regard for the writer he once described in a poem as "indefatigable alchemist." David Cecil writes, persuasively, that "Henry James was the high priest of Max's chosen and professed faith." Both writers were moral aesthetes, and, as Cecil nicely puts it, "Max's spiritual history may be described as a journey from the crude aestheticism preached by Oscar Wilde to the finer aestheticism—moral as well as literary—manifested in Henry James." Max Beerbohm's favorite line from James reads: "Be generous and delicate and pursue the prize." In New English translation this means: Keep your sympathy, keep your subtlety, and keep the ambition always to write as well as possible. Although Max remained critical of James on small points—he once compared James's penchant for revising his early work in the style of his later phase to "patching pale gray silk with snippets of very dark thick brown velvet"—it was to James, at the close of Max's life, that he returned again and again for replenishment of the ideal of the beauty and moral vision of art.

Does the august phrase "moral vision" seem too high-flown to apply to Max Beerbohm himself? It was Henry James who, in a tribute to Turgenev, said that the great question about any writer is, "How does he feel about life? What in the last analysis is his philosophy?" The word "philosophy" and the name "Max Beerbohm" seem to want to fly apart. In his essay "Laughter," Max allowed that he might have a certain mellow wisdom, but went on to say, "I suffer from a strong suspicion that things in general cannot be accounted for through any formula or set of formulae, and that any one philosophy, howsoever new, is no better than another. That is in itself a sort of philosophy, and I suspect it accordingly; but it has for me the merit of being the only one I can make head or tail of." I believe that in this anti-philosophy a philosophy can nonetheless be found; it is the philosophy held in common by nearly all the great essayists.

To be an essayist is to divest oneself of the belief in a general set or system of ideas. All the great essayists, from Montaigne through Hazlitt to Beerbohm to Mencken through Orwell are not so much anti-philosophical as a-philosophical. (Orwell, true, claimed to be a socialist, but he is never less convincing than when making that claim.) None is notably religious. The very form of the essay—discursive, tentative, enmeshed in the particular—seems to imply that, to life's great questions, there probably are no answers, only hints, shadows, fleeting moments of elucidation. Mencken once put it straight out, announcing that no one knows who created the universe, or what intentions lie behind natural laws, or why sin and suffering were sent into the world, and maintained that anyone who claimed to know the answers to these questions was a con man. The essayist is by nature a skeptic: in Montaigne's case, a truly philosophical skeptic; in Hazlitt's and Orwell's cases, passionate skeptics; in Mencken's and Beerbohm's cases, laughing skeptics.

Max Beerbohm's skepticism grew not only out of the forms in which he worked but out of the methods he applied to those forms. He was a past master at parody; his book *A Christmas Garland* is prized by all who adore parody. Yet isn't parody, despite the parodist's insistence that *on se moque ce qu'on aime,* a criticism of (and skepticism about) excess in style, joined, it is true, to a love of idiosyncrasy? He had the lightest loveliest ironic touch, yet isn't irony also the perfect medium for the skeptic—irony whose underlying assumption is that nothing is as it seems and hence that nothing may be taken at face value? The reason for Max Beerbohm's antipathy to genius is, I believe, genius's own antipathy to moderation and irony. Genius confidently knows what it knows; the skeptic knows that what genius is so confident it knows probably is wrong or not worth knowing. The fox nips at the hedgehog.

Yet it would be a mistake to leave the impression that Max Beerbohm was chiefly a nipper. While he is a writer who stressed limitation, his range as an essayist is surprisingly wide and he often struck surprisingly deep. His best single book of essays, which was also his final book of essays, is *And Even Now*. It displays his talent in its full flower. Some of these essays are built around a comic conceit ("How Shall I Word It?," "Kolniyatsch," "Hosts and Guests"), some are reminiscential ("A Relic," "No. 2 The Pines," "William and Mary"), and some are made sheerly out of reflection ignited by a minor incident or curious phenomenon.

In the latter class is a little essay entitled "Something Defeasible." It is about Max watching a small boy taking great pains to build a cottage out of sand at the seashore. Max exchanges a few sentences with the laconic young artist, then returns to his newspaper, about which he remarks (the year is 1919), "During the War one felt it a duty to know the worst before breakfast; now that the English polity is threatened merely from within one is apt to dally . . . ." (Quite a "merely"; Max won't permit speed-reading.) He comments on the changes within England; these have mostly to do with the slow destruction of English life as he knew it and loved it as a boy and young man. Meanwhile the sea is rolling in on the boy's sand cottage. Is the boy sad at the destruction of what he had worked so painstakingly to build? Quite the reverse:

> His face had flushed bright, and now, as the garden walls crumbled, and the paths and lawns were mingled by the waters' influence and confluence, and the walls of the cottage itself began to totter, and the gables sank, all, all was swallowed, his leaps were so high in air that they recalled to my memory those of a strange religious sect which once visited London; and the glare of his eyes was less indicative of a dreamer than of a triumphant fiend.

This is the first startling turn in the essay. The next comes in the sentence that follows it, which reads: "I myself was conscious of a certain wild enthusiasm within me." Yet it is "the boy's own enthusiasm that made me feel, as never before, how deep-rooted in the human heart the love of destruction, of mere destruction, is." Thinking back upon the destruction of England, he adds, "but I waived the question coming from that hypothesis, and other questions that would have followed; for I wished to be happy while I might."

So dark a note is far from the characteristic note in the artist whom Louis Kronenberger once called "The Perfect Trifler." Knowing that that note, too, played in Max Beerbohm's head makes the many lovely trifles he contrived all the more delightful, even dear, and their perfection all the more impressive. Max looked into the dark and, without underestimating its density by one jot, laughed, and his laughter has brought laughter to those of us who have discovered his splendor as an artist so that we, too, can be happy while we might.

(*September* 1985)

New tales for old wives

by Gloria G. Fromm

In the early, almost mythical, 1960s, Charlotte Payne-Townshend, the wife of George Bernard Shaw, was the subject of a thoroughly informative biography that managed to justify its existence while making only modest claims for Mrs. G. B. S.[1] Although some of the questions that it raised had their expected Freudian ring (What did she learn from her parents' unhappy marriage? Was there sex between the Shaws?), they were handled with care and delicacy, out of deference—one presumes—to the famous man as well as to the limits of then current knowledge. Since Charlotte Payne-Townshend had not herself done anything much more noteworthy than marry the skittish Shaw, there were no real surprises in *Mrs. G. B. S.,* except perhaps that Shaw's wife for nearly half a century seemed less recoverable than one would have thought. Janet Dunbar's vivid portrait of the early years of a restless, intelligent young woman faded after the marriage, as if to illustrate how unlikely it was that anyone could stand out in relation to G. B. S. himself.

That Shaw's wife did stand up to him is quite evident, nonetheless, and to some extent at least she followed her own non-Shavian interests. Like a number of others in the Twenties and Thirties with longings for the infinite, she came under the brief spell of the Russian philosopher Ouspensky, whose best-known work claimed to have found the key to the enigmas of the world, a claim that might have struck Mrs. Shaw as a welcome challenge to the omniscience at home. In any case, she had money of her own as well as cosmic yearnings, and apparently went out of her way to satisfy them. It is not clear how much success she had.

What does come through most clearly in this treatment of the Shaws is Dunbar's rueful recognition that, no matter how you twist and turn them, the proportions don't change: "Mrs. G. B. S." says it all. Once the marriage took place, Charlotte Payne-Townshend's identity was more or less fixed for the rest of her life, and neither she nor her biographer seemed unduly troubled by it. In her old age, moreover, bedridden by a crippling form of lumbago from which she was virtually doubled up, an increasingly difficult Charlotte Shaw was patiently tended by her equally old but still upright husband. One comes away, finally, with the image of a woman who may have been bent by wifehood but who was certainly not broken.

Since the days of *Mrs. G. B. S.,* women and biography have entered into a dramatic new relationship, significantly altering the presentation of great men's wives and very often of the great men themselves. Janet Dunbar's disposition toward accommodation and compromise has been gradually displaced by antagonism and assertiveness, as unsung wives, deprived wives, maligned wives become increasingly the subjects of current polemical

1 *Mrs. G. B. S.: A Portrait,* by Janet Dunbar, was published by Harper & Row in 1963.

biography. If most wives were traditionally ignored (or barely mentioned) in books about their husbands, then the obvious remedy was to give them more space and at the same time to fix the blame for the long-standing neglect where it belonged—not on the women, by any means. And while the iron was hot, a few deserving *sisters* of famous men could be taken care of as well. Lest this seem too harsh and premature an abstraction of what has happened during the last twenty years, a somewhat concrete sampling might be in order, beginning with Nancy Milford's *Zelda.*[2]

The story of the Scott Fitzgeralds and their "Twenties" marriage has been told so many times, most recently in James Mellow's *Invented Lives,*[3] that it needs no rehearsing here. All the "getting and spending," the Atlantic crossings, the adolescent antics at home and abroad, have been endlessly catalogued as though their fascination were eternal. Scott was always the center of interest, but the Fitzgeralds lived their public lives as a pair, and from the first Zelda's strangeness did not escape notice—and it would have been strange if it *had,* since her behavior and speech were at times positively bizarre. Among the witnesses to Zelda's numerous oddities—such as leaping across a restaurant table or asking Scott for a cigarette just as he was negotiating a mountain curve in their car—was John Dos Passos, who spent an afternoon with her in an amusement park and who was driven to conclude then and there that the woman was mad. That Scott was rapidly becoming an alcoholic merely added to the fun and made them a couple you definitely had to watch.

But singling out Zelda as the subject of a biography required a good deal more than watching. Nancy Milford related in her preface how she had travelled thousands of miles in search of Zelda, and how she had been moved as she had never been moved before by her letters to Scott, most of them written in the Thirties from various mental institutions. Milford made it clear, too, that the principal aim of her book was to find out why, after only ten years of marriage, Scott Fitzgerald's wife had broken down, why, that is, the Southern belle—with her "clean wild hair brushed back from her face"—had gone insane. Dazzled by her freshness and beauty, Milford saw the young Zelda as "the American girl living the American dream," a dream that something or somebody had turned into a nightmare. It goes without saying that the finger would point eventually to Scott and to the marriage, and that Zelda would be seen not as having the fixed identity of a Mrs. G. B. S. but as having no identity at all. This, Milford seemed to be suggesting, was what Scott had engineered and what finally drove Zelda mad. She had longed for her own accomplishments to match his, but whatever she took up—dancing, story writing, painting—he somehow managed to spoil.

In other words, the real project underlying Milford's biography was to construct the identity that Zelda *might have had* under other circumstances. It involved her, of course, in a detailed account of Zelda's early prewar years in Montgomery, Alabama, before she met and married Scott. They were privileged years, during which, as Milford seemed disinclined to notice, Zelda's unchecked willfulness and exhibitionism spelled trouble—foreshadowed not only the fabulous marriage to Scott and exhibitionism, *en duo,* on a grand scale, but also the private crash that came shortly after the big public one in '29 and that virtually put an end to their life together. In light of so graphic a picture—however unwittingly drawn—of Zelda's disturbed and disturbing girlhood, with its wild impulses and "acting out," one is frankly compelled to ask whether Zelda's greatest potential might not have been the breakdown she suffered at thirty.

As a matter of fact, while it is generally agreed that the marriage precipitated the breakdown, for Milford the breakdown

2 *Zelda: A Biography* was published by Harper & Row in 1970.

3 James Mellow's *Invented Lives,* originally published by Houghton Mifflin in 1984, was reprinted in paperback by Ballantine in 1986.

actually provided the strongest piece of evidence for what Zelda Fitzgerald might have been able to make of herself if the world—and Scott—had not stood in her way: a novel called *Save Me the Waltz,* written in something like six weeks while she was in a Baltimore psychiatric clinic. One of the many curiosities of the Fitzgerald relationship was the effect on Scott of this largely incoherent fiction. By all accounts (including his own), it made him frantic and hysterical because he saw Zelda encroaching on the matter of his own unfinished novel, the work long in the making that would finally appear as *Tender is the Night.* Without Zelda's original manuscript, which has been lost, it is hard to know just how much duplication there really was, but Scott's reaction seems excessive in any case, in light of both the surviving proofs and the text as published, which make all too plain Zelda's cracked shell of a mind. Fitzgerald, one suspects, could not help himself, but Milford took Zelda's book even more seriously than he, subjecting it to an extended critical analysis as though there were a readable narrative instead of raw data from a disordered psyche.

Scott's own behavior might well be explained as part of the "craziness" he and Zelda had in common, which Leon Edel has described—in the language of psychopathology—as *folie à deux,* where two people (often a married couple) share a delusional system. Milford's biography provides more than enough evidence to support Edel's point, but it also illustrates another brand of folly, that of the biographer who ignores her own findings, who takes her subject's wishes for deeds and her yearnings for accomplishments. Zelda certainly had a streak of talent (a "brilliant offbeat style" was how James Mellow put it in *Invented Lives*), and Scott mined it ruthlessly for his fiction. But to intimate that he, and not her own incapacities, prevented her from becoming a full-fledged artist is to misread all the psychological signs. Even Fitzgerald, in his last, worn-out years, when he tried to defend himself against her family's accusation that it was he who had caused her breakdown, finally seemed to understand how profoundly damaged Zelda had already been when he first met her.

Unwilling to admit the deep roots of Zelda's illness, Nancy Milford was not inclined to make very much of Scott's hard-earned understanding: her project called for a different brand of damages. Even so, she did not present Zelda as exclusively the victim-wife in the way Diane Johnson would process the first Mrs. Meredith a couple of years later, in the book generally known as *Lesser Lives.*[4] In this case, the challenge lay not so much in being able to imagine an alternate identity for her subject as in being able to create—out of whole cloth—an entire life. For if relatively little was known (then and now) about George Meredith, even less information was available about his first wife. Despite the fact that she was the favorite daughter of Thomas Love Peacock—satirist, skeptic, and great friend of Shelley—Mary Ellen Meredith left few traces behind: a handful of letters, a commonplace book, some food recipes, and two prose pieces about housewifery, published early in her short-lived marriage to Meredith. Quite undaunted by so small a store, Johnson proceeded to imagine what must have happened between a young ambitious writer (he was twenty-two) and an older woman (by seven years) who had not only been married before and already borne a child but had "educated herself," when a teenager, by reading French novels. With such bits and pieces—this particular one about novel-reading gleaned from a letter written by Mary Shelley that described Mary Ellen Peacock at fourteen—Johnson constructed an elaborate edifice of innuendo and surmise, held together by her firm belief that Peacock's daughter, brought up in a freethinking environment where advanced views about women and sex prevailed, could only have been ground to dust in the repressive Victo-

4 Diane Johnson's *The True History of the First Mrs. Meredith and Other Lesser Lives* was published in 1972 by Knopf.

rian world of George Meredith, the Portsmouth tailor's son.

Actually, neither George *nor* Mary Ellen had a chance in the courtroom set up by Johnson, though for *him,* of course, there were no tears shed: the fault, after all, lay deep in his character, while Mary Ellen's gender alone had determined her fate by forcing her into marriage. This—one of the few options open to a nineteenth-century woman—usually meant, as everyone knows by now, frequent debilitating pregnancies, and when the woman happened to be married to a man like George Meredith, sensitive, "high-strung," and "passionately ambitious" for a literary fame not to be jeopardized "by every day work" (which put them constantly in debt), her options had been reduced practically to zero. And, irony of ironies, Meredith's weak digestive system could not tolerate the gourmet meals his wife loved to cook. For Johnson, then, Mary Ellen's creativity was blocked on all sides, sacrificed to Meredith's delicate stomach as well as to his craving for fame. That she was driven to leave him after only six or seven years seemed to Johnson axiomatic.

The details of the first Mrs. Meredith's "elopement" from her husband are scanty, but the universal conclusion has been that she left with her lover, the painter Henry Wallis, who was also the father of the child born soon after. Taking issue with this received view as an all-too-conventional one that may have fit the circumstances but not her subject's character, Johnson thought it far more likely that Mary Ellen had left George in order to save her soul. Longing for independence (especially from him) and hoping to earn a livelihood by her own pen, she separated from her husband at the same time she just happened to be involved with Wallis. Put another way, to Johnson, Wallis was quite incidental, but even if she *had* gone off with him, it would simply mean that in the world of the 1850s a woman of Mary Ellen's class could not have acted alone. Alas, fate was dogging her steps. She died three years later when she was only forty, perhaps from an old kidney ailment aggravated by numerous pregnancies but certainly without having had the time or opportunity to prove herself. And, to Johnson's disgust, George Meredith went on to become a famous novelist, who never forgave his first wife for insulting him by leaving him and whose "books are full of erring wives." Johnson's own book, full of scorn for erring (and timid) biographers as well as for erring (and hard-hearted) husbands, was meant to evoke by every conceivable fictional means the world that had coldly and silently witnessed the sufferings of Mary Ellen Meredith, a world of sin and guilt that no mere Biographer—tied not only to Fact but also to inhibiting Convention—could possibly have reproduced. But like a postmodern novel calling attention to its own apparatus, *The True History of the First Mrs. Meredith and Other Lesser Lives* was an entirely self-conscious vehicle: fiction wrestling pretentiously with fact; footnotes vying with text; capital letters carrying the derogatory tone and meaning; the whole enterprise driven by an inflated sense of mission and directed mainly at those who shared the author's point of view, readers who would miss none of her innuendos and already felt they knew what a nineteenth-century woman's life had to be like.

Reconstructed along such preconceived lines, as though it lay there ready and waiting to emerge, the first Mrs. Meredith's life was turned into a political exemplum, duly illustrating a variety of sins against women. In contrast, the life of the second Mrs. Hardy, scrupulously researched and presented by Robert Gittings and Jo Manton (themselves a husband-and-wife team), became a curious study in understatement.[5] Avoiding the slightest temptation to claim for their subject more than ordinary abilities or "small talent," they produced a biography that seems a crossbreed, as though a life were being singled out for its *lack* of inter-

---

5 *The Second Mrs. Hardy,* by Robert Gittings and Jo Manton, was published by the University of Washington Press in 1979.

est. Perhaps this was precisely Gittings and Manton's point—that the ordinariness of Thomas Hardy's wife had never been fully documented. But it has certainly been proven now, beyond the shadow of a doubt.

Gittings himself, as Thomas Hardy's most recent biographer, knew only too well the background of his second marriage: how Hardy, nearly seventy and unhappy in his first marriage, struggling with *The Dynasts,* that vast epic in blank verse and prose, met Florence Dugdale and wooed her for seven years behind his wife's back. She was twenty-eight when they met, with just the kind of delicate beauty that appealed to him: a certified teacher who hated teaching and loved poetry, who had grown up in Enfield, a few miles north of London, where John Keats also went to school and where she was taught to revere "great authors." In Enfield, too, from her biographers' point of view, the great deception practiced on Florence Dugdale had its beginnings—in the "literary evenings and conversaziones" that fostered a taste for genteel verse and the expression of fine sentiments. Thus, already persuaded that she had some talent, when Hardy praised her writing she believed him; when he touched up one of her stories and sent it for her to the *Cornhill,* she thought it had been accepted on its merits; when he persuaded the editor of an illustrated paper to hire her, she assumed it was in recognition of her own skills. Grown used to Hardy's tender ministrations, Florence was completely unprepared for the change that came over the great author when his wife suddenly died. He had paid little attention for years, it would seem, to the ailing Emma, and her death took him by surprise—as did the manuscript he found among her papers, in which she affectingly recalled their early years together. The result was that Hardy could barely attend to Florence, so obsessed was he with the memory of Emma. In the months following—even after he and Florence were married—Hardy devoted himself almost exclusively to a series of poems that revealed, in his biographer's view, all the guilt and remorse activated by Emma's death.

Whether Gittings has read these poems rightly or not, the second marriage would certainly appear to have had its problems. Chief among them, however, had to be Florence Hardy's indisputable ordinariness. Led astray by false ideals as well as by Hardy's oblique eroticism—or the wayward muse of a genius—how could she have understood her own unhappiness? Or, for that matter, the irony in the fact that being Hardy's wife required an unexpected degree of selflessness and sacrifice, costing her—as Gittings and Manton show—the very beauty that had earned her Hardy's attention in the first place? Yet the marriage lasted fourteen years, until Hardy's death at the age of eighty-seven, and in the eyes of the world Florence Hardy was "the priestess of his cult."

She herself may have felt that her worst problems began after her husband died, since most of her two-volume biography of Hardy, published within two years of his death, had actually been written by him. To make matters worse, in the same year (1930) as her second volume, Somerset Maugham's satiric novel, *Cakes and Ale,* appeared, with its nasty portrait of an aged writer and his much younger wife, identified by virtually all the reviewers as Mr. and Mrs. Hardy. It is at this low point in her life that Gittings and Manton began their biography of Florence, with a view—as they themselves put it—to discovering "the real character of the second Mrs. Hardy" as opposed to the fictional, something no one had seen fit to inquire about until then. By the end of the book, not only had they documented her "real character," but they had also succeeded in showing why it had never aroused any interest. Yet they seem to have thought they were doing Florence Hardy double justice by ascribing her defects to the cultural environment in which she had grown up and by carefully distinguishing her own modest character from that of the calculating wife in *Cakes and Ale.* Surely this is a form of justice that comes perilously close to punishment. For all their stated intent to make Hardy's second wife *known* for the first time, obliging them to point out in the process his failings as man and husband, Gittings and Manton reveal—more clearly than anything else—the drastic limitations of the woman they chose as their subject.

In their most recent collaboration—on a new life of Dorothy Wordsworth—the same misplaced zeal is apparent, even though here the famous brother does not seem to have been, as Hardy was, a target.[6] On the contrary, he was left out as much as possible, with a view to giving Dorothy the space and attention she deserves. But once again, though fostered and endorsed by prevailing attitudes toward women and biography, the good intentions backfired, producing a life with its center neatly cut away. As Bruce Bawer noted in his review of *Dorothy Wordsworth* in these pages, omitting William and his poetry from Dorothy's life deprived it of the very meaning she intended it to have. So that instead of paying homage to an extraordinary woman, Gittings and Manton have actually set aside, *devalued* her own strongest feelings, just when even radical feminists, studying Dorothy's rich prose texts in order to intensify their value, have taken to regarding them as subtle interactions with her brother's poems. Professing to admire her, Gittings and Manton have succeeded in belittling her—by attempting what amounts to a reduction (for *her*) from dependent sisterhood to independent womanhood. Whether you deplore such submergence of self or not, whether you choose to call it absorption by the Other, or extreme passivity, or perhaps even arrested development, to rub out William the poet in an effort to highlight Dorothy the woman can only turn her into a far smaller person than the one she worked so hard to be.

Achieving results very different from those they intended would seem a hazard that biographers in particular are likely to run, especially when they tie themselves into cultural/political programs. For example, Jean Strouse's biography of Alice James, the chronically and mysteriously ailing younger sister of William and Henry, can be said to suffer from too close—and deterministic—a reading of the life.[7] The private struggles of Strouse's subject, both physical and mental, have been carefully placed in their nineteenth-century context, with causative connections made between the cultural environment of women and Alice's "invalid" existence. But these links have struck some readers as forced and questionable, and the portrait of Alice as overcharged with psychoanalytic doctrine, her life experience turned into a tale relentlessly plotted. Even more to the point, Alice comes through as painfully lacking in the creative energy that drove her older brothers to overcome their own personal disabilities. So that while explicitly denying that she was making Alice "a heroine (or victim-as-heroine)," Strouse could not help attributing her failure to the James family as well as to society at large. Paradoxically, Alice seemed to have been *incapacitated* by her sizable share of James talent. Perhaps with less, she might have managed to escape from herself, but along with the James gifts came the James will to power—exercised by Alice through illness, the only weapon she felt was available to her. Put differently, Alice was forced to devote virtually all her "fine intelligence" to resolving what Strouse presents as the "essential contradiction" of her life—the fact that she was both "a James and a girl." Such were the large modern terms in which Strouse argued for the meaning and value of Alice James's small, strangled life; and Strouse derived them, at least in part (as her introduction shows), from the celebrated essay by Virginia Woolf that has had more influence on biographies of women in the Seventies and Eighties—and has been more misused—than almost any other single work: "A Room of One's Own."

In this essay that has become a sacred text for large numbers of contemporary women, Woolf imagined the dire fate of a "wonder-

6 *Dorothy Wordsworth,* by Robert Gittings and Jo Manton, was published by Oxford University Press/Clarendon in 1985.

7 *Alice James: A Biography,* by Jean Strouse, was published by Houghton Mifflin in 1980.

fully gifted" younger sister of Shakespeare, a woman *consumed* by the urge to express herself and driven wild by the poetic sensibility she was not supposed to have by virtue of her sex. She would have had no encouragement from her family except to marry; and she might have run off to London expressly to avoid marriage. Once there, she would surely have gravitated to the theaters, caught the eye of an actor-manager, and in due course "found herself with child." From Virginia Woolf's point of view, this could have had but one result—suicide—for in her opinion "any woman born with a great gift in the sixteenth century would certainly have gone crazed, shot herself, or ended her days in some lonely cottage outside the village, half witch, half wizard, feared and mocked at." Chances are that Woolf was more right than not in her *feel* for the limitations operating on an inspired woman in the sixteenth century and that in all likelihood a sister of Shakespeare *would* have been undone by her anachronistic sensibility. But many of the actual women—including the highly verbal Alice James—who are fitted into the Woolfian paradigm as sisters under the skin have had little of the intensity and creative drive of the gifted being whose lineaments Woolf conjured up in her essay. It is almost as though, since Woolf's stirring vignette took hold, the impediments have counted far more than the gifts, as though frustration and suffering were now principal prerequisites for biographies of women, prerequisites all too often met by the wives of famous men precisely bcause so many of them have left little else to show for themselves.

Misery is certainly the abiding theme of the recently published lives of Jenny Marx and Sara Coleridge, with most of their suffering attributed to the great men themselves—to the extraordinary demands they made on their wives and the sacrifices that marriage to them entailed. As H. F. Peters baldly put it in the introduction to *Red Jenny,* his biography of Jenny Marx, "the woman behind every great man is the victim of his passions . . . ."[8] But Peters was also driven to confess that "during the seven years of [his] efforts to understand the life of Jenny Marx there were times when [he] felt that it could not be done, because so many personal documents, letters and diaries, had been destroyed or were being withheld." His solution, since he claimed not to want to "present an ideological thesis," was "to lay out the facts about her life with her husband and her children, as she herself gave them." In other words, he would provide what amounts to a doubly partial story. Yet, in spite of his disclaimer, the raison d'être of his biography is surely ideological, for it has come into being—with all its admitted handicaps—in a cultural climate that does not mind them, that does not object to incompleteness or partiality so long as it is on the right side—the wife's side. But when there is virtually no interpretation, no attempt at a translation of Jenny Marx's self-expressed feelings or their tones, her life can easily become one huge cliché. "[She] lived and died in the vortex of her husband's fateful gospel": so Peters was content to sum it up. And so at least one reviewer rightly complained that he had told Karl's life story and not Jenny's.

She has fared no better at the hands of an equally sympathetic, equally uninquiring woman, Edna Healey, who recites the events of Jenny Marx's life along with those of Mary Livingstone's and Emma Darwin's in a book called *Wives of Fame.*[9] Like Peters, Healey concentrates on the hardship and woe in a life with the absolutist Karl Marx: political exile, poverty, illness, births and deaths. The chronicle is grim indeed, and the moral all too obvious: such is "the fate of those who [choose to] live with demon-heroes." Mary Livingstone's sufferings turn out to have been even greater than Jenny's, married as she was to a religious fanatic who (unlike the thoroughly bourgeois Marx)

8 *Red Jenny: A Life with Karl Marx,* by H. F. Peters; St. Martin's Press, 208 pages, $14.95.

9 *Wives of Fame: Mary Livingstone, Jenny Marx, Emma Darwin,* by Edna Healey, was published in London in 1986 by Sidgwick and Jackson.

cared nothing for this world, so that she had to endure one pregnancy after another under the most primitive conditions, dying at an early age in the wilds of Africa. By contrast, Emma Darwin's secure, placid, and long-lived marriage to the dedicated scientist, which produced its own small army of children yet managed to provide a nurturing environment for them, is presented as an instance of great good luck for both husband and wife. But the book offers no comprehensive view of either nineteenth-century life or marriage, much less of sexuality. It seems to have come into being in order to point out that the world has completely forgotten the self-sacrificing wives of Livingstone, Marx, and Darwin—but without explaining *why* the world ought to remember them now.

When there is little to tell of a life beyond its pain and suffering (and these are shared by untold millions of men as well as women), when, in spite of voluminous archives, the biographical materials are thin and the individual consciousness remains closed and impenetrable, what drives the study of such a life? Molly Lefebure would claim, no doubt, that for *her* obscure subject, Sara Coleridge, "the most maligned of great men's wives," biography is the only corrective possible. It is certainly true that, since her own day, Coleridge's wife has borne the character of an ill-tempered, unloving ninny, a characterization Coleridge himself not only subscribed to but also apparently originated, hence the nearly universal readiness with which it has been handed down. No matter how many questions about the poet have come up over the years, no matter how many subtle shifts in the judgment on him have taken place, the verdict on Sara has remained substantially the same. Molly Lefebure set out to change that verdict, in effect, to clear Sara Coleridge's name at long last by examining all the surviving documents—every scrap—for information that might cast doubt on the received view of Sara and the marriage: biography, in other words, as a rescue mission.

Lefebure's book about Sara, *The Bondage of Love,*[10] grew out of her earlier study of Sara's husband, *The Bondage of Opium,* in which she argued at great length—and persuasively—for the disastrous effects on Coleridge of his drug addiction. In this new book she maintains, as one might expect, that Sara's own behavior could not have been unaffected by her husband's habit; and she tries to show how the strains in the marriage did in fact stem from opium—indeed, how living with Coleridge became more and more difficult, if not impossible, as even his loyal friends, the Wordsworths, finally had to admit. In Lefebure's view, then, opium (and not Wordsworth's sister-in-law, whom Coleridge claimed to love) came between the Coleridges, bringing out his worst tendencies, if not altering his personality; and yet despite its uncertain beginnings, with Coleridge attempting to retreat from his hasty proposal of marriage, their relationship was firmly based in strong, positive feeling on both sides.

Admittedly, the Coleridge marriage makes more sense seen this way instead of monochromatically, especially since after years of estrangement there was something of a rapprochement at the end, when his drug habit had been brought under control and he was being looked after in Highgate. So that even though Lefebure's demonstration involves some tenuous and inconclusive evidence—guessing at the contents of missing letters, for example, or presuming to know how S. T. and Sara actually felt at certain crucial moments, it has rendered the old picture of the marriage somewhat suspect. But does this mean that Sara was not as unsuitable a wife for a poet and a genius as everyone has always assumed? For whatever the poet's reasons for believing her unsuitable, believe it he did, and no biographer can alter those feelings, opium-induced or not. In the same

---

10 *The Bondage of Love: A Life of Mrs. Samuel Taylor Coleridge,* by Molly Lefebure, was published in London in 1986 by Victor Gollancz. Norton will publish the book here this month (287 pages, $17.95).

way, even if Sara's intelligence could actually be measured and shown to be considerably greater than people have thought, this would not change the perception of general incompetence—however unjust or inaccurate—that seemed to prevail throughout her life. Moreover, the life has already been lived—in circumstances whose complex causes and effects are scarcely recoverable. To argue for a new reading of a body of work is one thing; it is quite another to put Sara Coleridge's scant remains under the hermeneutic microscope, as though her painful experience with Coleridge could be treated like an accomplishment worth preserving. In truth, neither his part in the marriage *nor* hers can bear very close scrutiny. Sara Coleridge herself seemed to realize this, for after Coleridge's death she burned the accumulated correspondence of forty years—in order, she claimed, to protect her husband's reputation, but at the same time destroying the evidence that might have left no doubt about her own role in the relationship. And the question of motive remains, despite Lefebure's partisan certainty that the mistreated Sara Coleridge had only her husband's interests at heart after all.

The method of Lefebure's book, involving as it does the attempt to reconstruct a domestic life, is carried even further in *Pre-Raphaelite Sisterhood* by Jan Marsh, a biographical/historical study of the models who sat for the Pre-Raphaelite painters and became their mistresses and wives.[11] Since then, they have been mythologized as the faces and forms in the famous paintings, but with little or no attention paid to their real lives and background, which were always obscure in any case. What Marsh set out to do was to give these women—six of them—human dimensions, so that they could be moved out of the realm of male-dominated myth, where they have long been "viewed merely as satellites of the men," into a world that would recognize their own creative urges and ambitions as well as their separate personalities. She combed the Pre-Raphaelite source materials for information that would fill in her account of their daily lives as well as for evidence of undeveloped gifts and frustrated longings. There was Lizzie Siddall, for example, trying her hand at drawing, and Georgie Macdonald taking up wood-engraving. But neither one of them got very far, mainly because—as Marsh presents it—even the *support* of an untrained woman's artistic efforts in the mid-nineteenth century could become an impediment. Thus, Lizzie may have been too lavishly praised by Gabriel Rossetti and persuaded to paint before she had learned to draw; or perhaps, without the benefit of "life studies," she could not have mastered figures. Whatever the reason, the result was that "most of the people in her pictures have no legs . . . ." As for Georgie Macdonald, her marriage to Burne-Jones—in Marsh's view—prevented her from realizing her own ambitions. To support this view, Marsh describes how, "on the eve of her wedding, [Georgie] assessed their material goods: £30 in cash from Ned's earnings and her own 'small deal table with a drawer in it that held my wood-engraving tools.' This table, which appears to have been her only significant possession, was clearly valued as a solid symbol of her own aspirations. It tells us that, like her husband, Georgie had serious artistic ambitions, although as it turned out, Ned's brushes and pens were to eclipse her engraving-tools." Surely that table of Georgie's "tells us" nothing of the kind. Nor does the equally simplistic argument that is dominated by feminist ideals and that runs through Marsh's entire book make her case for the undeveloped powers she wants to claim: "women were denied opportunities and then defined as inferior"; this "makes it hard to assess their abilities." How do you know, in other words, what these women might have been capable of achieving if they had begun with the educational advantages of a Rossetti, a Burne-Jones, a William Morris, instead of growing up—as some of them did—in the slums of London? What if they

11 *Pre-Raphaelite Sisterhood,* by Jan Marsh, was published in 1985 in London by Quartet Books.

had *not* had "defeats and deficiencies imposed on their sex"? Still, whether "imposed" or not, the "defeats and deficiencies" are all too apparent, as Marsh's account cannot help but show, and in the last analysis they do make a difference, though it means that her subjects can scarcely be distinguished from the rest of humanity—unless, of course, all that matters is what might have been rather than what was.

Once again, an elaborate rescue operation has turned into demolition. Removed from the world of myth and transcendent value, the Pre-Raphaelite women are reduced to ordinary, insignificant human beings. And in her extraordinary postscript, Jan Marsh argues for the significance of the insignificant—for all the "details of [women's] emotional lives, domestic responsibilities, family relations and . . . social activities" that have never been deemed worthy of "serious attention" and are always dismissed at once as "trivialization." But it is Jan Marsh herself who has trivialized her subjects by crying their limitations and rationalizing their weaknesses, by studying meager endowments as though they were great gifts, by failing—in the very act of investigating the reality of these women's lives—to acknowledge and accept that reality for what it was. So, too, when women who were mainly wives, with no special gifts or achievements, are made biographical subjects in their own right, the effort required to give their lives equal significance as well as space makes a mockery of the delicate and humane art of biography. When praise demeans because it is undeserved; when to magnify is to diminish and to single out is to expose (but no one will admit this), we are truly in the land of political make-believe, where categories are more important than what is in them and where moral currencies have been so inverted that the wrongs of the past have become the "rights" of today.

(*April* 1987)

VI. The Contemporary Scene

Richard Serra at MOMA

by Hilton Kramer

The Richard Serra exhibition which has come to the Museum of Modern Art this spring is an event bound to disturb—perhaps even infuriate—a great many more people than it pleases.[1] In this respect, as in others, the exhibition is completely faithful to the spirit of Mr. Serra's work, which from the outset of his career—some twenty years ago—has been conceived of as a series of provocations. Yet it would be a mistake, I think, to allow this posture of provocation to set the terms of our response to the sculpture which we encounter in the MOMA exhibition. It would also, alas, be a mistake to discount it entirely. For the element of provocation is an integral part of Mr. Serra's artistic program. It would therefore be absurd to ignore it.

The problem, in Mr. Serra's case, is to determine exactly what *artistic* role the artist's posture of provocation plays in the creation of his sculpture. This is not an easy task, however, for the artist himself has done much to obscure the issue, and his many "activist" champions—no doubt taking their warrant from the artist's own attitudes and then raising the ante, so to speak, in their own political interests—have done even more. We need to be reminded, then, that it is as an *artist*—and not as something else—that Mr. Serra's primary claim on our attention rests. To see what that claim really amounts to, it is therefore essential that we separate the art from the artist's reputation. And this, in turn, means that on the occasion of the present exhibition at MOMA, we must separate the art from the texts describing it in the catalogue accompanying the show—texts which MOMA itself, in an extraordinary disclaimer, has all but disavowed but which it has obviously deemed politic to publish without interference.[2]

There is no mystery, of course, as to how this unusual situation, in which the museum finds itself publicly at odds with its own publication, has come about. The museum had apparently intended for some time to devote an exhibition to Mr. Serra's work. Before much headway could be made in that endeavor, however, Mr. Serra suddenly emerged as a figure of considerable controversy. The large outdoor sculpture called *Tilted Arc,* which he created for the plaza of the Jacob K. Javits Federal Building in lower Manhattan on a commission from the General Services Administration, became the focus of a fierce debate. A great many people who work in the Javits building—people who have to live with the sculpture every

1 "Richard Serra/Sculpture," organized by Laura Rosenstock and Rosalind E. Krauss, opened at the Museum of Modern Art on February 27 and closes on May 13.

2 *Richard Serra/Sculpture* by Rosalind E. Krauss. Edited and with an Introduction by Laura Rosenstock. Essay by Douglas Crimp. The Museum of Modern Art (clothbound, $40; paperback, $22.50).

working day—strongly objected to it. (The sculpture consists of a Cor-Ten steel wall, measuring one hundred and twenty feet in length and twelve feet in height, which bisects the building's plaza.) This led to a hearing on the suitability of the work. As a result of the hearing, a decision was made to order the removal of *Tilted Arc* to another site, and this prompted further debate. (It did not cause the work to be removed, by the way. At this writing, it remains in place.) Naturally, given the current climate of opinion, the whole episode made of Mr. Serra something of an artist-hero and, owing to the fact that *Tilted Arc* was a government commission, something of a political martyr as well.

As I have elsewhere given my opinion on this work and the controversy surrounding it, I do not propose to go into the matter again in any detail here.[3] Suffice to say that I was not one of those who succumbed to the charms of *Tilted Arc,* nor was I persuaded that the decision to order its removal from the Javits plaza constituted a crime against art, society, or anything else. On the contrary, it seems to me that there are legitimate reasons for objecting to the work and that the entire controversy has done much to illuminate the deeply problematic nature of the project which has come to be called public art—a vast and expensive program upon which the government embarked with a great deal of naïveté and a woeful paucity of serious thought about its implications or indeed its essential purposes.

What is of more direct concern here, however, is the role which the *Titled Arc* affair has played in the presentation of the MOMA exhibition. By its very nature, of course, *Tilted Arc* could not be included in the exhibition. There is, to be sure, a photograph of the work in the show, as there are of the artist's many other immense public sculptures both here and abroad. But photographs are not sculpture, and the photographs in question are in many cases extremely misleading. This is certainly the case with the photograph of *Tilted Arc.* It does not in any sense suggest what it is actually like to experience the sculpture ***in situ,*** which is what the controversy is really about. *Tilted Arc* is by no means the only work photographically misrepresented in this way in the MOMA show. A sculpture I very much admire—the construction called *Carnegie,* which was erected last fall outside the entrance of the Museum of Art at the Carnegie Institute in Pittsburg—is similarly misrepresented by an aerial view of a kind which is vouchsafed to almost no one but the birds (and professional photographers seeking bird's-eye views). We can hardly be surprised, then, that it is one of these aesthetically sanitized photographs of *Tilted Arc* which adorns the cover of the MOMA publication, which is not really a catalogue of the exhibition but a propaganda offering wholly devoted to exalting Mr. Serra in his role as artist-hero and political martyr.

The question which therefore most urgently needs to be asked about the sculpture of Richard Serra at this juncture is this: What is it we are left with when all the controversy and role-playing is put aside? With this question in mind, the MOMA exhibition turns out to be an event of exceptional artistic interest. By no means is everything in the exhibition an unqualified artistic success, in my opinion. But there is much that is. And there can be no question, I think, but that Mr. Serra has taken sculpture in a direction that is new, however much his work may owe to the ideas of his contemporaries. What is original in his work may not always to be to our liking, perhaps—but it nonetheless leaves the art of sculpture significantly altered.

Every artist is shaped to one degree or another by his moment of entry into the art scene, and Mr. Serra has proved to be no exception to the rule. His moment of entry came in the turmoil of the Sixties, and in his work there is still to be discerned some of the characteristic forms of that period and

---

3 See "Art Since the War: Who Will Write Its History?" in *The New Criterion,* Summer 1985, pages 7-8.

some of its characteristic attitudes, too (not all of which found their way directly into art at the time.) Much of the new art of that period—especially the new abstract art—was not only highly formalistic in spirit but cool and impersonal in feeling. Elementary shapes —geometric or at least straight-edged—predominated, and in sculpture there was a distinct preference for outsize scale and for an industrial or fabricated look in the finish of the work. Such were the established characteristics of Minimal sculpture when Mr. Serra arrived on the scene in the Sixties, and he very quickly made them his own. Minimalism became the "tradition" to which he attached himself.

To this tradition, however, was added something else: the notion that both the process by means of which the sculpture is executed and the specific space in which it is created must henceforth be regarded not merely as the circumstantial conditions of the work's realization but as essential, defining aspects of its artistic existence. Hence the emergence of so-called process art and site-specific sculpture, in both of which Mr. Serra played a much publicized role.

Not all of the influences which shaped Mr. Serra's outlook in the Sixties were strictly aesthetic, of course. There was also the *révolté* ethos of the counterculture, which called for a programmatic resistance to whatever could then be regarded as established social practice. The innovations inherent in both process art and site-specific sculpture were born of this spirit of resistance, but in themselves they proved to be feeble as well as temporary challenges to the artistic status quo—and no challenge whatever to the established social order. With few exceptions, they were easily assimilated into the patronage system they were ostensibly designed to challenge, and have remained a permanent feature of an expanded art world ever since. What began as a radical attack on established artistic conventions was very quickly embraced as a new artistic orthodoxy. Which is why a "radical" artist like Mr. Serra could so swiftly become the darling of cultural bureaucrats, bourgeois collectors, and highly placed academics throughout the Western world. It was not that he had failed to produce something new, but that within a decade of his debut he was clearly seen to be taking sculpture in a direction which, although new and in some respects startling, was nonetheless consistent with what prior modernist practice had prepared the way for.

I have already observed that Minimalism was the tradition to which Mr. Serra attached himself at the outset of his career, and he remains very much a Minimalist sculptor today—but a Minimalist with a difference. To the purely formalistic attributes of Minimalism he has added something odd and unexpected—an element of dread, or what might even be called fear, which I do not recall ever before encountering in a sculptural work in quite the same way. In much of Minimalist sculpture, no matter how elephantine the scale of the work may be, the highly simplified forms together with their impersonal surfaces and rigorously logical structures tend to have a rather benign, if not indeed a sedative, effect on any reasonably knowledgeable spectator. Just about the last thing in the world we expect to experience in the presence of these works is a sensation of dread. Far from posing either a physical or theoretical threat to our existence, Minimalist sculpture tends for the most part to relax the spirit and offer us the visual equivalent of nirvana—which is to say, deliverance from all sense of pain, anxiety, or trauma.

This is distinctly not the case with many of the steel constructions we encounter in the Serra exhibition at MOMA. For one thing, these sculptures occupy the museum's spaces with an authority which is all but indistinguishable from a certain mode of aggression. Their outsize forms tend either to impede or direct our movements in or around them; to take an interest in these works is, to some extent, to surrender to their scale, which is not so much a human scale as a scale designed to diminish our sense of autonomy and volition. I speak particularly of the room-size constructions which, by means of immense steel slabs, divide space in such a way as to hold us captive, direct our vision, and control our movements as a condition of seeing the work at all. I cannot speak for others, of course, but I doubt if I am the only spectator to find the experience of such works vaguely threatening. Enclosed in the vault-like spaces which the sculptor has created, one naturally wonders—not continuously, but from time to time—what would happen if one of these weighty steel members were suddenly to topple. Or rather, one doesn't wonder—one knows for certain that in such an event one would be crushed to death. Of course nothing does topple. Everything remains securely in place, and one is free to explore the work in perfect safety. And yet the implied threat is there—and it persists in remaining a constituent element in the experience of seeing Mr. Serra's work for as long as one lingers in its presence. Even with the constructions which one cannot enter—which are roped off from the viewer and which we therefore see from a space we do not share with the work itself—the delicate balances sustained by the huge steel plates give the impression of a precariousness that reinforces this sense of an implied threat and thus surrounds us with an atmosphere of dread.

I at least know of nothing quite like this in the history of sculpture. As Dr. Johnson famously said of the prospect of hanging, it is an experience that concentrates the mind. We leave this exhibition with a very vivid sense of having seen something and felt something we have never seen or felt before, and the memory of it is not soon dissipated. It remains fixed and unforgettable. Whether we like it or not—whether, indeed, we are meant to like it—is another question, and I very much doubt if this question of our "liking" the work is of compelling interest to Mr. Serra. I rather think he would believe he had failed in his mission if we were found to like it too quickly. (Which, if true, must make his current popularity among cultural bureaucrats something of a problem for him.) His primary aim (I gather) is to affect and manipulate our response, to impose a certain control on our perceptions, and thus to shatter our complacency in the face of the art experience, and in this he certainly succeeds. The marriage of Minimalist form and existential dread turns out to be a potent combination.

I note with interest, by the way, that neither of the two sculptures which MOMA has acquired for its permanent collection—*Cutting Device: Base Plate Measure* (1969), which is the first work we see on entering the exhibition, and *Modern Garden Arc* (1986), which reposes in the museum's elegant sculpture garden—can be said to generate this sense of dread. They belong to Mr. Serra's more purely formalistic works. Which is entirely understandable. Vastly more space would be required for one of Mr. Serra's room-size constructions than MOMA has, or will ever have, available in its permanent collection. And there are probably other reasons why the museum has settled for what is, in truth, only a token representation of the artist's work in its permanent collection. Mr. Serra is not, after all, primarily a museum artist. As that wall of photographs documenting Mr. Serra's many public commissions reminds us, his major works have mainly been created for large outdoor sites, and I very much doubt if MOMA is ever going to turn over its beautiful garden to something akin to the *Tilted Arc.* Were it ever to do so, the uproar likely to ensue would make the whole controversy which has raged over the commission for the Javits plaza look like a pastoral idyll.

Instead of this unpleasant and indeed unthinkable prospect, the museum has turned over its book on Richard Serra to two authors—Rosalind E. Krauss and Douglas Crimp, co-editor and managing editor, respectively, of *October* magazine—who, for the most part, completely ignore the exhibition which MOMA has mounted on this occasion and offer the museum's public absolutely nothing in the way of an intelligible guide to the artist's work. In the customary *October* manner, the one gives us a post-structuralist disquisition of insurmountable opacity while the other rides his political hobbyhorse for a replay of the *Tilted Arc* melodrama, grandly announcing that we have now, as a result of this controversy, witnessed "the redefinition of the site of the work of art as the site of political struggle." No wonder, then, that William Rubin, the director of the museum's Department of Painting and Sculpture, felt obliged in his preface to this publication to declare that "The Museum of Modern Art disagrees with the rhetorical tone and historical polemic of much that has been written about *Tilted Arc* here as elsewhere." We can assume that Mr. Serra got the publication he wanted and that getting it was one of the conditions he laid down for agreeing to this exhibition. That is the way it usually goes nowadays with artist-heroes, especially those honored few who have also been elevated to the status of political martyrs. They get everything they ask for. But the fact remains that this MOMA exhibition is itself in no sense a "site of political struggle," nor is Mr. Serra himself of any outstanding interest as a political figure. He *is* of great interest as a sculptor, however, and it is a pity that an institution of MOMA's stature could not bring itself to offer its public even a hint about what the real nature of that interest might be. Its abject surrender in this matter has surely set a precedent it will live to regret, for the next time around the ante will be raised to a degree guaranteed to be even more unpleasant than anything the museum might have faced on this occasion.

(*May* 1986)

Einstein's long march to Brooklyn
by Samuel Lipman

Brooklyn, though having lost a famous baseball team (and, before that, an infamous football team), need weep no longer: it now has the up-to-date Brooklyn Academy of Music, the national leader in the presentation of guaranteed media-succulent avant-garde theater-cum-dance-cum-"music" extravaganzas. Indeed, so successful has the institution been under the guidance of Harvey Lichtenstein, its President and Chief Executive Officer, that *Blam!*—the title chosen for an exhibition of Pop, Minimalist, and performance art at the Whitney Museum this fall—might have been thought to refer not to the famous 1960s (Roy) Lichtenstein cartoon painting but to the 1980s (Harvey) Lichtenstein Brooklyn Academy of Music.

Jokes aside, the Brooklyn Academy's record in presenting what it has chosen to call the "Next Wave" has been notable. A successful series sailing under this name took place in 1983; it featured eleven attractions, among them such icons of the new as dancers Trisha Brown, Lucinda Childs, Carolyn Carlson, and Molissa Fenley, and theatrical *animateurs* Lee Breuer (of Mabou Mines fame) and George Coates. This year—with one exception—the presentation roster seemed a bit slimmer in hype value; on the whole the names of the artists—dancers Remy Charlip, Bill T. Jones, Arnie Zane, Mark Morris, and Elisa Monte, videographer Tim Morris, far-out saxophonist Richard Landry, and even composer Steve Reich—appeared to come out of the debate within the experimental art world rather than to stand perched, as their predecessors of the year before had been, on what might be called the brink of true media stardom.

The one exception, of course, was the presentation of the now-mythic—at least in some circles—*Einstein on the Beach,* the mid-1970s collaboration between composer Philip Glass and director-designer-visual artist Robert Wilson. The 1983 Brooklyn festival had begun with Glass's *The Photographer,* a kind of tribute to the nineteenth-century figure Eadweard Muybridge, who first proved by the evidence of the camera that a horse, when trotting, has all four hooves off the ground at the same time. This work, in its static artificiality, seemed to impress even the composer's fans as something more of a whimper than a bang. *Einstein,* however, was different. Through its use of the terrifying images associated with the scientist's work, it had managed, in two 1976 performances at the (rented) Metropolitan Opera House, to enter into the consciousness of artistically knowing New Yorkers. A measure of the fame the work has gained with the passing of time is that so many people now claim to have been present that these performances must have been given, not at the Met, but at Madison Square Garden. The choice of *Einstein* to close the 1984 festival with some twelve performances thus seemed a deliberate attempt to end with strength, to make up once and for all for whatever was less than exciting in the earlier part of the season. Artistic merit aside, the effort succeeded at the box office: *Einstein* seems to have sold out every performance, in the process enabling the entire festival to gross over a million dollars.

Apart from their collaboration on *Einstein,* Glass and Wilson have separately made enviable public careers. Glass is the most visible of the musical Minimalists, those composers who have found a way out of both the complexities, disintegrations, and unpopularity of post-World-War-II modernism. Following in the footsteps of La Monte Young and Terry Riley, and evolving on a parallel course with Steve Reich, Glass used the simplest harmonic materials, iterated at stupefying length, and orchestrated for instruments sometimes electronic and always electrically amplified. Prior to the mid-1970s, his music was instrumental, written for and performed by an ensemble led by him and bearing his name. The result of all this was a growing reputation on the New York downtown music scene and several LPs available only in the more sophisticated record stores. In Europe, too, where Glass had worked with Nadia Boulanger and first become inspired to follow his present course through association with Ravi Shankar, a cult began to form around him and his ideas. This cult abroad was perhaps most interesting as yet another example of the European readiness to be charmed by American simplicities at once eccentric and divine.

Whereas Glass's artistic education at the Juilliard School in New York and with Boulanger in Paris was nothing if not establishment, Robert Wilson was from the beginning of his theater career in the 1960s something of an autodidact. Born in Texas in 1941, he had almost graduated from the University of Texas with a degree in business administration when he decided to come to New York to study architecture; though he did take a degree in it at Pratt Institute and even served as an apprentice with an architect, his interests lay more with the visual arts, and more specifically with body movements. For him, such movements were not "dance" but rather a means toward freeing blocked impulses and capacities. He had worked with handicapped, deprived, and disturbed children to support himself, and in the process developed an aesthetic of slow-motion gesture and action, wherein each detail carried a portentous but usually nonexplicit, quasi-symbolic meaning.

When Wilson's therapy-induced movements were grafted onto his background in architecture and his time spent in painting in New York during the yeasty mid-1960s, the result was a theatrical conception of painterly stage designs, massive constructed sets, and wordless dance, all unfolding without very much action but at heavenly length. Wilson's titles for his stage works all seemed to suggest more content than the works themselves made any attempt to provide: *The Life and Times of Sigmund Freud* (1969), *Deafman Glance* (1970), and *The Life and Times of Joseph Stalin* (1973). All were huge stage pageants using for the most part untrained actors and dancers who did Wilson's bidding more through the force of his personality, deployed during unlimited rehearsal time, than through any professional experience of their own. The critics—especially those of the avant-garde stripe—were interested, and audiences here and abroad attended in enough numbers to convince private and governmental backers that Wilson was indeed onto something.

Wilson likes to call his earlier works "operas," though the music that accompanied them was, by common consent, little more than trivial, even for those critics whose standards were anti-profundity. In this regard the collaboration with Glass on *Einstein* awakened expectations—which many critics later found wholly fulfilled—of a Wagnerian "Gesamtkunstwerk," that is, a unity of music, theater, and dance in which the aesthetic whole was vastly greater than the sum of its parts. Whatever the justice done in this instance to the wooly formulation ascribed to Wagner—his great *oeuvre,* after all, demonstrated nothing if not the primacy of music—the general feeling after the first performances of *Einstein* was that the multi-media avant-garde had at last come of age.

Even for those who were enthusiastic in saluting *Einstein* on its first appearance, the creative results from Wilson and Glass working separately thereafter—they had entered upon a period of strained relations that precluded their further collaboration for the time being—fell short of complete satisfaction. Wilson, for his part, retired to Europe, where funding, mostly from state sources, was easier to find than in America. He conceived and staged several less ambitious works on the Continent, and even turned his busy imagination to making video clips capable of being shown in any order and at any length. Then Wilson devoted the major part of his attention to a project grandiose even for him, an extravaganza that was to be the centerpiece of the cultural offerings at the 1984 Olympic Games in Los Angeles. It was designed to do nothing less than sum up the entire human world-historical experience.

In any case, *the CIVIL warS: a tree is best measured when it is down* was first conceived by Wilson as an agglomeration, lasting twelve hours, of six related theater pieces with music; the six parts were to be produced (and financed) in six different countries, then shipped to Los Angeles, where their assembling was to be funded by the Olympic Arts Committee and presented at the Shrine Auditorium. Though individual segments had been produced in Rotterdam, Cologne, Rome, and Minneapolis, their putting together at the Olympics defied even the financial abilities of the doughty Robert Fitzpatrick, President of the California Institute of the Arts (a school founded some years ago with Walt Disney money) and Director of the Olympic Arts Festival. The work was scaled down to eight hours, and further cuts were envisioned, but to no avail. Despite more than three million dollars from the producing countries, two hundred thousand dollars from Los Angeles, and almost a million and a half dollars from donations and projected ticket sales, the entire project was scrubbed amidst massive publicity. The French Communist Party daily, *l'Humanité* (as quoted by *American Theatre,* the magazine of the non-profit Theatre Communications Group) wrote that the cancelation was "a crime against the spirit."

Whatever the expert status of *l'Humanité* in matters of the spirit, the segment of *the CIVIL warS* produced last spring in Minneapolis suggested a different conclusion. There, in the small auditorium of the Walker Arts Center, one could hear and see a collection of entr'actes from *the CIVIL warS*. Wilson called these "knee plays" because they serve as the "joints" between the work's five acts.

It is doubtless less than fair to judge an art work lasting twelve hours (some estimates go as high as sixteen) by intervening excerpts alone. But a passage in the program notes, presumably written by Wilson, explicitly argues for these entr'actes' existing on their own: "*the Knee Plays* is like a substory that is woven through the tapestry of *the CIVIL warS* . . . . they serve in some cases as an introduction to the larger scenes, but on their own they tell a story together that can be seen separately." The knee plays include music composed and led by David Byrne (of Talking Heads fame) and played by seven musicians, six brass and one percussion. The narration was written and spoken by Byrne as well. The scenario and the direction were solely by Wilson; the design and lighting were by Wilson and a group of (presumably subordinate) collaborators. The choreography for the evening was by Suzushi Hanayagi, variously described in the program as "one of Japan's foremost classically trained Kabuki dancers" and as "one of Japan's foremost classical dancers." Rehearsal time for the Walker performances had apparently been generous: rehearsals had begun (after much planning here and abroad) fully one month before the opening.

There is no point in attempting to describe the story line of the knee plays, for it is part and parcel of Wilson's aesthetic that there is none. Instead, the watcher is confronted by a motley assortment of symbols drawn from the stock inventory of emotionally charged detritus floating about in every half-educated intellectual's mind. On this occasion, the material consisted of a tree becoming a boat becoming a book and then ending up once again a tree. More consequential for the viewer was the heavy oriental influence on the proceedings, an influence mostly enshrined in the choreography and in the *mise-en-scène.* To my Western and doubtless parochial eyes, it all seemed stiff, arbitrary, and unconvincing. The movements of the dancers, full of jerks and bodily poutings, seemed like some clumsy imitation of Japanese *samurai* movies on late-night television. The sets included bird-puppetry carried around the audience and a clumsily constructed boat that insisted (on the night I attended) on repeatedly falling apart. It was all creaky, and its minimalism extended well beyond its conception of its craftsmanship.

A special word, I suppose, is necessary to describe the music and the narration. Byrne's composition—it must be remembered that he wrote only the music for the knee plays: the music for the five major acts of the whole work came from other composers, including Glass—was a combination of charmless hymn tunes and the minimalist overworking of already thin material. And the narration, at least on the level of literary interest, added nothing to the evening's vitality. Seemingly heavily drawn from the deadpan monologues of performance artist Laurie Anderson—another icon of the new avant-garde artistic sensibility—Byrne's words would have been laconic had there not been quite so many of them. A quotation from the opening of the first knee play defines the curiously androgynous camp effect:

> Today is an important occasion.
> She thinks that she must wear the right clothes.
> The right combination of clothes
> . . . will make her lucky.

A quotation from the beginning of the fourth knee play adumbrates an element of schizoid alienation never very far from Wilson's work:

> I thought that if I ate the food of the area I was visiting
> That I might assimilate the point of view of the people there
> As if the point of view was somehow in the food
> So I would make no choices myself regarding what I ate.
> I would simply follow the examples of those around me.

The reception by the audience of Wilson partisans in Minneapolis fell short of delirium on the night I attended. Even *The New York Times*'s usually ebullient (at least on this subject) John Rockwell seemed to have some difficulty getting his praise started:

> Mr. Wilson is a creator of massive spectacles, and sometimes his more intimate work has looked schematic and simplistic. There was a bit of that during the first few "knee plays" on Thursday. But then Mr. Wilson exerted his spell, or one began to comprehend what he was about.

For my part, I found the whole effect both boring and amateurish, with remarkably little to show onstage for the month-long efforts of something like fifty people. Indeed, so aimless did everything seem that I could not help wondering later whether the key to both the aridity onstage in Minneapolis and the spectacular financial demands that caused the cancellation of the Olympic Arts Festival presentation was not simply Wilson's oft-trumpeted insistence on developing the final form of his works in rehearsal. This implies an emphasis on casualness and at the same time an inevitability of outcome too profound to be communicated to the participants in words. In artistic matters, after all, the line separating egoistic self-indulgence and merely not knowing what one wants is often a fine one indeed.

In the meantime, while Wilson had been preparing *the CIVIL warS,* Glass was devoting himself to opera. The first major fruit of his attempt to write for conventional opera houses was *Satyagraha,* a set of tableaux drawn from Gandhi's experiences in South Africa from 1893 to 1914. The work was commissioned by the city of Rotterdam and first performed by the Netherlands Opera in 1980; the American premiere took place in 1981 at Artpark in upstate New York; the New York premiere was given at the Brooklyn Academy in the fall of the same year. *Satyagraha*'s "libretto" was written by Glass and his associate and friend Constance DeJong, with sets and costumes by Robert Israel, and staging by Hans Nieuwenhuis.

Satyagraha's vocal text is completely drawn from the Indian *Bhagavad-Gita* and sung in Sanskrit, a language known neither by Glass nor by the participants in the performance. By Glass's own testimony he does not wish the audience to be distracted by understanding. The work's three acts are each overseen onstage by a different benevolent, totemic figure: Tolstoy, the Indian philosopher Rabindranath Tagore, and Martin Luther King, Jr. The mimed (in slow motion) Gandhi material is, of course, heavily fraught with anticipation of the American civil-rights struggles of the 1960s. The music is in Glass's repetitious and mostly motoric style, this time with the motor set on *Molto adagio.* Only the score's ingenious (though Broadway-commercial sounding) orchestration—and a moving theme at the end seemingly drawn from the apotheosis of Tchaikowsky's *Swan Lake*—saved the evening from the total tedium Glass's admirers call ecstasy. In fairness, it must be added that ten thousand tickets were purchased for the work's five sold-out Brooklyn performances.

Satyagraha was the second of what Glass calls his "portrait" operas, *Einstein* being the first. The third, and latest, of these is *Akhnaten,* a work based on *Oedipus and Akhnaton,* a 1960 book of psychoanalytic-historical speculations by Immanuel Velikovsky, a best-selling author famous for *Worlds in Collision,* an attempt to prove that the Red Sea actually did part. The work was first produced in Germany early last year. Its American performance was the result of a co-production by the Houston Grand Opera and the New York City Opera. *Akhnaten* thus arrived at the New York State Theater in November and, like all of Glass's recent operatic works, promptly sold out.

As far as my own experience of *Akhnaten* is concerned, I must confess that I only managed to last through the first act. Musically the work began with an endless arpeggiated A-minor chord. The number of notes in the arpeggios varied and sometimes quick repeated chords—also in A minor—were sounded. The stage was full of piles of sand, to which scantily clad Egyptians added water to make what one presumes were monotheistic mudpies; the eponymous hero throughout behaved in the manner of what Andrew Porter called in *The New Yorker* a hermaphrodite, a description which seems both kind and understated. The first act ended with several minutes—Andrew Porter, again displaying British caution, thought it seemed like only five—of what can only be dubbed a romp around the pyramid. At the end of the act the audience was either too stupefied or too moved or too exalted to do more than give a few rattlings of applause, which sounded like nothing so much—or so little—as the fluttering of aged pigeons' wings.

Donal Henahan in the *Times* and Peter Davis in *New York* hated it all. Henahan, no slouch with a cutting phrase, summed up the musical side of the evening this way:

> *Akhnaten* . . . is not a work whose music asks to be listened to seriously. Despite the publicity that Mr. Glass's works have received, his operas to date add up to little more than pageants with backgrounds of continually repeated, barely varied sound patterns. They stand to music as the sentence "See Spot run" stands to literature . . . .
>
> Considered strictly as an almost primitively tonal protest against the self-defeating complexity of most contemporary music, *Akhnaten* may act as a tonic, if you will forgive the pun. But it is one more example of going-nowhere music . . . .

Davis made his verdict into a prediction of the composer's future: "Glass may have reached the end of his limited resources and can think of nowhere else to go." Speaking for advanced opinion, Andrew Porter wrote respectfully and at some length on the opera, describing the work's sources and blaming the unsatisfactory nature of the outcome on the problems of the production. Porter even described the music, but the closest he could come to saying he liked it wasn't really very close at all:

> The only section of the score I've seen, the Akhnaten-Nefertiti love duet, is two hundred and seventy-five bars stuck in an arpeggiated E minor, colored by passing notes and added notes. There are pedals and some slow, occasionally dissonant counterpoints in the form of climbing chromatic scales. The lovers' voices shine out above this in a slow chorale-like melody, crossing, overlapping . . . and ending each phrase on a unison, octave, or fifth. The metres and the phrase lengths vary. It's a carefully composed, carefully proportioned stretch of music.

My own reaction to the third of *Akhnaten* I was able to endure will come as no surprise. It was rising boredom, passing through the various degrees of irritation to fidgets and anger. Is it that I was merely reacting to the presence of a strong creative personality? I hardly think so. Rather it was just the normal response of a Diogenes trying to find, not an honest man—that would by comparison be easy—but a performance of Glass or Wilson that would justify the hype. Neither man by himself had been able to bring it off. Would a collaboration succeed where each had failed?

So in the long run it all came down to *Einstein on the Beach* in Brooklyn. For months the buildup had been intense, and a veritable Niagara of printed material on the pair, all clearly produced with the cooperation of their busy subjects, had prepared the scene. The sets and the costumes from the 1976 performances had been stored, and so were available to re-create the original production. The lighting design, by Beverly Emmons, and the sound design, by Kurt Munkacsi, were repeats of 1976; many of the musicians, too, were back for the revival. The 1976 choreography (except for one dance at the beginning of Act I) had been the work of Andrew deGroat, a dancer much favored for his ability to twirl endlessly in one place; in the present performances, Lucinda Childs (who had been a lead dancer in the 1976 production and had choreographed the beginning of Act I) was the choreographer for the entire work. Several actors repeated their earlier roles; and most of the words they spoke were carried over from 1976.

The performance I attended was billed as the opening, though several performances, called previews, had been given earlier. While the news could hardly have been a total surprise, it still came as something of a shock to be informed by a sign in the lobby that the performance would last four and a half hours without intermission. Fortunately, this disciplined call to duty was leavened by a generous concession printed in the program:

> As *Einstein on the Beach* is performed without intermission, the audience is invited to leave and re-enter the auditorium quietly, as necessary. The food service will remain open during performances.

With comfort and nourishment thus assured, it was possible to settle down to the performance. Though the opera was scheduled to begin at two o'clock, the music seemed already to have started when I arrived ten minutes early. This music consisted of low organ-like tones, only slowly changing, coming out of an electronic console in the orchestra pit. Anyone not familiar with the recording of Glass's score made after the Met performances in 1976 might have been pardoned for assuming that this quasi-doodling was just pre-performance tuning.

Several minutes later—but still before the official starting time—the audience's filing into the hall was matched onstage by the appearance in front of the curtain, but to one side, of Childs and Sheryl Sutton, the two dancer-actresses who were to be onstage for almost the entire length of the marathon. They sat down in front of a table in the two chairs which had been prepared for them; their costumes, clearly chosen to awaken memories of Einstein's dowdy dress, consisted of men's pants, open-necked white shirts, and suspenders. Both wore telephone-operator headsets, complete with microphones. As they sat they began to make slow, laborious motions with their hands and arms, giving the impression of being in considerable pain. At the same time they began to count numbers very slowly; sometimes other words were audible, including the fascinating phrase "Take a Toyota." As this action went on before the closed curtain, a chorus, also dressed in Einstein costume, began to file stiffly into the orchestra pit. The chorus began to sing numbers as well.

Suddenly—it was now about 2:10, and the sold-out house was still only about two-thirds full—the curtain went up, and the music, which up till now had been quite delicate, came alive with an enormous amplified rush. Childs, repeating her dance from the 1976 production, kept up a constant movement diagonally from the back of the stage to the front, and then back again; her dancing was frenetic, as was the music. From the side a crudely schematic steam locomotive, looking like an enormous child's toy, advanced ever so slowly to the center of the stage. On the back curtain a narrow band of light, like some fugitive element from a Morris Louis or Kenneth Noland painting, descended from the top to the floor.

Now a violinist dressed—surprise!—like Einstein appeared on an elevated platform in the pit, and began to play an endless solo consisting of slow single notes, mostly in scales. From the many loudspeakers could be heard nonsense containing the name "Mr. Bojangles." The male judge began, in a sententious tone, to tell a story about a modest woman—so modest that she wore a blindfold when bathing—who gave a speech in Kalamazoo on the rights of women. After describing how the woman wanted to lead her listeners in singing the national women's song, the judge went on to quote her as recommending that women should tell men, if they don't behave right, to take "their kisses right back where they came from."[1]

Now there was a huge dance sequence, illuminated by a vaporous persimmon light, which proved for me by far the highlight of the entire event. Danced by the members of the Lucinda Childs Dance Company, the choreography seemed a brilliant evocation of the post-World-War-II New York dance scene in all its athleticism, buoyancy, and optimism. Though it all went on too long, and though Glass's music kept up a constant drumbeat of triviality, one could not help feeling that dance, as brought to Brooklyn by Lucinda Childs, had staked its claim to full artistic stature.

From this point on things went downhill. There was a jail scene featuring what looked like two male dancers, one of whom was stated in the program to be a woman. In this scene Childs went on muttering lines

1 Interestingly, this somewhat ambivalent pitch for women was not in the 1976 recording, and presumably not in the 1976 production either. In its place was an equally sententious speech devoted to what I suppose must be called equality of sexual choice:

> In Paris there is a number of young men who are very beautiful, very charming, and very lovable. Paris is called "the city of lights." But these young men who are very beautiful, very charming, and very lovable, prefer the darkness for their social activities . . . .
>
> One of the most beautiful things of Paris is a lady. She is not too broad, bordered with smiles, and very, very, very pleasant to look at. When a gentleman contemplates a lady of Paris, the gentleman is apt to exclaim "Oo la la," for the ladies of Paris are very charming. And the ladies of Paris are dedicated to the classic declaration, expressed in the words "L'amour, toujours l'amour!"

Whether or not the avant-garde is attempting to tell us that feminism has replaced free sexuality as a cause I leave to the reader to determine.

typical in their combination of nonsense and alienation:

> I was in this prematurely air-conditioned supermarket and there were all these aisles and there were these bathing caps you could buy that had these kind of Fourth of July plumes on them that were red and yellow and blue and I wasn't tempted to buy one but I was reminded of the fact that I had been avoiding the beach.

As if to show that the Third World guerilla movement is still with us, she picked up an automatic weapon and pointed it first at her colleagues onstage, then at the orchestra pit, and then finally at the paying customers.

Perhaps I tired, or perhaps the profusion of visual material and incessant music unmatched by any real story line made connected notetaking impossible. Much of the rest hardly seemed worth writing down. There was a long scene with a couple standing on the platform of a railway observation car, and another scene in which a long horizontal bar, lighted in front and meant to represent a bed, was raised ever so slowly by a cable at one side so that it became vertical; it was then raised into the flies. Toward the end of the afternoon, a little missile, perhaps two feet long, flew across the front of the stage on a guy wire against a sky-blue backdrop. This was succeeded by a nuclear explosion, and then by a new drop curtain which in the center depicted a mushroom cloud, on the top right an American bomber, and on the top left a detailed explanation in words of technical aspects of an atomic blast.

So here at last was the point of the whole work. Einstein, the shabby, music-loving, humble philosopher-scientist had come home to roost with a vengeance. The putative disaster of the century—the threat of annihilation which produces the alienation of the person—can now be seen to rest at the feet of the greatest scientific mind of the century. If this is what comes of logical thinking, I suppose the argument would run, who could condemn Robert Wilson for putting on a melodrama without a story line, and Philip Glass for writing hours of music using only a few harmonies and even fewer harmonic and rhythmic devices?

The end of the opera, on the stage as in the recording, found Childs and Sutton sitting on a bench, not touching, as a bus driver intoned drippy words expressive of young love. It was all frightfully maudlin, and the final words seemed risible indeed:

> Once more her voice was heard. "Kiss me, John," she implored. And leaning over, he pressed his lips warmly to hers in fervent osculation . . . .

At the final curtain almost all the seats in the house were still occupied, and the applause was deafening. John Rockwell wrote in *The New York Times* the next morning:

> I find it constantly involving and almost religiously moving. For thsoe who feel the same, the performances this week in Brooklyn will be experiences to cherish for a lifetime.

For those who do *not* feel the same, the problem will be to understand just what took place in *Einstein* and why this work appears to have such a powerful effect on certain people. The verdict on *Einstein* as an art work must be that, as a collaboration, it represents a vastly more interesting work than either has been able to achieve on his own. As music heard apart from the stage spectacle (and at low volume on one's home phonograph), Glass's score seems both harmless and even appealing, as if it were quite content to function as a sentimental pop anodyne; heard in the visual context of Wilson's shameless exploitation of contemporary anomie, the music takes on a character no more musically impressive, but vastly more evocative of a certain kind of cultural despair. As stage spectacle, Wilson's aimless cramming together of overworked metaphors is tied together and even integrated by the frenzied electronic sameness of the music. The result doubtless is the putting into art of a unique moment in modern culture: the moment in the 1970s when it had become clear to all the participants that the best, if not the only, causes were those undertaken strictly for oneself.

The social characteristics of the audience for *Einstein* are, I think, quite clear. Affluent, relatively educated, moderately successful in the professions, old enough to know about the 1960s, too young to know that the events of the 1960s had a historical context beyond personal concerns. The other side of this concentration on self is a loss of faith in a transcendent order, a loss which hardly renders less necessary the satisfaction of human needs for comfort and reassurance. It is about this situation that Stephen Holden wrote in the *Times* on the Sunday of the *Einstein* opening (in an admiring article titled "The Avant-Garde is Big Box Office"):

> Whether mystical or nonsensical, the idea of evoking a totality of experience is the essential thrust behind works like "Einstein on the Beach". . . . But that reality isn't a rarefied perception of truth and God toward which high art has traditionally directed audiences, but a multiplicity of images and sounds, from cartoons to Mozart. Its appeal may come from its attempt to embrace not only the familiar but—everything we don't know and can only imagine.

Doubtless *Einstein,* like other products of the counterculture and its fossil remnants, has a political cast attractive to its viewers. But those who are determined to find in this ideology manifestations of an orthodox left-wing, state-oriented disposition will be wrong: the politics of *Einstein* and its kindred is that beguiling, irresponsible variety of anarchism so endemic in an educated middle class which, no matter how existentially alienated, still wants someone else to pay for its amenities, whether these amenities be urban redevelopment or cultural offerings.

In this regard, it is significant that the requisite financial support for the entire range of Brooklyn Academy "Next Wave" offerings does not come from the audience, which pays only a part of the cost of mounting the various events. Even the huge gross for *Einstein* failed to cover the costs of reviving a previously paid-for production. It is significant, too, that it was not the audience that was to cover the expenses of *the CIVIL warS* at the Los Angeles Olympics. Indeed, in neither case was the lion's share of the money to come from private patrons of vast means. Rather the money was to come from corporations, foundations, and, most especially, governments. In the case of *the CIVIL warS,* most of the necessary money had already come from foreign governments via their own lavish support of culture. In the case of *Einstein* a glance at the acknowledgments page in the 1984 Next Wave souvenir booklet discloses that the first seven donor names saluted are the National Endowment for the Arts, the National Endowment for the Humanities, the Rockefeller Foundation, the Howard Gilman Foundation, the Ford Foundation, the Pew Memorial Trust, and AT&T.

If this analysis of the audience is correct, one can understand why *The New York Times,* Gotham's mission to (and trading post for) the Yuppies, is in the forefront of the publicity wave for the Next Wave festival, and also why *The Wall Street Journal,* that former bastion of bourgeois respectability, has published material extolling Glass on tour as well as the doings in Brooklyn. Whether the *Journal*'s writer is experimental music critic (and *Village Voice* regular) Gregory Sandow or opera and dance buff Dale Harris, the tone is one of wonder and gratitude for the new—and popular—riches being proffered. Clearly these newspapers have identified an audience, not just for a certain kind of culture, but for themselves.

Given the current success of *Einstein,* two questions about the movement it exemplifies remain to be discusseed: its future as box office and its future as art. Despite all the claims made for the burgeoning commerical success of this branch of the avant-garde, the fact remains that its productions, from solo appearances to fully staged events, require hefty subsidies from non-profit sources. The one example usually cited as showing the financial potential of this material is the hit English single "O Superman" by Laurie Anderson. Though it briefly was near the top of the English rock-singles charts and inspired Warner Bros. to sign her to a contract here, it has proved incapable of replication either by Anderson or any of her colleagues and imitators. The costs necessary to put these events on, whether in lighting, staging, dancing, or audio, are onerous, and audiences for intellectually trendy attractions are notoriously fickle. Furthermore, there is no sign that this material is capable of appealing to an uneducated mass audience on the one hand or to traditionally oriented music lovers on the other. It must be added, too, that any artistic product so tied up with the particular historical and personal experiences of its devotees tends to find it hard to attract new audiences who must come fresh to the offering.

None of the above considerations, of course, has any necessary relationship to artistic validity and potential. Whatever the stature of *Einstein on the Beach* as an art work in itself may be, it seems clear enough that it has not had progeny as successful as it was immediately upon its birth. It is equally clear, it bears repeating, that neither Wilson nor Glass, working separately, has been able to achieve the success on his own that they have earned together. Once again, we may take the word of John Rockwell that at least so far *Einstein* is *sui generis*: for him, "This Wilson-Glass collaboration is the major achievement in the performing arts of the minimalist esthetic." Wilson and Glass may, it is conceivable, decide to work together again on something new; it should be borne in mind, however, that sequels which have as their only purpose the repetition of an earlier success, usually fizzle.

And so, the 1984 Next Wave Festival in Brooklyn is history. But the grants go on, and the yards of favorable publicity already generated guarantee no shortage of future events in Brooklyn and elsewhere. Whether one calls *Einstein on the Beach* performance art or multimedia, there can be little doubt that it symbolizes the nearest we have yet come in this country to an art form crafted for the tastes of what has been called the new class, that group which, we are told, alone possesses the skills to run our society. The new class certainly will have progeny; will its art?

(*February* 1985)

Starring Cindy Sherman: notes on the new art world

by Jed Perl

At Metro Pictures

There are very few galleries in SoHo where one can have any expectation of seeing art of quality on a regular basis. I can think of fewer than a dozen: Washburn, Ingber, and the cooperatives at 121 Wooster Street come quickly to mind. But in general in SoHo the mise-en-scène surpasses in interest any of the art hanging on the walls. There's an obvious element of theater in the galleries, especially in the deluxe SoHo art palaces, where the immense spaces set the stage for many different gradations of chic and hauteur.

Art-as-spectacle: this is a very old idea whose time has once again come. The courtly culture of the Baroque, with its trompe l'oeil decor and elaborately composed gardens, made art and life into teasing mirror twins. One feels an echo of this theatrical idea—an echo as blurred and off-center as a color xerox copy—in the new ambitions of the art scene in SoHo and the East Village. Style in art and manners in life are viewed within the new art world as analogous. In art, as in life, the breaking of conventions and the adoption of antiquated modes are seen as spectacular, as contributions to the drama of the present. The gallery becomes, like the nightclub, a frame for action. And just as waiters and doormen set the mood for the adventure of an evening out, so the gallery staff—a few quietly refined young men and women—set the tone for the adventure of art. These gallery assistants are art world demigods of youth and fashion. They seem intent yet not overly absorbed; they go about their jobs at the telephone and the typewriter with a special superior air. I wonder how they manage to wear such elegant clothes when their weekly salaries couldn't rent a studio apartment for half a month. (Perhaps it's like one of those O. Henry stories—the single outfit, carefully pressed each night.) But the mysteries of looking good, of keeping up appearances, are an element in their role. They're cult followers, devoted as vestals. They guard the way to that wild genius: the artist.

Sometimes, when one of these fancy galleries has one of its less hot personalities hanging on the walls, you almost feel sorry for the staff. They're just putting a good face on things, and it becomes hard to know what all the fuss is really about. But at the right moment in the right gallery what amounts to an antique sense of decorum seems suddenly apropros. At Cindy Sherman's show at Metro Pictures this October you knew just what the staff was up to. The artist of the moment was in residence—up there on the walls in four-by-six-foot color glossies, acting crazy as can be. The space was full of visitors and the gallery folk were carrying themselves with perfect aplomb. They were fulfilled, and they could have balanced the whole world on the head of a pin.

The photographs

Cindy Sherman's new group of color self-portrait photographs—there were fourteen in the October Metro Pictures show—have the glossy, unreal look of commercial products. The printing, done in a professional color lab, is technical perfection: Sherman's blues and oranges and greens are screechy-loud, and her highlights have a greasy shine. In this recent group of portrait photographs Sherman (who's just over thirty) is acting the freaked-out female, cut off from normal life. She's got up in ghastly makeup and fake body parts, but the smoothness of the packaging makes it all seem remote and manageable and dull. Sherman has invented a photographic equivalent of the impersonal, licked surfaces of nineteenth-century academic painting. What's going on in the photographs is as out of reach as the doings in the Middle Eastern harems of academic painters like Gérôme. (Sherman includes in one photo or another a turban, a few swags of cloth, and some exotic-looking, overturned beakers and flasks.) Her photographs have the claustrophobic, back-lit feel of the images kids used to look at in Viewmaster stereo machines. The images are overwrought, hyped-up, and the color looks glacé.

Since Sherman began exhibiting in New York at the end of the 1970s, her photographs, which are all self-portraits, have presented a rogues' gallery of the many guises of a modern Everywoman. Sherman and her supporters take some pride in her refusal to quote directly from sources in movies or TV. Her photographs aren't pop rip-offs; they're supposed to be distillations, allegorical readings of the mass-culture gestalt. Sherman began in the late 1970s with a series of small black-and-white photos called "Untitled Film Stills," in which she photographed herself as a career girl, a housewife, a hitchhiker—as all the gals in 1950s movies and TV. The "Untitled Film Stills" series was shot "on location"—in houses, on highways, on city streets—and many of the images included the whole figure and a good deal of naturalistic background. Since finishing the "Untitled Film Stills" in the early Eighties, Sherman has moved into the studio and brought the camera closer in, so that now her face and figure fill up most of the images. She still wears wigs, makeup, and clothes, but she's now trying to convey a psychologically charged feeling, a sense that you're inside the woman's head. Roughly speaking, Sherman has evolved from Doris Day types to Joan Crawford types. In the recent work we're in the world of *Whatever Happened to Baby Jane?*

In the new photos—which began as an assignment from *Vanity Fair* magazine to create a fairy tale—Sherman is working over the fairy-tale tradition. She impersonates witches and assorted crazies crawling around in dirt or peeking out from behind ears of wheat. In some of the photos she's a victim, cringing at a danger lurking just beyond our field of vision; in others she's the one who's doing the scaring. What one can see of the settings is either outdoorsy, with hints of earth and vegetation and sky, or else boudoir-like, with pieces of sleazy fabric. Though the settings of Sherman's photos have looked less than naturalistic for the past few years, this show marks the first time she's really gone out of this world. Critics have seen here an interest, new to Sherman, in the primitive—maybe even a response to MOMA's "Primitivism" show. To me this sounds rather highfalutin, and Sherman's discussion of these photos in an interview in the October issue of *New York Talk* (a SoHo fashion and entertainment rag) puts them squarely within her usual range of concerns. I don't think she cares if mankind's oldest fears and obsessions are hidden, like sediment, at the bottom of modern culture. What fascinates her is the ridiculous takeoffs on primitive life that she finds in Grade-B movies and in the contraptions sold in novelty shops. Sherman tells the interviewer, Alan Jones (who edited a book of interviews called *The Art Dealers*), that

> [t]here's a great place on Broadway called Gordon's, a giant novelty shop. At first, I didn't use any of their really strange stuff. One

> transitional piece was vaguely based on a Hansel and Gretel sort of situation—a lost waif-type little girl lying in dirt and rocks. Pretty soon I got into more weird costumes. I love going through all the novelty catalogues. Unfortunately the handless arm stump was sold out when I tried to order it from Gordon's.

In the new series, Sherman wears in one image or another false breasts, buttocks, teeth, wounds, a false beard, and two false noses—a pig's snout and a witch's beak with warty chin attached. In the *New York Talk* piece Sherman says, "I was getting bored with just looking like a different *person.* Now it's much more fun to look like a *monster*! There's something I really like about being completely transformed physically." When you're at Metro Pictures you can't get away from the fact that you're looking at another photo of Cindy Sherman. In working out the costumes and personas, she may have experienced a personal catharsis. I believe her when she says that sometimes "I dance around and look at myself and can't *believe* it!" But what the viewer is conscious of is a SoHo artist putting on a lot of unusual trappings. We may feel a certain curiosity about Cindy Sherman's greasepaint world (how many of us have seen a pair of fake buttocks before?); and yet looking at her photographed performances is nothing like watching a good actor or actress take on some elaborate disguise. Actors have the time element; they can take you over the initial shock of the costume, draw you into the performance, and convince you they've been transformed. They can show the living being within. Sherman's photos are one-shot deals; they're vague and provisional, like the rough costume-sketches stage designers do.

Viewing Sherman's photographs makes me feel like a bored school teacher giving out grades. Sherman presents a neatly finished product—she's no slouch. But her creepy-crawly routines are photographed without a stitch of pictorial inventiveness. This artist is a compositional illiterate. Western art offers so many marvelous ways to pull us in and out of a composition—and so many models for the psychology of gesture—and Sherman misses them all. Maybe she wants us to feel that she's the first artist to use the human figure dramatically; maybe the awkward placements and croppings are meant to look unaffected. But Sherman is far too self-conscious about what she's doing to achieve anything like the intuitive simplicity of the untutored artist. She reminds me of the art student who's taken all the chic courses and then decided to play it primitive.

The photo artists

Cindy Sherman's one-woman psychodramas are extremely contrived; she glories in artificiality. But by presenting her fantasies in the form of photographs she avoids the fussed-over feeling that so many people nowadays attribute to painting. Sherman has invented Allegory Lite. Photographic art is instantaneous, and no matter how fanciful the thought processes that go into it, the final product has a quality of ease and speed. Apparently some artists now see the brevity of photography as a criticism of the older methods of picture making: photography makes painting seem laborious, heavy-handed. Sherman is one of a number of artists who in the past decade have used photographic methods while letting everyone know they're not photographers. They want to wed the ease of photography to the high-art cachet of painting.

For these artists photography is the all-purpose metaphor of modern life. It's at once fast, easy, commercial, chic, thought-provoking, sensational, banal. Photography can suggest the gaudy, glamorous fun of the contemporary city; but it can also make just about anything look ordinary and dull. Photography, which turns everything into pictures, can make us feel that nothing is real; it's the perfect medium for the artist who wants to tell us about the dehumanizing effects of modern mass culture. Some of the new photo art, such as Sherrie Levine's photographic reproductions of art-book reproductions of German Expressionist paintings (yes: you have read this statement correctly), seem to play, in the Dada vein, at being wittily obscure. There is as well a posturing, messagey side to this new photographic art —as in the work of Barbara Kruger, who juxtaposes images and words. Example: A close-up of the face of a Howdy-doody doll with, superimposed on it, the words: "When I hear the word culture I take out my checkbook." Many of the photo artists favor the cool, remote feel of old-fashioned black-and-white or the blurriness of crummy color shots. Sherman, however, makes no bones about her affection for the glamour of photography. Cindy Sherman is photo art at its lushest; her art is wickedly deluxe.

The new photo art has people standing up and taking notice; it seems to give gallery-goers something they've been craving. Sherman taps straight into the nerve ends of contemporary culture. For the past five years, she's been taking on the pop culture stereotypes one by one, and she's turned herself into a humorless, high-art Lily Tomlin. A counterculture comedienne like Tomlin offers the promise of catharsis: she shows how people bend to the real or imagined demands of the world, and audiences leave her performances feeling easier with themselves and their lives. I think viewers hope for a similar sense of release when they go to look at Sherman's work. Her "Untitled Film Stills" revealed the artist as a rootless independent who could walk in and out of any role society required of her. In her more recent work, Sherman comes on as the terrified or terrifying female, and people probably feel she's creating a wacky technicolor allegory out of all the disturbing feelings they keep bottled up inside. Sherman makes female psychodrama into art-world spectacle.

Sherman may be doing for the women's issues what two other photo artists—Gilbert and George, the British art team—are doing for homosexual issues. Gilbert and George's recent work, which consists of huge photo collages, is mostly about a world of seductively tough or soft working-class boys. If Sherman is playing dress-up-time with all the female clichés, Gilbert and George are playing cut-and-paste with the gay ones. Gilbert and George go so far in one collage *(Life without End)* as to represent themselves as boy worshippers. They kneel in prayer like the donors in some fifteenth-century altarpiece, only in place of the saint there's a working-class boy idol in regulation T-shirt and jeans. The lushness of Sherman's and Gilbert and George's recent work—the extravagant tableaux and brilliant colors—isn't artistically satisfying, but the work has a heat about it, and this is generated by the charged implications of the subjects. These artists are in touch with the outer reaches of contemporary society, the places where conventions and morals are being challenged and unraveled and changed. (Gilbert and George call their photographic pieces "Moral Works.") For viewers who have always been unsure about what they want from art, these photo works may be the perfect answer: you can't miss the connection to life.

Cindy Sherman, Gilbert and George, and some of the other photo artists are taking up the big issues many better artists stay away from. But picking up a hot topic isn't the same thing as making art. (Maybe the good artists have good reason for shying away from these issues, many of which can't—presto!—be turned into art.) The critic Peter Schjeldahl—whose 1982 *Art in America* piece, "Shermanettes," is the most convincing thing that's been written about Sherman—can make you feel Sherman is breaking through all the conventions and flying free. But when I stand in front of the photos at Metro Pictures, I don't feel I'm in the presence of an engaging artistic imagination. There's a tendency in talking about blatantly autobiographical artists like Sherman (and Gilbert and George) to become obsessed with their psychological profiles: are they good people? are they too narcissistic? have they suffered? What's lacking in the work, though, isn't psychological but artistic—the ability to ferret out of an image or a subject some key bit of form, some rhythmic idea.

What Baudelaire said

In almost all recent discussions of the relations between the artist and society one essay written about two generations ago looms as the classic text to be praised, embroidered, or overthrown. This is Clement Greenberg's 1939 piece, "Avant-Garde and Kitsch." Though Greenberg saw the artist as functioning more and more in a domain apart, he was hardly unconcerned with the texture of civilization as a whole. "Avant-Garde and Kitsch" is an essay written in the shadow of what looked to many like the end of Western urban civilization, and it's an essay edged in socialist dreams. At the end, Greenberg observes that "Capitalism in decline finds that whatever of quality it is still capable of producing becomes almost invariably a threat to its own existence. Advances in culture, no less than advances in science and industry, corrode the very society under whose aegis they are made possible. Here, as in every other question today, it becomes necessary to quote Marx word for word." Today, forty-five years later, neither the collapse of capitalism nor the rise of socialism appear imminent, and it seems as if Baudelaire, not Marx, is the nineteenth-century wise man we who are interested in art should be quoting "word for word." Baudelaire's *Salon of 1859*, in particular the section on "The Modern Public and Photography," strikes me as almost uncanny when considered in relation to Cindy Sherman and the new art world.

Baudelaire, who was writing only two decades after the coming of photography, had to see photography's significance somewhat differently than we do a hundred and twenty-five years later. And yet there doesn't appear to be a single element of the peculiar contemporary intermix between photography and art and reality that Baudelaire couldn't have predicted on the basis of what he saw around him in the 1850s. Baudelaire sees photography, with its easy relation to reality, as quelling the sense of yearning and struggle we feel when a painter reaches for the truth. What Baudelaire gets at is the curiously sedative aspect of so much of photography—and especially of artistic photography: its power to distance things, to trap them in amber. For the mass-market audience the revelations of photography become a substitute for the experiences cultured people used to look for in works of art. Baudelaire believes the public is lapping photography up for its cheap, prepackaged thrills. He tells the story of a gathering where an attempt was made to "discreetly conceal" some pornographic stereo photographs from a "beautiful woman, a woman of high society, not of mine." The lady's friends, Baudelaire explains, were "taking upon themselves some feeling of delicacy in her presence; but 'No,' she replied. 'Give them to me! Nothing is too strong for me.'" That's the sort of line you sense playing in the minds of all the elegantly dressed visitors to the picture palaces down in SoHo. Nothing is too strong for them! They're glad Cindy Sherman has gone hog-wild, because now they can prove they're up to watching a pleasant-looking young woman doing gross-out routines with a pig snout or fake buttocks. (A week after Sherman's show closed, the same crowd was at the Castelli Gallery on West Broadway watching Bruce Nauman's new neon jobs; male silhouettes that flashed on and off, every other flash bringing their limp penises erect and often into the waiting rears and mouths of other mostly male figures. The combination of expensiveness and porn was so flagrant it made me laugh out loud.)

Baudelaire's main argument in "The Modern Public and Photography" is that ordinary people prefer the truth of photography to the truth of imaginative art. And though it's become fashionable in recent decades to question the veracity of all photographs, the public still appreciates the relatively simple connection between a photographic image and the world outside. Baudelaire is quite sympathetic to what we would today call "straight" photography—the sort of portraiture and documentary work which his friend Nadar was famous for. What drives him to distraction and inspires his best venomous style is the artists who substitute for artistic imagination the frisson of photographic verisimilitude. Photo artists, he says, are trying "to strike, to surprise, to stupify [the public] by means of unworthy tricks, because they know that it is incapable of ecstasy in front of the natural devices of true art." I feel something like this cynical pandering in Cindy Sherman's work.

It's fashionable to say Cindy Sherman is a bad photographer—or that she's not a photographer at all. What these demurrals really tell us is that she's not to be regarded as nature's "humble servant"—which is how Baudelaire described the photographer's role. (The great photographers—Atget, Walker Evans—could be called the geniuses among the humble servants.) Sherman doesn't have a stitch of humility—it's not a SoHo virtue—and she's mucking together exactly those values Baudelaire said were irreconcilable: photographic truth and artistic imagination. Sherman's slick photographic effects are a come-on: they're the glamorous evidence of her imaginative prowess, and they're meant to make us believe in her as an artist. But in the wake of this photographic seduction (to quote Baudelaire) "strange abominations [take] form."

In "The Modern Public and Photography," Baudelaire reserved his deepest rage for the nineteenth-century art photographers who dressed people up in the costumes and poses of historic or literary folk. I find his description of these photographs rather Shermanesque. "By bringing together a group of male and female clowns, got up like butchers and laundry-maids in a carnival, and by begging these *heroes* to be so kind as to hold their chance grimaces for the time necessary for the performance, the operator flattered himself that he was reproducing tragic or elegant scenes from ancient history. Some democratic writer ought to have seen here a cheap method of disseminating a loathing for history and for painting among the people." This last part is most interesting. Baudelaire says the illusions of photographic truth can be used to convince us of untruths—to trash on the truth. This is what most of nineteenth-century art photography was about; and Sherman is really doing the same thing. The banality of the vision—with its rejection of the only truth an artist can ever depend on: the truth of the imagination—makes a capitulation to the most ordinary taste of the bourgeoisie. Baudelaire is hardly the only person who has described the failure of salon art, but he may be the first to connect the emptiness of official art to the mechanistic photographic forms of popular culture. When artists with old-fashioned ambitions adopt new-fangled techniques, the result—in 1985 as in 1859—can be an art that's comfortably shocking. It teaches us how to be shocked and not give a damn.

Pop go the Sixties

Cindy Sherman was born in 1954, and the work she's doing today obviously has a great deal to do with what was going on in the United States when she (and all of us baby boomers) were teenagers in the 1960s. In a way she's a latter day Pop Artist, and Pop was probably the first art to be not just comfortably but even cozily shocking. Cindy Sherman is so enormously successful, it's a little difficult to think of her as a confused artist. But her mental landscape—at least what you see of it in her work—seems like a case of the cool-cat ironies of Lichtenstein and Warhol gone haywire. It's as if Lichtenstein and Warhol and Sixties pop culture is the whole world to her: she seems a bit like the screwed-up adolescent that Paul Goodman describes in his 1963 novel, *Making Do.*

> He regarded the detritus of our culture, the world of TV or Hollywood or even the advertising, as if that were the normal lively world. He did not have enough common sense or confidence in himself to look directly at the street. If a scene was on the TV and had that official warrant and interpretation, he had the courage to think that it was real; otherwise he doubted it.
>
> But then when, inevitably, he became nauseated and disillusioned with such an unsatis-

> factory reality, he pathetically began to assume that there was a secret metaphysical truth in the disillusioned French and Italian movies, the stereotypes of Harlem and hipsters, the ideology of hasheesh. He desperately wanted these too to be on TV, in order to make sure!

Though there's nothing down-at-the-heels about Cindy Sherman's reputation, her sensibility has a desperate, almost deranged lack of focus.

If one wanted to make up a fantasy of a high-toned theoretical history of Pop, one might say that Warhol and Lichtenstein are Pop's pure, high, classical moment, and that with Sherman Pop is in a sort of crisis-wracked, neurotic, mannerist decline. Maybe bad art does recapitulate in ghastly parody the history of good art: certainly the particular savor of Sherman's photographs has to do with her having lived through Pop's classic moment and become too knowing about all the internal contradictions to be able to keep the forms and sentiments clear. Maybe Sherman suffers from overexposure to the entire hundred-year history of modernism's love affair with the pop world.

In the 1860s, Manet made painting out of the popular Parisian fashions for things Spanish and Japanese. And there have been, in the years since, more than a few attempts at painting and sculpting with one eye on the museum and the other on the underlife or fashionable life of contemporary culture. These attempts have had some happy results: in the work of Robert and Sonia Delaunay, in Schwitters and the other collagists, in Picasso's Ballets-Russes period. But it's never been clear whether the high energy of high art was just sponging up everything in its path, or if pop culture was, in fact, energizing the museum-art tradition.

People who enjoy both pop and high culture have always sensed that there is a sort of general analogy to be drawn between the methods of the two: all art achieves its effects by grabbing hold of a complex of traditions, and then going into them, reshaping them, and transforming them. It's probably this general sense of an analogy that turns so many painters and sculptors into connoisseurs and collectors of pop and folk art of all kinds. But it has always seemed to me that it was people who weren't terribly engaged in either high or popular art—who weren't creators or ardent consumers of either posters or paintings, pop tunes or lieder—who were interested in making the comparisons. If you're really involved in the conventions of an art form and how artists use them, you are just not going to be overly concerned with how one set of conventions ultimately sets up against another. It gets to be an artificial issue. The painter or sculptor who brings pop culture into his work has succeeded when we no longer think to make the better-or-worse comparisons. This is the difficulty for the artist who goes into pop: he's got to create an analogy to the vigor of the street that doesn't get hung up on dreary comparisons.

What Sherman is tying into isn't just Pop Art—it's an attitude toward mass culture in general which really first flowered when she (and this writer, as well) were young. No doubt people have enjoyed peeking beneath the conventions and formulas of popular culture for as long as commercial civilization has existed. Long before the Sixties people had looked into popular forms of art and seen there a hundred odd, bizarre, and occasionally endearing subtexts—it didn't take the Sixties to discover the surrealism in Busby Berkeley or the wildly anarchic sexual personalities of Mae West and Bogie. The Surrealists themselves had revealed pop's hidden texts to a degree. But their disclosures of the kinks in capitalist culture were couched in the best obscurantist language of modernism and were of interest only to a small avant-garde audience.

In the 1960s all the subtexts went public. There were new kinds of stores that sold new kinds of products. There were the poster-sized blow-ups of photographs of Bogie and Mae West, the red-white-and-blue striped and starred and union-jacked clothes and plastic doodads. Hitherto obscure historic styles, like Beardsley's and Tiffany's, were suddenly ubiquitous. A private, ironic way of looking at the world was transformed into a permanent public revelation. This felt exhilarating at first: who ever dreamed that so many people could be so knowingly ironic about bad taste and quirky good taste and old-fashioned nationalist sentiments? But then, fairly quickly, the context of taste and irony and discrimination that made all these odd things so interesting began to evaporate. The 1960s stumbled into a form of irony that had no perspective from which to be ironic. In Paul Goodman's 1971 book about poetry called *Speaking and Language,* he commented, in passing, on this phenomenon. "In a confused society," he said, obviously referring to his own, "avant-garde does not flourish very well. What is done in order to be idiotic can easily be co-opted as the idiotic standard." The Surrealists may have done certain things in order to be idiotic; but when you walk into Cindy Sherman's show, you know you're just being confronted by the idiotic standard.

Pop culture crops up most convincingly in Sixties art where we may least expect it. The vein of anarchic innocence that for some of us will always say "early Beatles" isn't felt in the heavy, museum-style of Lichtenstein's and Warhol's Pop Art. I find the spectacle of a prepackaged postwar America reflected in some of the more conservative branches of Sixties art, and it's refreshing to encounter artists who don't make a fuss about their pop culture borrowings. There's a bit of the Pop attitude in the opening lines of Randall Jarrell's poem "Next Day," published in *The Lost World* in 1964. We are with a woman in a supermarket.

> Moving from Cheer to Joy, from Joy
>   to All,
> I take a box
> And add it to my wild rice, my Cornish
>   game hens.
> The slacked or shorted, basketed, identical
> Food-gathering flocks
> Are selves I overlook.

The realist Fairfield Porter, who did much of his best work in the 1960s, also catches something of the surprising ways pop culture impinges on our lives. He will carefully include the present-tense look of a cereal box or a slightly-out-of-date car in the informally brushed "old-fashioned" vision of a still life or landscape. What's invigorating in Jarrell and Porter is the way high-art style seems to buckle and even get a trifle campy in order to include these pieces of the pop world. It's just this sense of high style clashing interestingly and amusingly with the pop scene that's missing in the more obviously modernist works of Warhol and Lichtenstein.

For all its cheekiness, Pop Art is an essentially world-weary and cynical style. In Pop Art the mass-culture images feel frozen and deracinated: they've lost their power to move us in odd, unexpected ways. The trick of basing paintings on photographic images began with the silk-screens of Rauschenberg and Warhol. The Pop Artists didn't enter into the uproar of pop culture, they snipped off bits of it. The method of Warhol and Lichtenstein and Rauschenberg is to take things out of context—this is what gives their work its dissociated, modern look. They've lost the plentitude, the richness of mass culture, and the new photo artists haven't regained it, either. For Cindy Sherman and the other photo artists, the modern look of the work is a function of the disappearance of the brushstroke, that irreducible token of the artist's hand. Sherman, like the Pop Artists before her, has meant to replace the old pleasures of touch and stroke—of the artist searching for a perfect balance as he concocts a fictional world—with the giddy pleasures of pop. There's something depressing about the trade-off.

Nostalgia

As the baby-boom generation heads, in the 1980s, toward grown-up status and even middle age, the 1950s and early 1960s are being transformed into a collection of sentimental vignettes. Nostalgia is one of Cindy Sherman's subjects; Fifties nostalgia is almost the lingua franca of the contemporary art scene. Lots of the new clothes are Fifties-ish in style; and a lot of the routines in the downtown clubs—the drag take-offs on female stereotypes and the Fifties movies, often run with the sound turned off—are paradistic gestures that reflect an extravagant love-hate relation with the days when we were young. The furnishings that those of us whose parents had "good taste" grew up with in the 1950s—the furniture of Charles Eames and Paul McCobb—is now exhibited and bought and sold and collected by people who are in their thirties. The more sophisticated of the rock videos are full of the bright color and sharp outlines of 1950s design, and the new painting is full of the poses and looks—the cigarette smoking and hair-sprayed coiffures—of the time.

This is all rather strange for those of us who were kids back then. I've now had the experience of seeing the dining-room table that I grew up eating at (a modest piece by Paul McCobb) sitting in the window of an antique shop on the Upper Westside. I find that the acquisitive side of my personality is a bit charmed and a bit put off by the way one can now collect the pieces of one's past as a materialized version of the possessiveness of memory. In the 1950s, Charles Eames concocted a deck of playing cards which, instead of the conventional markings, had on both sides collages of color photographs showing a mish-mash of charming and enchanting things.These handsome cards were slotted on each side so they could be put together to make large paper buildings. The set was called "house of cards." As a kid in Ann Arbor, Michigan, in the 1950s I bought a box of these at an artsy store called The Artisans, and they miraculously hung on in my parent's basement through many moves. Now I've reclaimed them. To look at that deck of cards is to engage in a sort of innocent narcissistic fantasy about one's own past—the past is packaged, commodified. And though there's nothing wrong with this as an impulse of the collector or the connoisseur, when narcissism becomes the driving force behind an artist's style, as it does seem to for many now, there is something wrong.

The critic Sanford Schwartz, who's in his thirties, recently touched on this generational ambivalence in a piece in *The New Yorker.* Schwartz was writing about a show of work by the Bay Area artist David Park, who died in 1960. He said he was surprised at "how much Park's best work recalls the fifties." Schwartz said he was "equivocal about this. Part of me thinks that there is something weak and commercial about this period look, that I'm drawn to the pictures for nostalgic reasons. But part of me is fascinated by it." What's missing in most of the new art treatments of Fifties nostalgia is just this element of ambivalence. The artists don't seem able to get at how equivocal we all feel about this recent past of ours.

The Fifties nostalgia that crops up in so much of the new art lacks a sense of detail. Cindy Sherman invokes suburban life and modern design in so broad a fashion that we can't get a handle on her attitude. You don't know what she really has in mind. The better design work of the 1950s had an optimistic spirit about it that's rarely conveyed in the pictures that evoke Fifties style. It was after the war that America first embraced the Bauhaus and biomorphic sensibilities of Europe. The sparkle of Paul Rand's graphic designs—those icons of Fifties style—comes from Rand's way of grabbing hold of the clarity of modern European design and giving it an American spin. (In 1957, Rand and his wife Ann published a children's book called *Sparkle and Spin.*) Rand occasionally used Victorian typefaces and collage snippets from photographs in his work, and these bits provide a taste of what is to come in 1960s design. But with Rand the chaos of mass culture is disciplined by the smart, spanking-new feel of the work—by the faith in modernism.

The Fifties were the last happy stand of modernist design. In Rand's work there's an easy, slightly unthinking optimism that connects with the clean-lined, ecstatic feeling that is one side of the suburban short stories John Cheever was writing at the time. None of the artists who have been playing with the Fifties recently have gotten at that clear-headed, perfect-Sunday-afternoon feeling. Nor have any of the younger artists been able to get at the other side of the Cheever world: the dark tones, the bleakness inside those two-kids, two-car suburban homes. It's as if the artists who were kids in the Fifties are unable or unwilling to admit that the Fifties were a living, breathing world. Artists in their thirties are turning their own past into a pop-culture cliché.

Toward a new theory of the picturesque

These words are from Rudolf, a one-name-only East Village nightclub entrepreneur: "As a mecca of creativity and craziness [New York] is in decline—this city is out. Rio is definitely happening. And Hong Kong—the lease expires in 1997—believe me those people are running wild." I take this as metaphoric: not so much a rejection of New York as an affirmation of the apocalyptic era so many artists and writers seem to feel in New York just now. The occupants of the new art scene are young and of the middle class. They went through adolescence in the 1960s and 1970s, with credit cards and computers, backyard pools and shopping centers. They grew up with the obviously false lilt of "I'm OK, you're OK" in their ears, and they are attracted to New York because here—despite gentrification, which is a form of suburbanization—they can still feel the contrasts of rich and poor, the elegantly dressed figure moving along the garbage-strewn streets. All this seems to confirm what they sensed beneath the seamlessness of freeway America when they were kids: some permanent disaster in contemporary civilization. The fascination with Hong Kong—or with Berlin—for art watchers is in the strange flowers of the dark, nether realms of civilization. Apparently where the kitsch of capitalism meets the kitsch of communism there's a savor in the air. The grinding dullness of totalitarian bureaucracy is seen to rhyme with the new boredom of an avant-garde with no more tricks up its sleeves.

The young of the middle class have always gone slumming among the real poor, and the margins of civilization have often struck artists as picturesque. Ruins gave the monied classes of the eighteenth and nineteenth centuries many opportunities for serene reflection on the passage of cultures and civilizations. We know from many nineteenth-century images this attractive view: in the foreground, a gentleman on a little hill; in the perfectly drawn middle distance, the Doric temples of Paestum or the broken tombs of the Appian Way; off to the side, a tumbledown farm, a mother with dark hair and ragged skirts, several children, an ancient but still usable well (the glory of Roman engineering). Poverty can, horrible to say, look picturesque, though only a deranged aesthete will find beauty in misery. In the East Village (hub of an art scene that is very hot, or maybe even past its prime), among the ruins of boarded-up tenements and graffitied walls around Avenues A and B and C, the old appreciation of ruins takes unexpected turns. Though there is still in pockets of the East Village the vitality of ethnic groups, where the real action is supposed to be—east of Second Avenue—a new theory of the pleasures of ruins has been taking form. These ruins aren't real ruins—they point to no previous glory, only to many episodes in an ever present, unremitting decay.

The class content of the taste for ruins hasn't changed completely since the nineteenth century. The comfortably ensconced still like to contemplate the world of the tumbledown. In the nineteenth century, when the "haves" were sure of the space between them and the others, there was room for the view—there was a gentle perspective from which the nicely dressed men and women watched the charming poor. In the contemporary East Village the clarity of class distinctions is gone, and though the poor are still poor—maybe even worse off—

the monied have lost or denied to themselves the peculiar moral elation of the composed view. On the streets of the East Village the view doesn't compose, and this is surely the heart of the new picturesque. These are the ruins you can't contemplate—it's all interminable, grinding foreground. For those who live there the neighborhood surely has a bit of the comfortable feeling one's neighborhood always has, no matter how bad it is. But speaking as a visitor (and most artists and gallery-goers are visitors) I find almost embarrassing the birth of art galleries in this world, where the rudiments of civilization (the privacy of one's apartment, the interchange of the street) dissolve for the real inhabitants—for those who see America as a dream on TV—into a rubbly nightmare. The middle class will either change the neighborhood or leave it; the underclass may have to leave, but wherever they go, for them it will be the same.

The scene casts quite a spell. The new connoisseurs and dandies sit in the night contemplating not the cameos and engravings of the old aesthete's study but the throwaways of capitalism. A taste for the graffitied ruins of old buildings is only an extreme case of a general passion for what mainstream culture has left behind or cast aside. The fashions and accessories of Fifties moderne, the lurid plastics of Canal Street, the novelty shop tricks and the gold and velvet Hispanic icons of Fourteenth Street are all desirable, for they embody a vague sense of dislocation and represent an unconscious, accidental critique of centrist values. Some of these objects carry real emotion: Hispanic religious kitsch, for example, is a genuine pop style. If you look at the technicolor madonnas printed on cardboard and listen to the pop gospel tunes (where sentimental AM radio love melodies combine with lyrics about Our Saviour) you feel that for the people who actually live with these things they're inspiring—like the dream of a better life, of an apartment somewhere else, probably in Queens. But when the popular forms find their way into the fancy art galleries the emotion goes awry. To love pop culture too much from too great a distance is to let connoisseurship get unhinged.

The image of Cindy Sherman shopping amidst the Halloween disguises of Gordon's novelty store on Broadway is a significant portrait of the artist as a new-style connoisseur of the picturesque. If you're looking for the kooky products of commercial civilization, you probably can't hope for much more than Gordon's. I believe Cindy Sherman has known the ecstasy of shlock. And her sense of the picturesque *is* finely tuned. What are her photos but ingenious dime-store recountings of the categories which the eighteenth-century English theorists of the picturesque liked to enumerate? Sherman's art encompasses, in parody form, the beautiful, the terrifying, and the sublime. The Cindy Sherman who goes to Gordon's is, like the Gilbert and George who photograph the low life of London, a connoisseur of the contemporary picturesque—an egotist furnishing her mind.

Today artists and critics are joined in an addiction to the new picturesque. Their god-protector is that painter of ruins, the late de Chirico. He is a better and a worse and above all a very different artist than his new admirers would have us believe, but the East Villagers are probably right to see in his moodily-lit late work the soul of a sentimental archeologist. To describe the impacted geological layerings of late twentieth-century culture, the new writers on art bring forth a dazzling array of texts. The articles that get written have cascades of wild, often erudite quotations—they can be beguiling. In these essays the figure of Baudelaire wandering through Paris a hundred and twenty-five years ago and of Walter Benjamin wandering through Baudelaire's Paris eighty years later, revolve like the images of infinite regress in some house of mirrors. Watteau also seems a figure with which to be obsessed now (the painter David Salle speaks of him). The paradoxes and delusions of contemporary commercial culture can be compared to the confused values of the late aristocracy which Watteau took as his subject. The illusions of class and the beauties of the confusion of the fêtes champetres are perhaps seen as related to the chaotic ambience of the new nightclubs. (In the fêtes, the musical men wear odd, dandified theatrical garb, as they do at the big club on Fourteenth Street, the Palladium, where the go-go dancers can be boys, dressed in Fifties costumes of pleated pants and button-down shirts.) *Gersaint's Shopsign*—the first masterpiece in which the art market becomes a subject for art, and the first example of an advertisement become a masterpiece—this is seen as the extraordinary precedent for many contemporary foibles.

Trompe l'oeil

In Cindy Sherman's photographs the layerings of make-believe and irony and insincerity are piled high. Who's to say what's a pose and what's not a pose? Even beauty, which was so often in the past a sign of goodness or heroism in art can now be presumed to be no more than a brilliant mask. Art's illusions seem more illusory than ever—a house of cards, thin and on the verge of falling down.

Trompe l'oeil—the fine art of fooling the eye and the mind—is the most popular art game in town. Fake masterpieces, fake artists, fake issues: we have them all, and they all have those charming, seductive surfaces. The new art world is a great movie set. No wonder one of its premier showcases is called Metro Pictures. This mocking Pop Art name evokes the old-time movie houses —the kind Edward Hopper might have painted. A gallery called Metro Pictures promises something other than ordinary works of art; it promises the glamour of the silver screen. The name seems to flirt with the vernacular; it has a jokey edge. And yet when you walk inside Metro Pictures the vast white spaces and the obvious smoothness of the whole operation lend an air of sobriety, almost of sanctity. Sherman's pictures have that same combination of the jokey and the serious. Though the costumes and the disguises can't but be a bit funny, in the photographs Sherman's face never reveals the pleasure in dressing up that she describes in the *New York Talk* interview. She always wears a far-off, grave expression. She looks unshockable, as haughty as the queen of some exotic tribe. Trompe l'oeil is serious business.

One can explore all around Cindy Sherman's art—look at her working methods, sources, attitudes. And yet it's in the nature of her photographs that such a search brings us no closer to her. It's like walking up to a picture of a window painted on a wall: the closer you get, the less you can believe in it. In Cindy Sherman's art the Fifties, the Sixties, the East Village, the Grade-B movies, the nightclubs: all of these form an imaginary set of Viewmaster slides that you can pick up and examine, one by one. The images wheel by, like the pictures on the stereo cards that were grabbed by the fine lady in Baudelaire's anecdote. We see some flesh, a masquerade, a memory, a bit of beauty—but it's all remote. The Cindy Sherman photos at Metro Pictures, in their trim, matte black frames, felt, like the images in the stereo machine, infinitely removed. Cindy Sherman, protected by sheets of plexiglass, was untouchable. She revealed nothing about herself; she remained a shadowy figure.

All photography is trompe l'oeil and all trompe l'oeil is tragicomic. There's the tragicomedy of the grand stage—of Rembrandt and Bernini and the Baroque ceiling painters—and then there's the tragicomedy of today. The new art world has turned trompe l'oeil, with its tradition of divine guessing games, into a TV drama of deceit. One expects an artist who wears masks to want to be unmasked; but maybe not. Cindy Sherman has taken on a hundred different roles, and yet you end up feeling there's really nobody there.

(*January* 1986)

The phenomenon of Allen Ginsberg

by Bruce Bawer

I'm so lucky to be nutty.
—Allen Ginsberg, "Bop Lyrics" (1949)

The very first poem in Allen Ginsberg's *Collected Poems 1947-1980*[1] seems, in a way, to prophesy Ginsberg's entire career. It is titled "In Society," and it dates from 1947, when the poet was twenty-one years old. The poem records a dream: Ginsberg is at a high-society cocktail party, is more or less ignored, and is told by a woman, "I don't like you." He screams at her:

> . . . "What!"
> in outrage. "Why you shit-faced fool!"
> This got everybody's attention.
> "Why you narcissistic bitch! How
> can you decide when you don't even
> know me," I continued in a violent
> and messianic voice, inspired at last,
> dominating the whole room.

Could Ginsberg have known, at that tender age, that he would spend much of his adult life dominating rooms in this manic, "messianic" manner—indeed, that his attention-getting tactics at poetry readings, political conventions, sit-ins, be-ins, protest marches, and Yippie Life Festivals would be a crucial catalyst in his rise to fame? Even Richard Howard, who in his no-nonsense survey of contemporary American poetry, *Alone with America*, begins forty of forty-one essays with a businesslike disquisition upon the poetic career at hand ("In 1960, Howard Moss selected an appropriate showing of poems from his first three volumes . . ."), makes an exception in the case of Allen Ginsberg. The long opening paragraph of Howard's essay on Ginsberg is devoted not to *explication de texte* but to an anecdote. The gist of it is that once, at a poetry conference attended by Howard, an elderly poet just back from Nigeria was "extol[ling] the rare privilege of moving among a race of women proudly nude," whereupon the bard of the Beat Generation rose from his seat, "stepped up onto the dais and without a word, without a smile, without a single deprecating gesture, Allen Ginsberg took off all his clothes."

You could fill a book with Ginsberg anecdotes of this sort. (The stories about him removing his clothing at one public gathering or another would by themselves make up a long chapter.) What is remarkable is not that Ginsberg has advertised himself with such arrogance and audacity, but that it has worked like a charm; thanks to such shameless scene-stealing antics, he has attained a measure of fame that he could never have secured by his poetry alone. He is, unarguably, the only poet in America who is not just a member of the august American Academy of Arts and Letters but a bona fide celebrity, the sort who appears on network

1 *Collected Poems 1947-1980,* by Allen Ginsberg; Harper & Row, 837 pages, $27.50.

talk shows. He is idolized by English professors as well as rock stars, and associates comfortably with both groups. He is truly famous.

The *Collected Poems 1947-1980* is the ultimate testimony to this fame. Two inches thick, clad in a bright, firetruck-red wrapper, this imposing tome, like its author, stands out big and brash among its fellows, demanding to be recognized. Its message could not be more obvious: that this poet, whose verse has heretofore been packed into numerous shoddy little small-press volumes, henceforth belongs to the ages. What's more, the *Collected Poems* is only the first step in what amounts to the mainstream press's canonization of Allen Ginsberg. In the words of the publicity flyer accompanying the review copy, Harper & Row will, in the fullness of time, "make available [Ginsberg's] journals, letters, literary essays, and lectures on American literature, as well as a new collection of poems scheduled to coincide with his sixtieth birthday in 1986." What poet, living or dead, has been treated so reverently by Publishers' Row? There can be no denying it hereafter: Allen Ginsberg, who rose to renown as the outspoken enemy of the Establishment, and the most prominent feature of whose poetry has always been its hostility to the order of things in the United States of America, is now the Republic's premier Establishment poet.

Ginsberg's parents, at least, would have been happy. And if there is anything in America that Allen Ginsberg has not rebelled against in his three decades as the amazingly tireless (and drearily tiresome) Poet of Protest, it is his parents. Ginsberg's father, Louis, was a poet—a premodernist rhymester, to be sure, but a poet; his mother, Naomi, was a Communist agitator whose paranoid psychosis (as any reader of "Kaddish" knows) eventually necessitated her commitment to a mental institution. Poetry, paranoia, protest: this was the mixed legacy of Ginsberg's parents, and it is a legacy to which Ginsberg—who has dedicated his *Collected Poems* to their memory—has been eternally and entirely faithful. When, at age sixteen, he left their Paterson, New Jersey, home to attend Columbia University, Ginsberg took up studies in literature, his father's field; and, just as loyally, he rejected the opportunity that Columbia offered to breathe sane air for the first time in his life. Rather—in a clear attempt to cultivate a Naomi Ginsberg-like rebelliousness—Ginsberg took up with the Beats.

Or, more precisely, the as-yet-unknown Beats-to-be. At first, in addition to Ginsberg, there were three of them: Jack Kerouac (a middle-class boy who lived with his mother in Ozone Park, Queens), William Burroughs (an heir to the gigantic corporation of the same name), and Lucien Carr (a slim, handsome student at Columbia). Though they looked harmless enough, Kerouac, Burroughs, and Carr had the same problem Ginsberg did: they craved chaos. They looked down upon the society in which they lived, for no other reason than that, like any other nonanarchic society, it had laws, a government, a way of life; they considered the classical, intellectually oriented education offered at Columbia to be pointless and stifling; and they romanticized poverty, criminality, and rootlessness in a way that only naïve, sheltered young men could do. They felt themselves to be geniuses—literary geniuses, to be precise—and disdained the "well-made" piece of writing as much as they did the well-ordered mind. Truly great minds, they insisted, were not sane and stable and logical, and did not express themselves in lucid, beautifully balanced sentences; instead, such minds soared above the surface of the earth, touched the stars, whirled and shook and spun erratically in the upper air. The great, in short, were always a little mad. Thus it was with genuine pride that the Beats asserted—at first to one another, and then, later, to an increasingly attentive world—their own madness.

The Beats have been spoken of as populist writers, as celebrators of the democratic spirit. But the truth is that they were confirmed elitists. Their collective self-image was nothing short of messianic; in their judgment, they were, by virtue of their self-proclaimed mental instability, incomparably superior to the civilization into which they had been born, to the professors who had been designated to instruct them, to the great authors that everybody read. The appeal of this anti-logic to the young Ginsberg, in particular, is obvious: what could bring more comfort to a sensitive young man who loved his mother than the idea that her mental illness, far from being a family tragedy, was, on the contrary, something to be proud of? It was this anti-logic, at any rate, that persuaded Ginsberg, when he was not yet twenty years old, to reject Lionel Trilling and the other too-sane "squares" of the Columbia English department as being utterly incapable of giving him a real education, and to allow the loosely bound Burroughs (who was twelve years older than he was) and the wacky Kerouac (four years his senior) to be his literary mentors. The Beats used the same anti-logic to determine which outsiders would be allowed to join their fraternity. Thus Herbert Huncke, a psychopathic burglar and drug addict who was known to New York police as "the Creep" (and whom Ginsberg once described as "the only sophisticated man in New York"), was heartily welcomed into the fold. (Huncke would make an enduring, if unwitting, contribution to American literature: he introduced his cronies to the word "beat," meaning worn-out, jaded; it was Kerouac who, in a deliberate echo of Gertrude Stein's "lost generation" remark, borrowed Huncke's word and coined the appelation "the Beat Generation.") And Neal Cassady, a dashing railway brakeman from Denver who arrived on the scene in 1946, was such an excellent specimen of the obsessive-compulsive type that the Beats not only let him into their charmed circle but, endlessly fascinated by his hyperkinetic hedonism, made a literary hero out of him. Kerouac would immortalize him as Dean Moriarty in *On the Road* (1956) and other novels, and Ginsberg (who fell in love with Cassady) would write numerous poems about him over the ensuing decades, one of the first being "Dakar Doldrums" (1947). The initial stanza of this poem not only demonstrates the intensity of Ginsberg's unrequited passion (Cassady had thrown him over for a woman, and a despondent Ginsberg had signed onto a freighter bound for Senegal) but provides a good illustration of his extremely imitative, pseudo-Elizabethan early style (the first of many extremely imitative Ginsberg styles):

> Most dear, and dearest at this moment most,
> Since this my love for thee is thus more free
> Than that I cherished more dear and lost;
> Most near, now nearest where I fly from thee:
> Thy love most consummated is in absence,
> Half for the trust I have for thee in mind,
> Half for the pleasures of thee in remembrance—
> Thou art most full and fair of all thy kind.

Amid all the *non compos mentis* carryings-on, then, there *was* some writing going on among the Beats. But, all in all, the history of Ginsberg's first years with his subterranean compeers bears less resemblance to a literary chronicle than it does to a textbook of case histories in schizophrenia. Two incidents stand out. The first, which took place in 1944, was the murder by Lucien Carr of a young man named David Kammerer, who, according to Carr, had made a pass at him. Since the crime was therefore an "honor slaying," Carr was let off with a relatively brief term in an Elmira, New York, reformatory. His fellow Beats, for their part, appear to have gotten a Norman Mailerish thrill out of the affair; the murder, one gathers from the many narratives that have touched on the crime, confirmed their image of themselves as a dangerous band of underground rebels. Then, in 1948 (the year he was finally graduated from Columbia), Ginsberg had his first brush with fame. He was implicated in one of Huncke's burglaries, got his picture on the cover of the *Daily News* as a result, and was sent to the Columbia Psychiatric Institute instead of prison. There he met and befriended Carl Solomon, a well-read maniac who (one gets the impression) made the Beats look like the Sitwells; upon release from the Institute,

Solomon immediately assumed the role of the group's so-called "lunatic saint." (He would also, in time, become the raving mad junkie-protagonist of Ginsberg's most famous poem, "Howl.") Solomon was, in the words of Beat historian John Tytell, something of a Platonic ideal of "the artist as outrage"—and therefore, obviously, a model of sorts for the outrageous public persona that Ginsberg was eventually to assume.[2]

Besides being the year that Ginsberg joined Carr in the pantheon of hipster hoods, 1948 was also the year of two supposedly epiphanic events in the life of the aspiring poet. The first involved William Blake. One day, Ginsberg was alone in his apartment, having just read "Ah! Sun-Flower" (a poem in *Songs of Experience*), when suddenly he heard a voice—that of Blake himself, he figured—reading the verses aloud. Over the next few weeks, the voice returned and read other Blake poems to him. The Ginsberg groupies have made much of this incident; Paul Portugés devotes a whole book *(The Visionary Poetics of Allen Ginsberg)* to an interpretation of Ginsberg's entire corpus in light of it, insisting that the auditory hallucination "revolutionized [Ginsberg's] ideas about poetry, his concept of self, and his perception of the quotidian world." Ginsberg himself (as quoted in Jane Kramer's book *Allen Ginsberg in America*) puts it this way:

> The thing I felt was that there was this big god over all, who was completely aware and completely conscious of everything, and at the same time completely the same as everybody, and that the whole purpose of being born was to wake up to Him . . . . I felt everything vibrating in one harmony—all past efforts and desires, all present realizations . . . . And I felt that even *my* previous ponderings had been harmoniously flower-petaled toward this final understanding of what it was all about and that all my poetic musings about supreme reality were prophetic, really, and just the sweet, well-intentioned strivings of a poor mind to reach what was already there.[3]

What it comes down to is that this "visitation" (which occurred, by the way, after Ginsberg had been smoking marijuana and inhaling Benzedrine regularly for several years) gave Ginsberg an abrupt push in the direction of the cosmic. It made him more of a transcendental poet than he had been before—the sort of poet, that is, who does not think of a poem as an object, a "made thing," but rather as the effusion of a poetic self that sees all, knows all, encompasses all. This was, then, the beginning of the end of whatever interest the twenty-two-year-old Ginsberg might have had in developing his poetic technique.

The second epiphanic event of 1948 was somewhat more down-to-earth. Ginsberg went to hear his fellow Patersonian, William Carlos Williams, read at the Museum of Modern Art, and when the older poet recited his poem "The Clouds," which at its end trails off in mid-sentence, the device struck Ginsberg with the force of a revelation: you could write the way you talk! Up to this point he had been, in his own words, "hung up on cats like Wyatt, Surrey, and Donne," and had churned out reams of pseudo-Elizabethan poems (and would continue to do so for a couple more years, finally abandoning the iamb—for a while, anyway—after "Ode: My Twenty-Fourth Year" in 1950-1951). Now, hung up on a cat named Williams, he began dividing entries from his prose journals into lines and calling them poems:

> I walked into the cocktail party
> room and found three or four queers
> talking together in queertalk.
> I tried to be friendly but heard

---

2 Tytell's book is *Naked Angels: The Lives and Literature of the Beat Generation* (McGraw-Hill, 1976).

3 *Allen Ginsberg in America*, by Jane Kramer (Random House, 1969), pages 72-73. Jane Kramer, a *New Yorker* writer, plays Boswell to Ginsberg's Johnson, reverently recording every "yeah," "like," "wow," and "om" that the poet uttered over a period of several months in 1967.

myself talking to one in hiptalk.
"I'm glad to see you," he said, and
looked away. "Hmn," I mused. The room
was small and had a double-decker
bed in it, and cooking apparatus:
icebox, cabinet, toasters, stove;
the hosts seemed to live with room
enough only for cooking and sleeping.

Now, *that* was the way to write a poem—no muss, no fuss! Williams, whom Ginsberg soon came to know quite well (and whom he would refer to in later years as his "guru"), was flattered by these imitative (if utterly unimaginative) verses and provided an introduction for the book in which Ginsberg planned to publish them.

That book, however—*Empty Mirror* was its title—would not find a publisher till 1961; so Williams obligingly contributed a second introduction to what became Ginsberg's debut volume, *Howl & Other Poems* (1956). Between the writing of *Empty Mirror* and of *Howl,* though, Williams's influence waned. There were (aside from the obvious incompatibility of Williams's "no-ideas-but-in-things" approach and Ginsberg's Blake-born neo-Platonism) several reasons for this decline in influence. One of them was Kerouac's new "theory" of spontaneous writing, to which Ginsberg subscribed enthusiastically upon its introduction in 1951. The idea, as set forth in Kerouac's essay "Essentials of Spontaneous Prose" (and applied in the fast-as-lightning composition of *On the Road*), was that, when one is writing, the first words to enter one's head are always the best ones for the purpose; revision is a deceitful process because it involves *thinking,* that dreaded enemy of honest feeling and consequently of true art. "First thought, best thought": it was a ridiculous concept, but one perfectly suited to the Beats, who were impatient, impulsive, and incomparably conceited, who hated order, and who didn't really want to spend all that much time writing anyway. (If they did, there wouldn't be any time left to be "hip.") Ginsberg, for one, would never be the same after "Essentials of Spontaneous Prose"; Kerouac, he was later to say (in one of the most dubious compliments in the history of American literature), "taught me everything I knew about writing."

But Kerouac was not the only member of the Beat Generation who was making discoveries. Sometime between the writing of *Empty Mirror* and of *Howl* Ginsberg made a big one: Walt Whitman. Here, he realized, was the perfect model for the spontaneous, transcendental poet he wanted to be. Ginsberg's Open Road was to be different from Whitman's, though; his journey down the "long brown path" of Whitmanian fame was not to be a lyrical, lighthearted hike but a bumpy, buffoonish protest march. "Paterson" (1949), his first poem in imitation of the Bard of Paumanok, not only made it clear that he had shamelessly appropriated the entire arsenal of Whitmanian devices—the vatic tone, the long lines, the comprehensive lists, the names of American places, the programmatic egocentrism, the rampant sensuality, the practice of beginning a series of lines with the same words or phrases, and the obsession with the past, present, and future of America—but established the distinctly un-Whitmanian uses to which he would put them. At the beginning of "Paterson," Ginsberg bluntly declares his hostility toward the American way of life: "What do I want in these rooms papered with visions of money?" He despises the idea of participating in an economic system governed by "the slobs and dumbbells of the ego with money and power/to hire and fire and make and break and fart and justify their reality of wrath/and rumor of wrath to wrath-weary man." What sort of life would Ginsberg prefer? A demented, disordered one, of course:

I would rather go mad, gone down the dark
road to Mexico, heroine dripping in my veins,
eyes and ears full of marijuana,
eating the god Peyote on the floor of a mudhut
on the border
or laying in a hotel room over the body of
some suffering man or woman;
rather jar my body down the road, crying by

a diner in the Western sun;
rather crawl on my naked belly over the tincans of Cincinnati;
rather drag a rotten railroad tie to a Golgotha in the Rockies;
rather, crowned with thorns in Galveston, nailed hand and foot in Los Angeles, raised up to die in Denver,
pierced in the side in Chicago, perished and tombed in New Orleans and resurrected in 1958 somewhere on Garrett Mountain,
come down roaring in a blaze of hot cars and garbage,
streetcorner Evangel in front of City Hall, surrounded by statues of agonized lions,
with a mouthful of shit, and the hair rising on my scalp,
screaming and dancing in praise of Eternity annihilating the sidewalk, annihilating reality,
screaming and dancing against the orchestra in the destructible ballroom of the world,
blood streaming from my belly and shoulders
flooding the city with its hideous ecstasy, rolling over the pavements and highways
by the bayoux and forests and derricks leaving my flesh and my bones hanging on the trees.

With "Paterson," then, Ginsberg set the course he would follow for the rest of his life: that of the self-proclaimed martyr and madman, the Hyde to Whitman's Jekyll, the prophet-poet turned enemy of the system.

Ginsberg made other significant "discoveries" besides Whitman, of course. From around 1952, the poet, in his own words, "experimented with poetic effect of psychedelic drugs." What this means is that he wrote "Howl" on peyote, "Wales Visitation" on LSD, "I Hate America" on heroin, "On Neal's Ashes" on morphine or marijuana, "Denver Doldrums" on Benzedrine, "Kaddish" on methadrine, "A Ghost May Come" on marijuana, "Death to Van Gogh's Ear!" on codeine. He composed a series of poems that take their titles from the name of the drug on which they were written: "Mescaline," "Laughing Gas," "Lysergic Acid." He went all the way to Peru just to bring back a hallucinogenic vine called *ayahuasca*. Portugés's book contains an interview in which Ginsberg discusses in depth the various effects of these substances on his work. "All mellow poems seem to emerge out of heroin. Endless metaphysical-political ravings in my journal and other stuff you've seen were written on morphine and heroin." He speaks of poems like "Marijuana Notation" and "Psalm I" as having a "grass-like clarity." He says of laughing gas: "It gives the appearance of enlarging perception to a point where the totality of the universe invades the individual entity and dissolves the individual entity into the blackness of space." These were not, of course, private "experiments"; Ginsberg, like his friend and fellow chemist Timothy Leary, proselytized long and hard for the use of psychedelic drugs, travelling from campus to campus reciting poems like "Aether," in which he asserts that "you can see/God by sniffing the/gas in a cotton . . . ."

Ginsberg also discovered Eastern religion. His full-dress involvement with it dates back to the early Sixties, when he went to Asia and found himself intrigued by Hinduism and Buddhism. What appealed to him most about these religions was their emphasis on the self-determination of the individual and their understanding of morality as a subjective consideration. Life was not a matter of objective right and wrong, it was a matter of being true to one's own karmic sense of things. No philosophy of life could have pleased Ginsberg more. His exploration of Eastern religions has continued ever since; in the autobiographical notes to his *Poems All Over the Place, Mostly Seventies* (1978), Ginsberg indicated that he was spending a good deal of his time practicing both "mantra-heart meditation" (with one Swami Muktananda) and Tibetan Buddhist meditation. The influence of Hinduism, Hare Krishna, and the various species of Buddhism on his work has been largely semantic; in his poems and journals, for instance, he habitually (and gratuitously) describes relationships in terms of karmas and yogas. This is not to suggest, of course, that the babas, swamis, gurus, and lamas have not had a substantial impact upon the way Ginsberg lives and writes; like his psychedelic drugs, they have helped him fight off the desire for intellectual order that exists in some corner of every conscious mind and to give even freer rein to his id. Ginsberg, in typical fashion, prefers to describe this process as the "holy divine yoga of losing ego."

Ginsberg's id, of course, was unusually healthy even without the help of the gods of the East. It was, in fact, years before he signed his soul over to them that Ginsberg and his id became famous. The setting for this historic occasion was a place called the Six Gallery in San Francisco; the poem—in which Ginsberg brought the mad-anarchist persona of "Paterson" into full bloom—was, needless to say, "Howl." Ginsberg had moved to the Bay City two years earlier, establishing connections with such local poets as Gary Snyder, Philip Whalen, Kenneth Rexroth, Philip Lamantia, Michael McClure, and Lawrence Ferlinghetti, and finding himself a twenty-year-old lover named Peter Orlovsky, who was (in Orlovsky's own words) "crazy as a wildflower" and who has lived with Ginsberg, on and off, ever since. (Like Ginsberg, Orlovsky had had a visionary epiphany: he had been walking down the street one day and the trees had bowed down to him.)

That evening in the Six Gallery all of the above were present—as were Kerouac and Cassady—as Ginsberg introduced "Howl" to the world in his best artist-as-outrage manner. The poem created a sensation, one that a brave reader (aware, perhaps, that Ginsberg had earned a living for a time as a "marketing research consultant") might ascribe not so much to its literary merits as to Ginsberg's truly impressive job of packaging—to his projection, both in print and in person, of a sharply defined, attention-getting persona. "Howl"—which, as Norman Podhoretz was to write soon afterward, "got the San Francisco renaissance off to a screaming start"—succeeded even better than "Paterson" in conveying the Beat movement's hatred of bourgeois life, its rejection of every known type of order (whether psychological, social, or aesthetic), and its conviction that America's best and brightest were to be found wherever the disturbed and the delinquent congregated. The extremity of the poem's point of view, the singular way in which Ginsberg delivered it, and the obscenity trial that followed its publication by City Lights Books fixed Ginsberg in the literary firmament in a way that a less outrageous piece of writing (however magnificent it might be) could never have done.

Ginsberg learned his lesson. Since "Howl," he has published (and read from a thousand platforms) over a dozen books of poetry, and the recipe has remained pretty much the same throughout: take one part anti-Establishment rhetoric, one part sexual indelicacy, one part scatology and general grubbiness, and mix rather sloppily. *Voilà*—a book of poetry. And a Guggenheim, a National Book Award, a membership in the American Academy of Arts and Letters, a *Collected Poems* issued by Harper & Row. Ginsberg is thought of as a radical poet, but in a sense he is anything but; like the most uncreative contributor to *Reader's Digest* or *Time* (the two magazines he most frequently maligns in his verse), he has always known his audience and has always given it exactly what it wanted. The one thing that can never be found in his poetry is the unexpected. He has, for instance, been carrying on about Americans and their money for decades, and the subtlety of his observations and the eloquence of his expression have failed to develop beyond the monotonous Moloch-chant of "Howl" ("Moloch! Moloch! Nightmare of Moloch! Moloch the loveless! Mental Moloch! Moloch the heavy judger of men!", etc.) or the sloppy superficiality of his 1957 poem, "Death to Van Gogh's Ear!":

> Money! Money! Money! shrieking mad
> celestial money of illusion! Money made of
> nothing, starvation, suicide! Money of
> failure! Money of death!
> Money against Eternity! and eternity's strong
> mills grind out vast paper of Illusion!

Money, he howls, "has reckoned the soul of America." Money has put

> millions of agitated fanatics in the bughouse
> for the sake of the screaming soprano
> of industry
> Money-chant of soapers—toothpaste apes in
> television sets—deodorizers on hypnotic
> chairs—
> petroleum mongers in Texas—jet plane
> streaks among the clouds—
> sky writers liars in the face of Divinity—
> fanged butchers of hats and shoes, all
> Owners! Owners! Owners! with obsession
> on property and vanishing Selfhood!

For awkwardness and lack of originality, the poem is hard to beat; but Ginsberg has valiantly spent the rest of his career trying. In a 1970 poem called "Friday the Thirteenth," he is still singing the same unmelodic, rhythmically ragged tune:

> Slaves of Plastic! Leather-shoe chino-pants
> prisoners! Haircut junkies! Dacron-sniffers!
> Striped tie addicts! short hair monkeys on
> their backs! Whiskey freaks bombed out on
> 530 billion cigarettes a year—
> twenty Billion dollar advertising Dealers!
> lipstick skin-poppers & syndicate Garbage
> telex-Heads!
> Star-striped scoundrelesque flag-dopers!
> Car-smog hookers Fiendish on
> superhighways!
> Growth rate trippers hallucinating Everglade
> real estate! Steak swallowers zonked on
> Television!
> Old ladies on Stockmarket habits—old Wall
> Street paper Money-pushers!

Yes, it certainly does sound like the literary equivalent of a *Pravda* cartoon, but for the past few decades there has been a substantial segment of the American literary public eager to applaud such brassy banalities. This is not to suggest that Wall Street and Madison Avenue are not excellent targets for satire. They are. But these collocations of anti-capitalist clichés are not satire. Satire requires wit, and these witless lines attest only to the extremity of Ginsberg's attitude toward America. Ginsberg simply cannot stand the fact that Americans purchase homes, buy clothing, eat well and regularly, use cars to get places. The orderliness of it all enrages him. That Americans do other things in the course of a day besides buy stock, wear synthetics, and watch television does not seem to occur to him; the only emotional depth or sensitivity of which he appears to be aware is his own and that of his cronies. These poems attack the supposed monomaniacal consumerism of the typical American, but it is Ginsberg who is the monomaniac: he cannot look at middle-class America without seeing a race of faceless, heartless, mass-consuming, polluting, war-mongering, credit-card-using, *Reader's Digest*-reading robots. That he himself watches television, buys property (a good deal of it, too), and eats well does not deter him in the least from waxing hysterical about the fact that others do. He knows *he's* okay—he sweats, drools, performs all the other bodily functions, and describes it all in graphic detail every chance he gets. And he knows his friends and lovers are okay, too. It's the rest of the country in whose loving, feeling, laughing, crying, thinking, breathing reality he is incapable of believing. It's as if you have to drag yourself through the negro streets at dawn looking for an angry fix, bite detectives in the neck and shriek with delight in police cars, and howl on your knees in the subway in order to be recognized by Ginsberg as having feelings.

One of Ginsberg's favorite themes is the FBI-CIA-Mafia-Pentagon-White House-Chase Manhattan-Standard Oil-ITT-NBC-ABC-CBS-*New York Times*-Reader's Digest cabal. In "Television Was a Baby Crawling Toward That Deathchamber" (1961), Ginsberg describes "the Presidential mike & all its starry bunting" as a "front for some mad BILLIONAIRES / who own United Fruits & Standard Oil and Hearst The Press and Texas NBC and someone owns the Radios owns vast Spheres of Air . . . ." He suggests secret and sinister connections among a multitude of American corporations, the Mutual Network and the *Reader's Digest,* and maintains that

> Six billionaires that control America are
> playing Scrabble with antique Tarot—
> they've just unearthed another Pyramid—
> in the bombproof Cellar at Fort Knox
> Not even the FBI knows who—They give
> orders to J. E. Hoover thru the metal
> phonegirl at the Robot Transmitter on
> top of RCA . . . .

And on and on it goes, in "'Have You Seen This Movie?'" (1970):

> . . . What Mafia runs N.J.? What Mafia knew
> J. Edgar FBI?
> What's Schenley's Whiskey trader
> Fleishmann's Hoover Institute?
> What opium's passed thru CIA Agents'
> airplane's luggage in Saigon, Bangkok,
> Athens, Washington?
> What narcotic agent's not dependent on Shit
> for a living?
> What Bank's money created ex nihil serves
> orphan, widow, monk, philosopher?
> or what Bank's money serves real Estate
> Asphalt over widow's garden? Serves old
> Nick in the Pentagon?

—and in "Anti-Vietnam War Peace Mobilization" (1970), wherein Ginsberg describes the White House as

> . . . filled with mustached Germans
> & police buttons, army telephones, CIA
> Buzzers, FBI bugs
> Secret Service walkie-talkies, Intercom
> squawkers to Narco
> Fuzz & Florida Mafia Real Estate Speculators.

—and in "Thoughts on a Breath" (1974), a meditation upon

> Police state, Students, Poetry open tongue,
> anger and fear of Cops,
> Oil Cops, Rockefeller Cops, Oswald Cops,
> Johnson Cops Nixon Cops
> president Cops
> SMU Cops Trustee Cops CIA Cops
> FBI Cops Goon Squads of Dope

—and in "Hadda Be Playing on the Jukebox (1975):

> Hadda be Central Intelligence The Family
> "Our Thing" the Agency Mafia Organized
> Crime FBI Dope Cops & Multinational
> Corporations
> one big set of Criminal gangs working
> together in Cahoots
>
> . . .
>
> Secret Police embraced for decades, NKVD &
> CIA keep eachother's secrets, OGPU & DIA
> never hit their own, KGB & FBI one mind—
> brute force

—and in "Birdbrain!" (1980):

> Birdbrain runs the World!
> Birdbrain is the ultimate product of
> Capitalism
> Birdbrain chief bureaucrat of Russia, yawning
> Birdbrain ran FBI 30 years appointed by
> F. D. Roosevelt and never chased
> Cosa Nostra!
>
> . . .
>
> Birdbrain runs the Pentagon his brother runs
> the CIA, Fatass Bucks!
> Birdbrain writes and edits *Time Newsweek*
> *Wall Street Journal Pravda Izvestia* . . . .

Does Ginsberg believe in the literal truth of all these accusations of conspiracy? Certainly not. He is showing us what runaway paranoia looks like. But to what purpose? Apparently, this is not meant to discredit *him,* to make him look ridiculous, but is intended rather as an eloquent condemnation of the American economic and political system. And critics and readers buy it in droves. It is as if Ginsberg's absurd, anarchistic paranoia is itself, to some people's way of thinking, evidence against "The System." Nor do Ginsberg's fans seem to be disturbed by the indiscriminateness of his put-downs. "In America it's Attica in Russia it's Lubianka Wall," he writes in "Capitol Air" (1980). Television and Nazi gas chambers, the mass media and Stalin's gulags: to Ginsberg, as far as one can tell, they are all equally horrible. He makes no distinctions at all—he is just *against, against, against*—and this is a significant failing, for perceptive, sensitive distinctions are the basis of all intelligent discourse and all worthwhile art. Such catalogue poems as "Capitol Air" and "Yes and It's Hopeless" and "Birdbrain!" lump the unpleasant in with the evil, link various phenomena of American popular culture with some of the more hateful manifestations of Soviet totalitarianism. Ginsberg's point is identical throughout: "The System the System in Russia & China the same." What he hates, patently, is the very idea of a *system*; and he sees absolutely no difference between a system that is essentially democratic and one that is out-and-out totalitarian.

To read such poems as these back-to-back in the *Collected Poems* is to be stunned by the oversimplification, the repetition, the self-indulgence, the egocentrism, the utter inability to develop a theme. Doesn't he ever, one wonders, get sick of reiterating these banalities? Doesn't he ever yearn to get beyond the surface cliché, to develop a more sophisticated view of the world, and to express it in more memorable and meticulously chosen words? How can he stand to keep drawing the same distorted picture of a psychedelic universe in which everyone conspires against Allen Ginsberg, rather than exploring and attempting to understand the complexities that make the actual world interesting and frustrating and *real*? Reading these poetically and intellectually vapid verses one after the other, one is constantly reminded that they were written not to be read in privacy but to be declaimed to an audience—an audience that is supposed to cheer, not think; to applaud opinions it already shares with Ginsberg, not to mull over unfamiliar ideas or admire a finely turned phrase.

Ginsberg's most famous subject, of course, is the Vietnam War. Now that his anti-war poems have been published in chronological sequence with the rest of his poetry in the *Collected Poems,* it is more obvious than ever that, to a substantial degree, the war was less a cause for Ginsberg than an opportunity. The peace movement provided him with an occasion, a focus, and a wider audience than ever for the anti-American anarchism that he had been peddling for a decade. Ginsberg's attitude toward Vietnam, as expressed in his poetry, was never that American military involvement in that part of the world was a bad idea, and that it would be in the best interests of the United States and of the ultimate cause of democracy to withdraw. No; to Ginsberg, the war was just another miserable manifestation—like television and *Time* magazine—of a system he despised. In "Returning North of Vortex" (1967), Ginsberg makes his position clear. "I hope we lose this war," he writes. "Let the Viet Cong win over the American Army!" Perhaps the most revealing lines are the following: "And if it were my wish, we'd lose & our will / be broken / & our armies scattered as we've scattered the airy guerrillas of our own yellow imagination." Scattered armies, broken wills: is this the dream of a man who wants genuine peace—that is, order, stability, tranquility—or of a connoisseur of chaos?

The answer seems obvious. And yet the literary critics of this country, in their infinite wisdom, have elevated Ginsberg to an unequaled stature among his poetry-writing contemporaries. What makes this situation all the more paradoxical is that surprisingly few of the critics who have celebrated Ginsberg in print seem honestly convinced that his poetry has any literary value at all. One critic after another, in fact, has gone out of his way to avoid remarking at any length upon the manifest mediocrity of most of Ginsberg's verse; repeatedly, one finds Ginsberg's partisans walking rhetorical tightropes, praising the poet while managing to avoid judging the poetry (or, at the very most, acknowledging its inadequacy as literature, but ingeniously discovering some nonliterary reason for admiring it). Oddest of all, many of the critics are in the habit of suggesting that it is just plain *wrong* to judge Ginsberg's poetry *qua* poetry. Richard Howard, for instance, writes in a recent issue of the *Boston Review* that the *Collected Poems* "may not be poetry at all, [but] it is always testimony, a kind of processional martyrology—in that martyrs are witnesses to the truth." John Malcolm Brinnin said much the same thing a decade ago in reviewing a book of Ginsberg's lectures and talks called *Allen Verbatim*: "As John Middleton Murry said of D. H. Lawrence, 'To charge him with a lack of form . . . is to be guilty of irrelevance. Art was not his aim.'" Gerrit Henry, writing in *Poetry* in 1974, observes admiringly that "the poems in *The Fall of America* aren't much as poems, but there's one whale of a *mensch* behind them." Is there any other American poet who gets reviews like this?

Not only does Ginsberg win Brownie points from his critics for being a *mensch* and a "martyr" (a martyr to what? fame? wealth? honors?); he actually gets credit for his courage. What courage? Why, the courage—believe it or not—to print such rubbish and call it poetry. Indeed, as Gerrit Henry sees it, Ginsberg's gutsiness on this account makes him nothing less than a "culture hero." "There's no doubt," Henry writes, "that Ginsberg takes an enormous risk in gathering the effect of that slapdash, patchwork sort of journalism-of-the-soul that he goes in for and calling it poetry, laying himself bare to all sorts of criticism and, indeed, mockery . . . ." Ginsberg, says Henry (in a repudiation of critical responsibility that is surprisingly common among Ginsberg's apologists), acts on a "messianic" impulse "which no critic of poetry is really empowered to judge." So there.

One of the more celebrated writers who prefer to discuss Ginsberg as messiah, rather than as poet, is Saul Bellow. In his recent story "Him with His Foot in His Mouth,"[4] Bellow, speaking through his protagonist, delivers a tribute to Ginsberg which is based entirely upon the image the poet has cultivated of himself as the twentieth century's answer to Whitman. America needs a transcendental poet, Bellow's speaker insists, and "the only authentic living representative of American Transcendentalism is that fat-breasted, bald, bearded homosexual in smeared goggles, innocent in his uncleanness." Ginsberg, the speaker suggests, "takes a stand for true tenderness and full candor. Real candor means excremental and genital literalness." (Does this mean that Euripides, Shakespeare, Dante, Goethe did not write with "real candor"? Conversely, is "excremental and genital literalness" all that "real candor" requires?) Bellow's speaker goes on:

> What Ginsberg opts for is the warmth of a freely copulating, manly, womanly, comradely, "open road" humanity which doesn't neglect to pray and to meditate. He speaks with horror of our "plastic culture," which he connects somewhat [!] obsessively with the CIA . . . . This psychopathic vision, so touching because there is, realistically, so much to be afraid of, and also because of the hunger for goodness reflected in it, a screwball defense of beauty, I value [highly] . . . . He is a faithful faggot Buddhist in America, the land of his birth. The petrochemical capitalist enemy (an enemy that needs sexual and religious redemption) is right here at home. Who could help loving such a comedian!

"The petrochemical capitalist enemy . . . such a comedian": what sort of logic is at work here? If the speaker is serious about capitalism being the enemy, what does being a comedian have to do with it? Or *is* he serious? One thing, at least, is clear about this bizarre passage: Ginsberg's poetry is not mentioned once. Bellow's speaker praises Ginsberg not because he is a fine poet but because he is a "comedian," because he holds the "correct" political views (that is, he is obsessive about the hazards of American capitalism and oblivious to the outrages of Soviet Communism), and (in-

4 The story appears in the recent collection, *Him With His Foot in His Mouth and Other Stories,* by Saul Bellow: Harper & Row, 294 pages, $15.95.

credibly) because he is "psychopathic," a "screwball." At the end of this tribute, Bellow's speaker (although by this point it is clearly Bellow speaking and no one else) pays Ginsberg the most peculiar compliment of all:

> I . . . refuse to overvalue the erotic life. I do not believe that the path of truth must pass through all the zones of masturbation and buggery. [Ginsberg] is consistent; to his credit, he goes all the way, which can't be said of me. Of the two of us, he is the more American.

This from the author of *The Adventures of Augie March*![5]

This seems to be *the* way to handle Ginsberg these days—call him the Atomic Age Whitman, but sidestep, as much as possible, the question of whether his poetry makes the grade. James Atlas, in his review of the *Collected Poems* for *The Atlantic,* obviously finds the poems, on the whole, offensive and mediocre, but, rather than letting the chips fall where they may, comes up with an assortment of excuses for them. Yes, he admits, some of the poems are nothing more than pornographic records of Ginsberg's pederastic revels—but, "lurid as they are, they belong to the convention of the horny old poet celebrating the transient beauty of youth." Yes, a lot of the poetry is "stoned babble" and "there aren't many memorable lines in even the best" of it—but at least "it's never dull. Crammed with gossip, anecdotes, and confessions of sexual miscreancy, his garrulous, untidy narratives read like a good novel." Yes, "these poems are uneven, to say the least"—but so are Williams's *Paterson,* Olson's *Maximus Poems,* Lowell's *Notebook.* Amid all these clever rationalizations, Atlas manages to describe Ginsberg as the "heir of Whitman" and to allude to the poet's "Whitmanesque lines"—and, of course, to title the piece "A Modern Whitman."

Then there is Francis X. Clines (who is —fittingly, somehow—the *Times*'s White House correspondent), the author of a profile of Ginsberg published recently in *The New York Times Magazine.* Clines makes a point of saying that Ginsberg "carefully claims no large place in American literature"; but he adds that "his labor and style alone, *regardless of the esthetic judgments of later generations* [my emphasis], currently put him [sic] as a major working writer in the nonclassical tradition of Walt Whitman and William Carlos Williams." What in the world does *this* mean? What it means, I think, is this: "Look, *you* know his poetry's terrible, and *I* know his poetry's terrible, but, heck, everybody knows that he's the modern Whitman, and who am I to buck the crowd?"

Such are the ways of personality cults. One of the many ironies of the Ginsberg cult is that this particular poet has profited hugely by his lack of originality. He began his career as a blatant imitator of Elizabethan poets, went on to become a rather faint xerox copy of William Carlos Williams, and finally settled on being a fourth-rate pseudo-Whitman. He has never learned selectively from his masters in the way most poets do—has never, that is, developed his own personal style by borrowing, in various subtle ways, from a number of poets; instead, he has simply copied styles wholesale. And, of course, to make the imitation worth the trouble, the former marketing research consultant has promoted himself more ingeniously than any American poet in history. By drawing attention to his combative, outrageous public personality and to his connections with Whitman, Williams, Blake, and other poets, Ginsberg has subtly steered the critics away from writing about this poetry as a literary phenomenon and has beguiled them into discussing him as a social

---

5 Interestingly enough, Louis Simpson—whose poetry, like Bellow's novels, has helped memorably to define the character of late twentieth-century America—says much the same thing at the end of the chapter on Ginsberg in *A Revolution in Taste* (Macmillan, 1978): "With his beard, bald head and intent brown eyes [Ginsberg] is definitely a personality, as American as apple pie and the flag."

force, a symbol, an heir to a tradition. Clines, for example, describes Ginsberg as "the celebrity poet who once piped a flood of hippie humanity into Golden Gate Park in the 1960's on the strength of 'flower power,'" as "the poet of resistance who once could rile authorities with the single syllable 'om,' his mantra chant against the Vietnam War sounding through the Chicago tear gas of '68," and as "the symbol of social iconoclasm and doctored mind expansion, one of the first to sing brazenly beyond the closet of homosexuality." Ginsberg has created such a myth about his person, in fact, that many of the people who write about him seem shocked, and a bit disappointed, that he lives pretty much the way the rest of us do. Clines describes Ginsberg and Orlovsky looking pensively over their financial accounts, and says, "It is startling to witness this mundane anxiety in two of the surviving souls of the Beats, the artists who were so refreshing in thumbing their nose [sic] at the materialist preoccupation of post-war America." Jane Kramer suffered a similar rude surprise: "I'm not sure what, exactly, I had expected of Ginsberg, but I remember coming home from our first day together astounded by the fact that he had gone to the bank to deposit a check and then slipped into a local diner for some bacon and eggs." Imagine—Ginsberg with a bank account! Ginsberg handling *money!*

How can one explain the eagerness of such reputable members of the literary establishment to embrace the Ginsberg myth? Clearly, these writers and critics (not to mention the people who give out Guggenheims and major book awards) don't despise America; in some sense they *are* America, or at least its cultural representatives. But for some reason they are nonetheless comforted by the fact that somewhere in these states there is an Allen Ginsberg who *does* despise America—who has, in fact, spent most of his life thumbing his nose at everything they represent. One suspects that by admiring Ginsberg, many of these Establishment writers and critics are simply playing mind games with themselves. They know that they are bourgeois, and they know that being bourgeois is very unhip; applauding the revolutionary ravings of an Allen Ginsberg is one easy way to remove that bad old bourgeois stigma—for a brief interval, anyway—and to feel a bit like a madman oneself. What this amounts to, in other words, is radical politics as a form of entertainment—dissent-as-diversion. Those apologists for Ginsberg who are not attracted to the poet as a sort of polemical performance artist are, one supposes, simply living up to their notion of liberalism; for among many members of the intellectual and artistic classes in postmodern America, it is considered a sign of true enlightenment not only to tolerate but to celebrate the writer-as-radical—however bad his writing, however inane and irresponsible his radicalism. Few Americans have benefited more from such naïve, nonsensical "everybody-loves-a-radical" ways of thinking than Allen Ginsberg. What makes it all especially despicable is that although these writers and critics glorify Ginsberg for his supposed "candor" and "honesty," they cannot even be honest with themselves; for the only reason they are willing to cheer Ginsberg on is that they know very well that however much he propagandizes for the overthrow of the status quo, he will never achieve it. Applauding Ginsberg, in short, costs them nothing.

This is not to suggest, of course, that Ginsberg is harmless. Thanks to the support he has received from the literary establishment, he has been in a position to do—and *has* done—considerable damage to both American society and American literary culture. Besides being largely responsible for making drug use fashionable among this country's educated young (the tragic results of which hardly need to be explained here), Ginsberg has helped to promulgate the ridiculous notion, now regarded as dogma by all too many young people in the United States, that a poem is whatever you pour, unedited, onto a page. He has been the model for countless aspiring writers to whom the distinctive characteristics of a good contemporary poet are his disdain for literary tradition, his refusal (and often inability) to write in conventional forms, his lack of attention to matters of craft, his vulgar exhibitionism, and his preoccupation with knee-jerk political dissent. Ginsberg is, in short, the father of a generation of Americans to whom "culture" is a word most often used immediately following the word "drug"—a generation to whom poetry is something marked not by intelligence, sensitivity, and an imaginatively expressed apperception of natural order, but by incoherent egoism, fashionable anarchistic platitudes, and put-on paranoia. This is the legacy of Allen Ginsberg, the legacy to which Harper & Row has chosen to raise a substantial monument in the form of the *Collected Poems 1947-1980*. With all due respect to that venerable publishing firm, it is not a legacy to celebrate.

(*February* 1985)

"The battle it was born to lose": the poetry of Geoffrey Hill

by Robert Richman

The life of an honest man must be a perpetual infidelity. For the man who wishes to remain faithful to truth must make himself continually unfaithful to all the continual, successive, indefatigable renascent errors. And the man who wishes to remain faithful to justice must make himself continually unfaithful to inexhaustibly triumphant injustices.
—Charles Péguy, in *Bar-Cochebas*

The tongue's atrocities.
—Geoffrey Hill, in "History as Poetry"

When a major new work appears by one of the best poets now writing it is reason enough to command our attention. But when the work marks a significant departure in the poet's career, it is cause for our most careful scrutiny. When Geoffrey Hill's long poem, *The Mystery of the Charity of Charles Péguy,*[1] was published in Britain last year, it was immediately apparent to readers familiar with Hill's career that the poet was, at the age of fifty, striking out in a new direction. For thirty years, Hill had written poems whose central characteristic was a deep unease with the whole idea of writing poetry. Indeed, so fiercely had Hill's work questioned itself that at times it often seemed as if he would cease writing altogether. With the publication of *Tenebrae,* in 1978, Hill's hand was so palsied by a near-nihilistic despair that his career seemed expended. But with *Péguy,* he has burst forth with one hundred quatrains of expansive, and in some ways vigorous, homage. *Péguy* is a moving rebellion against Hill's own previous work, the product of a very different kind of obsession. If we have learned anything from this poet's brilliant and fastidious career, it is that we should not underestimate the intelligence behind his every gesture. What is it about the French poet and patriot Charles Péguy (1873-1914) that kept one of our great contemporary poets from falling silent?

To get at the answer to this question, and thus at a proper sense of the question's importance, we must first examine the curious history of Geoffrey Hill's career. The task of understanding his difficult poetry is alleviated somewhat by the small amount one has to contend with. In thirty years of writing, only four thin volumes have appeared prior to *Péguy*: *For the Unfallen* (1959), *King Log* (1968), *Mercian Hymns* (1971), and *Tenebrae* (1978). *Péguy* is Hill's longest sequence to date.

Whether Hill has written about the difficult attraction of love, the paradox of a God unknowable but known, or the gruesome spectacle of history (holocausts and holo-

---

1 *The Mystery of the Charity of Charles Péguy,* by Geoffrey Hill. Agenda Editions/André Deutsch, 31 pp., £3. The poem was also published, in its entirety, in *The Paris Review,* Summer, 1983.

caust victims play a large part in his work), the poetry has always been grim, clipped, infrequent. On top of this, Hill's subjects are often played out against the inability of poetry to do justice to the experience it wishes to relate. Indeed, Hill's moral sensibility has been so anguished by the effrontery of writing about profound spiritual and physical pain that he has seemed to reject what he saw as poetry's often indulgent beauty. If Wordsworth, in high Romantic fashion, could confidently feel that "Over his own sweet voice the stock-dove broods," Hill has felt compelled to give the opposite view. In many of the early poems, "the Word," as he calls it, is castigated outright. In other poems he dramatizes the gap between poetry and experience by foiling our expectations of how a poem should read. Yet other, later, poems diminish to the point of threatening their own extinction. Either they grow impenetrably opaque or they simply disintegrate. The scarcely articulated bursts of energy and choked cries of grief in *Tenebrae* are Hill's most extreme examples of feeling and experience swallowing up their expression on the page.

Whether Hill's despair has manifested itself in strict, formal sonnets or in the shrinking black holes of the later poetry, all his poems, to some degree, are "Consumed with that which they were nourished by." Shakespeare was referring to the way the passions that feed life eventually conspire in its demise, but the paradox also applies to Hill's poetry: the experience that brings the poem to life sets up a standard the poem cannot do justice to. Indeed, the denial of fulfillment is a theme central to Hill's work.

All this would seem to be a surefire recipe for poetic nihilism. Unfortunately, for many poets—often American—who have pursued similar ideas, it is. We observe in their work a tendency toward loose forms, aggressively subjective eruptions, and the kind of ironic reversal that descends into a bland disparaging of the whole idea of poetry. Hill's achievement—and it has been one of the most substantial in contemporary English poetry—has been to create, out of this quasi-nihilistic obsession, true works of poetry: profound, deeply crafted, and eloquent. Needless to say, the task of producing poetry of refinement and power from this creative-destructive paradox has not been easy. Given the kind of interior battle Hill's poetry wages—between a distrust of poetry itself and an allegiance to poetic tradition—it is not surprising that Hill has written so few poems in the past thirty years. His oeuvre is spare and brutal, and extraordinarily powerful.

How does Hill achieve this power in his work? The first poem of Hill's first book, called "Genesis," contains the seeds of a good many of his major themes:

I
Against the burly air I strode,
Where the tight ocean heaves its load,
Crying the miracles of God.

And first I brought the sea to bear
Upon the dead weight of the land;
And the waves flourished at my prayer,
The rivers spawned their sand.

And where the streams were salt and full
The tough pig-headed salmon strove,
Curbing the ebb and the tide's pull,
To reach the steady hills above.

II
The second day I stood and saw
The osprey plunge with triggered claw,
Feathering blood along the shore,
To lay the living sinew bare.

And the third day I cried: "Beware
The soft-voiced owl, the ferret's smile,
The hawk's deliberate stoop in air,
Cold eyes, and bodies hooped in steel,
Forever bent upon the kill."

III
And I renounced, on the fourth day,
This fierce and unregenerate clay,

Building as a huge myth for man
The watery Leviathan.

And made the glove-winged albatross
Scour the ashes of the sea
Where Capricorn and Zero cross,
A brooding immortality—
Such as the charmed phoenix has
In the unwithering tree.

IV
The phoenix burns as cold as frost;
And, like a legendary ghost,
The phantom-bird goes wild and lost,
Upon a pointless ocean tossed.

So, the fifth day, I turned again
To flesh and blood and the blood's pain.

V
On the sixth day, as I rode
In haste about the works of God,
With spurs I plucked the horse's blood.

By blood we live, the hot, the cold,
To ravage and redeem the world:
There is no bloodless myth will hold.

And by Christ's blood are men made free
Though in close shrouds their bodies lie
Under the rough pelt of the sea;

Though earth has rolled beneath her weight
The bones that cannot bear the light.

Hill views his subject, the creation of the world, through the eyes of a contemporary man, someone stung by the horrors that have taken place on this "fierce and unregenerate clay" since its genesis. The poem's mood, darkened by the "burly air" of history's pain and suffering, is unrelievedly bleak. "Genesis" is an exploration of the dark side of the creation myth. And because it is a vision "created" by the knowledge of the destruction the event will wreak ("By blood we live . . ."), the line "Crying the miracles of God" does not refer to the redemptive miracles of a benevolent God. On the contrary, the speaker is announcing, with irony, the "miracles" of destruction and pain, accompanied by the "crying" of real tears. The poem is, in its essence, a deeply felt questioning of the idea of redemption.

In its fatalism Hill's sensibility is almost Hardyesque, but Hardy's poems resolve themselves in a way Hill's do not. "Genesis" draws its bleak picture through displacement, a refusal on the poet's part to abide by the formal, musical, and to some degree intellectual principles of a more traditional kind of poetry. It uses gnarly, palpable sounds, surprising half-rhymes, plodding rhythms (as if the poem were being made to bear some incredible weight), and juxtapositions that purposefully set our sense awry. Although grounded in poetic tradition, "Genesis" resists lyrical mellifluousness and poetic catharsis. Although moving, it withholds some essential idea of artistic "beauty." The poem's power—which grows as we reread it—derives from the way it refuses to resolve itself in an expected fashion. This refusal of resolution is the formal equivalent of the poem's theme, the impossibility of redemption on earth.

More readily understandable, more fully "resolved," poems in *For the Unfallen* illuminate the difficult poems of displacement. One such "easy" poem, often anthologized, is "In Memory of Jane Fraser."

When snow like sheep lay in the fold
And winds went begging at each door,
And the far hills were blue with cold,
And a cold shroud lay on the moor,

She kept the siege. And every day
We watched her brooding over death
Like a strong bird above its prey.
The room filled with the kettle's breath.

Damp curtains glued against the pane
Sealed time away. Her body froze
As if to freeze us all, and chain
Creation to a stunned repose.

She died before the world could stir.
In March the ice unloosed the brook
And water ruffled the sun's hair.
Dead cones upon the alder shook.

Though Hill's bleakness is plain—nature is

not seen as vibrant and colorful but as the pallid reflection of a dying woman—this poem does not question itself by means of deflection of obscurity. Its music and form offer the reader a feeling of hope—a stay against the darkness of its vision.

There is an element common to both the obscure and "easy" poems that gives us the sense that all is not lost in the world of poetry. This is Hill's high rhetoric. It constitutes the poet's central connection to the English poetic tradition, and it is what distinguishes him so sharply from his contemporaries. It is the quality against which all Hill's self-questioning experimentalism must be placed. Donald Hall has written of Hill's debt to Allen Tate, and of the way both Hill and Robert Lowell (Tate's disciple) departed—in opposite directions—from their master. While Lowell broke free of tradition into a more immediate, day-by-day sense of "history," Hill immersed himself deeper into the past and tradition. Hill took as his subjects mythology, English culture, wars, holocausts, martyrs, and poets; and his poetry became, as a result, tighter, densely impacted, and even more allusive than Tate's. By the early Sixties, it was as difficult to conceive of Hill writing a poem about the mundane occurrences in a day's routine—indeed, anything about himself or about the present—as it was to imagine Lowell adopting the creation myth as his subject. The divergence of the two poets probably had much to do with the differences between the English and the American temperament. Whatever the reason, Hill's poetry has a moral depth that makes American experiments along the same lines appear almost gratuitous. And his obsession with tradition and history makes his "radicalism" appear, to American eyes, anything but radical. Indeed, because of its allusiveness, Hill's voice seems to resemble that of the Metaphysical poets of the seventeenth century more than that of his contemporaries.

But the more tradition becomes inescapable for Hill, the more ambivalent about it he feels. If he is unable to ignore the litany of pain and despair on "this fierce and unregenerate clay," he is just as incapable of writing a poem that makes it into an aesthetic object. In "Two Formal Elegies," written "for the Jews in Europe," Hill transforms those killed in the holocaust into accusing figures who refuse to yield "their abused/Bodies" to the poet recollecting them in tranquility:

> Knowing the dead, and how some are disposed:
> Subdued under rubble, water, sand graves,
> In clenched cinders not yielding their abused
> Bodies and bonds to those whom war's chance saves
> Without the law: we grasp, roughly in song.
> Arrogant acceptance from which song derives
> Is bedded with their blood, makes flourish young
> Roots in ashes. The wilderness revives,
>
> Deceives with sweetness harshness . . . .

If, as survivors of the war, the young (a metaphor for poets) permit the "wilderness" to "revive" and deceive "with sweetness harshness," they become, Hill suggests, complicitous in the destruction themselves. For to "sing" a deceptively sweet song is, in his view, an "arrogant acceptance" of the suffering of these martyrs. Among other things, the reviving wilderness cannot but mean here a normally resolving poem—one that, in its "beauty," tramples on death and pain. "Grass resurrects to mask, to strangle," says Hill in another poem, and those being strangled by nature's—and the poet's—renewing beauty are the dead.

The danger of falsifying and distorting history by making it poetically beautiful, objectified, something "out there," is a major theme in Hill's poetry. In "Annunciations," he attacks the "cleansing" properties of poetry, which make the "stiffening-mire" of history into objects "clean to the touch."

> The Word has been abroad, is back, with a tanned look
> From its subsistence in the stiffening-mire.
> Cleansing has become killing, the reward
> Touchable, overt, clean to the touch.

Hill's dim view of the creation myth in "Genesis," we can now see, is also an assault on poetic creation as such: "'Beware / The soft-voiced owl . . . . The hawk's deliberate stoop in air, / Cold eyes, and bodies hooped in steel, / Forever bent upon the kill.'"

When Hill questions, in the eighth poem of "Funeral Music," what seems to be the idea of an afterlife (the "timeless colloquy . . . beyond us"), the repository of souls he really has in mind is the realm of poetry. It constitutes, after all, a "distant sphere of harmony" where "all echoes" of individual, particular suffering "are the same." Poetry, like religion, "objectifies" and therefore falsifies life.

> Not as we are but as we must appear,
> Contractual ghosts of pity; not as we
> Desire life but as they would have us live,
> Set apart in timeless colloquy:
> So it is required; so we bear witness,
> Despite ourselves, to what is beyond us,
> Each distant sphere of harmony forever
> Poised, unanswerable . . . .

"There are silences," says Hill in "The Guardians," and the remark reflects his own feelings of helplessness before the inability of poetry to do justice to the enormity of history. The "bones" that "cannot bear the light" in "Genesis"—the dead—begin to slip out of the poet's grasp entirely. Thus do Hill's poems often seem to shrink before our eyes. This is all he can muster by way of an elegy for yet another holocaust victim:

> SEPTEMBER SONG
>
> *born 19.6.32—deported 24.9.42*
>
> Undesirable you may have been, untouchable
> you were not. Not forgotten
> or passed over at the proper time.
>
> As estimated, you died. Things marched,
> sufficient, to that end.
> Just so much Zyklon and leather, patented
> terror, so many routine cries.
>
> (I have made
> an elegy for myself it
> is true)
>
> September fattens on vines. Roses
> flake from the wall. The smoke
> of harmless fires drifts to my eyes.
>
> This is plenty. This is more than enough.

There is here a clear, if humble, identification of the poet with the victim he is eulogizing; characteristically, the extinction in the poem extends to poetry itself.

The poem's of *King Log* resemble "September Song." In many respects, *King Log*'s extreme difficulty and relentless excision is an act of revenge on the more fully resolved poems of *For the Unfallen.* Indeed, each book of Hill's career is a rebellion against its predecessor, a refusal to follow through or resolve the expectations aroused by an earlier book. In this way Hill enacts within his own poetic development the generational struggle between the old and the young, the dead and the living, that is the theme of his poetry. In "The Guardians" the old men watch "the safe / Packed harbours topple under sudden gales," while the young, "having risen early, had gone, / Some with excursions beyond the bay-mouth . . . ."

Thus, in *King Log,* Hill goes about methodically excluding the kind of historical detail that might have survived in a poem from *For the Unfallen.* In an essay appended to the sequence called "Funeral Music," Hill includes what the poems omit. "Without attempting factual detail," he explains, "I had in mind the battle of Towton, fought on Palm Sunday, 1461," and then proceeds to give a fairly comprehensive account of the incident. As a result, the poems carry the deflection first observed in "Genesis" to an extreme, emptying themselves of any trace of narrative content.

It is important for us to understand that many of the poems in *King Log* remain close to tradition nonetheless. They are still products—especially "Funeral Music," which is one of Hill's great achievements—of the dialectic between the poet and his precursors. Tradition remains the all powerful principle in even the most experimentally disjunct poems. As Hill's career progresses, tradition becomes so powerful, so admonishing that it threatens to silence the poet altogether. In "The Songbook of Sebastian Arrurruz," for instance, the "storm" of tradition "Broods over the dry earth" of Hill's own creative power, arresting his ability to pull himself out of the trap of self-referentiality.

> Love, oh my love, it will come
> Sure enough! A storm
> Broods over the dry earth all day.
> At night the shutters throb in its downpour.
>
> The metaphor holds; is a snug house.
> You are outside, lost somewhere. I find myself
> Devouring verses of stranger passion
> And exile. The exact words
>
> Are fed into my blank hunger for you.

And when Hill does momentarily overcome the obstacle of tradition's "downpour," the result is tiny bits of metaphor unattached to anything resembling a poem.

> i
> Darkness
> above all things
> the Sun
> makes
> rise
>
> ii
> Vultures
> salute their meat
> at noon
> (Hell is
> silent)
>
> iii
> Blind Sun
> our ravager
> bless us
> so that
> we sleep.

This is one of "Four Poems Regarding the Endurance of Poets." It is a desperately moving testament to the unendurability of poetry. Hence, *King Log* ends with the poet

> Scarcely speaking: it becomes as a
> Coolness between neighbours. Often
> There is this orgy of sleep. I wake
> To caress propriety with odd words
> And enjoy abstinence in a vocation
> Of now-almost-meaningless despair.
>
> ("The Songbook of Sebastian Arrurruz")

Hill roused himself out of this "orgy of sleep" with the writing of *Mercian Hymns* in 1971. The book is an explosion. Gone are the formal stanzas, the rhymes, thematic consistency, and the structure of allusion. In their place is a radical obliquity that is deflection carried to an extreme. The paralyzing weight of tradition has been largely shucked; history, or what is left of it, is scattered in fragments throughout a series of thirty short prose-poems. The central consciousness of the poem is an eighth-century Midlands king named Offa. His reveries (which constitute the poems) are a dimensionless void of subjectivity where the tension between past and present, tradition and creation, is lost. The result is anachronism and confusion aplenty.

The danger of this experiment—which Hill is perfectly aware of—is that poetry becomes a formless repository of everything. The "garden" of "Sequence XII" is clearly the garden of verse; it wants upkeep, and "festers for attention": "telluric cultures enriched with shards, corms, nodules, the sunk solids of gravity." "I have accrued," says the poet, "a golden and stinking blaze."

As impenetrable as the poems in *Mercian Hymns* sometimes are, one thing is clear: their subject is an individual. The *Hymns* consist almost entirely of the meandering of Offa's mind. Through Offa, Hill seems to represent the individual ego breaking the shackles of history and tradition that so restricted utterance in *King Log*. The poet, in other words, no longer content to exercise his ego through deflection, lets loose one long scream of bloody revenge against the power of the past. Perhaps the culture-at-large abetted the radical break of the "staggeringly gifted child," as Hill says in one poem, from its "outclassed forefathers." Hill wrote these poems between 1968 and 1971.

Offa parades his liberated self, but he is not as free of the past as he would have us think; and neither, by extension, is the poet. At the end of *Mercian Hymns* this unshackled ego "vanish[es]," leaving "behind coins, for his lodging, and traces of red mud." Coins: poems, creative acts. Red mud: the blood of the inescapable earth.

"I cannot turn aside from what I do," announces Hill in "Lachrimae," a sonnet sequence in *Tenebrae* (1978) and the painful struggle with tradition and history that *Mercian Hymns* attempted to abandon begins again, in some of Hill's strictest forms yet. The subjects explored in these poems are familiar: the failed gods of poetry and love, and the false hope of staying "amid the things that will not stay." The artificial relief of religion is under especially pitiless scrutiny in *Tenebrae*. "Crucified Lord, you swim upon your cross / and never move."

> You are the castaway of drowned remorse,
> you are the world's atonement on the hill.
> This is your body twisted by our skill
> into a patience proper for redress.
>
> ("Lachrimae")

Hill finds discomfort in the comfort of God's "timeless colloquy," and the bleats of agony are exquisite.

> Christ the deceiver
> took all I had
> his darkness ever
> my fair reward
>
> ("The Pentecost Castle")

Such poems turn in on themselves—black holes of despair that swallow their tremendous internal energy before it can escape. They constitute some of contemporary poetry's most powerful moments.

Like religion, love also holds out a promise of fulfillment—a perfect realm—that it cannot satisfy. It too comes under a cold and merciless and unerring scrutiny. Whatever we taste of love's pleasure, says Hill, it will be gone tomorrow, and our sorrow will be deeper for love's having tortured us with the illusion of permanence and happiness.

> The crocus armies from the dead
> rise up; the realm of love renews
> the battle it was born to lose,
> though for a time the snows have fled . . . .

Hill leaves us without any hope of release from this predicament; even the poet's escape from the pain of love into the "abstinence" of his chosen art form is unmasked as yet another fraud:

> and abstinence crowns all our care
> with martyr-laurels for this day.
> Towers and steeples rise away
> into the towering gulfs of air.
>
> ("Veni Coronaberis")

With savage irony (note the sing-song quality of the first two lines), Hill suggests that even abstinence can be fulfilled; hence the extraordinary image of unsatisfied, misguided lust in the last two lines. To Geoffrey Hill, the faintest whisper of possible consummation cheats life of its despair.

The subject of Hill's newest book is Charles Péguy—an odd choice, considering what we know of Hill's interests.

At first glance, there is nothing in Hill's earlier work to prepare us for this *hommage* to one of the strangest characters in the history of French poetry. When the forty-one-year-old Péguy was killed leading his company into battle at the Marne during the second week of World War I—according to legend he was shouting *Vive la France* the moment the fatal bullet struck the middle of his forehead—he was already a prime candidate for canonization as an intellectual martyr. The author of polemical essays and strangely beautiful poetry, and the editor, from 1900 to 1914, of the journal *Les Cahiers de la Quinzaine,* Péguy was an embattled, controversial figure. Brashly mixing socialism and nationalism, Catholic faith and anti-clericalism, militarism and a hatred of military authority, Péguy was a staunchly independent thinker, someone who endlessly frustrated those wanting to enlist him in what he saw as their corrupt causes. Péguy honed a sharp paradoxical style to go with his beliefs. "The life of an honest man must be a perpetual infidelity," he said, and it was only one of many remarks designed to rankle his contemporaries. Indeed, his final *Vive la France* notwithstanding, this "bag of contradictions," as one historian called him, even distrusted patriotism—at least the caricature of it that had emerged in France during the Dreyfus Affair.

But in an ironic twist that would not have amused the *sérieux* Péguy, the many groups, causes, and intellectual petitioners he had held at bay during his lifetime returned after his death to stake claims on his spirit. Perhaps it was the usefulness of having a "purist" on one's side. Whatever the case, Catholic groups that had bridled at his many "sins" while Péguy was alive extolled his ideas after his death, and in one case took his name; fascist groups of the Twenties and Thirties, whose anti-semitism Péguy would have excoriated, pointed to him as an intellectual precursor; and socialists whose ideologies Péguy would have mocked also found him useful for a footnote or two. The Vatican, which had considered Péguy a heretic while he lived, only recently bought his papers. Statues have been erected, squares named, even the building which housed *Les Cahiers* has been given a plaque—all in a futile effort to capture the spirit of a man whose essence was his refusal to be captured.

The Mystery of the Charity of Charles Péguy, like the books that preceded it, metes out a harsh sentence to its predecessor. The rapid-fire bursts of *Tenebrae,* which superseded the gnomic mélange of *Mercian Hymns,* have been overtaken by an expansive voice—a voice largely unafraid of itself.

Vistas of richness and reward. The cedar
uprears its lawns of black cirrus. You have
found
hundred-fold return though in the land
of exile. You are Joseph the Provider;

and in the fable this is your proper home;
three sides of a courtyard where the bees thrum
in the crimped hedges and the pigeons flirt
and paddle, and sunlight pierces the heart-

shaped shutter-patterns in the afternoon,
shadows of fleurs-de-lys on the stone floors.
Here life is labour and pastime and orison
like something from a simple book of hours;

and immortality, your measured task,
inscribes its antique scars on the new desk
among your relics, bits of ivory quartz
and dented snuffbox won at Austerlitz.

The proofs pile up; the dead are made alive
to their posthumous fame. Here is the archive
of your stewardship; here is your true domaine,
its fields of discourse ripening to the Marne.

But for all the "vistas of richness and reward" such lines represent in Hill's oeuvre, one of the major characteristics of Hill's work remains: deflection and resistance to resolution. In the one-hundred quatrains of *Péguy* (divided into ten sections with varying numbers of stanzas), our vision is constantly deflected away from the "heroic" figure that was born with Péguy's death on the Marne (perpetrated by, among others, "church and civic dignitaries," as Hill puts it in a Note). Instead, we are pointed in the direction of a more subtle and far more important essence. The deliberately infelicitous, often rough iambic pentameter, the qualified half-rhymes, the confusing shifts of person, place, and perspective, the disorienting selection of another country's patriot, and the pervasive irony all conspire to shield this shadowy essence from distortion and abuse. Like the dead in "Two Formal Elegies" that withhold their bodies from the poet's aesthetic violation, Péguy's complex sensibility must be locked away for safekeeping, too. The crucial difference is that Péguy is guarded not from the poet's potential distortion, but from the distortion of others. "The bones that cannot bear the light" are certainly the bones of Charles Péguy, but the "light" comes from Péguy's too-fervent admirers, not Geoffrey Hill.

Péguy begins with the murder of Jean Jaurès, the socialist deputy whom Péguy deeply admired during the Dreyfus Affair but later came to loathe for his corrupt socialism. After Péguy had (metaphorically) called for Jaurès's blood in *Les Cahiers,* a "young madman," as Hill recounts in his Note, "who may or may not have been over-susceptible to metaphor, almost immediately shot Jaurès through the head."

> Crack of a starting-pistol. Jean Jaurès
> dies in a wine-puddle. Who or what stares
> through the café-window crêped in powder
> smoke?
> The bill for the new farce reads *Sleepers Awake.*

Hill relates this incident (the first of but three historical events included in the poem) because, like Péguy's death at the Marne, it helped "define" Péguy—albeit mistakenly—for generations of men. This particular incident promoted the popular image of Péguy as a prophet, while the battlefield-death supplied him his heroic cast. Hence, the "who or what" staring at the scene are those waiting in the wings, preparing to concoct the mythical Charles Péguy. The next stanza begins: "History commands the stage wielding a toy gun," suggesting that these fashioners of Péguy-icons for the delectation of "lame patriots" are making a threat (that is, presenting a false likeness) they really cannot make good on.

The real Charles Péguy is absent from the scene. Indeed, he does not appear at all until the last section of the poem—and then only in death. Hill seems to suggest that Péguy is simply too susceptible to distortion to be drawn from behind the curtain of this poem. When, in the fourth stanza, Hill asks, "Did Péguy kill Jaurès? Did he incite / the assassin? Must men stand by what they write . . . ?" we know that Péguy is not available to respond. (Given Péguy's loquaciousness in life, this is especially ironic.) Instead, Hill conjures up alternate witnesses, the "fools and scoundrels" whose vision it is the poem's intention to confound.

> Truth's pedagogue, braving an entrenched
> class
> of fools and scoundrels, children of the world,
> his eyes caged and hostile behind glass—
> still Péguy said that Hope is a little child.

It is the hidden man, "hostile behind glass," however, who retains the vision of hope.

In the poem's third section Péguy's absence is filled by a brilliant and sustained rendering of his "dream of France, militant-pastoral," including, among other things, Péguy's courtyard, his "dented snuffbox," the "shadows of fleurs-de-lys on the stone floors," Chateau de Trie, Chartres, and Colombey-les-deux-Eglises. This misty vision of prewar France certainly seems tangential to any serious consideration of Péguy—except in Hill's oblique homage. At the end of the section, Hill enjoins Péguy to "bid the grim bonne-femme / defend your door: 'M'sieur is not at home.'"

In the fourth part of the poem Hill elaborates on still another side issue—the new men of the twentieth century Péguy feared and hated so much.

> This world is different, belongs to them—
> the lords of limit and of contumely.
> It matters little whether you go tamely
> or with rage and defiance to your doom.
>
> This is your enemies' country which they took
> in the small hours an age before you woke,
> went to the window, saw the mist-hewn
> statues of the lean kine emerge at dawn.
>
> Outflanked again, too bad! You still have pride,
> haggard obliquities . . . .

Yet these "enemies" too help define, in this poem of deflective definitions and "haggard obliquities," Charles Péguy. If they "outflanked" Péguy when he was alive, and in the years since his death, it is Hill's chance to help Péguy's spirit outflank them now.

In the fifth, and longest, section of *Péguy,* we are again "constrained/to leave [him] sleeping . . . to turn away and contemplate the working/of the radical soul . . . ." Hill then scans, with satisfying and appropriate unpredictability, the "Hedgers and ditchers, quarrymen, thick-shod/curés de campagne, each with his load" and "coifed girls like geese, labourers cap in hand,/and walled gardens espaliered with angels" of the France Péguy loved and represented. Slowly, ever so slowly, Hill's portrait without a face emerges, through the accumulation of external detail, a creation mysteriously appropriate to Péguy's rugged and uncompromising nature.

With irresistible irony, Hill reminds us, in the sixth section, what the ordinary celebration of military valor requires—but what this extraordinary celebration must omit.

> Here there should be a section without words
> for military band alone: "Sambre et Meuse,"
> the "Sidi Brahim" or "Le Roi s'Amuse". . . .

This introduces the second historical event of the poem: Dreyfus's court martial. Hill presents this scene with all the hostility he can muster for the "patriots" responsible for this act of vicious cowardice. They are the forebears of our century's "lame patriots" who, in their own way, betrayed Péguy.

> A puffy satrap prances on one leg
>
> to snap the traitor's sword, his ordered
> rage
> bursting with "cran et gloire" and gouts of
> rouge.
> The chargers click and shiver . . . .
>
> . . . No wonder why
> we fall to violence out of apathy . . . .

This last phrase could have been uttered by Péguy. He certainly made his share of remarks about the Affair, all eminently quotable. But again Hill's ephemeral hero must remain silent. Hence we find ourselves walking up yet another divergent path.

> But who are "we," since history is law,
> clad in our skins of silver, steel and hide,
> or in our rags, with rotten teeth askew,
> heroes or knaves as Clio shall decide?

This diverting question enables Hill to continue in the same vein, rather amusingly, for four stanzas more. Remarkably, however, the farther from view Hill positions Péguy, the clearer his significance becomes.

In part seven Hill lets loose some devastating irony for those who "still dutifully read/'heureux ceux qui sont morts.'" This line, from *Ève* (published in 1913), has established itself in the years since Péguy's death as the centerpiece of the standard French eulogy for those fallen in battle—fallen, as Hill scathingly writes, "'pour la patrie,' according to the book." And, in the eighth section,

> . . . Death does you proud,
> every heroic commonplace, "Amor,"
> "Fidelitas," polished like old armour,
> stamped forever into the featureless mud.

In the ninth section we encounter more irony. The "ancient landscape of green branches" in France is not, Hill suggests, as innocently beautiful as it seems to be. For as long as the landscape—like Péguy, like authentic patriotic feelings—is subject to the distortion and abuse of the "lords of limit and contumely" who so casually, hypocritically, and for their own devious purposes invoke it, we cannot permit ourselves to enjoy its beauty. Plainly, Hill is "reviving" another "wilderness" (as he does in "Two Formal Elegies") to show how it deceives with "sweetness harshness," but the poet is no longer committing the crime. The "lame patriots" of France—along with the Church, the socialists, and the fascists—are the evildoers. "Ah, such a land/the Ile de France once was . . ." says Hill, and his nostalgia is shot through with irony. To present the Ile de France any other way would make one complicitous with those who have exulted in its beauty at the expense of the "haggardly oblique" dead, like Péguy.

In the last section Péguy finally appears—only to fall dead in the field of beetroot. The wound in his forehead is, says Hill, "a simple lesion of the complex brain." The metaphor is apt. The utter "simplicity" of labeling Péguy a hero is indeed a "lesion" on the brain of Péguy's real complexity and intelligence. Similarly, the necessary transformation that landscape, innocence, beauty, and nostalgia (to name only a few this poem conjures up) have experienced in our century is nothing if not a bleeding lesion that can only be stanched, temporarily, with irony. Hill scarcely relishes this dark scenario: if anything, *Péguy* registers his unfathomable disgust with this world created by the "lords of limit and contumely."

The hope—and there is hope—lies with Péguy, who is still, at the poem's end, hidden: "his arm over his face as though in sleep/or to ward off the sun." His resistance to the sun, the "light" of which disables so severely, seems to be a triumphant gesture, a gesture of self-protection and disobedience. It shields Péguy's quirky patriotism and subtle mind from the narrow notions of "patriotism" and "intelligence" that are common currency today.

Hill has time for one final, consummate irony in the poem's last lines. He assures the "lords of limit" that they are able to

> . . . come to the salute
> at every hole-and-corner burial-rite
> bellowed with hoarse dignity to the wind.
>
> Take that for your example! But still mourn,
> being so moved: éloge and elegy
> so moving on the scene as if to cry
> "in memory of those things these words were
> born."

Take that for your example: Hill heaves the popular, heroic version of Péguy, "bellowed with hoarse dignity to the wind," back at its creators. *Take that for your example,* says Hill, for we have a better one, hidden behind Péguy's arm on the beetroot field, safely shrouded in Hill's oblique poem. We can even "still mourn" for our hidden Péguy, on the condition that our mournful, elegiac feeling—expressed in the plainly nostalgic last line—is kept in ironical, distancing quotation marks. We can be moved by elegy, we can feel nostalgia, we can cry for Péguy—only "as if" we are experiencing them. The emotional fraudulence of our century runs so deep that we must continually question feelings as seemingly harmless as nostalgia for the past and reverence for nature.

Péguy is an extraordinary achievement for many reasons. For one thing, the execution of the conception is flawless. This is not surprising from Hill; what is surprising is that he sustains it over such a long poem. But most astonishing of all is the way *Péguy* emerges, for all its endless qualification, deflection, and irony, as a patriotic song for a fallen hero. But isn't this what Hill wished to avoid? Yes, but in the same remarkable way Hill's earlier poetry was successful *as poetry* while in a deep sense *refusing to be poetry,* so Hill's patriotic homage succeeds while continually indicating that such an effort is impossible. This sort of paradox has always been at the center of Geoffrey Hill's work. It has been largely responsible for Hill's scarce output. Yet in *Péguy* this paradox has been conducted over an immensely broad canvas—one with space enough to explore the dilemma of paying proper homage in an age rife with false or compromised homages. All of this makes *Péguy* one of the most serious and important long poems written in recent memory.

Yet the question remains: what is it about Charles Péguy that gives Hill the courage to create his own homage in such a hopelessly impure environment? It is not simply that Péguy himself has stimulated so many inauthentic homages springing from impure motives. For an answer we must turn to some of the details Hill was required to omit from the poem itself.

When Charles Péguy published his long poem *Le Mystère de la Charité de Jeanne d'Arc* in 1910[2] he was an isolated man. For years he had been upbraiding everyone he could lay hold of in the pages of *Les Cahiers*: politicians, theologians, intellectuals. Even close friends had come under attack. Whether he wrote about the holiness of poverty, the sanctity of tradition, the hypocrisy of the idea of equality, or the shallowness of the Church's believers (he called them "ready-made souls"), someone was bound to be offended.

But if Péguy was alone it was hardly his fault. (At least, so he felt.) It was the fault of the modern age. Péguy believed that the twentieth century's lack of spirituality—he called it *mystique*—had forced men to adopt rigid, narrow views. (The "lords of limit" and contumely, in Hill's poem.) These professional politicians, professional theologians, and professional intellectuals who had come into power took no interest in Péguy's little world of contradiction and paradox, where deep spiritual belief was at the root of every action and every word and gave things of the earth such richness and dimension.

It was this atmosphere of imminent crisis that led Péguy to think that the *mystique* which had withered away during the nineteenth century was about to re-emerge to bring France to life again. He felt it would happen soon, and when it did, all the corrupt Church Fathers, the bought-off socialists, and the anti-Semitic nationalists would have to come clean. France would then rise up out of the doldrums (Péguy always claimed he was living in an *epoch*—during which nothing interesting happened—rather than an *era*—which was historically significant), and he, Charles Péguy, might even be vindicated. Subscribers to *Les Cahiers* might even start reading it.

But the return to spirituality—to Péguy's *mystique*—never happened. Péguy thought it would occur when the Dreyfus case was reopened (to street battles) in 1898, but that hope was dashed. "I shall always remain inconsolable," said Péguy with reference to the Affair. Then Péguy thought that if spiritual rejuvenation could not take place in France, he would write a poem about such a previous rejuvenation in history. Although he chose Joan of Arc as his exemplar of spiritual renewal, he hoped readers would see her as the kind of prophet needed by the twentieth century. The complaint made to God in the poem, "There is never anything . . . if only we could see the daybreak of your kingdom," is as much about Péguy's time as it is about Joan's. Divine intervention in the form of voices heard by Joan was precisely the way *mystique* manifested itself. Péguy, needless to say, believed his own poetic voice carried forth the tradition of a re-emergent *mystique*, learned from Joan. At any rate, this explained to Péguy (and Péguy alone, since no one else was by now listening) why he suffered such isolation. He, like Joan, was misunderstood, and a perfect candidate for martyrdom.

Péguy knew that the resurgence of *mystique* in twentieth-century France would be, as it had been five hundred years earlier, a revolutionary event. Unlike secular revolutions (which, Péguy felt, were always cynical and misguided), this would be a crusade for truth. To paraphrase Péguy, the real Church was revolutionary, designed to overthrow the pagan order. And it was the job of an embattled "infidel" in the pagan order to correct the "renascent error" of the pagan past.

Now Geoffrey Hill scarcely believes in the re-emergence of *mystique*. What he does believe in—and what Péguy's martyrdom at the hands of the groups and causes he shunned during his life signifies—is the paradoxical command within tradition to revolt. Hill's career has been, above all, a rebellion against the "orthodoxy" of that which precedes him[3]

2 Originally published in *Les Cahiers de la Quinzaine*, January 16, 1910. Julien Green's English translation, entitled *The Mystery of the Charity of Joan of Arc*, was published in the U.S. by Pantheon Books in 1950.

3 Not that any of the early work should be revalued. On the contrary, it becomes even more important. As Péguy said, in one of his best paradoxes ever, "The sinner is at the very heart of Christianity." Why? "Because the sinner can make the best prayer."

—right down to his deflective lines. With *Péguy,* Hill revolts against the silencing, self-referential obsession with "the Word." If *Péguy* means anything in this sense, it is as testament to the endless process of renewal, the drama of generations, that is at the center of man and his world—and of the poetry of Geoffrey Hill. If the spiritual core animating this renewing process—found in the writings of Péguy—must be masked by Hill by means of endless deflection and displacement and the "haggard obliquities" of the *Péguy* poem, it only shows how much of an "infidelity" such a rebellion can be. All Hill can do is write a poem inspired *by* his latest rebellion, not *about* it.

The central nugget in Charles Péguy's writing that sparked Hill's latest rebellion is charity. To Péguy, a Catholic, Christian charity meant that giving without receiving, creating without demanding redemption, and loving without requiring fulfillment were all earthly reflections of the selfless love of God. Hill, for his part, is in all likelihood not a practitioner of Christian charity. But another kind of charity, a secular version of what Péguy practiced, seems very much to have inspired Hill in the writing of *Péguy.* In "Annunciations," Hill wrote:

> O Love, subject of the mere diurnal grind,
> Forever being pledged to be redeemed,
> Expose yourself to charity; be assured
> The body is but husk and excrement . . . .

When this poem was written, love demanded fulfillment, but was incapable of achieving it. And Hill's poetry reflected this impossibility of fulfillment by continually deflecting away from normal aesthetic resolution. Indeed, to write a poem that achieved resolution was to Hill an act of fraud; hence his subjection of it to such debilitating, scorching scrutiny. But Charles Péguy, who derived a comparable inspiration from Joan, has revealed charity to Hill, which allows Hill, if not entirely to escape this deflective procedure, then at least to divert it away from himself and his own creations. The self-referential obsession is no longer the source and object of Hill's high, moral castigation: the bad creations of others are. And the "creation" of the Péguy-myth was the natural object to undo, since it was Péguy's example that permitted Hill to escape continued self-laceration.

If Hill cannot entirely give up deflection and obliquity as methods, it is because this would be too radical a break with his own past as a poet. They still function usefully as a mode of expression for Hill. And as Péguy said, "Charity," which is "full of war," is "at once deeply conservative and deeply revolutionary." It is this paradoxical truth that allows Hill both to break with his past and to remain true to his vision. It is, in other words, what allows him to continue to create some of the most significant poetry of our time.

(*April* 1984)

In search of the good Shepard

by Mimi Kramer

Sam Shepard has been "goin' down big" in New York this year. In addition to the off-off-Broadway revival of *Tooth of Crime* earlier this year, Shepard's *Fool for Love* opened to rave reviews this summer at the Circle Repertory Company a few streets away from where the Cherry Lane's revival of *True West* has been playing all year. And two more Shepard plays are scheduled to open at La Mama in September. For a playwright who has insisted, for the last ten years, that he doesn't want to be a playwright at all, Sam Shepard has become an oddly permanent fixture on the American theatrical scene.

An aura of mysticism surrounds Shepard's plays. Just as they seem to find their way to New York almost against their author's will, so their form and genesis has been attributed to some other-than-human force: "The stuff would just come out," as Shepard put it in a 1974 interview, "and I wasn't really trying to shape it or make it into any big thing." But "disciplined" is a word the critics also use to describe his plays, and Stanley Kauffmann labels Shepard our "best practicing American playwright."

This mysticism, in fact, seems to hover over almost everything written about Shepard to date. The vocabulary of Shepard criticism—among people who write seriously about drama as literature—comprises words like "shamanism," "totemism," and "mythology." But the most mysterious feature in all this is the inability of critics who think Shepard is good to say *why* he is good.

Take, for example, a hefty volume of criticism from a couple of years ago entitled *American Dreams: The Imagination of Sam Shepard.*[1] With its wide-angle cover photo of a sky-blue Packard coming at you from out of several thousand kilowatts of sunset, *American Dreams* is the sort of book that really makes you wish you had a coffee table. The introduction, "Alphabetical Shepard," is not a sustained piece of prose on a set topic (such as: "Why Sam Shepard is Worth Two Hundred Nineteen Pages of Your Time") but instead a collection of the editor's spasmodic thoughts. Here is a typical example:

> The jazz artist teases the audience into following his rhythm for as long as he can keep it going, lifting them to a tantalizing high, taking them down, bringing them up again, one tempo to another, a little bit at a time as if they were caught in a sexual embrace with music that continually forestalls the orgasmic response of applause and shouts. The most powerful solo parts in Shepard's plays have that same erotic effect which is what makes his writing sexy though there's no actual sex in them: it's the rhythm of sex not the representation of it. Shepard's seduction is linguistic—a coming to language than [*sic*] to speech.

---

1 *American Dreams: The Imagination of Sam Shepard,* edited by Bonnie Marranca. Performing Arts Journal Publications, 1981.

This is but a foretaste of the insights to come. Inside we are told by one critic that "This sense of 'nowness' celebrates in a personal way the human scale of the theatrical experience." One academic locates in Shepard

> a series of constantly changing dramatic images, each of them carrying at least the promise of emotional content—audience empathy as *coitus interruptus.*

The director of the Playwrights' Program at Juilliard discloses that "Shepard's passion for dark, ominous visions and greater abstractions runs a clear course back to Hawthorne and Melville." And we meet a professor of English at the University of Pennsylvania for whom the "scene in [*Buried*] *Child* in which Tilden cleans the corn and then gently covers his sleeping father with the shucks" was "one of the most remarkable scenes" that he can remember having seen on the stage.

American Dreams, as its editor points out, is not "one long monologue in praise of Sam Shepard"; it is a series of long monologues in his praise. But nowhere in the book—amid the articles, essays, and interviews, the solemn treatises on how aspects of his life reflect "recurrent themes" in Shepard's work, the accounts of how various Shepard *opera* came to fruition—is there a single word addressed to the question of whether Shepard's work really merits all this attention. The subject has not even been touched on. In the realm of question-begging, *American Dreams,* I think, is down on its knees.

The position of a book like *American Dreams* is not by any means unique in the canon of Shepard criticism. What seems to have set the tone for current attitudes toward Shepard (and unwittingly excused him from having to be a better playwright than he is) was Elizabeth Hardwick's review in 1967 of an early Shepard play, *La Turista.* Hardwick's review, like so much else that has been written about Shepard since, consisted more of description than of exegesis—plot summary interspersed with observations about contemporary life extrapolated from the play, rather than a discussion of the play itself. More important, though, Hardwick's review assumed a value in Shepard's work without seeming to recognize any need to demonstrate it. In fact, far from wanting to analyze Shepard's play, Hardwick maintained that its very interest lay in its obscurity, in our inability to explain the play, even to ourselves. For Hardwick, the value in Shepard's work was that it lacked the "order" that had "been the heart of European fiction and drama."

> Incident after incident, each growing out of the other, united in a chain of significant motivation, of cause and effect—moments of human destiny strung out like beads on a string. This is what we mean, perhaps, when we say we "understand" a work of literary art. Yet each decade brings us the conviction that this order is no longer present to the serious writer.

Such an assertion, unaccompanied by argument or explanation, takes criticism out of the realm of rational discourse. But Hardwick's review did more. By putting the burden of proof on the audience to appreciate the play rather than on the playwright to affect the audience or the critic to persuade, Hardwick placed Shepard, by means of tone and implication, above criticism. She did not spare the unappreciative audience, however:

> The night I saw *La Turista* the American Place audience was, for the most part, utterly depressing; middle-aged, middle class and rather aggressively indifferent: a dead weight of alligators, dozing and grunting before muddily sliding away . . . . But, indeed, what good does it do a man to go and see something he won't like just because the reviewers have told him to do so? He would be better off at home.

It was an *ad hominem* approach: I think Sam Shepard is good and anyone who doesn't like him is a philistine. Well, now the wheel has come full circle: "If you don't like this play," threatens Clive Barnes in this morning's *New York Times* advertisement for a play currently running on off-off Broadway, "I don't like you." His tongue is in his cheek, of course, but the play for which he saved this particular gag was Shepard's *Fool for Love.*

Sam Shepard is not as good a playwright as everyone says. On the other hand, he is a far better playwright than one might be led to suppose from the quality of his followers' thought. What makes Shepard seem so much better than he actually is, I think, is the fact that what he does well is precisely what American playwrights—great and mediocre alike—have consistently done badly if they bothered to do it at all: to use the form of theater to artistic advantage.

For most of our "great American plays," the stage is an embarrassment. Take an example from a recent piece of widely acclaimed theater: Marsha Norman's Pulitzer-Prize-winning play *'night, Mother.* It requires one naturalistic set and takes place in the space of time taken to enact it, yet the extent of Norman's achievement was to prove that preserving the theatrical unities is not enough. The set, so ostentatiously detailed in all its ghastly accuracy, was put to no physical or metaphorical use by the playwright—it was not a battleground for the conflicting values of life and death, it was not a place where anything had happened. It was simply the setting for a play. Consequently, like the clock so prominently displayed on its wall and so carefully synchronized to accord with "real time," it just sat there, a pointless monument to the waste and folly of theatrical contrivance.

Shepard's *True West* at the Cherry Lane Theater is an example of a play that uses theatrical space well. In it two brothers squabble in a suburban kitchen in Southern California. One is a Hollywood screenwriter with a family upstate, the other a desert rat who makes his living stealing home appliances from people's houses. In the course of the play we watch the brothers alternate between envy and derision toward one another, exchanging (in addition to blows) wistful fantasies of each other's chosen way of life. Each brother voices a half-formed plan to invade the other's world and each challenges himself to try the other's trade. The desert rat tries spinning fantasies for mass consumption and the screenwriter tries breaking into houses. In the space of what seems like a single night a perfectly good typewriter is destroyed and all the toasters in the neighborhood wind up on "Mom's" kitchen floor. Also, "Mom's" kitchen itself, is completely trashed.

The Cherry Lane Theatre is not always an easy place to be while all this is going on. But the space created and then destroyed there is used to good economy. "Mom's kitchen" is an ambiguous territory, neutral but violently contested. Neither brother actually belongs in this house, but each has an equal claim to be there. Because Shepard is not primarily interested in the psychological realism of sibling rivalry, however, "Mom's kitchen" takes on a sense of place on an ironic level. Neither brother really wants to lay claim to this territory. For each it is a worthless stopping place on the way to some fantasy or away from some regret. Even the monstrous Lee, who cannot seem to remember from one moment to the next what he was saying, when he was last on the desert, or what he was doing there, has, we find, a vision. To Lee a "real nice" house is one that doesn't have a watchdog. But the house outside of which he lurked threateningly on one of his nightly "tours" was, he says,

> like a paradise. Kinda' place that sorta' kills ya' inside. Warm yellow lights. Mexican tiles all around. Copper pots hangin' over the stove. Ya' know like they got in the magazines. Blonde people movin' in and outa' the rooms, talkin' to each other. (*Pause*) Kinda' place you wish you sorta' grew up in, ya' know.

The wimp-like Austin, meanwhile, has an equally unrealistic vision of what life on the desert is all about. Its naïveté enrages Lee:

> Hey, do you actually think I choose to live out in middle a' nowhere? Do ya'? Ya' think it's

> some kinda' philosophical decision I took or somethin'? I'm livin' out there 'cause I can't make it here!

What keeps these revelations, unlike the endless series of revelations in *'night, Mother,* from seeming simplistic or contrived is that they do not form the substance of the dramatic action. They are merely sideswipes in a larger conflict raised by a single dramatic action: Lee's boast that he can write a better story treatment than Austin, better because it would be "real."

At the end of Scene 2 Austin asks Lee to make himself scarce the next day because he is planning to meet with a producer over the project he is working on. "No sweat," says Lee. He blackmails Austin for the keys to Austin's car and on his way out tosses over his shoulder,

> Hey, ya' know, if that uh—story of yours doesn't go over with the guy—tell him I got a couple a' "projects" he might be interested in. Real commercial . . . . True-to-life stuff.

Needless to say, Lee comes back early the next day, bearing a stolen television set. We think he's about to ruin everything for Austin: he pockets the producer's lighter, rambles on about Kirk Douglas, claims to be a keen golfer, and chats the producer up about a story idea. But the producer leaves with a vague promise about lunch and a game with Lee next day and a suggestion that Lee get his brother to help him write the treatment for the story.

Later that night Austin, over the typewriter, is pleased to be contemptuous about Lee's story. According to Austin, people

> don't end up chasing each other across the Panhandle. Through "Tornado Country." . . . And they don't have horses conveniently along with them when they run out of gas.

But the producer's judgment, the following day, is that Lee's story "has a ring of truth . . . . Something about the real West." To Austin, "There's no such thing as the West anymore! It's a dead issue." But because the disputed territory of "Mom's kitchen" is the setting for a battle over another "disputed territory," it is fitting for us to be trapped there. We may not love being there, but we are there for a reason.

"So they take off after each other straight into an endless black prairie," Lee dictates to Austin as the lights go down on Act I:

> Each one separately thinks that he's the only one that's afraid. And they keep riding like that straight into the night. Not knowing. And the one who's chasin' doesn't know where the other is taking him. And the one who's being chased doesn't know where he's going.

"It was *them,*" said the woman from Scarsdale standing outside the Cherry Lane during the intermission. "The ones he was talking about just before the lights went out. All that stuff he was saying in the story, you remember? About chasing each other and not knowing that the other one was afraid? Well he was talking about *them*!"

Where are the obscurities of yesteryear? In 1967 Elizabeth Hardwick wanted to defend Shepard's genius against ravening hordes of women from Scarsdale and their indifference. In those days—the late Sixties and early Seventies—Shepard was engaged in writing avant-garde theater. The purpose of avant-garde theater, of course, is to push back the limits of an audience's capacity to be shocked or upset, and accordingly Shepard's plays during this period were not what you might call "audience-friendly." They weren't hostile to the audience; they just weren't particularly concerned with being accessible. Shepard's plays, during this period—highly influenced by the experimental theater groups in whose midst Shepard began writing—tended to present words, images, characters, and events bearing no relation to one another and little relation to reality. "Surreal," people called them; they allegedly had a quality of "mythic realism." Shepard himself and some of his followers maintained that his work was meaningless, that, as one director put it, "It's always hard to tell what, if anything, Sam's plays are 'about'—although they are unmistakably alive." To try to locate meaning in Shepard's work was, according to Shepard, "a dangerous area" because "once it goes off into the so-called meaning of it, then it's lost, it's gone away." Elizabeth Hardwick, on the other hand, maintained that the kinds of plays Shepard was writing—"the episodic, the obscurely related, the collection of images, moods"—were the only "serious" kind of writing one could do for the theater because "the connections . . . in drama" had "become like those in poetry."

In 1967 it must have been hard to tell how good a playwright Sam Shepard was; but in the mid-Seventies Shepard declared his intention of trying to write a different kind of play, "very stark and not so flashy and not full of a lot of mythic figures and everything." The plays that followed, did, in fact, become increasingly conventional, increasingly "not full of a lot of mythic figures and everything." Stripped of the jargon of the avant-garde, *True West* and *Fool for Love* give us a chance to see how breathtakingly banal Shepard really is.

I saw *True West* twice. The first time John Malkovich played the part of Lee, and sitting in the first row of the tiny theater I felt properly menaced. But even directly under the vacant stare of Malkovich's mindless smiling violence, I found the degree of anxiety produced by what was happening on stage to be roughly equivalent to the anxiety I usually suffer during the chase scene at the end of *Never Give a Sucker an Even Break.* The second time round Lee was miscast: Bruce Lyons, though he played well, was too young and unthreatening. He was rather cute, in fact. On this occasion the audience seemed to be enjoying themselves much more: shrieking with laughter and practically falling into the aisles. On second viewing I realized that *True West* reminded me of nothing so much as situation comedy.

What partly gives the play this quality of middlebrow family entertainment (and one could almost imagine it adapted into a prime-time television series) is its structure and the nature of its comedy. The crude level of irony at which the gags are pitched, the general reliance for comic effect in each scene on cheating the expectations raised in the preceding one, the short scenes framed by punchy opening and closing lines: it all seemed to cry out for commercial interruptions. But even more distinguishing was its ability to find a conflict so harmless that it poses no threat to the audience: nothing is at stake. Throughout *True West* one's interest is engaged by the problem of which brother has the upper hand. This keeps changing and Shepard turns the tables on us skillfully. But to what end—for what is there, ultimately, to choose between a desert rat and a writer of made-for-TV screenplays?

Shepard's use of stage space promises to make some point about the nature of fantasy. In the published version of the play he warns that the set for *True West must* be a realistic kitchen not stylized in its design. The stage set for *True West* at the Cherry Lane is marvelous: you know that kitchen; you have seen it a million times. But with the opening line—"So Mom took off for Alaska, huh?"—you also know that you are someplace between the normal and the bizarre, a world where kitchens are familiar but where people just take off for Alaska without raising comment. In the course of the play Shepard will manipulate our assumptions and expectations so as to make us doubt the normalcy of the situation. Incredible things begin happening and because we hear them from an unreliable source—Lee—we wonder whether they are true. It turns out that they are; but all the while that the brothers' situation is becoming increasingly "unrealistic," there is always that realistic stage set falling, scene by scene, into a deeper state of dilapidation.

The implicit promise in the tension Shepard has created here is that, with the return of "Mom," who, as Lee puts it, "don't like even a single tea-leaf in the sink," some reference point will be restored to the world of the play and will demand of us some judgment on the problems of reality that the play has posed. Of course, this never happens. "Mom," when she appears, turns out to be half again as flaky as anything going on in the play. The brothers' behavior and the state of the kitchen barely provoke comment, and she is soon gone again, leaving Lee and Austin to resume their battle to the death. The play even ends with the brothers facing it off in freeze-frame.

Shepard is certainly aware that he has reneged on his play's promises and it is even clear why: he simply does not see the mechanism of a moral or metaphysical reference point as a necessary part of theater. Shepard is not interested in judgments any more than he is interested in irony and delusion; consequently his play performs the same function for his audience as *I Love Lucy* did: it passes the time.

Like *True West, Fool for Love,* at the Circle Repertory Theater, promises to make some comment on the nature of reality and fantasy. The promise is implicit in the play's very title: the word "fool," after all, implies the recognition of some error or deception. But, like *True West, Fool for Love* never gets beyond a trite statement that fantasies exist.

In *Fool for Love* we encounter a pair of star-crossed lovers whose romance is awkwardly tinged with incest. On the surface, the main focus of the play seems to be the fate of May and Eddie's stormy and steamy relationship—or rather its ontological status. "How many times have you done this to me?" challenges May. "Suckered me into some dumb little fantasy and then dropped me like a hot rock." "It's no fantasy," Eddie assures her; and, sententiously, May replies, "It's all a fantasy." Eddie—with his soiled jeans, his tragic limp, and his cowboy boots stuck together with duct tape—is apparently having an affair with some sort of "countess." For May, only the jealous fantasy is important:

> I can't even see you now. All I see is a picture of you. You and her. I don't even know if the picture's real anymore. I don't even care. It's a made-up picture.

But as May and Eddie rehearse and rehash the long passage of their meetings, we find that the central dramatic action consists in an attempt to establish the truth not of the present, but of the past. The arrival of another character, Martin, the "date" whom May has spoken of and whose existence we have been led to doubt, provides May and Eddie with an occasion for offering accounts of how a half-brother and half-sister could innocently become lovers. May and Eddie, like Austin and Lee in *True West,* are fond of spinning yarns; but since each story is discredited almost as soon as it is told, the central conflict in the play is a sort of contest over "truth" in storytelling.

Like *True West, Fool for Love* requires a single set and uses theatrical space well, to a point. Throughout the action of the play an old man sits in a rocking chair to stage left, nursing a bottle of Tennessee whiskey and watching the play. That he is or may be Eddie and May's father (by two different women) gradually emerges and the Old Man becomes a central figure in the stories they tell of the past. The use of lighting and stage space makes clear that the Old Man and the pair of lovers exist on two different planes of reality: one exists only as a figment of the other's imagination. The underlying question of the play is: *Whose* imagination? Sometimes Eddie smiles at the Old Man, pours him a drink, or addresses him directly; at other times both May and Eddie seem unaware of his existence. But, always, the Old Man is smiling or chuckling, and finally, when he doesn't like the story being told, he becomes involved in the action of the play. At the end of *Fool for Love,* when May and Eddie have left separately, the Old Man goes back to his rocker and delivers the final pronouncement. Addressing no one in particular and pointing at a blank wall, he says:

> Ya' see that picture over there? Ya' see that? Ya' know who that is? That's the woman of my dreams. That's who that is. And she's mine. She's all mine. Forever.

As a statement about delusion this leaves

something to be desired; as a *demonstration* of delusion it is a total failure for the simple reason that, intriguing as all this is, we have not a clue how the different levels of reality are meant to relate to one another. The Carrollian question, "Which dreamed it?" has never been answered.

I assumed that the ambiguity, though irritating, was intentional. But the soon-to-be-published playscript explicitly states in the stage directions that the Old Man "exists only in the minds of May and Eddie." I saw the play twice and thought it was the other way around. So did all the people I spoke to who saw the play. So did all the people whose reviews of *Fool for Love* I read. What would Sam Shepard say about this? Would he fault his play? the audience? Or would he say it doesn't really matter because the audience's response is of no importance and the play has no meaning anyway?

The question is worth asking since the tie that seems to bind the Shepard "school" together is a view of theater which diminishes the importance of the audience's role in the theatrical experience. When Elizabeth Hardwick chose for rhetorical purposes to deprecate the audience and make their response seem of little consequence, the particular kind of theater she was championing had already done that very thing. Sam Shepard and the experimental theater groups around which he "grew up" as a playwright were the heirs to a movement in avant-garde theater that had sought to disturb the traditional audience-actor relationship and replace it with something else. The alternatives found by groups like The Living Theatre, The Open Theatre, The Polish Laboratory Theatre, and the Performance Theatre Group ranged from making the audience victims of open harassment to making them participants in a sort of mystic religious experience. Somewhere between the two extremes emerged an approach to theater that did not effectively seem to care whether an audience was there or not. Each of these (largely improvisational) groups claimed to be searching for the one salient characteristic of the theatrical form, the thing that made theater itself; and ironically that was the first thing to go: for historically the only thing that defines theater and separates it from its roots in religious ritual is the presence of an involved but nonparticipating audience. It is the audience that transforms theater from a spiritual experience to an intellectual one, and it is the premise that the playwright has something to communicate to the audience that keeps theater from regressing to religion.

Shepard's early affiliation with Joseph Chaikin's Open Theatre may go a long way toward explaining some of the contradictions in Shepard's ostensible views of theater and the role of the playwright. For there are contradictions. The early Shepard made it clear that he viewed theater as a private experience and the presence of the audience as an intrusion. This no longer seems to be the case: precisely what the inane comedy and wistful visions of plays like *True West, Fool for Love,* and *Buried Child* do so well is to locate and control the audience's feelings and frame of reference. But to what end? Ultimately, Sam Shepard has precious little to say.

Shepard is not a playwright who can dispense with an audience or with "so-called meaning." He cannot afford to. Already, for all his sense of theatricality, his ear for language, and his skill at handling conflict, Shepard's brand of theater teeters dangerously on the brink of ritualism. A playwright who cares to do no more than control his audience's feelings is merely a priest in borrowed robes.

(*October* 1983)

Di Suvero and constructivism

by Eric Gibson

From the beginning of his career twenty-five years ago the figure of Mark di Suvero has loomed large on the artistic landscape. Indeed, he is one of the few sculptors of his generation to have become something of a myth. In 1960 he made a dramatic debut at the Green Gallery with an exhibition of oversized sculptures. In the same year he was in a near-fatal elevator accident which for some time dramatically limited the range of his artistic activity. By the late Sixties, however, he was back in full possession of his powers, making sculptures on an even bolder scale than before. In the early Seventies he caused a sensation by going into self-exile, to protest the Vietnam War. And when he returned in 1975 he was greeted by a triumphant retrospective of his work at the Whitney Museum. All of this by now has helped to confer upon di Suvero a legendary status. Even his media image is that of the artist-superman—bare-chested, hard-hatted, working the controls of a crane or battling a resistant work-in-progress.

The Whitney Museum's retrospective was really the crest of the wave. It marked the return of the artist-exile at the moment when America was ending its commitments in Southeast Asia. It also presented di Suvero as both the legitimate heir of David Smith in the tradition of constructed sculpture and a younger, brasher rival to the Englishman Anthony Caro, whose own retrospective at the Museum of Modern Art had closed only a few months before. As such the Whitney retrospective signaled the end of one phase of di Suvero's career—its long, troubled beginning—and the opening of another in which one anticipated that di Suvero would be able to give full rein to his formidable creative powers, undistracted by physical disabilities or political interests. Ten years have passed since then, and now another di Suvero retrospective is on view, this one at the Storm King Art Center in Mountainville, New York.[1] How does di Suvero's work look now that all the hoopla is behind us?

The new exhibition, it must be said, is somewhat misleading. Comprising twenty-one sculptures indoors and eighteen outdoors, it omits the large-scale early works, such as *Barrel, Hankchampion,* and *Che Faro senza Eurydice,* that did so much to establish di Suvero's early reputation and announce his sculptural concerns and intentions. From the late Fifties the exhibition presents only the expressionistic, Rodin-inspired *Hand* sculptures; it then moves on to the post-accident pieces of 1961-67 without acknowledging in any way the important work that came between.

At the outset, then, we are given a dis-

1 "Mark di Suvero: Twenty-five Years of Sculpture and Drawings," which will be on view until October 31, was organized by David R. Collens, the Director of the Storm King Art Center. The exhibition's catalogue-brochure ($4.00) contains an essay by Phyllis Tuchman.

torted view. As it stands, the visitor unfamiliar with di Suvero's sculpture is likely to come away from Storm King with the impression that his early works were part of a protracted "warming up" period during which he experimented with many different modes of sculptural expression before finally finding his true artistic self in the later (post-1967), large-scale outdoor sculptures.

The truth is very different. These small-scale works—at least those from 1961-1967—represent what I believe to be an interim phase of di Suvero's work. It consists of work executed during the long period of convalescence, that is, the period before he felt sufficiently recovered to *return* to making large-scale, gestural sculpture. Thus if we are to get any accurate sense of the inner logic of di Suvero's work over the years—surely the purpose of a retrospective of this kind—it is vital that we have these early pieces before us.

Di Suvero's early works (happily two are on view at the Modern and at the Whitney) were striking at the time, and remain so today, for the manner in which they fused the language of constructivism and the sensibility of Abstract Expressionism. They were six or seven feet high and formed from worn planks and pilings scavenged from the wharves of lower Manhattan; occasionally they incorporated more recognizable objects, such as ladders or barrels. These disparate elements were held together—and apart—by steel rods and chains in a manner which suggested forces held in permanent tension. While constructivist in their use of discrete, found forms and in their vestigial Cubist syntax, they were without the traditional Cubist "core" which would normally order and lock disparate parts. Instead, all the elements thrust away from the center, creating voids which di Suvero worked as eloquently as his solids. The result was sculpture whose drama resided in both its size and its vigorous, gestural character.

Much was made at the time—and in the years following—of the similarities between this phase of di Suvero's career and Abstract Expressionist painting, that of Franz Kline in particular. The cantilevered lengths of wood were seen as sculptural analogues to Kline's bold, black paint swaths, forms which likewise appeared arrested in space.

Yet far more important—and, as far as I know, little noticed at the time—was the way di Suvero altered the formal vocabulary of constructivism as it had existed from Picasso down through David Smith and, later, Anthony Caro. For in using battered pieces of wood and readily recognizable objects, di Suvero departed from the more tailored, elegant look of orthodox constructivist sculpture.

Artists such as Smith and Caro strove continually to de-emphasize—within certain limits, to be sure—the industrial origin of their forms, the better to accommodate them to the overall aesthetic program. Smith, even when using something as distinct as a wrench or a pair of tongs, achieved this accommodation by articulating the form's purely sculptural qualities—its mass or lack of it, its contours, its spaces. Caro, in turn, eschewed recognizably industrial elements—except for I-beams—preferring more generalized forms. And of course he painted his work. Both men consistently attempted to put a certain amount of distance between their finished sculpture and the scrapyard or the steel mill that was its source. "De-naturing," as this was referred to at the time, was nothing more—and nothing less—than the passage from nature to culture. The world of things was drawn upon and the object transfigured and so made part of the world of art. Such a transfiguration was vital to the success of constructed sculpture as it had existed prior to di Suvero. David Smith acknowledged this fact when he spoke disparagingly of "stopped images"—sculptures in which the borrowed industrial forms violated the integrity of the whole by affirming too explicitly its identity in "nature."

Di Suvero, in making no concessions to such refinements, in effect "de-aestheticized" constructed sculpture, bringing it down from the loftier realms of good taste in order to give it a rawer, more direct expressive charge and relation to the viewer. (In this there is a small element of irony, for it reflects the belief that constructivism, originally thought radical in its use of common or debased materials, needed the very sort of *bouleversement* it had administered to the established practice of its time.)

Nowhere was this "de-aesthetization" more evident than in di Suvero's unadulterated use of large, recognizable objects—ladders, barrels, and the like. In their consciously incongruous, "look-at-me" character they had a quality of artistic subversiveness and daring that suggested the artist's willingness to take enormous risks and his desire to make a brash gesture in the interests of making sculpture more "real."

All of this gave a populist dimension to di Suvero's work. He used whatever materials came to hand, as opposed to restricting himself to certain "ideal" forms, the implication being that anything is admissible in the making of art. The more direct, down-to-earth mode of address to the viewer implied a more democratic outlook, one deliberately opposed to the more rarefied, "fine art" creations of earlier constructed sculpture.

Di Suvero's 1960 accident—he was riding atop an elevator that crushed him when it failed to stop—brought his artistic activity to a halt. When he was well enough to sit in a wheelchair, he could only work by welding pieces of metal in his lap, or by using assistants to move modestly larger forms. These sculptures form an eclectic mix—not surprisingly, really, since they are the work of someone trying to get used to another order, another scale of sculptural operation. They make one realize how much the earlier works were scaled to an upright body. What we have in these works is di Suvero trying to teach himself a new language—new to him, anyway—but without leaving behind the old vocabulary.

Thus among this group there are works which come across as "drawing room" pieces—overly elegant, precious things made of overlapping and intersecting arcs of stainless steel, such as *Moonrise* (1961-62). Or there is *Bachpiece* (1962), a masterpiece of sculptural illusionism—admittedly a curious thing in di Suvero—in which a tilted chunk of beaten-up wood and three or four vertical nails stand at opposite ends of a sloping steel "hill," the tense, charged relation between the disparately scaled groups vividly suggesting four persons confronting a giant monolith. And there is *For Giacometti* (1962), a moderately large-sized floor piece (four feet high, six feet wide) in which, at opposite ends of a platform, a section of wooden beam wrapped in chain and another with a metal ring projecting from its top tilt away from each other. In its poise, dynamic tension, charged interior space, and gestural character, *For Giacometti* is closest to the earlier large-scale works. It conflates the essential qualities into what is almost a landscape configuration.

Not until di Suvero gets fully mobile again does he truly recover his sculptural momentum. When he does, it is in a manner even more vigorous and expansive than before.

In 1967 the artist shifted from wood construction to metal and embarked on a succession of enormous sculptures (thirty to forty feet high) made of extended I-beams and cables, apparently in an effort to recapture the impressive gestural style of his earlier phase. Owing to the attenuation of the I-beams, these later sculptures have reduced, linear silhouettes that make them look somewhat fragile and give them a surprising grace and elegance; in relation to their rougher forebears, they are almost refined. The earliest, *Are Years What? (For Marianne Moore)* (1967), carries over the staccato rhythms of the prior phase and so stands as a perfect point of transition. It is as if the accident had never happened and di Suvero was indeed simply moving on from what he had done before. What differentiates these sculptures, more than their size, is the introduction of an element that will soon become the artist's signature: the suspended or balanced form. Here it is two I-beam sections joined to form a "V," and hung by one end so that the "V" floats and rotates in space midway up the sculpture.

If in these sculptures di Suvero does return to his former gestural manner, it is gesture with a new artistic center. This is understandable, for there can be no doubt of the causal link between this new campaign and di Suvero's full recovery from the accident seven years before. So sudden, and so extreme, is the shift in size, and so aggressively do these sculptures stake their claim to their environment, that they suggest a sudden release, an exultation at the onset of free, unfettered mobility—exactly what one might expect of an artist recently emerged from a period of prolonged physical debility and confinement, particularly an artist whose earlier work had been so animated and physical in character. All at once, it seems, di Suvero moves from a generalized, aesthetic expressionism to one that is personal, even autobiographical.

In the sculptures following *Are Years What? (For Marianne Moore)* the balancing element is no longer incidental: it is central to the entire work—in a way similar to Calder's stabiles, where forms are also suspended from firm structural supports. Additionally, these sculptures are not the spreading configurations of old: they are architectonic, structural affairs divided into two parts, "support" and "action."

It goes without saying that at such a scale, such feats as di Suvero performs are highly dramatic. The sight of *Mon Père, Mon Père* (1973-75)—with its enormous "V" form suspended horizontally some twenty feet in the air—is captivating, and not a little terrifying. Yet once one has gotten past the drama, these aspects strike one as gestures undertaken for their own sake. They have a decided attention-attracting character to them, a character one had seen earlier in di Suvero's work but now isolated and made the "subject" or point of the work. Other sculptors, notably George Rickey, have made balancing their "subject," but in Rickey's work it has a symbolic as well as plastic *raison d'être,* expressing continuity, stability, equilibrium. Di Suvero's balancing, by contrast, has no meaning outside itself. Even as an expressive gesture it falls flat, functioning as a diluted, more genteel version of the dynamic tension of the earlier works. What we have here, then, is not the coordinated set of aesthetic relations we associate with orthodox constructivism but instead a heroic demonstration—a demonstration of freedom from physical considerations and principles.

With this freedom comes another development in di Suvero's form vocabulary, again an outgrowth of tendencies seen in the earlier sculpture. If previously the artist used whole, recognizable objects in his work in order to "de-aestheticize" the constructivist language, to make it more "real" and accessible, in the large, post-1967 outdoor works he uses recognizable objects without giving them even vestigial aesthetic roles. Thus, suspended from the middle of *She* (1977-78)—a low, laterally spreading sculpture—is a steamroller drum. It hangs there inert, with no relation to anything else around it. Similarly, affixed to one end of *Sunflowers for Vincent* (1978-83)—a bright yellow, horizontal sculpture—is a stainless steel ship's propeller.

In these sculptures di Suvero's populist stance becomes more pronounced. The directness and relative ease of access of the early works—always, it should be stressed, existing on an *aesthetic* plane—is transferred to the physical realm as the artist increasingly makes sculptures with parts that can be pushed, rotated, or otherwise maneuvered by the spectator. The ultimate version of this is his increasingly frequent practice of suspending low platforms off his sculptures—there is one suspended from *She*—designed for the viewer to sit or recline on. In di Suvero's exhibition of recent work this summer at the Oil & Steel Gallery in New York there was even a piece whose "sculptural" members were *only* supporting such a platform. Clearly here the imperatives of constructed sculpture have been overturned and put in the service of a kind of "playground sculpture."

The emphasis on demonstration as the principal artistic statement, the increasingly explicit use of recognizable objects, and the more physical, interactive aspects of his sculpture tell us that di Suvero has moved a long way from the tradition of orthodox, constructivist sculpture. Indeed one might say that at this point di Suvero's sculptures are not so much constructivist as simply *constructed.* He has tried to extend into these monumental works the vernacular expressionism of his early pieces, but he has succeeded only in emptying them of any but the most transitory satisfactions. By renouncing his earlier aesthetic logic and formal rigor he has left us with the casual, the utilitarian, the entertaining.

As such di Suvero's sculptures represent not the vital extension of a tradition but the playing out of one. They anticipate, even clear the ground for, a figure like R. M. Fischer, who combines discarded industrial forms to make not abstract sculpture but "abstract" lamps, domesticating the constructivist impulse and taking the anti-aestheticism announced in di Suvero's work to its ultimate conclusion. Di Suvero's work thus stands as an important benchmark in the journey from late modernism to the formulation of the so-called postmodern canons of irony and the commonplace.

What a difference a decade makes! Ten years ago it would have been unthinkable to suggest that di Suvero stood in anything but the mainstream of modernist sculpture. That we can no longer hold this view is a consequence of the passage of time and the displacement effected by new art. No doubt di Suvero's artistic persona is robust enough to withstand these changes. Still, it is unlikely that we will ever again look upon his sculpture with the same innocent enthusiasm as we did before.

(*September* 1985)

Three musical eminences

by Samuel Lipman

Boulez at Columbia

It will probably not have escaped the diligent reader's attention that there is in fact one distinguished performer today who does compose at a level of ambition consistent with the celebrity of his performing career. This rare bird is, of course, Pierre Boulez (born 1925), the distinguished French composer and conductor who is by all odds the most important creative musician his country has produced since Poulenc and Messiaen. Boulez has recently been making a performing tour of the United States, his first since his departure from the New York Philharmonic in 1977. He has been conducting American orchestras as well as the Ensemble InterContemporain, his group from IRCAM (Institut de Récherche et de Coordination Acoustique/Musique), the new music component of the Beaubourg project in Paris.

Boulez and his ensemble came into New York at the beginning of March to the accompaniment of much printed material—and even giant cloth banners at Lincoln Center—emblazoned "Boulez is Back!" The schedule of Boulez and Boulez-associated events included three concerts of the Ensemble InterContemporain conductd by Boulez; one set of Philharmonic subscription concerts conducted by Zubin Mehta and containing Boulez's important work *Rituel* (in addition to works of Mozart); another set of Philharmonic concerts conducted by Boulez and containing works by Stravinsky and Debussy in addition to his own *Improvisations sur Mallarmé I, II, & III*; a concert performed by ensembles from the Philharmonic, with the Suite from Stravinsky's *L'Histoire du Soldat* conducted by Boulez; and finally a public conversation with Boulez at Symphony Space, an old movie theater on upper Broadway now used for avant-garde and "innovative" musical presentations.

This flurry of activity seemed altogether a belated making of amends to Boulez, whose six-year tenure with the Philharmonic has increasingly bulked larger—and better—in the memories of New York music-lovers. Just what went wrong during Boulez's leadership of the Philharmonic remains slightly unclear even now. At the time there was a widespread impression that the orchestra's subscriptions weren't selling; certainly there was vastly less interest in the records made by the orchestra with Boulez than there had been in those made by his predecessor, Leonard Bernstein. The audience which did find its way to the concerts—and it must be remembered that much of the time Boulez was at the Philharmonic he conducted in Philharmonic Hall, the earlier and even more acoustically unsatisfactory state of what is now called Fisher Hall—seemed unsympathetic to Boulez's readings of familiar repertory and to his choice of difficult new music. Though he did conduct the music of quite a few Americans, Boulez seemed deeply out of touch with the earlier nativist music which to this day marks America's proudest achievement in composition. Perhaps as a result of all these factors, Boulez evidently didn't want to spend very much time in New York when he wasn't actually performing. And one unhappy outcome seems even more important than all the foregoing: Boulez the composer at no time seemed to make a favorable impression on the orchestra, the audience, or on New York critical opinion.

There were, however, positive features of Boulez's activity at the Philharmonic. The New York audience received a conspectus of the most important new music being written, as well as of some parts of the nineteenth-century repertory usually ignored by celebrity music directors. The audience itself began to change; it came to include some younger elements, perhaps more willing than their elders to have artistic risks taken on their behalf. As for the orchestra, despite the coarsening of tone attendant on playing so much new music, so much unfamiliar old music, and so much familiar old music in unfamiliar conceptions, the Philharmonic learned new standards of playing together and in tune. Above all, unlike the situation today after eight seasons of Mehta, there was no doubt while Boulez was running the Philharmonic that someone was musically and intellectually in charge, and that what went on in Philharmonic concerts was worthy of respect and honor even when it seemed uninviting and, on occasion, actually ugly.

It was most assuredly the positive, not the negative, features of Boulez's achievement which seemed uppermost as the capacity audience assembled at the Columbia University gymnasium on the evening of March 5 to hear the first Boulez event, a concert by the Ensemble InterContemporain. The idea of seeing Boulez conduct seemed like a throwback to the past. The crowd on hand was an uneasy mixture of music-business notables, avant-garde composers and artists and their groupies, and just plain music lovers come to have their ears and minds stimulated. It was a fascinating combination, of a kind one never sees anymore at New York Philharmonic concerts.

Musical-world gossip has it that Boulez turned down the nearby Cathedral of St. John the Divine because of its boomy acoustics in favor of the surprisingly clear-sounding Columbia gymnasium. In any case, the sound heard by the audience, seated on the playing floor, was produced not just by the ambient acoustics of the gymnasium but also by the loudspeakers hung from the ceiling and posted at the corners of the room.

The loudspeakers were in their way the stars—certainly they were the loudest performers—of the evening. The short program contained only two works, *Dialogue de l'Ombre Double* ("Dialogue of the Double Shadow") and *Répons* ("Response"). Although very different from each other, both works were as much creatures of late twentieth-century electronic technology as of their composer's undoubtedly fertile mind.

Dialogue de l'Ombre Double—the title is drawn from Paul Claudel's drama *Le Soulier de satin (The Satin Slipper)*—was written in 1985 for the composer Luciano Berio's sixtieth birthday. It is a seventeen-minute piece for a solo clarinettist, playing both live (but amplified) from the stage and on a pre-recorded tape. The work alternates between its pre-recorded and live sections; the room lights, including spotlights focused on the stage, are turned off for the pre-recorded sections, on for the live.

The musical material of *Dialogue* comprises improvisatory gestures made up of leaping passages utilizing the full range of the clarinet, and tremolos between intervals of varying sizes. Some relief from the thinness of the monodic musical line is provided by the clarinettist when he begins to play live before his pre-recorded double has quite finished; rather more relief is provided by the use of computer-generated procedures to pick out and lengthen individual notes and their overtone components.

The musical effect of all this legerdemain was, at least on this listener, meager. What sounds very much like clarinet improvisation—especially when the instrument is played in as refined a manner as it was here by Alain Damiens—is not unpleasant at all. But more is required to sustain interest over a quarter-hour than a clarinet playing in conversation with itself. At its best, Boulez's *Dialogue* seemed to partake of the atmosphere of French impressionist music, most notably the opening of Debussy's *Prélude à l'après midi d'un faune* (1894), and *Syrinx* (1913) for solo flute. But Debussy's works seem pointed and never too long, and *Dialogue,* alas, went on and on.

It cannot be denied, however, that what the composer did not supply in *Dialogue* by way of music was supplied by technology. The live clarinet, amplified though it was, sounded remarkably lifelike; the taped clarinet, though clearly recorded in a different acoustic, still sounded real. The exciting passage of the taped sounds from speaker to speaker around the gymnasium evoked nostalgic memories of demonstrations of quadraphonic sound—even, three decades ago, of early stereo. But the sounds at the Columbia gymnasium were so full-bodied and so distortion-free that one could appreciate the technology for the thrilling scientific and engineering miracle it is.

Répons, forty-five minutes long, was conducted by Boulez. From the first measures it was clear that it is compositionally a weightier piece by far than *Dialogue.* The program notes for the Columbia concert described in admirably succinct terms the work's scoring and the instrumental set-up:

> *Répons* is conceived on two distinct but intercommunicating planes. Seated in the middle of the auditorium is a chamber orchestra . . . : nine woodwinds, seven brass and eight strings, all treated as soloists, all allowed to make their music without electronic intervention. Then, positioned around the audience there are six players who each have a principal instrument and some adjunct: a pianist with a celesta, another pianist with an electric organ, a harpist with two harps differently tuned, and performers on cymbalon (the large trapezoidal Hungarian dulcimer on legs), vibraphone and xylophone, each with percussion. These six soloists also have tape recorders carrying "background" music, and their instrumental playing is fed via microphones to the electronic equipment for amplification, transformation and diffusion around the hall.

And so it was at Columbia, except that there seemed to be only one harp. It was soon clear that *Répons* is also technologically more imposing than *Dialogue.* Its sophisticated electronic equipment, which was not visible from where I sat, was also described in the program notes:

> . . . the essential equipment consists of the 4X machine developed at IRCAM by Giuseppe de Giugno, and the halaphone invented by Hans Peter Haller in the studios of Southwest German Radio . . . . The system is able to alter the timbre of any sound before sending it on to the loudspeakers; it can also store an event and perhaps repeat it several times with programmed changes of pitch. Therefore, the electronic element is not merely passive, accepting and transmitting what the instrumentalists produce; rather, it has an active role in the music's unfolding, and the computer technicians are "performers" of *Répons* quite as much as are the players of the more usual instruments.

With the first blocks of dissonantal chords that came from the chamber orchestra it was clear that Boulez as conductor was exerting a magisterial presence over the performance. As the instruments from around the hall were heard, adding to the heavy impasto of sound, Boulez seemed to dominate everything, presiding over what seemed like infinite separate planes of sound with spare, sharp, and decisive motions. When he gave cues, the response from the musicians was immediate and precise; he seemed a master of even the wild passages emanating from the two pianos as they played their cavorting figurations. Like his conductorial manner, the sound was rhythmically alive, hard-edged, at least superficially expressionless, and often brutal.

So triumphant was Boulez's conducting that even the brilliant technology was thrown into the shade. I wish I could report that the triumph was not just that of Boulez the conductor but also that of Boulez the composer. But once again, as in *Dialogue,* it seemed that the musical material was mostly gesture and manner, and therefore essentially trivial. One can only admire Boulez's skill in creating sounds which over a long period of time seem stylistically consistent and integrated. He surely has passed the test of finding his own style.

But there is more in music composition than finding a consistent style. There is the absolute necessity of giving the listener in some way the impression that he is hearing what for want of a better term must be called *music*—sound that through some miracle becomes euphony. Boulez's blocks of dissonances, even when, as in *Répons,* they verge on lush, Messiaen-like harmonies, seem all too rarely to break through the noise barrier. It is not that his dissonances are extreme; and it is not that he uses more of them than, for example, the American composer Elliott Carter. But familiarity with Boulez's materials does not, contrary to the case with Carter, render them musical. Whether because of the pitch intervals he uses, the density of their occurrence, the registers in which they are employed, the particular instrumental timbres for which he writes, or the attacks he asks his musicians to use, his dissonances do not seem to live, and his music does not seem to live either—as music.

But the music—or something—does live in Boulez's own performance of it. Perhaps what Pierre Boulez presented on this night at the Columbia University gymnasium cannot be adequately described as music composition, any more than what he did can be adequately described as mere conducting. Perhaps the combination can only be described by that much-abused term, performance art. If such is the case, this was for once performance art done by an artist in full intellectual command of the most sophisticated musical techniques. Whatever one chooses to call it, by once again demonstrating the power of the performer as composer Pierre Boulez was the cause of what must surely be one of the most important events to have taken place in New York City musical life for many years.

(*April* 1986)

A dissent on Menotti

By most standards, a banner event in the history of American opera was scheduled to take place this past November. Everything seemed in place: a major work on the subject of one of the greatest painters of the Western tradition, written (libretto as well as music) by a composer rich in years and in innumerable popularly successful performances of his previous operas, presenting in the title role one of the most celebrated tenors of the last half century, conducted by a major European conductor and produced (under the composer's direction) by the distinguished opera company resident in our nation's capital, with the whole package to be broadcast (on a delayed basis) by PBS on network television.

Curiously, the result was called a disaster. Gian Carlo Menotti's *Goya* was premiered, in the year of the composer's seventy-fifth birthday, on November 15 (and broadcast on PBS on November 28) at the Kennedy Center Opera House in Washington, D.C., by the Washington Opera. The work—starring the great Placido Domingo in a brilliant and well-nigh unsurpassable performance of the title role, and featuring the distinguished conductor Rafael Frühbeck de Burgos in the pit—was largely condemned, when not ignored altogether, by major critical opinion and relegated to the garbage heap of operatic history. It is painful to quote from the journalistic barrage, but for the record two quotations will give the flavor of the onslaught:

> . . ."Goya," as soon became clear, had everything in its favor except a composer and a

librettist capable of dealing in depth with its operatically promising subject. Mr. Menotti, functioning as usual in both capacities, has produced a rather stupefying exercise in banality, similar in its superficiality to his other recent works, though on a larger canvas . . . . This time Mr. Menotti has composed a parody of a Menotti opera.

—Donal Henahan, in *The New York Times*

. . . it's hard to imagine how such an experienced, if chronically uninspired, opera fabricator, libretto as well as music—the best of which are minor but viable achievements—could have signed his name to the sad exhibit that was unveiled November 15 at the Kennedy Center Opera House. How are the mediocre fallen!

—Leighton Kerner, in *The Village Voice*

As negative as these verdicts are, they are in fact an accurate reflection of other reviews, and of private, not-for-publication, expert opinion as well.

And so a compositional career which began with the youthful 1937 *Amelia Goes to the Ball,* a work so successful on its initial performances in Philadelphia and New York that it was immediately picked up for production in the 1937-38 season by the Metropolitan Opera, now seems to have described that most tragic of artistic trajectories, the descent from initial triumph to final failure. Of little account now, or so educated opinion would have it, is an achievement that along the way produced the long-running Broadway successes of *The Medium* (1946), *The Telephone* (1947), and *The Consul* (1951); into the discard pile (at least for intellectual opinion) is thrown the NBC-commissioned television opera *Amahl and the Night Visitors* (1950), perhaps the most performed operatic work written in the twentieth century. Even Menotti's current performance statistics seem of curiously little weight: the fact that (according to the most recent *Opera News* survey) in the 1985-86 season *The Medium, The Telephone,* and *Amahl* together racked up *798* performances in the United States alone is a datum good only for proving how much opera activity there is in the United States. It apparently does not serve to prove the staying power of Menotti.

I cannot say that in the past my own opinion of Menotti has been different from the prevailing critical rejection of him which seemed to set in during the 1960s, and which seems to have gained strength ever since. When *Menotti,* John Gruen's interesting biography of the composer, came out in 1978, I bought such records of Menotti's works as were then available—and in truth, except for his most popular operas, there is little to be purchased—only to find myself unwilling to accept as authentic a music which seemed so purposeful in its pursuit of an easily flowing vein of melody and in its rejection of all the developments in music of the last half century and more.

Nor was my opinion of the composer's works better when I experienced them in live performance. I found the extravagant and often hysterical *Juana La Loca* (1979), written as a vehicle for Beverly Sills's operatic farewell and produced first in San Diego and then at the New York City Opera, fragmented and unimpressive; the 1980 performance of the sardonic and distanced *The Hero* (1971) by the Juilliard American Opera Center struck me as trivial and jejune; the easy sentiment of *Amahl* has always been difficult for me to accept.

When I received a request at the beginning of November from the Voice of America to give an interview about Menotti, to be broadcast on a special program in connection with the *Goya* premiere in Washington, my initial reaction was to say that Menotti was a composer who had wasted whatever talent he had in an attempt to be popular, and that in the process he had been unable to go beyond rewriting Puccini for television. Fused with this moral judgment was an intellectual conviction that to turn one's back on the present, as Menotti surely had done, was to guarantee one's irrelevance. But even one's own cherished critical opinions ought not to be taken as holy writ. And so, before actually giving the interview, I returned once more to the recordings—augmented by some new acquisitions and by a tape of the City Opera broadcast of *La Loca*—of the music I had previously found so unconvincing.

This time around, I found ample evidence for a more positive view of Menotti, not just as a master of theater-*cum*-music, but as a musician and composer. Even a not very well played 1955 Leopold Stokowski recording of the Suite from the ballet *Sebastian (*1944)[1] now managed to convey the composer's great melodic power. The gripping original cast recording (made about the time of the work's 1947 Broadway run) of *The Medium*[2] made a persuasive case for the composer's ability to weld drama (in this case melodrama) with music so that the quintessentially nagging observation about twentieth-century opera did not arise: namely, that if the libretto is theatrically first-rate, the music is hardly needed, but if the libretto isn't independently distinguished, then the music somehow doesn't seem strong enough to stand on its own. Sad to say, I found that the original cast recording of *The Telephone*[3] didn't change my original opinion of the arch and campy nature of the work. What was a surprise to me, however, was the tremendous lyrical power of Magda Sorel's great aria from *The Consul,* Menotti's 1949 protest against the bureaucratized police state. Heard in Patricia Neway's glorious performance from the original cast recording,[4] this excerpt—written to Menotti's lines, "To this we've come / that men withhold the world from men"—is in itself proof that newly written opera cast in traditional molds continues to have the power to move our emotions.

When I returned to the impressive 1955 recording of *The Saint of Bleecker Street* (1954),[5] I heard evidence of a growing musical solidity which was present throughout the work and not limited, as it had been, to climactic dramatic moments. The prevailing texture of musical writing seemed increasingly characterized by melodic as well as rhetorical power. The music, singing voices, and orchestra seemed to carry more weight, and the conversational patter (something for which Menotti was much admired in his first triumphs on Broadway) less. Only one important attribute of musical value (in my opinion) was still missing: the ability of musical phrases in themselves, not just in connection with the dramatic scenes they accompany, to stick in the listener's mind.

With this newly favorable opinion in mind, I listened to the tape of *La Loca,* made as it was at a time of Beverly Sills's decline as a singing artist. I immediately realized that much of my negative opinion of the work had been based upon an adverse judgment of Miss Sills's singing, a singing which for vocal spread and pitchless shrieks can have few parallels in recent New York operatic history. But a determined attempt on my part to isolate this admittedly basic element of the performance enabled me to recognize that Menotti's work was now marked by a new and powerful lyricism, complete with memorable melodic passages. One can only regret that a well-sung production of *La Loca* has not yet been mounted in New York

1 This recording was originally released on RCA LM-1858, and re-released—but now deleted—on RCA ARL 1-2715.

2 This recording, with the inimitable Marie Powers in the title role, is fortunately still available on CBS Odyssey Y2-35239.

3 This recording, conducted by Emanuel Balaban (as was the original cast recording of *The Medium*), is currently available on CBS Odyssey Y2-35239, packaged with *The Medium.*

4 This excerpt, along with fascinating passages sung by other artists from works by Victor Herbert, Deems Taylor, Louis Gruenberg, Aaron Copland, and Howard Hanson, is available on New World Records NW241, under the title *Toward an American Opera 1911-1954.*

5 Excellently conducted by the late Thomas Schippers, Menotti's onetime protégé, this recording was first available on RCA LM-6032 and later on RCA CBM-2-2714. It is now no longer listed in the Schwann catalogue.

to correct the performance-bound impression created by the 1979 City Opera version; that a new verdict on this much-maligned opera might be possible for the independent in spirit was suggested by a tantalizingly short excerpt from *La Loca,* hardly more than a few seconds long, which was shown, along with several other valuable film clips of Menotti's operas, on a recent ninety-minute PBS special devoted to the composer's career.

The television showing of *Goya* at the end of November impressed me not as the nadir of Menotti's compositional career, as the reviews would have it, but rather as its triumph. Here, in approximately one hundred minutes of music, was a complete world of rich emotion and gorgeous melody. Indeed, not since Puccini's *Turandot* has there been Italian operatic song of this density and uninterrupted flow. In *Goya,* Menotti has managed to strip from his creation every irrelevant, merely diverting element, and to concentrate upon the pure vein of music which he possesses.

Fortunately, Menotti decided to make an opera, not a historical treatise. The story is simple, and makes no pretense to historical accuracy. The five scenes of the opera, divided into three acts, show the painter in a tavern, meeting the beautiful Duchess of Alba who was disguised as a chambermaid, falling in love with her over again when he meets her in the splendor of her palace, spurning the advice of the King of Spain to throw her over, losing her to the Queen's poison plot, and then as an old man, blind and deaf, judging his past and finding that his life had been well spent for art. Along the way there are opportunities for Spanish dances in the tavern, pageantry in the royal palace, a mad scene as Goya realizes that he is going deaf, a ballet in which, now aged, he recollects the demons of his life, and the confrontation between the young Goya and what Menotti calls the painter's "deaf and blind carcass."

There will be no pedantic scholarship, of the kind now so fashionable in operatic criticism, expended on the libretto of *Goya.* The plot makes sense, not as history, but as a portrayal (in a musical setting) of the heights —and the depths—of an artist's life. At the very beginning of the Prelude to *Goya* we hear the great melody which throughout the opera most often represents the hero's love for the Duchess; again and again it returns, often in alternation with another theme, which seems to represent the Duchess herself and which is sounded to moving effect upon her death. Though these two themes are the cornerstones of the opera, the writing throughout is melodically distinguished and memorable, with great tenor and soprano arias as well as immensely attractive passages of dance music both popular (as in the tavern scene) and stately (as in the Act II entrance music for the Queen and for the Duchess of Alba).

The point of the opera, of course, is Goya's love, not just for the Duchess and for women, but for art. And so, fittingly, the greatest moments of the opera occur at the end as the specter of the Duchess appears to Goya as he is about to die. She sings, to the melody which has accompanied her progress through the opera, a hymn of forgiveness and blessing:

> I am the guilty one, I understood too late.
> Too late I prized your love,
> I filled your heart with pain.
> The silent cry of your raging brush,
> More than the soldier or the priest,
> will forever fight the fiend.
> Join the immortal company!
> Come, receive your crown, your glorious
> rest.

To these words Goya answers, in soaring melodic phrases:

> Oh Art! Oh Beauty!
> My only truth, my only love.
> Pity the artist's humanity,
> And lead him to God's perfection.

And then he dies.

Some words must be given to the transcendent performance of Placido Domingo in the title role. Ringing high notes, faultless legato production, what seemed to be immense stamina, believable acting (though some critics found it wooden) consistently beautiful vocal quality—all these, on this night, were his. It must be stressed that the role, written as it was at his suggestion, is grateful (for the right artist) beyond measure. If there is one factor alone which makes the opera difficult to produce, it is the need for a great tenor to sing Goya—a need all the greater because of Domingo's *tour de force* in the premiere.

Elsewhere the televised performance was of remarkably high quality. Victoria Vergara, as the Duchess of Alba, sang beautifully and touchingly; the other vocal roles, too, were well filled. The conducting of Frühbeck de Burgos was splendid, as was the playing of the orchestra. A particular commendation must be given to everyone involved for the excellence of the performance because of the usual lateness with which the composer finished his work. It seems that the week preceding the premiere found all the best New York music copyists in Washington, laboring around the clock to have the orchestra parts ready in time for opening night. I must say, too, that I found the television image of the sets and costumes consistently satisfying, and Menotti's direction edifying.

It remains, I suppose, to explain just why so moving a work was so unsuccessful with educated opinion. Much of the reason lies with Menotti's ostentatiously rich melodic and harmonic vocabulary. It is not, of course, that one is not allowed to write in a pastiche of bygone compositional styles; Dominick Argento, to name just one example, has recently done so to the greatest success in his *Casanova,* given for the first time last season at the City Opera.[6] But it cannot be too strongly emphasized that Menotti is *not* a writer of pastiche, for pastiche connotes a distanced, and usually mocking, treatment of that which is copied.

Menotti, by contrast, possesses a deeply authentic style, a style continuous with Puccini and other masters of late Italian opera. For our writers on music, alas, everything can be forgiven in a composer save sincerity. Because Menotti so clearly loves the immediate past out of which he writes, he stands condemned in the court of critical opinion.

I suppose something of the violence of the rejection of *Goya* can be traced to the conventional nature of the sentiments the opera's admittedly conventional music enshrines. In a time of flaunted anti-conventionalism, Menotti's opera has a lot to answer for: an artist gaining his renown through attendance upon the aristocracy, a lover shamelessly indulging his pursuit of beautiful women, and a life justified—and highly valued—in terms of its production of great art. And yet, the fact remains that it is Menotti's sentiments which carry on the great tradition of operatic rhetoric: his musical exploitation of the dramatic conventions of love and art tie him firmly to a past in which opera was at once popular and refined, at once for the masses and for the *cognoscenti.*

To pay such a high tribute to Gian Carlo Menotti is hardly to say that his music, any more than his drama, is up-to-date. It is even less to say that Puccini is a viable model for others who wish to write serious music in general or opera in particular. It is still less to demand that the music of the present or of the future contain lush melodies and warmly appealing harmonies. To admire *Goya* highly does not mean that one cannot ardently wish to see works produced, whether by Schoenberg or Hindemith, Busoni or Milhaud, Sessions or Weisgall, that engage modern culture and society on its own terms.

To be capable of liking *Goya,* I trust, is not to be reactionary. It is simply to be able to listen with open ears to a beautiful piece of lyric theater. To reject *Goya,* as I suspect it is now being rejected, merely *because* it is

6 For my discussion of *Casanova* and its production at the City Opera, see *The New Criterion,* January, 1986.

beautiful at a time when musical art does not have the right to be beautiful is itself to be more than reactionary; it is to be obscurantist. Such obscurantism raises a fundamental question about music and its reception in our time: can any new music, or any possible new music, satisfy the demands our seasoned observers place upon it? The reception of *Goya* goes far to suggest a dismal answer to this most dismal question.

(*January* 1987)

Sad thoughts on Walter Busterkeys, a.k.a. Liberace

Musical success, it has often been noted, is hardly a respecter of the high-minded. For composers and performers alike, the brass rings of fame and money are often not at the disposal of the noble in aspiration or even the uncommonly attractive, but rather of the attractively common.

And so it was, I am afraid, with the pianist Wladziu Valentino Liberace, who was born in West Allis, Wisconsin, in 1919, and who died in Palm Springs, California, this past February. As I write these words, the newspapers are full of stories that the pianist was indeed a victim of the dreaded disease AIDS, despite what his personal physician wrote on the death certificate.

This embarrassment to Liberace's memory seems only a pendant to a career that thrived on another, and quite different, kind of shame. For the embarrassment of Liberace's life was that of a success without respect, a success achieved through flouting the very idea of earning the respect of one's colleagues or of a sophisticated audience. What Liberace courted, and won, was the love of the world out of which he grew, and whose faithful son he remained to the end of his life.

But first some facts about Liberace, culled from a long *New York Times* obituary. His father was a musician in the Sousa concert band; his mother played the piano. He began piano lessons when he was four. As a teenager, he worked as a pianist in silent-movie theaters, and when he was fourteen he played, under the scarcely believable pseudonym of Walter Busterkeys, in a Wausau, Wisconsin, cocktail lounge. According to *The New Grove Dictionary of American Music,* he also played in an ice-cream parlor. Hard as it may be to imagine, he appeared with the Chicago Symphony Orchestra as a soloist (according to the *Times*) under the *echtmusikalisch* Frederick Stock in 1936, playing the Liszt First Concerto; according to the *Grove Dictionary* article, the concert (conductor unnamed) took place in 1940, and the piece was the Liszt Second Concerto. In the *Grove Dictionary* account, he adopted the name Walter Busterkeys after moving to New York in 1940 to perform in nightclubs.

Most performing musicians, like the specialists they are trained to be, continue assiduously to cultivate their failures even when the evidence for those failures is overwhelming. Not so Liberace. According to the *Times,* three years after his Chicago Symphony debut, he "stumbled onto the musical formula that made him famous":

> It happened at a recital in La Crosse, Wis. The audience yelled for Liberace to play the popular novelty song "Three Little Fishies" as an encore, and he did. This break with concert tradition "really shook 'em up," Liberace said later, and he realized he was on the road to riches, rhinestones, and Rolls-Royces.

Whatever his initial progress on the road to fame, Liberace hit the jackpot in the mid-1950s with weekly programs on national television, combining his playing of arrangements of classical pieces with a line of patter so sugary-sweet as to seem hostile to those outside the social context of his charm. He often spoke in hyperbolic terms of his mother and of his close relationship to her. And what one can only call Liberace's *mise-en-scène* always included gaudy costumes, which in the end became gowns, and a quasi-votive candelabrum on the piano.

As a young pianist in the 1950s, I could hardly avoid being aware of Liberace. What thrust him to my attention was not simply his success, for television (like pop music and the movies before) was always unearthing assorted phenomena for the worship of the masses and the spiteful delectation of the elite. Liberace, alas, quickly became a personal matter for me everywhere I went outside the limited musical circles in which I moved, for his very success—often he played compositions I had played myself, among them demanding works of Chopin—was a shining model of what a pianist might aspire to, and a mocking example of what no classical pianist might attain.

Had Liberace played badly, my discomfiture might have been easily handled: serious artists can always reassure themselves by pointing to the triumph of the incompetent. Unfortunately for my feelings, Liberace played rather well. He displayed at all times a large, accurate, and brilliant technique, even indulging himself from time to time in impressive displays of octaves, scales, and complicated passagework. His tone, it is true, was prevailingly hard-edged, but that could easily be explained by the hard-edged tone of the piano he had chosen to play. All in all, his playing purled and glittered just the way an accomplished pianist's should. As for his meretricious choice of repertory and the lack of any spiritual quality in his playing, his rapturous audience reception had a curious way of putting such metaphysical deficiencies into limbo.

What now in retrospect seems clear to me is that Liberace's great commercial success from 1956 on—using as it did television and hyped personal appearances to sell a debased version of classical music—made possible the great commercial success two years later of a vastly more traditional crowd-pleasing pianist. It will be remembered that Van Cliburn—born in Louisiana and raised in Texas—won the International Tchaikowsky Competition in Moscow in April of 1958, and was suddenly catapulted into national prominence not only as a great pianist but as a *popular* pianist. Cliburn's initial repertory was the famous Tchaikowsky B-flat minor Concerto and the Rachmaninoff Third Concerto, both high-Romantic works hugely appealing to an enormous public. Cliburn's manner on and off the platform, at once soft-spoken and easy, seemed not just authentically American but, like Liberace's, authentically non-New York American. Cliburn's mother, like Liberace's, had been a pianist, and indeed was his only teacher until he was seventeen. She remained a constant presence in his life as he toured the country. Though Cliburn did (somewhat stiffly) essay Beethoven and Brahms, it was as a performer of Tchaikowsky, Rachmaninoff, and, of course, Chopin, that his career was made. While many serious musicians respected his unpretentious musicality and his unforced piano tone, his greatest personal success was made with those who had hitherto been strangers to concert halls. It is difficult to avoid the conclusion that Cliburn's fans, like Liberace's, have remained strangers to concert halls ever since, at least when those concert halls are occupied by serious musical programs.

If the legacy of Liberace has been the power of television to make great careers on the fringes of classical music (a power which has recently been displayed in the case of Luciano Pavarotti), the most important legacy of Cliburn, undoubtedly stemming from the size of his post-Moscow career, has been the contest mania among young performers all over the world. This mania, which places more emphasis on contest competition than on mature artistry, has resulted in an explosion of contests and winners, and a dearth of interesting performers growing up at their own pace.

And so it is easy now to see the different but also curiously similar careers of Liberace and Cliburn—the one ended by death and the other by what one can only assume is a combination of physical and emotional problems (Cliburn has not played in public since 1978)—as having provided spectacularly inapplicable models for the careers of serious musicians. Such is the tragedy of it all. There is also a strange irony in these two great but ultimately ephemeral reputations.

The irony is simply that both Liberace and Cliburn were able to capitalize—and were perhaps the last pianists to do so—on the splendid epoch of the piano as *the* musical instrument par excellence. That epoch lasted from the beginning of the nineteenth century to World War II. During those one hundred and forty years the piano was indispensable to creators and performers for the making of both music and careers; it was indispensable, too, across middle-class society as the carrier of a music serious in origin and popular in reception. The piano in the living room, like the candelabrum (so beloved by Liberace and his fans) in the dining room, became an emblem of cultural advancement and participation. It was this touching aspiration which made possible two huge successes, one now ended and the other, we can only hope, in abeyance. Whatever the future holds in store for music in general, the piano will probably never again enjoy such popularity and prestige.

(*April* 1987)

Mark Morris Superstar

by Eva Resnikova

In his short career as a choreographer—he began creating dances for his own company in 1980—Mark Morris has produced a body of work prodigious in its volume and scope, and troubling in the elusiveness of its intentions. New Yorkers were offered a smorgasbord of Morrisiana this autumn during a month-long period that saw a "Great Performances" broadcast on PBS, the local premiere of a ballet commissioned by the Joffrey, the Batsheva Dance Company of Israel's performance of a piece originally created for his own company, and the Mark Morris Dance Group's mixed bill at the Brooklyn Academy of Music's Next Wave Festival.

The dozen works these programs comprised form a dizzying array that seems almost purposely devised to defy categorization. Yet several genres can be distinguished within Morris's oeuvre. There are the mimed vocal pieces (*Robe of White,* to a 1950s country-western ballad; *Love, You Have Won,* to a Vivaldi aria; *Jealousy,* to a Handel chorus; *Tamil Film Songs,* to an excerpt from an "unknown Indian film score"; *Dogtown,* to songs of Yoko Ono); the parodies (*Pièces en Concert,* to Couperin, which sends up baroque dance; *Canonic 3/4 Studies,* to a taped montage of clichéd ballet-class music, which does the same to classical ballet); the religious modern-dance opuses (*Gloria,* to Vivaldi, in the ecstatic mode of Doris Humphrey; *Stabat Mater,* to Pergolesi, in the long-woolen-underwear mode of Mary Wigman); the music visualizations (*Prelude,* to a harpsichord and violin miniature by the early avant-garde American composer Henry Cowell; *Marble Halls,* to J. S. Bach's familiar double-harpsichord concerto; *Esteemed Guests,* a classical ballet, danced on pointe, to a C. P. E. Bach cello concerto). Notably absent from this autumn's offerings were any examples of Morris's *épater les bourgeois* genre, which includes such works as *Striptease* and his drag solo *10 Suggestions.*

Morris's past is as eclectic as his present. Born in 1956 in Seattle, he began his dance training with flamenco, then added ballet lessons, and by age thirteen was performing with a Balkan folk-dance ensemble. After high school he journeyed to Madrid to continue his studies of Spanish dance but found the homophobia there intolerable. He returned to Seattle for more ballet lessons, and in 1976 he moved to New York. Following a stint with the Feld Ballet, he decided to concentrate on modern dance, and over the next few years he performed in the companies of Lar Lubovich, Laura Dean, Hannah Kahn, and, briefly, Twyla Tharp.

In 1980 Morris gathered together some dancers and gave his debut recital at the Cunningham studio in New York. The following year a reformulated group gave the first of what would be three annual seasons at Dance Theater Workshop. Morris now began attracting major attention in the press. In January 1984 he received the imprimatur of Arlene Croce of *The New*

Yorker, the doyenne of dance critics, who devoted a thoughtful, somewhat guarded essay to Morris, declaring him a talented and serious choreographer. A year later, following Morris's sold-out performances at the 1984 Next Wave Festival, she pulled out all the stops, proclaiming him a "master" and "our guide to the future." It had already apparently become a bit much for the twenty-eight-year-old choreographer, who had retreated to his hometown of Seattle late in 1983.

Unlike most modern-dance choreographers, who prefer to think of themselves as prime movers, Morris is generous in acknowledging his artistic influences. These run the gamut from the early moderns (including, amusingly, those he couldn't possibly have seen) to the postmoderns, and he claims to revere Balanchine. His only harsh judgments are reserved for boring minimalists, self-absorbed performance artists, and recent Tharp, whose work he considers "mean-spirited." Morris just as freely admits to borrowing from whomever he admires. This unabashed raiding of dance history is generally taken as an indication of his assimilation of the past—the necessary prelude to his assuming responsibility for the dance of the future.

Much attention has focused on Morris's physical appearance. (Croce began her first *New Yorker* review with a description of his mop of brown ringlets, since shorn; another critic begins his interview in a recent issue of *Dance Magazine,* "Why did you cut off those beautiful curls?") Morris is unfailingly described as androgynous: a puzzling locution, since he does not exhibit any apparent female sexual characteristics—and we've seen all of him. He is, however, effeminate to a degree difficult to stomach even for a veteran dancegoer largely inured to this *déformation professionnelle.*

Just thirty, Morris has allowed his prettiness to deteriorate badly over the last few years. He was always unusually fleshy for a dancer, and now he has developed premature middle-age spread and an incipient double chin. Like the sacrifice of his curls, Morris's seeming lack of concern with physical perfection appears calculated to encourage viewers to focus on the edge of roughness he has always favored, both in his own dancing and in that of his company, who are similarly atypical physical specimens for dancers: a motley group of bottom-heavy, rather mature persons (some of his men are quite bald). Morris has said that he choreographs quickly and avoids over-rehearsing, preferring the amateur fervor of folk dancing to the professional polish of ballet.

Morris's strong points as a dancer are innate rather than learned: a fine rhythmic sense and the ability to vary the impetus of a phrase. But his greatest skill—also a gift—is as a mime. This is what allows him to zero in on the essence of a dance form he has not mastered (baroque, Indian, classical ballet) and come up with a simulacrum that is instantly recognizable, and obviously inauthentic—like a kinetic version of Sid Caesar's ability to give the impression that he is speaking French or Japanese.

It is all great fun and highly entertaining, but Morris's legerdemain is no more proof of his "assimilation" of these forms than Caesar's is. The moments of real dance interest in the predominantly mime pieces are rare and, when they do occur, largely ancillary. Morris's formal skills as a choreographer must be judged in the music visualizations and in the religious works, which are basically music visualizations with some programmatic content. In *Marble Halls* (a gratuitous title), Morris attempts a formal interpretation of Bach's double-harpsichord concerto in C minor in the manner of Balanchine, whose *Concerto Barocco,* set to the same composer's double-violin concerto in D minor, Morris inevitably evokes. The work ultimately fails: Morris's limited movement vocabulary cannot express the music's complexities, nor can his cultivated crudeness reflect its subtleties.

The most disturbing moment in the dance occurs just after the last strains of the exquisite second-movement adagio have died away, when one of the dancers suddenly falls forward. Morris's use of slapstick here is evidently intended as irony: the visual equivalent of the currently fashionable wisecracking school of contemporary fiction epitomized by Lorrie Moore, whose characters communicate about their wrenchingly painful lives in one-liners in order to intimate depths of feeling so great as to be incapable of direct expression. It is also a shameful bit of coyness on Morris's part that serves to protect him from comparison with the creator of *Concerto Barocco.*

The deliberate restriction of Morris's language is partly an anti-elitist—read anti-ballet—bias that has a time-honored place in the history of modern dance. In Morris's case, though, the rejection of ballet has an added dimension: one of the reasons he turned to modern dance, he has said, was that he "got tired of pretending to be a straight guy in love with a ballerina." In his own works Morris treats men and women as if they were interchangeable. Since any language, verbal or visual, increases in eloquence according to its ability to make distinctions, Morris has sacrificed a powerful expressive resource in order to make a political statement.

When this distinction is forced upon him, however, as it is when he works with classically trained dancers, the effect appears to be salutary. In *Esteemed Guests* (another gratuitous title), to C. P. E. Bach's cello concerto in A major, Morris has succeeded in creating a truly original contemporary classical style. Its hallmark is a rigidity in the arms and torso that, astonishingly, brings to mind the calm center of Bournonville rather than bad ballet training. It is a rejection not of classical ballet but of a certain saccharine pseudo-lyricism typified by the works of resident Joffrey choreographer Gerald Arpino. (Morris actually makes the Joffrey dancers appear elegant.) This rigidity is carried to its ultimate expression in an extraordinary moment in the Largo, when the female corps dancers, supported in second position on pointe by their partners, fall slowly forward, until they are actually lying flat on their faces on the ground—an extreme image that Morris is able to render not only dignified but moving.

In *Esteemed Guests,* working with a received vocabulary that he makes his own, Morris is witty without being wisecracking, serious without being solemn. In his setting of Pergolesi's forty-minute *Stabat Mater,* he is not only solemn but sanctimonious. Here not a moment of levity or vulgarity is admitted. The movements are echt modern-dance angst, performed by dancers dressed in plain gray leotards and tights. There are three successive backdrops that progressively open up the stage space when they are raised. Each features a cross: the first is flame-red; the last, glowing white. It is the same image used to end *Robe of White,* the country-western mime piece, which recounts the story of a mother receiving the news, via registered letter, that her son has died in battle.

The sincerity of Morris's spiritual beliefs is not our concern. One must, however, question the artistic intentions of a choreographer who stages pratfalls to Bach but treats a Fifties inspirational pop-music ballad with respect. Morris's attitude could be an affectation, in which case he would be guilty of camp. Or it could be genuine; but then serious questions must be raised concerning his much-vaunted musical sensitivity.

If Morris wears his heart on his sleeve (as Croce aptly puts it in her most recent assessment, in which Morris seems to have been quietly demoted from "guide to the future" to "choreographer of the year"), he wears his religiosity on his chest. An oversized silver cross adorned this part of Morris's anatomy when he came out to take his curtain call in Brooklyn following the premiere of *Stabat Mater.* He acknowledged the applause in his characteristic fashion, by placing the palms of his hands together and moving his outstretched arms up and down in front of him in a gesture of benediction simultaneously vaguely Eastern and Western, which he bestowed alternately on cheering audience and beaming dancers. One might have suspected oneself present at the Second Coming rather than just Mark Morris's second appearance at the Next Wave Festival.

Is it mere coincidence that Morris's elevation to major-choreographer status occurred just as George Balanchine became inactive and died? There seems almost an unwitting collusion between new young choreographer and bereft audience and critics. Balanchine's self-appointed apostles may have allowed despair to color their perceptions of a talented and promising, if still somewhat undisciplined and self-indulgent, aspirant, who is not, alas, the savior of the dance.

(*January* 1987)

"The Common Pursuit" in New York

by James Atlas

Simon Gray's new play, *The Common Pursuit,* has been something of a literary event in New York this season. Or perhaps I should say a New York event. The night I went to see it at the newly renovated Promenade Theatre on Upper Broadway, a significant proportion of the audience consisted of celebrities. I spotted Lorne Michaels, the director of *Saturday Night Live,* in the company of Paul Simon; Robert Bernstein, the president of Random House; and Claus von Bülow, accompanied by his mistress and his daughter, Cosima, in a leopard-skin leotard. A disparate group, united only by their visibility on the scene; but sufficiently notable to establish that something of importance was happening at the Promenade.

The reviews had been good (or is it enough to say that Frank Rich liked it?), but I'd grown wary of New York theater after a few recent experiences—Wallace Shawn's boring *Aunt Dan and Lemon,* Marsha Norman's lugubrious *'night Mother,* Neil Simon's puerile *Brighton Beach Memoirs.* I don't know if they were good or bad; they were definitely no fun. What intrigued me about *The Common Pursuit* was the subject: literary life in England. It's hard to imagine such a play being written by an American, or about American literary life. For one thing, there is no American literary life. Writers in America are scattered all over the land; New York no longer dominates the scene (if it ever did). In England, where writers tend to congregate around the Cambridge/Oxford/London axis, it's hard to imagine a play these days that's about anything else. Tom Stoppard's *The Real Thing,* Harold Pinter's *Betrayal,* and virtually Gray's entire oeuvre dwell in that comfortable, bookish world, a world populated by moderately scruffy, moderately well-off writers, publishers, BBC sorts, people in the arts. They live in North London—Hampstead, say, or Maida Vale—write for *Encounter* and *TLS,* know a very good French restaurant in Soho. They wear tweed jackets patched at the elbows and have an opinion about the poetry of Philip Larkin. Generally they don't teach—there are few writing programs in English universities. Instead they cobble together a career out of free-lance journalism, the odd anthology, a book every two or three years.

Americans in the literary profession regard this world with ambivalence, envying its coziness while reserving a vague contempt for its insularity and self-absorption. There isn't that monstrous, huge ambition that impels American novelists toward the great book, with all the rewards it bestows in money, status, fame. "When success happens to an English writer, he acquires a new typewriter," Martin Amis has observed. "When success happens to an American writer, he acquires a new life." With British writers, the attitude is: write a lot, as much as you can, and show some improvement with every book. William Boyd, Beryl Bainbridge, Anita Brookner are defiantly prolific. In his mid-thirties, A. N. Wilson has published more novels than Saul Bellow. Minor novels, but novels nonetheless; no one objects. Large ambition is looked upon as vulgar; it's not done. David Lodge's latest academic satire sums it up: *Small World.* The only novelists with any claim to greatness in contemporary England—Salman Rushdie and V. S. Naipaul—aren't English. Indeed, they're distinctly foreign—Third Worlders, as it were. And ill-mannered ones at that, pushing with their big important books.

Simon Gray is very much in the *Small World* tradition. The one play of his I'd seen, *Butley,* about a down-at-the-heels English professor at London University who manages to lose both his wife and his male lover in the course of a single day, was indefatigably witty, but never really capitalized on the pathos of the situation. Butley is a sad figure, bitter, alcoholic, vicious, never at a loss for the devastating rejoinder. Himself a professor at Queen Mary College, London, Gray has gotten the seediness of academic life exactly right. The contemporary-novels syllabus ("Burroughs, Genet, Roth, etc."); the language of student papers ("In this sense it might be said that Leontes represents the affliction that is a universal, and so contingently human evil . . ."); the photograph of T. S. Eliot in the dingy office: as a portrait of stifling pedantry, *Butley* is an effective play, as unremittingly bleak as Malcolm Bradbury's *The History Man.*

As a portrait of human relationships, however, it's a bit sketchy. Butley's wife has a walk-on role; we never learn much about that marriage, or where it went wrong, except that Butley doesn't like women. (So why did he get married?) His lover, Joey, is a pale wallflower of a fellow: a pansy. The other characters—Joey's new lover, Reg Nuttall, a working-class bloke who's made his way up in the publishing world; their fussy colleague, Edna Shaft—are stereotypes. That's the trouble with writing plays; once characters are introduced, you've somehow got to deal with them. Gray never does; he makes everyone a foil for Butley's witticisms. When I saw *Butley* in London, the audience roared. It's the kind of play one thoroughly enjoys, and never thinks about again.

The Common Pursuit is a more complicated play. The story of a group of literary undergraduates at Cambridge in the mid-Sixties, it involves five characters, and all of them *are* characters: Stuart, the editor of a literary magazine he's preparing to launch; Martin, a mild-mannered English major willing to do the drudge work on the magazine; Nick, who openly declares his intention of becoming "a big-name theatre reviewer when I grow up, like Ken what's-it"; Peter, the studious one, "Senior scholar in history, an inevitable First"; and Humphrey, a poet concentrating in philosophy, or "Moral Sciences." (Marigold, the one woman in the play, is scarcely more than an object of competition among the men.)

When we first encounter them, in Stuart's rooms at Cambridge, they're typically callow undergraduates, one-upping each other in a dispute over whether it's Bach or Vivaldi on the record player (*gramophone,* in Cambridge parlance), indulging in salacious banter about pricks and big breasts and who's queer and who isn't—the usual adolescent smirking of virgins. By Scene Two, nine years later, Stuart is set up in an office in Holborn, struggling to keep afloat his marriage and his magazine, *New Literary Review*; Peter's a shabby adulterer; Nick is noisily selling out, lunching with editors from *Vogue*; and so on, each messing up his life in his own way.

Gray is a perfect mimic of London literary talk, the nattering gossip that serves as a disguise for envy and resentment—gossip enlivened in this case by its authenticity. When the play opened in London, critics were quick to point out that Stuart was in actual fact Ian Hamilton, Robert Lowell's biographer and former editor of *The New Review,* the glossy, high-toned magazine he presided over during the early Seventies; the ostentatiously chain-smoking Nick was obviously the late drama critic Kenneth Tynan. The name of Clive James, critic, journalist, television personality, also surfaced in the press, though no one was quite sure how he figures in—unless as "Nappies," an offstage presence in competition with Nick for a TV interviewer's job. Humphrey, who loiters about the homosexual underworld and ends up getting murdered by a piece of rough trade, was based (I read somewhere) on a classmate of Gray's at Cambridge who dropped out of sight, became a carpenter, and died in his forties. Everyone is clearly *someone.*

This all makes for a very amusing play, if you happen to be interested in the intricacies of the London lit. scene. Gray's account of Stuart's politicking with the Arts Council for grant money is a clever and comic rehearsal of Ian Hamilton's efforts on behalf of *The New Review,* and he has a good deal to say about Hamilton's relationship with Robert Lowell, whose *Notebook* poems he published in the magazine. In the play, Lowell (not Philip Larkin, as some reviewers supposed) is Hubert Parkin, "our greatest living poet figure," first glimpsed through the window of Stuart's college rooms and later on his main exhibit in the *New Literary Review.* Though he never appears onstage, Parkin is a significant presence in the play; Stuart visits him in the hospital, where he's gone bonkers (as Gray might have put it), scribbling poems that turn out to be shopping lists. "Seeing him like this," Stuart says, "is a—a contamination." Appointed Parkin's authorized biographer, Stuart goes off to New York to flog his book, only to discover that people are less interested in Parkin's poetry than in his life—"especially in its brutal beginning and its spectacular degeneration." Well, yes, that is what happens. "You didn't care for him very much, did you?" remarks Peter. "Not as much as I hoped when I began." Such are the perils of discipleship.

By the end of the play, nothing has quite measured up—for Stuart or for anyone else. Humphrey is dead, Nick is on his way to an early death from emphysema (the disease that killed Tynan); and Peter is an academic hack exiled to Leeds. Only Martin, now a successful independent publisher and married to Marigold, seems mildly content; but then, he's not creative like the others, so what does he know about suffering? The epilogue finds Gray's five characters back in Cambridge, once again the smarmy, bantering undergraduates they were before life cut them down to size, gabbling on about their bright futures—in Martin's line that closes the play, "What we were about to give the world."

Gray has gotten hold of a very good subject—the diminished expectations and forfeited ideals that go by the name of growing up—and he handles it with engaging verve. I wish he had delivered more on the drama within a drama he sets up involving Stuart, whose marriage to Marigold founders on the issue of children—she wants them, he doesn't—and her eventual happy union with the less obsessed Martin; but you can't have everything. As it is, Gray has managed to depict the sadness of life's whittling down, how undramatic failure is. Only the great and tragic are destroyed; the rest of us just shrink until we fit our characters. Humphrey gives up his book on Wagner when he discovers that he doesn't have the imagination to grasp his genius. "Everything I've written about him reduces him to my own sort of size," he explains to Martin. "Which makes him too small to be interesting to me."

Critics have faulted Gray for confining himself to the literary/academic world—a world, complained one London critic, "of limited, incestuous appeal." His plays *are* pretty cramped: *Quartermaine's Terms* is set in a school for foreign-language students in Cambridge; *Man in a Sidecar* is about a well-known lady novelist; *Dog Days* is about a literary editor's mid-life crisis. The one play where Gray has ventured somewhat far afield, *Rear Column,* which deals with a platoon of men stranded in the Congo and their descent into savagery, was a critical disaster. Loitering about the jungle waiting for their leader, the famous explorer H. M. Stanley, to return, they sound remarkably like the undergraduates in *The Common Pursuit.* But never mind. It's not the subject itself that matters, it seems to me; after all,

Lucky Jim was about academic life. It's a life with as much inherent pathos as any other. Besides, as the playwright himself says plaintively to interviewers, "It's the world I know best." You write about what you know.

Why, then, having been entertained by *The Common Pursuit,* having been flattered by Gray's assumption that his audience would know all about the London literary world, having enjoyed the clever dialogue and the fine performances and the impressive set, did I come away feeling as if I hadn't been told the whole truth? The answer, I suspect, can be found in the title itself. Appropriated from F. R. Leavis—*The Common Pursuit* was one of his most influential books—it conjures up a figure who would seem at first glance remote from Gray's somber but innocent play. Severe, reclusive, invested by his disciples with an almost religious authority, Leavis had an immense influence on the life of Cambridge. Gray once called him "the only great man I have met." The director Peter Hall, a near-contemporary of Gray's, claimed in his *Diaries* that Leavis was "the inspiration of my Cambridge years."

Reading over *The Common Pursuit*—Leavis's, that is—I could see why. His critical voice is stern, resolute, unwavering from its single purpose: to determine what is important in English literature, and why. Yet I could also see why he had so many enemies. His besetting flaw, as many of his critics have noted, was his bullying high-mindedness, his insistence upon defining a canon of great literature that excluded whatever Leavis considered second-rate. The English novel consisted of Jane Austen, George Eliot, James, and Conrad (he later included D. H. Lawrence), and that was that. There was no middle ground. It was either literature or it was nothing. John Gross, in his brilliant chapter on Leavis in *The Rise and Fall of the Man of Letters,* called him a "salvationist," afflicted with a messianic compulsion to impose his own ideas upon others, so obsessed with "the value of Value that he makes the critical act an end in itself."

All this is true, but reading him is still an exhilarating experience. In his preface to *The Common Pursuit,* Leavis acknowledges that he's borrowed his title from a passage in Eliot's "The Function of Criticism" where Eliot calls upon critics to collaborate in "the common pursuit of true judgment"—and true judgment is what you feel you're getting from Leavis. He reads with a vigilant attention, a sensitivity to style, and an informed scholarly knowledge of what made Swift or Johnson or Pope significant to the public of their day—why and in what spirit their work was applauded or condemned. If he's at times polemical, willing to quote a work of literature to illustrate a moral point, he's still an effective close reader, and deeply sympathetic toward authors he admires. The two essays on Hopkins in *The Common Pursuit* are generous and eloquent; more than any criticism I know, they bring out Hopkins's poetic vitality, a vitality that survived intolerable neglect. Angry, vehement, even punitive Leavis may have been; but he was equally fervent in appreciation.

Gray studied with Leavis, and was impressed, as Hall was, by his unremitting seriousness. It wasn't only—or even mainly—as a teacher of literature that he was held in awe; it was as a moralist. As Hall puts it: "He somehow inculcated a feeling that art was to do with better standards of life and better behaviour." It wasn't a popular approach. Leavis was detested by the English faculty at Cambridge, and never awarded tenure; to the end of his life, he remained a Fellow of the University. It was a bitter experience. *Scrutiny,* the journal he edited for many years, gave over considerable space to the fulminations of his wife Queenie (Q. D. Leavis) against Cambridge literary politics. They stood alone against the world, proud to worship before the shrine of High Culture.

Leavis couldn't have been a more unlikely ally for the ambitious, opportunistic young men depicted in Gray's version of *The Common Pursuit.* In a memoir of his Cambridge years, Gray admits that he didn't dare make reference to Leavis when he was sitting for his exams—which made him, the playwright says lightly, "an accomplished liar." Now, all this might have made for interesting drama. Standards of the sort Leavis espoused are rare; to fall short of them is to be human. Gray sensed this dramatic potential—the way expedience gets in the way of ideals. But he didn't make it explicit. In the London version of the play—or in the published text, anyway—his only reference to Leavis was in the title. Those who knew its source could infer the connection; those who didn't . . . well, no big deal. Lately, though, Gray has been engaged in a spate of rewriting—at the Promenade the night I was there, he was lurking about the aisles with a notepad, still tinkering—and he's now dragged Leavis in at the very beginning. Stuart's magazine is called *The Common Pursuit,* and there's much business about the great critic: Stuart has in hand a letter from Leavis promising to support the "embattled and beleaguered" magazine—rhetoric that troubles the young editor. "He makes it sound as if I'm about to surrender."

Not much chance of that. Gray's play, if you think about it long enough, isn't about failure at all. It's about success. Sure, there are reversals, stumblings, the odd minor tragedy along the way. But all's right in the end, isn't it? Or as all right as things get in this world. *The Common Pursuit* reminded me of its much-touted precursor, Frederic Raphael's *The Glittering Prizes,* which had a nearly identical scenario. For Raphael's smug protagonist, Adam Morris, Cambridge is "the city of perspiring dreams"—a pun on Cardinal Newman's evocation of the "dreaming spires" of Oxford. Life after Cambridge is drab, banal, corrupt—betrayals and affairs and marital spats and the humiliation of selling out to Hollywood (I'm referring to the novel, or "novelization," not having seen the televised version); but in the end Adam's book gets rave reviews and a lucrative movie deal. Just like the way it happens in life.

The Common Pursuit is less exuberant than *The Glittering Prizes,* and a good deal less crass, but it doesn't end so badly either. Peter fails to get a chair at Oxford; still, he gets a chair. Stuart is somewhat reduced in stature, chastened by the loss of Marigold, but an eminent biographer; Nick even wants to have him on his show. And Nick, emphysematous Nick, is a literary man-about-town. The only one who suffers is the Leavis-like moralist Humphrey, who refuses to publish his poems because they're not good enough and abandons his book on Wagner because he's not up to it. "What partly killed him was that he couldn't perform his worldly task," according to Nick. "At least to his standards." Is there a lesson in this?

Unfailingly self-deprecating in his interviews and published writings, Gray works to give an impression of humility. The prefaces to the Penguin collection of his plays are tirelessly abject. They stress the loneliness, the fear of failure, the "purple patch between March 1969 and February 1971" when he suffered "three flops in a row." "I seem in retrospect to have spent most of this period with my head down, to conceal as I went about my daily business cheeks that flamed easily and eyes that watered over trifles." Yet what emerges from Gray's journal of the London production, *An Unnatural Pursuit & Other Pieces* (St. Martin's, 1985), is how pleased with himself he really is. For nearly two hundred pages, he recounts the daily crises he endured—finding actors, revising the script, wrangling with producers, dining at restaurants called L'Épicure with Harold Pinter. Not to worry; in the end, it goes off without a hitch. Nothing really troubles Gray; he doesn't even take his own play seriously. He frets about the "delicate, and melancholy and quite amusing (I hope) scene in which Humphrey's death is announced," afraid the audience won't feel sad. But his confidence is irrepressible. Watching the scene where Nick predicts that the Arts Council will turn down a grant to his magazine on the grounds that it's elitist, the playwright begins to wonder if perhaps his own play is elitist. "I observed to Harold, on the way back to the car, that the same charge would probably be made about the play. He agreed cheerfully. So, in a spirit of *je-m'en-fou*ism (fuck-'em-allism), we drove elitely back to Holland Park in Harold's Mercedes to a glass of our usual tipple, champagne." I find this a little nauseating, to put it plainly.

Reading Leavis's *The Common Pursuit*—the real one, I'm tempted to say—I came across an essay that clarified the uneasiness Gray's play had induced in me. Entitled "Keynes, Lawrence, and Cambridge," it purports to be a review of Keynes's memoirs, but it's really a dissection of what could be called the Cambridge mentality—the aura of brilliance and precocious accomplishment that defined Bloomsbury. Members of a highly select society known as The Apostles, the group assembled in Cambridge around the turn of the century—Keynes, Leonard Woolf, Lytton Strachey, and (somewhat earlier) Roger Fry—were exceptional minds, everyone agreed. What troubles Leavis is their self-delight, ill-disguised as irony. What infuriates him is Keynes's claim that D. H. Lawrence was "jealous" of the Cambridge group. Why should Lawrence be jealous? He was a member of an even more exclusive club, Leavis's own Great Tradition; and, like Leavis, originally a working-class boy. What Lawrence was reacting against—and Leavis's defense of him illustrates how movingly sympathetic he could be toward those he perceived as, like himself, outsiders—was the "Cambridge-Bloomsbury ethos," with its covert self-congratulation, its "virtually intact complacency." Here is Leavis on Bloomsbury:

> Articulateness and unreality cultivated together; callowness disguised from itself in articulateness; conceit casing itself safely in a confirmed sense of high sophistication; the uncertainty as to whether one is serious or not taking itself for ironic poise . . . .

Sound familiar?

In his memoir of Cambridge, Gray recalls those years as a mostly painful experience. Beset by financial difficulties, his father emigrated to Halifax just as Gray was preparing to attend Oxford. Instead he ended up in Nova Scotia, at Dalhousie University. By the time he got to Cambridge, determined to study with Leavis, he was in his twenties—not a youthful undergraduate at all and by no means part of the idyllic undergraduate scene. Life at Cambridge for Gray wasn't punting on the Cam; it was "a cold little warren of rooms above a coffeeshop" that he shared with "two other outcasts," and a Christmas dinner of sardines on bread. What if, instead of writing a play about witty young men in their snug, well-appointed college rooms, Gray had written about that Christmas dinner? He might have gotten at the truth of his experience. You never know. But that one dolorous image leaped out at me with more force than anything in the play.

In his journal about *The Common Pursuit,* Gray finds himself worrying about whether his work is too special, too narrow in scope: "But we are, I console myself, what we are." It's the *console* that bothers me.

(*February* 1987)

The death of Andy Warhol

by Hilton Kramer

The death of Andy Warhol was bound to be a media event, and so it was. For the media, after all, it was like a death in the family. Here was a figure who was famous for being famous, for knowing the famous, and for serving as an avatar of fame, and nothing so pleases the media as an opportunity to celebrate one of their own creations. The front-page obituary in *The New York Times,* the special segment on the MacNeil-Lehrer News Hour, the cover story in *New York* magazine, not to mention the many pictures and news stories in the daily tabloids and on the network news programs—the coverage could hardly have been better (or worse) if Warhol himself had orchestrated it. Which, in a sense, he had. The most distinguishing characteristic of this prodigious outpouring of commentary, homage, and celebrity-worship was the way it confined itself to the terms which Warhol himself had set for the discussion of his life and work. Even writers who, on other occasions, find it appropriate to apply more elevated standards to art (and life) proved ready and eager to suspend them in discussing Warhol and his significance. It was as if no language but Warhol's own—the language of hype—could be expected to have any meaning when it came to explaining just what it was that made him important.

All the same, it is my impression that Warhol's death caused some of these volunteer laureates of hype and celebrity a good deal of uneasiness. Suddenly they were on the spot. They couldn't in good conscience bring themselves to say that Warhol had been a great artist even though they had often written about him as if he were. They couldn't, in many cases, even bring themselves to explain why he should be considered an important artist even though they had long taken it for granted that he was. No one is under oath, of course, in writing obituary notices. Even so, there was a general tendency on this occasion to take refuge in the subject's fame, in his personality, in his business affairs and his entourage, even his wig, and leave the art more or less unexamined. Amid the expected encomiums, there was in fact a discernible hedge and wariness to be observed in the claims advanced for Warhol's artistic achievement. It turned out that almost no one could bring any conviction to the task of specifying what that achievement had consisted of.

The truth is, even among his friends and admirers it was widely recognized—even if seldom admitted—that, although being an artist was essential to his social position, Warhol was far more important as a social phenomenon that he ever was or could be *as* an artist. That was what gave him his special aura, after all—and his influence. *As* an artist he ended his career exactly as he began it—as a gifted *commercial* artist with a flair for the arresting graphic image and skillful layout. He was never much of a painter, and as a sculptor he didn't exist. (As for his movies, it is probably enough to observe that, having served their purpose—which was to propagate the Warhol myth—they had long ago predeceased their creator. Of aesthetic merit they had none whatever.) Warhol's "genius" (if it can be called that) consisted of his shrewdness in parlaying this essentially commercial talent into a career in an art world that no longer had the moral stamina to resist it: a career that would have been unthinkable, for example, ten years earlier.

To an extent that was unrivaled among his contemporaries in the Pop Art movement, if only because they knew so much less than he did about the dynamics of the fashion world, Warhol understood that something momentous had happened to the art scene in the late Fifties—that the relation which had formerly obtained between art and fashion (and hence between art and publicity, and between art and money) had undergone a decisive change. Which is to say that he understood the success of Robert Rauschenberg and Jasper Johns better than they did. (Not that they were slow to catch on—but that is another story.) Their success owed much to the international acclaim which Abstract Expressionism, having passed through its avant-garde phase, was receiving for the first time, and to their putative role as both the heirs and the rebels of that movement. Warhol understood that something else was involved; that with the success of Rauschenberg and Johns, the age of the avant-garde had drawn to a close. Their success had been, initially, an art world success, but it quickly developed into a much larger phenomenon. A boundary separating art and fashion had been breached, and never again would the really big successes of the art world be confined to that world. Henceforth success in that art world would be played on a much larger stage.

Rauschenberg and Johns came out of the school of Marcel Duchamp. They stood in relation to Abstract Expressionism very much as Duchamp had stood to Cubism—as plenipotentiaries to the world of publicity and chic, agents of "advanced" styles that offered just the right dash of scandal (the stuffed goat, the paint-splattered bed, the targets and flags, etc.) to excite a taste that had wearied of the rigors of abstract art. Warhol, on the other hand, belonged to the school of Condé Nast, where such "scandals" are recognized as marketable commodities and routinely processed as the materials of fashion. In moving from a career in fashion illustration to a career in this swiftly expanding art world, Warhol saw that the product needed only the most superficial modification to win attention and garner rewards—rewards far greater than any to be found in the realm of fashion illustration. Art, no matter how debased, still offered a kind of status that was denied to advertising, but otherwise there were now fewer and fewer differences separating the art world from the advertising world. The ethos was getting to be essentially the same. Success was the goal, the media would provide the means of achieving it, and what the media loved more than anything else—certainly more than art—was a product based on their own stock-in-trade. And that, from his "Marilyns" to his "Maos," is what Warhol mainly specialized in giving them. Considering the magnitude of his accomplishment in this respect, it would be churlish to deny that he did indeed have genius of a sort. No ordinary talent could have done it—but the talent, alas, was not primarily an artistic talent.

As everyone knows, the art world never really recovered from this fateful incursion. As a movement Pop Art came and went in a flash, but it was the kind of flash that left everything changed. The art public was now a different public—larger, to be sure, but less serious, less introspective, less willing or able to distinguish between achievement and its trashy simulacrum. Moreover, everything connected with the life of art—everything, anyway, that might have been expected to offer some resistance to this wholesale vulgarization and demoralization—was now cheapened and corrupted. The museums began their rapid descent into show biz and the retail trade. Their exhibitions were now mounted like Broadway shows, complete with set designers and lighting consultants, and their directors pressed into service as hucksters, promoting their wares in radio and television spots and selling their facilities for cocktail parties and other entertainments, while their so-called "education" programs likewise degenerated into sundry forms of entertainment and promotion. The critics were co-opted, the art magazines commercialized, and the academy, which had once taken a certain pride in remaining aloof from the blandishments of the cultural marketplace, now proved eager to join the crowd—for there was no longer any standard in the name of which a sellout could be rejected. When the boundary separating art and fashion was breached, so was the dividing line between high art and popular culture, and upon all those institutions and professions which had been painstakingly created to preserve high art from the corruptions of popular culture the effect was devastating. Some surrendered their standards with greater alacrity than others, but the drift was unmistakable and all in the same direction—and the momentum has only accelerated with the passage of time.

There was no more telling symbol of this surrender of standards than Warhol himself, the cheerful nihilist who became the unlikely culture-hero of a new era. Anyone who was around at the time will remember exactly when it was that we were given our first taste of its lethal character. It came, of course, in the early Sixties with the false dawn and specious glamour of the Kennedy administration—the media-fabricated glamour that in retrospect has turned out to be the perfect political analogue for what was occurring on the cultural scene. There is an important book to be written about the cultural fallout of the Kennedy years, and Warhol's would by no means be the only significant career that would require a place in the story. So, among many others, would Norman Mailer's and Arthur Schlesinger, Jr.'s and George Plimpton's, and so too, in their own spheres, would the history of *New York, The New Yorker,* and *The New York Review of Books,* not to mention less exalted branches of the media. Still, in any such study a special place would have to be reserved for the Warhol phenomenon, which gave to the art world—but not to the art world alone—a model that has proved to be so irresistible that it is now a permanent, and permanently disabling, component of cultural life. It was really that ghastly model, rather than the man or his art, that the media celebrated so copiously in their obituary notices of Andy Warhol—a model that continues to exhibit a potency his art could never achieve.

(*May* 1987)

Contributors

James Atlas is a novelist *(The Great Pretender)*, biographer *(Delmore Schwartz: The Life of an American Poet)*, and critic whose articles and reviews are widely published. He is a regular contributor to *Vanity Fair*.

Bruce Bawer has been a regular contributor to *The New Criterion* since 1983. He is the author of two books, *The Middle Generation: The Lives and Poetry of Delmore Schwartz, Randall Jarrell, John Berryman, and Robert Lowell* and *The Contemporary Stylist*. He is the regular film critic for *The American Spectator* and has published poems in *Poetry, Boulevard,* and *The Hudson Review*.

Cleanth Brooks is Gray Professor of Rhetoric Emeritus at Yale University. His most recent book is *The Language of the American South*.

Frederick Brown is professor of French literature at the State University of New York at Stony Brook and the author of *Theater and Revolution: The Culture of the French Stage*. He is writing a biography of Emile Zola.

Hortense Calisher is a widely published novelist and short-story writer. She is president of the American Academy of Arts and Letters. Her article on Barbara Pym appeared in the inaugural (September 1982) issue of *The New Criterion*.

W. S. Di Piero has contributed both prose and poetry to *The New Criterion*. He has published two volumes of poetry, *Solstice* and *Early Light*, and a translation of the *Pensieri* of Giacomo Leopardi. He is a member of the English faculty at Stanford University.

Rackstraw Downes is a painter and writer. He shows regularly at Hirschl & Adler Galleries and is the editor of *Fairfield Porter: Art in Its Own Terms* (1979).

Fernanda Eberstadt is a novelist (*Low Tide*) and a critic whose articles appear regularly in *The New Criterion, Commentary*, and other publications.

Joseph Epstein has been a regular contributor to *The New Criterion* since its inaugural issue and is the editor of *The American Scholar*. His recent books have included *Plausible Prejudices, The Middle of My Tether,* and *Once More Around the Block*.

Gloria G. Fromm is the author of *Dorothy Richardson: A Biography* and professor of English at the University of Illinois at Chicago.

Eric Gibson has been a regular contributor of art criticism to *The New Criterion* since 1984. He is the New York correspondent for *Studio International* (London) and teaches at the Parsons School of Design.

Creighton Gilbert is professor of art history at Yale University and a regular contributor to *The New Criterion*. His most recent book is *The Works of Girolamo Savoldo*.

David Gress is a senior research fellow at the Hoover Institution and author of *Peace and Survival: West Germany, the Peace Movement, and European Security*.

Donald Hall, the distinguished poet and critic, is the author, most recently, of *The Ideal Bakery*, a collection of stories. His most recent volume of poetry is *The Happy Man.*

Dan Hofstadter has been a regular contributor to *The New Criterion* since 1983. He is a painter, translator, biographer, and critic. His most recent book is *The Despot and the Slave.*

William H. Jordy, Henry Ledyard Goddard Professor of Art History Emeritus at Brown University, has been a regular contributor of architectural criticism to *The New Criterion* since its inaugural issue. He is the author of two volumes in the American Buildings and Their Architects series, published by Doubleday.

Roger Kimball has been a regular contributor to *The New Criterion* since 1983. He has contributed criticism and reviews to a variety of publications, among them *Architectural Record*, the London *Times Literary Supplement, Commentary*, and *The American Scholar.*

Hilton Kramer is the editor of *The New Criterion*. He is the author of two volumes of art criticism, *The Age of the Avant-Garde* (1973) and *The Revenge of the Philistines* (1985), and was formerly the chief art critic of *The New York Times*. He is currently at work on a book to be called *Abstract Art: A Cultural History.*

Mimi Kramer was *The New Criterion*'s theater critic from December 1982 to September 1986. Her writings have also appeared in *Vogue, Vanity Fair, Spy,* and *The Wall Street Journal*, and she writes regularly on theater for *The New Yorker.*

Brad Leithauser is the author of two volumes of poetry, *Hundreds of Fireflies* and *Cats of the Temple*, and a novel, *Equal Distance*. He has also written for *The New York Review of Books, The New Yorker,* and *The New York Times Book Review.*

Samuel Lipman, the publisher of *The New Criterion*, is the regular music critic for *Commentary* and the author of two volumes of music criticism, *Music After Modernism* (1979) and *The House of Music* (1984). He is a member of the National Council on the Arts and the artistic director of the Waterloo Music Festival.

James Lord is the author of *A Giacometti Portrait* (1965) and *Giacometti: A Biography* (1985). He is currently at work on a volume of memoirs.

Cynthia Ozick is a novelist, short-story writer, and critic. Her most recent novel is *The Messiah of Stockholm* (1987), and her essays are collected in *Art & Ardor* (1983).

Jed Perl has been a regular contributor of art criticism to *The New Criterion* since October 1982. His study of French art since World War One, *Paris Without End*, is scheduled for publication in February 1988. He writes for *Vogue, The New Republic,* and other publications.

Ronald Radosh is professor of history at Queensborough Community College and the Graduate Center, City University of New York, and the co-author (with Joyce Milton) of *The Rosenberg File.*

Eva Resnikova has written on dance for *The New Criterion* since September 1983. She has also written for *The New Republic.*

Robert Richman is the poetry editor of *The New Criterion*, to which he also regularly contributes critical essays and reviews. His anthology, *The Direction of Poetry*, will be published in 1988.

James W. Tuttleton, professor of English at New York University, is the author of *The Novel of Manners in America* and editor of the Washington Irving volume in the Library of America series.

René Wellek, Sterling Professor Emeritus at Yale University, has recently published volumes five and six of *A History of Modern Criticism,* 1750–1950. He is currently at work on volume seven, which will deal with literary criticism in Europe in the twentieth century.

Index

A

D

E

F

G

H

I

J

M

N

O

P

Q

R

V

W

Y

Z